THE ESSENTIAL
GARDENER

THE ESSENTIAL
GARDENER

ANNUALS, PERENNIALS, BULBS, ROSES, TREES, SHRUBS, HERBS, VEGETABLES

The Best Plants for Design and Cultivation

Text and Photography by Derek Fell

CRESCENT BOOKS
NEW YORK • AVENEL, NEW JERSEY

A FRIEDMAN GROUP BOOK

This 1993 edition published by Crescent Books, distributed by Outlet Book Company, Inc., a Random House Company, 40 Engelhard Avenue, Avenel, New Jersey 07001.

Random House
New York • Toronto • London • Sydney • Auckland

ISBN 0-517-69339-9

THE ESSENTIAL GARDENER
The Best Plants for Design and Cultivation
was prepared and produced by
Michael Friedman Publishing Group, Inc.
15 West 26th Street
New York, New York 10010

Editor: Sharon Kalman
Art Director: Jeff Batzli
Designer: Robert W. Kosturko
Layout: Beverly Bergman
Photography Editor: Christopher C. Bain

Printed and bound in China by Leefung-Asco Printers Ltd.

8   7

Thie book is intended as a reference only. The information presented here is not to substitute for any treatment prescribed by a physician.

DEDICATION

For O. D. Gallagher, who taught me how to write; Harry Smith, who taught me how to photograph; and David Burpee, who taught me how to garden.

ACKNOWLEDGMENTS

A great many people must be thanked for helping me photograph and write such a comprehensive garden book. They include Jack Aprill of Leaming's Run, a beautiful garden of annuals near Cape May, New Jersey; Charles H. Mueller, of Lentenboden Bulb Garden, near New Hope, Pennsylvania; Goldsmith Seeds, owners of a beautiful display garden and test garden for annuals, near Gilroy, California; Snipes Nursery, Wrightstown, Pennsylvania, owners of a model garden featuring annuals; Earl Jamison, owner of Peddlers Village, near New Hope, Pennsylvania; the Netherlands Flower Bulb Institute for providing help in locating many photogenic bulb gardens; Sir John Thouron, for allowing me to photograph his magnificent perennial garden near Unionville, Pennsylvania; Ruth Levitan, for inviting me to photograph her beautiful perennial garden near Stamford Connecticut; Oehme, van Sweden & Associates, of Washington, D.C., for allowing me to photograph perennial gardens they designed. Ed Toth, whose vegetable garden in New Jersey was the most productive and aesthetically pleasing I have ever photographed; Jackson & Perkins and Conard Pyle Company (Star Roses), both quality rose breeders, for help in photographing roses; Well Sweep Herb Garden, Port Murray, New Jersey, for allowing me access to their display gardens; Drayton Hastie, owner of Magnolia Plantation and Garden, Charleston South Carolina; plus many other owners of gardens—both great and small—who shared not only their gardens at the peak of perfection, but also many tips and planting secrets.

A special thanks to Kathy Nelson, for typing much of the manuscript, to Wendy Fields for helping me to grow many of the plants in my own garden, and to Peggy Fisher and Elizabeth Murray, both of whom helped with research and garden plans for portions of the book. Also to Springhill Nurseries, the Daffodil Mart, Klehm Nurseries, and other growers for providing me with plants to photograph in my "photography gardens."

Derek Fell
    Cedaridge Farm
    Bucks County, Pennsylvania.

TABLE OF CONTENTS

AUTHOR'S NOTE

THIS BOOK REPRESENTS A COMPENDIUM OF the most important plants for North American gardens, with an emphasis on those that are relatively carefree, easy to obtain, and most likely to add the strongest visual interest to your landscape.

Most of the plants are "survivors"—some prominent in the North American landscape and others not so prominent, but worthy of attention. The book is conveniently divided into annuals, perennials, flowering bulbs, roses, trees and shrubs, and vegetables and herbs. Specific "how-to-do-it" information is given for each plant group, and a complete chapter of garden designs suggests how to use the plants in a home landscape.

Even if you don't have space for a garden plot, many of the plants featured here are suitable for growing in containers to decorate patios, decks, balconies, and windowboxes.

Annuals are the first plant group we can turn to for "instant" color. Many can be purchased locally from garden centers, ready-grown in convenient transplant pots. Many annuals will bloom nonstop for ten weeks or more, right up until fall frost when they die down, having finally completed their life cycle. Many annuals are easily raised from seed.

Perennials live from year to year, and though they need no replanting, color is not normally produced from seed until the second season unless year-old plants in large-size transplant pots are purchased from local nurseries and garden centers. Also, the color span of most perennials is a few weeks, compared to months for many annuals.

Flowering bulbs are highly dependable and easy to plant. Just pop them in the soil to their required depth and, like hardy perennials, hardy bulbs will come up year after year. The more exotic kinds that are tender can be lifted from the soil and held over winter in a dormant state until after spring frost. Then they can be planted outdoors again. Bulbs are distinctly different from true perennials in that they have an underground swollen stem or root segment—the bulb—with built-in reserves of energy, allowing the plant to survive hardships such as freezing weather or drought.

Shrubs bridge the gap between perennials and trees. Though there is no botanical difference between a tree and a shrub (they are both classified as woody plants, forming a strong cell structure called wood), a shrub tends to be multiple-stemmed, while a tree grows a single trunk. Also, shrubs tend to stay under 15 feet in height. Trees and shrubs carry their ornamental effect higher into the sky than annuals or perennials, which are classified as herbaceous plants, their common trait being the formation of soft stems.

Though roses are classified as woody plants and are generally grouped with shrubs, they are separated in this book into a special section of their own because they are so popular and so important as ornamental landscape plants. Also, they are extremely versatile in the landscape, useful as specimen shrubs, massed in a bed, and climbing high into the sky. There are also low-growing species of roses for containers and groundcover effects.

Herbs and vegetables are grouped together because they are generally not grown for ornamental effect so much as for culinary use, either as a flavoring (in the case of many herbs) or as a complete food (in the case of plants we commonly call vegetables).

All things considered, these are the plant categories most people want to grow in their home gardens. This book, therefore, aims to cut through a lot of confusion, present the most worthwhile kinds for dramatic impact, and those readily available commercially.

So please sit back, relax, and enjoy the show with this veritable feast of ideas for making the most out of your home landscape.

Derek Fell

PART ONE

ESSENTIAL
ANNUALS

INTRODUCTION

INSTANT COLOR, CONTINUOUS BLOOM

COMPARED TO OTHER TYPES OF ORNAMEN-tal plants, flowering annuals provide an abundance of bloom quickly, but all for a minimal investment of time and money. They are the easiest flowering plants to grow—far more dependable than perennials, flowering bulbs, and flowering shrubs. A packet of seeds costing a dollar or less can produce thousands of plants. Even if you prefer to let a professional bedding plant grower start the seeds for you, and buy transplants from a garden center, it's possible to purchase annuals for as little as twenty-five cents each when you buy them in flats.

Many people feel a much greater sense of accomplishment when they grow their own annuals from seed. To see how easy it can be—even with small seeds—turn to page 19 where a variety of seed starting techniques are presented.

Annuals are undemanding plants that can be fully grown in one season, usually flowering within six to twelve weeks from the time they are sown. Depending on the climate you live in and the varieties you choose, annuals can produce a bold, brilliant floral display lasting from four weeks to seven months. A large selection of young plants already in flower is available from local garden centers in early spring, so the impatient gardener can add instant color to the garden.

It is amazing how versatile annuals can be. Displays of annuals can be used exclusively in beds and borders; they can be mixed with perennials to fill the gaps of a perennial border, offering color continuity as the perennials come in and out of bloom; and many annuals can be planted in containers, especially hanging baskets, making it possible even for city gardeners to decorate confined areas and hard-to-plant spaces like balconies, terraces, and patios. For more information about container gardening, see page 26.

Some annuals—like marigolds and snapdragons—are so versatile that they grow in every state, from Florida to Alaska to Hawaii. Whether you have cool or hot summers, rich or poor soil, moist or dry soil, sun or shade, you will find a wide range of annuals to fit every need of your garden and produce a colorful display. The lists starting on page 83 will help you choose the right varieties for your particular needs.

Whatever your garden design requirements, there are annuals to meet them. Annuals that creep along the ground, such as alyssum and *Zinnia angustifolia* (Classic zinnia), are suitable to use as ground-cover plants, and they have an added bonus of flowers; annuals that stand tall and erect, such as cleome and sunflowers, are suitable for backgrounds and structural highlights; annuals that cascade and spill over the edges, such as lobelia and petunias, are suitable for raised beds, pots, and balconies; annuals with long stems are suitable for cutting so you can fill your home with fresh flowers, many with the added attraction of a pleasant fragrance. Again, the lists starting on page 83 will provide specific information.

Perhaps the biggest advantage of annuals is their extensive color range, making them suitable for creative garden designs, particularly gardens of a single color theme, such as "white gardens," "golden gardens," "blue gardens," and even "green gardens." Gardens that cover large expanses can emulate the French Renaissance style of "carpet bedding," in which generous swatches of color are planted in swirls and flourishes, or in more formal geometric shapes. The color schemes can be dramatic, using strong colors such as yellow, orange, and red, or subtle and sophisticated, using subdued colors such as blue, white, and pink. To help you devise some effective garden designs using annuals, a number of garden plans are featured, beginning on page 614, with specific planting ideas for both sunny and shady locations.

When planning to include annuals in your garden, don't be put off by garden writers who describe annuals as "boring." Anyone who thinks of them this way hasn't traveled enough and seen annuals displayed in beautiful and imaginative ways. To prove how stimulating and exciting annuals can be, the photographs chosen show a variety of appealing garden uses. Even in the encyclopedia section, the specimens selected are shown as an integral part of a garden.

Opposite page, far left, above: Claude Monet's garden at Giverney, France is famous for its "Grand Allee," featuring annual nasturtiums that creep across a gravel walk way.

Opposite page, far left, below: This fence features a morning glory vine and a border of wax begonias.

Opposite page, left: An effective companion-planting of perennial scarlet sage and annual vinca.

Left: Pansies and alyssum define a serpentine border at a Tucson, Arizona home in early spring.

CHAPTER ONE

ANNUAL BASICS

THE SEEDS OF MOST ANNUALS ARE extremely easy to germinate, requiring little more than moist potting soil that maintains a temperature of 70°F. Generally speaking, if a seed is tiny—such as begonias and petunias—it should not be completely covered with soil, but pressed into the upper soil surface (just enough to anchor it), since exposure to light improves the rate of germination.

With such fine seeds lying on the soil's surface, it is extremely difficult to prevent them from drying out; a good practice is to enclose the seed-starting unit (see pages 19 to 23) in a plastic bag, away from direct sunlight. The plastic helps create a humid microclimate, allowing moisture to condense on the inner wall, thus keeping the seeds from dehydrating.

Once seedlings are up, they should be watered on a regular basis to keep the soil moist, and placed in a location with bright, constant light. If moisture is infrequent or sunlight comes only from one direction, then the plants will "stretch," producing poor transplants. When growing seedlings on a windowsill, raise the level of the seed-starting unit so the seedlings are closer to the light, and also consider placing a reflector on the side of the seed-starting unit that receives the least amount of light. A handy reflector can be made by simply wrapping aluminum foil around a piece of cardboard and propping it against the unit.

Different varieties of annuals require different periods of time in which to germinate and grow into useful transplants. Slow-growing plants such as begonias may need as many as ten to twelve weeks to be large enough to transplant, while French marigolds can be ready to transplant in four weeks. The seed packet will generally advise you as to how long it should take to start a variety from seed, and whether the variety can tolerate frost (hardy annual) or is killed by frost (tender annual).

A large number of flowering annuals dislike being transplanted and prefer to be sown directly into the garden; Shirley poppies are a good example. However, many people still prefer to start them indoors in order to get earlier blooms in the garden. In this case, it is vital to choose a method of seed starting that prevents root disturbance at transplant time.

Seed-Starting Techniques

Basically, there are two types of seed-starting techniques: the *one-step* and the *two-step*. These two methods (plus two others), as well as information on starting hard-to-start seeds are illustrated for you. In a one-step system the seeds are sown directly into a pot, such as a Jiffy-pot, Jiffy pellet, Fertl-cube, Maxi-pot, or other brands. As the seeds germinate, the seedlings are thinned, leaving just one strong seedling to grow to transplant size. There is no transfer to another pot.

With the two-step method (mostly used with fine-seeded varieties such as begonias and petunias and wherever very large quantities of transplants are desired), the seed is first sown into a seed tray—or a seed flat—either scattered over the entire surface and pressed in, or else sown into furrows made by a straight edge.

The seeds should be allowed to germinate thick and fast (heat from a heating cable under the seed tray will encourage rapid germination), but as soon as they are large enough to handle, the best-looking seedlings should be pulled out gently and transferred to individual pots until they have reached transplant size.

When growing seedlings it is extremely important to use sterile materials—both potting soil and pots. Don't use soil dumped out from other pots or garden soil, and if you are recycling old pots make sure they are thoroughly cleaned

The illustrations on the opposite page show various seed-starting techniques.

1. Scatter seeds thinly over soil surface in seed tray.

2. Thin out seedlings to leave only the healthiest plants.

3. Transfer to individual pots when large enough to handle.

4. Place a group of seeds in the planting hole of a peat pellet.

5. Thin seedlings to a single strong plant.

6. Gently remove netting to free roots at time of transplanting.

with soapy water. This kind of hygiene is extremely important in order to avoid a common fungus disease called "damping-off" that attacks young seedlings. A symptom of this disease is a tendency for the seedling to keel over, weakened at the soil line. As an extra precaution against the disease a fungicide like Benomyl or Benlate can be sprayed over the soil surface of newly seeded containers.

It is also extremely important to subject all seedlings to a period of "hardening-off" before they are transferred from a comfortable indoor environment to a relatively cold, exposed, outdoor environment. The hardening-off process requires several days in a cold frame so that when the transplants finally make the full transition to their garden locations, they can withstand unexpected temperature fluctuations. A cold frame—usually consisting of an aluminum frame with a vented glass top that opens automatically on warm, sunny days so the seedlings don't burn—can be purchased from mail-order garden suppliers and local garden centers. A makeshift cold frame can be easily constructed by using plastic sheeting stretched over wire hoops. Or, seedlings can simply be left in an unheated porch area for several days before going into the garden.

Today, there are many seed-starting units available. Below is an evaluation of each one.

Peat Pellets These consist of compressed peat, and come in two types: the Jiffy-7 peat pellet, the peat being bound together with a plastic netting, and the Jiffy-9 peat pellet, which has no netting and is held together with an invisible "binder." You place both types in a shallow tray of water where they soak up the moisture and expand to several times their original height. They become soft and have a depression in the top for sowing seeds. Both kinds have a tendency to dry out rather quickly unless kept out of direct sunlight and enclosed in plastic bags. Also, plants grown in the Jiffy-7 peat pellets generally do better if the netting is gently removed, otherwise it can inhibit root development. These peat pellets are inexpensive and available in kit form with watering tray and plastic dome included.

Peat Pots These are either square or round. The square pots are joined at the lip, and choosing them over the round pots allows you to fill a large number at a time with potting soil. These pots need to be filled with planting soil and kept

moist. As the plants grow, the roots will actually penetrate the sides of the pot; soon after transplanting, the peat decomposes to give the roots freedom to grow. However, even with this feature of rapidly biodegradable peat sides, it is still a good practice to gently tear out the bottom of these peat pots to allow the roots greater freedom, so the plant becomes more quickly established in its outdoor location.

Preplanters If you don't want to fuss with potting soil and filling pots, then you may want to buy preplanters. These are sold under different brand names, such as Seed 'n Start and Punch 'n Grow, and can be found at garden centers. They are simply compartmented seed trays already filled with potting soil, with seeds sown into the upper soil surface. All that's required is that you place the unit in a sunny indoor location and add water. This is not the most economical way to grow a lot of annuals, since you are paying for a lot of convenience and very little seed.

Seed Tapes are another example of a product that is very convenient, but grows little seed in comparison to a traditional seed packet. The seed is prespaced along a biodegradable tape. As soon as the tape is covered over and moistened it decomposes, giving the seeds freedom to germinate at uniform distances. This system is fine if you want to grow all your flowers in straight lines—as in a cutting garden—but if you prefer to grow them in clumps or drifts of color, there isn't much benefit in using seed tape.

Plastic Pots, like peat pots, can be round or square, with the square pots generally taking up less room than the round pots. If the pots are not connected, they fit comfortably into a square seed flat. Plastic pots can be obtained in groups of six, often referred to as a "six-pack." It is quite an easy matter to detach the pots one at a time by turning them over and, by tapping sharply, the root ball will slip out for easy transplanting. Plastic pots are inexpensive, especially when bought in quantity, and they are an economical way to grow large numbers of annuals.

Plastic and Peat Seed Trays When you are fussing with starting fine seeds such as petunias and begonias, plastic and peat seed trays are the preferred choice. You simply fill them with potting soil, sow the seeds thinly over the surface, and then transfer the strongest plants into individual pots as soon as they are large enough to handle (you will be able to pull

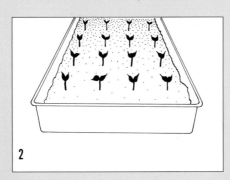

1

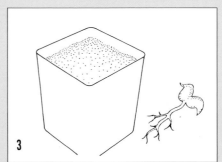

2

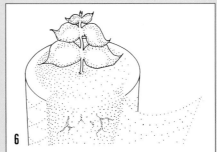

3

1. Place seeds in individual compartments of a plastic six-pack.

2. Thin seedlings to one per compartment.

3. Press bottom of flexible plastic compartment to pop out each root ball for transplanting.

SEED-STARTING METHOD #3

1. Place seeds in fiber or peat pot.

2. Thin to one plant per pot. Let roots penetrate sides.

3. Tear out bottom of pot prior to planting.

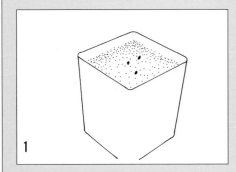

4

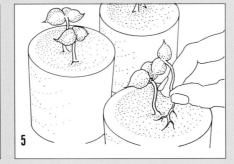

5

6

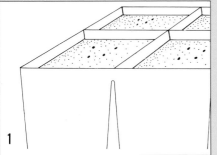

1

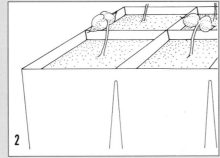

2

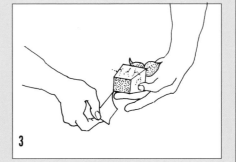

3

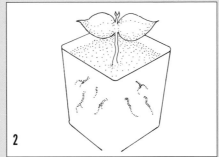

1

2

3

A. M. Georgens

SMALL SEEDS—STARTING METHOD #1

1. Pour seeds into teaspoon directly from packet.

2. Pick up seeds individually with the end of a moist pencil.

3. Place seeds in rows on a moist paper towel.

4. Roll towel loosely. Keep warm and moist. Most fine seeds need light to germinate.

5. Examine towel after required germination period.

6. Use end of moist pencil and forefinger to pick seedlings off towel. Transfer to individual peat pots.

A. M. Georgens

them up using a pencil and forefinger). Avoid watering with a strong flow of water, such as from a watering can, because this will disturb the soil surface and hamper germination. It is better to keep the soil moist with a "mister" or a bottle that applies droplets of water.

Direct-Seeding of certain fast-growing flowering annuals is an easy system. Marigolds (*tagetes*), zinnias, calendula, alyssum, and celosia are examples of annuals which can be sown directly onto bare soil, lightly covered, and left to germinate without any need for starting indoors. The hardy varieties, such as calendula, can be sown several weeks before the last frost date in your area, and tender varieties, such as zinnias and marigolds can be sown after the last frost date. Before sowing the seed outdoors, take a stick or handful of flour and mark out the area designated for each different type of seed. Then take the seeds from your seed packet and scatter them so they fill the space. In the absence of natural rainfall, set a lawn sprinkler in position so that the area gets a good drink of water. Water anytime the soil looks dry, until the seedlings are up and well established.

BUYING QUALITY TRANSPLANTS

Ready-grown transplants from bedding plant outlets, such as garden centers, are a strong temptation for many good reasons, primarily the time, effort, and expense saved from fussing with seeds. However, the selection offered by these outlets is a fraction of what you might expect to find in a good mail-order seed catalog, and you will probably not be able to find anything rare or unusual. But, buying bedding plants is the closest you can come to instant color in your garden. In fact, the majority of varieties offered are likely to have at least a few flowers, so you will be able to make accurate color selections and judge the shape and size of the blooms.

Actually, the best transplants to buy are those that are not yet in bloom. Buy green and the resulting plant in your garden is likely to overcome transplant shock more easily, put on a growth spurt that catches up with the flowering transplants, and produce a greater density of color over a longer period of time.

Also, look for stocky plants rather than those that are long and lanky. When a plant is under stress—either from infrequent watering, poor light, or disease—it will often become stretched, and when transplanted to the garden may droop from transplant shock and take a long time to recover.

The best transplants are generally compact and stocky, with a dark green leaf color. Examine the leaf undersides for any signs of pest colonies such as aphids or mealybugs. Feel the potting soil and determine if it is moist or bone dry: Plants in bone dry soil may already have suffered root damage.

After you load up your car with bedding plants, go straight home and transplant your purchases as soon as possible. Do not go to the grocery store and shop, leaving the plants in a hot car where they can wilt and burn quickly once the car starts to overheat.

If any of the plants you purchase have a lead shoot that is doing all of the growing, pinch it back after you transplant so that the plant is encouraged to branch sideways and grow bushier. After transplanting, water all your plants. Be careful! that tender varieties are transplanted after all danger of frost is over. If frost threatens, consider covering them with floating row covers—inexpensive, lightweight, see-through covers that rest on top of the plants and offer protection against unexpected light frost.

SOIL PREPARATION FOR ANNUALS

The most important requirement for a successful garden of annuals is proper soil preparation. Although many annuals are native to desert regions and can survive in impoverished soils, the best displays are produced by ensuring that the soil is reasonably fertile and well drained. The soil texture should be crumbly and allow freedom of root movement to a depth of at least twelve inches. Clay loam or sandy loam are both good for growing annuals, but in soil that contains a large amount of clay, adding organic matter will improve its texture. Similarly, if soil is too sandy—allowing moisture and plant nutrients to drain away too quickly—then adding liberal amounts of organic matter is essential. The best kind of organic matter is garden compost, but bales of peat, leaf

SMALL SEEDS—STARTING METHOD #2

1. Sprinkle seeds on surface of peat pellet so surface is covered. Press seeds into surface lightly, but do not cover. Keep moist and warm.

2. When seeds have all sprouted, tear away the pellet netting.

3. Submerge pellet in bowl of water. Soil and seedlings will separate. Seedling will float.

4. Using moist pencil point and forefinger, gently lift seedlings individually.

5. Transfer to individual peat pots filled with planting mix.

6. When plants reach transplanting size, peat pot can be planted directly into the garden to allow freedom for roots.

mold, and well-decomposed animal manure are also suitable.

Soil Test

A soil test will help you determine the nature of your soil. Your county cooperative extension office can test soil for you to determine its pH and the nutrients you should add. Mix the needed organic matter into the soil by digging it over and raking in the organic ingredients. If the soil needs lime (in highly acidic soils) or sulphur (in highly alkaline soils), you can add them when you are working in the organic material.

SITE SELECTION, IRRIGATION, AND AFTER CARE

Once the soil has been improved so that it is loose and fertile, and has a pH content as close to neutral as possible, you must keep it in good condition by applying compost. If the soil is not in good condition the following suggestions may help: modify the light, provide sufficient moisture, booster the applications of fertilizer, control pests and diseases, and weed the soil.

Site selection greatly depends on light, since an open meadow will produce more light than a wooded lot. However, even the removal of a single tree limb on a shaded site can be sufficient to turn a shady spot into a sunny one.

Irrigation and water retention can also make a big difference in the performance of plants that like cool conditions. If the soil is kept cool by a high humus content and watered regularly to keep it moist, shade-loving annuals, such as impatiens, coleus, and begonias, will grow in a sunny location.

Sun or Shade

Most flowering annuals prefer full sun, although there are some shade-loving varieties, such as impatiens and coleus (check list on page 91). Annuals can also be divided into cool-season annuals and warm-season annuals. Generally speaking, cool-season annuals, such as antirrhinum and calendula, are hardy and flower best during spring and early summer when the nights are still cool, or in coastal areas and high elevations where summers are mild. Conversely, warm-season annuals, such as impatiens and zinnias, are generally tender, and are damaged by frost. They grow best when the soil temperature rises and the hours of sunlight are extended. Check the individual variety descriptions, starting on page 91 to determine whether a variety is tender or hardy, warm-season or cool-season.

Irrigation

Regular amounts of water are especially important in the early stages of growth as transplants are struggling to become established. Most flowering annuals should not be watered by overhead sprinklers, since this encourages mildew and other fungal diseases; but, in the event of a drought it is better than nothing. Drip irrigation, whereby soaker hoses lay along the soil surface, covered over with a protective mulch, is the best way to irrigate flowering annuals in the absence of natural rainfall.

After Care

Fertilizer Flowering annuals are not heavy feeders in comparison to vegetables and flowering perennials. A granular, general purpose fertilizer—such as 10-10-10—raked into the upper soil surface at the start of the season, is generally sufficient to provide all the nourishment annuals need to maintain continuous bloom. (The numbers on a package of fertilizer tell you the percentages of each major plant nutrient. In this case, the fertilizer is composed of 10 percent nitrogen, 10 percent phosphorus, and 10 percent potassium. The rest is "filler," which serves as a distributing agent.) In addition to granular fertilizers, liquid fertilizers applied to the soil surface work just as well. Care should be taken that beds and borders are not overloaded with nitrogen, since this can stimulate excessive foliage growth at the expense of flowers. Nasturtiums and marigolds, for example, are particularly susceptible to excessive nitrogen.

Compost is a wonderful product to add to flower beds or borders. Well made compost not only acts as a soil conditioner so the soil is always loose and crumbly, but it also acts as a natural fertilizer. Start a compost pile in a corner of your garden simply by piling garden and kitchen waste into a heap. The best compost is made from a balance of fresh green material (such as grass clippings, leafy green hedge trimmings, potato peels, and freshly pulled weeds) plus "dead" material (such as wood ashes, sawdust, dried leaves, animal manure, and bone meal). The fresh green material provides mostly nitrogen, while the dead material produces phosphorus (especially bone meal) and potassium (especially wood ashes). Compost made from a balance of organic wastes also provides desirable trace elements, such as calcium, and when well decomposed has a pH close to neutral. Add compost to your soil twice a year if possible—in spring before transplanting, and again in autumn after the beds are cleared.

Diseases It is impossible to protect annuals from every potential disease problem. However, in areas of the country where mildew and botrytis can be problematic, consider a general purpose fungicide, such as Benlate or Benomyl. Spraying every three to four weeks can make a tremendous difference in the health and vitality of your plants—especially zinnias and geraniums which are quite vulnerable to fungus attacks. Be careful when choosing sprays, as many are hazardous to the environment. Many fungicides, however, are "organic" and after they lose their effectiveness decompose without leaving toxic substances in the atmosphere or the soil. Certain insect sprays are also "organic" (such as sprays made from rotenone, pyrethrum, or a combination of the two), and break down into harmless compost a short time after application. However, it is important to read the label of even "organic" controls to determine whether they must be kept away from children, pets, or fish, and how to dispose of unused portions.

Pests Probably the two most troublesome pests are slugs, which attack transplants during periods of wet weather, and deer (or other foraging animals), which feast on a flower bed as nonchalantly as if it were a field of corn. Slugs are best brought under control by using slug bait, available from garden centers.

Deer—and other hungry animals—are best kept out of flower beds by spraying them with a product such as Ropel, which makes the plants distasteful. Ropel must not be used on edible plants, but for ornamentals it is really the only effective deer control short of building a high fence around your property. The spray acts as a systemic, making all parts of the plant unpalatable, yet it has no odor. It remains effective up to three months.

Weeding Beds and borders for flowering annuals must be kept clear of weeds, otherwise the weeds will take over. The most effective method of weed control is a mulch applied to the soil surface after transplants are set into position; this way the annuals can grow but the weeds are suffocated. Organic mulches, such as shredded bark, cocoa-bean hulls, and shredded leaves, are both decorative and effective, though they may need topping-up as wind and weather wears the layer thin. A durable alternative is a mulch blanket that rests on top of the soil and is colored brown to look like soil. Mulch blankets are anchored at the edges with soil, and annuals are planted through it by cutting holes with scissors. Black plastic is popular as a mulch blanket because it is inexpensive; to hide its ugly appearance a thin layer of organic mulch can be spread over the top of it.

GROWING ANNUALS IN CONTAINERS

No flowering plants thrive better in containers than flowering annuals. In comparison to flowering perennials, flowering bulbs, vegetables, and small shrubs, annuals require less room for roots and they bloom for far longer periods. Even people who have plenty of room for an in-ground garden use containers because they can decorate concrete patios and wood decks, bringing color much closer to the house. Windows too can be filled with color by using window boxes and hanging baskets.

Generally speaking, the bigger the container the easier it is to grow annuals. Small containers have a tendency to dry out too quickly, so choose units with adequate space and soil depth. Generally speaking, anything less than a one gallon capacity will need watering daily. Garden centers offer a wide

choice of containers, but it's a lot more fun to rummage through flea markets and secondhand stores for some offbeat containers, such as rusty old cauldrons and horse troughs. Select containers with drainage holes in them, since the roots will rot if water doesn't drain freely. If drainage holes don't exist—and you cannot bore them into the container yourself—then consider a layer of crushed stones and charcoal in the bottom as a "drainage field," taking care that you don't apply more water than the drainage area can hold.

Select only containers made of problem-free materials. For example, unless they are situated in a shaded area, plastic and steel can overheat and burn delicate root hairs on hot, sunny days. Better alternatives to these two are clay, ceramic, or wood, since all of these materials tend to keep the soil cool.

The best soil for containers is a blend of a commercial peat-based potting soil, such as Pro-Mix, with some good garden loam. This combination provides good anchorage and moisture holding capacity. If you are using wooden containers—such as whiskey half barrels—consider lining the inside with a plastic garbage bag so the soil is kept clear of the wood to resist rotting.

Unless hanging baskets are in a cool, shady area plastic is not as good as a wire basket that has moist sphagnum moss lining the edges. Hanging baskets are especially prone to overheating and drying out, because of the free air circulation around them, but the moist sphagnum helps prevent rapid evaporation. Also, plants can be pushed through the sides of the basket to give a rounded, well filled look compared to a plastic basket that can only be planted around the upper rim.

Although just about every kind of annual can be grown in some kind of container, plant breeders have developed special kinds of annuals to look extremely attractive in both pots and hanging baskets. When considering annuals for containers, pay particular attention to those described as "cascading," for example cascading lobelia and cascading petunias. Instead of growing up, they tend to grow sideways and spill down over the edges of a pot or hanging basket so that the container can be completely hidden with foliage or flowers.

Beds & Borders Annuals can be displayed at their best in beds and borders. Generally, a bed is any plot of soil surrounded on all sides by paving or lawn, and is capable of

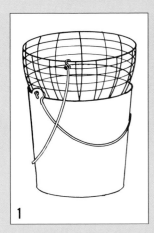 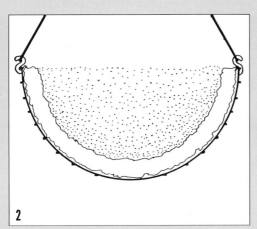 

A. M. Georgens

Opposite page: The 'Futura' variety of impatiens makes a beautiful, colorful hanging basket in a partially shaded location.
Left: Three stages of preparing a hanging basket: (1) place wire basket over a bucket to keep it stable while filling; (2) line inside of wire basket with moist sphagnum moss like a nest, then fill the nest with potting soil; (3) the finished basket is shown here planted with an assortment of annuals.

being viewed from many directions. Beds can be round, square, rectangular, oval, or kidney-shaped. A border usually backs up to something vertical—such as a hedge, fence, or wall—and it is most often viewed from one direction, or from an angle.

To facilitate drainage, beds are often mounded in the middle, and for best display the tallest plants are also situated in the middle. In a bed, the shortest plants—called "edging" plants—are placed around the perimeter. With borders the soil is usually highest in back, and that is where the tallest plants are placed. Edging plants are placed at the front of the border, with medium-height plants sandwiched between the tall background plants and low edging plants.

Annuals are frequently mixed with perennials in perennial borders, rock gardens, and water gardens in order to maintain color throughout the season as the perennials come in and out of bloom. For example, in a perennial border alyssum, ageratum, and dwarf begonias are popular to use for edging, while cleome, sunflowers (*Helianthus annuus*), and snapdragons (*Antirrhinum majus*) are popular for tall highlights. Cosmos, salvia farinacea, and American marigolds (*Tagetes erecta*) are examples of medium-height annuals that combine well with perennials.

In rock gardens, low-growing plants like verbena, alyssum, dahlberg daisy (*Dyssodia tenuilobia*), and nasturtiums can turn an average planting of perennials into something vibrant and special.

For making water gardens more colorful—especially the margins of ponds and streambanks—try some of the new mixtures of mimulus (monkey flowers), along with impatients, coleus, begonias, and browallia.

Cutting Garden Many people like to grow annuals solely for the sake of cutting them to make lovely indoor flower arrangements, but dislike taking them from beds and borders. It makes sense, therefore, to set aside a special area to grow plants specially for cutting. Usually, this area is located near the vegetable garden so that flowers for the house and edibles for the kitchen can be gathered together.

A good layout for cutting gardens is the "straight-row" system often used in vegetable gardens. Annuals can be grown in fifteen foot rows (or longer), with walkways between each row to make gathering the flowers easy. The best cutting gardens have a balance between long-stemmed flowers suitable for fresh arrangements—such as marigolds (*Tagetes*), zinnias, and snapdragons (*Antirrhinum*)—and "everlastings,"—such as strawflowers (*Helichrysum*), immortelle (*Xeranthemum*), and globe amaranth (*Gomphrena*)—which are easily dried to make dried flower arrangements.

CHAPTER TWO

THE ENCYCLOPEDIA OF ESSENTIAL ANNUALS

THE FOLLOWING 100 SUPERLATIVE ANNUALS for garden display have been chosen mostly for their ornamental value.

They are listed alphabetically by their botanical (Latin) name because this most consistently identifies garden annuals better than their common names. While many annuals have popular common names—'French Marigold' for *Tagetes patula*—others do not have such familiar common names or else are widely known by two or more common names—*Impatiens wallerana,* for example is often called plain 'Impatiens,' 'Busy Lizzies,' or 'Patience Plant.'

To find a description for any annual where you know only the common name, simply turn to the index for a quick cross-reference.

The heights given are mostly mature heights when the plants start to flower. Often, with good soil or prolonged rainfall, or late in the season, plants may exceed the heights stated here.

BOTANICAL NAME *Ageratum houstonianum*

COMMON NAME Floss Flower

RANGE Native to Central America. Tender annual.

HEIGHT 12 inches; mounded habit.

CULTURE Easy to grow in well-drained, garden loam soil in full sun. Start seeds indoors at 70° to 75°F and set 8-week-old transplants, spaced 8 inches apart, into the soil after all danger of frost.

DESCRIPTION Fluffy mauve-pink, blue, or white flower clusters bloom all summer on compact plants. Leaves are broad, oval, pointed, dark green. Excellent for edging beds and borders.

RECOMMENDED VARIETY Blue Danube, a lovely blue hybrid variety.

BOTANICAL NAME *Amaranthus tricolor*

COMMON NAME Joseph's-coat

RANGE Native to Mexico. Tender annual.

HEIGHT 3 to 4 feet; erect habit.

CULTURE Easy to grow in any well-drained, garden loam soil in full sun. Start seed indoors at 70° to 75°F and set 6-week-old-transplants, spaced 12 inches apart, into the garden after all danger of frost.

DESCRIPTION The top most leaves, colored red, orange, green, and yellow, arch out like a fountain. A popular accent for mixed beds and borders.

RECOMMENDED VARIETY 'Illumination' old leaves are chocolate colored; new leaves are brilliant orange-red.

BOTANICAL NAME *Anchusa capensis*

COMMON NAME Summer Forget-me-not

RANGE Native to South America. Biennial grown as hardy annual.

HEIGHT 12 inches; low, mounded habit.

CULTURE Easy to grow in any well-drained loam soil in full sun. Start seed at 60°F and set out 6- to 8-week-old transplants, spaced 6 to 12 inches apart, several weeks before the last frost date. Flowers best when nights are cool.

DESCRIPTION Blue flowers are clustered on branching stems. Leaves are bright green, lancelike. Good to use for edging beds and borders.

BOTANICAL NAME *Antirrhinum majus*

COMMON NAME Snapdragon

RANGE Native to the Mediterranean. Hardy annual.

HEIGHT Up to 3 feet; erect, spirelike habit.

CULTURE Start seed indoors at 70° to 75°F and set 8-week-old transplants, spaced 12 inches apart, into the garden after danger of heavy frosts.

DESCRIPTION Tubular flowers are arranged in spikes, some with closed mouths, others with open throats. Colors include red, yellow, orange, pink, white, and bicolors. Leaves are narrow, lancelike, dark green. Excellent for mass plantings in beds and borders. Tall kinds, such as the 'Rockets' are good for cutting. Dwarf kinds, such as 'Floral Carpet' are excellent for edging and low beds.

BOTANICAL NAME *Arctotis stoechadifolia*

COMMON NAME African Daisy

RANGE Native to South Africa. Tender annual.

HEIGHT 12 to 15 inches; clump-forming habit.

CULTURE Easy to grow in any fertile, well-drained loam soil in full sun. Prefers cool nights. Start seed indoors with the soil temperature at 60° to 70°F, and set 6- to 8-week-old transplants, spaced 12 inches apart, into the garden after all danger of frost. Also can be direct-seeded.

DESCRIPTION Daisy-like flowers are borne on slender stems in yellow, orange, red, and pink, plus bicolors. Leaves are bright green, toothed. Popular for mixed beds and borders, especially in coastal gardens. Good for cutting.

BOTANICAL NAME *Begonia* x *semperflorens*

COMMON NAME Wax Begonia

RANGE Native to South America. Tender annual.

HEIGHT 8 to 12 inches; low, compact habit.

CULTURE Prefers moist, humus-rich, fertile loam soil in partial shade. Hybrids will tolerate full sun. Start seed indoors at 70° to 85°F soil temperature and set 10- to 12-week-old transplants, spaced 6 to 10 inches apart, into the garden after all danger of frost.

DESCRIPTION Masses of white, pink, or red flowers cover mound-shaped plants, with either bright green or bronze foliage, depending on variety. Exceptional for massing in beds and borders. Also good for containers, including hanging baskets.

RECOMMENDED VARIETY 'Cocktail' series, featuring bronze foliage.

BOTANICAL NAME *Brachycome iberidifolia*

COMMON NAME Swan River Daisy

RANGE Native to Australia. Tender annual.

HEIGHT 12 inches; bushy, mounded habit.

CULTURE Prefers a moist, fertile, humus-rich loam soil in full sun. Flowers best when nights are cool. Start seeds indoors at 60° to 70°F soil temperature and set 6-week-old transplants, spaced 12 inches apart, into the garden after all danger of frost.

DESCRIPTION Covers itself in blue or white daisy-like flowers. Leaves are small, toothed, dark green. Good for massing in mixed beds and borders. Popular in coastal gardens.

BOTANICAL NAME *Brassica oleracea*

COMMON NAME Ornamental Cabbage; Ornamental Kale

RANGE Developed from species native to Europe. Hardy annual.

HEIGHT 12 inches; low, mound-shaped habit.

CULTURE Easy to grow in any well-drained, fertile loam soil in full sun. Does best when nights are cool. Start seeds indoors at 65° to 85°F soil temperature and plant 6- to 8-week-old transplants, spaced 12 inches apart, in the garden several weeks before the last expected frost date.

DESCRIPTION Mostly white or pink frilly leaves form a decorative rosette at the center of cabbagelike plants; all other leaves are blue-green. Popular for edging beds and borders and for massing. Good for fall color since the plants like cool temperatures and withstand heavy frosts.

BOTANICAL NAME *Browallia speciosa*

COMMON NAME Lovely Browallia

RANGE Native to South America. Tender annual.

HEIGHT 12 inches; mounded, bushy habit.

CULTURE Prefers a moist, fertile, humus-rich soil in partial shade. Start seed indoors at 70° to 85°F soil temperature and set 8- to 10-week-old transplants, spaced 12 inches apart, into the garden after all danger of frost.

DESCRIPTION Masses of blue or white flowers resembling small petunias cover the plants all summer. Leaves are lancelike, delicate, bright green. Suitable for massing in shady beds and borders. Popular for containers, especially hanging baskets.

RECOMMENDED VARIETY 'Blue Bells Improved.'

BOTANICAL NAME *Calendula officinalis*

COMMON NAME Pot-marigold

RANGE Native to the Mediterranean. Hardy annual.

HEIGHT 12 inches; bushy habit.

CULTURE Easy to grow in any well-drained loam soil in full sun. Does best when nights are cool. Start seeds indoors at 70°F soil temperature and set 6-week-old transplants, spaced 12 inches apart, into the garden several weeks before the last expected frost. Also can be direct-seeded.

DESCRIPTION Mostly yellow and orange double flowers held erect on stiff stems. Leaves are dark green, indented, have a spicy odor. Suitable for mixed beds and borders.

RECOMMENDED VARIETY: 'Pacific Beauty.'

BOTANICAL NAME *Callistephus chinensis*

COMMON NAME China Aster

RANGE Native to China. Tender annual.

HEIGHT 1 to 3 feet; upright, branching habit.

CULTURE Easy to grow in any fertile, well-drained loam soil in full sun. Start seed indoors at 60° to 70°F soil temperature and set out 6-week-old transplants, spaced 12 inches apart, after all danger of frost. Flowers best when nights are cool.

DESCRIPTION Double- and semi-double chrysanthemum-like flowers are mostly red, pink, white, and blue. Leaves are dark green, serrated. Popular as an accent in beds and borders. Dwarf types, such as 'Dwarf Queen' are suitable for edging. Tall kinds, such as 'Giant Perfection' are excellent for cutting.

BOTANICAL NAME *Capsicum annuum*

COMMON NAME Ornamental Pepper

RANGE Native to South America. Tender annual.

HEIGHT 10 inches; compact, bushy habit.

CULTURE Prefers fertile, well-drained, sandy loam soil in full sun. Start seeds indoors at 70° to 85°F soil temperature and set 8 to 10 week-old transplants into the garden, spaced 8 inches apart, after all danger of frost.

DESCRIPTION Low, mounded plants cover themselves with round or cone-shaped fruits that ripen from green to orange and red. Excellent for edging beds and borders, also for growing in containers.

RECOMMENDED VARIETY 'Holiday Cheer' bears round, marble-size fruit.

BOTANICAL NAME *Catharanthus roseus*

COMMON NAME Vinca; Periwinkle

RANGE Native to Madagascar. Tender annual.

HEIGHT 12 inches; low, spreading habit.

CULTURE Easy to grow in any well-drained, fertile loam soil in full sun or partial shade. Drought tolerant. Start seeds indoors at 70° to 85°F and set 10-week-old transplants into the garden, spaced 12 inches apart, after all danger of frost.

DESCRIPTION Star-shaped flowers are flowering continuously. Blossoms are mostly white, pink, or purple with contrasting red centers on plants that freely branch sideways. Glossy, dark green, broad, pointed leaves look like evergreen needles. Popular for edging beds and borders, also as a ground cover and for cascading from window boxes.

RECOMMENDED VARIETY 'Little Linda' is a prolific, flowering purple.

BOTANICAL NAME *Celosia cristata*

COMMON NAME Crested Cockscomb

RANGE Native to Asia. Tender annual.

HEIGHT Up to 3 feet; erect, bushy habit.

CULTURE Easy to grow in any fertile, well-drained loam soil in full sun. Start seeds indoors at 70° to 85°F soil temperature and set 5-week-old transplants into the garden, spaced 12 inches apart, after all danger of frost. Older transplants tend to suffer shock. Also can be direct-seeded.

DESCRIPTION The flowers of crested cockscomb resemble lumps of brain coral held erect above long, spear-shaped, green leaves. Good for massing in beds and borders. Excellent for cutting and drying for arrangements.

RECOMMENDED VARIETY 'Floradale' bears large globular heads on compact plants.

RELATED SPECIES *C. plumosa* bears flowers that resemble feathery plumes.

BOTANICAL NAME *Centaurea cyanus*

COMMON NAME Bachelor's-button; Cornflower

RANGE Native to Europe. Hardy annual.

HEIGHT 3 feet; erect habit.

CULTURE Easy to grow in any well-drained loam soil in full sun. Start seed indoors at 70°F soil temperature and set 4-week-old transplants into the garden. Older transplants tend to wilt. Also can be direct-seeded.

DESCRIPTION Mostly blue, white, pink, or red flowers are held erect on slender stems. Leaves are dark green, lancelike. Popular for mixed beds and borders, also for wildflower meadow gardens. Excellent for cutting.

RECOMMENDED VARIETY 'Blue Diadem' bears large blue flowers.

BOTANICAL NAME *Chrysanthemum carinatum*

COMMON NAME Painted Daisy

RANGE Native to Morocco. Hardy annual.

HEIGHT 3 feet; erect, bushy habit.

CULTURE Easy to grow in any well-drained, fertile loam soil in full sun. Start seed indoors at 60° to 70°F soil temperature and set 6-week-old transplants into the garden, spaced 12 inches apart, 3 weeks before the last expected frost date. Also can be direct-seeded.

DESCRIPTION Daisy-like flowers are ringed with several bands of contrasting colors, mostly in variations of red, white, and yellow. Leaves are dark green, toothed. Good for mixed beds and borders. Often included in wildflower meadow mixtures. Excellent for cutting.

RECOMMENDED VARIETY 'Rainbow Mixed Colors.'

BOTANICAL NAME *Clarkia amoena*

COMMON NAME Godetia; Satin Flower

RANGE Native to California. Hardy annual.

HEIGHT 12 inches; bushy, clump-forming habit.

CULTURE Easy to grow in any well-drained loam soil in full sun. Thrives best when direct-seeded. If desired, start seed indoors at 60°F soil temperature and set out 6-week-old transplants, spaced 12 inches apart, several weeks before the last frost date. Older plants suffer transplant shock. Flowers best when nights are cool.

DESCRIPTION Lovely, cup-shaped flowers with crinkled petals and a satinlike sheen cover the plants in early summer. Colors include white, pink, red, purple, and bicolors. Leaves are narrow, pointed, dark green. Popular in coastal gardens for beds and borders.

RECOMMENDED VARIETY 'Dwarf Mixed Colors.'

BOTANICAL NAME *Cleome hasslerana*

COMMON NAME Spiderflower

RANGE Native to Central America. Tender annual.

HEIGHT Up to 5 feet; tall, spirelike habit.

CULTURE Easy to grow in any well-drained loam soil in full sun. Start seed indoors at 70° to 85°F soil temperature and set out 6-week-old transplants, spaced 12 inches apart, after all danger of frost.

DESCRIPTION Ball-shaped flower heads have a spidery appearance from long, slender filaments that support the flowers, and pointed seed pods that project beyond the flowers. Color range includes pink, white, and purple. Leaves are deeply indented, dark green. Popular as a background in beds and borders. Also suitable for cutting.

BOTANICAL NAME *Cobaea scandens*

COMMON NAME Cup-and-saucer vine

RANGE Native to Central America. Tender annual.

HEIGHT Up to 10 feet; vining habit.

CULTURE Easy to grow in any fertile, well-drained loam soil in full sun. Start seeds indoors at 70° to 85°F soil temperature and set out 6- to 8-week-old transplants, spaced 3 feet apart, after all danger of frost. Needs support to climb.

DESCRIPTION Unusual flowers resemble Canterbury Bells, and are pollinated by bats in their native lands. Colors include violet-blue, purple, and white-tinted pink or green. Mostly used to cover chain-link fences or train on a trellis or wall.

BOTANICAL NAME *Coleus* x *hybrida*

COMMON NAME Coleus

RANGE Native to Indonesia. Tender annual.

HEIGHT 2 feet; bushy habit.

CULTURE Prefers fertile, humus-rich, moist loam soil in partial shade. Start seed indoors at 70° to 85°F soil temperature and set out 8- to 10-week-old transplants, spaced 12 inches apart, after all danger of frost, in partial shade.

DESCRIPTION Grown mostly for the vibrant color of its leaves, sometimes three contrasting colors appear together, with no two leaves exactly alike. Colors include yellow, red, orange, lime green, dark green, and mahogany. The decorative appearance of the leaves is often enhanced by scalloped or ruffled margins. Popular for beds and borders, also containers, including hanging baskets.

BOTANICAL NAME *Consolida ambigua*

COMMON NAME Larkspur

RANGE Native to Southern Europe. Hardy annual.

HEIGHT 3 feet; upright, spirelike habit.

CULTURE Easy to grow in any fertile, well-drained loam soil in full sun. Start seed indoors at 60° to 70°F and set out 6- to 8-week-old transplants, spaced 12 inches apart, after danger of frost. Also can be direct-seeded. May need staking.

DESCRIPTION Beautiful flower spikes resemble small delphinium. Color range includes white, blue, purple, and pink. Leaves are fern-like. Good as tall backgrounds for beds and borders. Excellent for cutting, and for dried flower arrangements.

BOTANICAL NAME *Coreopsis tinctoria*

COMMON NAME Calliopsis

RANGE Native to North America. Hardy annual.

HEIGHT 1 to 2 feet; bushy habit.

CULTURE Easy to grow in any fertile, well-drained loam soil in full sun. Start seed indoors at 70°F soil temperature and set out 6-week-old transplants, spaced 12 inches apart, after all danger of frost.

DESCRIPTION Produces an abundance of daisy-like flowers on airy plants with fine, green leaves. Colors include yellow, orange, red, and mahogany, plus bicolors. Good for beds and borders, also for wildflower meadows. Tall kinds suitable for cutting.

RECOMMENDED VARIETY 'Dwarf Mixed Colors' grow compact, mound plants (6 to 8 inches) suitable for edging.

BOTANICAL NAME *Cosmos bipinnatus*

COMMON NAME Cosmos

RANGE Native to Mexico. Tender annual.

HEIGHT 3 to 5 feet; upright, branching habit.

CULTURE Easy to grow in any fertile, well-drained loam soil in full sun. Start seed indoors at 70° to 85°F soil temperature and set out 6-week-old transplants, spaced 12 inches apart, after all danger of frost. Also can be direct-seeded.

DESCRIPTION Flowers resemble single-flowered Dahlias on airy plants with fine, feathery leaves. Color range includes red, white, pink, and bicolors. Good for tall backgrounds in beds and borders, also for wildflower meadows. Excellent for cutting.

RECOMMENDED VARIETY 'Sensation' mixed colors.

RELATED SPECIES *C. sulphureus*, including 'Diablo' with deep orange flowers and 'Sunny Gold,' a dwarf yellow just 12 inches high.

BOTANICAL NAME *Cucurbita pepo*

COMMON NAME Ornamental Gourds

RANGE Native to South America. Tender annual.

HEIGHT 10 feet; vining habit.

CULTURE Easy to grow in any well-drained loam soil in full sun. Start seed at 70° to 85°F and set out 4-week-old transplants, spaced at least 3 feet apart, after danger of frost.

DESCRIPTION Vigorous vines with heart-shaped leaves are grown mostly for the decorative fruit, which vary not only in shape but also in their color combinations. Some fruit are shaped like apples, pears, and oranges with beige, yellow, orange, and green coloring. Flowers are yellow, inconspicuous. Good for covering trellises and fences. A similar gourd species *Lagenaria siceria* ('Bottle Gourds') are popular for making bird houses and dippers.

BOTANICAL NAME *Cynoglossum amabile*

COMMON NAME Chinese Forget-me-not

RANGE Native to China. Hardy annual.

HEIGHT 2 feet; clump-forming habit.

CULTURE Easy to grow in any fertile, well-drained loam soil. Start seed at 70° to 85°F and set out 8-week-old transplants, spaced 12 inches apart, several weeks before the last expected frost date.

DESCRIPTION Dainty, star-shaped flowers resemble forget-me-nots, vary in color from deep blue to pale blue to white. Good accent for mixed beds and borders. Suitable for cutting.

BOTANICAL NAME *Dahlia* x *hybrida*

COMMON NAME Bedding Dahlias

RANGE Native to Mexico. Tender annual.

HEIGHT 1 to 3 feet; upright, bushy habit.

CULTURE Prefers a moist, fertile, humus-rich loam soil in full sun. Start seeds indoors at 60°F soil temperature and set out 8-week-old transplants, spaced 12 inches apart, after all danger of frost.

DESCRIPTION Single or double flowers have mostly rounded petals. Color range includes yellow, white, orange, pink, red, and mahogany. Leaves can be bright green or bronze in color. Good for massing in beds and borders. Excellent for cutting.

RECOMMENDED VARIETY 'Rigoletto,' with a dwarf, compact habit and wide color range. Not to be confused with tuberous dahlias which are taller and capable of growing flowers the size of dinner plates.

BOTANICAL NAME *Datura metel*

COMMON NAME Angel's Trumpet

RANGE Native to South America. Tender annual.

HEIGHT 2 to 3 feet; mounded, sprawling habit.

CULTURE Easy to grow in any well-drained loam or sandy soil in full sun. Start seed at 70° to 85°F and set out 6-week-old transplants, spaced at least 2 feet apart, after all danger of frost.

DESCRIPTION White trumpet-shaped flowers up to 6 inches long are borne freely all summer. Dark green leaves are spear-shaped. Good accent for mixed beds and borders. Suitable for growing in containers. **Caution:** all parts are poisonous.

BOTANICAL NAME *Delphinium elatum*

COMMON NAME Delphinium

RANGE Native to Northern Europe. Biennials best treated as hardy annuals.

HEIGHT 3 to 5 feet; spirelike habit.

CULTURE Prefers a moist, fertile, humus-rich loam soil in full sun and sheltered from winds. Start seed indoors at 70° to 80°F soil temperature and set out 12-week-old transplants several weeks before the last expected frost date. Usually needs staking. Flowers best when nights are cool, and in coastal locations.

DESCRIPTION Columnlike flower spikes are studded with flat flowers that have contrasting centers called "bees," which are usually black or white. The flowers' color range includes white, blue, purple, and pink. Excellent for tall backgrounds in beds and borders. Superb cut flower.

RECOMMENDED VARIETY 'Pacific Giants' grow to a height of 6 feet. Seedsmen also offer a strain known as *Belladonna* hybrids, such as 'Connecticut Yankees,' which grow compact and bushy (2½ feet).

BOTANICAL NAME *Dianthus caryophyllus*

COMMON NAME Carnation

RANGE Native to Europe. Tender perennial best grown as tender annual.

HEIGHT 2 feet; upright, bushy habit.

CULTURE Easy to grow in any fertile, well-drained loam soil in full sun. Start seed at 70°F soil temperature and set out 8-week-old transplants, spaced 12 inches apart, after danger of frost.

DESCRIPTION Fragrant double flowers are white, yellow, red, pink, and mahogany on slender stems. Gray-green leaves are slender, pointed. Tall kinds such as 'Chabaud Giants' are good for cutting. Dwarf varieties such as the 'Knights' are suitable for massing in beds and borders.

BOTANICAL NAME *Dianthus chinensis*

COMMON NAME Dianthus

RANGE Native to China. Hardy annual.

HEIGHT 12 inches; compact, mounded habit.

CULTURE Easy to grow in any well-drained loam soil in full sun. Start seed indoors at 70°F and set out 8-week-old transplants, spaced 6 to 12 inches apart, several weeks before the last frost date.

DESCRIPTION Fragrant flowers with frilly petal edges are borne in profusion. Color range includes red, white, and pink—sometimes with a contrasting red eye at the petal center. Gray-green leaves are narrow, pointed. Popular for massing in low beds and borders; also for edging and rock gardens. Tall kinds are good for cutting.

RECOMMENDED VARIETY 'Magic Charms,' an early, free flowering (having abundant growth spurts) plant.

BOTANICAL NAME *Dimorphotheca sinuata*

COMMON NAME Cape Marigold; African Daisy

RANGE Native to South Africa. Tender annual.

HEIGHT 12 inches; compact, mounded habit.

CULTURE Easy to grow in any well-drained loam soil in full sun. Start seeds indoors at 60° to 70°F and set out 4-week-old transplants, spaced 12 inches apart, after all danger of frost. Also can be direct-seeded.

DESCRIPTION Daisy-like flowers have shimmering petals in white, yellow, orange, and pink with prominent black eyes. Dark green leaves are small, serrated. Good for edging low beds and borders. Especially popular for rock gardens in coastal areas.

BOTANICAL NAME *Dorotheanus bellidiformis*

COMMON NAME Livingstone Daisy

RANGE Native to South Africa. Tender annual.

HEIGHT 6 inches; low, spreading habit.

CULTURE Easy to grow in any well-drained loam or sandy soil in full sun. Start seed indoors at 60°F soil temperature and set out 8-week-old transplants, spaced 8 inches apart, after all danger of frost. Also can be direct-seeded in mild climates. Flowers best when nights are cool.

DESCRIPTION Flowers have shimmering petals, borne in such profusion that they can completely hide the foliage. Colors include purple, pink, orange, apricot, and yellow, plus bicolors. Good for edging low beds and borders.

RECOMMENDED VARIETY 'Yellow Ice,' an early flowering yellow.

BOTANICAL NAME *Dyssodia tenuiloba*

COMMON NAME Dahlberg Daisy

RANGE Native to Mexico. Tender annual.

HEIGHT 6 inches; low, spreading habit.

CULTURE Easy to grow in any well-drained, fertile loam soil in full sun. Start seed indoors at 60° to 80°F soil temperature and set out 6- to 8-week-old transplants, spaced at least 6 inches apart, after all danger of frost. Also can be direct-seeded. Drought resistant.

DESCRIPTION Dainty yellow flowers are borne in great profusion all summer on airy plants that hug the ground. Excellent for edging beds and borders. Makes a good temporary ground cover and is suitable for containers.

BOTANICAL NAME *Eschscholzia californica*

COMMON NAME California-poppy

RANGE Native to California. Hardy annual.

HEIGHT 12 inches; compact, mounded habit.

CULTURE Easy to grow in any well-drained loam soil in full sun. Start seeds indoors at 60°F soil temperature and set out 4-week-old transplants, spaces 12 inches apart, several weeks before the last frost date. Older transplants suffer shock. Can be direct-seeded. Self-seeds easily. Flowers best when nights are cool.

DESCRIPTION Poppy-like flowers have a satin sheen. Colors include yellow, orange, pink, white, and red. Leaves are narrow, pointed. Popular for massing in beds and borders, also wildflower meadows.

RECOMMENDED VARIETY 'Ballerina,' a rich mixture with crinkled petals.

BOTANICAL NAME *Euphorbia marginata*

COMMON NAME Snow-on-the-Mountain

RANGE Native to North America. Tender annual.

HEIGHT 2 to 3 feet; erect, bushy habit.

CULTURE Easy to grow in any well-drained loam soil in full sun. Tolerates drought and sandy soil. Start seed indoors at 70°F and set out 6- to 8-week-old transplants, spaced 12 inches apart, after danger of frost. Also can be direct-seeded.

DESCRIPTION The attractive silvery green foliage becomes even more ornamental when the leaf tips produce clusters of white-edged leaves with tiny white flowers clustered in the middle of each whorl. Popular as an accent in mixed beds and borders. **Caution:** A milky sap that seeps from the stem when cut may cause skin irritation.

BOTANICAL NAME *Gaillardia pulchella*

COMMON NAME Blanket Flower

RANGE Native to North America. Tender annual.

HEIGHT 3 feet; erect, bushy habit.

CULTURE Easy to grow in any well-drained loam soil in full sun. Start seed indoors 70° to 85°F and set out 6-week-old transplants, spaced 12 inches apart, after danger of frost. Also can be direct-seeded.

DESCRIPTION Double- and semi-double flowers are yellow, orange, and red, plus bicolors. Leaves are dark green, narrow, serrated. Good for massing in beds and borders. Popular for wildflower meadows. Suitable for cutting.

BOTANICAL NAME *Gazania ringens*

COMMON NAME Rainbow Daisy

RANGE Native to South Africa. Tender annual.

HEIGHT 12 inches; low, spreading habit.

CULTURE Easy to grow in any well-drained loam soil in full sun. Start seed indoors at 60°F soil temperature and set out 6-week-old transplants, spaced 12 inches apart, after danger of frost. Flowers close up on cloudy days.

DESCRIPTION Shimmering flowers are mostly yellow, orange, pink, red, and mahogany with black zone around the petal center. Dark green leaves are narrow, pointed. Good for mixed beds and borders.

RECOMMENDED VARIETY 'Mini Star,' a dwarf compact variety good for rock gardens and for creating a ground cover effect.

BOTANICAL NAME *Gomphrena globosa*

COMMON NAME Globe Amaranth

RANGE Native to India. Tender annual.

HEIGHT Up to 2 feet; bushy, mounded habit.

CULTURE Easy to grow in any well-drained loam soil in full sun. Start seed indoors at 70° to 85°F and set out 6-week-old transplants, spaced 12 inches apart, after danger of frost. Also can be direct-seeded. Extremely drought resistant.

DESCRIPTION Clover-like flowers are mostly white, orange, pink, and purple. Dark green leaves are spear shaped. Good for massing in beds and borders. Popular both as a fresh cut flower and for dried arrangements.

BOTANICAL NAME *Gypsophila elegans*

COMMON NAME Baby's-breath

RANGE Native to Europe. Tender annual.

HEIGHT 2 feet; bushy, cloudlike habit.

CULTURE Easy to grow in any well-drained loam soil in full sun. Start seed indoors at 70°F and set out 4- to 5-week-old transplants, spaced 12 inches apart, after all danger of frost. Also can be direct-seeded. Drought tolerant.

DESCRIPTION Dainty white or light pink aspirin-size flowers are borne in such profusion on billowing plants that they appear to be a cloud of mist when seen from a distance. Stems and leaves are delicate, wispy. Popular as an accent in mixed beds and borders. Excellent for cutting.

RECOMMENDED VARIETY: 'Covent Garden.'

BOTANICAL NAME *Helianthus annuus*

COMMON NAME Sunflower

RANGE Native to North America. Tender annual.

HEIGHT Up to 8 feet; upright habit.

CULTURE Easy to grow in any well-drained loam soil in full sun. Start seed indoors at 70° to 85°F and set out 4-week-old transplants, spaced 3 feet apart, after all danger of frost. Generally flowers just as fast from direct-seeding.

DESCRIPTION Some varieties of sunflowers have the largest flowers in the plant kingdom, with individual flower heads up to 24 inches across. Their centers are full of edible nutlike seeds, which are surrounded by golden yellow petals. Dwarf or branching varieties with smaller flowers are more popular for ornamental display, such as 'Teddy Bear,' with full double flowers resembling those in the famous Van Gogh painting, and 'Color Fashion,' a tall mixture of yellow, bronze, red, and purple single-flowered types good for cutting and backgrounds.

BOTANICAL NAME *Helichrysum bracteatum*

COMMON NAME Strawflower

RANGE Native to Western Australia. Tender annual.

HEIGHT Up to 5 feet; upright, bushy habit.

CULTURE Easy to grow in any well-drained loam soil in full sun. Start seed indoors at 60° to 70°F soil temperature and set out 6-week-old transplants, spaced 12 inches apart, after all danger of frost. Also can be direct-seeded.

DESCRIPTION Papery flowers are semi-double in white, yellow, orange, red, and pink. Dark green leaves are narrow, pointed. Popular as an accent in mixed beds and borders. Extremely popular for cutting to use in dried flower arrangements. Dwarf varieties, such as 'Dwarf Spangle' (12 inches tall) are good for edging and rock gardens.

BOTANICAL NAME *Hunnemannia fumariifolia*

COMMON NAME Mexican Tulip Poppy

RANGE Native to Mexico. Tender annual.

HEIGHT 2 feet; upright, branching habit.

CULTURE Easy to grow in any well-drained loam or sandy soil in full sun. Start seed indoors at 70° to 85°F and set out 4 to 5-week-old transplants, spaced 12 inches apart, after all danger of frost. Also can be direct-seeded. Drought resistant.

DESCRIPTION Shimmering yellow flowers are borne on slender stems. Dark green leaves are deeply indented. Popular accent in mixed beds and borders. Often included in meadow wildflower plantings.

BOTANICAL NAME *Iberis umbellata*

COMMON NAME Candytuft

RANGE Native to Spain. Hardy annual.

HEIGHT 12 inches; low, mounded habit.

CULTURE Easy to grow in any well-drained loam soil in full sun. Start seeds indoors at 60°F soil temperature and set out 6-week-old transplants, spaced 6 inches apart, several weeks before the last expected frost date. Also likes to be direct-seeded in early spring or late summer for fall blooms. Flowers best when nights are cool.

DESCRIPTION Clusters of dainty flowers form flat umbels in white, pink, and red. Dark green leaves are narrow, pointed. Popular for edging beds and borders. Dried seed pods are used in dried flower arrangements.

BOTANICAL NAME *Impatiens balsamina*

COMMON NAME Balsam

RANGE Native to India. Tender annual.

HEIGHT 2 to 3 feet; upright, bushy habit.

CULTURE Prefers moist, fertile, humus-rich soil in full sun or partial shade. Start seed indoors at 70° to 85°F and set out 6- to 8-week-old transplants, spaced 12 inches apart, after danger of frost.

DESCRIPTION Camellia-like flowers are mostly white, pink, red, and purple, in some varieties borne along the stems, in others on top of the foliage. Leaves are bright green, serrated, spear shaped. Suitable for massing in beds and borders.

BOTANICAL NAME *Impatiens wallerana*

COMMON NAME Patience plant

RANGE Native to Asia. Tender annual.

HEIGHT Up to 3 feet; bushy, spreading habit.

CULTURE Prefers moist, fertile, humus-rich soil in partial shade. Start seed indoors at 70° to 80°F and set out 10-week-old transplants, spaced 12 inches apart, after danger of frost.

DESCRIPTION Plants bloom continuously and are covered with single and double flowers, some varieties having solid colors and others possessing bicolored flowers. Leaves are dark green, broad, pointed. Popular for massing in beds and borders. Some varieties good for container planting, including hanging baskets. Dwarf varieties make sensational ground covers. Most widely planted flowering annual for shade.

RECOMMENDED VARIETIES 'Super Elfins' and 'Futura' grow just 12 inches high.

BOTANICAL NAME *Ipomoea alba*

COMMON NAME Moonflower

RANGE Native to South America. Tender annual.

HEIGHT Up to 10 feet; vining habit.

CULTURE Prefers moist, fertile, humus-rich soil in full sun. Start seeds indoors at 70° to 85°F. Soak seeds overnight to speed germination. Set out 6-week-old transplants, spaced 3 feet apart. Plants need strong support. Flowers open in the late afternoon, bloom at night, and close by noon the following day.

DESCRIPTION White trumpet-shaped flowers are borne on vining plants with dense foliage cover. Leaves are attractive, dark green, and heart shaped. Popular for decorating fences, trellises, and posts.

BOTANICAL NAME *Ipomoea tricolor*

COMMON NAME Morning Glory

RANGE Native to South America. Tender annual.

HEIGHT Up to 10 feet; vining habit.

CULTURE Easy to grow in any well-drained loam soil. Start seed at 70° to 85°F. Soak the hard-coated seeds overnight to aid germination. Set out 4-week-old transplants, spaced 3 feet apart, after danger of frost. Plants need strong support. Flowers open in the morning, generally close by afternoon except on cloudy days.

DESCRIPTION Wide trumpet-shaped flowers are mostly blue, white, red, pink, and bicolors. Leaves are dark green, heart shaped. Probably the most popular of all flowering vines, they climb by means of tendrils, making them suitable for covering fences, trellises, and posts.

RECOMMENDED VARIETY 'Heavenly Blue.'

BOTANICAL NAME *Kochia scoparia*

COMMON NAME Burning Bush

RANGE Native to Mexico. Tender annual.

HEIGHT 3 feet; bushy, upright habit.

CULTURE Easy to grow in any well-drained loam soil in full sun. Start seeds at 70° to 85°F and set out 4- to 6-week-old transplants, spaced 1 to 2 feet apart, after danger of frost.

DESCRIPTION Dense, feathery foliage forms an upright oval form resembling an Evergreen Cypress. Grown mostly for its bushy habit, it is popular for creating a hedge effect for beds and borders. Bright green summer foliage develops reddish tones in autumn.

BOTANICAL NAME *Lathyrus odoratus*

COMMON NAME Sweet Pea

RANGE Native to Sicily. Hardy annual.

HEIGHT Up to 6 feet; vining, upright habit.

CULTURE Prefers fertile, humus-rich, well-drained loam soil in full sun. Soak seeds overnight to aid germination and start them indoors at 60° to 75°F. Set out 4-week-old transplants, spaced 12 inches apart, several weeks before the last frost date. Can be direct-seeded where summers are cool. Flowers best when nights are cool. The tallest growing varieties need support.

DESCRIPTION Fragrant ruffled flowers with prominent keels are borne on strong vines with clover-like leaves and tendrils that allow the plants to climb. Tall kinds such as 'Galaxy' are popular for backgrounds in mixed beds and borders, also for decorating fences and trellises. Dwarf kinds such as 'Snoopea' do not need support (they possess no tendrils) and are useful for bedding in areas with cool summers. Sweet peas are among the finest flowers for cutting to make fresh flower arrangements.

BOTANICAL NAME *Lavatera trimestris*

COMMON NAME Rose-mallow

RANGE Native to the Mediterranean. Hardy annual.

HEIGHT Up to 3 feet; upright, bushy habit.

CULTURE Easy to grow in any well-drained loam soil in full sun. Start seed indoors at 70°F and set out 4-week-old transplants, spaced at least 12 inches apart, several weeks before the last frost date. Also can be direct-seeded.

DESCRIPTION The lovely hibiscus-like flowers with their shimmering petals are borne in such profusion that they almost completely hide the foliage. Colors include pink, white, and red. The dark green leaves resemble English ivy. Popular accent for mixed beds and borders. Also makes a spectacular temporary flowering hedge.

BOTANICAL NAME *Limnanthes douglasii*

COMMON NAME Scrambled Eggs; Meadow-foam

RANGE Native to California. Hardy annual.

HEIGHT 4 inches; low, ground-hugging habit.

CULTURE Easy to grow in any moist, well-drained loam soil in full sun. Plants tolerate crowding and direct-seeding is preferred. Seeds may be started at 60° to 70°F and set out 4-week-old transplants, spaced 6 inches apart, several weeks before the last frost date. Flowers best when nights are cool.

DESCRIPTION Dainty flowers are yellow in the middle with white petal edges. At peak bloom, the dazzling flowers are so numerous they completely hide the foliage. Mostly used as an edging for beds and borders; also as a temporary ground cover in areas with cool summers.

BOTANICAL NAME *Limonium sinuatum*

COMMON NAME Statice

RANGE Native to the Mediterranean. Tender annual.

HEIGHT 2 to 3 feet; upright, bushy habit.

CULTURE Easy to grow in any well-drained loam soil in full sun. Start seeds at 60° to 70°F soil temperature and set 8-week-old transplants, spaced 12 inches apart, after danger of frost.

DESCRIPTION Papery flower clusters are held erect on stiff stems. Color range includes white, yellow, pink, lavender, and blue. Leaves are lancelike. Suitable for mixed beds and borders. Popular for cutting and creating dried arrangements.

BOTANICAL NAME *Linaria maroccana*

COMMON NAME Toadflax

RANGE Native to Morocco. Hardy annual.

HEIGHT 12 inches; upright, spirelike habit.

CULTURE Prefers a fertile, well-drained loam soil in full sun. Start seed indoors at 65° to 80°F soil temperature and set out 8-week-old transplants, spaced 12 inches apart, after danger of frost. Pinch lead shoot after transplanting to encourage bushier habit.

DESCRIPTION Cup-shaped flowers are mostly blue, pink, or white. Leaves are blue-green, heart shaped, fleshy. A double form, 'Prima Donna,' is available. Good accent for mixed beds and borders. Excellent for cutting. Good pot plant.

RECOMMENDED VARIETY 'Fairy Bouquet.'

BOTANICAL NAME *Lisianthus russulanus*
(Sometimes listed as Eustoma grandiflorum)

COMMON NAME Prairie Gentian

RANGE Native to Texas. Tender annual.

HEIGHT 1 to 2 feet; upright habit.

CULTURE Prefers a fertile, well-drained loam soil in full sun. Start seed indoors at 65° to 80°F soil temperature and set 8-to-10-week-old transplant, spaced 12 inches apart, after danger of frost. Pinch lead shoot after transplanting to encourage bushier habit.

DESCRIPTION Cup-shaped flowers are mostly blue, pink, or white. Leaves are blue-green, heart shaped, fleshy. A double form, Prima Donna, is available. Good accent for mixed beds and borders. Excellent for cutting. Good pot plant.

BOTANICAL NAME *Lobelia erinus*

COMMON NAME Lobelia erinus

RANGE Native to South Africa. Tender annual.

HEIGHT 6 inches; compact, mounded habit.

CULTURE Prefers fertile, moist, well-drained loam soil. Flowers best when nights are cool. Start seed at 70° to 80°F and set out 10-week-old transplants, spaced 6 inches apart, after all danger of frost.

DESCRIPTION Dainty flowers are borne in profusion on airy plants. Colors include blue, rose pink, red, and white. Bright green leaves are small, needlelike. Popular as an edging for beds and borders. Excellent for hanging baskets and other containers.

RECOMMENDED VARIETY 'Blue Heaven.'

BOTANICAL NAME *Lobularia maritima*

COMMON NAME Alyssum

RANGE Native to the Mediterranean. Hardy annual.

HEIGHT 6 inches; low, mounded, spreading habit.

CULTURE Easy to grow in any well-drained loam soil in full sun. Tolerates crowding and is most often direct-seeded. If transplanting is preferred, start seed at 60° to 70°F and set out 4-week-old transplants, spaced 6 inches apart, several weeks before the last expected frost date.

DESCRIPTION Masses of dainty white, pink, or purple flowers are borne in such profusion they often completely hide the foliage. Bright green leaves are small, narrow, pointed. Extremely popular as an edging for beds and borders. Also good for hanging baskets and other container plantings. Grows among paving stones and along dry walls.

RECOMMENDED VARIETIES 'Carpet of Snow' (white) and 'Wonderland' (deep pink).

BOTANICAL NAME *Machaeranthera tanacetifolia*

COMMON NAME Tahoka-daisy

RANGE Native to Texas. Hardy annual.

HEIGHT 1 to 2 feet; low, bushy habit.

CULTURE Easy to grow in any well-drained loam soil in full sun. Start seed at 60°F soil temperature and set out 6-week-old transplants, spaced 12 inches apart, several weeks before the last expected frost date.

DESCRIPTION Blue flowers have golden yellow centers, resemble Michaelmas Daisies. Leaves are bright green, deeply indented. Good accent for mixed beds and borders. Popular for rock gardens. Suitable for cutting.

BOTANICAL NAME *Matthiola incana*

COMMON NAME Stocks

RANGE Native to Southern Europe. Hardy Annual.

HEIGHT 3 feet; erect, spirelike habit.

CULTURE Prefers moist, fertile, humus-rich soil in full sun. Start seed at 65° to 75°F soil temperature, but after seeds germinate plants should not be subjected to air temperatures higher than 65°F. If plants are exposed to temperatures any higher than 65°F they are unlikely to bloom. Set out 6-week-old transplants, spaced 12 inches apart, several weeks before the last expected frost date. Pinch lead shoot to encourage side branching.

DESCRIPTION Fragrant, ruffled flowers are studded in a column along strong stems. Colors include white, yellow, pink, red, and purple. Leaves are straplike. Popular for beds and borders where 4 to 5 months of cool temperatures prevail. Excellent for cutting.

RECOMMENDED VARIETY '7-Weeks Tyrsomic,' early flowering.

RELATED SPECIES *M. bicornis* ('Night-Scented Stocks').

BOTANICAL NAME *Mimulus* x *hybridus*

COMMON NAME Monkey Flower

RANGE Native to Chile. Hardy annual.

HEIGHT 12 inches; low, mounded habit.

CULTURE Prefers moist, fertile, humus-rich soil in sun or partial shade. Start seed at 60°F soil temperature and set out 8- to 10-week-old transplants, spaced 6 to 12 inches apart, several weeks before the last expected frost date. Flowers best during cool weather.

DESCRIPTION Tubular flowers have heavily freckled faces and a velvety texture. Colors include white, yellow, orange, red, and pink. Leaves are broad, serrated, bright green. Suitable for massing in beds and borders. Good for container planting, especially beside garden pools.

BOTANICAL NAME *Mirabilis jalapa*

COMMON NAME Four-o'-clock

RANGE Native to Peru. Perennials grown as tender annuals.

HEIGHT 3 feet; bushy habit.

CULTURE Easy to grow in any well-drained loam or sandy soil in full sun. Start seed at 70° to 85°F and set out 6-week-old transplants, spaced 1 to 2 feet apart, after danger of frost. Also can be direct-seeded.

DESCRIPTION Tubular flowers bloom continuously all summer; they stay closed during the morning on sunny days, but remain open all day on cloudy days. Colors are variable from plant to plant and on individual plants; a single flower may have white, yellow, orange, and pink blossoms, some of them even bicolored. Leaves are heart shaped. Popular accent for mixed beds and borders.

BOTANICAL NAME *Moluccella laevis*

COMMON NAME Bells-of-Ireland

RANGE Native to Asia. Tender annual.

HEIGHT 2 to 3 feet; bushy, spreading habit.

CULTURE Easy to grow in any well-drained loam soil. Soak seeds overnight to aid germination, and start them at 70° to 85°F. Set out 6-to-8-week old transplants, spaced 12 inches apart, after danger of frost. Also can be direct-seeded after danger of frost.

DESCRIPTION Slender flower spikes are crowded with ornamental, bell-shaped, green flower bracts. Leaves are broad, indented. Popular accent in beds and borders. Valued for cutting and dried flower arrangements.

BOTANICAL NAME *Myosotis sylvatica*

COMMON NAME Forget-me-not

RANGE Native to Europe. Biennial grown as hardy annual.

HEIGHT 12 inches; low, mounded habit.

CULTURE Prefers moist, fertile loam soil in sun or partial shade. Start seed at 70°F and set out 8-week-old transplants, spaced 6 to 12 inches apart, several weeks before the last expected frost date. Flowers best when nights are cool.

DESCRIPTION Dainty, blue, star-shaped flowers cover the plants in early summer. Leaves are dark green, straplike. Popular for edging beds and borders, also for massing along pond margins and stream banks. Plants reseed themselves readily. A bed of Forget-me-nots mixed with tulips make a particularly effective planting combination.

BOTANICAL NAME *Nemesia strumosa*

COMMON NAME Nemesia

RANGE Native to South Africa. Tender annual.

HEIGHT 12 inches; mounded habit.

CULTURE Prefers moist, fertile, well-drained loam soil in full sun. Start seed at 60°F and set out 6-to 8-week old transplants, spaced 12 inches apart. Flowers best when nights are cool.

DESCRIPTION Orchid-like flowers, arranged in clusters, have a prominent lower lip. Colors include yellow, red, white, pink, and orange. Leaves are narrow, pointed. Popular for massing in beds and borders in areas with cool summers. Good for containers. A blue Nemesia, 'Blue Gem,' is grown separately and not generally included in seed mixtures.

BOTANICAL NAME *Nemophila menziesii*

COMMON NAME Baby-Blue-Eyes

RANGE Native to California. Hardy annual.

HEIGHT 9 inches; low, mounded habit.

CULTURE Easy to grow in any well-drained loam soil in full sun. Start seed at 60°F and set out 6-week-old transplants, spaced 6 inches apart, several weeks before the last expected frost date. Also can be direct-seeded. Flowers best when nights are cool.

DESCRIPTION Dainty, cup-shaped blue flowers have white centers. Bright green leaves are delicate, fern-like. Good edging for beds and borders. Popular for rock gardens and growing in wildflower meadow mixtures. Self-seeds readily.

BOTANICAL NAME *Nicotiana alata*

COMMON NAME Flowering Tobacco

RANGE Native to South America. Tender annual.

HEIGHT 3 feet; erect, bushy habit.

CULTURE Easy to grow in any well-drained loam soil in full sun. Start seed indoors at 70° to 85°F and set out 8-week-old transplants, spaced 12 inches apart, after all danger of frost.

DESCRIPTION Borne in profusion on long stems, the tubular flowers can be white, pink, red, yellow, or green. Leaves are dark green, oval. Popular for massing as a background in mixed beds and borders.

RECOMMENDED VARIETY 'Nicki' hybrids, a semi-dwarf strain growing 18 inches high that does not close up in the afternoon like other varieties.

BOTANICAL NAME *Nierembergia hippomanica*

COMMON NAME Cupflower

RANGE Native to South America. Perennial best grown as tender annual.

HEIGHT 12 inches; low, mounded habit.

CULTURE Easy to grow in any well-drained loam soil in full sun. Start seeds at 70° to 85°F and set out 10-week-old transplants, spaced 6 inches apart, after all danger of frost.

DESCRIPTION Small cup-shaped purple flowers are produced in such abundance they almost hide the foliage, which is delicate and needlelike. Good for edging beds and borders. Popular as a flowering pot plant.

BOTANICAL NAME *Nolana napiformis*

COMMON NAME Nolana

RANGE Native to Peru and Chile. Tender annual.

HEIGHT 4 to 12 inches; low, mounded habit.

CULTURE Easy to grow in any well-drained loam soil. Start seeds at 70° to 85° F and set out 6-week old transplants, spaced 12 inches apart, after all danger of frost, in full sun.

DESCRIPTION A creeping plant that covers itself in cheerful blue flowers with yellow and white throats, resembling small morning glories. Soft, fleshy green leaves are indented. Good to use for edging and as a temporary ground cover.

BOTANICAL NAME *Papaver nudicaule*

COMMON NAME Iceland Poppy

RANGE Native to Canada. Hardy annual.

HEIGHT 3 feet; erect habit.

CULTURE Easy to grow in any well-drained loam soil in full sun. Flowers best when nights are cool. Direct-seeding is generally preferred since transplants are subject to shock. Even where plants generally grow better from direct-seeding, some gardeners still prefer to transplant. In this case, start seed at 55° to 65°F and set out 4-week-old transplants, spaced 12 inches apart, several weeks before the last expected frost date in spring.

DESCRIPTION Flowers are mostly orange, yellow, pink, and white on slender, wiry stems. Bright green leaves are serrated, forming a rosette. Good accent for beds and borders. Popular for wildflower meadows. Excellent cut flower, especially when cut stems are held over a flame to seal them and prevent wilting.

BOTANICAL NAME *Papaver rhoeas*

COMMON NAME Shirley Poppy

RANGE Native to Europe. Hardy annual.

HEIGHT 3 feet; upright, clump-forming habit.

CULTURE Easy to grow in any well-drained loam or sandy soil in full sun. Direct-seeding is generally preferred since plants tolerate crowding. Even though plants grow better from direct-seeding, some gardeners still prefer to transplant. In this case, start seeds at 60° to 70°F and set out 4-week-old transplants, spaced 12 inches apart, several weeks before the last expected frost date.

DESCRIPTION Flowers are mostly red, white, and pink with black markings at the base of each petal, growing on top of wiry stems. Leaves are hairy, serrated. Popular as accents in beds and borders, also for wildflower meadows. Suitable for cutting if cut stems are held over a flame immediately after picking to seal the ends and prevent wilting.

BOTANICAL NAME *Pelargonium* x *hortorum*

COMMON NAME Geranium

RANGE Native to South Africa. Perennial best grown as tender annual.

HEIGHT 12 inches; erect habit.

CULTURE Easy to grow in any well-drained loam soil in full sun. Start seed at 70° to 85°F and set out 8- to 10-week-old transplants, spaced 12 inches apart, after danger of frost.

DESCRIPTION Flowers are borne in clusters on strong, slender stems. Color ranges from red, pink, and salmon to white and bicolors. Leaves are usually brown around the margin and rounded with ruffled edges. Popular for massing in beds and borders. Suitable for containers.

RECOMMENDED VARIETY 'Orbits,' an early flowering dwarf strain with conspicuous leaf-zone patterns and a natural tendency to branch freely from the base.

BOTANICAL NAME *Penstemon gloxinioides*

COMMON NAME Bearded Tongue

RANGE Native to Mexico. Perennial best treated as tender annual.

HEIGHT 2 feet; erect, spirelike habit.

CULTURE Easy to grow in any well-drained loam soil in full sun. Start seed at 60°F and set out 8- to 10-week-old transplants, spaced 12 inches apart, after all danger of frost. Flowers best when nights are cool.

DESCRIPTION Tubular flowers form long spikes. Color range includes white, red, pink, and purple. Leaves are bright green, lancelike. Useful accent in beds and borders. Good for cutting.

RECOMMENDED VARIETY 'Giant Floradale' has large flowers.

BOTANICAL NAME *Petunia* x *hybrida*

COMMON NAME Petunia

RANGE Native to South America. Tender annual.

HEIGHT 12 inches; mounded habit.

CULTURE Easy to grow in any well-drained loam soil in full sun. Start seeds at 70° to 85°F and set out 8- to 10-week-old transplants, spaced 12 inches apart, after all danger of frost.

DESCRIPTION Two types are most popular among home gardeners: 'multi-floras' have relatively small and numerous flowers, and 'grandifloras' with their large, ruffled flowers. Color range includes red, white, blue, yellow, pink, purple, and bicolors. Popular for massing in beds and borders. Good for hanging baskets and other kinds of containers.

BOTANICAL NAME *Phlox drummondii*

COMMON NAME Phlox

RANGE Native to Texas. Hardy annual.

HEIGHT 12 inches; low, spreading habit.

CULTURE Easy to grow in any well-drained loam soil in full sun. Start seed at 55° to 65°F and set out 6- to 8-week-old transplants, spaced 12 inches apart, several weeks before the last expected frost date in spring. Flowers best when nights are cool.

DESCRIPTION Flowers are produced in clusters on short stems. Colors include red, white, pink, and purple plus bicolors. Leaves are bright green, spear shaped. Popular for massing in beds and borders, also rock gardens.

RECOMMENDED VARIETY 'Twinkle' mixed colors, a dwarf with pointed petals.

BOTANICAL NAME *Portulaca grandiflora*

COMMON NAME Moss Rose

RANGE Native to South America. Tender annual.

HEIGHT 6 inches; low, spreading habit.

CULTURE Easy to grow in any well-drained sandy or loam soil in full sun. Start seeds at 70° to 85°F and set out 4-week-old transplants, spaced 12 inches apart, after all danger of frost. Also, can be direct-seeded.

DESCRIPTION Shimmering rose-like flowers are borne in profusion on succulent plants. Bright green leaves are narrow, plump, pointed. Color range includes red, white, yellow, orange, and purple. Popular for edging beds and borders. Also suitable for window boxes and other container plantings.

RECOMMENDED VARIETY 'Calypso' hybrid mixed colors, containing a high percentage of double flowers that remain open all day.

BOTANICAL NAME *Reseda odorata*

COMMON NAME Mignonette

RANGE Native to Egypt. Hardy annual.

HEIGHT 12 inches; erect, bushy habit.

CULTURE Easy to grow in any well-drained loam soil in full sun. Start seed at 70° to 85°F and set out 6-week-old transplants, spaced 6 inches apart, several weeks before the last expected frost date of spring. Also can be direct-seeded.

DESCRIPTION Fragrant orange flowers cluster, forming an inconspicuous, though not very ornamental, flower spike. The heavy, pleasant fragrance is reason enough to find a small spot for it in mixed beds and borders. Good for cutting. A good choice for window boxes.

BOTANICAL NAME *Ricinus communis*

COMMON NAME Castor Bean Plant

RANGE Native to Africa. Perennial grown as tender annual.

HEIGHT Up to 8 feet; erect, branching habit.

CULTURE Easy to grow in any well-drained loam soil in full sun. Start seed at 70° to 85°F soil temperature and set out 6-week-old transplants, spaced at least 3 feet apart, after danger of frost.

DESCRIPTION Grown for its spectacular tropical foliage. Gigantic, glossy, deeply indented leaves can measure up to 3 feet across. Creates a dramatic accent in beds and borders, particularly island beds and foundation plantings. The bean-size seeds have speckled markings and are used to make necklaces **Caution:** seeds and other parts are poisonous.

Right: A beautiful free-form lawn surrounded by borders of annuals. Salvia 'Evening Glow' flowers prolifically in the foreground.

BOTANICAL NAME *Rudbeckia hirta burpeeii*

COMMON NAME Gloriosa Daisy; Black-eyed Susan

RANGE Native to North America. Perennial grown as hardy annual.

HEIGHT 3 feet; erect, branching habit.

CULTURE Easy to grow in any well-drained loam soil in full sun. Start seed at 65° to 75°F and set out 8-week-old transplants, spaced 12 inches apart, several weeks before the last expected frost date of spring. Also can be direct-seeded.

DESCRIPTION Large, daisy-like flowers can be single or double. Color range includes yellow, orange, and mahogany plus bicolors, all with contrasting black or green eyes, depending on variety. Popular for massing in beds and borders, also for wildflower meadows.

RECOMMENDED VARIETIES 'Double Gold,' spectacular yellow double flower excellent for backgrounds and 'Marmalade,' a single-flowered orange dwarf that flowers abundantly, just 12 inches high.

BOTANICAL NAME *Salpiglossis sinuata*

COMMON NAME Painted Tongue; Velvet Flower

RANGE Native to South America. Tender annual.

HEIGHT 3 feet; upright, bushy habit.

CULTURE Prefers a fertile, well-drained, humus-rich soil in full sun. Start seed at 70° to 85°F and set out 8-week-old transplants, spaced 12 inches apart, after all danger of frost. Flowers best when nights are cool.

DESCRIPTION Petunia-like flowers have an incredibly diverse color range including red, white, blue, purple, pink, yellow, and brown, usually with conspicuous petal veins and contrasting freckles. Bright green leaves are pointed, notched. Good accent for mixed beds and borders where summers are cool. Popular pot plant for the greenhouse and conservatory.

BOTANICAL NAME *Salvia farinacea*

COMMON NAME Blue Salvia

RANGE Native to Texas. Perennial grown as tender annual.

HEIGHT 3 feet; upright, bushy habit.

CULTURE Easy to grow in any well-drained loam soil in sun or partial shade. Start seed at 70°F and set out 8-week-old transplants, spaced 12 inches apart, after all danger of frost. Drought resistant.

DESCRIPTION Small florets form erect flower spikes on slender stems. Favored color is blue though white is also available. Leaves are dark green or gray-green, spear shaped. Valuable for backgrounds in mixed beds and borders.

RECOMMENDED VARIETY 'Catima,' an intense, deep blue.

BOTANICAL NAME *Salvia splendens*

COMMON NAME Scarlet Sage

RANGE Native to South America. Tender annual.

HEIGHT 1 to 3 feet; bushy habit.

CULTURE Easy to grow in any well-drained garden loam in sun or partial shade. Start seed at 70° to 85°F and set out 8-week-old transplants, spaced 12 inches apart, after all danger of frost. Flowers best when nights are cool.

DESCRIPTION Tubular florets are arranged into a spectacular flower spike. Favored color is red, though pink, white, and purple are available. Dark green leaves are spear shaped. Extremely popular for massing in beds and borders, also for container growing.

RECOMMENDED VARIETY 'Carabiniere,' an intense fiery red with solid spikes that grow 12 inches high.

BOTANICAL NAME *Sanvitalia procumbens*

COMMON NAME Creeping Zinnia

RANGE Native to Mexico. Tender annual.

HEIGHT 6 inches; low, spreading habit.

CULTURE Easy to grow in well-drained loam soil in full sun. Start seed at 70° to 85°F and set out 4-week-old transplants, spaced 12 inches apart, after all danger of frost. Also can be direct-seeded.

DESCRIPTION Dainty daisy-like flowers are bright yellow with black centers. Leaves are bright green, spear shaped. Creates a beautiful ground cover. Popular for edging beds and borders. Suitable for window boxes and rock gardens since plants will cascade.

BOTANICAL NAME *Scabiosa atropurpurea*

COMMON NAME Sweet Scabious; Pincushion Flower

RANGE Native to Europe. Hardy annual.

HEIGHT 3 feet; erect, branching habit.

CULTURE Easy to grow in any well-drained loam soil in full sun. Start seed at 70°F and set out 4- to 5-week-old transplants, spaced 12 inches apart, in mid-April.

DESCRIPTION Flowers resemble tight pincushions, rounded and fully double. Colors include blue, white, red, pink, and black. Good accent for mixed beds and borders. Excellent for cutting.

RECOMMENDED VARIETY 'Giant Imperial.'

BOTANICAL NAME *Schizanthus* x *wisetonensis*

COMMON NAME Butterfly Flower; Poor Man's Orchid

RANGE Native to Chile. Tender annual.

HEIGHT 2 feet; upright, bushy habit.

CULTURE Prefers fertile, well-drained, humus-rich soil in full sun. Start seed at 60° to 70°F and set out 10- to 12-week-old transplants, spaced 12 inches apart, several weeks before the last expected frost date. The taller varieties may need staking. Flowers best when nights are cool.

DESCRIPTION Orchid-like flowers are clustered into a long flower spike held erect on slender stems. Color range includes white, yellow, orange, pink, and purple, usually with freckled throats. Good for massing in beds and borders where summers are cool and moist. Popular for growing as a flowering pot plant in greenhouses and conservatories.

RECOMMENDED VARIETY 'Hit Parade,' a compact dwarf growing just 12 inches high; excellent for bedding.

BOTANICAL NAME *Senecio cineraria*

COMMON NAME Dusty Miller

RANGE Native to the Mediterranean. Perennial grown as tender annual.

HEIGHT 12 inches; low, mounded habit.

CULTURE Easy to grow in any well-drained loam soil in full sun. Start seed at 60° to 70°F and set out 10-week-old transplants, spacing them 6 inches apart, after danger of frost.

DESCRIPTION One of several plant species commonly called 'Dusty Miller,' grown purely for the ornamental value of their silvery gray indented leaves. Extremely popular for edging beds and borders and combining with other plants in containers.

RECOMMENDED VARIETY 'Silverdust,' which displays finely indented, velvetlike leaves.

BOTANICAL NAME *Tagetes erecta*

COMMON NAME American Marigold; African Marigold

RANGE Native to Mexico. Tender annual.

HEIGHT Up to 3 feet; erect, bushy habit.

CULTURE Easy to grow in any well-drained loam soil in full sun. Start seed at 70° to 85°F and set out 6-week-old transplants, spaced 12 inches apart, after all danger of frost. Also can be direct-seeded.

DESCRIPTION Flowers are mostly double in yellow, orange, gold, and white. Leaves are feathery, with a spicy fragrance, though odorless kinds are available. Popular for massing in beds and borders. Good for cutting.

RECOMMENDED VARIETY 'First Lady,' a primrose-yellow, semi-dwarf.

BOTANICAL NAME *Tagetes patula*

COMMON NAME French Marigold

RANGE Native to Mexico. Tender annual.

HEIGHT 12 inches; low, mounded habit.

CULTURE Easy to grow in any well-drained loam soil in full sun. Start seed at 70° to 85°F and set out 6-week-old transplants, spaced 12 inches apart, after danger of frost. Also can be direct-seeded.

DESCRIPTION Flowers can be single or double, the doubles often featuring a crest—a raised center of petals. Color range includes yellow, orange, red, and gold. Leaves are feathery and have a spicy odor that repels many insects. Popular for massing in beds and borders, also for edging paths. Good for container plantings, especially window boxes.

RECOMMENDED VARIETY 'Boy' series. A cross between the dwarf French and tall American called 'Triploid hybrids' is an exceptional class of dwarf marigold that is free flowering.

BOTANICAL NAME *Tagetes tenuifolia*

COMMON NAME Striped Marigold

RANGE Native to Mexico. Tender annual.

HEIGHT 12 inches; cushionlike habit.

CULTURE Easy to grow in any well-drained loam soil in full sun. Start seeds at 70° to 85°F and set out 6-week-old transplants, spaced 12 inches apart, after all danger of frost. Also can be direct-seeded.

DESCRIPTION Dainty daisy-like flowers are mostly yellow, orange, or rusty red, borne in such profusion they almost completely hide the foliage. Leaves are finely cut, fern-like, and have a spicy odor that repels many insects. Mostly used for edging beds and borders. Also good for containers and rock gardens.

RECOMMENDED VARIETIES 'Lemon Gem' (lemon yellow) and 'Paprika' (rusty red with yellow center).

BOTANICAL NAME *Thunbergia alata*

COMMON NAME Black-eyed Susan Vine

RANGE Native to Africa. Tender annual.

HEIGHT Up to 10 feet; vining habit.

CULTURE Easy to grow in any well-drained loam soil in full sun. Start seed at 70° to 85°F and set out 6-week-old transplants, spaced 12 inches apart, after danger of frost. Also can be direct-seeded.

DESCRIPTION Mostly orange flowers have black eyes. Bright green leaves are broad, pointed. Good to cover fences and climb up trellises. A dwarf strain, 'Susie,' is especially suitable for hanging baskets and window boxes and is available in orange, yellow, and white (all with black eyes).

BOTANICAL NAME *Tithonia rotundifolia*

COMMON NAME Mexican Sunflower

RANGE Native to Mexico. Tender annual.

HEIGHT 5 feet; erect, branching habit.

CULTURE Easy to grow in any well-drained loam soil in full sun. Start seed at 70° to 85°F and set out 6-week-old transplants, spaced at least 12 inches apart, after all danger of frost. Also can be direct-seeded.

DESCRIPTION Dahlia-like flowers are bright orange. Dark green leaves are broad, pointed, serrated. Useful background for beds and borders. Can create a hedge effect with its thick foliage cover. Good cut flower if cut in bud stage.

BOTANICAL NAME *Torenia fournieri*

COMMON NAME Wishbone Flower

RANGE Native to North Africa. Tender annual.

HEIGHT 12 inches; low, mounded habit.

CULTURE Prefers fertile, moist, humus-rich soil in partial shade. Start seeds at 70° to 85°F and set out 10-week-old transplants, spaced 8 inches apart, after all danger of frost.

DESCRIPTION Flowers resemble small pansies with an unusual arrangement of stamens in the throat in the shape of a wishbone. Colors are mostly violet-blue and pink. Leaves are bright green, serrated. Popular for edging beds and borders. Also grown as a flowering pot plant.

BOTANICAL NAME *Tropaeolum majus*

COMMON NAME Nasturtium

RANGE Native to South America. Hardy annual.

HEIGHT 12 inches; low, spreading habit.

CULTURE Easy to grow in any well-drained loam soil in full sun. Start seed at 65°F and set out 5- to 6-week-old transplants, spaced 12 inches apart, several weeks before the last expected frost date in spring. Flowers best when nights are cool. Can be trained to climb. Also can be direct-seeded.

DESCRIPTION Flowers can be single- or double-flowered, with or without spurs. Plants with spurless flowers (such as 'Whirlybird') tend to display better because the flowers always face up. Color range includes red, yellow, orange, apricot, white, pink, and mahogany. Leaves are shaped like parasols. Suitable for low beds and borders, also containers. Tall kinds can be used to cover trellises and fences.

BOTANICAL NAME *Venidium fastuosum*

COMMON NAME Monarch-of-the-veldt

RANGE Native to South Africa. Tender annual.

HEIGHT 2 feet; bushy habit.

CULTURE Easy to grow in any well-drained loam soil in full sun. Start seed at 70° to 80°F and set out 6-week-old transplants, spaced 12 inches apart, after danger of frost. Also can be direct-seeded. Flowers best when nights are cool.

DESCRIPTION Daisy-like, semi-double flowers are golden yellow with a black center encircled by an attractive brown zone. Bright green leaves are serrated. Good accent for beds and borders. Excellent for cutting.

BOTANICAL NAME *Verbena* x *hybrida*

COMMON NAME Summer Verbena

RANGE Native to South America. Tender annual.

HEIGHT 12 inches; low, spreading habit.

CULTURE Easy to grow in any well-drained loam soil in full sun. Start seed at 70° to 85°F and set out 8-week-old transplants, spaced 12 inches apart, after all danger of frost.

DESCRIPTION Primrose-like florets are arranged in flat clusters. Color range includes white, red, pink, blue, and purple with white centers. Leaves are dark green, narrow, serrated. Popular for massing in beds and borders, and for edging. Suitable for containers, especially window boxes.

RECOMMENDED VARIETY 'Springtime,' a good mixture that branches freely.

BOTANICAL NAME *Viola tricolor*

COMMON NAME Pansy

RANGE Native to Europe. Biennial grown as an annual.

HEIGHT 8 inches; low, mounded habit.

CULTURE Prefers moist, fertile, humus-rich soil in sun or partial shade. Start seed at 70°F and set out 10-week-old transplants, spaced 6 inches apart, either in fall or several weeks before the last expected spring frost date. Flowers best when nights are cool.

DESCRIPTION Cheerful flowers often have markings that resemble human facial characteristics. Color range includes red, white, blue, yellow, and orange with black blotches or black "whiskers," depending on the variety. Extremely popular for massing in beds and borders for early spring bloom. Also suitable for containers (especially window boxes) and rock gardens.

RECOMMENDED VARIETY 'Majestic Giants' or any hybrid mixture since hybrids are earliest-flowering and heat-resistant.

BOTANICAL NAME *Xeranthemum annuum*

COMMON NAME Immortelle

RANGE Native to the Mediterranean. Hardy annual.

HEIGHT 2 feet; erect habit.

CULTURE Easy to grow in any well-drained loam soil in full sun. Start seed at 70° to 85°F and set out 6-week-old transplants, spaced 12 inches apart, several weeks before the last expected spring frost date. Also can be direct-seeded.

DESCRIPTION Papery flowers have pointed petals. Colors include pink and white. Good accent for mixed beds and borders. Mostly grown for cutting and dried flower arrangements.

BOTANICAL NAME *Zinnia angustifolia*

COMMON NAME Classic Zinnia

RANGE Native to Mexico. Tender annual.

HEIGHT 12 inches; spreading habit.

CULTURE Easy to grow in any well-drained loam soil in full sun. Start seed at 70° to 85°F and set out 4-week-old transplants, spaced 12 inches apart, after danger of frost. Also can be direct-seeded. Tolerates dry soil.

DESCRIPTION Small, single orange flowers are borne in profusion on low-growing, ground-hugging plants. Leaves are smooth, pointed. Popular for edging beds and borders and as a ground cover to decorate dry slopes. Good for containers, particularly window boxes.

BOTANICAL NAME *Zinnia elegans*

COMMON NAME Zinnia

RANGE Native to Mexico. Tender annual.

HEIGHT Up to 3 feet; upright, branching habit.

CULTURE Easy to grow in any well-drained loam soil in full sun. Start seed at 70° to 85°F and set out 4- to 5-week-old transplants, spaced 12 inches apart, after danger of frost. Also can be direct-seeded.

DESCRIPTION Flowers are mostly divided into two kinds: dahlia-flowered with rounded petals and cactus-flowered with quilled petals. Color range includes white, yellow, orange, red, pink, purple, and green, plus bicolors. Popular massed in beds and borders. Good for cutting. Special dwarf varieties, such as the 'Peter Pans' are best for bedding.

Left: A bed of 'Majestic Giants' hybrid pansies flowers profusely during the cool weather of late spring.

Right: A window decorated with morning glory 'Heavenly Blue'.

CHAPTER THREE

PLANT SELECTION GUIDE

ANNUALS ARE AN EXTREMELY VERSATILE group of plants, some low-growing and suitable for creating flowering ground covers; others tall and spire-like for sensational backgrounds. There are annuals for sun and shade, dry and moist soils, plus many other uses and conditions.

ANNUALS WITH BLUE TO PURPLE FLOWERS

Ageratum houstonianum (Flossflower)
Anchusa capensis (Cape forget-me-not)
Browallia speciosa (Amtheyst flower)
Callistephus chinensis (China aster)
Campanula medium (Canterbury bells)
Centaurea cyanus (Bachelor's button)
Consolida ambigua (Rocket larkspur)
Convolvulus tricolor (Dwarf morning glory)
Cynoglossum amabile (Chinese forget-me-not)
Gomphrena globosa (Globe amaranth)
Heliotropium arborescens (Heliotrope)
Ipomoea tricolor (Morning glory vine)
Lathyrus odoratus (Sweet pea)
Limonium sinuatum (Sea lavender)
Lisianthus russulanus (Prairie gentian)
Lobelia erinus (Edging lobelia)
Myosotis sylvatica (Forget-me-not)
Nemophila menziesii (Baby-blue eyes)

Nierembergia hippomanica (Cup flower)
Petunia x *hybrida* (Petunia)
Phlox drummondii (Annual phlox)
Salpiglossis sinuata (Painted tongue)
Salvia farinacea (Blue sage)
Salvia splendens (Scarlet sage)
Scabiosa atropurpurea (Pincushion flower)
Torenia fournieri (Wishbone flower)
Trachymene coerulea (Blue lace flower)
Verbena x *hybrida* (Garden verbena)
Viola tricolor (Pansy)

ANNUALS WITH RED TO PINK FLOWERS

Amaranthus tricolor (Joseph's coat)
Alcea rosea (Hollyhock)
Antirrhinum majus (Snapdragon)
Begonia x *semperflorens* (Wax begonia)
Callistephus chinensis (China aster)
Capsicum annuum (Ornamental pepper)
Catharanthus roseus (Vinca, Periwinkle)
Celosia cristata (Cockscomb)
Clarkia hybrids (Godetia)
Cleome hasslerana (Spider flower)
Coleus x *hybridus* (Coleus)
Consolida ambigua (Larkspur)
Cosmos bipinnatus (Mexican aster)
Dahlia hybrids (Dahlia)
Dianthus species (China pink)
Digitalis purpurea (Foxglove)
Dimorphotheca sinuata (Cape marigold)
Eschscholzia californica (California poppy)
Gaillardia pulchella (Blanket flower)
Gazania ringens (Gazania)
Gypsophila elegans (Baby's-breath)
Helichrysum bracteatum (Strawflower)
Hibiscus moscheutos (Swamp mallow)
Iberis species (Candytuft)
Impatiens species (Balsam, Patience plant)
Lathyrus odoratus (Sweet pea)
Lavatera hybrids (Tree mallow)
Linaria maroccana (Toadflax)
Lisianthus russulanus (Prairie gentian)
Matthiola incana (Stock)
Mimulus x *hybridus* (Monkey flower)
Nemesia strumosa (Nemesia)
Nicotiana alata (Flowering tobacco)
Papaver species (Iceland poppy, Shirley poppy)
Pelargonium x *hortorum* (Geranium)
Petunia x *hybrida* (Petunia)

Phlox drummondii (Annual phlox)
Portulaca grandiflora (Rose moss)
Salpiglossis sinuata (Painted tongue)
Salvia splendens (Scarlet sage)
Scabiosa atropurpurea (Pincushion flower)
Schizanthus x *wisetonesis* (Butterfly flower)
Tropaeolum majus (Nasturtium)
Verbena x *hybrida* (Garden verbena)
Viola tricolor (Pansy)
Xeranthemum annuum (Immortelle)
Zinnia elegans (Zinnia)

ANNUALS WITH GREEN FLOWERS

Coleus hybrids (variety, Saber Lime Green)
Moluccella laevis (Bells-of-Ireland)
Nicotiana alata (variety, Limelight)
Zinnia elegans (variety, Envy)

ANNUALS WITH BLACK OR BROWN FLOWERS

Viola tricolor (Pansy variety, Jet Black)
Salpiglossis sinuata (Velvet flower)

Right: Red salvia and impatiens decorate a slope at Leaming's Run, New Jersey.

ANNUALS WITH YELLOW AND ORANGE FLOWERS

Alcea rosea (Hollyhock)
Calendula officinalis (Pot marigold)
Celosia cristata (Cockscomb)
Coreopsis tinctoria (Calliopsis)
Cosmos sulphureus (Orange cosmos)
Dahlia hybrids (Dahlia)
Dimorphotheca sinuata (Cape marigold)
Dyssodia tenuiloba (Dahlberg daisy)
Eschscholzia californica (California poppy)
Gaillardia pulchella (Blanket flower)
Gazania ringens (Gazania)
Gomphrena globosa (Globe amaranth)
Helianthus species (Sunflower)
Linaria maroccana (Toadflax)
Matthiola incana (Stock)
Mimulus x *hybridus* (Monkey flower)
Nemesia strumosa (Nemesia)
Papaver nudicaule (Iceland poppy)
Pelargonium x *hortorum* (Geranium)
Portulaca grandiflora (Rose moss)
Rudbeckia hirta (Gloriosa daisy)
Sanvitalia procumbens (Creeping zinnia)
Tagetes species (Marigolds)
Thunbergia alata (Black-eyed Susan vine)
Tithonia rotundifolia (Mexican sunflower)
Tropaeolum majus (Nasturtium)
Vendium fastuosum (Monarch-of-the-veldt)
Verbena x *hybrida* (Garden verbena)
Viola tricolor (Pansy)
Zinnia species (Zinnia)

ANNUALS WITH WHITE FLOWERS

Ageratum houstonianum (Flossflower)
Alcea rosea (Hollyhock)
Antirrhinum majus (Snapdragon)
Arctotis stoechadifolia (African daisy)
Begonia x *semperflorens* (Wax begonia)
Callistephus chinensis (China aster)
Catharanthrus roseus (Madagascar periwinkle)
Cleome hasslerana (Spider flower)
Dahlia hybrid (Dahlia)
Dianthus species (China pink)
Dimorphotheca sinuata (Cape marigold)
Eschscholzia californica (California poppy)
Gypsophila elegans (Baby's-breath)
Helichrysum bracteatum (Strawflower)

Iberis species (Candytuft)
Impatiens balsamina (Balsam)
Impatiens wallerana (Patience plant)
Ipomoea alba (Moonflower vine)
Lathyrus odoratus (Sweet pea)
Lobelia erinus (Edging lobelia)
Lobularia maritima (Sweet alyssum)
Matthiola incana (Stock)
Nicotiana alata (Flowering tobacco)
Papaver species (Iceland poppy, Shirley poppy)
Pelargonium x *hortorum* (Geranium)
Petunia x *hybrida* (Petunia)
Phlox drummondii (Annual phlox)
Salvia splendens (Scarlet sage)
Scabiosa atropurpurea (Pincushion flower)
Thunbergia alata (Black-eyed Susan vine)
Verbena x *hybrida* (Garden verbena)
Viola tricolor (Pansy)

Opposite page: A large formal bed featuring mostly petunias, marigolds, and dusty miller is planted to form a huge star design.
Left: White vinca makes a good companion in a border.

Opposite page: This spectacular flower border features pale pink spider plants, rose pink zinnias, scarlet cockscomb, and lime green coleus.

LOW-GROWING ANNUALS

Ageratum houstonianum (Flossflower)
Antirrhinum majus, dwarf cultivars (Snapdragon)
Arctotis stoechadifolia (African Daisy)
Begonia x *semperflorens* (Wax begonia)
Calendula officinalis (Pot marigold)
Capsicum annuum (Ornamental pepper)
Catharanthus roseus (Madagascar periwinkle)
Celosia cristata (Cockscomb)
Coleus x *hybridus* (Coleus)
Dahlia hybrids (Dahlia)
Dimorphotheca sinuata (Cape marigold)
Dyssodia tenuiloba (Dahlberg daisy)
Gaillardia pulchella (Blanket flower)
Gazania ringens (Gazania)
Iberis species (Candytuft)
Impatiens wallerana (Patience plant)
Limnanthes douglasii (Meadow foam)
Linaria maroccana (Toadflax)
Lobelia erinus (Edging lobelia)
Lobularia maritima (Sweet alyssum)
Myosotis sylvatica (Forget-me-not)
Nemesia strumosa (Nemesia)
Nemophila menziesii (Baby-blue eyes)
Nicotiana alata (Flowering tobacco)
Nierembergia hippomanica (Cup flower)
Pelargonium x *hortorum* (Geranium)
Petunia x *hybrida* (Petunia)
Phlox drummondii (Annual phlox)
Portulaca grandiflora (Rose moss)
Salvia species (Sage)
Sanvitalia procumbens (Creeping zinnia)
Schizanthus x *wisetonensis* (Butterfly flower)
Senecio cineraria (Dusty miller)
Tagetes species (Marigolds)
Tropaeolum majus (Nasturtium)
Verbena x *hybrida* (Garden verbena)
Viola tricolor (Pansy)
Zinnia species (Zinnia)

MEDIUM-GROWING ANNUALS

Anchusa capensis (Cape forget-me-not)
Amaranthus tricolor (Joseph's coat)
Calendula officinalis (Pot marigold)
Callistephus chinensis (China aster)
Catharanthus roseus (Madagascar periwinkle)
Clarkia hybrids (Godetia)
Cleome hasslerana (Spider flower)
Coleus x *hybridus* (Coleus)
Dahlia hybrids (Dahlia)
Eschscholzia californica (California poppy)
Euphorbia marginata (Snow-on-the-mountain)
Gomphrena globosa (Globe amaranth)
Helianthus species, dwarf cultivars (Sunflowers)
Helichrysum bracteatum (Strawflower)
Impatiens wallerana (Patience plant)
Kochia scoparia (Burning bush)
Lavatera hybrids (Tree mallow)
Limonium species (Algerian sea lavender, statice)
Mirabilis jalapa (Four-o'clock)
Pelargonium x *hortorum* (Geranium)
Petunia x *hybrida* (Petunia)
Papaver species (Poppies)
Rudbeckia hirta (Gloriosa daisy)
Schizanthus x *wisetonensis* (Butterfly flower)
Tagetes species (Marigolds)
Zinnia elegans (Zinnia)

TALL-GROWING ANNUALS

Alcea rosea (Hollyhock)
Amaranthus tricolor (Joseph's coat)
Antirrhinum majus (Tall snapdragon)
Celosia cristata (Plumed cockscomb)
Cleome hasslerana (Spider flower)
Consolida ambigua (Rocket larkspur)
Cosmos bipinnatus (Cosmos)
Delphinium elatum (Delphinium)
Digitalis purpurea (Foxglove)
Helianthus species (Sunflower)
Hibiscus moscheutos (Swamp mallow)
Tithonia rotundifolia (Mexican sunflower)
Zinnia elegans, tallest cultivars (Zinnia)

HEAT-TOLERANT ANNUALS

Amaranthus tricolor (Joseph's coat)
Begonia x *semperflorens-cultorum* (Wax begonia)
Capsicum annuum (Ornamental pepper)
Catharanthus roseus (Madagascar periwinkle)
Celosia cristata (Cockscomb)
Convolvulus tricolor (Dwarf morning glory)
Coreopsis tinctoria (Calliopsis)
Dahlia hybrids (Dahlia)
Dyssodia tenuiloba (Dahlberg daisy)
Euphorbia marginata (Snow-on-the-mountain)
Gomphrena globosa (Globe amaranth)
Helianthus species (Sunflowers)
Kochia scoparia (Burning bush)
Mirabilis jalapa (Four-o'clock)
Petunia x *hybrida* (Petunia)
Portulaca grandiflora (Rose moss)
Rudbeckia hirta (Gloriosa daisy)
Salvia species (Sage)
Sanvitalia procumbens (Creeping zinnia)
Senecio cineraria (Dusty miller)
Tagetes species (Marigold)
Tithonia rotundifolia (Mexican sunflower)
Verbena x *hybrida* (Garden verbena)
Zinnia species (Zinnia)

ANNUALS FOR MOIST SOIL

Cleome hasslerana (Spider flower)
Euphorbia marginata (Snow-on-the-mountain)
Hibiscus moscheutos (Swamp mallow)
Limnanthes douglasii (Meadow foam)
Mimulus x *hybridus* (Monkey flower)
Myosotis sylvatica (Forget-me-not)
Senecio x *hybridus* (Cineraria)
Torenia fournieri (Wishbone flower)
Tropaeolum majus (Nasturtium)
Viola tricolor (Pansy)

ANNUALS FOR SHADE

Begonia x *semperflorens* (Wax begonia)
Browallia speciosa (Amethyst flower)
Coleus x *hybridus* (Coleus)
Impatiens wallerana (Patience plant)
Mimulus x *hybridus* (Monkey flower)
Myosotis sylvatica (Forget-me-not)
Nemophilia menziesii (Baby-blue eyes)
Nicotiana alata (Flowering tobacco)
Senecio x *hybridus* (Cineraria)
Thunbergia alata (Black-eyed Susan vine)
Torenia fournieri (Wishbone flower)
Viola tricolor (Pansy)

ANNUALS FOR INDOORS

Begonia x *semperflorens* (Wax begonia)
Browallia speciosa (Amethyst flower)
Capsicum annuum (Ornamental pepper)
Catharanthus roseus (Madagascar periwinkle)
Coleus x *hybridus* (Coleus)
Impatiens wallerana (Patience plant)
Nierembergia hippomanica (Cup flower)
Pelargonium x *hortorum* (Geranium)
Thunbergia alata (Black-eyed Susan vine)
Torenia fournieri (Wishbone flower)

Left, above: A bed featuring snapdragons and coleus; the snapdragons are lighted by morning sun, the coleus can be seen in the shade of a tree.

Left, below: The gloriosa daisy, 'Pinwheel.'

Opposite page: Dwarf 'Peter Pan' orange zinnia begins flowering spectacularly in early summer.

ANNUALS FOR EDGING

Ageratum houstonianum (Floss flower)
Antirrhinum majus (Snapdragon)
Begonia x *semperflorens* (Wax begonia)
Brassica olereacea (Ornamental kale)
Browallia speciosa (Amethyst flower)
Callistephus chinensis (China aster)
Capsicum annuum (Ornamental pepper)
Celosia plumosa (Cockscomb)
Dianthus chinensis (China pink)
Iberis species (Candytuff)
Impatiens wallerana (Patience plant)
Linaria maroccana (Toadflax)
Lobelia erinus (Edging lobelia)
Nierembergia hippomanica (Cup flower)
Petunia x *hybrida* (Petunia)
Phlox drummondii (Annual phlox)
Portulaca grandiflora (Rose moss)
Senecio cineraria (Dusty miller)
Tagetes signata (Signet marigold)
Tagetes patula (French marigold)
Torenia fournieri (Wishbone flower)
Viola tricolor (Pansy)
Zinnia, dwarf cultivars (Zinnia)

ANNUALS FOR FRAGRANCE

Dianthus caryophyllus (Carnation)
Lathyrus odoratus (Sweet pea)
Lobularia maritima (Sweet alyssum)
Matthiola incana (Stock)
Mirabilis jalapa (Four-o'clock)
Nicotiana alata (Flowering tobacco)
Petunia x *hybrida* (Petunia)
Reseda odorata (Mignonette)
Scabiosa atropurpurea (Sweet scabious)

ANNUALS FOR HANGING BASKETS

Browallia speciosa (Amethyst flower)
Coleus x *hybrida* (Coleus)
Impatiens wallerana (Patience plant)
Lobelia erinus (Edging lobelia)
Lobularia maritima (Sweet alyssum)
Nemesia strumosa (Nemesia)
Pelargonium x *hortorum* (Geranium)
Petunia x *hybrida* (Petunia)
Sanvitalia procumbens (Creeping zinnia)
Schizanthus x *wisetonensis* (Butterly flower)
Thunbergia alata (Black-eyed Susan vine)
Tropaeolum majus (Nasturtium)
Verbena x *hybrida* (Garden verbena)
Viola tricolor (Pansy)

VINING ANNUALS

Cobaea scandens (Cup and saucer vine)
Cucurbita pepo (Gourds)
Ipomoea alba (Moonflower vine)
Ipomoea x *multifida* (Cardinal climber)
Lathyrus odoratus (Sweet pea)
Thunbergia alata (Black-eyed Susan vine)
Tropaeolum majus (Nasturtium) if trained

Opposite page: This color border features a mixtures of giant-flowered zinnias against an evergreen hedge.

ANNUALS FOR CUTTING

*Asterisked varieties make good everlastings.

Antirrhinum majis (Snapdragon)
Calendula officinalis (Pot marigold)
Callistephus chinensis (China aster)
Celosia cristata (Cockscomb)
Centaurea cyanus (Cornflower)
Chrysanthemum carinatum (Painted daisy)
Consolida ambigua (Larkspur)
Cosmos bipinnatus (Cosmos)
Dahlia x *hybrida* (Dahlia)
Delphinium elatum (Delphinium)
Dianthus caryophyllus (Carnation)
Digitalis purpurea (Foxglove)
Gaillardia pulchella (Gayflower)
* *Gomphrena globosa* (Globe flower)
Gypsophila elegans (Baby's-breath)
Helianthus annuus (Sunflower)
* *Helichrysum bracteatum* (Strawflower)
Lathyrus odoratus (Sweet pea)
* *Limonium sinuatum* (Statice)
Lisianthus russulanus (Prairie gentian)
Matthiola incana (Stocks)
* *Molucella laevis* (Bells of Ireland)
Papaver nudicaule (Iceland poppy)
Penstemon gloxiniodes (Beard tongue)
Rudbeckia hirta (Gloriosa daisy)
Salvia farinacea (Blue salvia)
Scabiosa atropurpurea (Sweet scabious)
Tagetes erecta (American marigold)
Venidium fastuosum (Monarch-of-the-veldt)
* *Xeranthemum annuum* (Immortelle)
Zinnia elegans (Zinnia)

ANNUALS THAT NATURALIZE

Alcea rosea (Hollyhock)
Anchusa capensis (Cape forget-me-not)
Calendula officinalis (Pot marigold)
Centaurea cyanus (Cornflower)
Coreopsis tinctoria (Calliopsis)
Cosmos bipinnatus (Cosmos)
Cosmos sulphureus (Orange cosmos)
Cynoglossum amabile (Chinese forget-me-not)
Dianthus chinensis (China pink)
Dyssodia tenuiloba (Dahlberg daisy)
Eschscholzia californica (California poppy)
Euphorbia marginata (Snow-on-the-mountain)
Limnanthes douglasii (Meadow foam)
Linaria maroccana (Toadflax)
Lobularia maritima (Sweet alyssum)
Mirabilis jalapa (Four-o'clock)
Moluccella laevis (Bells of Ireland)
Myosotis sylvatica (Forget-me-not)
Papaver nudicaule (Iceland poppy)
Papaver rhoeas (Shirley poppy)
Portulaca grandiflora (Rose moss)
Rudbeckia hirta (Gloriosa daisy)

ANNUALS WITH DECORATIVE FOLIAGE

Amaranthus tricolor (Joseph's coat)
Begonia x *semperflorens* (Wax begonia)
Brassica olereacea (Ornamental cabbage)
Coleux x *hybridus* (Coleus)
Euphorbia marginata (Snow-on-the-mountain)
Ipomoea species (Morning glory)
Kochia scoparia (Burning bush)
Pelargonium x *hortorum* (Geranium)
Senecio cineraria (Dusty miller)
Tagetes 'Irish Lace' (Irish lace marigold)

ANNUAL FLOWERING GUIDE

		Jan	Feb	Mar	Apr	May	Jun	Jul	Aug	Sep	Oct	Nov	Dec
Ageratum houstonianum	(Floss flower)						■	■	■	■			
Amaranthus tricolor	(Josephs-coat)						■						
Anchusa capensis	(Summer Forget-me-not)							■					
Antirrhinum majus	(Snapdragon)									■			
Arctotis stoechadifolia	(African Daisy)						■						
Begonia x *semperflorens*	(Wax Begonia)						■	■	■	■			
Brachycome iberidifolia	(Swan River Daisy)						■						
Brassica oleracea	(Ornamental Kale)										■	■	■
Browallia speciosa	(Lovely Browalia)							■	■	■			
Calendula officinalis	(Pot-Marigold)					■	■			■			
Callistephus chinensis	(China Aster)							■					
Capsicum annuum	(Ornamental Pepper)								■	■	■		
Catharanthus roseus	(Vinca, Periwinkle)						■	■	■	■	■		
Celosia cristata	(Crested Cockscomb)												
Centaurea cyanus	(Cornflower)							■					
Chrysanthemum carinatum	(Painted Daisy)												
Clarkia amoena	(Godetia, Satin Flower)						■						
Cleome hasslerana	(Spiderflower)								■	■	■		
Cobaea scandens	(Cup-and-saucer Vine)												
Coleus x *hybrida*	(Flame Nettle)					■	■			■			
Consolida ambigua	(Larkspur)												
Coreopsis tinctoria	(Plains Coreopsis)												
Cosmos bipinnatus	(Cosmos)							■	■	■			
Cucurbita pepo	(Ornamental Gourds							■	■	■			

		January	February	March	April	May	June	July	August	September	October	November	December
Cynoglossum amabile	(Chinese Forget-me-not)							■	■				
Dahlia x *hybrida*	(Bedding Dahlias)						■	■	■	■	■		
Datura metel	(Angel's Trumpet)							■	■	■	■		
Delphinium elatum	(Candle Larkspur)						■	■					
Dianthus caryophyllus	(Carnation)							■	■	■			
Dianthus chinensis	(Dianthus)					■	■	■					
Dimorphotheca sinuata	(Cape Marigold, African Daisy)												
Dorotheanus bellidiformis	(Livingstone Daisy)												
Eschscholzia californica	(California-poppy)					■	■						
Euphorbia marginata	(Snow-on-the-Mountain)							■	■	■			
Gaillardia pulchella	(Blanket Flower)						■	■	■	■			
Gazania ringens	(Rainbow Daisy)							■	■	■			
Gomphrena globosa	(Globe Amaranth)							■	■	■	■		
Gypsophila elegans	(Baby's-breath)						■	■					
Helianthus annuus	(Sunflower)								■	■			
Helichrysum bracteatum	(Straw-flower)							■	■	■			
Hunnemannia fumariifolia	(Mexican Tulip Poppy)												
Iberis umbellata	(Candytuft)					■	■	■					
Impatiens balsamina	(Balsam)						■	■	■				
Impatiens wallerana	(Patience-plant)					■	■	■	■	■	■		
Ipomoea alba	(Moonflower)							■	■	■			
Ipomoea tricolor	(Morning Glory)							■	■	■	■		
Kochia scoparia	(Burning Bush)							■	■	■	■		
Lathyrus odoratus	(Sweet Pea)							■	■				

	January	February	March	April	May	June	July	August	September	October	November	December
Lavatera trimestris (Rose-mallow)							X	X				
Limnathes douglasii (Meadow-foam)					X	X						
Limonium sinuatum (Statice)							X	X				
Linaria maroccana (Toadflax)							X					
Lisianthus russulanus (*Eustoma grandiflorum*) (Prairie-gentian)								X	X			
Lobelia erinus (Lobelia)							X	X	X			
Lobularia maritima (Alyssum)				X	X	X				X		
Machaeranthera tanacetifolia (Tahoka-daisy)							X	X	X			
Matthiola incana (Common Stocks)							X	X	X			
Mimulus x *hybridus* (Monkey-flower)							X		X			
Mirabilis jalapa (Four-O'clock)							X	X				
Moluccella laevis (Bells-of-Ireland)												
Myosotis sylvatica (Forget-me-not)					X							
Nemesia strumosa (Nemesia)							X		X			
Nemophilia menziensii (Baby-blue-eyes)												
Nicotiana alata (Flowering Tobacco)								X	X			
Nierembergia hippomanica (Capflower)												
Papaver nudicaule (Iceland Poppy)					X	X	X					
Papaver rhoeas (Shirley Poppy)						X	X					
Pelargonium x *hortorum* (Geranium)							X	X	X	X		
Penstemon gloxiniodes (Bearded Tongue)								X				
Petunia x *hybrida* (Petunia)						X	X	X	X	X		
Phlox drummondii (Phlox)						X	X					

		January	February	March	April	May	June	July	August	September	October	November	December
Portulaca grandiflora	(Moss Rose)						■	■	■	■			
Reseda odorata	(Mignonette)						■	■	■	■			
Ricinus communis	(Castor-bean Plant)						■	■	■	■	■		
Rudbeckia hirta burpeeii	(Black-eyed-Susan)						■	■	■	■			
Salpiglossis sinuata	(Velvet-flower)						■	■					
Salvia farinacea	(Blue Salvia)						■	■	■	■	■		
Salvia splendens	(Scarlet Sage)							■	■	■	■		
Sanvitalia procumbens	(Creeping Zinnia)						■	■	■	■	■		
Scabiosa atropurpurea	(Sweet Scabious)						■	■	■	■			
Schiznathus x *wisetonensis*	(Butterfly-flower)					■	■						
Senecio cineraria	(Dusty Miller)					■	■	■	■	■			
Tagetes erecta	(American Marigold)						■	■	■	■	■		
Tagetes patula	(French Marigold)						■	■	■	■	■		
Tagetes tenuifolia	(Striped Marigold)						■	■	■	■	■		
Thunbergia alata	(Black-eyed Susan Vine)						■	■	■	■			
Tithonia rotundifolia	(Mexican Sunflower)						■	■	■	■			
Torenia fournieri	(Wishbone flower)							■	■	■	■		
Tropaeolium majus	(Nasturtium)						■	■	■	■	■		
Venidium fastuosum	(Monarch-of-the-veldt)							■	■	■			
Verbena x *hybrida*	(Summer Verbena)							■	■	■			
Viola tricolor	(Pansy)					■	■						
Xeranthemium annuum	(Immortelle)						■	■					
Zinnia angustifolia	(Classic Zinnia)							■	■	■			
Zinnia elegans	(Zinnia)							■	■	■			

Left: This sensible planting scheme features tall cosmos as a background, blue salvia in the middle, and dwarf French marigolds in the foreground.

PART TWO

ESSENTIAL
PERENNIALS

INTRODUCTION

FLORAL BEAUTY YEAR AFTER YEAR

A COLORFUL PERENNIAL BORDER IS A HIGHLY popular garden feature. It not only provides an old-fashioned accent, but, when properly planted, brings a sophisticated beauty to the garden that no other group of herbaceous plants can match. Not as gaudy as beds of annuals, not as short-flowering as most bulb plantings, perennials offer extensive design possibilities.

First, it's important to know what a perennial is in comparison to other groups of plants, such as *annuals*, which complete their life cycle in a year, and *biennials*, which complete their life cycle in two years. However, biennials often give the appearance of being perennials because they generally seed themselves freely, and so seedlings are always springing up in the bed to replace the older plants. Broadly defined, a perennial can be any plant that lives for more than two years, producing foliage the first year and flowering the next, then under favorable conditions, continues to flower year after year. Based on this definition, all shrubs and bulbs could be considered perennials. However, in horticultural circles true perennials are considered different from bulbs because bulbs have a unique ability to survive periods of stress—such as severe cold or drought—because of their swollen underground food store, called a bulb (also called a rhizome, corm, or tuber, depending on its composition). True perennials are also distinguished from most shrubs because shrubs develop a special, durable cell structure known as "wood." A small group of plants called "subshrubs" bridge the gap between perennials and shrubs. Although they are similar to perennials, subshrubs do in time grow a woody cell structure. Tree peonies, lavender, and rosemary are examples of subshrubs that are frequently classified as perennials and grown in perennial gardens.

True perennials are often referred to as "herbaceous perennials," with stems that are soft and fleshy rather than woody. In this book, we will deal mostly with herbaceous perennials. Some are evergreen, maintaining green leaves throughout winter, but most have top growth that dies down to the ground, surviving winter weather by means of vigorous roots that are better adapted for longevity than those of annuals or biennials. There is a large group of true perennials that can be grown as annuals to flower the first year, providing the seed is sown early enough. Some varieties of rudbeckias, such as gloriosa daisies, are examples of perennials that will flower the first year. The same is true with some varieties of delphinium, dianthus, and hollyhock *(Alcea rosea)*. The best example of a native perennial that plant breeders have developed to bloom the first year is the hardy hibiscus, 'Southern Belle.' Developed from *Hibiscus moscheutos,* native to southern swamps, Southern Belle grows flowers up to ten inches across in white, pink, or red, providing the seed is started early indoors and four-inch transplants can be set into the garden after the last frost date in spring. Though the seedlings are tender to frost, once established the plant will survive severe winter weather by means of its hardy root system, producing fresh green growth and an abundance of new flowers year after year.

Perennials are most often considered for beds and borders where an informal, natural look is desired in the landscape. Perennials can be mixed to obtain a succession of color from spring through autumn, or one kind can be planted in a mass to make a dramatic impact over a shorter period of time. Though most perennials are valued for their colorful flowers, a vast number are prized for their ornamental leaves. Foliage color in perennials is especially treasured because it generally lasts much longer than the fleeting beauty of other flowers. Ornamental grasses and ferns are good examples of this group. The color of the leaves is not the only facet to consider when planting mixed perennial beds and borders; texture and form are also important. The heavily veined leaves of some hostas, for example, are extremely attractive, while the wispy, graceful leaves of fountain grass are a beautiful highlight among perennials with broader leaves, such as hostas and lamb's ears *(Stachys byzantina)*.

© Elizabeth Murray

Opposite page, left: In autumn, Claude Monet's garden at Giverney, France, features this border of perennial yellow sunflowers and purple Michaelmas daisies, plus annual nasturtiums and tuberous red dahlias.

Opposite page, right: Mixed beds of summer-flowering perennials interplanted with salad greens.

Right: Drifts of perennial sedum cover a sunny slope at Ohme Gardens, Wenatchee, Washington State.

CHAPTER ONE

DESIGNING WITH PERENNIALS

THERE ARE TWO WAYS TO PLANT PERENNIALS for color impact. One is to concentrate color for a particular season, such as early summer when most perennials reach peak bloom. Another is to spread color over an extended period so that something new is always coming into bloom. The latter is the most difficult to achieve—except in large gardens—without the help of annuals and flowering bulbs to fill in during the early and later months of the growing season.

Perennials are versatile plants for decorating a landscape, far more adaptable to a large range of soil types and light conditions than annuals or flowering bulbs. Only among perennials, for example, will you find flowering plants suitable for boggy soils and water gardens. Also, there is a far greater choice of flowering perennials suitable for shade.

To help you in your selections, see the chart on page 194 which gives approximate blooming times for the 100 choice perennial plants featured in this book.

Beds and Borders are the traditional way to effectively display perennials. Beds are usually planted in circular, oval, square, rectangular, or kidney shapes. Sometimes, they are triangular or pie-shaped when part of a cartwheel design. They are basically islands of soil, usually surrounded by lawn or paving material, with the soil mounded in the center to facilitate drainage and to provide a better display contour than a simple flat surface would. Borders have a backdrop—usually a wall, fence, or hedge with the soil elevated, sloping up to the rear.

One of the most impressive ways to use perennials in a garden is in a "double border," where parallel borders are divided by a path, ending in a focal point such as a gazebo, fountain, or bench. The effect is particularly attractive if the dividing strip is grass: but, where foot traffic is heavy, a paving material—such as brick or flagstone—can be used.

Since perennials come in a vast range of heights, varying from ground-hugging plants to tall plants, care must be taken so that the shorter ones are not screened by the taller ones. In island beds, concentrate tall plants in the middle and shorter ones around the edge. In a border, the tall plants should be placed in the rear and the short ones in the front.

Perennials generally have vigorous root systems, and therefore the soil for beds and borders should be dug deeply (to at least two feet) and enriched with plenty of organic material, such as well-decomposed animal manure, leaf mold, garden compost, or peat (for more on how to prepare soil for planting perennials, see page 123).

Both beds and borders can be easily cared for by installing drip irrigation systems to provide moisture during dry spells, and by applying a weed-suffocating mulch to hide and protect the drip lines.

Rock Gardens are popular places to grow perennials, especially when there is a good balance between the color of the perennial plants and other design elements such as evergreen shrubs, rocks, and water. Perennials that creep and cascade over rough terrain are especially good to plant in rock gardens, particularly those that are drought tolerant, such as mountain phlox *(Phlox subulata),* sedum, and echevaria. However, an easy-care form of rock garden is a dry wall, where large perennials can be planted along the top and smaller ones inserted between stones down the side. Low, spreading perennials—such as yellow alyssum and rock cress—are especially good for rock gardens and dry walls since they have the ability to drape over ledges and boulders.

Water Gardens take the form of an informal pond or a formal pool, where plants can be positioned on dry ground around the water to provide the drainage they need. There is also a large group of perennials called "bog plants" that thrive in permanently wet soil. In designing water gardens you should divide your plants into two distinct groups: those that like wet roots and those that are better suited to higher ground around the margin.

In formal pools, perennial plants are generally used sparingly if the architectural lines of the pool must complement other design elements, such as a nearby building. In this case, perennials are usually grown in containers sunk into the pool at strategic places so there is enough clear water between the plants to produce reflections.

In informal pools it is much more effective if the edges blur, with perennial plants spilling over into the water, billowing foliage contrasting with spiky foliage, creating a type of organized chaos.

Cutting Garden Many perennials with long stems are valued for the beautiful indoor floral arrangements that can be created with them. Though cutting flowers can be taken from display beds and borders, the overall color impact of the border will be reduced. Thus, many people prefer to have a special area set apart from the display area specifically for cutting, with flowers planted in regimented rows to make picking easy. Often, this area is adjacent to a vegetable garden since vegetables for the kitchen and perennials for arrangements can be conveniently picked at the same time.

Cut perennials will last a long time simply by immersing them in water soon after cutting. Lilies *(Lilium),* gay feather *(Liatris spicata),* asters, and shasta daisies *(Chrysanthemum* x *superbum)* are especially valued for cutting. Others—such as sea holly *(Eryngium maritimum)* and globe thistle *(Echinops ritro)*—are suitable for drying to create longer-lasting dried flower arrangements. A small group quickly wilt after cutting.

Left: This intensively planted perennial garden features pink 'Autumn Joy' sedum, yellow rudbeckia, mauve astilbe, and blue hosta on both sides of a small stream.
Opposite page, left: a large mixed flower arrangement of garden perennials.
Opposite page, right: A small, simple, fresh flower arrangement of mixed varieties of chrysanthemums.

This can be stopped by sealing the cut end either by steeping it in boiling water for a few seconds or by scorching the ends. Poppies and dahlias are notable examples.

Don't just cut perennials for their flowers. Many have interesting foliage shapes, textures, and colors that can make floral arrangements more dramatic.

Shade Garden There are many different kinds of shade, from light shade where many different plants can grow, to deep shade where the choice of plant types is much more limited. The time of day that shade falls on a garden is also important. Some plants will flower poorly if shaded at noon, but will perform reasonably well when shaded during the morning or late afternoon. Likewise, many perennial wildflowers will bloom spectacularly in spring before the leaves are in full leaf, but woodland shade may be too heavy during mid-summer for many perennial varieties.

When shade is too great, measures can be taken to adjust the perennials to the environment. Even the removal of a single overhanging tree limb can make a noticeable difference. In fact, tests in light laboratories have shown that even 1 percent more light can mean a 100 percent improvement in plant performance.

The addition of brightly colored walls can help increase the amount of reflected light into a problem shade area; also, laying down a highly reflective mulch, such as white pebbles or landscape chips, can produce spectacular results.

In a heavily wooded area, don't be afraid to thin out the overhead tree canopy by selectively removing mature trees if too much shade is preventing the growth of your plants. If you cannot bring yourself to do this and would rather keep the area densely shaded, then consider an understory (a growth of plants low to the ground) of mostly foliage plants, such as ferns and hostas. The diversity of shapes, colors, and textures that can be obtained from just these two large perennial plant families is remarkable.

Opposite page: This coastal garden on Long Island, New York, features a rich assortment of ornamental grasses, plus clump-forming perennials with colorful foliage.
Far left: Perennial white physostegia, yellow rudbeckia, and annual red salvia create a colorful flower bed in late summer.
Left: A dry wall richly planted with sun-loving perennials, including blue companula, yellow and red rock rose, and purple fleabane.

Meadow Gardens   Grasses and weeds are tenacious competition for a meadow garden. Many grasses are too aggressive and will crowd out cultivated perennials. However, some perennials can persist against grass competition. In a meadow garden it is possible to create spaces where clumps of perennials can be kept free of the encroaching grass. Some very good persistent perennials include species of tickseed (*Coreopsis*), cone flower (*Echinacea*), daylilies (*Hemerocallis*), loosestrife (*Lythrum*), gay feather (*Liatris*), and blackeyed Susan (*Rudbeckia*). It's also possible to highlight a meadow garden by introducing some clump-forming ornamental grasses into it.

Don't expect to create a meadow garden by broadcasting perennial seeds like chicken feed among tall grasses and expect a harmonious field of wildflowers. Usually, it is far more successful if the entire area is plowed first. Then scatter a mixture containing both annual and perennial wildflower species onto bare soil. The annuals will bloom the first season and complete their life cycle, while the perennials will establish themselves during their first season and bloom strongly the next and subsequent years. Eventually, stubborn grasses and noxious weeds may begin to dominate and deplete the perennial flowering display, at which time the area can be plowed up and the process repeated.

Perennial Grass Garden   Ornamental grass gardens have become extremely popular in recent years, particularly in places that are exposed to climatic extremes such as high winds and arid soil. At first, a border or garden of ornamental grasses may seem rather a boring prospect, but it is amazing how colorful a grass garden can be if the right varieties are chosen. For example, Japanese blood grass *(Imperata cylindrica rubra)* turns a brilliant crimson red color in autumn that is especially attractive when backlit by a rising or setting sun. Blue fescue *(Festuca glauca)* is a wonderful powder blue color that is accentuated even more dramatically on rainy days. Plus, there are many yellow and silver variegated forms of grasses.

In addition to the leaf colors, it's important to consider the flowering display some ornamental grasses produce. Most striking are the fluffy white plumes of pampas plume *(Cortadera selloana)* and the arching pink plumes of fountain grass *(Pennisetum setaceum)*.

Opposite page: This late-summer perennial border features orange helenium, yellow rudbeckia, and blue-mist shrubs.

Left: This rock garden successfully blends dwarf conifers with colorful perennials, including pink stonecrop sedum, red dragon's blood sedum, silvery lamb's ears, and yellow rudbeckia.

It's also possible to create striking contours with ornamental grasses by placing them in the landscape like cushions on a sofa. Many have billowing, cascading silhouettes with long, slender, arching leaves. Others have leaves that stand stiff and upright, while yet another group will lie prostrate to make a dense ground cover. Ornamental grasses can be planted to create hedges and screens, particularly for swimming pools and patios where the slightest rustle of leaves in the breeze can create the illusion of living in a serene and peaceful wilderness.

Most ornamental grass gardens undergo dramatic transformations in autumn, as their dried seed heads, shimmering in the sunlight, change color to wonderful shades of beige, russet, brown, and silver.

Perennial Fern Garden Consider fern gardens for shady places, especially under trees that cast high shade and beside water features such as streams, ponds, and pools. Though ferns are widely distributed throughout the world, surviving in both desert and arctic environments, the widest selection is best grown in a cool, moist environment. Even if you live in a region with severe winters where tropical ferns cannot survive outdoors, you can plant a tropical fern garden in tubs so they can be moved indoors during the winter. Two particularly good tree ferns are the Australian tree fern *(Alsophila australis)* and the Hawaiian tree fern *(Cybotium splendens)*, both of which grow a healthy crown of fronds atop slender, dark brown trunks. Unfortunately, there are no hardy tree ferns. But, frost-exclusion is all that's necessary to keep the Australian tree fern healthy throughout the winter.

Ferns are best planted in groups, with each variety allowed a special territory within which to spread. Paths mulched with pine needles can wind through the clumps of ferns.

A water feature is particularly suited for a fern garden, especially a waterfall with ferns planted in pockets of soil among boulders, so that the droplets of splashing water soak the fern fronds.

Cushions of moss and clumps of hostas among ferns create a soothing, cooling environment.

Left: This colorful corner planting features red Maltese cross, yellow yarrow, and purple sage.

CHAPTER TWO

GROWING PERENNIALS

THERE ARE MANY WAYS THAT PERENNIALS can regenerate themselves. The least expensive and most popular method is generally by seed; this method of propagation allows hundreds—or even thousands—of plants to be reproduced for a fraction of a penny apiece. Sometimes a good method is to sow the seed in a specially prepared seed bed. When the seedlings are large enough to transplant they can be moved to permanent quarters in the garden. In this manner, you don't have to bother with starter pots or potting soil. However, it is advisable to locate the special seedling bed in a lightly shaded location to protect the young seedlings from sunburn. An alternate source of irrigation is also needed so that in case of insufficient rainfall, the seedlings can still be watered. Perennials can be sown into the soil from about mid-spring to mid-summer, allowing the majority of them to grow to a sturdy size by the time fall frosts occur and winter weather makes them dormant. Transplanted to their flowering positions in fall, perennials will remain dormant through the winter and then burst into glorious bloom in spring and summer.

Another seed-starting method is to grow perennials in starter pots during spring or summer, and transplant them to the garden in late summer, early fall, or the following spring if you can provide some protection, such as a cold frame, during severe winter weather. A cold frame is a miniature greenhouse—made of wood or aluminum—partially sunk into the soil, with a glass or plastic cover that can be vented during sunny days.

To grow perennials in starter pots, it's first necessary to germinate the seeds in a seed flat or a seed tray. Different perennials have different optimum temperature needs (and other idiosyncrasies), which normally will be printed on the seed packet. Once the seeds have germinated and are large enough to handle, they should be removed from the seed flat and individually potted. Two kinds of starter pots are popular—those made of plastic with a flexible bottom so that the soil and root ball can be popped up easily when you transplant, and those made of compressed peat. Roots will grow through the peat and, providing the bottom is torn loose to release the lower roots, the entire pot can be planted with minimum root disturbance and transplant shock.

BUYING PERENNIAL PLANTS

Many people do not have the time or the inclination to fuss with seeds, and would much rather buy started plants from a garden center or specialist mail-order nursery. In this case, there are distinct differences between the two sources of supply. Generally speaking, if you buy perennial plants from a local garden center your choice will be limited solely to the most popular types and varieties offered. To have access to more sophisticated varieties, and a much larger offering of hard-to-find species, you will have to turn to the list of sources on page 679.

Perennials offered by mail are usually quite different from perennials you purchase in pots at a garden center. Mail-order perennials are generally supplied "bare-root"—wrapped in moist paper to keep the root from drying out. Or, the perennial will be growing in a small "plug"—a cone of soil with the roots forming a mesh that holds the soil together. These should be transplanted into the garden as soon as possible and watered regularly until they are well established. At the time of planting, you may need to gently open the root mass and pack soil in and around it to give the roots breathing space. Although spring is an ideal time to plant perennials, so, too, is fall since the cool conditions and the abundant moisture that prevail at that time of year generally allow the roots to grow strong before extremely cold weather makes them dormant.

ROOT DIVISIONS

A large group of perennials—such as daylilies *(Hemerocallis)*, bearded iris *(Iris germanica)*, and peonies *(Paeonia)*— take a long time to produce flowering-sized plants from seed, and in many cases the resulting progeny may be a mixture of different colors. If you do not want to wait, root division is a quicker way to increase your stock of this particular group of perennials. After several years, most perennials will form thick clumps of roots or bulbs that are easily divided in the spring or fall. Depending on the size of the mother clump, you will normally need a garden fork to dig up the root mass and separate it into smaller clumps. Usually, the clump will show growing tips where new foliage will appear. Providing each division has a minimum of three growing points, the clump is likely to make good progress when transplanted.

Some perennials have such vigorous root systems that all it takes to grow a new plant is a small piece of root, called a root cutting. But, it can be tedious cutting roots so small, and simple division will ensure a higher rate of success.

Left, above: Bearded iris rhizomes prior to dividing. *Left, below:* The same bearded iris rhizomes after dividing and ready for transplanting.

Root Divisions

1. Thick perennial clumps may need separating into smaller clumps by using garden forks to make divisions.

2. Separate smaller clumps by hand, ensuring each clump has a healthy growing crown and roots.

3. Lift clump with fork or spade. Wash away large clumps of soil. Pull and separate into divisions, each division containing new growth or buds, old stems, and a root system.

4. In the ground, a typical perennial clump will look like this—with the thick root ball hollow in the middle. Sometimes new growth is not as obvious as shown here, especially in fall after frost.

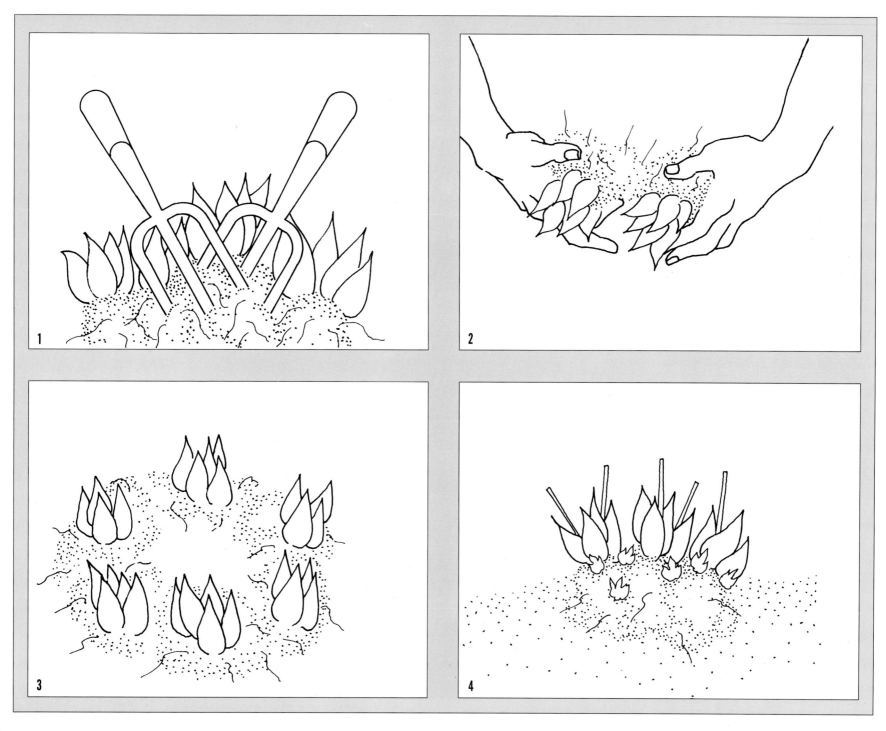

STEM CUTTINGS

A vast number of perennials readily root themselves from stem sections, called stem cuttings. Carnations (*Dianthus caryophyllus*), asters, and chrysanthemums are popular perennials frequently increased by stem cuttings. Usually, a four- to six-inch section of new growth on side shoots is cut on a slant just below the leaf joint. Leaves in the lower half are removed so that just a crown of leaves at the top of the cutting remains. The bare stem section is treated with a rooting hormone (available from garden centers) and inserted into a moist potting soil, such as a peat-perlite mixture. Normally, a seed flat is used so that dozens of cuttings can be rooted at one time. Place the flat under light shade in a cold frame or under a plastic cover for protection until the cuttings are well rooted. Keep the soil moist. After a period of about four to six weeks you should be able to tug on one of the cuttings to find if it has developed a healthy root system along the bare section of stem.

On a smaller scale, cuttings can be rooted in eight- or ten-inch clay pots placed on a bright windowsill indoors. Avoid direct sunlight since cuttings are easily burned, especially under glass, and do not allow the soil to dry out.

Left: This dramatic perennial border features perennial white shasta daisies, plumes of white salvia, blue globe bellflower, and orange-flowered annual cosmos.

Stem Cuttings

1. Cut off a 5-inch-long side shoot.

2. Remove lower leaves.

3. Dip end in rooting hormone.

4. Set firmly in soil mix.

5. and 6. Place cuttings in propagator, made from seed flat, with plastic cover.

7. Alternatively, use deep box covered with glass.

8. Set out in cold frames during winter.

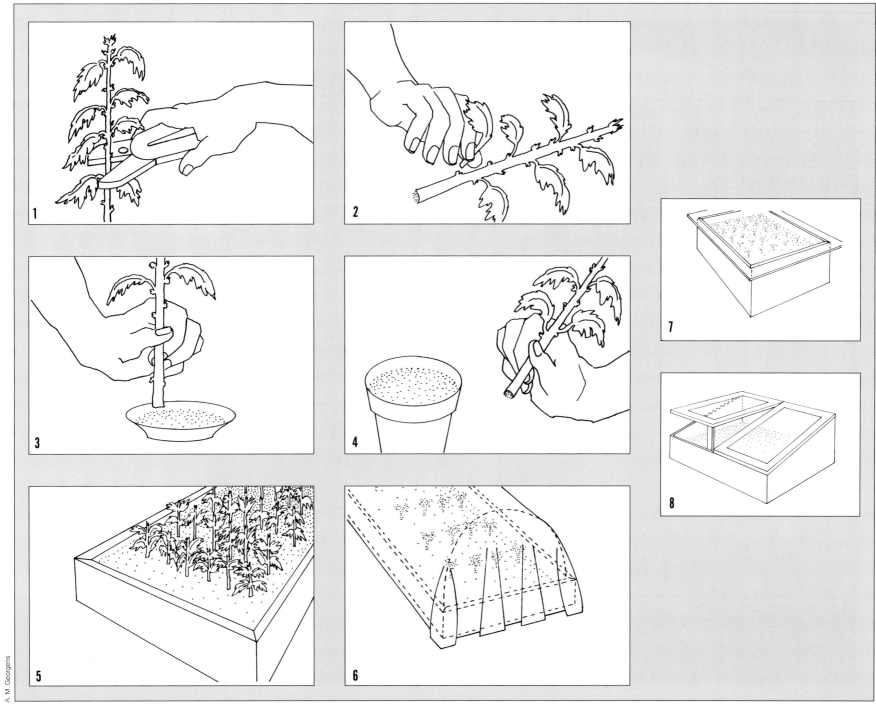

A. M. Georgens

Left: Perennial phlox light up this perennial border in early summer.

Opposite page, left: Here, perennial lavender is protected in the winter by a mulch of pine needles applied after the first frost.

Opposite page, above: Viola plants set out into their flowering positions in autumn are protected with a mulch of attractive pine needles so they will bloom early in spring.

Opposite page, below: Here, perennial plants have been mulched with decorative pine bark to deter weeds and conserve soil moisture.

SOIL PREPARATION

Perennials are mostly planted in beds and borders. Although many are tolerant of poor soil and dry conditions, generally they are heavy feeders, requiring not only a fertile soil high in organic matter, but also one that is crumbly to a depth of at least two feet, with good moisture retention and good drainage of excess moisture. Soil that is excessively sandy or contains a lot of clay is not good for perennials. In both cases, the addition of large amounts of well-decomposed animal manure, compost, leaf mold, or peat moss may be necessary to bring the soil up to standard.

In soil with high acidity (generally found in areas with high rainfall) the addition of lime may be necessary every three years at the rate of 5 pounds per 100 square feet. In soil that contains high alkaline it may be necessary to build a raised bed of stones or landscape ties above the indigenous soil, and truck in a soil with low alkalinity or neutral pH.

A good way to get the necessary soil depth for beds and borders is to raise the planting area. Mound the soil so it stands about twelve inches above the original soil level, and edge the bed with stone or landscape ties to keep it in place.

To conserve soil moisture it is a good practice to incorporate some kind of "mulch"—a covering over the soil that deters weeds and retains moisture—into it. Good mulch materials for perennials include shredded bark, wood chips, straw, shredded leaves, leaf mold, and garden compost. A soil that is topped each year with compost will generally keep perennials in good health. Where compost is not available to do this, a general-purpose granular fertilizer—such as 10–10–10—should be scattered over the soil in early spring and carefully raked into the upper inch of the soil. The numbers 10–10–10 refer to the percentages of major plant nutrients in a fertilizer formula. In this case: 10 percent nitrogen, 10 percent phosphorus, and 10 percent potash. The remaining 70 percent of this fertilizer is "filler" that acts as a distributing agent.

CHAPTER THREE

THE ENCYCLOPEDIA OF ESSENTIAL PERENNIALS

T HE FOLLOWING SUPERLATIVE PERENNIALS for garden display have been chosen for their ornamental value, many with gorgeous flowering displays, others for their decorative leaves.

They are listed alphabetically by their botanical (Latin) name because this most consistently identifies garden perennials better than their common names. While many have popular common names—'Johnny Jump-up' for *Viola tricolor*—others are not as common or are known by two or more common names— *Yucca filamentosa,* for example, is often called 'Yucca,' 'Desert Candle,' or 'Adam's Needle.'

To find a description for any perennial where you know only the common name, simply refer to the index for a quick cross-reference.

The heights given are mostly mature heights, when the plants start to flower. Often, with good soil or abundant rainfall, or late in the season, plants may exceed the heights stated here.

BOTANICAL NAME *Acanthus mollis*

COMMON NAME Bear's-breech

RANGE Native to Mediterranean. Hardy zone 8 south.

HEIGHT 4 feet; spreading habit.

CULTURE Tender. Needs cool, moist soil in sun or shade. Propagated by root division. Blooms in early summer.

DESCRIPTION Large, deeply indented, glossy green leaves are highly ornamental, creating a tropical, shrublike appearance. Flowers are pale purple, borne on long, slender flower spikes. Popular in coastal locations. Good garden accent used singly; also useful as a ground cover for large expanses of moist soil. Flower spikes make good dried arrangements.

BOTANICAL NAME *Achillea filipendulina*

COMMON NAME Yellow Yarrow

RANGE Native to Europe and Asia. Hardy zone 4 south.

HEIGHT 3 to 4 feet; upright, spreading habit.

CULTURE Easy to grow in any well-drained garden soil in full sun. Propagated by root division. Blooms in spring.

DESCRIPTION An invasive plant forming dense clumps of fern-like, aromatic leaves. Flat flower panicles are borne on slender stems in shades of yellow, mostly golden yellow and pale yellow. A related species, *A. millefolium* has rosy red flowers. Effective in mixed beds and borders. Good for cutting and adding fragrance to potpourris.

RECOMMENDED VARIETY 'Moonshine.'

BOTANICAL NAME *Aegopodium podagraria* 'variegatum'

COMMON NAME Bishop's-weed

RANGE Native to Europe and Asia. Hardy zone 4 south.

HEIGHT 12 inches; low, spreading habit.

CULTURE Easy to grow in any well-drained garden soil in full sun. Propagated by root division in spring or fall. Blooms early summer, but grown more for its attractive leaves.

DESCRIPTION Ivy-shaped leaves form a dense mat, making this an ideal ground cover, especially for edging paths. Light green leaves have a white margin. Flowers are white like Queen Anne's Lace, borne on long, slender stems. Flower stems can be used as a cut flower.

BOTANICAL NAME *Ajuga reptans*

COMMON NAME Blue Bugle

RANGE Native to Europe. Hardy zone 3 south.

HEIGHT 3 to 6 inches; low, rosette-forming habit.

CULTURE Easy to grow in any well-drained garden soil. Propagated by division of offsets in spring or fall. Spring-blooming.

DESCRIPTION Plants form attractive ground-hugging rosettes of evergreen, dark green, crinkled leaves. Bronze leaf and variegated forms are also available. Attractive blue or white flower spikes appear in spring. Best used as a ground cover for edging paths and as drifts in rock gardens.

RECOMMENDED VARIETY 'Burgundy Glow' with white and pink variegated foliage.

BOTANICAL NAME *Alcea rosea*

COMMON NAME Hollyhocks

RANGE Native to China. Hardy zone 4 south.

HEIGHT 6 feet; upright habit.

CULTURE Prefers moist, fertile loam soil in full sun. Propagated mostly by seed. Summer-flowering.

DESCRIPTION Tall flower spikes are studded with cup-size satinlike flowers in red, pink, yellow, and white. Both single and double flower forms are popular. Leaves are large, green, ivy-shaped. Good to use for tall backgrounds in mixed borders. Also popular to grow against walls, along fence rows, and beside garden structures such as tool sheds.

BOTANICAL NAME *Alchemilla mollis*

COMMON NAME Lady's-mantle

RANGE Native to Europe. Hardy zone 4 south.

HEIGHT 1 to 2 feet; prostrate, spreading habit.

CULTURE Prefers moist, humus-rich soil in sun or partial shade. Propagated by root division. Spring-blooming.

DESCRIPTION Yellow flowers are borne in dense clusters and are highly ornamental, though plants are also grown for their silvery leaves that form bushy clumps. Popular for edging garden pools and as an accent in mixed beds and borders.

BOTANICAL NAME *Amsonia tabernaemontana*

COMMON NAME Blue-star

RANGE Native to North America. Hardy zone 4 south.

HEIGHT 2 feet; bushy habit.

CULTURE Prefers moist, well-drained loam soil in full sun. Propagated by root division. Spring-flowering.

DESCRIPTION Masses of pale blue flowers are borne in clusters on long stems. The willow-like leaves give the plants a graceful appearance. Good accent for mixed beds and borders. Suitable for cutting.

BOTANICAL NAME *Anchusa azurea*

COMMON NAME Italian Bugloss

RANGE Native to Europe. Hardy zone 4 south.

HEIGHT 3 to 5 feet; erect habit.

CULTURE Prefers moist, well-drained loam soil in full sun. Propagated mostly by seed and root division. May need staking. Early summer-flowering.

DESCRIPTION Flowers resemble a large Forget-me-not, azure blue, clustered at the top of slender stems. Leaves are long, pointed. Popular as an accent in mixed beds and borders. Good for cutting. The variety 'Little John' is a dwarf, compact type producing a 12-inch high mound suitable for mass planting.

BOTANICAL NAME *Anemone* x *hybrida*

COMMON NAME Japanese Anemone

RANGE Hybrids of species native to Japan. Hardy zone 5 south.

HEIGHT Up to 5 feet; upright, clump-forming habit.

CULTURE Prefers moist, humus-rich loam soil in sun or partial shade. Propagated by root division in spring. May need staking. Late summer-flowering.

DESCRIPTION Masses of lovely white and pink flowers resembling single and semi-double roses are held erect on slender stems. Leaves are dark green, sharply indented. Popular accent in mixed beds and borders. Good for cutting.

RECOMMENDED VARIETIES 'Whirlwind,' a semi-double white. These plants are sometimes sold as *A. japonica*.

BOTANICAL NAME *Anemone pulsatilla*

COMMON NAME Pasqueflower

RANGE Native to Europe and Asia. Hardy zone 5 south.

HEIGHT 12 inches; low, mound-shaped habit.

CULTURE Prefers well-drained alkaline or neutral soil in full sun. Propagated by seed and division in early spring. Early spring-flowering.

DESCRIPTION Lovely bell-shaped purple flowers are borne on arching stems above a clump of silvery, finely dissected leaves. Hybrid forms are available in white, rose red, and pink. Wonderful accent for rock gardens, especially planted in drifts among creeping phlox to create a miniature alpine meadow.

BOTANICAL NAME *Anthemis tinctoria*

COMMON NAME Golden Marguerite

RANGE Native to Europe. Hardy zone 4 south.

HEIGHT 3 feet; bushy habit.

CULTURE Tolerates a wide range of soils with good drainage in sun or partial shade. Propagated by seed and root division. Summer-flowering.

DESCRIPTION Yellow, daisy-like flowers are formed in abundance on long stems. Leaves are finely toothed, fragrant, fern-like. Popular for mixed beds and borders. Good for cutting.

RECOMMENDED VARIETY 'Kelwayi,' a golden yellow.

RELATED SPECIES *A. nobilis* ('Chamomile'), forming dark green cushions with yellow, buttonlike flowers.

BOTANICAL NAME *Aquilegia* hybrids

COMMON NAME Columbine

RANGE Developed from species native to North America. Hardy zone 5 south.

HEIGHT 2 to 3 feet; upright, airy habit.

CULTURE Prefers fertile loam soil in sun or partial shade. Propagated mostly by seed. Spring-flowering.

DESCRIPTION Unusual nodding flowers are shaped like granny's bonnets, with elegant, long spurs, held high above the foliage on slender stems. Leaves are gray green, deeply indented. Popular for mixed beds and borders. Exquisite cut flower.

RECOMMENDED VARIETY "McKana Giants,' which will bloom the first year if sown in January or February.

RELATED SPECIES *A. caerulea* (a gorgeous blue and white bicolor) and *A. canadensis* (a red and yellow bicolor).

BOTANICAL NAME *Arabis caucasica*

COMMON NAME Rock-cress; Wall-cress

RANGE Native to Europe. Hardy zone 4 south.

HEIGHT 12 inches; low, ground-hugging habit.

CULTURE Easy to grow in any well-drained garden soil in sun or partial shade. Propagated by seed and root division. Early spring-flowering.

DESCRIPTION Dainty, white, four-petaled flowers cover the spreading plants. Dark green leaves are spear-shaped. Popular for rock gardens and dry walls, also edging paths, beds, and borders.

BOTANICAL NAME *Armeria maritima*

COMMON NAME Common Thrift

RANGE Native to coastlines of Europe. Hardy zone 4 south.

HEIGHT 12 inches; mounded, ground-hugging habit.

CULTURE Prefers well-drained, sandy soil. Salt tolerant. Propagated by seed and division. Spring-flowering.

DESCRIPTION Globular pink or white flower clusters grow atop slender stems above a cushion of gray-green evergreen needlelike leaves. Excellent for seaside gardens. Creates a good ground cover planted in a mass. Useful to edge beds and borders. Popular in rock gardens and dry walls.

BOTANICAL NAME *Artemesia ludoviciana*

COMMON NAME Silver King

RANGE Native to North America. Hardy zone 5 south.

HEIGHT 3 feet; erect, bushy habit.

CULTURE Easy to grow in any well-drained soil in full sun. Propagated mostly by root division. Grown mostly for its foliage color.

DESCRIPTION Silver King artemesia has inconspicuous white flowers and is grown mainly for its silvery foliage that remains colorful all summer and into autumn. Plants are especially effective when mixed with pink flowers to give an old-fashioned look to perennial beds and borders. The leaves are narrow, toothed. Popular for cutting both fresh and dried.

RELATED SPECIES *A. schmidtiana*, resembling a silver cushion.

BOTANICAL NAME *Arum italicum*

COMMON NAME Italian Arum

RANGE Native to the Mediterranean. Hardy zone 6 south.

HEIGHT 12 inches; low, mounded habit.

CULTURE Prefers moist, acidic, humus-rich soil in partial shade. Propagated by seed and by division of dormant tubers. Grown mostly for its leaf shape and late summer berry display.

DESCRIPTION Attractive arrow-shaped leaves appear in spring, immediately following the appearance of a greenish white flower spathe resembling a small Calla Lily or Jack-in-the-pulpit. However, its principal ornamental value is the cluster of bright red berries that ripens on top of each flower stalk in late summer and persists into early autumn. Good to grow in woodland gardens along stream banks or pond margins.

RECOMMENDED VARIETY 'Pictum' with green and white variegated leaves.

Right: This perennial garden at Van Dusen Botanical Gardens, Vancouver, British Columbia, blends yellow and pink flowers in a striking color combination. Plants include yellow verbascum, rose campion, and pink fleabane.

BOTANICAL NAME *Asclepias tuberosa*

COMMON NAME Butterfly Milkweed

RANGE Native to North America. Hardy zone 4 south.

HEIGHT 2 to 3 feet; upright, clump-forming habit.

CULTURE Prefers well-drained loam or sandy soil in full sun. Propagated by seed or root division. Drought resistant. Summer-flowering.

DESCRIPTION Brilliant clusters of orange flowers freely produced on bushy plants. Slender stems have narrow, pointed green leaves. Popular for growing in meadows where it competes favorably with grasses. Also good to grow in mixed beds and borders. Excellent for cutting.

RECOMMENDED VARIETY 'Gay Butterflies,' a mixture that includes yellow, red, and pink.

BOTANICAL NAME *Aster novae-angliae*

COMMON NAME Michaelmas Daisy

RANGE Native to New England. Hardy zone 4 south.

HEIGHT 3 to 5 feet; erect, billowing habit.

CULTURE Prefers moist, fertile, well-drained loam soil. Propagated by root division. May need staking. Late summer-flowering.

DESCRIPTION Daisy-like pink, purple, and white flowers have golden yellow centers, are borne in profusion on bushy plants with finely toothed green leaves. Excellent for garden display in mixed beds and borders. Tall kinds especially good for backgrounds. Suitable for cutting.

RECOMMENDED VARIETY 'Alma Potschke' (deep pink).

RELATED SPECIES AND HYBRIDS *A.* x *frikartii* 'Wonder of Staffa' (lavender blue) and *A. tartaricus* (violet blue from Siberia).

BOTANICAL NAME *Astilbe* x *arendsii*

COMMON NAME False Spirea

RANGE Hybrids of species native to China. Hardy zone 5 south.

HEIGHT 2 to 4 feet; upright, clump-forming habit.

CULTURE Prefers moist, fertile, loam soil in partial shade. Propagated by root division. Early summer-flowering.

DESCRIPTION Spires of pink, red, and white flower clusters are borne in profusion above shrublike plants with sharply indented leaves. Popular for mixed beds and borders, and for the margins of ponds and steams. Excellent for cutting.

RECOMMENDED VARIETY 'Fanal' (dark red) and 'Ostrich Plume' (coral pink).

RELATED SPECIES *A. chinensis* 'Pumila' (dwarf, light pink) and *A. taquetii* ('Superba' tall, deep pink with extra-long flower plumes).

BOTANICAL NAME *Aubrieta deltoidea*

COMMON NAME False Rock-cress

RANGE Native to Europe. Hardy zone 5 south.

HEIGHT 6 inches; low, spreading habit.

CULTURE Tolerates poor soils providing drainage is good in sun or partial shade. Propagated by seed and root division. Spring-flowering.

DESCRIPTION Dainty, four-petaled flowers cover the mound-shaped plants in pink or purple. Leaves are oval, pointed. Very popular in rock gardens and dry walls. Also good for edging paths, beds, and borders.

BOTANICAL NAME *Aurinia saxatilis*

COMMON NAME Basket of Gold; Perennial Alyssum

RANGE Native to Europe. Hardy zone 4 south.

HEIGHT 12 inches; mounded, clump-forming habit.

CULTURE Prefers well-drained sandy or gritty soil in full sun. Propagated by seed and stem cuttings. Flowers in early spring.

DESCRIPTION Tiny golden yellow flowers are formed in dense clusters on spreading plants with gray-green narrow, pointed leaves. Popular for dry walls and rock gardens; also good for edging beds and borders. The variety 'Citrina' has pale yellow flowers.

BOTANICAL NAME *Baptisia australis*

COMMON NAME Blue Wild Indigo

RANGE Native to North America. Hardy zone 4 south.

HEIGHT 3 to 4 feet; upright, bushy habit.

CULTURE Prefers a sandy loam soil with excellent drainage in full sun. Drought tolerant. Propagated by seed and root division. Spring-flowering.

DESCRIPTION Lupin-like blue flowers are formed on strong stems. Clover-like leaves are bright green. Useful as an accent in mixed beds and borders. Excellent for cutting.

BOTANICAL NAME *Bergenia cordifolia*

COMMON NAME Heartleaf Bergenia

RANGE Native to Siberia. Hardy zone 3 south.

HEIGHT 12 inches; rosette, ground-hugging habit.

CULTURE Prefers moist, humus-rich loam soil in partial shade. Propagated mostly by root division. Early spring-flowering.

DESCRIPTION Clusters of pink flowers are produced on long stems above a rosette of fleshy, cabbage-like evergreen leaves that are usually tinted red. Popular for creating a ground cover under trees and along stream banks or pond margins. Also used in rock gardens. Many good hybrids have been introduced, such as 'Silver Light' (white-flowered) and 'Sunningdale' with carmine flowers.

BOTANICAL NAME *Caltha palustris*

COMMON NAME Marsh-marigold

RANGE Native to Northern Europe. Hardy zone 4 south.

HEIGHT 12 inches; mounded, clump-forming habit.

CULTURE Prefers moist, fertile, humus-rich soil in partial shade. Tolerates boggy conditions. Propagated by seed and root division. Early spring-flowering.

DESCRIPTION Conspicuous buttercup-like flowers are shimmering golden yellow, in single or double forms. Leaves are glossy dark green, heart-shaped. Popular in woodland gardens where soil remains moist. Excellent accent for pond margins and stream banks.

RECOMMENDED VARIETY 'Flore Pleno' with large, double flowers.

BOTANICAL NAME *Campanula glomerata*

COMMON NAME Globe Bellflower

RANGE Native to Europe. Hardy zone 4 south.

HEIGHT 2 to 3 feet; upright habit.

CULTURE Prefers moist, fertile loam soil in full sun. Propagated by seed or root division. Early summer-flowering.

DESCRIPTION Beautiful blue or white bell-shaped flowers are clustered into a globe shape on slender stems. Mint green leaves are narrow, pointed. Popular in mixed beds and borders. Excellent for cutting.

BOTANICAL NAME *Campanula percisifolia*

COMMON NAME Willow-leaf Bellflower

RANGE Native to Europe. Hardy zone 4 south.

HEIGHT 2 to 3 feet; erect, clump-forming habit.

CULTURE Easy to grow in any moist, well-drained garden soil in full sun. Propagated by seed and root division. Spring-flowering.

DESCRIPTION Large bell-shaped flowers in blue or white are crowded along slender stems. Leaves are narrow, willow-like. Popular in mixed beds and borders. Good for cutting.

RELATED SPECIES *C. latifolia* ('Great Bellflower').

BOTANICAL NAME *Catananche caerulea*

COMMON NAME Cupid's-dart

RANGE Native to the Mediterranean. Hardy zone 5 south.

HEIGHT 2 to 3 feet; upright clump-forming habit.

CULTURE Easy to grow in any well-drained garden soil in full sun. Drought-resistant. Propagated by seed or root division. Summer-flowering.

DESCRIPTION Pale blue cornflower-like blooms are held erect on slender stems. Leaves are gray-green, grasslike. Popular for mixed beds and borders. Excellent for cutting in both fresh and dried arrangements.

BOTANICAL NAME *Centranthus ruber*

COMMON NAME Red Valerian

RANGE Native to the Mediterranean. Hardy zone 5 south.

HEIGHT 2 to 3 feet; upright, bushy habit.

CULTURE Thrives in a wide range of well-drained soils in full sun. Propagated by seeds and root cuttings. Spring- and early summer-flowering.

DESCRIPTION Small red, pink, or white flowers form showy clusters on long, slender stems. Leaves are gray-green, narrow, pointed. Does best in cool coastal locations where it self-sows readily. Good for rock gardens and dry walls, also mixed beds and borders. Excellent cut flower.

BOTANICAL NAME *Cerastium tomentosum*

COMMON NAME Snow-in-summer

RANGE Native to Europe. Hardy zone 4 south.

HEIGHT 6 inches; ground hugging, spreading habit.

CULTURE Easy to grow in any well-drained soil in full sun. Propagated by seed and root division. Late spring-, early summer-flowering.

DESCRIPTION Small white flowers almost smother the foliage, creating a carpet of white, like drifts of snow. Gray, narrow leaves are covered with silvery hairs. Popular for rock gardens and dry walls. Also good for edging mixed beds and borders.

BOTANICAL NAME *Chrysanthemum* x *morifolium*

COMMON NAME Garden Mum; Cushion Mum

RANGE Hybrids of species mostly native to China. Hardy zone 5 south.

HEIGHT 1 to 2 feet; mounded habit.

CULTURE Prefers moist, fertile well-drained loam soil in full sun. Propagated by stem cuttings and root division. To maintain a good dome shape with lots of basal branches, growing tip should be pinched in spring and summer. Winter hardiness is highly variable depending on variety. Mostly autumn-flowering.

DESCRIPTION Flower shape and color among garden chrysanthemums is extremely varied, from pompom flowers and daisy flowers to "spiders" and "spoons," in yellow, red, orange, bronze, purple, and white. Leaves are dark green, narrow, and toothed. Popular for massing in beds, edging borders, and container planting. Tall types are good for cutting.

BOTANICAL NAME *Chrysanthemum parthenium*

COMMON NAME Feverfew

RANGE Native to Mediterranean. Hardy zone 4 south.

HEIGHT 2 to 3 feet; erect, bushy habit.

CULTURE Easy to grow in any well-drained garden soil in full sun. Self-seeds readily and needs rigorous thinning to keep it in bounds. Propagated by seed and root division. Late spring- and summer-flowering.

DESCRIPTION Small, white, daisy-like flowers have conspicuous yellow centers. Double, buttonlike forms also available. Leaves are typical chrysanthemum shape, finely toothed. Popular in mixed beds and borders as a cloudlike accent. Excellent cut flower.

BOTANICAL NAME *Chrysanthemum* x *superbum*

COMMON NAME Shasta Daisy

RANGE Native to Europe. Hardy zone 5 south.

HEIGHT 1 to 3 feet; upright, bushy habit.

CULTURE Prefers moist, fertile, well-drained loam soil in full sun. Propagated by seed and root divisions. Young plants need the tip growth pinching to encourage bushy habit. Summer-flowering.

DESCRIPTION White, daisy-like flowers have golden yellow centers. Some varieties are double flowered. Individual flowers can measure up to 5 inches across. Sometimes confused with *C. leucanthemum* ('Ox-Eye Daisy'), which is smaller flowered and blooms a month earlier than Shasta Daisy. Dark green leaves are slender, toothed. Popular for display in mixed beds and borders. Excellent for cutting. Dwarf varieties, such as 'Miss Muffet,' are suitable for containers and edging.

BOTANICAL NAME *Cimicifuga racemosa*

COMMON NAME Snakeroot

RANGE Native to North America. Hardy zone 3 south.

HEIGHT 6 feet; towering, erect, spirelike habit.

CULTURE Prefers moist, fertile, humus-rich soil in partial shade. Propagated by root division. May need staking. Summer-flowering.

DESCRIPTION Beautiful, tall, flower spikes are crowded with tiny white or creamy flowers. Leaves are dark green, fern-like, finely toothed. Popular for woodland gardens and as a background in mixed beds and borders.

RELATED SPECIES *C. simplex*, only 4 feet tall and flowers later.

BOTANICAL NAME *Coreopsis lanceolata*

COMMON NAME Lance-Leaf Coreopsis

RANGE Native to North America. Hardy zone 4 south.

HEIGHT 2 to 3 feet; upright habit.

CULTURE Easy to grow in any well-drained soil in full sun. Propagated by seed and root division. May need staking in fertile soils. Summer-flowering.

DESCRIPTION Bright yellow, daisy-like flowers are borne in profusion on long, slender stems. Leaves are narrow, spear-shaped. Popular for mixed beds and borders. Also wildflower meadows.

RECOMMENDED VARIETY 'Goldfink' (dwarf, compact). Good for cutting.

RELATED SPECIES *C. verticillata* ('Thread-leaf Coreopsis') growing mounds of airy foliage and yellow, star-shaped flowers.

BOTANICAL NAME *Dianthus plumarius*

COMMON NAME Cottage Pinks

RANGE Native to Europe. Hardy zone 4 south.

HEIGHT 12 inches; low, mounded, ground-hugging habit.

CULTURE Easy to grow in any well-drained soil in full sun. Propagated by seed and root division. Spring-flowering.

DESCRIPTION Fragrant, carnation-like double flowers, mostly with fringed petals. Colors include white, pink, rose red, and purple. Often bicolored. Leaves blue-gray, evergreen, grasslike. Popular for rock gardens and dry walls, also for edging mixed beds and borders. Superb cut flowers. Many beautiful hybrids have been created.

RELATED SPECIES *D. deltoides* ('Maiden Pinks'), *D. gratianopolitanus* ('Cheddar Pinks') and *D.* x *allwoodii* ('Allwood Pinks')—all of which are smaller-flowered and generally more dwarf and compact, making them suitable for rock gardens.

BOTANICAL NAME *Dicentra spectabilis*

COMMON NAME Japanese Bleeding-heart

RANGE Native to Japan. Hardy zone 2 south.

HEIGHT 2 to 3 feet; bushy habit.

CULTURE Prefers light, acidic, well-drained soil in sun or partial shade. Propagated by root division in spring. Spring-flowering.

DESCRIPTION Heart-shaped pink or white flowers are borne on graceful arching stems. The finely cut, gray-green leaves die down during hot weather but the roots remain viable and survive. Winters in dormant condition. Excellent display plant for shady mixed borders.

RELATED SPECIES *D. eximia* ('Eastern Bleeding Heart') and *D. formosa* ('Western Bleeding Heart') are native to the United States, more compact in habit, also popular for beds and borders.

BOTANICAL NAME *Digitalis purpurea*

COMMON NAME English Foxglove

RANGE Native to Europe. Hardy zone 4 south.

HEIGHT 5 feet; towering, erect habit.

CULTURE Prefers moist, fertile, humus-rich soil in partial shade. Propagated by seeds. Early summer-flowering.

DESCRIPTION Though truly a biennial, English Foxgloves appear to be perennial since they reseed themselves so easily and generally come back year after year. Purple, tubular flowers with handsome freckles in the throats are crowded along tall, slender, flower spikes. Leaves are thick, coarse, pointed. Excellent for backgrounds in mixed beds and borders. Also popular in woodland wildflower gardens. A hybrid variety, 'Excelsior,' has white, pink, and yellow flowers.

RELATED SPECIES *D. grandiflora* ('Yellow Foxglove') is a true perennial form propagated by division, producing lovely yellow flower spikes. All species are excellent for cutting.

BOTANICAL NAME *Doronicum caucasicum*

COMMON NAME Dogbane

RANGE Native to China. Hardy zone 3 south.

HEIGHT 2 feet; upright, spreading habit.

CULTURE Prefers rich, moist, loam soil in full sun. Propagated by seed and by root division in early spring. Early spring-flowering.

DESCRIPTION Golden yellow, daisy-like flowers appear on long stems. Coarse, pointed, toothed leaves form dense, spreading mats that may need dividing after several years. Popular for mixed borders and rock gardens. Excellent for cutting.

Left: A beautiful mass planting of delphinium enjoy cool conditions in the rose garden at Butchart Gardens, Victoria, British Columbia.

BOTANICAL NAME *Echinacea purpurea*

COMMON NAME Purple Coneflower

RANGE Native to North America. Hardy zone 3 south.

HEIGHT 3 to 6 feet; upright habit.

CULTURE Tolerates poor soil; may need staking if soil is moist and fertile. Prefers full sun. Propagated by seed and by root division. Forms clumps that may need dividing after several years. Summer-flowering.

DESCRIPTION Flowers have a rakish profile pointing skyward. A large cone-shaped crown of brown anthers has purple petals that sweep back. Good for garden display, especially in mixed borders.

BOTANICAL NAME *Echinops ritro*

COMMON NAME Small Globe-thistle

RANGE Native to the Mediterranean. Hardy zone 3 south.

HEIGHT 3 to 5 feet; billowing habit.

CULTURE Prefers fertile loam soil in full sun. Generally needs staking. Propagated mostly by seed and root division. Summer-flowering.

DESCRIPTION Steel blue, globe-shaped flowers are borne in profusion on long stems. Popular for mixed borders. Beloved by flower arrangers for fresh flower arrangements and as dried flowers.

RECOMMENDED VARIETY 'Taplow Blue.'

BOTANICAL NAME *Erigeron* hybrids

COMMON NAME Fleabane

RANGE Native species grow from Southern California to the Pacific Northwest. Hardy zone 6 south.

HEIGHT 1 to 2 feet; bushy, spreading habit.

CULTURE Tolerates salt spray and light, sandy soil. Prefers full sun. Propagated by root division in spring. Summer-flowering.

DESCRIPTION Lavender or pink daisy-like flowers have golden yellow centers. Excellent for garden display in mixed borders and rock gardens. Good for cutting.

RECOMMENDED VARIETY Hybrids of *E. speciosus* and *E. glaucus*.

BOTANICAL NAME *Eryngium giganteum*

COMMON NAME Giant Sea-holly

RANGE Native to Mexico. Hardy zone 5 south.

HEIGHT 2 to 3 feet; upright, bushy habit.

CULTURE Prefers sandy, fertile soil in full sun. Propagated by seed. Plants die after flowering but generally self-seed. Summer-flowering.

DESCRIPTION Silver flowers resemble thistles, with a high crown surrounded by a spiky collar that is highly ornamental. Best used in mixed borders. Excellent for cutting to use in fresh and dried arrangements.

RELATED SPECIES *E. amethystinum* has steel blue flowers and is hardy from zone 2 south.

BOTANICAL NAME *Eupatorium coelestinum*

COMMON NAME Perennial Ageratum

RANGE Native to North America. Hardy zone 5 south.

HEIGHT 2 feet; bushy, spreading habit.

CULTURE Easy to grow in any well-drained soil in sun or partial shade. Propagated by seed and root division. Summer-flowering.

DESCRIPTION Fluffy flower heads are mostly powder blue. Leaves are dark green, spear shaped. Popular for mixed beds and borders. Also useful for wild gardens, either woodland or meadow.

RELATED SPECIES *E. fistulosum* ('Joe-pye Weed') with tall, 8 feet flower spikes and massive, fluffy pink flower clusters.

BOTANICAL NAME *Euphorbia epithymoides*

COMMON NAME Cushion Spurge

RANGE Native to Europe. Hardy zone 4 south.

HEIGHT 12 inches; low, mounded habit.

CULTURE Easy to grow in any well-drained soil in full sun. Propagated mostly by root division. Drought resistant; prefers a dry summer climate. Early summer-flowering.

DESCRIPTION Creates a cushion of bright yellow flowers. Leaves are succulent, green, oval. Popular for planting among rock gardens and dry walls, also edging paths.

RELATED SPECIES *E. myrsinites* ('Myrtle Euphorbia'), has yellow flowers and prostrate, sprawling stems suitable for dry slopes. Many other species are used in perennial gardens.

BOTANICAL NAME *Gaillardia* x *grandiflora*

COMMON NAME Blanket-flower

RANGE Native to North America. Hardy zone 4 south.

HEIGHT 2 to 3 feet; erect, bushy habit.

CULTURE Prefers sandy, well-drained soil in full sun. Propagated by seed and root division. Summer-flowering.

DESCRIPTION Mostly red, daisy-like flowers with yellow petal tips. Other colors include yellow and burgundy. Gray-green leaves are deeply indented. Popular for wildflower meadows, also mixed beds and borders. Excellent cut flower. Dwarf varieties like 'Goblin' and 'Baby Cole' are suitable for rock gardens and edging.

BOTANICAL NAME *Geranium himaleyense*

COMMON NAME Blue Cranesbill

RANGE Native to the Himalayas. Hardy zone 4 south.

HEIGHT 12 inches; mounded, spreading habit.

CULTURE Easy to grow in any well-drained soil in sun or partial shade. Propagated by seed and root division. Spring- and early summer-flowering.

DESCRIPTION Gorgeous lilac blue, saucer-shaped flowers bloom profusely on light, airy foliage that is deeply serrated. Largest flowered of the cranesbill geraniums. Popular for mixed beds and borders, also rock gardens.

RECOMMENDED VARIETY 'Johnson's Blue' an extremely profuse blooming hybrid.

RELATED SPECIES *G. sanguineum* with pink or rose flowers, and *G. psilostemon* exhibiting a bushy, erect habit and rose flowers with black centers.

BOTANICAL NAME *Geum chiloense*

COMMON NAME Chilean Avens

RANGE Native to South America. Hardy zone 5 south.

HEIGHT 2 feet; erect, airy habit.

CULTURE Prefers fertile, moist, well-drained loam in sun or partial shade. Propagated by seed and root division. Early spring-flowering.

DESCRIPTION Flowers resemble miniature roses, usually semi-double in orange, red, and yellow. Leaves are deeply indented, strawberry-like. Popular for mixed beds and borders. Good for cutting.

RECOMMENDED VARIETIES 'Mrs. Bradshaw' (orange-scarlet) and 'Lady Stratheden' (yellow).

BOTANICAL NAME *Gypsophila paniculata*

COMMON NAME Baby's-breath

RANGE Native to Europe. Hardy zone 3 south.

HEIGHT 2 to 3 feet; billowing habit.

CULTURE Prefers alkaline, moist, well-drained soil in full sun. Propagated mostly by seeds. Summer-flowering.

DESCRIPTION Dainty white or pale pink flowers are borne in such profusion on brittle, slender stems, that the whole plant looks like a cloud or patch of mist. Good for garden display in mixed borders, also for cutting in fresh arrangements and as a dried flower.

RECOMMENDED VARIETIES 'Bristol Fairy' (white, double flowers) and 'Pink Fairy' (light pink, double flowers).

BOTANICAL NAME *Helianthemum nummularium*

COMMON NAME Rock Rose

RANGE Native to Europe. Hardy zone 6 south.

HEIGHT 12 inches; ground-hugging habit.

CULTURE Tolerates a wide range of soils with good drainage in full sun. Propagated mostly from seeds. Spring-flowering.

DESCRIPTION Spreading, evergreen plants are smothered with delicate pill-sized flowers with petals that look like crèpe paper, in yellow, orange, white, pink, and rose red. Popular for rock gardens and dry walls.

BOTANICAL NAME *Helenium autumnale*

COMMON NAME Sneezeweed

RANGE Native to North America. Hardy zone 4 south.

HEIGHT 5 feet; upright, bushy habit.

CULTURE Prefers moist, fertile, loam soil in full sun. Propagated by root division in spring. May need staking. Late summer-flowering.

DESCRIPTION Daisy-like flowers are produced in abundance on tall stems. Color range includes yellow, orange, and rusty red, some bicolored. Leaves are green, narrow, pointed. Popular for mixed beds and borders. Good for cutting.

BOTANICAL NAME *Helianthus* x *multiflorus*

COMMON NAME Perennial Sunflower

RANGE Native to North America. Hardy zone 5 south.

HEIGHT 5 to 6 feet; upright, bushy habit.

CULTURE Prefers moist, fertile, loam soil in full sun. Propagated by seed and root division. May need staking. Summer-flowering.

DESCRIPTION Golden yellow daisy-like flowers can be single or double, held high on stiff, slender stems. Leaves are dark green, spear shaped. Popular as an accent in mixed beds and borders.

RECOMMENDED VARIETY 'Flore pleno' has a full double flower. Good for cutting.

RELATED SPECIES *Helianthus angustifolius* ('Swamp Sunflower') is a familiar sight along waysides in late summer, tolerating boggy conditions.

BOTANICAL NAME *Heliopsis helianthoides*

COMMON NAME False Sunflower

RANGE Native to North America. Hardy zone 4 south.

HEIGHT 4 feet; erect, bushy habit.

CULTURE Easy to grow in any well-drained soil in full sun. Propagated by seed and root division. Late summer-flowering.

DESCRIPTION Golden yellow daisy-like flowers are mostly single and semi-double. Dark green, spear-shaped leaves. Highly popular as an accent for mixed beds and borders. Excellent for cutting.

RECOMMENDED VARIETY 'Incomparabilis' grows single and semi-double flowers.

BOTANICAL NAME *Helleborus niger*

COMMON NAME Christmas-rose

RANGE Native to Europe. Hardy zone 4 south.

HEIGHT 6 to 12 inches; low, spreading habit.

CULTURE Prefers moist, loam, or humus-rich soil in partial shade. Propagated by seed (must be fresh) and root division. Winter- and early spring-flowering.

DESCRIPTION Pure white flowers resemble single flowered roses, change to green with age, have golden yellow centers. Leaves are leathery, toothed, appear after the flowers die. Good to use in rock gardens, woodland gardens, and edging mixed beds and borders.

RELATED SPECIES *H. orientalis* ('Lenten Rose') is very similar but with a wider color range, including purple, pink, white, and cream, some with freckles.

BOTANICAL NAME *Hemerocallis* hybrids

COMMON NAME Daylilies

RANGE Developed from species native to Asia. Hardy zone 4 south.

HEIGHT 3 to 4 feet; tufted, clump-forming habit.

CULTURE Easy to grow in any well-drained garden soil in sun or partial shade. Drought tolerant. Propagated by root division. Summer-flowering.

DESCRIPTION Orange, red, yellow, mahogany, pink, and lilac blue trumpet-shaped flowers are borne on long stems. Popular as an accent in mixed beds and borders, also massed as a ground cover for erosion control of dry slopes.

RECOMMENDED VARIETIES 'Pink Dawn,' 'Hyperion' (yellow), and 'Stella di Oro' (orange).

BOTANICAL NAME *Heuchera sanguinea*

COMMON NAME Coral-bells

RANGE Native to North America. Hardy from zone 4 south.

HEIGHT 2 feet; rosette-forming habit.

CULTURE Prefers fertile, well-drained, humus-rich soil in sun or partial shade. Propagated by seed and root division. Early summer-flowering.

DESCRIPTION Tiny red or pink bell-shaped flowers clustered at the top of slender, wiry stems, held well above the ivy-shaped leaves. Popular for rock gardens, also as accents in mixed beds and borders. Good for cutting. Heuchera has been crossed with *Tiarella* ('Foamflower'), a North American woodland wildflower, to produce a more spirelike hybrid called *Heucharella*.

BOTANICAL NAME *Hibiscus moscheutos*

COMMON NAME Rose Mallow

RANGE Native to North America. Hardy zone 5 south.

HEIGHT 4 to 5 feet; erect habit.

CULTURE Prefers moist, fertile, loam soil in full sun. Tolerates boggy conditions. Propagated mostly by seeds. May need staking. Summer-flowering.

DESCRIPTION Flowers of hybrid varieties are unusually large—the size of dinner plates—in white, crimson, and pink, many with a contrasting center. Flowers last only a day, but plants flower continuously from mid-summer to fall frost. The large green leaves are attractively heart shaped. Popular for mixed borders and edging stream banks.

RECOMMENDED VARIETIES 'Southern Belle' (blooms first year from seed sown in January or February) and 'Super Giants' (largest flowers).

BOTANICAL NAME *Hosta seiboldiana*

COMMON NAME Plantain-lily

RANGE Native to Japan. Hardy zone 4 south.

HEIGHT 2 to 3 feet; low, rosette-forming habit.

CULTURE Prefers moist, humus-rich loam soil in partial shade. Propagated by root division. Where snails or slugs are a problem, bait heavily to avoid unsightly leaf damage. Summer-flowering.

DESCRIPTION Mostly admired for its large, blue-green, paddle-shaped leaves that are heavily textured and blistered, with prominent leaf veins. Foliage turns a lovely golden color in autumn. Lilac flowers are borne on long stems high above the foliage. Popular for edging shaded walkways, also stream banks and pond margins in woodland settings.

RECOMMENDED VARIETY 'Frances William.'

RELATED SPECIES *H. fortunei, H. lancifolia,* and *H. undulata* are also popular perennials with different leaf colorings and leaf shapes.

BOTANICAL NAME *Iberis sempervirens*

COMMON NAME Perennial Candytuft

RANGE Native to Mediterranean. Hardy zone 4 south.

HEIGHT 12 inches; mounded, spreading habit.

CULTURE Tolerates a wide range of soils providing drainage is good. Propagated by seed and root division. Spring-flowering.

DESCRIPTION Dense, white flower clusters cover the low, ground-hugging plants. Dark green leaves are evergreen, narrow, pointed. Popular for rock gardens and dry walls; also for edging mixed beds and borders.

BOTANICAL NAME *Iris germanica*

COMMON NAME Bearded Iris

RANGE Native to Europe. Hardy zone 4 south.

HEIGHT 2 to 4 feet; upright, clump-forming habit.

CULTURE Easy to grow in any well-drained garden soil in full sun. Propagated by division of rhizomes any time of year. Blooms spring and early summer.

DESCRIPTION Slender, sword-shaped leaves emerge in spring from fleshy roots called rhizomes. Flowers are large and showy, usually featuring a prominent arching petal called a "lip" and an eye-catching yellow arrangement of stamens known as the "beard." Color range includes white, yellow, orange, pink, red, blue, purple, and black, plus bicolors. Good for mixed beds and borders, creating a temporary hedge effect. Also good for large floral arrangements. Spicy fragrance. Numerous hybrids have been created, including dwarfs suitable for rock gardens.

BOTANICAL NAME *Iris sibirica*

COMMON NAME Siberian Iris

RANGE Native to North-central Europe. Hardy zone 4 south.

HEIGHT 2 to 4 feet; upright, clump-forming habit.

CULTURE Prefers acidic, moist soil in full sun. Propagated by root division in spring or autumn. Blooms in late spring.

DESCRIPTION Long, slender leaves emerge in spring, remain decorative all summer. Flowers are numerous on tall, slender stems. Color range is mostly shades of blue and white. Good for mixed beds and borders. Especially attractive massed along stream banks and pond margins. Excellent for cutting. A number of good hybrids have expanded the color range to include yellow.

RELATED SPECIES *I. pseudacorus* ('Flag Iris'), *I. kaempferi* ('Japanese Iris'), and *I. cristata* ('Crested Iris').

BOTANICAL NAME *Kniphofia uvaria*

COMMON NAME Red-hot Poker

RANGE Native to South Africa. Hardy zone 5 south.

HEIGHT 3 to 4 feet; erect, clump-forming habit.

CULTURE Prefers fertile, well-drained loam soil in full sun. Drought resistant. Propagated mainly by root division and offsets. Summer-flowering.

DESCRIPTION Tubular flowers in red and yellow are clustered at the top of a poker-straight, thick, succulent stem held high above the leaves which are spiky, arching up and out in a clump. Popular for mixed beds and borders, also rock gardens. Excellent for cutting.

BOTANICAL NAME *Lathyrus latifolius*

COMMON NAME Perennial Sweet Pea

RANGE Native to Europe. Hardy zone 4 south.

HEIGHT 6 to 9 feet; vining habit.

CULTURE Tolerates a wide range of soils providing drainage is good, in full sun. Propagated mostly by seeds. Needs staking to climb. Summer-flowering.

DESCRIPTION Easy to grow, vigorous climber with stems and flowers like Sweet Peas, but a more limited color range—mostly pink, white, and rose red. Popular for covering unsightly slopes as a ground cover and for training up posts or walls as a tall, decorative vine.

BOTANICAL NAME *Liatris spicata*

COMMON NAME Bottlebrush; Gayfeather

RANGE Native to North America. Hardy from zone 4 south.

HEIGHT 4 to 5 feet; erect, bushy habit.

CULTURE Easy to grow in any well-drained garden soil in full sun. Propagated by seed and root division. Summer-flowering.

DESCRIPTION Purple or white flower spikes resemble bottle brushes, stand erect like pokers held well above the narrow-leafed foliage. Popular as an accent in mixed beds and borders. Excellent for both fresh and dried arrangements.

RECOMMENDED VARIETY 'Kobold' displays deep purple flowers.

BOTANICAL NAME *Ligularia* x *prezèwalskii*

COMMON NAME Rocket Ligularia

RANGE Native to Asia. Hardy zone 4 south.

HEIGHT 6 feet; erect, spirelike habit.

CULTURE Demands a moist, humus-rich, fertile soil in partial shade. Leaves wilt as soon as soil dries out and during direct afternoon sunlight. Propagated by root division. Early summer-flowering.

DESCRIPTION Towering flower spikes are crowded with bright golden yellow flowers on slender black stems that contrast spectacularly with large, sharply indented, highly decorative leaves. Popular as a background for mixed beds and borders; also stream banks and pond margins. Good for cutting.

RECOMMENDED VARIETY 'The Rocket' with a slight bronze cast to the leaves.

BOTANICAL NAME *Lilium lancifolium*

COMMON NAME Tiger Lilies

RANGE Native to Asia. Hardy zone 4 south.

HEIGHT 4 to 6 feet; erect habit.

CULTURE Prefers moist, fertile, humus-rich soil in sun or partial shade. Propagated mostly by bulbils that form in the leaf axils or division of bulbous roots. May need staking. Summer-flowering.

DESCRIPTION Nodding orange flowers are exotically spotted, hang from the top of tall, slender stems. Leaves are narrow, lancelike. Naturalizes easily. Popular for backgrounds in mixed beds and borders. Excellent for cutting. There are hundreds of other related species of lilies. Also known as *L. Tigrinum*.

BOTANICAL NAME *Linum perenne*

COMMON NAME Blue Flax

RANGE Native to Europe. Hardy zone 5 south.

HEIGHT 1 to 2 feet; billowing habit.

CULTURE Easy to grow in a wide range of soils with good drainage in full sun. Propagated by seed and cuttings. Spring-flowering.

DESCRIPTION Dainty blue flowers are borne in abundance on light, airy stems with narrow leaves. Popular in mixed beds and borders, also wildflower meadows. Not a long lasting perennial, but self-seeds.

BOTANICAL NAME *Liriope muscari*

COMMON NAME Lily-turf

RANGE Native to Asia. Hardy zone 6 south.

HEIGHT 18 inches; compact, clump-forming habit.

CULTURE Prefers fertile, humus-rich loam soil in sun or partial shade. Propagated by root division. Summer-flowering.

DESCRIPTION Mostly grown for its grasslike evergreen leaves which can be dark green or variegated green and cream. Lavender-blue or white flower spikes appear among the foliage. Mostly used for edging walkways, beds, and borders. Also popular as a ground cover.

BOTANICAL NAME *Lobelia cardinalis*

COMMON NAME Scarlet Lobelia

RANGE Native to North America. Hardy zone 3 south.

HEIGHT 4 to 5 feet; erect, spirelike habit.

CULTURE Prefers moist, humus-rich, acidic soil in partial shade. Propagated by seed and root division. Tolerates boggy conditions. Summer-flowering.

DESCRIPTION Striking spires of cardinal red flowers, contrasting well with the dark green, serrated spear-shaped leaves. Plants are short-lived, but readily seed themselves. Popular in mixed beds and borders, also woodland gardens and along stream banks. Good for cutting.

BOTANICAL NAME *Lupinus* hybrids

COMMON NAME Russell Lupines

RANGE Developed in England from native North American species. Hardy zone 5 south.

HEIGHT 3 feet; erect, clump-forming habit.

CULTURE Prefers moist, sandy soil or well-drained loam. Propagated mostly from seeds. Best treated as a biennial. Self-sows easily. Spring-flowering.

DESCRIPTION Spires of fragrant, pea-like flowers are white, yellow, red, pink, blue, and purple, many bicolored. Leaves are dark green, like splayed fingers. Lupines thrive best in cool, coastal gardens since they cannot tolerate hot, dry summers. Popular for mixed beds and borders, also meadow wildflower gardens.

RELATED SPECIES: *L. perennis* (yellow flowering), native to the East Coast and the similar *L. arboreus*, native to the West Coast. Good for cutting, but flower spikes will wilt unless wired.

BOTANICAL NAME *Lychnis chalcedonica*

COMMON NAME Maltese Cross

RANGE Native to Siberia. Hardy zone 4 south.

HEIGHT 2 to 3 feet; erect habit.

CULTURE Easy to grow in any well-drained garden soil in sun or partial shade. Propagated by seed or root division. Summer-flowering.

DESCRIPTION Clusters of scarlet red flowers are borne on slender stems, each floret the shape of a Maltese cross. Leaves are dark green, spear shaped. Popular as an accent in mixed beds and borders. Excellent for cutting.

RELATED SPECIES *L. coronaria* ('Rose campion').

BOTANICAL NAME *Lysimachia punctata*

COMMON NAME Yellow Loosestrife

RANGE Native to Europe. Hardy zone 5 south.

HEIGHT 2 to 3 feet; spirelike habit.

CULTURE Prefers moist loam soil in sun or partial shade. Propagated by root division. Tolerates boggy conditions. Early summer-flowering.

DESCRIPTION Erect spikes of yellow flowers grow in clumps. Spear-shaped, ruffled green leaves. Popular as an accent in mixed beds and borders, also pond margins and stream banks.

RELATED SPECIES *L. clethroides* ('Gooseneck') has small, terminal spikes of white flowers with a curious twist at the tips. Both species are suitable for cutting.

BOTANICAL NAME *Lythrum salicaria*

COMMON NAME Purple Loosestrife

RANGE Native to North America. Hardy zone 4 south.

HEIGHT 2 to 5 feet; erect, spirelike habit.

CULTURE Prefers moist, fertile, loam soil in full sun. Tolerates boggy conditions. Propagated by root division. Summer-flowering.

DESCRIPTION Thousands of small, purple flowers are crowded along slender stems, resembling rockets. Leaves are dark green, willowlike. Popular as an accent in mixed beds and borders, also for planting along pond margins and stream banks. The wild types are a familiar sight in swampy areas, spreading across acres of marsh. Cultivated varieties do not readily naturalize.

RECOMMENDED VARIETY 'Morden's Pink' is suitable for cutting.

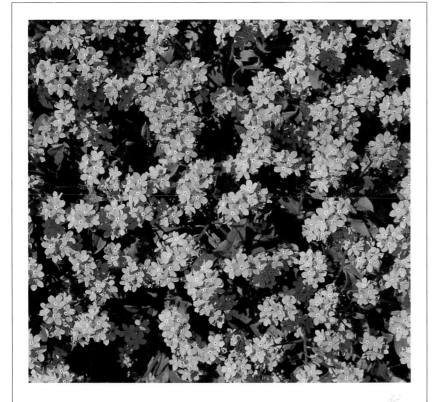

BOTANICAL NAME *Myosotis scorpioides*

COMMON NAME Forget-me-not

RANGE Native to Europe. Hardy zone 5 south.

HEIGHT 6 to 12 inches; low, mounded habit.

CULTURE Prefers moist, fertile, humus-rich loam soil in sun or partial shade. Propagated by seed and root division in early spring. Early spring-flowering.

DESCRIPTION Myriad, small blue flowers with yellow centers are borne in airy clusters creating a misty appearance. Leaves are paddle shaped. Popular for massing in a bed, especially among tulips. Good for edging walkways and woodland paths. Also suitable for pond margins and stream banks.

BOTANICAL NAME *Nepeta mussinii*

COMMON NAME Ornamental Catmint

RANGE Native to Europe. Hardy zone 4 south.

HEIGHT 2 to 3 feet; bushy habit.

CULTURE Prefers moist, fertile, loam soil in full sun. Propagated by seed and root division. A hybrid, *N.* x *faasenii*, does not set seed and generally produces the best flowering display. Summer-flowering.

DESCRIPTION Mintlike plants produce dense clusters of mauve blue flowers. Leaves are dark green, heart-shaped. Creates a hedge effect and therefore is popular for lining walkways. Also used in mixed beds and borders.

RELATED SPECIES *N. cataria*, ('Catmint'). These plants attract cats.

BOTANICAL NAME *Oenothera tetragona*

COMMON NAME Sundrop

RANGE Native to North America. Hardy zone 5 south.

HEIGHT 18 to 24 inches; upright, clump-forming habit.

CULTURE Prefers sandy or well-drained loam soil in full sun. Propagated by root division. Early summer-flowering.

DESCRIPTION Cup-shaped yellow flowers shimmer like satin. Leaves are green, spear shaped. Popular for mixed beds and borders. Forms a dense, spreading mass of brilliant yellow.

RELATED SPECIES The taller *O. missourensis* ('Evening Primrose') and pink-flowered *O. speciosa* 'Texas Wine Cup'.

BOTANICAL NAME *Opuntia humifusa*

COMMON NAME Hardy Prickly-pear

RANGE Native to North America. Hardy zone 5 south.

HEIGHT 6 inches; prostrate, ground-hugging habit.

CULTURE Easy to grow in any well-drained garden soil in full sun. Propagated by rooting the leaves (pads) in moist sand. Drought resistant. Early summer-flowering.

DESCRIPTION This true cactus has oblong pads bristling with sharp spines, producing shimmering yellow flowers up to 3 inches across. When the flowers die, the plant's edible red fruits develop and ripen in autumn. Popular for rock gardens and dry walls.

BOTANICAL NAME *Paeonia officinalis*

COMMON NAME Herbaceous Peony

RANGE Native to Europe and Asia. Hardy zone 5 south.

HEIGHT 3 to 4 feet; bushy habit.

CULTURE Prefers cool, moist, humus-rich loam soil that drains well. Best in full sun. Propagated by root division. Blooms in late spring.

DESCRIPTION Handsome shrublike plants have large single and double flowers up to 6 inches across in white, pink, and red. Leaves are dark green, deeply indented. Good accent in mixed beds or borders; also planted en masse as a hedge. Good for cutting.

RECOMMENDED VARIETIES 'Estate Hybrids' developed by an Illinois peony breeder.

BOTANICAL NAME *Papaver orientale*

COMMON NAME Oriental Poppy

RANGE Native to Asia. Hardy zone 4 south.

HEIGHT 3 to 4 feet; upright habit.

CULTURE Easy to grow in any well-drained garden soil in full sun. Propagated by seed and root division. Blooms in spring.

DESCRIPTION Shimmering satinlike flowers up to 10 inches across, single- and double-flowered, with a mass of powdery black stamens at the center. Colors include red, orange, pink, purple, and white, mostly with attractive black blotches at the petal base. Leaves are green, fernlike, and hairy. Popular for mixed beds and borders, or massed alone. Striking cut flower if ends are quickly scorched or boiled to prevent wilting.

BOTANICAL NAME *Perovskia atripicifolia*

COMMON NAME Russian Sage

RANGE Native to Asia. Hardy zone 5 south.

HEIGHT 3 to 4 feet; upright, shrubby habit.

CULTURE Easy to grow in any well-drained garden soil in full sun. Propagated by cuttings taken in summer. Summer-flowering.

DESCRIPTION Small blue flowers form showy spikes. Twiggy stems have small, narrow gray leaves which when bruised are highly aromatic. A good background in mixed beds and borders. Excellent cut flower, both fresh and dried.

BOTANICAL NAME *Phlox paniculata*

COMMON NAME Summer Phlox

RANGE Native to North America. Hardy zone 4 south.

HEIGHT 3 to 4 feet; upright habit.

CULTURE Prefers deeply cultivated, fertile loam soil in full sun. Propagated by seed and root division. Susceptible to powdery mildew controlled by fungicidal spray. May need staking. Summer-flowering.

DESCRIPTION Bold flower clusters grow to 9 inches long in white and shades of red, pink, salmon, lavender, and blue. Good for tall backgrounds in mixed borders. Popular for cutting. 'Pinafore' is an excellent dwarf with clear pink flowers.

BOTANICAL NAME *Phlox subulata*

COMMON NAME Moss-pinks

RANGE Native to North America. Hardy zone 4 south.

HEIGHT 6 inches; low, ground-hugging habit.

CULTURE Requires excellent drainage and full sun. Propagated by seed and root division. Spring-flowering.

DESCRIPTION Small, star-shaped flowers are crowded closely together to form a cushion of color in pink, red, blue, and white. Narrow, gray-green leaves are evergreen. Good for rock gardens and dry walls. Creates an attractive ground cover when planted in a mass. Useful for edging beds and borders.

BOTANICAL NAME *Physalis alkekengi*

COMMON NAME Chinese Lanterns

RANGE Native to the Orient. Hardy zone 5 south.

HEIGHT 2 feet; spreading, sprawling habit.

CULTURE Tolerates poor soil, providing drainage is good, in full sun. Propagated mostly by seed and division of its invasive underground roots. Late-summer flowering.

DESCRIPTION Inconspicious, cream colored star-shaped flowers are replaced by ornamental lantern-shaped seed cases that turn orange-red in late summer. Leaves are spear shaped. Generally grown massed in a bed by themselves. The stems are best gathered in autumn, air-dried and used for cheerful, long-lasting dried arrangements during winter months. Also known as *P. franchetii*.

BOTANICAL NAME *Physostegia virginiana*

COMMON NAME Obedient Plant

RANGE Native to North America. Hardy zone 4 south.

HEIGHT 3 to 5 feet; upright, clump forming habit.

CULTURE Prefers moist soil, full sun. Propagated by seed and root division. Late summer-flowering.

DESCRIPTION Pink or white flowers resemble Snapdragons, form spikes at the top of long, slender stems. Leaves are narrow, pointed. A member of the mint family, the stems are square. Good for late-flowering garden display in mixed beds and borders. Spreading roots may need thinning each year to prevent them from becoming invasive. Called 'Obedient Plant' because flower heads can be twisted into different positions.

BOTANICAL NAME *Platycodon grandiflorus*

COMMON NAME Balloonflower

RANGE Native to China. Hardy zone 4 south.

HEIGHT 2 feet; upright habit.

CULTURE Prefers acidic, loam, fertile soil in full sun or partial shade. Propagated by seeds. Blooms in summer.

DESCRIPTION Beautiful, clear blue bell-shaped flowers up to 3 inches across on erect stems. White and pink forms, double and semi-double are also available. Leaves are narrow, pointed. Gets its common name, 'Balloonflower', from the appearance of inflated flower buds. Excellent for mixed beds and borders and for rock gardens. Good for cutting.

BOTANICAL NAME *Polemonium reptans*

COMMON NAME Jacob's-ladder

RANGE Native to North America. Hardy zone 4 south.

HEIGHT 12 inches; low, spreading habit.

CULTURE Prefers moist, humus-rich, loam soil in sun or partial shade. Propagated by root division in spring. Spring-flowering.

DESCRIPTION Small, light blue bell-shaped flowers are crowded in loose clusters. Leaves are made up of oval leaflets symmetrically arranged like a ladder. Useful for edging walkways and as a ground cover in woodland gardens.

RELATED SPECIES *P. caeruleum,* taller growing (to 3 feet) and useful as a border accent.

BOTANICAL NAME *Polygonum bistorta*

COMMON NAME Knotweed

RANGE Native to Europe. Hardy zone 4 south.

HEIGHT 2 to 3 feet; erect, clump-forming habit.

CULTURE Prefers moist, fertile, loam soil in partial shade. Propagated by seed, cuttings, and root division. Summer-flowering.

DESCRIPTION Pokerlike pink flowers are held well above the green, straplike foliage. Popular for mixed beds and borders, particularly as an edging. Good for cutting.

RECOMMENDED VARIETY 'Superbum' with extra large flowers.

BOTANICAL NAME *Primula japonica*

COMMON NAME Japanese Primrose; Candelabra Primrose

RANGE Native to China and Japan. Hardy zone 6 south.

HEIGHT 1 to 2 feet; rosette-forming habit.

CULTURE Prefers moist, acidic, humus-rich soil in light shade. Propagated by seed and root division. Blooms in spring.

DESCRIPTION Plants form dark green clumps of succulent crinkled, veined leaves. Flowers are borne in clusters on slender stems. Colors include white, red, pink, and purple. Good for massing along stream banks, pond margins, and wherever soil remains moist all year.

RELATED SPECIES *P. beesianum* ('Bees Primrose') has yellow and orange flowers. Cannot tolerate hot or dry summers.

BOTANICAL NAME *Primula* x *polyantha*

COMMON NAME Polyantha Primrose

RANGE A hybrid species native to Europe. Hardy zone 5 south.

HEIGHT 12 inches; rosette-forming habit.

CULTURE Prefers moist, acidic, humus-rich soil in partial shade. Propagated by seed and root division. Blooms in spring.

DESCRIPTION Primrose-like flowers are borne in clusters on slender stems. Color range includes yellow, red, white, and blue. Leaves are fleshy, green, crinkled. Excellent for shade gardens, especially in woodland. 'Pacific Giants' have the largest flowers and widest color range, though not long-lived.

RELATED SPECIES *P. vulgaris* ('English Primrose') and *P. veris* ('Cowslip').

BOTANICAL NAME *Rudbeckia fulgida*

COMMON NAME Black-eyed Susans

RANGE Native to North America. Hardy zone 4 south.

HEIGHT 2 to 3 feet; upright habit.

CULTURE Easy to grow even in poor soils. Prefers moist loam soil in full sun. Propagated by seed and root division in early spring. Summer-flowering.

DESCRIPTION Yellow, daisy-like flowers have dark brown centers up to 3 inches wide, produced in profusion. Leaves are gray-green, pointed, and narrow. Good for meadow gardens, mixed beds, and borders.

RECOMMENDED VARIETY 'Goldsturm,' a compact form that produces an especially brilliant floral display.

BOTANICAL NAME *Salvia* x *superba*

COMMON NAME Violet Sage

RANGE A hybrid of species native to Europe. Hardy zone 5 south.

HEIGHT 2 feet; upright, spreading habit.

CULTURE Prefers sandy, fertile soil in full sun or light shade. Propagated by root division. Blooms in summer.

DESCRIPTION Violet-blue flowers are borne on long spikes, densely crowded together, making a strong display in mixed borders or massed alone in beds. Slender stems have narrow pointed leaves.

RECOMMENDED VARIETY 'East Friesland.'

RELATED SPECIES *S. farinacea* ('Mealy-Cup Sage') with blue and white flowers; *S. pratensis* ('Meadow Clary') with lavender blue flowers.

BOTANICAL NAME *Saponaria ocymoides*

COMMON NAME Soapwort

RANGE Native to Europe. Hardy zone 4 south.

HEIGHT 6 inches; low, ground-hugging habit.

CULTURE Easy to grow in any well-drained soil in sun or partial shade. Drought resistant. Propagated by seed and root division. Spring-flowering.

DESCRIPTION Dainty, bright pink star-shaped flowers are produced in profusion on trailing plants. Dark green lance-shaped leaves are small, pointed. Excellent choice for rock gardens and dry walls.

BOTANICAL NAME *Scabiosa caucasica*

COMMON NAME Pincushion Flower

RANGE Native to Europe. Hardy zone 4 south.

HEIGHT 3 feet; upright, spreading habit.

CULTURE Easy to grow in any well-drained garden soil in full sun. Propagated by seed or root division. May need staking. Summer-flowering.

DESCRIPTION The flat, ruffled blue flowers have a pale crest in the center, held erect on long, slender stems. Leaves are narrow, indented. Popular as an accent in mixed beds and borders. Superb for cutting.

BOTANICAL NAME *Sedum spectabile*

COMMON NAME Stonecrop

RANGE Native to China and Japan. Hardy zone 4 south.

HEIGHT 2 feet; upright, clump-forming habit.

CULTURE Tolerates poor soil, but prefers fertile loam in full sun. Drought resistant. Propagated by cuttings and root division. Late summer-flowering.

DESCRIPTION Bright pink flower clusters are flattened, circular. The individual star-shaped flowers are small, but are crowded together in a tight mass up to 6 inches wide. Leaves are blue-gray, succulent, smooth, and pointed. Plants are excellent for garden display in mixed borders and rock gardens or massed alone in beds. 'Autumn Joy,' a hybrid of *S. spectabile*, has deep, rosy red flowers that turn bronze when they die. Color will persist in a dried state well into winter, making this a valued plant for dried-flower arrangements.

BOTANICAL NAME *Stokesia laevis*

COMMON NAME Stoke's Aster

RANGE Native to North America. Hardy zone 5 south.

HEIGHT 2 feet; bushy, spreading habit.

CULTURE Easy to grow in any well-drained garden soil in sun or partial shade. Propagated by seed or root division. Spring-flowering.

DESCRIPTION Powder blue flowers resemble giant Cornflowers, up to 4 inches across. Leaves are narrow and serrated like China Asters. Good for mixed beds and borders. Suitable for cutting.

BOTANICAL NAME *Trollius europaeus*

COMMON NAME Globeflower

RANGE Native to Europe. Hardy zone 5 south.

HEIGHT 2 feet; upright, clump-forming habit.

CULTURE Prefers moist, fertile, humus-rich loam soil in sun or partial shade. Tolerates boggy conditions. Propagated by seed or root division. Spring-flowering.

DESCRIPTION Buttercup yellow globular flowers are borne erect on slender stems. Leaves are dark green, serrated. Popular for stream banks and pond margins. Suitable for cutting.

BOTANICAL NAME *Veronica longifolia*

COMMON NAME Speedwell

RANGE Native to Europe. Hardy zone 4 south.

HEIGHT 3 feet; erect, bushy habit.

CULTURE Easy to grow in any well-drained garden soil in full sun. Propagated by seed and root division. May need staking. Early summer-flowering.

DESCRIPTION Elegant spires of blue, white, or pink flowers. Leaves lance-like, dark green. Popular accent for mixed beds and borders.

RECOMMENDED VARIETIES 'Blue Spires,' 'White Icicle,' and 'Red Fox,' (which is actually a deep pink).

RELATED SPECIES *V. teucrium*, a dwarf, compact plant with bright blue flowers.

BOTANICAL NAME *Yucca filamentosa*

COMMON NAME Spanish Dagger; Adam's Needle

RANGE Native to Mexico and southern U.S. Hardy zone 5 east.

HEIGHT 6 feet; spiky, clump-forming habit.

CULTURE Easy to grow in any well-drained soil in full sun. Drought tolerant. Propagated by division of offsets. Summer-flowering.

DESCRIPTION Each clump of spiny leaves sends up a flower spike resembling a huge asparagus spear, which opens out into a fountain of creamy white flowers. The leaves have nasty points as sharp as nails. Plants are best used as accents at the back of beds and borders. Also popular massed together on dry slopes for erosion control and in rock gardens. The flowers are edible in salads and taste like Belgian endive. Variegated forms with golden stripes are available, such as 'Golden Sword.'

RELATED SPECIES *Y. glauca* ('Soapweed') has narrower leaves and is more ornamental when used in containers.

CHAPTER FOUR

PLANT SELECTION GUIDE

Whether your garden is in the sun or the shade, your soil moist or dry, whether you prefer a cutting garden or a display garden that will be the envy of your neighborhood, there are perennial plants to suit every need. The following lists are intended as a helpful, easy reference. They are not all-inclusive, and by consulting specialist catalogs you will be able to find additions to these lists. Throughout this section, unless otherwise noted, any member of the species can be used. Or, check the encyclopedia section for specific varieties.

PERENNIALS FOR CUTTING

Achillea filipendulina (Yellow Yarrow)
Anchusa azurea (Italian Bugloss)
Anemone x *hybrida* (Japanese Anemone)
Anthemis tinctoria (Golden Marguerite)
Aquilegia hybrids (Columbine)
Artemisia ludoviciana (Silver King)
Asclepias tuberosa (Butterfly Milkweed)

Aster novae-angliae (Michaelmas Daisy)
Astilbe x *arendsii* (False Spirea)
Baptisia australis (Blue Wild Indigo)
Catananche caerulea (Cupid's-dart)
Centranthus ruber (Red Valerian)
Chrysanthemum species (Mum)
Cimicifuga racemosa (Snakeroot)
Coreopsis lanceolata (Lance-leaf Coreopsis)
Dianthus plumarius (Cottage Pinks)
Doronicum caucasicum (Dogbane)
Echinacea purpurea (Purple Coneflower)
Echinops ritro (Small Globe-thistle)
Eryngium giganteum (Sea-holly)
Eupatorium coelestinum (Perennial Ageratum)
Gaillardia x *grandiflora* (Blanket-flower)
Gypsophila paniculata (Baby's-breath)
Helenium autumnale (Sneezeweed)
Helianthus x *multifloras* (Perennial Sunflower)
Heliopsis helianthoides (False Sunflower)
Heucherea sanguinea (Coral-bells)
Iris germanica (Bearded Iris)
Iris sibirica (Siberian Iris)
Kniphofia uvaria (Red-hot poker)

PERENNIALS FOR CUTTING (cont.)

Liatris spicata (Gayfeather)
Lilium species (Lily)
Lychnis chalcedonica (Maltese Cross)
Lysimachia punctata (Yelllow Loosestrife)
Lythrum salicaria (Purple Loosestrife)
Papaver species (Poppies)
Phlox paniculata (Summer Phlox)
Physostegia virginiana (Obedient Plant)
Rudbeckia fulgida (Black-eyed Susan)
Scabiosa caucasica (Pincushion Flower)
Stokesia laevis (Stoke's Aster)
Veronica longifolia (Speedwell)

PERENNIALS FOR MEADOW GARDENS

Alcea rosea (Hollyhock)
Achillea filipendulina (Yellow Yarrow)
Anthemis tinctoria (Golden Marguerite)
Asclepias tuberosa (Butterfly Milkweed)
Baptisia australis (Blue Wild Indigo)
Catananche caerulea (Cupid's-dart)
Chrysanthemum x *superbum* (Shasta Daisy)
Coreopsis lanceolata (Lance-leaf Coreopsis)
Echinacea purpurea (Purple Coneflower)
Eupatorium coelestinum (Perennial Ageratum)
Gaillardia x *grandiflora* (Blanket-flower)
Gyposphila paniculata (Baby's-breath)
Helenium autumnale (Sneezeweed)
Helianthus x *multiflorus* (Perennial Sunflower)
Heliopsis helianthoides (False Sunflower)
Hemerocallis hybrids (Daylily)
Hibiscus moscheutos (Rose mallow)
Iris sibirica (Siberian Iris)
Liatris spicata (Gayfeather)
Lilium species (Lily)
Lupinus hybrids (Russell Lupines)
Lythrum salicaria (Purple Loosestrife)
Papaver orientale (Oriental Poppy)
Phlox paniculata (Summer Phlox)
Rudbeckia fulgida (Black-eyed Susan)

Opposite page: This small city sidewalk perennial border features a handsome clump of pink stonecrop sedum, plus plantings of hosta, rudbeckia, and gaillardia; annual alyssum is used as an edging.
Left: Straw-colored flower plumes of feather reed grass and golden yellow rudbeckia are star performers in this meadow garden.

PERENNIALS FOR ROCK GARDENS

Aegopodium podagraria (Bishop's weed)
Ajuga reptans (Bluebugle)
Alchemilla mollis (Lady's Mantle)
Anemone pulsatilla (Pasqueflower)
Anthemis tinctoria (Golden Marguerite)
Aquilegia hybrids (Columbine)
Arabis caucasica (Rock-cress)
Armeria maritima (Common Thrift)
Aubrietia deltoide (Flower Rock-Cress)
Aurinia saxatilis (Perennial Alyssum)
Bergenia cordifolia (Heartleaf Bergenia)
Campanula percisifolia, dwarf species
   (Willow-leaf Bellflower)
Cerastium tomentosum (Snow-in-summer)
Dianthus plumarius (Cottage Pinks)
Dicentra spectabilis, dwarf species
   (Japanese-Bleeding-heart)
Doronicum caucasicum (Dogbane)
Erigeron hybrids (Fleabane)
Euphorbia epithymoides, dwarf species (Cushion Spurge)
Geranium himaleyense, dwarf species (Blue Cranesbill)
Heuchera sanguinea (Coral-bells)
Iberis sempervivens (Perennial Candytuft)
Linum perenne (Blue Flax)
Liriope muscari (Lily-turf)
Nepeta mussinii (Ornamental Catmint)
Oenothera tetagona (Sundrop)
Opuntia humifusa (Hardy Prickly-pear)
Phlox subulata (Moss-pinks)
Platycodon grandiflorus (Balloon flower)
Polygonum bistorta (Knotweed)
Saponaria ocymoides (Soapwort)
Sedum spectabile (Stonecrop)
Stokesia laevis (Stoke's Aster)
Veronica longifolia (Speedwell)
Yucca filamentosa (Spanish dagger)

PERENNIALS FOR DAMP AND MOIST PLACES

Alchemilla mollis (Lady's mantle)
Arum italicum (Italian Arum)
Astilbe x *arendsii* (False Spirea)
Caltha palustris (Marsh-marigold)
Eupatorium coelestinum (Perennial Ageratum)
Hosta seiboldiana (Plantain-lily)
Helenium autumnale (Sneezeweed)
Hibiscus moscheutos (Rose mallow)
Iris sibirica (Siberian Iris)
Ligularia x *prezewalskii* (Rocket Ligularia)
Lobelia cardinalis (Scarlet Lobelia)
Lysimachia punctata (Yellow Loosestrife)
Lythrum salicaria (Purple Loosestrife)
Myosotis scarpioides (Forget-me-not)
Polygonum bistorta (Knotweed)
Primula japonica (Japanese Primrose)
Trollius europaeus (Globeflower)

Left: A clump of *Lysimachus punctata* (Yellow Loosestrife) thrives in moist soil.

PERENNIALS FOR FOLIAGE EFFECTS

Acanthus mollis (Bear's Breach)
Aegopodium podagraria (Bishop's weed)
Ajuga reptans (Bluebugle)
Artemisia ludoviciana (Silver King)
Arum italicum (Italian Arum)
Bergenia cordifolia (Heartleaf Bergenia)
Cerastium tomentosum (Snow-in-summer)
Dianthus plumarius (Cottage Pinks)
Hosta seiboldiana (Plantain-lily)
Liriope muscaria (Lily-turf)
Yucca filamentosa (Spanish Dagger)

PERENNIALS FOR WOODLAND GARDENS

Aquilegia hybrids (Columbine)
Arum italicum (Italian Arum)
Astilbe x *arendsii* (False Spirea)
Bergenia cordifolia (Heartleaf Bergenia)
Cimicifuga racemosa (Snakeroot)
Dicentra spectabilis (Japanese Bleeding-heart)
Digitalis purpurea (English Foxglove)
Helleborus niger (Christmas-rose)
Hosta seiboldiana (Plantain-lily)
Lilium species (Lily)
Lobelia cardinalis (Scarlet Lobelia)
Myosotis scarpioides (Forget-me-not)
Polemonium reptans (Jacob's-ladder)
Primula species (Primrose)

Left: Blue-foiliaged *Hosta seiboldiana* and white-speared *Cimifuga racemosa* are good companions in this mixed border that also uses shrubs and annuals for dramatic impact.

PERENNIAL FERN GARDEN

The following popular and easy-to-grow ferns are readily available through specialist perennial growers. Ferns are especially valuable for shade gardens and wherever cool, moist conditions prevail, such as surrounding a pool or beside a stream.

Those marked with an asterisk are tender; others are hardy to frost.

Adiantum pedatum
(Maidenhair fern)
*Asplenium nidus-avis
(Bird's nest fern)
Asplenium platyneuron
(Ebony spleenwort)
Athyrium filix-femina
(Lady fern)
*Cyrtomium falcatum
(Holly fern)
Dennstaedtia punctilobula
(Hay-scented fern)
*Dicksonia antartica
(Australian tree fern)

Dryopteris erythrosora
(Japanese sword fern)
Matteuccia Struthiopteris pensylvanica (Ostrich fern)
Osmunda cinnamomea
(Cinnamon fern)
Polypodium virginianum
(Polypody fern)
Polystichum acrostichoides
(Christmas fern)
*Woodwardia species
(Chain ferns)

Right: This exquisite Victorian-style fern garden features both tender and hardy kinds in a small conservatory at the Morris Arboretum.

PERENNIALS FOR SHADE

Aquilegia hybrids (Columbine)
Cimicifuga racemosa (Snakeroot)
Dicentra spectabilis (Japanese Bleeding-heart)
Helleborus niger (Christmas-rose)
Hosta seiboldiana (Plantain-lily)
Lobelia cardinalis (Scarlet Lobelia)
Liriope muscari (Lily-turf)
Polemonium reptans (Jacob's-ladder)
Primula species (Primrose)

(See also list of recommended ferns)

Right: Bleeding hearts are excellent flowering perennials for light shade.

PERENNIAL GRASSES

Briza Media (Quaking Grass)
Calamagrostis acutiflora stricta (Feather Reed Grass)
Cortadera selloana (Pampas Grass)
Deschampsia caespitosa (Tufted Hair Grass)
Elymus glaucus (European Dune Grass)
Erianthus ravennae (Ravennae Grass)
Festuca ovina 'glauca' (Blue Fescue)
Glyceria maxima 'variegata' (Manna Grass)
Imperata cylindra rubra (Japanese Blood Grass)
Miscanthus sinensis (Chinese Silver Grass)
Miscanthus sinensis 'Gracillimus' (Maiden Grass)
Miscanthus sinensis 'Zebrinus' (Zebra Grass)
Panicum virgatum (Switch Grass)
Pennisetum alopecuroides (Australian Fountain Grass)
Pennisetum setaceum (Crimson Fountain Grass)
Pennisetum villosum (Feather Top)
Phalaris arundinacea picta (Ribbon Grass)

PERENNIALS FOR HOT, DRY SOIL

Achillea filipendulina (Yellow Yarrow)
Anthemis tinctoria (Golden Marguerite)
Arabis caucasica (Rock-cress)
Artemisia ludoviciana (Silver King)
Asclepias tuberosa (Butterfly Milkweed)
Aurinia saxatilis (Perennial Alyssum)
Campanula percisifolia (Willow-leaf Bellflower)
Catananche caerulea (Cupid's-dart)
Cerastium tomentosum (Snow-in-summer)
Coreopsis lanceolata (Lance-leaf Coreopis)
Dianthus plumarius (Cottage Pinks)
Echinacea purpurea (Purple Coneflower)
Echinops ritro (Small Globe-thistle)
Eryngium giganteum (Sea-holly)
Euphorbia epithymoides (Cushion Spurge)
Gaillardia x *grandiflora* (Blanket-flower)
Gypsophila paniculata (Baby's-breath)
Helianthemum nummularium (Rock Rose)
Hemerocallis hybrids (Daylily)
Iberis sempervivens (Perennial Candytuft)
Kniphofia uvaria (Red-hot poker)
Liatris spicata (Gayfeather)
Linum perenne (Blue Flax)
Lychnis chalcedonica (Maltese Cross)
Opuntia humifusa (Hardy Prickly-pear)
Veronica longifolia (Speedwell)
Yucca filamentosa (Spanish dagger)

PERENNIALS FOR GROUND COVER

Aegopodium podagraria 'variegatum' (Bishop's-weed)
Ajuga reptans (Bluebugle)
Alchemilla mollis (Lady's Mantle)
Bergenia cordifolia (Heartleaf Bergenia)
Cerastium tomentosum (Snow-in-summer)
Hosta seiboldiana (Plantain-lily)
Iberis sempervirens (Perennial Candytuft)
Liriope muscari (Lily-turf)
Lysimachia punctata (Yellow Loosestrife)
Myosotis scarpioides (Forget-me-Not)
Opuntia humifusa (Hardy Prickly-pear)
Sedum species (Stonecrop)

Opposite page: A close-up view of ribbon grass shows beautiful bands of green and white along the leaf blades, creating a decorative effect in perennial borders from spring until fall frosts.

RED PERENNIALS

Alcea rosea (Hollyhocks)
Achillea filipendulina (Yellow Yarrow)
Aquilegia hybrids (Columbine)
Armeria maritima (Common Thrift)
Arum italicum (Italian Arum)
Asclepias tuberosa (Butterfly Milkweed)
Aster novae-angliae (Michaelmas Daisy)
Astilbe x *arendsii* (False Spirea)
Aubrieta deltoide (Flower Rock-Cress)
Bergenia cordifolia (Heartleaf Bergenia)
Centranthus ruber (Red Valerian)
Chrysanthemum morifolium (Cushion Mum)
Dianthus plumarius (Cottage Pinks)
Digitalis purpurea (English Foxglove)
Erigeron hybrids (Fleabane)
Gaillardia x *grandiflora* (Blanket-flower)
Helenium autumnale (Sneezeweed)
Hemerocallis hybrids (Daylily)
Heuchera sanguinea (Coral-bells)
Hibiscus moscheutos (Rose mallow)
Iris germanica (Bearded Iris)
Kniphofia uvaria (Red-hot poker)
Liatris spicata (Gayfeather)
Lilium species (Lilies)
Lobelia cardinalis (Scarlet Lobelia)
Lupinus hybrids (Russell Lupine)
Lychnis chalcedonica (Maltese Cross)
Papaver orientale (Oriental Poppy)
Phlox paniculata (Summer Phlox)
Phlox subulata (Moss-pinks)
Primula x *polyantha* (Polyanthus Primrose)

PINK PERENNIALS

Alcea rosea (Hollyhocks)
Anemone japonica (Japanese Anemone)
Aquilegia hybrids (Columbine)
Armeria maritima (Common Thrift)
Aster novae-angliae (Michaelmas Daisy)
Astilbe x *arendsii* (False Spirea)
Aubrieta deltoide (Flower Rock-Cress)
Bergenia cordifolia (Heartleaf Bergenia)
Campanula species (Bellflower)
Centranthus ruber (Red Valerian)
Chrysanthemum x *morifolium* (Cushion Mum)
Dianthus plumarius (Cottage Pinks)
Dicentra spectabilis (Japanese Bleeding-heart)
Digitalis purpurea (English Foxglove)
Echinacea purpurea (Purble Coneflower)
Erigeron hybrids (Fleabane)
Eupatorium coelestinum (Perennial Ageratum)
Gypsophila paniculata (Baby's-breath)
Helianthemum nummularium (Rock Rose)
Helleborus niger (Christmas-rose)
Heuchera sanguinea (Coral-bells)
Hibiscus moscheutos (Rose mallow)
Iris germanica (Bearded Iris)
Lathyrus latifolius (Perennial Sweet Pea)
Liatris spicata (Gayfeather)
Lilium species (Tiger Lilies)
Liriope muscari (Lily-turf)
Lupinus hybrids (Russell Lupine)
Lythrum salicaria (Purple Loosestrife)
Myosotis scarpioides (Forget-me-not)
Papaver orientale (Oriental Poppy)
Phlox paniculata (Summer Phlox)
Phlox subulata (Moss-pinks)
Physostegia virginiana (Obedient Plant)
Primula japonica (Japanese Primrose)
Primula polyantha (Polyanthus Primrose)
Saponaria ocymoides (Soapwort)
Sedum spectabiles (Stonecrop)
Veronica longifolia (Speedwell)

Opposite page: This woodland garden uses sky blue forget-me-nots, yellow alyssum, and pale blue woodland phlox to create color low to the ground, under a canopy of flowering dogwoods.
Left: A single plant of hollyhock makes a good structural highlight against a dry wall.

Right: This Colonial-style perennial garden, featuring yellow yarrow, purple foxglove, and blue delphinium, includes a gazebo as a strong design element.

Opposite page: A portion of the Iris Garden at Ladew Topiary Gardens, near Monkton, Maryland, uses mostly bearded iris, plus a variegated form of lily turf for edging.

BLUE PERENNIALS

Amsonia tabernaemontana (Bluestar)
Anemone pulsatilla (Pasqueflower)
Ajuga reptans (Bluebugle)
Acanthus mollis (Bear's breach)
Anchusa azurea (Italian bugloss)
Aquilegia hybrids (Columbine)
Aster novae-angliae (Michaelmas Daisy)
Baptisia australis (Blue Wild Indigo)
Campanula percisifolia (Willow-leaf Bellflower)
Catananche caerulea (Cupid's-dart)
Echinops ritro (Small Globe-thistle)
Eryngium giganteum (Sea-holly)
Geranium species (Blue Cranesbill)
Hosta seiboldiana (Plantain-lily)
Iris germanica (Bearded Iris)
Iris sibirica (Siberian Iris)
Linum perenne (Blue Flax)
Liriope muscari (Lily-turf)
Lupinus hybrids (Russell Lupine)
Myosotis scarpioides (Forget-me-not)
Nepeta mussinii (Ornamental Catmint)
Perovskia atripicifolia (Russian Sage)
Phlox subulata (Moss-pinks)
Platycodon grandiflorus (Balloon Flower)
Polemonium reptans (Jacob's-ladder)
Primula polyantha (Polyanthus Primrose)
Salvia x *superba* (Violet Sage)
Scabiosa caucasica (Pincushion Flower)
Stokesia laevis (Stoke's Aster)
Veronica longifolia (Speedwell)

WHITE PERENNIALS
(INCLUDING SILVER-FOLIAGED)

Acanthus mollis (Bear's breach)
Aegopodium podagraria (Bishop's weed)
Ajuga reptans (Bluebugle)
Alcea rosea (Hollyhock)
Amsonia tabernaemontana (Bluestar)
Anchusa azurea (Italian bugloss)
Anemone japonica (Japanese Anemone)
Aquilegia hybrids (Columbine)
Arabis caucasica (Rock-cress)
Artemesia ludoviciana (Silver King)
Aster novae-angliae (Michaelmas Daisy)
Astilbe x *arendsii* (False Spirea)
Aubrieta deltoide (Flower Rock-Cress)
Campanula percisifolia (Willow-leaf Bellflower)
Centranthus ruber (Red Valerian)
Chrysanthemum morifolium (Cushion Mum)
Chrysanthemum parthenium (Feverfew)
Chrysanthemum superbum (Shasta Daisy)
Cimicifuga racemosa (Snakeroot)
Delphinium elatum (English Delphinium)
Dicenetra spectabilis (Japanese Bleeding-heart)
Digitalis purpurea (English Foxglove)
Echinacea purpurea (Purple Coneflower)
Eryngium giganteum (Sea-holly)
Gypsophila paniculata (Baby's-breath)
Helleborus niger (Christmas-rose)
Hemerocallis hybrids (Daylily)
Heuchera sanguinea (Coral-bells)
Hosta seiboldiana (Plantain-lily)
Iberis sempervivens (Perennial Candytuft)
Iris germanica (Bearded Iris)
Iris sibirica (Siberian Iris)
Liatris spicata (Gayfeather)
Lilium species (Tiger Lilies)
Liriope muscari (Lily-turf)
Phlox paniculata (Summer Phlox)
Phlox subulata (Moss-pinks)
Physostegia virginiana (Obedient Plant)
Platycodon grandiflorus (Balloon Flower)
Polygonum bistorta (Knotweed)
Primula polyanthus (Polyanthus Primrose)
Stokesia laevis (Stoke's Aster)

YELLOW AND ORANGE PERENNIALS

Alcea rosea (Hollyhocks)
Alchemilla mollis (Lady's mantle)
Aegopodium podagraria (Bishop's weed)
Achillea filipendulina (Yellow Yarrow)
Anthemis tinctoria (Golden Marguerite)
Aquilegia hybrids (Columbine)
Asclepias tuberosa (Butterfly Milkweed)
Aurinia saxatilis (Perennial Alyssum)
Caltha palustris (Marsh-marigold)
Chrysanthemum morifolium (Cushion Mum)
Chrysanthemum parthenium (Feverfew)
Coreopsis lanceolata (Lance-leaf Coreopsis)
Digitalis purpurea (English Foxglove)
Doronicum caucasicum (Dogbane)
Euphorbia epithymoides (Cushion Spurge)
Gaillardia x *grandifloria* (Blanket-flower)
Geum chiloense (Chilean Avens)
Helianthemum nummularium (Rock Rose)
Helenium autumnale (Sneezeweed)
Helianthus x *multifloras* (Perennial Sunflower)
Heliopsis helianthoides (False Sunflower)
Hemerocallis hybrids (Daylily)
Iris germanica (Bearded Iris)
Kniphofia uvaria (Red-hot poker)
Ligularia x *prezewalskii* (Rocket Ligularia)
Lilium species (Tiger Lilies)
Lysimachia punctata (Yellow Loosestrife)
Oenothera tetragona (Sundrop)
Opuntia humifusa (Hardy Prickly-pear)
Physalis alkekengi (Chinese Lantern)
Primula polyanthus (Polyanthus Primrose)
Rudbeckia fulgida (Black-eyed Susan)
Trollius europaeus (Globeflower)

Opposite page: Here, yellow bearded iris is used to make a bold splash of color at Old Westbury Gardens, on Long Island.
Above: A red-hot poker plant and white shasta daisies are perfect companions in this sunny island bed.
Below: Yellow coreopsis and scarlet red cardinal flowers help to create an "old-fashioned" look in this Colonial garden at Pennsbury Manor, near Philadelphia, Pennsylvania.

PERENNIAL FLOWERING GUIDE

		Jan	Feb	Mar	Apr	May	Jun	Jul	Aug	Sep	Oct	Nov	Dec
Acanthus mollis	(Bear's breach)							■					
Achillea filipendulina	(Yarrow)						■						
Aegopodium podagravia	(Bishop's weed)					■	■	■	■	■			
Ajuga reptans	(Bluebugle)					■							
Alcea rosea	(Hollyhock)								■				
Alchemilla mollis	(Lady's mantle)						■						
Amsonia tabernaemontana	(Bluestar)					■							
Anchusa azurea	(Italian bugloss)						■						
Anemone x *hybrida*	(Japanese Anemone)									■			
Anemone pulsatilla	(Pasqueflower)				■								
Anthemis tinctoria	(Golden Marguerite)						■						
Aquilegia hybrids	(Columbine)						■						
Arabis caucasica	(Rock-cress)				■								
Armeria maritima	(Common Thrift)				■								
Artemisia ludoviciana	(Silver King)					■	■	■	■	■			
Arum italicum	(Italian Arum)								■	■			
Asclepias tuberosa	(Butterfly Milkweed)						■						
Aster novae-angliae	(Michaelmas Daisy)						■	■	■	■	■		
Astilbe x *arendsii*	(False Spirea)												
Aubrieta deltoide	(Flower Rock-Cress)				■								
Aurinia saxatilis	(Perennial Alyssum)												
Baptisia australis	(Blue wild Indigo)					■							
Bergenia cordifolia	(Heartleaf Bergenia)			■									
Caltha palustris	(Marsh-marigold)				■								

	January	February	March	April	May	June	July	August	September	October	November	December
Campanula percisifolia (Willow-leaf Bellflower)						■						
Catananche caerulea (Cupid's-dart)							■					
Centranthus ruber (Red Valerian)						■						
Cerastium tomentosum (Snow-in-summer)					■							
Chrysanthemum x *morifolium* (Cushion Mum)									■	■		
Chrysanthemum parthenium (Feverfew)						■						
Chrysanthemum x *superbum* (Shasta Daisy)								■				
Cimicifuga racemosa (Snakeroot)								■				
Coreopsis lanceolata (Lance-leaf Coreopsis)						■						
Dianthus plumarius (Cottage Pinks)						■						
Dicentra spectabilis (Japanese Bleeding-heart)						■						
Digitalis purpurea (English Foxglove)						■						
Doronicum caucasicum (Dogbane)					■							
Echinacea purpurea (Purple Coneflower)						■	■	■				
Echinops vitro (Small Globe-thistle)						■	■					
Erigeron hybrids (Fleabane)							■					
Eryngium giganteum (Sea-holly)						■	■					
Eupatorium coelestinum (Perennial Ageratum)								■				
Euphorbia epithymoides (Cushion Spurge)						■						
Gaillardia x *grandiflora* (Blanket-flower)								■				
Geranium himaleyense (Blue Cranesbill)						■						
Geum chiloense (Chilean Avens)					■							
Gypsophila paniculata (Baby's breath)							■	■				
Helianthemum nummularium (Rock Rose)									■	■		

	January	February	March	April	May	June	July	August	September	October	November	December
Helenium autumnale (Sneezeweed)									▓			
Helianthus x *multifloras* (Perrennial Sunflower)									▓			
Heliopsis helianthoides (False Sunflower)								▓				
Helleborus niger (Christmas-rose)			▓	▓								
Hemerocallis hybrids (Daylily)						▓	▓	▓				
Heucherea sanguinea (Coral-bells)					▓							
Hibiscus moscheutos (Rose mallow)							▓	▓	▓			
Hosta seiboldiana (Plantain lily)					▓	▓	▓	▓				
Iberis sempervivens (Perennial Candytuft)			▓									
Iris germanica (Bearded Iris)					▓							
Iris siberica (Siberian Iris)					▓							
Kniphofia uvaria (Red-hot poker)					▓							
Lathyrus latifolius (Perennial Sweet Pea)						▓						
Liatris spicata (Gayfeather)												
Ligularia x *prezewalski* (Rocket Ligularia)							▓					
Lilium lancifolium (Tiger Lilies)							▓					
Linum perenne (Blue Flax)				▓	▓							
Liriope muscari (Lily-turf)				▓	▓	▓	▓	▓				
Lobelia cardinalis (Scarlet Lobelia)							▓					
Lupinus hybrids (Russell Lupine)					▓							
Lychnis chalcedonica (Maltese Cross)						▓						
Lysimachia punctata (Yellow Loosestrife)						▓						
Lythrum salicaria (Purple Loosestrife)								▓				
Myosotis scarpioides (Forget-me-not)				▓	▓							

Right: Blue mountain phlox (foreground), yellow alyssum, and blue forget-me-nots (background) create sweeps of color in spring, while white flowering dogwoods carry color high into the sky.

		January	February	March	April	May	June	July	August	September	October	November	December
Nepeta mussinii	(Ornamental Catmint)						■						
Oenothera tetragona	(Sundrop)							■					
Opuntia humifusa	(Hardy Prickly-pear)						■						
Paeonia officinalis	(Herbaceous Peony)					■							
Papaver orientale	(Oriental Poppy)					■							
Perovskia atripicifolia	(Russian Sage)								■				
Phlox paniculata	(Summer Phlox)							■					
Phlox subulata	(Moss-pinks)					■							
Physostegia virginiana	(Obedient Plant)								■	■			
Platycodon grandiflorus	(Balloon flower)						■	■	■				
Physalis alkekengi	(Chinese Lantern)								■	■	■		
Polemonium reptans	(Jacob's-ladder)					■							
Polygonum bistorta	(Knotweed)						■						
Primula japonica	(Japanese Primrose)					■							
Primula x polyantha	(Polyanthus Primrose)				■								
Rudbeckia fulgida	(Black-eyed Susan)							■	■				
Salvia x superba	(Violet Sage)							■	■				
Saponaria ocymoides	(Soapwort)					■							
Scabiosa caucasica	(Pincushion Flower)							■	■				
Sedum spectabile	(Stonecrop)									■			
Stokesia laevis	(Stoke's Aster)						■						
Trollius europaeus	(Globeflower)				■	■							
Veronica longifolia	(Speedwell)					■	■						
Yucca filamentosa	(Spanish dagger)							■					

Left: The main components of this early spring perennial border are sky blue forget-me-nots, pale blue woodland phlox, and yellow alyssum.

ESSENTIAL
BULBS

INTRODUCTION

A Big Bang For The Buck

IT IS DIFFICULT TO HAVE A SATISFYING ORNAmental garden without taking advantage of the wide variety of flowering bulbs. Many bulbs have the color impact of annuals *and* the staying power of perennials. In addition to coming back year after year, many hardy types can survive arcticlike winters, while tender varieties will survive long periods of drought.

Bulbs can establish a garden's reputation like few other plant groups. At Keukenhoff, in Holland, displays of springflowering bulbs attract thousands of visitors from all over the world each year. In North America, at the estate garden of Winterthur (Delaware), the late Henry F. du Pont planted bulbs in vast quantities across meadows and among woodland. Hundreds of thousands of daffodils, bluebells, lilies, and colchicums were planted so thickly that du Pont literally painted the landscape with flowering bulbs, much like an artist daubing paint on a canvas.

Of course, gardeners do not need hundreds of acres or thousands of a single variety to enjoy the beauty of flowering bulbs. As few as fifteen bulbs clustered together can create a bold splash of color in a small bed or border.

The varieties presented here represent the best bulbs for today's gardens. Many are hardy and will grow in most of the colder regions of Canada. Others are tender. In the northern United States tender bulbs can be planted outdoors in the spring to flower in summer or fall. They must, however, be lifted from the ground soon after frost kills the top growth and be stored in a cool, frost-free basement over winter. In areas of the country with mild winters, such as the Gulf States, the Southwest, and California, many tender varieties can be grown outdoors year-round.

Bulbs serve many different purposes. Some are good for naturalizing, multiplying year after year; others make beautiful houseplants when grown in pots. An important section of this book presents useful lists and charts—grouping plants by color, height, bloom period, and other designations.

In addition, there is a unique design section presenting garden plans for different situations—island beds, shady borders, rock gardens, and cutting gardens, for example. These plans are easily adapted to individual preferences and site restrictions.

Finally, *Essential Bulbs* closes with a list of sources, including general bulb suppliers who sell a wide assortment of bulbs as well as bulb specialists who sometimes offer over 1,000 varieties of a particular bulb group—turn to them when you want to build a bulb collection or seek the rare and unusual.

The big attraction to bulbs among home gardeners is the ease with which they can be planted and the high probability that they will flower the following season without a lot of care. Even the smallest bulbs, such as snowdrops and aconites, are larger than most bean seeds and contain enough stored energy within their fleshy interiors to propel themselves into full flower with the merest covering of soil and moisture. With larger bulbs, such as daffodils and tulips, the task of planting is even easier. Simply stated, bulbs are a gardener's dream come true: a big bang for the buck with a minimum of effort.

HISTORY OF BULB GROWING

Primitive civilizations first valued bulbs for food and medicine. Though many are poisonous—such as daffodils and hyacinths—a large number are edible either raw (onions), cooked (dahlia tubers), or pounded into a pasty substance (elephant ears or "taro"—a source of poi, the Polynesian food staple). The autumn-flowering saffron crocus yields golden yellow, powdery stigmas and has been cultivated for centuries as a valuable source of flavoring and dye. Evidence of its early use appears on a jar from the island of Crete, dating to 1500 B.C. Colchicums yield a valuable medicinal substance called *colchicine*. The rhizome of an iris produces *orris* used in cosmetics as a scent, and North American Indians fiercely guarded tribal rights to vast meadows of *camassias* whose bulbs were a vital food.

The first mention of using bulbs in gardens appears in the writings of Theophrastus, a Greek philosopher, who lived around 300 B.C. In his book, *A History of Plants and Theoretical Botany,* he describes anemones, crocus, gladiolus, grape hyacinths, lilies, and ranunculus. Dioscorides, a Greek physician, and Pliny, a Roman scholar, further describe alliums, daffodils, hyacinths, and scillas.

By the mid-sixteenth century, tulips had found their way into Austrian gardens through trade with Turkey. Carolus Clusias, curator of Emperor Maximillian the Second's medicinal garden, collected many unusual flowering bulbs, including the tulip. When he lost his position after the Emperor's death in 1576, he emigrated to Holland, taking with him a large assortment of plants, including tulips. He was appointed curator of the Hortus Medicus medicinal garden in Leyden. The tulips he planted there aroused great interest among the Dutch. The flowers were so richly colored,

everyone wanted to grow them. Moreover, the tulip had an inherent tendency to produce color mutations—sometimes in solid colors, but also streaked with a contrasting color.

When a tulip produced a distinctive mutation, it could be further propagated from bulblets. First, the wealthy classes wanted new tulip varieties to grow in their gardens, and then the masses became obsessed with growing them. Speculators paid huge prices for a single bulb of a new variety if they thought it would generate a popular following. During the early seventeenth century tulips could be traded like stocks, and they changed hands by the cartload. The crash came suddenly in 1637 when public demand waned. Investors found themselves stuck with bulbs that could fetch only 5 percent of the purchase price, and political cartoonists delighted in portraying tulip traders as baboons.

In spite of their tarnished image, tulips continued to be produced in Holland by a core of growers who specialized in the breeding, propagating, and exporting of bulbs. The cool climate and sandy soil were perfect for growing tulips, and to this day Holland has remained the preeminent breeder and producer of tulips.

Holland also produces vast quantities of daffodils, hyacinths, and "minor bulbs" such as iris, grape hyacinths, aconites, and crocus; however, several other nations compete with Holland. In North America, the Pacific Northwest possesses ideal conditions for breeding and producing daffodils, dahlias, and lilies. Parts of Michigan have proven especially favorable for daylilies. Scotland, Ireland, and England all actively breed and produce daffodils and dahlias. Some Japanese growers have become expert producers of tulips and irises.

For the American gardener, bulbs are readily available from a multitude of local sources. Garden centers offer selections of popular varieties: summer-flowering bulbs on sale in spring for spring planting and spring-flowering bulbs on sale in fall for fall planting. A larger selection is available from catalog houses, a list of which is featured at the back of this book. Traditionally, mail-order bulb suppliers have published their bulb catalogs in summer to give gardeners ample time to order for fall planting. However, several companies now publish their bulb catalogs in spring and offer substantial "pre-season" discounts for early orders.

CHAPTER ONE

BULB BASICS

THE BULB IS ONE OF NATURE'S INGENIOUS inventions. It enables the plants to lie dormant, withstanding long periods of harsh conditions (usually severe temperatures or dry summers) until the plants bloom again. Generally, a bulb is an enlarged portion of root or stem comprised of a storehouse of energy that is released when certain favorable conditions cause it to break dormancy. It then sprouts leaves, produces flowers, sets seeds, and grows bulblets, ensuring a new generation of the plant. The favorable conditions that are needed to break dormancy are generally a combination of moisture, sunlight, and warm temperatures.

Some bulbs are extremely hardy, withstanding severe frosts; others are tender and are killed by freezing temperatures. Most bulbs require good drainage to survive from year to year, but a few, such as calla lilies, will tolerate permanently moist soil. Bulbs include spring-flowering, summer-flowering, and autumn-flowering kinds. Many can be flowered indoors or under glass during winter months by a special "forcing" technique (see page 213).

True Bulbs, such as tulips and daffodils, are essentially underground "buds" formed by a swollen portion of stem. Each bulb has a growing point and is composed of fleshy layers, like an onion. The layers are wrapped around the growing point, as with tulips, or the layers are composed of scales, as with lilies. At the bottom of true bulbs is a disk from which roots emerge. Bulbs also produce bulblets, which can produce a new plant.

Corms, such as crocus and gladiolus, are solid. As the food supply in the corm is used up it shrivels away and is replaced by a new corm that forms on the top of the old one. Like bulbs, corms have a basal disk from which roots emerge. Corms also produce cormlets.

Tubers, such as dahlias and caladiums, are similar to corms in that they are solid. They can be stem tubers, like caladiums, or root tubers, like dahlias. Neither has a basal disk, but are covered with "eyes," which are buds on the surface of the tuber or concentrated near the stem section.

Rhizomes, such as irises and calla lilies, are horizontal sections of swollen stem that lie on or below the ground. Buds on top of the rhizome produce new green growth, while roots develop along the underside.

One of the advantages of using bulbs, corms, tubers, and rhizomes is that they are large and easy to handle compared to other means of reproduction, such as seeds and cuttings. Bulbs also are easily planted, dependable, and capable of producing a bold splash of color quite quickly. Because of their similarities, most garden supply houses classify bulbs, corms, tubers, and rhizomes simply as "bulbs."

By their nature, all bulbs—corms, tubers, and rhizomes—are "perennials." If their cultural needs are met, they will come up faithfully year after year. Also, like most garden perennials, their floral display can be short-lived, although there are exceptions, such as tuberous begonias and dahlias.

A careful selection of bulbs can provide nine months of color, starting with aconites and snowdrops that bloom in early spring and ending with autumn-flowering crocus.

WHEN TO PLANT

Most bulbs can be categorized by their flowering period. When and how to plant these bulbs depends solely on when they flower. See the encyclopedia chapter for more detailed planting information for each bulb. In order to ensure a long bloom period throughout the season, plant a good mixture of spring-, summer-, and fall-flowering bulbs.

Spring-Flowering Bulbs

Plant the bulbs when the soil cools to below 60° F (15°C). In northern regions, plant in either late September or early October.

In warm climates, store the bulbs in an open container in the vegetable compartment of your refrigerator for six to eight weeks before planting. Don't place the bulbs next to fruit such as tomatoes, apples, or pears, since these give off a gas harmful to bulbs. This cold period simulates the chilling they would normally receive in the ground. Plant the bulbs on a cool day in late November or December.

Summer- and Fall-Flowering Bulbs

Plant the bulbs in spring when the danger of heavy frosts is past. Generally, in northern regions summer-flowering bulbs can be planted as late as the beginning of June. Fall-flowering bulbs are best planted before the end of June. Many of them produce leaves that die before the plants flower.

HOW TO NATURALIZE SPRING-FLOWERING BULBS

Perhaps nothing is more symbolic of spring than a sunny slope full of daffodils tossing their golden trumpets in the wind. Many spring-flowering bulbs, such as daffodils, will give a good show the first flowering season, but will flower progressively less in subsequent years until they completely peter out. Unfortunately, there is more to naturalizing a landscape than popping bulbs into the ground and hoping they will take care of themselves.

In most cases where bulbs fail to naturalize, the problem is poor feeding. With most flowering bulbs the most essential fertilizer nutrient is phosphorous. This is why experts recommend bone meal—phosphorous-rich fertilizer—for fall plantings. However, for naturalized plantings bone meal can be prohibitively expensive. Super phosphate provides a more economical substitute. (For more details on fertilizing, see page 216.)

Where soils are deficient in phosphorous, try two applications (one in the spring—before the bulbs flower—and one in the fall) of super phosphate mixed with a soil conditioner such as compost, dehydrated manure, peat moss, or leaf mold. Combine these two basic ingredients at the ratio of 1 to 1 by weight and apply 10 pounds of the mixture per 100 bulbs.

The daffodil is without doubt the most dependable bulb for naturalizing wherever cold winter temperatures can be relied on to provide a dormant period. Best of all, the bulbs are large and easy to handle. They will naturalize in open, sunny locations such as meadows, as well as in lightly shaded areas such as under deciduous trees. More importantly, daffodil bulbs are poisonous to rodents, who are notoriously destructive to naturalized plantings.

Classic naturalized settings for daffodils include areas alongside a sparkling stream, at the edge of a pond, on a sunny bank, or clustered around a clump of silver birch on an open lawn. To gain a naturalized effect, you can choose the less expensive bulb mixtures, and some catalogs will even feature a "naturalized collection" at a special low rate.

SPRING-FLOWERING BULBS SUITABLE FOR NATURALIZING

*Asterisked varieties are tender

VARIETY	LOCATION
Amaryllis belladonna	Sun, meadow
Camassia	Sun, meadow
Chionodoxa	Sun or shade, rock garden, woodland
Clivia miniata	Shade
Crocus	Sun or shade, lawn or meadow
Eranthis	Sun or shade, woodland
Erythronium	Sun or shade, rock garden
Fritillaria imperialis	Sun or shade, edge of woodland
Galanthus	Sun or shade, woodland, rock garden
Hyacinthoides	Shade, woodland
Iris cristata	Sun or shade, woodland
Iris reticulata	Sun, rock garden
Muscari	Sun or shade, rock garden
Narcissus	Sun or shade, woodland, meadow, lawn
Ornithogalum species	Sun, meadow, rock garden
Oxalis species	Sun, meadow
Tulipa species	Sun or shade, rock garden
Zephyranthes atamasco	Sun or shade, woodland, meadow

When planting, it is best to gently scatter the bulbs on the ground, and plant them where they fall. Leaf mold, peat moss, or well-decomposed animal manure and garden compost scattered onto the surface of the garden in the fall will work its way into the subsoil and benefit the bulb plantings.

Never mow a naturalized area until the leaves of the plantings have completely died away, since the leaves enable the new season's bulb to properly mature and multiply. Good drainage, of course, is essential to avoid waterlogging, which will rot the bulbs.

Some of the most effective daffodils for naturalizing include the dainty Hoop Petticoat *(Narcissus bulbocodium);* miniature daffodils *(Narcissus minimum)* such as Dove Wings and February Gold; the Poeticus class, such as Pheasant's Eye and Actaea; and the large trumpet daffodils *(Narcissus hybrida* ' Trumpet-flowered '), King Alfred (all yellow), Music Hall (white petals, yellow trumpet), and Beersheba (all white). These are all old-fashioned varieties, but thoroughly dependable, still widely available, and relatively inexpensive for naturalizing when planted in color groups.

Planting depths for daffodils vary according to the size of the bulb, but for the giant trumpet daffodils, six inches, measuring from the tip of the bulb, is about right. Recommended spacing is six inches apart. (For more spring-flowering bulbs suitable for naturalizing, see page 209.)

You must be more selective when choosing varieties of tulips for naturalizing, since the majority of varieties in catalogs will not naturalize, and those that do will not normally naturalize through sod. For tulips, a rock garden is ideal.

Another problem with tulips is their susceptibility to rodent damage. Even chipmunks and squirrels will search them out and destroy a new planting even before it has time to flower in the first season. Planting rodent repellent flakes helps protect the bulbs through the first season. Once the bulbs are established, rodent damage is usually not so great. Outdoor cats also provide effective control against rodents.

For smaller naturalized areas the *kaufmanniana* (or water-lily) tulips are dependable; also tulip species *chrysantha, turkestanica, sylvestris, dasystemons* and *clusiana.* The *kaufmannianas* are the earliest to bloom, opening their petals out flat when the sun shines, just like a water lily. *Clusiana* resembles a miniature candlestick tulip, since it holds its red

Opposite page, above: Iris germanica rhizomes before dividing.

Opposite page, below: Iris germanica rhizomes after dividing, but prior to replanting.

Left: Dwarf blue bearded iris grows easily and healthily in a rock garden.

and white striped petals upright. The *dasystemon* has a beautiful star shape, flowering close to the ground, with a distinctive yellow center and white petal edge.

In the rock garden, these species of tulips are effective when planted among rocky outcrops and dwarf conifers; however, the soil should be mulched with some natural-looking fibrous material to keep down the weeds.

Crocus are a favorite for naturalizing in a lawn. For extra-early blooms, choose yellow, and for largest size, choose purple varieties. Mixtures, of course, are effective and less expensive than buying separate colors, but once you have seen a lawn planted exclusively with bright yellow crocus or the striped Pickwick, you will realize how effective and well worth the extra cost a single-color planting can be.

To naturalize crocus in a lawn it is best to remove areas of sod, plant the bulbs two inches into the bare soil, and replace the sod after planting. This is generally easier and more effective than trying to plant the small bulbs through the grass with a trowel or bulb planter. By repeating this procedure in several areas, you will soon have beautiful, naturalized patches. Remember to feed twice a year and never mow until the spiky leaves have withered. Rodents consider crocus an extra tasty tidbit—rabbits will eat the tops—so where these pests present a potential problem, it is sometimes better to stick to the more dependable daffodil for naturalizing.

Winter aconite is a very dependable bulb for naturalizing. It is a good companion to snowdrops in a naturalized landscape, since the two bloom at about the same time—the yellow aconite contrasting with the pure white snowdrops. These two grow especially well at the edge of lightly wooded areas, where plenty of leaf mold enriches the soil.

Siberian squill, grape hyacinth, snow crocus, and *chionodoxa* will brighten up similar locations. A rock garden where they can be planted in thick clumps or bold drifts among boulders and driftwood is also a perfect place for these charming beauties.

GROWING BULBS INDOORS

There is a special pleasure in having rooms in the house filled with the color and fragrance of flowering bulbs, especially during winter months when the world outdoors is bleak and cold. The most popular varieties for fragrance are hyacinths and paperwhites, which can be forced into bloom using water alone. For sheer color impact, nothing can outshine the spectacular giant-flowering amaryllis, grown in a pot with soil. Tulips, daffodils, crocus, and grape hyacinths are also easily forced into early bloom in a pot of soil. Some varieties are easier to force than others, and usually the label on a bulb package (or the catalog description) will tell you which varieties are recommended and how to do the forcing.

Some bulbs need a "precooling" treatment in order to bloom indoors. Hyacinths, tulips, and daffodils, for example, generally need twelve weeks at 45° F or cooler in a dark place before transferring them to a room environment. To achieve this, place the bulbs in an unheated basement, a cold frame, or bury them in a trench in the ground. Cover the pots with an insulating material such as straw or pine bark, and check on them periodically to be sure they are moist but not soaked in water.

In warmer climates, refrigerate the bulbs. It is best to first plant them in a pot and refrigerate the whole package. If you don't have room for this, refrigerate just the bulbs in an open container for twelve weeks. Then pot them and place the pots in the coolest place you have while the roots grow—perhaps in a garage, utility room, or closet.

Mark your calendar when you begin cooling the bulbs so you will know when it is time to move them out into the light. By the end of the cooling period, shoots will appear. If you potted many bulbs and want them to flower over a period of time, remove them one at a time over several weeks.

Potting the Bulbs

Hyacinths are often grown in a specially shaped hyacinth glass that holds the bulb just above the water, with plenty of room for the roots to grow. Everyone seems to enjoy watching the white roots grow inside the crystal glass, finally leading up to a cluster of fragrant flowers.

Hyacinths and paperwhites can also be grown in a dish of pebbles (used for support) with water in the bottom. Any sort of container that holds water will do, but a low, shallow dish is best. A clear container will help you check the water level and

Opposite page: A crocus corn in flower, uprooted to show the structure of the entire plant.

Left, top: An amaryllis bulb planted in a plastic pot. After watering, the bulb will sprout and bloom within three weeks.

Left, bottom: A group of three paperwhite narcissus bulbs planted in a special pot that suspends them above the water, allowing the roots to drink, but the bulbs to remain dry.

the progress of the roots. It is important to keep the water level just below the bulb base. Any lower and the roots may dry out, any higher and the bulb may rot. A little charcoal in the container keeps the water clean.

Paperwhites do not need a cooling period. They need only to be potted and then put in the sun, and they'll bloom in three to five weeks.

Most bulbs, including hyacinths and paperwhites, are best grown in a pot with soil. Either plastic or clay pots will do, but the container must have a drainage hole in the bottom. The shape of the pot is not critical, but a low bulb pan provides a sturdy shape for growing a group of tall flowers.

Plant the bulbs in a commercial potting soil or a mixture of one part peat, one part perlite, and one part garden soil. (Garden soil alone will pack down too hard in the pot and should not be used.)

Be generous with the number of bulbs you put in each pot; however, avoid crowding the flowers. In a six-inch pot you can plant three hyacinths, six tulips, five daffodils, or twelve crocus bulbs. When planting tulips, place the flat side toward the edge of the pot so the large first leaf will grow outward over the edge. Plant the bulbs deep enough so that only their tips are above the soil and water them thoroughly after planting. (Of course, if you were planting these bulbs outside in the garden you would plant them much deeper and farther apart. See page 208.)

Flowering on a Sunny Windowsill

For shoot and flower development, bulbs need bright light. Place them in a south or west window or on a sun porch. In mild climates, put them outside in the sun. Temperatures should range from 55° to 65°F (12° to 18° C). Growth is rapid from this point, and flower buds will soon emerge. Then place the flowers wherever they will be enjoyed most. They will last longer if temperatures are on the cool side.

Bulbs that have been forced will not likely bloom the next year, and it is best to discard them when the blooms fade. If you wish, you can plant them in an out of the way spot in the garden.

Amaryllis

The amaryllis is a popular houseplant for indoor growing because of its big, bold flowers and ease of culture. It is a tropical plant that needs only a slight cooling period. Just plant the bulb in a six-inch pot with potting soil so that the top third of the bulb is above the soil line. To start amaryllis, place the pot in a warm location (70° to 75°F [21° to 24°C]) until the flowers begin to color. Watering should be light at first. After the flower stalk is one inch tall, water it enough to keep the soil moist but not soggy. When the bulbs flower, put the pot in a cool place to prolong the life of the flower.

To rejuvenate an amaryllis after it has flowered, keep the bulb indoors in its pot until the danger of frost is past. Keep the long, green leaves healthy for as long as possible by continuing to water. Then transfer the bulb outdoors to a shady part of the garden with fertile soil. Usually the leaves will remain green until fall frost, at which time the bulb should be lifted and stored for a minimum of ten weeks in a cool basement. After this period of cold treatment, the bulb can then be potted, brought into the light, and watered to reflower.

GROWING BULBS OUTDOORS

First loosen the soil by digging at least eight inches below the eventual depth of the bulbs. Mix in some lime and organic matter to improve the soil as needed. Lime lowers the pH in acidic soil, while organic matter improves clay or sandy soil. For bigger, more vigorous blooms, fertilize the area with a high-phosphorus fertilizer, such as Bulb Booster, according to the directions on the bag. Bulb Booster is made especially for bulbs and releases plant nutrients at just the right times in the bulb's growth cycle.

Plant the bulbs with the pointed end up—large bulbs about eight inches deep, small bulbs about five inches deep. Space the bulbs far enough apart so that the flowers will not be

Left: The Queen of Sheba, a lily-flowered tulip, makes an attractive border at the edge of a lawn.

crowded, but close enough that the planting will look full. (See the individual plant descriptions for suggested planting depths and spacing.)

After preparing the soil, use a bulb planter or trowel to dig individual holes for each bulb. For even flowering, be sure all the bulbs of the same kind are at the same depth.

After planting, water thoroughly and place three inches of mulch over the bed to deter weeds and to provide winter protection for fall-planted bulbs.

The bulbs continue to grow after blooming, storing food and forming next year's flowers. Good care at this time is very important for vigorous blooms the following spring. Remove the dead flowers so the bulbs won't use energy making seeds. Allow the foliage to yellow and wither naturally. Never cut the leaves off until they are completely brown. Leave the bulbs in the ground through the summer and fertilize again in fall.

For naturalized plantings it is important to get an informal look. To do this, mark out the area you want to plant with flour, lime, or string, and gently scatter the bulbs onto the ground, planting them where they fall. If bulbs are planted through sod, it is important to fertilize them twice a year so they remain sufficiently vigorous and can compete with the grass and grow through the sod. Fertilize in spring before the bulbs bloom, and again in fall.

Fertilizing Bulbs

To keep bulbs healthy and coming back each year, feeding is essential. The most important plant nutrients are nitrogen, phosphorus, and potash. Because they are essential to the healthy development of cultivated plants, all fertilizer formulas by law must show the percentage of each major nutrient. These are expressed in a nitrogen-phosphorus-potash ratio, such as 5-10-5 or 10-20-10. In a 5-10-5 formula, a total of 20 percent is active nutrient; the rest is "filler" that acts as a distributing agent. This is helpful to know when deciding comparative values, since a one pound package of 5-10-5 (twenty percent total nutrient content) at the same price as a one pound package of 10-20-10 (forty percent) would not be as good a buy. Phosphorus is the most important ingredient since it is responsible for healthy root and bulb development.

For outdoor bulb plantings it is best to feed bulbs twice a year—in autumn after planting and again in spring before they bloom. If you only have time to feed them once a year do it after planting, in autumn, and again the following year in early autumn. For summer-flowering bulbs, feed in spring.

For the best results, sprinkle the fertilizer on the soil surface and rake it into the topsoil at the rate recommended on the label. (For special instructions concerning naturalized plantings, see page 208.)

Composting can also supply food for bulb plantings, eliminating the need for packaged fertilizer. However, unless properly made, garden compost may supply too much nitrogen, causing leaves to develop at the expense of flowers. If compost is made mostly from decomposed animal manure, kitchen and garden waste, lawn clippings, sawdust, shredded leaves, and similar materials, then bone meal or superphosphate (high-phosphorus ingredients) should be mixed in at the time of application.

Soil Conditioning

Soil can be classified as clay, loam, or sand. Clay is heavy, cold, and forms a sticky mass when it is squeezed. It is impervious to water, which "puddles" on the surface. Sand—at the other extreme—is granular, doesn't bind together when squeezed, has poor moisture-holding capacity, and allows nutrients to drain quickly. Loam is a balanced mixture of clay, sand, and organic matter. The addition of organic matter will improve both clay and sandy soil. You will not improve sand by adding clay, nor improve clay by adding sand. Only the introduction of organic material—with its fluffy texture and aeration qualities—will break down clay or add body to sand.

Opposite page: At the Presby Iris Garden, near Montclair, New Jersey, hybrids of *Iris germanica* (bearded iris) create a rainbow border. *Left:* Clumps of Siberian iris foliage changing color in the fall. The rhizomes remain dormant in the soil throughout the winter and prior to flowering, sprout fresh green leaves in the spring.

Right: To create leaf mold, fallen leaves can be stored in an enclosure of chicken wire and left to decompose.

The Value of Leaf Mold

Leaf mold, the product of leaf litter, is the most important soil conditioner for improving the growth of bulbs. It can be found in both deciduous and evergreen wooded areas under the surface layer of dried fallen leaves. It is usually black or dark brown in color, fluffy in texture, and rich in nutrients—particularly trace elements. Moreover, its moisture-holding capacity is enormous—up to ten times better than unimproved garden topsoil.

The best way to obtain leaf mold is to create a leaf pile using chicken wire to form a holding area. Small leaves, such as pine needles and willow leaves, can be piled into the bin as they are collected, but larger leaves, such as oak and maple,

need to be shredded first, either by using a leaf shredder or a lawn mower.

Shredded leaves not only take up less volume than unshredded leaves, but also decompose much faster. Unshredded leaves can take a year or more to decompose, while shredded leaves can be useable as leaf mold within several months, particularly in warm weather and if an "activator" is mixed into the pile. An activator is any source of nitrogen. Nitrogen occurs naturally in green plant material, such as grass clippings, as well as blood meal, animal manure, and greensand. Packaged activators are also available from garden centers.

Leaf mold should be applied to bulb beds in spring after the plants bloom and then again in autumn. Either spread it on top of the soil as a mulch or rake it into the upper soil surface.

Protection from Pests and Diseases

In general, bulbs are remarkably free of pests and diseases. Many are poisonous, such as daffodils and hyacinths, and therefore are naturally repellent to damage by rodents. Tulips can present a problem wherever rodents or deer are prolific, since squirrels and mice find the tubers particularly tasty, and the leaves are a favorite food of deer. To discourage rodent damage, sprinkle rodent-repellent flakes or moth balls over the soil where bulbs are planted. To discourage deer from eating the top growth of flowering bulbs, spray the emerging leaves with Repel. This is absorbed by the leaves, making the plant distasteful past the blooming period.

Some bulbs are susceptible to maggot damage and other harmful worms that work their way into the soil. Others, like dahlias, have such succulent foliage growth that they are susceptible to attack by slugs, aphids, thrips, mites, and other chewing insects. Soil pests are extremely difficult to exterminate completely; however, chewing insects are easily controlled by insecticidal sprays that can be purchased from garden centers.

Two good organic insecticides to consider are insecticidal soap and those that combine rotenone and pyrethrum. Rotenone is a natural insecticide made from the roots of a tropical tree; pyrethrum is made from the petals of an African daisy. Together, they offer broad and effective control.

CHAPTER TWO

THE ENCYCLOPEDIA OF ESSENTIAL BULBS

THE FOLLOWING SECTION DESCRIBES 100 bulbs for spring, summer, or autumn display. Most of them are hardy, but some of them are tender. Many hardy varieties will not survive the winter in frost-free areas, and many tender varieties will not survive the winter in areas where the ground freezes. Often, hardy varieties can be grown in the south by treating them as annuals, while tender varieties can be grown in the north by lifting them in autumn, after frost has killed the tops, and storing the bulbs in a cool, frost-free area.

Each bulb featured here is listed first by its botanical (Latin) name, since this consistently identifies the bulb better than does its common name. While many bulbs have popular common names—'Daffodils' for *Narcissus* species—others do not have such familiar common names or else are widely known by two or more common names—*Lycoris squamigera*, for example, is often called 'Naked Ladies' or 'Magic Lily.'

To find a description for any bulb where you know only the common name, simply refer to the index for a quick cross-reference.

The heights given are mostly mature heights, when the plants start to flower. Often, in good soil or after abundant rainfall, plants may exceed the heights stated here.

BOTANICAL NAME *Acidanthera bicolor*

COMMON NAME Peacock Flower

RANGE Native to South Africa. Hardy zone 6 south.

HEIGHT 2 to 3 feet; erect habit.

CULTURE Easy to grow in any well-drained garden soil in full sun. The brown corms are 1 to 2 inches across. Plant in spring, 2 to 3 inches deep, 3 to 6 inches apart. Summer-flowering.

DESCRIPTION The orchid-like flowers are pure white with handsome purple-brown markings at the petal base. The leaves are long, slender, and iris-like. Best grown as an accent in mixed beds and borders. Excellent for cutting. Similar to gladiolus in habit and appearance.

BOTANICAL NAME *Agapanthus africanus*

COMMON NAME African Lily; Lily-of-the Nile

RANGE Native to South Africa. Hardy zone 8 south.

HEIGHT 3 feet; erect habit.

CULTURE Prefers fertile, moist, sandy soil in sun or partial shade. Plant the rhizomes in the fall, 2 inches deep, 12 to 24 inches apart. Summer-flowering.

DESCRIPTION Large terminal flowers. Clusters can be 10 inches across in shades of blue plus white. Leaves are straplike, forming a thick clump. Best grown in a mass in beds and borders. Popular as a patio or greenhouse pot plant.

RECOMMENDED VARIETIES 'Peter Pan', a dwarf hybrid 2 feet high; also 'Headbourne Hybrids' for increased hardiness.

BOTANICAL NAME *Allium christophii*

COMMON NAME Star-of-Persia

RANGE Native to Turkestan. Hardy zone 4 south to zone 8.

HEIGHT 2 feet; erect habit.

CULTURE Easy to grow in any well-drained garden soil in full sun. Requires warm, dry conditions during its summer rest period. Plant bulbs in fall, 4 inches deep above the bulb, spaced 12 inches apart. Spring-flowering.

DESCRIPTION Purple, starlike flowers form a large umbel up to 8 inches across. Blue-green, fleshy leaves are flat and straplike. Good for massing in mixed beds and borders. Good for cutting and for dried-flower arrangements. Planted in a mass, the flowers produce a billowing, cloudlike effect that is especially dramatic when seen against a background of evergreens.

BOTANICAL NAME *Allium giganteum*

COMMON NAME Giant Allium

RANGE Native to the Himalaya Mountains. Hardy zone 4 south to zone 8.

HEIGHT 4 to 5 feet; erect habit.

CULTURE Prefers fertile, humus-rich loam soil in full sun. Plant bulbs in fall, 6 inches deep above the bulb nose, spaced 12 inches apart. Spring-flowering.

DESCRIPTION Clusters of purple, star-shaped flowers form perfect globes up to 6 inches across on tall, slender stems. The fleshy, blue-green leaves are strap-shaped. Popular planted en masse in mixed beds and borders. Good for cutting. A mass planting of about 8 to 15 bulbs in a mixed bulb and perennial border is a real traffic-stopper.

BOTANICAL NAME *Allium moly*

COMMON NAME Lily Leek

RANGE Native to Southern Europe. Hardy zone 4 south to zone 7.

HEIGHT 12 inches; low-growing, clump-forming habit.

CULTURE Prefers well-drained, fertile, humus-rich loam soil in sun or partial shade. Plant bulbs in fall, 2 inches deep above bulb nose, spaced 6 inches apart. Spring-flowering.

DESCRIPTION Masses of starry yellow flowers form in clusters on slender stems, among onion-like leaves. Popular for edging paths, beds, and borders; also suitable for rock gardens. With its tendency to cluster, this is a good choice for creating a ground cover effect.

BOTANICAL NAME *Alstroemeria aurantiaca*

COMMON NAME Peruvian Lily

RANGE Native to South America. Hardy zone 7 south.

HEIGHT 2 to 3 feet; erect, clump-forming habit.

CULTURE Prefers a fertile, sandy loam soil in sun or partial shade. Plant tubers 6 inches deep from the tops, 12 inches apart in spring or fall. Summer-flowering.

DESCRIPTION Orange flower clusters have conspicuous orange-red stripes towards the petal centers. Hybrids include a color range of white, pink, red, and purple. Leaves are narrow, arching, and swordlike. Popular for massing in mixed beds and borders. Excellent for cutting. Suitable for growing in containers under glass in the northern United States. Other popular types of Peruvian Lily include *A. pelegrina* (lavender flowers resembling azaleas) and 'Ligtu' hybrids in a rich assortment of bold colors, including red, yellow, and orange.

BOTANICAL NAME *Amaryllis belladonna*

COMMON NAME Naked Ladies; Belladonna Lilly

RANGE Native to South Africa. Hardy zone 9.

HEIGHT 2 feet; erect, colony-forming habit.

CULTURE Prefers sandy loam soil in full sun. Plant bulbs in spring, 4 inches deep above bulb nose. Fall-flowering.

DESCRIPTION There is much confusion between the genus *Amaryllis* and *Hippeastrum*, which are often referred to as amaryllis. *A. belladonna* bears a cluster of funnel-shaped, pink flowers on fleshy, slender, leafless stems, similar to *Lycoris squamigera*, also known as Naked Ladies. After the flowers die, green, straplike leaves emerge and thrive until midsummer. Mostly used for naturalizing in open meadows and rock gardens in mild climate areas.

BOTANICAL NAME *Anemone blanda*

COMMON NAME Grecian Windflower

RANGE Native to Asia Minor. Hardy zone 4 south to zone 8.

HEIGHT 4 inches; low, spreading habit.

CULTURE Prefers a moist, humus-rich loam soil in sun or partial shade. Plant tubers 4 inches deep above the tuber, spaced $2^{1}/_{2}$ inches apart in fall. Early spring-flowering.

DESCRIPTION Purple, rose, and white daisy-like flowers close at dusk and during bad weather. With its dainty, fern-like foliage, they are mostly planted in colonies to produce a mass of bloom over several weeks. Good for naturalizing.

RECOMMENDED VARIETIES 'Rosea' (pink) and 'White Splendor.' Suitable for rock gardens, especially planted in a crescent around a boulder.

BOTANICAL NAME *Anemone coronaria*

COMMON NAME French Anemone; Poppy Anemone

RANGE Native to the Mediterranean. Hardy zone 8 south.

HEIGHT 9 inches; erect habit.

CULTURE Prefers a well-drained, humus-rich sandy or loam soil in sun or partial shade. Plant tubers 4 inches from top of tuber, spaced 3 inches apart in fall. In northern climates, can be grown only under cold frames. Spring-flowering.

DESCRIPTION Poppy-like flowers are red, blue, or white with a conspicuous crown of powdery black anthers at the petal center.

RECOMMENDED VARIETIES 'de Caen' (single-flowered) and 'St. Brigid' (double-flowered). Popular for mass planting in mixed beds and borders, and also as a pot plant. 'Mona Lisa,' a special large-flowered strain, is grown from seed under glass for cutting.

BOTANICAL NAME *Babiana stricta*

COMMON NAME Baboon Flower

RANGE Native to South Africa. Hardy zone 8 south.

HEIGHT 8 inches; clump-forming habit.

CULTURE Easy to grow in any well-drained loam or sandy soil, in full sun. Plant bulbs in fall, 3 inches deep, spaced 3 inches apart. Spring-flowering.

DESCRIPTION Clusters of sweetly scented flowers in blue, rose, and pink are produced freely over several weeks. Foliage is sword-shaped, dark green, and velvety. Exquisite in rock gardens and mixed beds and borders. Protected and mulched during winter, the tender bulbs can be left outdoors up to zone 6.

BOTANICAL NAME *Begonia* x *tuberhybrida*

COMMON NAME Tuberous Begonia

RANGE Native to the Andes. Hardy zone 10.

HEIGHT 18 inches; erect, bushy habit.

CULTURE Prefers moist, humus-rich soil in partial shade. Plant corms in spring after danger of frost, 1 inch deep above crown, spaced 12 inches apart. In areas subject to frost, corms must be lifted in fall and stored in a cool, frost-free area. Summer-flowering.

DESCRIPTION Large, rounded flowers up to 8 inches across, held erect on fleshy stems. Leaves are heart-shaped and toothed. Color range includes red, pink, yellow, orange, and white—some are bicolored. Popular for planting in shady beds and borders, also in window boxes and tubs. Some varieties suitable for hanging baskets. Excellent pot plant for growing under glass.

BOTANICAL NAME *Belamcanda chinensis*

COMMON NAME Blackberry-Lily

RANGE Native to China. Hardy zone 5 south.

HEIGHT 3 feet; erect, clump-forming habit.

CULTURE Easy to grow in any well-drained loam soil in full sun. Plant rhizomes 2 inches deep, spaced 6 inches apart in spring or fall. Summer-flowering.

DESCRIPTION Exotic orange flowers are spotted red and cluster at the top of strong, slender stems. Leaves are narrow, arching, and grasslike. After flowers fade, decorative seed pods form, revealing shiny black seeds as the pods dry. Popular for massing in mixed beds and borders. Both the flowers and the dried pods with seeds are good for cutting. A hybrid between *Belamcanda* and *Pardanthopsis*, called 'Candy Lilies,' has an extremely rich color range, including yellow, orange, pink, and white.

BOTANICAL NAME *Bletilla striata*

COMMON NAME Chinese Orchid

RANGE Native to China. Hardy zone 8 south.

HEIGHT 2 feet; upright habit.

CULTURE Outdoors, prefers moist, humus-rich, fertile, loam soil in partial shade. Indoors, grow in a 6-inch pot, using a peat-based potting soil. Plant rhizomes 4 inches deep, 4 to 6 inches apart in the fall. Spring-flowering.

DESCRIPTION The flowers are perfect miniatures of purple or white "Cattleya Orchids." Leaves are dark green, ribbed, broad, and pointed. Popular for woodland wildflower gardens and shady borders in mild climate areas. Easy-to-grow, flowering pot plant for northern states.

BOTANICAL NAME *Caladium* x *hortulanum*

COMMON NAME Rainbow Plant

RANGE Native to South America. Hardy zone 9 south.

HEIGHT 2 to 3 feet; arching, clump-forming habit.

CULTURE Prefers fertile, moist, humus-rich soil in partial shade. Plant tubers, with bumps up, 2 inches deep above the crown, spaced 4 inches apart in fall in frost-free areas; spring elsewhere. Summer-flowering.

DESCRIPTION Heart-shaped, heavily veined leaves, mostly in combinations of white, red, pink, and green, remain decorative all summer. White Jack-in-the-pulpit-like flower spathe is inconspicuous. Popular for massing in beds and borders. Excellent for containers. Plants are tender, must be set outside after danger of spring frost, and lifted for storage indoors before heavy fall frost.

RECOMMENDED VARIETIES 'Candidum' (white with green veins), 'Rosebud' (pink, white, and green), and 'Postman Joyner' (crimson with green edge).

BOTANICAL NAME *Camassia scilloides*

COMMON NAME Wild Hyacinth

RANGE Native to Oregon and British Columbia. Hardy zone 5 south to zone 8.

HEIGHT 12 inches; erect, spirelike habit.

CULTURE Prefers a well-drained, humus-rich soil in full sun. Plant bulbs 4 inches deep above bulb nose, spaced 3 inches apart in fall. Spring-flowering.

DESCRIPTION Blue starlike flowers form a loose flower spike. Grasslike leaves die down soon after flowering. Planted mostly in groups in mixed beds and borders. Good for naturalizing, especially in meadows and rock gardens. *C. esculenta* ('Quamash'), a closely related species is also good for garden display and produces edible bulbs used by Native North Americans as a food staple.

BOTANICAL NAME *Canna* x *generalis*

COMMON NAME Canna

RANGE Hybrids of species native to South America. Hardy zone 8 south.

HEIGHT 4 to 6 feet; erect, towering habit.

CULTURE Prefers moist, humus-rich, well-drained soil in full sun. Plant bulbs 4 inches deep above bulb nose, spaced 12 inches apart after danger of frost in spring. In areas subject to freezing, bulbs must be lifted in fall and stored in a dark, cool, frost-free room. Summer-flowering.

DESCRIPTION Huge, gladiolus-like flowers form terminal flower spikes on strong, erect stems with green or bronze leaves that are tropical in appearance, resembling banana leaves. Color range includes red, pink, orange, yellow, and cream. Popular as an accent in mixed beds and borders, particularly as a background.

RECOMMENDED VARIEITES 'The President,' a large-flowering red.

BOTANICAL NAME *Cardiocrinum giganteum*

COMMON NAME Himalayan Lily

RANGE Native to the Himalayas. Hardy zone 7 south.

HEIGHT 6 to 12 feet; erect, spirelike habit.

CULTURE Prefers moist, well-drained, humus-rich soil loaded with leaf mold in partial shade. Plant bulbs in fall, placing the crown just below soil surface, 2 to 3 feet apart. Early summer-flowering.

DESCRIPTION Gleaming white, trumpet-shaped, lily-like flowers have maroon stripes inside the petals. Borne in clusters, they form a spike on top of a tall, fleshy stem. Large, heart-shaped leaves are glossy dark green, forming rosettes until the flower spike elongates. Mostly grown as a tall background among azaleas and rhododendrons in woodland.

BOTANICAL NAME *Chionodoxa luciliae*

COMMON NAME Glory-of-the-snow

RANGE Native to Asia Minor. Hardy zone 4 south to zone 7.

HEIGHT 4 inches; low, clump-forming habit.

CULTURE Easy to grow in any well-drained garden soil in sun or partial shade. Plant bulbs 4 inches deep above the bulb nose in fall. Early spring-flowering.

DESCRIPTION Dainty blue or pink starlike flowers have white centers, 6 to 12 flowers crowded to a stem. Leaves are smooth and slender. Popular for planting drifts in rock gardens. Also can be naturalized in woodland under deciduous trees.

BOTANICAL NAME *Clivia miniata*

COMMON NAME Kafir-Lily

RANGE Native to South Africa. Hardy zone 9 south.

HEIGHT 2 feet; low-growing, colony-forming habit.

CULTURE Prefers moist, well-drained, fertile, humus-rich loam soil in partial shade. Plant bulbs (actually fleshy roots) in fall, 6 inches deep from the base of the roots with the crown just below soil surface, and 12 inches apart or in 12-inch pots. Spring- and early summer-flowering.

DESCRIPTION Trumpet-shaped flowers are clustered to make a dome on top of a thick stalk. Leaves are dark green, straplike, arching, and evergreen. Colors include orange, orange-red, and yellow. Popular in mild climate areas for growing under trees. In northern states mostly grown in pots. Likes to be pot-bound.

BOTANICAL NAME *Colchicum autumnale*

COMMON NAME Autumn-Crocus

RANGE Native to Europe and Africa. Hardy zone 5 south.

HEIGHT 8 inches; low-growing, clump-forming habit.

CULTURE Prefers fertile, moist, well-drained, humus-rich soil in sun or partial shade. Plant corms 3 to 4 inches deep from the crown, spaced 6 to 9 inches apart in summer. Late summer- and early fall-flowering.

DESCRIPTION Plants resemble giant crocus with rose-pink flowers, which appear after the large, straplike leaves have died. Double-flowered forms are available. Popular for edging paths, beds, and borders. Can be naturalized in rock gardens and grassy slopes.

RECOMMENDED VARIETY *C. speciosum*, with flowers that resemble pink water lilies.

BOTANICAL NAME *Colocasia esculenta*

COMMON NAME Elephant's Ear; Giant Taro

RANGE Native to tropical Pacific. Hardy zone 10 only.

HEIGHT 6 to 7 feet; erect, clump-forming habit.

CULTURE Prefers moist, fertile, humus-rich soil in partial shade. Plant corms 3 to 4 inches deep from the nose, spaced at least 4 feet apart after all danger of frost in spring. Corms must be lifted in the fall after frost and stored indoors until the following spring. Summer-flowering.

DESCRIPTION Massive heart-shaped green leaves can grow 5 feet long and 3 feet across. Popular as accents in beds and borders, and in large containers. Especially attractive planted along stream banks and pond margins. Corms are edible, used to make poi, a Polynesian food staple.

BOTANICAL NAME *Convallaria majalis*

COMMON NAME Lily-of-the-valley

RANGE Native to Europe. Hardy zone 3 south to 7.

HEIGHT 6 inches; low, spreading habit.

CULTURE Easy to grow in any well-drained soil in sun or partial shade. Tolerates drought. Plant rhizomes 1 inch deep, 4 inches apart in fall. Spring-flowering.

DESCRIPTION Highly fragrant, white or pink bell-shaped flowers are borne on arching stems, which are produced among the broad, pointed, bright green leaves. Popular as a ground cover to edge paths and borders. Commonly forced in pots to flower indoors in winter. Good for cutting to make dainty flower arrangements.

BOTANICAL NAME *Crinum* x *powellii*

COMMON NAME Summer Amaryllis

RANGE Native to Central and South America. Hardy zone 8 south.

HEIGHT 2 feet; upright habit.

CULTURE Easy to grow in any well-drained loam or sandy soil in full sun. Plant bulbs 6 inches deep from the top of the bulb, spaced 12 inches apart in fall. Summer-flowering.

DESCRIPTION Clusters of large pink or white trumpet-shaped flowers are borne on succulent stems, surrounded by arching, straplike, bright green leaves. Popular for seaside gardens in mild climate areas, where it may naturalize. Makes an attractive accent in mixed beds and borders.

BOTANICAL NAME *Crocosmia* x *crocosmiiflora*

COMMON NAME Montbretia

RANGE Native to South Africa. Hardy zone 6 south.

HEIGHT 3 to 4 feet; erect, clump-forming habit.

CULTURE Prefers a fertile, well-drained, humus-rich soil in sun or partial shade. Plant corms in fall or spring, 3 inches deep, spaced 4 inches apart. Summer-flowering.

DESCRIPTION Orange-red, freesia-like flowers are borne on slender, arching stems. Bright green leaves are swordlike. Popular for massing in mixed beds and borders. Excellent for cutting. Forms thick clumps, which may need dividing after three years.

BOTANICAL NAME *Crocus chrysanthus*

COMMON NAME Snow Crocus

RANGE Native to Greece. Hardy zone 4 south.

HEIGHT 3 inches; low, clump-forming habit.

CULTURE Easy to grow in any well-drained garden soil in full sun. Plant corms 4 inches deep above the corm, spaced 2½ inches apart in fall. Early spring-flowering.

DESCRIPTION Yellow, white, and violet-blue flowers are borne on short stalks above narrow, green, grasslike leaves. Popular for mass planting in rock gardens and as an edging for walks, beds, and borders. Good for naturalizing and pot culture.

RECOMMENDED VARIETIES 'Snow Bunting' (white), 'Blue Pearl,' and 'E.P. Bowles' (yellow).

BOTANICAL NAME *Crocus flavus*

COMMON NAME Yellow Crocus

RANGE Native to Greece and Yugoslavia. Hardy zone 4 south to 8.

HEIGHT 4 inches; low, colony-forming habit.

CULTURE Easy to grow in any well-drained garden soil in full sun. Plant corms 4 inches deep, spaced 2½ inches apart in fall. Early spring-flowering.

DESCRIPTION Golden yellow flowers, clustered several to each corm. Leaves are green, spiky, and upright. This species is often mixed with *C. vernus*, the common crocus, to make a mixture that includes yellow, as well as white and purple. Popular for edging paths, beds, and borders. Suitable for naturalizing in lawns. Good for pot culture.

RECOMMENDED VARIETY 'Yellow Mammoth.'

BOTANICAL NAME *Crocus tomasinianus*

COMMON NAME Snow Crocus

RANGE Native to Dalmatia. Hardy zone 4 south to zone 8.

HEIGHT 3 inches; low, colony-forming habit.

CULTURE Prefers well-drained, humus-rich loam soil in sun or partial shade. Plant corms in fall, 4 inches deep above the corm, spaced 2½ inches. Early spring-flowering.

DESCRIPTION Purple flowers from each bulb are produced in small clusters. Petals with prominent orange-yellow stamens open almost flat on sunny days. Leaves are dark green with a prominent white midrib. Self-seeds to form extensive colonies. Good for rock gardens and woodland. Will grow and bloom through grass.

BOTANICAL NAME *Crocus vernus*

COMMON NAME Common Crocus; Dutch Crocus

RANGE Native to the Pyrenees, Alps, and Carpathian Mountains. Hardy zone 4 south to zone 8.

HEIGHT 4 inches; low, colony-forming habit.

CULTURE Easy to grow in any well-drained garden soil in full sun. Plant corms in fall, 4 inches deep above corm, spaced 2½ inches apart. Early spring-flowering.

DESCRIPTION Purple, white, and bicolor striped flowers clustered several to each corm. Dark green with white midribs, the leaves appear after flowers fade. Popular for edging paths, beds, and borders. Suitable for naturalizing in lawns. Good for pot culture. It is a parent of many large-flowering varieties.

RECOMMENDED VARIETY 'Pickwick' (striped).

BOTANICAL NAME *Cyclamen neopolitanum*

COMMON NAME Hardy Cyclamen

RANGE Native to Greece. Hardy zone 6 south to zone 8.

HEIGHT 6 inches; low-growing, colony-forming habit.

CULTURE Prefers moist, humus-rich loam soil in partial shade. Plant corms in spring, 2 inches deep above crown, spaced 3 inches apart. Fall-flowering.

DESCRIPTION Flowers in pink or white are perfect miniatures of florists' cyclamen. Leaves are ivy-shaped, with silver markings. Popular for naturalizing in shady wildflower gardens and in sink gardens.

RELATED SPECIES *C. purpurascens* and *C. coum,* both spring-flowering.

BOTANICAL NAME *Cyclamen persicum*

COMMON NAME Florists' Cyclamen

RANGE Native to Greece. Hardy zone 9 south.

HEIGHT 6 to 12 inches; low-growing, clump-forming habit.

CULTURE Mostly grown indoors as a pot plant. Prefers moist, humus-rich (peat-based) soil in sun or shade. Plant corms so the crown is just below the soil surface, spaced 3 inches apart. Blooms in early spring from fall-planted bulbs when grown outdoors. Winter-flowering when grown indoors in a cool window or greenhouse.

DESCRIPTION Flowers have swept-back petals that face down and are borne at the top of slender stems. Leaves are decorative, heart-shaped, and sometimes bicolored green and silver. Colors include red, rose-pink, purple, and white. Popular for growing in beds and borders outdoors in frost-free areas. Excellent pot plant.

BOTANICAL NAME *Dahlia pinnata* hybrids

COMMON NAME Dahlia

RANGE Native to Mexico. Hardy zone 9 south.

HEIGHT Up to 6 feet; erect, shrubby habit.

CULTURE Plant tubers in spring after all danger of frost, 6 inches deep from the nose, spaced at least 12 inches apart for dwarf varieties, 2 to 3 feet apart for tall or giant flowering kinds. Tall kinds need strong stakes. Tubers must be lifted after first fall frost and stored indoors until following spring. Summer-flowering.

DESCRIPTION Flowers are highly variable among varieties, including formal decorative types with rounded, double heads and smooth petals to cactus-flowered types with narrow, quill-like petals. Flower size varies from 2-inch pompon type to dinner-plate size, up to 14 inches across. Color range includes white, yellow, orange, purple, pink, red, and bicolors. Stems are fleshy; leaves are bright green and indented. Popular as an accent in mixed beds and borders. Good for cutting if cut ends are scorched.

RECOMMENDED VARIETIES: 'Mary Elizabeth' (cherry red blooms up to 14 inches across) and 'Croydon Ace' (yellow flowers up to 12 inches across).

BOTANICAL NAME *Eranthis hyemalis*

COMMON NAME Winter Aconite

RANGE Native to Europe. Hardy zones 4 to 7.

HEIGHT 2 inches; low, clump-forming habit.

CULTURE Prefers a well-drained, humus-rich soil in sun or partial shade. Especially likes leaf mold. Plant tubers in fall, 4 inches deep above the tuber, spaced 2¹/₂ inches apart. Early spring-flowering.

DESCRIPTION Shimmering yellow flowers resembling buttercups appear before the leaves. Leaves are dark green and deeply indented. Popular for planting in woodland where it naturalizes freely from self-seeding. Often blooms during early spring thaws when snow still covers the ground.

BOTANICAL NAME *Eremurus elwesii*

COMMON NAME Foxtail Lily

RANGE Native to Asia. Hardy zone 5 south.

HEIGHT 6 to 10 feet; erect, spirelike habit.

CULTURE Prefers fertile, well-drained loam soil in full sun. Plant the tuberous roots in early fall, splayed out like an octopus with crown covered by 3 inches of soil. Summer-flowering.

DESCRIPTION Fringed white florets form a towering, pointed flower spike, held erect by a strong, slender stem. Leaves are sword-shaped, like a yucca. Popular for tall backgrounds in mixed beds and borders (especially with a tall hedge behind to provide shelter from wind). Other species include yellow and pink flowers.

RECOMMENDED VARIETY 'Shelford Hybrids' a dwarf form 4 to 5 feet in lovely pastel shades.

BOTANICAL NAME *Erythronium* 'Pagoda'

COMMON NAME Dogtooth Violet

RANGE Hybrid of species native to West Coast of North America. Hardy zone 4 south to zone 9.

HEIGHT 10 inches; erect, colony-forming habit.

CULTURE Prefers a well-drained, humus-rich soil in sun or partial shade. Plant tubers in fall, 4 inches deep above crown, spaced 4 inches apart. Early spring-flowering.

DESCRIPTION Yellow flowers have swept-back petals on a slender stem. Leaves are broad and pointed. Popular for rock gardens and woodland wildflower gardens.

RELATED SPECIES *E. montanum* ('Glacier Lily'), white with orange throat; *E. grandiflorum* ('Avalanche Lily'), yellow with white throat.

BOTANICAL NAME *Eucharis grandiflora*

COMMON NAME Amazon-Lily

RANGE Native to South America. Hardy zone 9 south.

HEIGHT 2 feet; erect habit.

CULTURE Prefers well-drained, moist, humus-rich soil in partial shade or under glass in pots. Plant bulbs in fall, with tops showing through the soil. Spring-flowering outdoors, winter-flowering indoors.

DESCRIPTION Nodding white flowers resemble small-cupped daffodils, opening in an umbel at the top of a slender stem. Leaves are broad, pointed, and glossy dark green. Mostly grown in pots under glass in northern states. In mild climate areas they are grown in shady beds and borders. Excellent for cutting.

BOTANICAL NAME *Eucomis comosa*

COMMON NAME Pineapple Lily

RANGE Native to South Africa. Hardy zone 7 south.

HEIGHT 2 feet; erect, colony-forming habit.

CULTURE Prefers moist, fertile, sandy soil in full sun. Plant bulbs in spring, 3 inches deep from nose of bulb, spaced 12 inches. Summer-flowering.

DESCRIPTION Star-shaped, lime green florets are densely clustered at the top of a strong, slender flower spike with a top-knot of spiky leaves resembling a pineapple. Leaves are dark green and straplike. In mild climate areas they are good for mixed beds and borders. Popular in northern states for growing in pots under glass.

BOTANICAL NAME *Freesia* x *hybrida*

COMMON NAME Freesia

RANGE Native to South Africa. Hardy zone 9 south.

HEIGHT 1 1/2 to 2 feet; arching habit.

CULTURE Prefers to be grown in 6-inch pots under glass, using a peat-based potting soil. Plant corms in fall with the point just below the soil surface, 6 to a pot. Store in a cool, dark place for 4 weeks, then move to a sunny location for flowering (10 to 12 weeks later). Lift and store corms through summer months. Spring-flowering.

DESCRIPTION Arching flower spikes are crowded with fragrant crocus-like florets in white, yellow, orange, pink, red, and purple. Leaves are narrow, long, and sword-shaped.

BOTANICAL NAME *Fritillaria imperialis*

COMMON NAME Crown Imperial

RANGE Native to Iran. Hardy zone 4 south to zone 6.

HEIGHT 2 feet; erect habit.

CULTURE Prefers well-drained, fertile, humus-rich soil in sun or partial shade. Plant bulbs in fall, 6 inches deep above the bulb nose, spaced 12 inches apart. The bulbs should be planted on their sides to keep water from collecting in the hollow on top of the bulb and rotting it. Spring-flowering.

DESCRIPTION Orange and yellow bell-shaped flowers hang from thick, succulent stalks. A tuft of green, spiky leaves crown the flower head. Longer pointed leaves crowd the stem. If cut or bruised the leaves produce a smell that pervades the air with a skunklike odor. Popular for mixed beds and borders; also planted at the edge of woodland.

BOTANICAL NAME *Fritillaria meleagris*

COMMON NAME Checkered Lily

RANGE Native to Europe. Hardy zone 4 south to zone 8.

HEIGHT 8 inches; erect, clump-forming habit.

CULTURE Easy to grow in any well-drained garden soil in sun or partial shade. Plant bulbs in fall, 4 inches deep above the bulb nose, 2¹/₂ inches apart. Spring-flowering.

DESCRIPTION Nodding, bell-shaped, white or purple flowers with a dark, checkered pattern on the petals. Leaves are thin, inconspicuous, and grasslike. Popular for rock gardens, wildflower meadows, and woodland gardens.

BOTANICAL NAME *Galanthus elwesii*

COMMON NAME Snowdrop

RANGE Native to Europe and West Asia. Hardy zone 4 south to zone 7.

HEIGHT 4 to 6 inches; low-growing, clump-forming habit.

CULTURE Prefers a well-drained, fertile, humus-rich soil, particularly one with leaf mold. Plant bulbs in fall, 4 inches deep above the bulb nose, spaced 2¹/₂ inches apart. Early spring-flowering.

DESCRIPTION Nodding white tear-drop-shaped flowers are held above the slender green foliage on erect stems. There is a double form, 'Flore Pleno.' Good for edging paths, beds, and borders, and for naturalizing in woodland. Bulbs increase readily by division and also self-seed.

BOTANICAL NAME *Gladiolus* x *hortulanus*

COMMON NAME Gladiolus

RANGE Native to South Africa. Hardy zone 6 south to zone 8.

HEIGHT 3 to 4 feet; erect, spirelike habit.

CULTURE Prefers fertile, well-drained loam soil in full sun. Plant corms 2 to 3 inches deep from the crown, spaced 12 inches apart in spring after ground has thawed. Plants may need staking. North of zone 6, gladiolus corms can be lifted in fall and stored indoors to survive winter. Summer-flowering.

DESCRIPTION Ruffled, open-throated florets are studded along tall, slender stems, forming beautiful flower spikes. Leaves are sword-shaped and ribbed, like irises. Color range includes yellow, white, orange, pink, red, purple, and bicolors. Popular for mixed beds and borders as a background. Excellent for cutting.

RECOMMENDED VARIETIES 'St. Patrick's' (green flowers) and 'Red Spire' (dark red).

BOTANICAL NAME *Gloriosa rothschildiana*

COMMON NAME Rothchild Gloriosa-Lily

RANGE Native to Africa. Hardy zone 10.

HEIGHT 3 to 8 feet; vining, climbing habit.

CULTURE Prefers a fertile, well-drained loam soil in full sun. Plant tubers in 6-inch pots covered with 2 inches of soil in a heated greenhouse or sun room. After flowering, withhold water to induce dormancy, lift bulbs and store among dry woodshavings for 3 months, then repot and water. Several flowering cycles can be had each year. Needs staking. Can be planted outdoors in northern climates after danger of frost for summer-flowering.

DESCRIPTION Crimson flowers have ruffled, yellow petal edges and prominent yellow stamens projecting forward. Leaves are dark green and spear-shaped. Popular for growing under glass in pots.

BOTANICAL NAME *Haemanthus katharinae*

COMMON NAME Katharine Blood-Lily

RANGE Native to South Africa. Hardy zone 10.

HEIGHT 12 inches; erect habit.

CULTURE Best grown in 6-inch pots using a peat-based, well-drained potting soil in full sun. Plant bulbs in fall, one to a pot, with the bulb nose projecting through the soil surface. When foliage withers in summer, withhold water to induce dormancy and revive its growth cycle in early fall. Winter- and early spring-flowering.

DESCRIPTION Globular, bristlelike, bright red flower heads up to 9 inches across are borne on top of a strong, slender stem. White and pink kinds also available. Spectacular pot plant for growing under glass.

BOTANICAL NAME *Hippeastrum hybrida*

COMMON NAME Amaryllis

RANGE Hybrids of species native to South America. Hardy zone 9 south.

CULTURE Prefers a fertile, well-drained, humus-rich garden soil or peat-based potting soil when grown in pots. Plant bulbs in fall, so that the nose is slightly above soil surface, spaced 12 inches apart. Winter-flowering indoors, spring-flowering outdoors in mild climates.

DESCRIPTION Huge trumpet-shaped flowers, up to 10 inches across, bloom 4 to a stem atop fleshy, hollow stalks. Leaves are broad, arching, and straplike. Color range includes red, white, orange, pink, and bicolors. Mostly grown in 6-inch pots in northern states. Popular in beds and borders in southern gardens.

BOTANICAL NAME *Hyacinthoides hispanica*

COMMON NAME Spanish Bluebell

RANGE Native to Europe. Hardy zone 6 south.

HEIGHT 15 inches; erect habit.

CULTURE Prefers fertile, moist, humus-rich soil in partial shade. Plant bulbs in fall, 3 inches deep above the bulb nose, spaced 6 inches apart. Spring-flowering.

DESCRIPTION Nodding, blue, bell-shaped flowers are highly fragrant and clustered at the top of arching stems. Leaves are green and sword-shaped. Popular for woodland gardens, where they will naturalize. Excellent for cutting. Similar in appearance to English Bluebells *(H. non-scriptus)*, but generally a little more showy and more reliable for North America.

BOTANICAL NAME *Hyacinthus orientalis*

COMMON NAME Dutch Hyacinth

RANGE Native to Mediterranean countries. Hardy zone 4 south to zone 8.

HEIGHT 8 to 10 inches; erect habit.

CULTURE Prefers fertile, humus-rich loam soil in full sun. Plant bulbs in fall, 6 inches deep from the bulb nose, spaced 6 inches apart. Spring-flowering.

DESCRIPTION Highly fragrant, star-shaped florets are closely set around a thick, fleshy stem, producing an erect flower column above several green, straplike leaves. Color range includes red, blue, pink, yellow, white, and purple. Good for massing in beds and borders. Popular for pot culture. Prechilled bulbs are offered by many bulb dealers for growing in special hyacinth vases, filled only with water.

RECOMMENDED VARIETIES 'Delft Blue,' 'Haarlem' (yellow), 'Lady Derby' (rose-pink), and 'Jan Bos' (red).

BOTANICAL NAME *Hymenocallis narcissiflora*

COMMON NAME Peruvian Daffodil; Ismene

RANGE Native to Peru. Hardy zone 8 south.

HEIGHT 2 feet; upright habit.

CULTURE Prefers a fertile, humus-rich, well-drained soil in sun or partial shade. North of their hardiness range, plant bulbs in spring after the ground thaws, 3 to 4 inches deep above the crown, spaced 12 inches apart. Summer-flowering.

DESCRIPTION Fragrant white flowers have long, reflexed petals and a daffodil-like trumpet at the petal center. The flowers are borne on top of slender stems among arching, straplike leaves. Popular for mixed beds and borders, also as a flowering pot plant. Naturalizes freely and creates colonies in frost-free areas.

BOTANICAL NAME *Incarvillea delvayii*

COMMON NAME Hardy Gloxinia

RANGE Native to China. Hardy zone 6 south.

HEIGHT 12 inches; low, rosette-forming habit.

CULTURE Prefers well-drained, fertile, humus-rich acid soil in sun or partial shade. Plant tubers in fall with tips angled down just below the soil surface, spaced 8 inches apart. Spring-flowering.

DESCRIPTION Lovely trumpet-shaped, pink or rosy red blooms have purple and yellow throats and are clustered at the top of slender stems. Leaves are glossy, dark green, heavily veined, and indented. Popular for rock gardens.

BOTANICAL NAME *Iris cristata*

COMMON NAME Crested Iris

RANGE Native to North America. Hardy zone 5 south to zone 8.

HEIGHT 6 inches; low, spreading habit.

CULTURE Prefers well-drained, humus-rich loam soil in sun or shade. Plant rhizomes in fall, with tips just below soil surface, spaced 6 inches apart. Spring-flowering.

DESCRIPTION Blue or white flowers carpet the ground among broad, spear-shaped, green leaves. Popular for rock gardens and edging woodland paths. Naturalizes freely.

BOTANICAL NAME *Iris danfordiae*

COMMON NAME Danford Iris

RANGE Native to Asia Minor. Hardy zone 4 south to zone 8.

HEIGHT 4 to 6 inches; low, erect, colony-forming habit.

CULTURE Prefers well-drained, humus-rich loam soil in full sun. Plant bulbs in fall, 4 inches deep above the bulb nose, spaced 2 to 5 inches apart. Early spring-flowering.

DESCRIPTION Typical iris flowers are golden yellow, striking through the soil even before the last snowfall. Narrow, pointed leaves appear after flowering. Mostly planted in small drifts in rock gardens.

BOTANICAL NAME *Iris hollandica*

COMMON NAME Dutch Iris

RANGE Developed from species native to Spain and North Africa. Hardy zone 8 south to zone 9.

HEIGHT 2 to 3 feet; erect habit.

CULTURE Prefers moist, fertile, humus-rich soil in sun or partial shade. Plant bulbs in fall, 3 inches deep, 4 inches apart. Spring-flowering.

DESCRIPTION Mostly blue, yellow, and white flowers, which are held erect on slender stems with spiky green leaves. They are graceful plants and extremely popular for cutting. Mostly massed in beds and borders.

BOTANICAL NAME *Iris kaempferi*

COMMON NAME Japanese Iris

RANGE Native to Japan. Hardy zone 5 south.

HEIGHT 2 to 3 feet; erect habit.

CULTURE Prefers moist, fertile, humus-rich loam soil in full sun. Plant rhizomes in fall, the tips just below the soil surface and spaced 12 inches apart. Tolerates boggy conditions. Early summer-flowering.

DESCRIPTION Mostly blue, purple, and white flowers with flattened heads (compared to other irises), on stiff stems among handsome, green, sword-shaped leaves. Popular for massing in beds and borders. Especially beautiful when planted along stream beds and pond margins.

BOTANICAL NAME *Iris reticulata*

COMMON NAME Dwarf Blue Iris

RANGE Native to the Caucasus Mountains. Hardy zone 4 south to zone 8.

HEIGHT 6 inches; low, colony-forming habit.

CULTURE Prefers well-drained, fertile, humus-rich soil in full sun. Plant bulbs in fall, 4 inches deep above the bulb nose, spaced 2¹/₂ inches apart. Spring-flowering.

DESCRIPTION Mostly purple and blue flowers, typically iris in shape. Sometimes sold in a mixture with *I. danfordiae* to introduce yellow into the color range. Leaves are narrow, green, and spiky. Popular planted in small drifts for rock gardens, also for forcing in containers.

BOTANICAL NAME *Ixia maculata*

COMMON NAME Corn-Lily

RANGE Native to South Africa. Hardy zone 7 south to zone 9.

HEIGHT 15 inches; erect, spreading habit.

CULTURE Prefers a fertile, humus-rich loam soil in full sun. Plant corms in fall, 4 inches deep above the crown, spaced 2¹/₂ inches apart. Spring-flowering.

DESCRIPTION Starlike flowers on tall, wiry stems with swordlike leaves. Color range includes cream, yellow, purple, and rose. Popular for mixed beds and borders and for rock gardens. Hardy in mild climate areas.

BOTANICAL NAME *Leucojum vernum*

COMMON NAME Spring Snowflake

RANGE Native to Europe. Hardy zone 4 south.

HEIGHT 9 inches; low-growing, clump-forming habit.

CULTURE Prefers a moist, well-drained, humus-rich soil in partial shade. Plant bulbs in fall, 3 inches deep above bulb nose, spaced 3 inches apart. Spring-flowering.

DESCRIPTION Dainty, pendulous, white flowers cluster along short, arching stems with narrow, pointed leaves. Popular for naturalizing in woodland and shade gardens. Often flowers before the last snowfalls of spring.

RELATED SPECIES *L. aestivum* ('Summer Snowflake') growing to 2 feet with larger flowers, especially in the variety 'Graveyte Giant.'

BOTANICAL NAME *Lilium auratum*

COMMON NAME Oriental Lily

RANGE Native to Japan. Hardy zone 5 south.

HEIGHT 4 to 6 feet; erect habit.

CULTURE Prefers fertile, well-drained, humus-rich soil in partial shade. Plant bulbs in fall, 4 inches deep above the crown, spaced 2 feet apart. Summer-flowering.

DESCRIPTION Magnificent white flowers with flared, reflexed petals measure up to 10 inches across, have yellow stripes down the center of each petal and exotic red spots. Prominent red stamens protrude far from the petals. Leaves are green and lance-shaped. Popular accent to mixed beds and borders. Exquisite for cutting. Hybrids such as the superlative 'Imperial' strain have been developed from *L. auratum*, including red and pink flowering kinds.

BOTANICAL NAME *Lilium candidum*

COMMON NAME Madonna Lily; Bermuda Lily

RANGE Place of origin unknown though probably Asia. Hardy zone 4 south.

HEIGHT 38 inches; erect, spirelike habit.

CULTURE Prefers a well-drained, humus-rich, sandy soil in full sun. Plant bulbs in fall, 4 inches deep above bulb nose, spaced 12 inches apart. Summer-flowering.

DESCRIPTION Large, white, trumpet-shaped blooms are borne at the top of a thick, fleshy stem with green, straplike leaves. Though considered hardy, *L. candidum* can be difficult to establish unless drainage is perfect. Popular for mixed beds and borders and for mass plantings. Good for cutting. Can be forced in pots.

BOTANICAL NAME *Lilium hybrida 'asiatic'*

COMMON NAME Asiatic Hybrid Lilies

RANGE Developed from species native to Asia. Hardy zone 4 to zone 7.

HEIGHT 2 to 5 feet; erect habit.

CULTURE Prefers moist, well-drained, humus-rich soil in partial shade. Plant bulbs in fall, 4 inches deep above the crown, spaced 12 inches apart. Summer-flowering.

DESCRIPTION The 'Mid-Century' strain of asiatic hybrid lilies is especially beautiful. The upward facing flowers measure up to 6 inches across in a wide assortment of colors, including red, yellow, white, orange, pink, lavender, and mahogany. Strong, slender stems have lancelike leaves. Popular for naturalizing in woodland gardens. Also planted as accents in mixed beds and borders. Superb for cutting.

RECOMMENDED VARIETY 'Enchantment,' which possesses a lovely range of colors.

BOTANICAL NAME *Lilium longiflorum*

COMMON NAME White Trumpet Lily

RANGE Native to Japan. Hardy zone 8 south.

HEIGHT 3 to 4 feet; erect habit.

CULTURE Prefers well-drained, humus-rich soil in full sun. Plant bulbs in fall, 4 inches deep above the crown, spaced 12 inches apart. Summer-flowering.

DESCRIPTION Fragrant and elegant, pure white, trumpet-shaped flowers are clustered at the top of slender stems. Leaves are lancelike. Popular for massing in mixed beds and borders. Exquisite for cutting. The variety *'eximium'* is especially well known as the Easter Lily, which is forced under glass in pots in time for Easter.

BOTANICAL NAME *Lilium superbum*

COMMON NAME Turkscap Lily

RANGE Native to North America. Hardy zone 5 south.

HEIGHT 5 to 6 feet; erect habit.

CULTURE Prefers moist, fertile, humus-rich loam soil in sun or partial shade. Plant bulbs in fall, 3 inches deep above the crown, spaced 12 inches apart. May need staking. Summer-flowering.

DESCRIPTION Orange-red flowers with recurved petals have yellow throats and exotic red spots. Its nodding flowers are clustered on top of a slender stem. Leaves are dark green and lancelike. Popular for massing in mixed beds and borders. Good for cutting.

BOTANICAL NAME *Lycoris radiata*

COMMON NAME Red Spider Lily

RANGE Native to Japan. Hardy zone 7 south.

HEIGHT 12 to 18 inches; erect habit.

CULTURE Easy to grow in any well-drained garden soil in sun or partial shade. Plant bulbs in spring, 3 inches deep, spaced 6 inches apart. Fall-flowering.

DESCRIPTION Rich red florets have narrow, reflexed petals and prominent, arching anthers, which give the flower clusters a spidery appearance. These flowers are borne on top of slender, naked stems. Leaves are narrow, pointed, and straplike. Popular for edging paths, beds, and borders. Also grown in containers. Excellent for cutting.

BOTANICAL NAME *Lycoris squamigera*

COMMON NAME Naked Ladies

RANGE Native to Japan. Hardy zone 5 south.

HEIGHT 2 feet; erect, colony-forming habit.

CULTURE Prefers well-drained, fertile, sandy soil in full sun. Plant bulbs in spring or fall, 4 inches deep from bulb nose, spaced 6 inches apart. Summer-flowering.

DESCRIPTION Pink, trumpet-shaped flowers appear at the top of a thick, fleshy stem after the straplike leaves have died. Popular as an accent in mixed beds and borders, and for naturalizing in drifts. Closely related to amaryllis.

BOTANICAL NAME *Muscari armeniacum*

COMMON NAME Grape Hyacinth

RANGE Native to Asia Minor. Hardy zone 4 south to zone 8.

HEIGHT 5 inches; low, clump-forming habit.

CULTURE Easy to grow in any well-drained garden soil in sun or partial shade. Plant bulbs in fall, 4 inches deep above the bulb nose, spaced 3 inches apart. Spring-flowering.

DESCRIPTION Tiny, bell-shaped, blue flowers are clustered on top of slender stems above narrow, pointed leaves. Readily increases by division of the bulbs and by self-seeding. Popular for edging paths, beds, and borders, also for naturalizing in rock gardens.

BOTANICAL NAME *Narcissus* x *hybrida* 'Double-flowered'

COMMON NAME Double-Flowered Daffodil

RANGE Developed from species native to Europe. Hardy zone 3 south to zone 9.

HEIGHT 20 inches; erect, clump-forming habit.

CULTURE Easy to grow in any fertile, well-drained loam soil in sun or partial shade. Plant bulbs in fall, 4 inches deep above the bulb nose, spaced 6 inches apart. Spring-flowering.

DESCRIPTION Fragrant flowers are mostly yellow or white and fully double, with a contrasting yellow or orange bicolor effect towards the petal center. Good as accents in mixed beds and borders. Sensational cut flower; also good for forcing in pots.

BOTANICAL NAME *Narcissus* x *hybrida* 'Trumpet-flowered'

COMMON NAME Trumpet Daffodil

RANGE Developed from species native to Europe. Hardy zone 3 south to zone 9.

HEIGHT 20 inches; erect, clump-forming habit.

CULTURE Easy to grow in any well-drained, fertile, garden loam in sun or partial shade. Plant bulbs in fall, 4 inches deep above the bulb nose, spaced 6 inches apart. Spring-flowering.

DESCRIPTION Mostly golden yellow or white, plus bicolored flowers with a prominent trumpet. The most popular of all daffodils for massing in beds and borders or naturalizing in meadows, lawns, and along stream banks and pond margins. Wonderful cut flower. Good for forcing in pots.

BOTANICAL NAME *Narcissus minimum*

COMMON NAME Miniature Daffodil

RANGE Native to Europe. Hardy zone 4 south to zone 8.

HEIGHT 6 inches; clump-forming habit.

CULTURE Easy to grow in any well-drained loam soil in sun or partial shade. Plant bulbs in fall, 4 inches deep from the top of the bulb, spaced 4 inches apart. Early spring-flowering.

DESCRIPTION Clusters of dainty, golden yellow, trumpet blooms are borne above long, pointed leaves. They are perfect miniatures of their larger cousins, the golden trumpet-flowered daffodil, excellent for naturalizing, and also popular for growing in pots. Other popular small-flowered species include *N. bulbocodium* ('Hoop Petticoat Daffodils') and *N. cyclamineus*, having reflexed, outer petals.

BOTANICAL NAME *Narcissus poeticus*

COMMON NAME Poet's Daffodil; Pheasant's Eye

RANGE Native to Greece. Hardy zone 3 south to zone 8.

HEIGHT 20 inches; erect, clump-forming habit.

CULTURE Easy to grow in any fertile, well-drained loam soil in sun or partial shade. Plant bulbs in fall, 4 inches deep above the bulb nose, spaced 6 inches apart. Spring-flowering.

DESCRIPTION White flowers have small, white or yellow frilly cup with orange rim. Leaves are narrow and pointed. Popular for naturalizing in deciduous woodland and along stream banks and pond margins. Superb for cutting.

BOTANICAL NAME *Narcissus triandrus*

COMMON NAME Daffodil; Angel's-Tears

RANGE Native to Spain. Hardy zone 4 to zone 8.

HEIGHT 12 inches; erect, clump-forming habit.

CULTURE Easy to grow in any well-drained garden soil in sun or partial shade. Plant bulbs in fall, 4 inches deep above bulb nose, and 4 inches apart. To grow in zone 9 south, precool bulbs 8 to 10 weeks at 40° to 45°F prior to planting in early December. Early spring-flowering.

DESCRIPTION White or yellow flowers clustered on slender stems. Leaves are long and narrow. Popular for mixed beds and borders. Excellent for cutting. Can be naturalized if fed a high-phosphorus fertilizer in spring before bulbs bloom and again in fall.

RECOMMENDED VARIETY 'Thalia,' a gleaming white.

BOTANICAL NAME *Nerine bowdenii*

COMMON NAME Nerine

RANGE Native to South Africa. Hardy zone 9 south.

HEIGHT 12 inches; erect habit.

CULTURE Easy to grow in any fertile, well-drained soil or sandy potting soil in sun or partial shade. Outdoors, plant bulbs in spring, leaving the bulb tips above the soil surface, spaced 3 to 4 inches apart. Indoors, plant in fall under glass. Summer-flowering outdoors, winter-flowering indoors.

DESCRIPTION Funnel-shaped flowers form terminal umbels on slender stalks above straplike green leaves. Colors include white, pink, and red. Popular for pot culture in the North and rock gardens in mild climate areas.

BOTANICAL NAME *Ornithogalum thyrsoides*

COMMON NAME Chincherinchee

RANGE Native to South Africa. Hardy zone 8 south.

HEIGHT 12 to 18 inches; erect, colony-forming habit.

CULTURE Prefers sandy loam soil in full sun. Plant bulbs in fall, 2 inches deep above the bulb nose, and spaced 2 inches apart. Spring-flowering.

DESCRIPTION White, starlike florets have dark centers and form a pointed cluster on top of a slender stem. Leaves are narrow, pointed, and grass-like. Naturalizes easily in mild climates. Popular for mixed beds and borders. Good for containers. Excellent for cutting.

BOTANICAL NAME *Ornithogalum umbellatum*

COMMON NAME Star of Bethlehem

RANGE Native to Europe; naturalized throughout North America. Hardy zone 4 south.

HEIGHT 6 inches; low, clump-forming habit.

CULTURE Easy to grow in any well-drained garden soil in sun or partial shade. Plant bulbs in fall, 4 inches deep above the bulb nose, and spaced 2½ inches apart. Spring-flowering.

DESCRIPTION Starlike flowers are white; leaves are narrow and pointed. Usually forms dense clumps by division of bulbs and self-seeding. Popular for edging paths and naturalizing in rock gardens.

BOTANICAL NAME *Oxalis pes-caprae*

COMMON NAME Bermuda Buttercup

RANGE Native to South Africa. Hardy zone 9 south.

HEIGHT 12 inches; low-growing, spreading habit.

CULTURE Easy to grow in any well-drained garden soil in full sun. Outdoors, plant bulbs in fall, 2 inches deep above the bulb nose, and spaced 3 inches apart. Outdoors, early spring-flowering in mild climate areas; indoor, winter-flowering under glass.

DESCRIPTION Bright yellow, buttercup-like flowers are borne on slender stems above shamrock-like plants. Suitable for pots and hanging baskets. Naturalizes freely in open, sunny locations.

BOTANICAL NAME *Pleione formosa*

COMMON NAME Fairy Orchid

RANGE Native to Formosa and China. Hardy zone 9 south.

HEIGHT 6 inches; low, colony-forming habit.

CULTURE Outdoors, prefers moist, humus-rich, fertile loam soil in partial shade. Indoors, best grown in 4-inch pots, using a peat-based potting soil. Plant corms in fall, 2 inches deep above the crown, and spaced 4 inches apart. Corms remain dormant from October through February. Spring-flowering.

DESCRIPTION Lovely pink or white orchid flowers have speckled throats and an exotic fringed lip. They are borne on slender stems above arching, pointed leaves. Good for growing massed in beds under deciduous shrubs that provide bright light in spring and cool shade in summer Popular for growing in pots.

BOTANICAL NAME *Polianthus* x *tuberosa*

COMMON NAME Tuberose

RANGE Native to Mexico. Hardy zone 7 south.

HEIGHT 2 to 3 feet; erect, spirelike habit.

CULTURE Prefers moist, fertile, humus-rich loam soil in full sun. Plant rhizomes in spring, 2 inches deep above the crown and spaced at least 6 inches apart. Lift rhizomes after flowering and store indoors even in areas where they are considered hardy. Late summer-flowering.

DESCRIPTION Highly fragrant, gardenia-like white flowers are clustered in a spike on top of a slender stem. Dark green leaves are broad and long, like gladiolus. Popular for mixed beds and borders. Exceptional for cutting.

BOTANICAL NAME *Puschkinia scilloides*

COMMON NAME Striped Squill

RANGE Native of Caucasus Mountains and Asia Minor. Hardy zone 4 south to zone 8.

HEIGHT 6 inches; upright, clump-forming habit.

CULTURE Easy to grow in any well-drained garden soil in full sun. Plant bulbs in fall, 4 inches deep above the bulb nose, and spaced 2½ inches apart. Spring-flowering.

DESCRIPTION Bluish white flowers are star-shaped and clustered at the top of a slender stem. Green leaves are straplike. Popular for naturalizing in rock gardens. Increases by division of bulbs and self-seeding.

BOTANICAL NAME *Ranunculus asiaticus*

COMMON NAME Persian Buttercup

RANGE Native to Greece, Turkey, and Persia. Hardy zone 8 south.

HEIGHT 12 to 18 inches; erect habit.

CULTURE Outdoors in mild climates, plant tubers in fall in any well-drained, humus-rich, garden soil in full sun. Cover with 3 inches of soil, spacing tubers 6 inches apart. Indoors, grow in a peat-based potting soil, with sand added for good drainage, 4 tubers to each 5-inch pot. After flowering, lift bulbs and store for 3 to 4 months before repotting. Outdoors, early spring-flowering; indoors, winter-flowering.

DESCRIPTION Lovely double flowers have petals that look like crèpe paper, in a rich color range that includes yellow, white, orange, pink, and red. The flowers are held erect on long stems. Leaves are deeply indented and fern-like. Popular in mild climates for mixed beds and borders. Good for cutting and containers.

BOTANICAL NAME *Scilla peruviana*

COMMON NAME Peruvian Squill

RANGE Native to South America. Hardy zone 8 south.

HEIGHT 12 inches; clump-forming habit.

CULTURE Easy to grow in any well-drained loam or sandy soil in sun or partial shade. Plant bulbs in fall, 4 inches deep from the top of the bulb, and spaced 4 inches apart. Spring-flowering.

DESCRIPTION Umbels of star-shaped blue flowers are borne on slender stems among bright green, straplike leaves. Mostly grown as a pot plant under glass. Resembles a miniature Blue Agapanthus.

BOTANICAL NAME *Scilla siberica*

COMMON NAME Siberian Squill

RANGE Native to the Caucasus Mountains. Hardy zone 4 south.

HEIGHT 5 inches; low-growing, erect, clump-forming habit.

CULTURE Easy to grow in any well-drained garden soil in sun or partial shade. Plant bulbs in fall, 4 inches deep above the bulb nose, and spaced 3 inches apart. Early spring-flowering.

DESCRIPTION Each bulb bears several stems of nodding, bell-shaped blue flowers above straplike leaves. Popular for forming drifts in rock gardens and naturalizing in woodland to form a dense, blue carpet. Increases by bulb division and self-seeding. Often blooms during a thaw while snow is still on the ground.

RECOMMENDED VARIETY 'Spring Beauty,' a sterile selection with extra-large flowers.

BOTANICAL NAME *Sinningia speciosa*

COMMON NAME Gloxinia

RANGE Native to South America. Hardy only indoors.

HEIGHT 12 inches; compact, rosette-forming habit.

CULTURE Best grown indoors as a flowering pot plant. Plant in spring, one tuber to a 6-inch pot, using a peat-based potting soil in partial shade. Plant tubers 1 inch deep above the crown. Keep soil moist at all times. After flowering, the plants may go dormant. Water sparingly until renewed growth begins. Summer-flowering.

DESCRIPTION Magnificent trumpet-shaped flowers can be single or double in mostly white, red, pink, purple, blue, and bicolors with conspicuous speckles in the throat. Leaves are spear-shaped, heavily veined, and velvety in texture. Excellent for growing under lights.

RECOMMENDED VARIETIES 'Emperor Frederick' (red flowers, bordered with white), 'Princess Elizabeth' (rich purple with white throat).

BOTANICAL NAME *Sparaxis tricolor*

COMMON NAME Harlequin Flower

RANGE Native to South Africa. Hardy zone 6 south.

HEIGHT 8 to 10 inches; erect, clump-forming habit.

CULTURE Prefers a well-drained, fertile sandy soil in full sun. Plant corms in fall, 4 inches deep above the crown, and spaced $2^1/_2$ inches apart. Needs a sheltered, south-facing exposure. Spring-flowering.

DESCRIPTION Six-petaled, starlike flowers are mostly bicolored and tricolored in white, yellow, red, and purple, with handsome dark brown zoning at the petal center. Popular for mixed beds, borders, and containers. Good for cutting.

BOTANICAL NAME *Sprekelia formosissima*

COMMON NAME Jacobean-Lily

RANGE Native to Mexico. Hardy zone 9 south.

HEIGHT 12 inches; erect habit.

CULTURE Easy to grow in any well-drained garden or potting soil. Plant bulbs in fall, with the neck protruding above the soil, and 4 inches apart. Planted in fall to bloom during winter or early spring. Spring-flowering outdoors; winter-flowering under glass.

DESCRIPTION Orchid-like, red flower is borne on a slender stem above a cluster of grasslike green leaves. Popular for growing in rock gardens in mild climates, but mostly grown as a pot plant under glass.

BOTANICAL NAME *Sternbergia lutea*

COMMON NAME Fall crocus

RANGE Native to Asia Minor. Hardy zone 7 south.

HEIGHT 6 inches; low-growing, clump-forming habit.

CULTURE Prefers fertile, humus-rich loam soil in full sun. Plant bulbs in summer, 4 inches deep from the bulb nose, and spaced 3 to 4 inches apart. Fall- and winter-flowering.

DESCRIPTION Crocus-like yellow flowers are borne on slender stems among grasslike leaves. Foliage persists through winter, and withers away as plants go dormant in spring. Popular for edging paths, beds, and borders. Also good for naturalizing on sunny slopes.

BOTANICAL NAME *Tigridia pavonia*

COMMON NAME Tiger-Flowers; Shell-Flowers

RANGE Native to Mexico. Hardy zone 7 south.

HEIGHT 2 feet; erect habit.

CULTURE Easy to grow in any fertile, well-drained garden soil in full sun. Plant bulbs in spring after danger of frost, 4 inches deep from the bulb nose, and spaced 6 inches apart. Summer-flowering.

DESCRIPTION Exotic, three-petaled flowers are iridescent with handsome red freckles at the petal centers. The leaves are sword-shaped and resemble iris leaves. Color range includes yellow, red, pink, orange, purple, and bicolors. Popular for mixed beds and borders, also pond margins and stream banks. Good for cutting, but the flowers last only a day.

BOTANICAL NAME *Triteleia uniflora*

COMMON NAME Star flower

RANGE Native to Argentina. Hardy zone 6 south to zone 9.

HEIGHT 5 inches; low, colony-forming habit.

CULTURE Easy to grow in any well-drained garden soil in sun or partial shade. Plant bulbs in fall, 4 inches deep from the bulb nose, and spaced 2½ inches apart. Spring-flowering.

DESCRIPTION Six-petaled, light blue, star-shaped, lightly fragrant flowers. Leaves are narrow, grasslike, and emit an onion odor when bruised. Popular for rock gardens. In warm, sunny, sheltered locations clumps can spread rapidly from bulb division and self-seeding.

BOTANICAL NAME *Tulbaghia violacea*

COMMON NAME Society Garlic

RANGE Native to South Africa. Hardy zone 9 south.

HEIGHT 2 feet; erect, clump-forming habit.

CULTURE Easy to grow in any well-drained garden soil. Plant corms in fall, with crowns just below soil surface in sun or partial shade, spaced 12 inches apart. Summer-flowering.

DESCRIPTION Pink, star-shaped flowers are clustered at the top of a slender stem. Evergreen leaves are narrow, pointed, onion-like, and emit an onion odor when bruised. Popular for creating an evergreen ground cover in mild climate areas. Also effective in mixed beds and borders.

BOTANICAL NAME *Tulipa clusiana*

COMMON NAME Candlestick Tulip; Peppermint Stick

RANGE Native to Iran. Hardy zone 4 to zone 8.

HEIGHT 12 inches; upright habit.

CULTURE Prefers fertile, humus-rich loam soil in partial shade. Plant bulbs in fall, 2 inches deep above the bulb nose, spaced 6 inches apart. Early spring-flowering.

DESCRIPTION White, urn-shaped flowers have rose-pink undersides and sharply pointed petals. Leaves are long, narrow, and pointed. Popular for massing in rock gardens and mixed borders. Naturalizes freely.

BOTANICAL NAME *Tulipa dasystemon, Tulipa tarda*

COMMON NAME Tulip species

RANGE Native to Asia. Hardy to zone 4 south to zone 8.

HEIGHT 6 inches; low-growing, colony-forming habit.

CULTURE Easy to grow in any well-drained garden soil in full sun. Plant bulbs in fall, 2 inches deep above the bulb nose and 6 inches apart. Early spring-flowering.

DESCRIPTION Bright yellow, star-shaped flowers open out flat on sunny days. Shimmering petals and narrow pointed leaves. Popular for rock gardens and edging mixed borders. Naturalizes freely.

BOTANICAL NAME *Tulipa fosteriana*

COMMON NAME Foster Tulip

RANGE Native to Turkestan. Hardy zone 4 south to zone 8.

HEIGHT 18 inches; erect habit.

CULTURE Prefers fertile, humus-rich, well-drained loam soil in full sun. Plant bulbs in fall, 6 inches deep above the bulb nose, and 6 inches apart. To grow in zone 9 south, precool bulbs 8 to 10 weeks at 40° to 45°F prior to planting in late November. Early spring-flowering.

DESCRIPTION Shimmering red flowers open out flat in full sun, display a black zone near the petal center, and remain closed on cloudy days. Hybrid varieties expand the color range to yellow, orange, red, and pink. Popular for massing in beds and borders, also good for rock gardens. Plants will naturalize by bulb division if fed with a high-phosphorus fertilizer in spring before flowering and again in fall.

RECOMMENDED VARIETIES 'Red Emperor' and 'Princeps,' both scarlet-flowered.

BOTANICAL NAME *Tulipa greigii*

COMMON NAME Peacock Tulip

RANGE Native to Turkestan. Hardy zone 4 south to zone 8.

HEIGHT 6 to 9 inches; erect habit.

CULTURE Prefers well-drained, humus-rich, fertile loam soil in full sun. Plant bulbs in fall, 3 inches deep above bulb nose, and spaced 4 inches apart. Early spring-flowering.

DESCRIPTION Flowers are iridescent, mostly opening out flat with pointed petals in sunlight. Leaves are distinctive among tulips—mostly striped green and purple, broad, wavy, pointed, and rosette-forming. Color range includes yellow, red, white, and bicolors. Popular for rock gardens, and for mixed beds and borders.

BOTANICAL NAME *Tulipa* x *hybrida* 'Darwin'

COMMON NAME Darwin Hybrid Tulips

RANGE Hybrids of species native to Asia Minor. Hardy zone 4 south to zone 9.

HEIGHT 2 feet; erect habit.

CULTURE Prefers well-drained, fertile, humus-rich loam soil in full sun. Plant bulbs in fall, 4 inches deep above bulb nose, and spaced 6 inches apart. Early spring-flowering.

DESCRIPTION Huge, urn-shaped, iridescent blooms are the largest among the tulips—the result of crossing regular Darwin tulips and *Fosteriana* tulips. Color range includes white, yellow, red, orange, pink, and bicolors. Leaves are broad and pointed. The most popular of all tulips for bedding. Though not as long-lasting as regular Darwin tulips, Cottage and Triumph Tulips—which they resemble—are unequaled for sheer brilliance.

BOTANICAL NAME *Tulipa* x *hybrida* 'Lily-Flowered'

COMMON NAME Lily-Flowered Tulip

RANGE Hybrids of species mostly native to Asia. Hardy zone 4 south.

HEIGHT 3 feet; erect habit.

CULTURE Prefers well-drained, fertile, humus-rich loam soil in full sun. Plant bulbs in fall, 4 inches deep above bulb nose, and spaced 8 inches apart. Spring-flowering.

DESCRIPTION Urn-shaped flowers have elegantly pointed petals in white, yellow, pink, red, orange, and purple. Leaves are broad and pointed. Popular as an accent planted in beds and borders.

RECOMMENDED VARIETIES 'Queen of Sheba' (orange-red with yellow petal tips) and 'White Triumphator' (a magnificent pure white).

BOTANICAL NAME *Tulipa* x *hybrida* 'Parrot'

COMMON NAME Parrot-Flowered Tulip

RANGE Hybrids of species native to Asia. Hardy zone 4 to zone 9.

HEIGHT 2 feet; erect habit.

CULTURE Prefers well-drained, fertile, humus-rich loam soil in full sun. Plant bulbs in fall, 4 inches deep above bulb nose, and spaced 8 inches apart. Spring-flowering.

DESCRIPTION Huge flowers have laciniated petals in yellow, pink, red, white, purple, and bicolors. Leaves are broad and pointed. Mostly massed in groups as an accent in beds and borders. Good for cutting.

BOTANICAL NAME *Tulipa* x *hybrida* 'Peony-flowered'

COMMON NAME Peony-Flowered Tulip

RANGE Hybrids of species mostly native to Asia. Hardy zone 4 south.

CULTURE Prefers well-drained, fertile, humus-rich loam soil in full sun. Plant bulbs in fall, 4 inches deep above bulb nose, and spaced 8 inches apart. Late spring-flowering.

DESCRIPTION Large, fully, double, peony-like flowers are borne facing up among broad, pointed leaves. Color range includes white, yellow, red, pink, orange, purple, and bicolors. Popular for massing in beds and borders.

RECOMMENDED VARIETIES 'Mount Tacoma' (white), 'Angelique' (pink). They are similar to—but with larger flowers that bloom later—Early Double Tulips, which bloom up to 4 weeks earlier in the season.

BOTANICAL NAME *Tulipa kaufmanniana*

COMMON NAME Water-Lily Tulip

RANGE Native to Turkestan. Hardy zone 4 south to zone 8.

HEIGHT 9 inches; low-growing, colony-forming habit.

CULTURE Easy to grow in any well-drained, fertile loam soil in full sun. Plant bulbs in fall, 4 inches deep above the bulb nose, and spaced 4 inches apart. Early spring-flowering.

DESCRIPTION Exceptionally beautiful flowers resembling water lilies. Color range includes white, yellow, red, and a few bicolors with black zoning. Petals remain closed on cloudy days, but open out flat in full sun. Popular for rock gardens and massing in beds and borders. Naturalizes by division of bulbs if fed with high-phosphorus fertilizer in spring before plants bloom and again in fall.

RECOMMENDED VARIETY 'Stresa' (yellow and red).

BOTANICAL NAME *Tulipa praestans*

COMMON NAME Leather-Bulb Tulip

RANGE Native to Bukhara (Russia). Hardy zone 4 south.

HEIGHT 12 inches; low-growing habit.

CULTURE Easy to grow in any fertile, well-drained loam soil in full sun. Plant bulbs in fall, 3 inches deep above the bulb nose, and spaced 6 inches apart. Spring-flowering.

DESCRIPTION Red flowers with pointed petals are borne in clusters of up to four and open at one time among broad, pointed, lancelike leaves. An eye-catching accent for low beds and rock gardens.

RECOMMENDED VARIETY 'Fusilier.'

BOTANICAL NAME *Veltheimia viridifolia*

COMMON NAME Cape Lily

RANGE Native to South Africa. Hardy zone 9 south.

HEIGHT 2 to 3 feet; erect habit.

CULTURE Easy to grow in any fertile, well-drained garden soil or potting soil in full sun. Plant bulbs in mid-summer or early fall, so tops protrude through soil. Space them 6 inches apart. Winter-flowering under glass; spring-flowering outdoors in mild climates.

DESCRIPTION Tubular yellow or pink flowers are clustered on top of a long, slender stem, resembling a 'Red-hot-poker' plant. Leaves are attractively scalloped, forming a rosette. Good as an accent massed in beds and borders. Popular for containers and for growing under glass in northern states. Excellent for cutting.

BOTANICAL NAME *Watsonia pyramidata*

COMMON NAME Bugle Flower

RANGE Native to South Africa. Hardy zone 8 south.

HEIGHT Up to 5 feet; erect habit.

CULTURE Prefers well-drained, fertile, sandy loam soil in full sun. Plant corms in fall, 4 inches deep above the crown, and spaced 6 inches apart. Summer-flowering.

DESCRIPTION Rosy red tubular florets form a flower spike on strong slender stems. Leaves are sword-shaped. Popular in mild climates for massing in mixed beds and borders. Good for cutting. Hybridization has expanded the color range to include white, pink, orange-red, and lavender.

BOTANICAL NAME *Zantedeschia aethiopica*

COMMON NAME Calla Lily

RANGE Native to Africa. Hardy zone 8 south.

HEIGHT 3 feet; erect, clump-forming habit.

CULTURE Prefers moist, fertile, humus-rich soil in sun or partial shade. Tolerates boggy conditions. Plant rhizomes in summer or fall, 4 inches deep above bulb nose, and spaced at least 12 inches apart. Late spring- and early-summer-flowering.

DESCRIPTION Pristine, fragrant, white flower spathes have powdery yellow pistils protruding from the petal center, which grows from thick, long stems. Leaves are green, wavy, and spear-shaped. Good for planting beside streams and pond margins in mild climates. Naturalizes freely in swampy soil. Popular for growing in 6-inch pots or tubs under glass in northern states. Hybridization has expanded the color range to include yellow, orange, pink, red, and maroon. Variety 'Green Goddess' has an unusual green tip.

BOTANICAL NAME *Zephyranthes atamasco*

COMMON NAME Atamasco Lily; Zephyr Lily

RANGE Native to southern United States. Hardy zone 7 south.

HEIGHT 12 inches; erect, colony-forming habit.

CULTURE Easy to grow in any fertile, well-drained garden soil in sun or partial shade. Plant bulbs in fall, 2 inches deep from bulb nose, and spaced 2 inches apart. Spring-flowering.

DESCRIPTION White, trumpetlike flowers are sometimes tinted pink, and are borne erect on slender stems above narrow, pointed, grasslike leaves. Popular in southern United States for naturalizing in lawns and along stream banks and pond margins. Suitable for pots under glass in northern states.

CHAPTER THREE

PLANT SELECTION GUIDE

Following is a quick reference guide to selecting bulbs for different situations. It is not absolute and the absence of a plant from a particular list does not mean it cannot be used for that specific purpose. For complete information on plant uses, see the encyclopedia section.

*marginally hardy

HARDY

Acidanthera bicolor (Peacock Flower)
Allium christophii (Star-of-Persia)
Allium giganteum (Giant Allium)
Allium moly (Lily Leek)
Allium schoenoprasum (Chives)
Anemone blanda (Grecian windflower)
Belamcanda chinensis (Blackberry Lily)
Camassia scilloides (Wild Hyacinth)
Chinodoxa luciliae (Glory-of-the Snow)
Colchicum autumnale (Autumn Crocus)
Convallaria majalis (Lily-of-the Valley)
Crocosmia x *crocosmiiflora* (Montbretia)

Crocus chrysanthus (Snow Crocus)
Crocus tomasinianus (Snow Crocus)
Crocus vernus (Common Crocus)
Cyclamen neopolitanum (Hardy Cyclamen)
Cyclamen persicum (Florist's Cyclamen)
Eranthis hyemalis (Winter Aconite)
Erythronium 'Pagoda' (Dogtooth Violet)
Fritillaria imperialis (Crown Imperialis)
Fritillaria meleagris (Checkered Lily)
Galanthus elwesii (Snowdrop)
Gladiolus x *hortulanus* (Gladiolus)
Hemerocallis fulva (Tawny Daylily)
Hyacinthoides hispanica (Spanish Bluebell)
Hyacinthus orientalis (Dutch Hyacinth)
Hymenocallis narcissiflora (Peruvian Daffodil)
Incarvillea delvanyii (Hardy Glosinia)
Iris species (Iris)
Leucojum vernum (Spring Snowflake)
Lilium species (Lily)
Muscari armeniacum (Grape Hyacinth)
Narcissus species (Lily)
Ornithogalum umbellatum (Star of Bethlehem)
Puschkinia scilloides (Striped Squill)
Scilla siberica (Siberian Squill)
Sternbergia lutea (Fall Crocus)
Tritelia uniflora (Star flower)
Tulipa species (Tulip)

TENDER

Agapanthus africanus (African Lily)
Alstroemeria aurantiaca (Peruvian Lily)
Amaryllis belladonna (Belladonna Lily)
Anemone coronaria (French Anemone)
Babiana stricta (Baboon Flower)
Begonia x *tuberhybrida* (Tuberous Begonia)
Bletilla striata (Chinese Orchid)
Caladium x *hortulanum* (Rainbow Plant)
Canna x *generalis* (Canna)
Cardiocrinum giganteum (Himalayan Lily)
Clivia miniata (Kafir Lily)
Colocasia esculaneta (Elephant's Ear)
Crinum x *powellii* (Summer Amaryllis)
Dahlia pinnata hybrids (Dahlia)
Eremurus elwesii (Foxtail Lily)
Eucharis grandiflora (Amazon-lily)
Eucomis comosa (Pineapple Lily)
Gloriosa rothschildiana (Rothchild Gloriosa-lily)
Hippeastrum hybrida (Amaryllis)
Ixia maculata (Corn-lily)
Lycoris squamigera (Naked Ladies)
Nerine bowdenii (Nerine)
Oxalis pes-caprae (Bermuda buttercup)
Sinningia speciosa (Gloxinia)
Sparaxis tricolor (Harlequin Flower)
Spreklelia formosissima (Jacobean Lily)
Tigridia pavonia (Tiger-flower)
Tulbaghia violacea (Society Garlic)
Velthemia viridofolia (Cape Lily)
Watsonia pyramidata (Bugle Flower)
Zantedeschia aethiopica (Calla Lily)
Zephyranthes atamasco (Atamasco Lily)

FALL COLOR

*tender to frost
Caladium x *hortulanum* (Rainbow Plant)
Canna x *generalis* (Canna)
 Colchicum autumnale (Autumn-Crocus)
Colocasia esculenta (Elephant's Ear)
 Cyclamen neopolitanum (Hardy Cyclamen)
Dahlia pinnata hybrids (Dahlia)
Gladiolus x *hortulanus* (Gladiolus)
Haemanthus katharinae (Katharine Blood-Lily)
Lycoris radiata (Red Spider Lily)
Polianthus x *tuberosa* (Tuberose)
 Sternbergia lutea (Fall Crocus)

ORNAMENTAL FOLIAGE

Begonia x *tuberhybrida* (Tuberous Begonia)
Caladium x *hortulanum* (Rainbow Plant)
Colocasia esculenta (Elephant's Ear)
 Cyclamen persicum (Florists' Cyclamen)
 Iris kaempferi (Japanese Iris)
Zantedeschia aethiopica (Calla Lily)

SUMMER FLOWER

Acidanthera bicolor (Peacock Flower)
Agapanthus africanus (African Lily)
Alstroemeria aurantiaca (Peruvian Lily)
Begonia x *tuberhybrida* (Tuberous Begonia)
 Belamcanda chinensis (Blackberry-Lily)
Canna x *generalis* (Canna)
 Crocosmia x *crocosmiiflora* (Montbretia)
Dahlia pinnata hybrids (Dahlia)
Eremurus elwesii (Foxtail Lily)
Eucomis comosa (Pineapple Lily)
Gladiolus x *hortulanus* (Gladiolus)
 Iris kaempferi (Japanese Iris)
 Lilium species and hybrids (Lily)
 Nerine bowdenii (Nerine)
 Polyanthus x *tuberosa* (Tuberose)
Sinningia speciosa (Gloxinia)
Tigridia pavonia (Tiger-Flowers)
Tulbaghia violacea (Society Garlic)
 Watsonia pyramidata (Bugle Flower)

SPRING FLOWER

Amaryllis belladonna (Belladonna Lily)
Anemone blanda (Grecian Windflower)
Anemone coronaria (French Anemone)
Bletilla striata (Chinese Orchid)
Camassia scilloides (Wild Hyacinth)
Cardiocrinum giganteum (Himalayan Lily)
Chionodoxa luciliae (Glory-of-the-Snow)
Clivia miniata (Kafir Lily)
Convallaria majalis (Lily-of-the-Valley)
Crinum x *powellii* (Summer Amaryllis)
Crocus species (Crocus)
Cyclamen persicum (Florists' Cyclamen)
Eranthis hyemalis (Winter Aconite)
Eucharis grandiflora (Amazon-Lily)
Erythronium 'Pagoda' (Dogtooth Violet)
Fritillaria imperialis (Crown Imperial)
Fritallaria meleagris (Checkered Lily)
Galanthus elwesii (Snowdrop)
Gloriosa rothschildiana (Rothchild Gloriosa-Lily)
Hyacinthoides hispanica (Spanish Bluebell)
Ixia maculata (Corn-Lily)
Leucojum vernum (Spring Snowflake)
Muscari armeniacum (Grape Hyacinth)
Narcissus species and hybrids (Daffodil)
Ornithogalum thrysoides (Chincherinchee)
Ornithogalum umbellatum (Star of Bethlehem)
Oxalis pes-caprae (Bermuda Buttercup)
Pleione formosa (Fairy Orchid)
Puschkinia scilloides (Stripped Squill)
Ranunculus asiaticus (Peruvian Buttercup)
Scilla peruviana (Peruvian Squill)
Scilla siberica (Siberian Squill)
Sparaxis tricolor (Harleqin Flower)
Sprekelia formosissima (Jacobean-Lily)
Tritelia uniflora (Star Flower)
Tulipa species and hybrids (Tulip)
Veltheimia viridifolia (Cape Lily)
Zantedeschia aethiopica (Calla Lily)
Zephyranthes atamasco (Atamasco Lily)

SHADE TOLERANT

Amaryllis belladonna (Belladonna Lily)
Begonia x *tuberhybrida* (Tuberous Begonia)
Bletilla striata (Chinese Orchid)
Caladium x *hortulanum* (Rainbow Plant)
Chionodoxa luciliae (Glory-of-the-Snow)
Cyclamen neopolitanum (Hardy Cyclamen)
Eranthis hyemalis (Winter Aconite)
Eucharis grandiflora (Amazon-lily)
Erythronium 'Pagoda' (Dogtooth Violet)
Fritillaria imperialis (Crown Imperial)
Fritillaria meleagris (Checkered Lily)
Galanthus elwesii (Snowdrop)
Hyacinthoides hispanica (Spanish Bluebell)
Lilium auratum (Oriental Lily)
Lilium hybrida 'asiatic' (Asiatic Hybrid Lilies)
Narcissus species and hybrids (Daffodil)
Scilla peruviana (Peruvian Squill)
Scilla siberica (Siberian Squill)
Sinningia speciosa (Gloxinia)
Zantedeschia aethiopica.(Calla Lily)
Zephyranthes atamasco (Atamasco Lily)

MOISTURE TOLERANT

Canna x *generalis* (Canna)
Colocasia esculenta (Elephant's Ear)
Iris kaempferi (Japanese Iris)
Zantedeschia aethiopica (Calla Lily)

ROADSIDE

Agapanthus africanus (African Lily)
Hemerocallis fulva (Tawny Daylily)
Lycoris squamigera (Naked Ladies)
Narcissus species (Daffodil)
Ornithogalum umbellatum (Star of Bethlehem)
Oxalis pes-caprae (Bermuda Buttercup)
Zephyranthes atamasco (Atamasco Lily)

Opposite page: Mass plantings of early double tulips in a rich mixture of colors. No other class of tulip looks as good planted in a mixture.

NATURALIZING

Agapanthus africanus (African Lily)
Alstroemeria aurantiaca (Peruvian Lily)
Anemone blanda (Grecian Windflower)
Camassia scilloides (Wild Hyacinth)
Chionodoxa luciliae (Glory-of-the-Snow)
Colchicum autumnale (Autumn-Crocus)
Convallaria majalis (Lily-of-the-Valley)
Crinum x *powellii* (Summer Amaryllis)
Crocus chrysanthus (Snow Crocus)
Crocus vernus (Common Crocus)
Cyclamen neopolitanum (Hardy Cyclamen)
Eranthis hyemalis (Winter Aconite)
Erythronium 'Pagoda' (Dogtooth Violet)
Galanthus elwesii (Snowdrop)
Hemerocallis fulva (Tawny Daylily)
Hyacinthoides hispanica (Spanish Bluebell)
Iris cristata (Crested Iris)
Lilium hybrida 'asiatic' (Asiatic Hybrid Lilies)
Lycoris squamigera (Naked Ladies)
Muscari armeniacum (Grape Hyacinth)
Ornithogalum thrysoides (Chincherinchee)
Scilla siberica (Siberian Squill)
Tulipa species and hybrids (Tulip)
Zantedeschia aethiopica (Calla Lily)
Zephyranthes atamasco (Atamasco Lily)

SEASIDE GARDENS

Agapanthus africanus (African Lily)
Amaryllis belladonna (Belladonna Lily)
Anemone coronaria (French Anemone)
Crinum x *powellii* (Summer Amaryllis)
Gladiolus x *hortulanus* (Gladiolus)
Hippeastrum hybrida (Amaryllis)
Hymenocallis narcissiflora (Peruvian Daffodil)
Iris kaempferi (Japanese Iris)
Ixia maculata (Corn-Lily)
Lycoris squamigera (Naked Ladies)
Nerine bowdenii (Nerine)
Ranunculus asiaticus (Persian Buttercup)
Veltheimia viridifolia (Cape Lily)
Zantedeschia aethiopica (Calla Lily)

DRIED ARRANGEMENTS

Allium giganteum (Giant Allium)
Belamcanda chinensis (Blackberry-Lily)

CUT FLOWERS

Acidanthera bicolor (Peacock Flower)
Agapanthus africanus (African Lily)
Allium christophii (Star-of-Persia)
Allium giganteum (Giant Allium)
Alstroemeria aurantiaca (Peruvian Lily)
Crocosmia x *crocosmiiflora* (Montbretia)
Dahlia pinnata hybrids (Dahlia)
Eremurus elwesii (Foxtail Lily)
Gladiolus x *hortulanus* (Gladiolus)
Iris species (Iris)
Ixia maculata (Corn-Lily)
Lilium species (Lily)
Narcissus species (Daffodil)
Ranunculus asiaticus (Persian Buttercup)
Tigridia pavonia (Tiger-Flowers)
Tulipa species (Tulip)
Veltheimia viridifolia (Cape Lily)
Watsonia pyramidata (Bugle Flower)
Zantedeschia aethiopica (Calla Lily)

GROUND COVER

Agapanthus africanus (African Lily)
Convallaria majalis (Lily-of-the-Valley)
Cyclamen persicum (Florists' Cyclamen)
Hemerocallis fulva (Tawny Daylily)
Iris cristata (Crested Iris)
Oxalis pes-caprae (Bermuda Buttercup)

FORCING

Agapanthus africanus (African Lily)
Amaryllis belladonna (Belladonna Lily)
Begonia x *tuberhybrida* (Tuberous Begonia)
Bletilla striata (Chinese Orchid)
Caladium x *hortulanum* (Rainbow Plant)
Clivia miniata (Kafir Lily)
Convallaria majalis (Lily-of-the-Valley)
Crocus species (Crocus)
Cyclamen persicum (Florists' Cyclamen)
Eranthis hyemalis (Winter Aconite)
Eucharis grandiflora (Amazon-Lily)
Eucomis comosa (Pineapple Lily)
Galanthus elwesii (Snowdrop)
Gloriosa rothschildiana (Rothchild Gloriosa-Lily)
Haemanthus katharinae (Katharine Blood-Lily)
Hippeastrum hybrida (Amaryllis)
Hyacinthus orientalis (Dutch Hyacinth)
Iris reticulata (Dwarf Blue Iris)
Lilium candidum (Madonna Lily)
Lilium longiflorum (White Trumpet Lily)
Narcissus x *hybrida* 'Double-flowered'
   (Double-flowered Daffodil)
Narcissus x *hybrida* 'Trumpet-flowered'
   (Trumpet Daffodil)
Nerine bowdenii (Nerine)
Pleione formosa (Fairy Orchid)
Ranunculus asiaticus (Persian Buttercup)
Scilla peruviana (Peruvian Squill)
Sprekelia formosissima (Jacobean-Lily)
Tulipa species (Tulip)
Veltheimia viridifolia (Cape Lily)
Zantedeschia aethiopica (Calla Lily)

BULBS FOR FRAGRANCE

Acidanthera bicolor (Peacock Flower)
Convallaria majalis (Lily-of-the-Valley)
Freesia x *hybrida* (Freesia)
Hyacinthoides hispanica (Spanish Bluebell)
Hyacinthus orientalis (Dutch Hyacinth)
Iris germanica (Bearded Iris)
Lilium longiflorum (White Trumpet Lily)
Narcissus x *hybrida* 'Double-flowered'
   (Double-flowered Daffodil)
Polianthus x *tuberosa* (Tuberose)

BULBS ACCORDING TO HEIGHT

DWARF HABIT

Allium moly (Lily Leek)
Anemone blanda (Grecian Windflower)
Babiana stricta (Baboon Flower)
Chionodoxa luciliae (Glory-of-the-Snow)
Colchicum autumnale (Autumn-Crocus)
Convallaria majalis (Lily-of-the-Valley)
Crocus species (Crocus)
Cyclamen species (Cyclamen)
Eranthis hyemalis (Winter Aconite)
Erythronium 'Pagoda' (Dogtooth Violet)
Eucharis grandiflora (Amazon-Lily)
Fritillaria meleagris (Checkered Lily)
Galanthus elwesii (Snowdrop)
Iris cristata (Crested Iris)
Iris danfordiae (Danford Iris)
Iris reticulata (Dwarf Blue Iris)
Leucojum vernum (Spring Snowflake)
Muscari armeniacum (Grape Hyacinth)
Narcissus species and hybrids (Daffodil)
Ornithogalum umbellatum (Star of Bethlehem)
Pleione formosa (Fairy Orchid)
Puschkinia scilloides (Striped Squill)
Sinningia speciosa (Gloxinia)
Sternbergia lutea (Fall Crocus)
Tulipa species (Tulips)
Zephyranthes atamasco (Atamasco Lily)

BULBS

MEDIUM HEIGHT

Acidanthera bicolor (Peacock Flower)
Allium christophii (Star-of-Persia)
Alstromeria aurantiaca (Peruvian Lily)
Amaryllis belladonna (Belladonna Lily)
Anemone coronaria (French Anemone)
Begonia x *tuberhybrida* (Tuberous Begonia)
Bletilla striata (Chinese Orchid)
Caladium hortulanum (Rainbow Plant)
Camassia scilloides (Wild Hyacinth)
Clivia miniata (Kafir Lily)
Dahlia pinnata (Dahlia)
Freesia hybrida (Freesia)
Haemanthus katharinae (Katherine Blood-Lily)
Hymenocallis narcissiflora (Peruvian Daffodil)
Iris hollandica (Dutch Iris)
Ixia maculata (Corn-Lily)
Leucojum vernum (Spring Snowflake)
Lilium hybrida 'asiatic' (Asiatic Hybrid Lilies)
Lycoris radiata (Red Spider Lily)
Narcissus species (Daffodil)
Nerine bowdenii (Nerine)
Sparaxis tricolor (Harlequin Flower)
Sprekelia formosissima (Jacobean-Lily)
Tigridia pavonia (Tiger-Flowers)
Tulbaghia violacea (Society Garlic)
Tulipa hybrids (Tulip)
Veltheimia viridifolia (Cape Lily)
Zantedeschia aethiopica (Calla Lily)

Opposite page: A simple, early-flowering bulb border featuring King Alfred daffodils, Red Emperor tulips, and a mixture of Dutch hyacinths.

TALL HABIT

Agapanthus africanus (African Lily)
Allium giganteum (Giant Allium)
Alstroemeria aurantiaca (Peruvian Lily)
Belamcanda chinensis (Blackberry-Lily)
Canna generalis (Canna)
Cardiocrinum giganteum (Himalayan Lily)
Colocasia esculenta (Elephant's Ear)
Dahlia pinnata (Dahlia)
Eremurus elwesii (Foxtail Lily)
Fritillaira imperialis (Crown Imperial)
Gladiolus hortulanus (Gladiolus)
Gloriosa rothschildiana (Rothchild Gloriosa-Lily)
Hemerocallis fulva (Tawny Daylily)
Iris germanica (Bearded Iris)
Iris kaempferi (Japanese Iris)
Lilium species (Lily)
Lycoris squamigera (Naked Ladies)

COLOR GUIDE

PURPLE

Allium christophii (Star-of-Persia)
Allium ginganteum (Giant Allium)
Anemone blanda (Grecian Windflower)
Anemone coronaria (French Anemone)
Bletilla striata (Chinese Orchid)
Colchicum autumnale (Autumn-Crocus)
Crocus tomasinianus (Snow Crocus)
Crocus vernus (Common Crocus)
Dahlia pinnata hybrids (Dahlia)
Fritillaria meleagris (Checkered Lily)
Gladiolus x *hortulanus* (Gladiolus)
Hemerocallis fulva (Tawny Daylily)
Hyacinthus orientalis (Dutch Hyacinth)
Iris kaempferi (Japanese Iris)
Iris reticulata (Dwarf Blue Iris)
Nerine bowdenii (Nerine)
Pleione formosa (Fairy Orchid)
Sinningia speciosa (Gloxinia)
Tulbaghia violacea (Society Garlic)
Tulipa species and hybrids (Tulip)

WHITE

Acidanthera bicolor (Peacock Flower)
Agapanthus africanus (African Lily)
Amaryllis belladonna (Belladonna Lily)
Anemone blanda (Grecian Windflower)
Begonia x *tuberhybrida* (Tuberous Begonia)
Caladium x *hortulanum* (Rainbow Plant)
Cardiocrinum giganteum (Himalayan Lily)
Convallaria majalis (Lily-of-the-valley)
Crinum x *powellii* (Summer Amaryllis)
Crocus chrysanthus (Snow Crocus)
Crocus vernus (Common Crocus)
Cyclamen neopolitanum (Hardy Cyclamen)
Cyclamen persicum (Florists' Cyclamen)
Dahlia pinnata hybrids (Dahlia)
Eremurus elwesii (Foxtail Lily)
Eucharis grandiflora (Amazon-Lily)
Erythronium 'Pagoda' (Dogtooth Violet)
Fritillaria meleagris (Checkered Lily)
Galanthus elwesii (Snowdrop)
Gladiolus x *hortulanus* (Gladiolus)
Hippeastrum hybrida (Amaryllis)
Hyacinthoides hispanica (Spanish Bluebell)
Hyacinthus orientalis (Dutch Hyacinth)
Hymenocallis narcissiflora (Peruvian Daffodil)
Iris cristata (Crested Iris)
Iris hollandica (Dutch Iris)
Iris kaempferi (Japanese Iris)
Ixia maculata (Corn-Lily)
Leucojum vernum (Spring Snowflake)
Lilium auratum (Oriental Lily)
Lilium candidum (Madonna Lily)
Lilium longiflorum (White Trumpet Lily)
Muscari armeniacum (Grape Hyacinth)
Narcissus x *hybrida* 'Double-flowered'
   (Double-flowered Daffodil)
Narcissus x *hybrida* 'Trumpet-flowered'
   (Trumpet Daffodil)
Narcissus poeticus (Poet's Daffodil)
Nerine bowdenii (Nerine)
Ornithogalum thyrsoides (Chincherinchee)
Ornithogalum umbellatum (Star-of-Bethlehem)
Pleione formosa (Fairy Orchid)
Polianthes x *tuberosa* (Tuberose)
Pushkinia scilloides (Striped Squill)
Ranunculus asiaticus (Persian Buttercup)

Sinningia speciosa (Gloxinia)
Sparaxis tricolor (Harlequin Flower)
Tigridia pavonia (Tiger-Flowers)
Tritelia uniflora (Star flower)
Tulipa species and hybrids (Tulip)
Watsonia pyramidata (Bugle Flower)
Zantedeschia aethiopica (Calla Lily)
Zephyranthes atamasco (Atamasco Lily)

RED/PINK

Alstroemeria aurantiaca (Peruvian Lily)
Amaryllis belladonna (Belladonna Lily)
Anemone coronaria (French Anemone)
Begonia x *tuberhybrida* (Tuberous Begonia)
Caladium x *hortulanum* (Rainbow Plant)
Crinum x *powellii* (Summer Amaryllis)
Crocosmia x *crocosmiiflora* (Montbretia)
Cyclamen neopolitanum (Hardy Cyclamen)
Cyclamen persicum (Florists' Cyclamen)
Dahlia pinnata hybrids (Dahlia)
Gladiolus x *hortulanus* (Gladiolus)
Gloriosa rothschildiana (Rothchild Gloriosa-Lily)
Haemanthus katharinae (Katharine Blood-Lily)
Hemerocallis fulva (Tawny Daylily)
Hippeastrum hybrida (Amaryllis)
Hyacinthus orientalis (Dutch Hyacinth)
Incarvillea delvayii (Hardy Gloxinia)
Ixia maculata (Corn-Lily)
Lilium hybrida 'asiatic' (Asiatic Hybrid Lilies)
Lycoris squamigera (Naked Ladies)
Nerine bowdenii (Nerine)
Oxalis pes-caprae (Bermuda Buttercup)
Sinningia speciosa (Gloxinia)
Sparaxis tricolor (Harlequin Flower)
Sprekelia formosissima (Jacobean-Lily)
Tulipa species and hybrids (Tulip)
Veltheimia viridifolia (Cape Lily)
Watsonia pyramidata (Bugle Flower)
Zantedeschia aethiopica (Calla Lily)
Zephyranthes atamasco (Atamasco Lily)

BLUE

Agapanthus africanus (African Lily)
Anemone blanda (Grecian Windflower)

Camassia scilloides (Wild Hyacinth)
Chionodoxa luciliae (Glory-of-the-snow)
Crocus chrysanthus (Snow Crocus)
Hyacinthoides hispanica (Spanish Bluebell)
Hyacinthus orientalis (Dutch Hyacinth)
Iris cristata (Crested Iris)
Iris hollandica (Dutch Iris)
Iris kaempferi (Japanese Iris)
Iris reticulata (Dwarf Blue Iris)
Muscari armeniacum (Grape Hyacinth)
Scilla peruviana (Peruvian Squill)
Scilla siberica (Siberian Squill)
Tritelia uniflora (Star flower)

YELLOW-ORANGE

Allium moly (Lily Leek)
Alstroemeria aurantiaca (Peruvian Lily)
Begonia x *tuberhybrida* (Tuberous Begonia)
Belamcanda chinensis (Blackberry-Lily)
Canna x *generalis* (Canna)
Clivia miniata (Kafir Lily)
Crocus chrysanthus (Snow Crocus)
Crocus flavus (Yellow Crocus)
Dahlia pinnata hybrids (Dahlia)
Eranthis hyemalis (Winter Aconite)
Eremurus elwesii (Foxtail Lily)
Erythronium 'Pagoda' (Dogtooth Violet)
Eucomis comosa (Pineapple Lily)
Fritillaria imperialis (Crown Imperial)
Gladiolus x *hortulanus* (Gladiolus)
Hemerocallis fulva (Tawny Daylily)
Iris danfordiae (Danford Iris)
Iris hollandica (Dutch Iris)
Ixia maculata (Corn-Lily)
Lilium hybrida 'asiatic' (Asiatic Hybrid Lilies)
Lilium candidum (Madonna Lily)
Narcissus species and hybrids (Daffodil)
Oxalis pes-caprae (Bermuda Buttercup)
Ranunculus asiaticus (Persian Buttercup)
Sparaxis tricolor (Harlequin Flower)
Sternbergia lutea (Fall Crocus)
Tulipa species and hybrids (Tulip)
Zantedeschia aethiopica (Calla Lily)
Zephyranthes atamasco (Atamasco Lily)

BULB PLANTING CHARTS

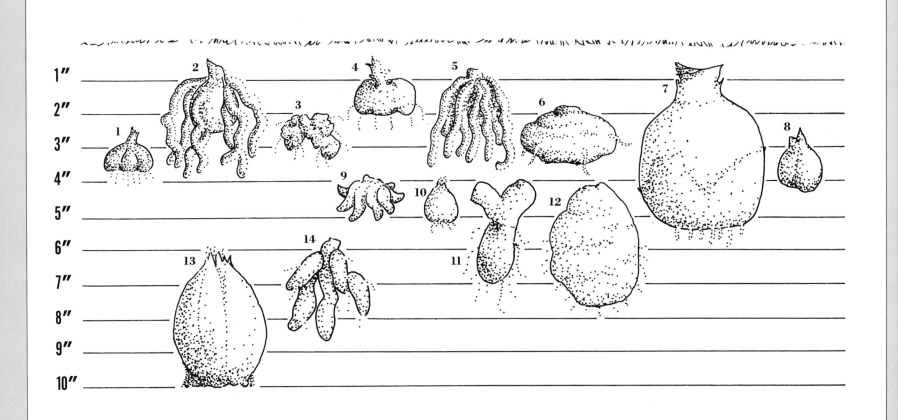

1"
2"
3"
4"
5"
6"
7"
8"
9"
10"

1—Acidanthera
2—Agapanthus
3—Anemone

4—Begonia
5—Belamcanda
6—Caladium

7—Cardiocrinum
8—Colchicum
9—Bletilla

10—Camassia
11—Canna
12—Colocasia

13—Allium giganteum
14—Alstroemeria

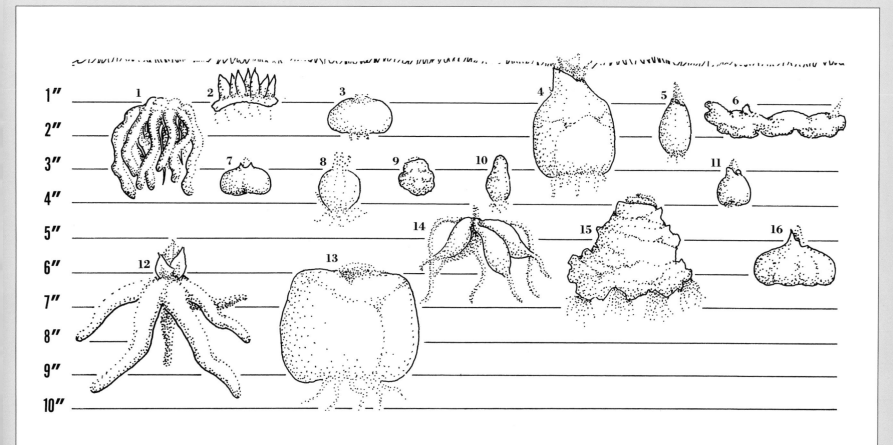

1"

2"

3"

4"

5"

6"

7"

8"

9"

10"

1—Clivia   4—Eucharis   7—Crocus   10—Erythronium   13—Fritallaria imperialis

2—Convallaria   5—Freesia   8—Crocosmia   11—Galanthus   14—Dahlia

3—Cyclamen   6—Gloriosa   9—Eranthis   12—Eremurus   15—Eucomis

                                                                       16—Gladiolus

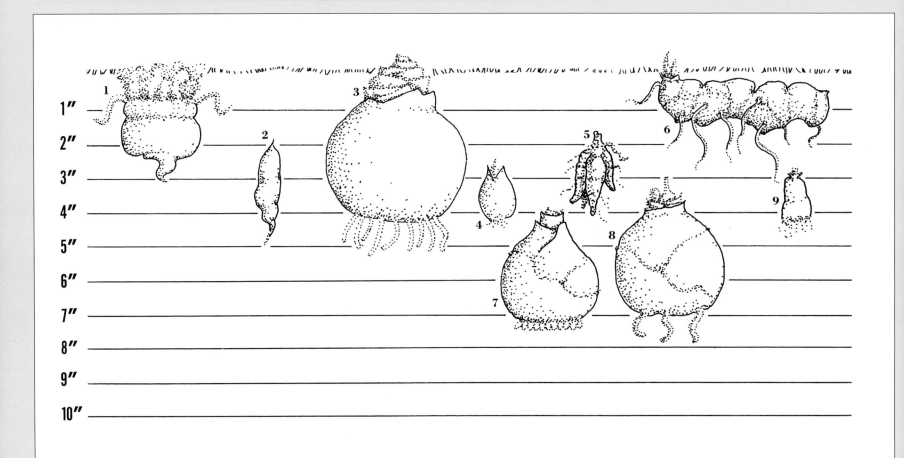

1"
2"
3"
4"
5"
6"
7"
8"
9"
10"

1—Haemanthus   3—Hippeastrum   5—Incarvillea   7—Hyacinthus   9—Ipheion
2—Hemerocallis   4—Hyacinthoides   6—Iris germanica   8—Hymenocallis

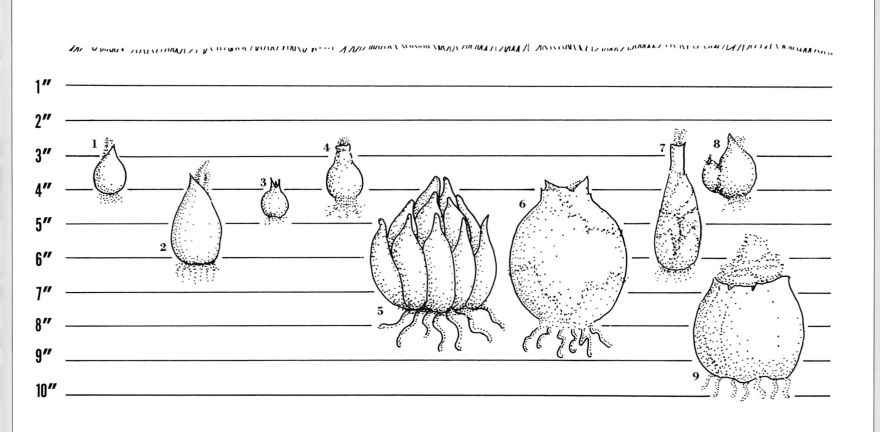

1"
2"
3"
4"
5"
6"
7"
8"
9"
10"

1—Iris reticulata   3—Ixia   5—Lilium   7—Lycoris   9—Narcissus
2—Iris hollandicus   4—Leucojum   6—Ismene   8—Muscari

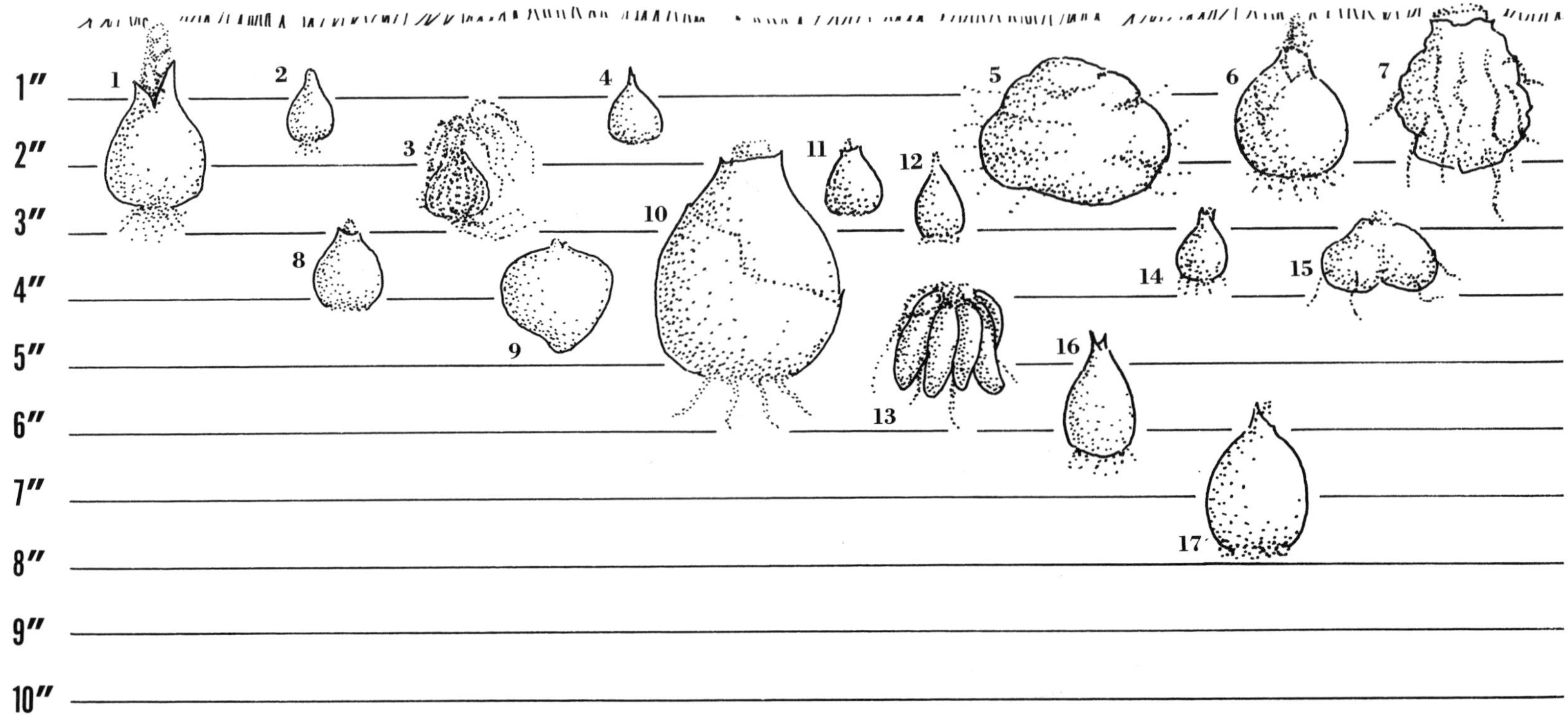

1—Nerine
2—Ornithogalum
3—Oxalis
4—Pleione
5—Sinningia
6—Sprekelia
7—Veltheima
8—Scilla sibirica
9—Zantedeschia
10—Poli anthes
11—Zephyranthus
12—Puschkinia
13—Ranunculus
14—Sparaxis
15—Watsonia
16—Sternbergia
17—Tulipa

A. M. Georgens

Left: Here, mixed tulips border a grassy walkway, adding brilliant color to this bulb garden.

BULB FLOWERING GUIDE

		Jan	Feb	Mar	Apr	May	Jun	Jul	Aug	Sep	Oct	Nov	Dec
Acidanthera bicolor	(Peacock Flower)							▓	▓				
Agapanthus africanus	(African Lily)					▓	▓						
Allium christophii	(Star-of-Persia)						▓						
Allium giganteum	(Giant Allium)						▓						
Allium moly	(Lily Leek)				▓	▓							
Alstroemeria aurantiaca	(Peruvian Lily)							▓					
Amaryllis belladonna	(Naked Ladies, Belladonna Lily)										▓		
Anemone blanda	(Grecian Windflower)				▓								
Anemone coronaria	(French Anemone)				▓								
Begonia x *tuberhybrida*	(Tuberous Begonia)							▓	▓	▓			
Belamcanda chinensis	(Blackberry-Lily)												
Bletilla striata	(Chinese Orchid)				▓								
Caladium x *hortulanum*	(Rainbow Plant)							▓	▓				
Camassia scilloides	(Wild Hyacinth)				▓								
Canna x *generalis*	(Canna)							▓	▓				
Cardiocrinum scilloides	(Wild Hyacinth)						▓						
Chionodoxa luciliae	(Glory-of-the-Snow)				▓	▓							
Clivia miniata	(Kafir-Lily)				▓								
Colchicum autumnale	(Autumn-Crocus)									▓			
Colocasia esculenta	(Elephant's Ear, Giant Taro)							▓	▓	▓			
Convallaria majalis	(Lily-of-the-valley)					▓							
Crocosmia x *crocosmiiflora*	(Montbretia)								▓				
Crocus chrysanthus	(Snow Crocus)				▓								
Crocus flavus	(Yellow Crocus)										▓		

		January	February	March	April	May	June	July	August	September	October	November	December
Crocus tomasinianus	(Common Crocus)			■	■								
Cyclamen neapolitanum	(Hardy Cyclamen)				■	■							
Cyclamen persicum	(Florists' Cyclamen)	■	■									■	■
Dahlia pinnata hybrids	(Dahlia)							■	■	■			
Eranthis hyemalis	(Winter Aconite)		■	■									
Eremurus elwesii	(Foxtail Lily)						■	■					
Erythronium 'Pagoda'	(Dogtooth Violet)				■	■							
Eucharis grandiflora	(Amazon-Lily)			■	■								
Eucomis comosa	(Pineapple Lily)							■	■	■			
Freesia x *hybrida*	(Freesia)					■	■						
Fritillaria imperialis	(Crown Imperial)					■	■						
Fritillaria meleagris	(Checkered Lily)					■	■						
Galanthus elwesii	(Snowdrop)		■										
Gladiolus x *hortulanus*	(Gladiolus)							■	■	■			
Gloriosa rothschildiana	(Rothschild Gloriosa-Lily)				■	■				■	■		
Haemanthus katharinae	(Katharine Blood-Lily)						■						
Hippeastrum hybrida	(Amaryllis)		■	■	■								
Hyacinthus orientalis	(Dutch Hyacinth)				■								
Hyacinthoides hispanica	(Spanish Bluebell)					■							
Hymenocallis narcissiflora	(Peruvian Daffodil)					■							
Hyacinthoides hispanica	(Spanish Bluebells)												
Hymenocallis narcissiflora	(Peruvian Daffodil)												
Incarvillea delvayii	(Hardy Gloxinia)						■						
Iris cristata	(Crested Iris					■							

		January	February	March	April	May	June	July	August	September	October	November	December
Iris danfordiae	(Danford Iris)			■									
Ixia maculata	(Corn-Lily)				■								
Leucojum vernum	(Spring Snowflake)				■								
Lilium auratum	(Oriental Lily)							■					
Lilium candidum	(Madonna Lily, Bermuda Lily)						■						
Lilium hybrida 'asiatic'	(Asiatic Hybrid Lilies)							■					
Lilium longiflorum	(White Trumpet Lily)								■	■			
Lycoris radiata	(Red Spider Lily)								■				
Lycoris squamigera	(Naked Ladies)									■			
Muscari armeniacum	(Grape hyacinth)				■								
Narcissus poeticus	(Poet's Daffodil)				■								
Narcissus triandrus	(Daffodil, Angel's Tears)				■								
Ornithogalum umbellatum	(Star of Bethlehem)					■							
Oxalis pres-caprae	(Bermuda Buttercup)				■								
Pleione formosa	(Fairy Orchid)												
Polianthes x tuberosa	(Tuberose)									■			
Puschkinia scilloides	(Striped Squill)					■	■						
Ranunculus asiaticus	(Persian Buttercup)			■	■								
Scilla campanulata	(Spanish Bluebell)					■							
Scilla siberica	(Siberian squill)				■								
Sinningia speciosa	(Gloxinia)						■	■					
Sparaxis tricolor	(Harlequin flower)				■								
Sprekelia formosissima	(Jakobean Lily)					■							
Sternbergia lutea	(Fall Crocus)									■			

	January	February	March	April	May	June	July	August	September	October	November	December
Trigrida pavonia (Tiger-Flowers, Shell-Flowers))							■	■				
Triteleia uniflora (Star Flower)				■	■							
Tulbaghia viloacea (Society Garlic)					■	■						
Tulipa clusiana (Candlestick Tulip, Peppermint Stick)				■								
Tulipa dasystemon (Tulip)				■								
Tulipa fosteriana (Foster Tulip)				■								
Tulipa greigii (Peacock Tulip)				■								
Tulipa x *hybrida Darwin* (Darwin Hybrid Tulip)				■	■							
Tulipa x *hybrida 'Lily-Flowered'* (Lily-Flowered Tulip)				■								
Tulipa kaufmanniana (Water-Lily Tulip)				■								
Tulip x *hybrida 'Parrot'* (Parrot-Flowered Tulip)				■	■							
Tulipa x *hybrida 'Peony-Flowered'* (Peony-Flowered Tulip)				■	■							
Tulipa praestans (Leather-Bulb Tulip)				■								
Veltheimia viridifolia (Cape Lily)				■								
Watsonia pyramidata (Bugle Flower)								■				
Zantedeschia aethiopica (Calla Lily)					■							
Zephyranthes atamasco (Atamasco Lily, Zephyr Lily)				■								

ESSENTIAL
ROSES

INTRODUCTION

A SALUTE TO THE ROSE

T HE ROSE WAS MADE THE OFFICIAL FLORAL emblem of the United States in 1986 in spite of very strong competition from the marigold, a native North American flowering annual. Rose leaf fossils have been found in Montana and Oregon showing that roses existed on the North American continent 35 to 40 million years ago. The country rejoiced in a well-chosen official flower.

According to mythology, roses were born of the tears shed by the broken-hearted Venus as she wept over her lover, the slain Adonis. Morphologically, the rose is a wonderful example of survival of the fittest, possessing not only thorns for protection against foraging animals, but a cast-iron constitution, beautiful flowers, and wide adaptation. Botanically, garden roses are classified as woody plants—a class that also includes shrubs and trees. Roses belong in the *Rosaceae* family, which includes blackberries, strawberries, cherries, crab apples, firethorn, and hawthorns among its distinguished members.

The rose is believed to be the first flower cultivated by humans. There is evidence that a rose garden was cultivated in Greece in the fifth century BC.

Throughout history, the presence of roses has been recorded at special events. When Christopher Columbus was close to despair at ever finding land during his first voyage to America, his crew picked a rose branch from the water and rejoiced at the possibility that land must be near. It is recorded that when the *Mayflower* landed at Plymouth, Massachusetts, "the shore was fragrant like the smell of a rose garden, and the happy children gathered strawberries and wild roses."

Roses have been cultivated by the Chinese since the Shen Nung Dynasty (2737–2697 BC). However, it was not until the 1700s, when Empress Josephine of France began the first garden—at Malmaison, near Paris—devoted entirely to roses, that roses gained mass appeal in the West. In all, about 250 varieties of roses were planted, and she commissioned a talented artist, Redoute, to paint a magnificent portfolio of the garden. Unfortunately, after the Napoleonic War the garden was neglected, even though interest in roses continued to climb.

It was not until 1910 that efforts were made to restore the rose garden, collecting together as many of the original species and varieties that comprised the original collection as possible.

Modern roses are descended from four wild roses—*Rosa centifolia* (the Cabbage Rose) from Asia, was crossed in 1840 with *R. Chinensis* (the China Rose), producing the first hybrid, called a hybrid perpetual for its ability to bloom more than once. This in turn was crossed with *R. odorata* (the Tea Rose), resulting in a variety called "La France" the first hybrid tea rose.

Roses have the ability to live for a very long time, representing a good investment to the home gardener. A rose bush in Hildesheim, West Germany, is estimated to be at least 300 years old, while the United States can claim to possess the world's largest rose bush. It is a yellow-flowering Lady Banks Rose in Tombstone, Arizona. Standing 9 feet high with a trunk diameter of 40 inches, it covers an area of 5,380 square feet, supported on a framework of sixty-eight posts. The original cutting came from Scotland in 1884.

This book is intended as a salute to this beautiful plant, with an emphasis on care, planting ideas, and recommended selections for what can be described as "the world's most beautiful flower".

CHAPTER ONE

A ROSE BY ANY OTHER NAME

ROSES ARE SOLD THROUGH RETAIL STORES, such as garden centers, and by mail order from catalogs. They are available either "bare-root" or "potted". If you buy a bare-root rose, the canes are cut short and may have a wax coating that acts as an anti-desiccant to resist dehydration. The roots are washed clean of soil, packed in moist sphagnum moss, and enclosed in a plastic wrapper.

There are three grades of bare-root roses, but in general the home gardener should choose #1 grade. The other grades (#1 $\frac{1}{2}$ and #2) are inferior and not worth risking the time and effort needed for planting and care.

Potted plants are grown in a disposable container rooted in a potting soil. Though potted plants may appear to offer a higher survival rate, the better buy is usually a dormant bare-root plant, planted during the bare-root season, which generally runs October through April in cold climates and December through February in areas where freezing does not occur. Outside the bare-root season, roses can be bought potted for transplanting into the garden in the spring.

To help make selections, even if you intend buying from a local retail store, obtain some rose catalogs and study the descriptions. They generally list the name, type, growth habit, color, and price. Some may indicate specific climatic

requirements, but for specific information on the best roses for your particular area, visit local rose gardens, attend a meeting of the local Rose Society, or consult a friend with growing experience.

A list of mail order sources is given in the source section, page 679.

Two excellent sources of worthwhile, old-fashioned roses are Tillotson's (also called Roses of Yesterday and Today) and the Antique Rose Emporium; see listings in the source section, page 679.

Height Standards For the purpose of describing relative heights among roses, the American Rose Society has designated three groups:

Low: Under 30 inches (1½ feet)
Medium: 30 to 48 inches (1½ to 4 feet)
Tall: Over 48 inches (4 feet)

It must be realized that these broad designations are based on national averages, and under optimum conditions a rose described as medium height may in fact exceed 4 feet, while a rose described as low-growing may exceed 1½ feet.

National Ratings The American Rose Society conducts a rating system from 1 to 10 for all roses available to buy and publishes the list annually. Because of climatic differences in North America, some chapters of the American Rose Society (such as the San Francisco Rose Society) have established rating systems independent of the National system, and wherever possible gardeners should seek local ratings. However, the National ratings system does help to show those plants that are generally widely adaptable. The roses are judged by the following categories: novelty, bud form, flower form, color opening, color finishing, substance, fragrance, habit, vigor, foliage, disease resistance, flowering effect, and overall value. The ratings are scored as follows:

10.0 Perfect (to date, no rose is rated 10)
9.9-9.0 Outstanding
8.9-8.0 Excellent
7.9-7.0 Good
6.9-6.0 Fair
5.9 or less   Poor, of questionable value

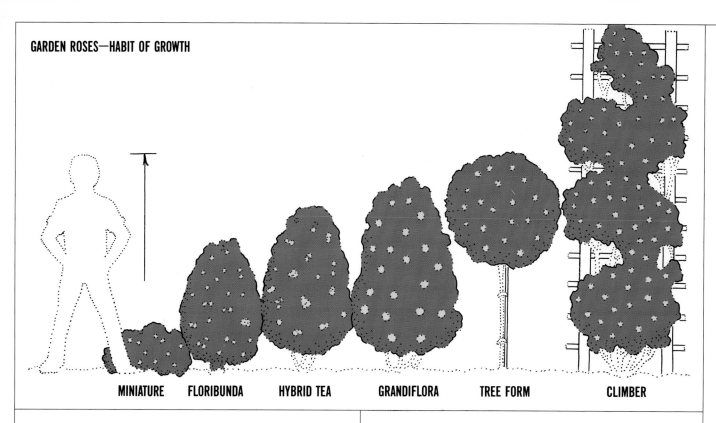

GARDEN ROSES—HABIT OF GROWTH

MINIATURE   FLORIBUNDA   HYBRID TEA   GRANDIFLORA   TREE FORM   CLIMBER

Opposite page: The climbing rose, Constance Spry, decorates the side of a barn. Flower arrangers love this rose for its heavenly fragrance and double, cupped, old-fashioned flowers.
Left: This drawing illustrates the approximate growing sizes of roses. Climbing roses will continue to grow upward as long as they have something to anchor onto.

ROSE CLASSIFICATIONS

The American Rose Society has established standards for classifying roses. In addition to categorizing roses by plant habit (grandifloras, floribundas, climbers, etc.), the Society has standardized color classifications, height comparisons, and has devised a rating system from 1 to 10 of overall performance as a result of tests conducted by rose growers throughout the country.

The following classifications describe roses by type:

Hybrid Teas are large-flowered roses growing one bloom to a stem. The term "tea" comes from their derivation from the "tea rose of China," which possesses a distinctive tealike fragrance. They are called hybrids because they are all the product of man-made crosses (hybridizing) between selected parents. Hybrid teas are mostly used as specimens for garden display and for cutting.

Grandifloras resemble hybrid teas with their large flower size, but their flowers differ in that they are held above the plant in clusters, rather than atop long, single stems. Grandifloras tend to grow tall and are best used as backgrounds.

Polyanthas are a strain of old-fashioned roses that date back hundreds of years. They bear small flowers that are produced in dense clusters. Many are highly subject to mildew, but are important parents in the development of the next classification, floribundas. Polyanthas are mostly used for hedges and singly to produce a shrub effect.

Floribundas have larger flowers than polyanthas, but not as large as grandifloras or hybrid teas, and they produce their flowers in clusters. Floribundas are excellent for massing in beds and borders.

Climbers are mostly mutations of polyanthas, grandifloras, hybrid teas, and floribundas, producing abnormally long canes that can be trained to climb. They can be trained vertically and horizontally.

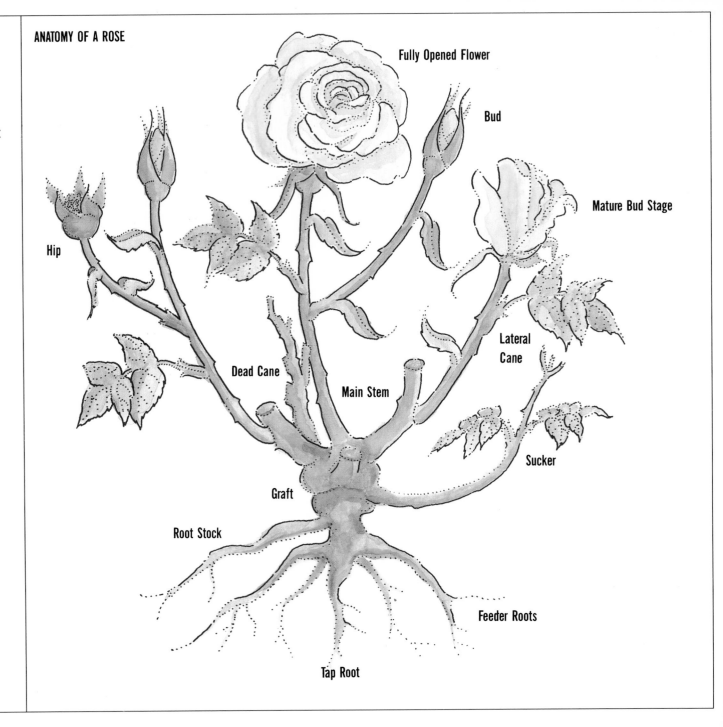

Right: This drawing illustrates the anatomy of the rose. Basically, all roses have the same anatomy.

Opposite page: This drawing represents the eight types of rose blossoms typical to most garden roses.

ANATOMY OF A ROSE

Fully Opened Flower

Bud

Mature Bud Stage

Hip

Lateral Cane

Dead Cane

Main Stem

Sucker

Graft

Root Stock

Feeder Roots

Tap Root

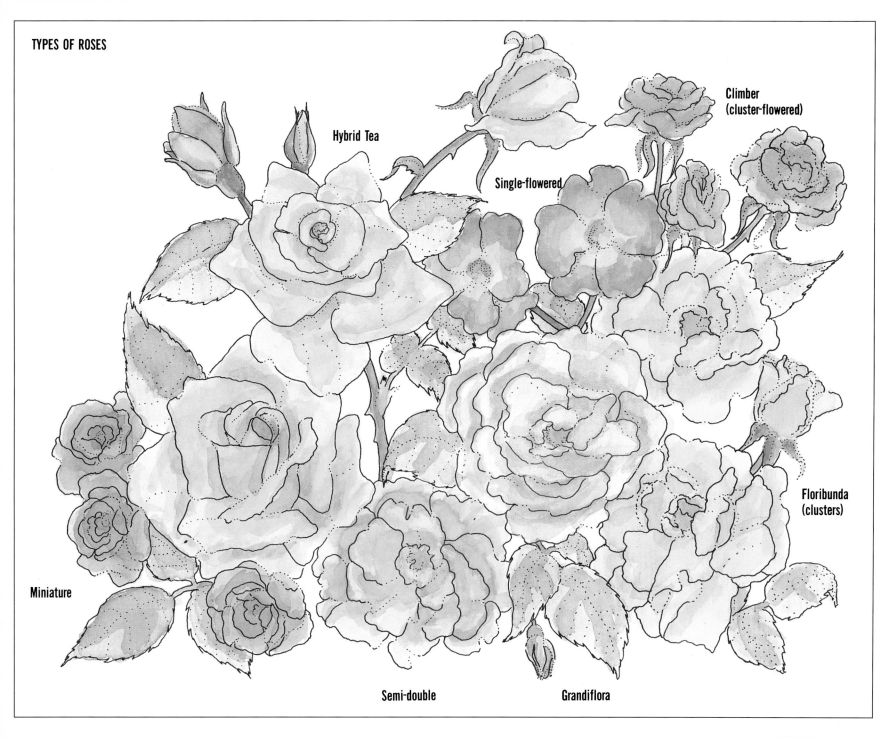

Hybrid Tea

Single-flowered

Climber
(cluster-flowered)

Floribunda
(clusters)

Miniature

Semi-double

Grandiflora

Right: The dainty miniature rose, Woman's Day, makes a beautiful, informal floral arrangement.
Opposite page, above: An overview of the famous rose garden at Hershey, Pennsylvania, in late June.
Opposite page, below: Here, a hedge of hybrid tea roses surround a bird bath.

Minatures are tiny roses that grow on dwarf, compact plants, developed from a sophisticated breeding program involving old polyanthas, floribundas, and wild roses with especially small flower forms. They are excellent for growing in containers, creating a low ground cover effect, and decorating sunny rooms as houseplants.

Miscellaneous Shrub Roses is a "catch-all" category for roses that generally do not seem to fit into the other main groups. Some of these include Pillar roses (short climbers) and some hedge roses that are too tall to be called miniatures and too small to be called polyanthas or floribundas.

In addition to these six basic rose classifications, we hear a lot about other designations. For example, there are species roses, which are roses found in the wild. Some of the most popular for garden culture are *Rosa centifolia* (Cherokee Rose), *Rosa rugosa* (Rugosa Rose) and *Rosa banksea* (Lady Banks Rose).

Old-fashioned Roses lump together a whole host of old cultivated roses with an obscure parentage. These include Moss Roses, with a mosslike covering on the flower buds, Damask Roses, named for their heady fragrance, and Gallicas, famous in Tudor times as the Rose of York (a pink) and the Rose of Lancaster (a white), the floral symbols used by opposing armies in Britain's Civil War, known as the War of the Roses. Few old-fashioned roses are grown in home gardens because of their relatively sparse flowers and rangy habit, but they still make their ways into historic gardens and special rose collections. There are a few exceptions to this generalization, including Roi de Victoria (a pink) and Cardinal de Richelieu (a purple). They are reasonably free-flowering with cup-shaped, fragrant, multi-layered flowers liked especially by flower arrangers. The individual rose descriptions in Chapter Three list the ratings from the National Rose Society.

All-American Rose Selections is a non-profit organization consisting of judges with rose test gardens. These gardens are located in different climatic regions of North America. Each year the judges grow and evaluate new roses sent from breeders in different countries. They grow the entries alongside roses already in commerce and give them points in comparison to these. The points are totalled and those with the required number of points receive either a bronze, silver, or gold medal and are introduced to the general public with a fanfare of publicity. All-America Selections does not test miniatures, but the American Rose Society makes "Awards of Excellence" in this category. A list of All-America Award winners appears on pages 386–387.

THE STORY OF PEACE ROSE:

French Breeding Expertise and American Salesmanship Combine to Create the Rose Sensation of All Time

The story of Peace Rose, the most famous rose in the history of modern rose breeding, began in 1935 when Papa Meilland, head of the French rose breeding concern of Meilland & Son, helped his son, Francis, select fifty promising seedlings for evaluation from a cross-pollination program. These fifty were culled from a total of eight hundred that had been patiently grown from seed to flower. They assigned each seedling a number so that they could refer to their notebooks and tell what particular cross produced any one of the fifty seedlings.

As was customary, at the start of every blooming season the Meillands invited a group of rose experts from around the world to inspect their test plots. From these visits the Meillands could often tell if a particular rose caught their fancy and helped the family decide which to introduce into cultivation.

The date was June 1939—three months before the outbreak of World War II. The star of the show was a plant innocuously labelled 3-35-40. The blooms of 3-35-40 were an incredible size—bigger than anything previously seen in a hybrid tea. The stems were strong, the leaves exuded health and vigor, a shimmering dark green, but most important of all was its enchanting color, marked by its romantic aura. The light yellow petals were shaded from pale ivory at the center to clear golden yellow at the edges, the tips were suffused with a touch of pink deepening to carmine. Every flower that opened, from bud to petal drop, was pure perfection, fully double, high pointed in the bud stage; it unfolded slowly, and outlasted every other rose in cultivation. To crown it all, the plants were extraordinarily hardy.

In spite of the dark political situation that was threatening the world with war, the success of 3-35-40 among the visiting rose experts suffused the Meilland family with a sense of happiness and tranquility. They knew that they had an extraordinary world-class rose on their hands. All it needed now was to be islolated and propagated into dozens, then hundreds, and finally thousands of cuttings so enough plants could be sold to start giving the family a return on their investment.

Unfortunately, war was not a good time to be selling roses, and by the day rose shipments were embargoed (a result of the outbreak of World War II) only three shipments of 3-35-40 had been sent out: one to a rose grower in Germany, another to a grower in Italy, and a third to Mr. Robert Pyle, head of the Conard Pyle Company, a rose grower located near Philadelphia, Pennsylvania. In the rush to send out these precious shipments, rose 3-35-40 had no name, even

though the Meilland family had decided, in one of their brainstorming sessions, to call the new rose Madame A. Meilland after Papa Meilland's mother.

As news came back about the shipments, the Meillands learned that the German grower had bestowed on the new rose the name, Gloria Dei (Glory be to God) while the Italian grower had called it Gioia!, meaning Joy; no immediate news was received of the American shipment. To survive the war, they devoted most of their rose fields to raising vegetables.

Finally, a month to the day after the liberation of France, a letter arrived at the Meilland household from America. It was from Robert Pyle, and his words were like music. He wrote: "My eyes are fixed in fascinated admiration on a glorious rose, its pale gold, cream and ivory petals blending to a lightly ruffled edge of delicate carmine . . . I am convinced it will be the greatest rose of the century."

Pyle had arranged a "Name Giving Ceremony" for the new rose at the Pacific Rose Society's Exhibition at Pasadena, California on Sunday, April 29, 1945. The war still raged in Europe, and after consulting with other rose growers, Pyle drafted a statement that was to be read at the Exhibition. It said: "We are decided that this greatest new rose of our time should be named for the world's greatest desire: PEACE."

Sunday, April 29, 1945 dawned bright and clear in Pasadena for the conference of rose growers. As the name for the new rose was declared, two white doves were set free. Miraculously, in war-weary Europe, after six long years, a truce was declared. The bombs stopped. On the day the Peace Rose was named, World War II ended and the world was at peace.

More coincidences followed. On the day that the judges for All-America Rose Selections met and honored Peace with an award, the war in Japan ended. A month later, on the day a peace treaty was signed in Japan, the American Rose Society bestowed its highest award on the Peace Rose: a gold medal.

Within a period of nine years, thirty million Peace Roses were planted throughout the world, each of them the progeny of a single seed no bigger than a pinhead, that produced a seedling known simply as 3-35-40 until it flowered 5,000 miles away on a Pennsylvania farm, inspiring a conservative Quaker businessman, Robert Pyle, to grant it a name nobody could ever forget, the Peace Rose.

THE TEN MOST OFTEN ASKED QUESTIONS ABOUT ROSES

1. **WHAT IS THE MOST POPULAR ROSE VARIETY OF ALL?**
The yellow-and-pink hybrid tea rose called Peace, developed by the firm of Meilland in France. However, in recent years, there has been extraordinary interest in climbing roses and in hedge roses. The climber, Blaze, has started to exceed sales of Peace, as has the hedge rose Simplicity.

2. **HOW SOON AFTER PLANTING WILL ROSES BE IN BLOOM?**
Floribunda, hybrid tea, and hedge roses will bloom just six to eight weeks after planting. Climbers will bloom a little during the first season, but are at their best by the second year. For more on planting roses, see pages 307–308.

3. **CAN I GROW ROSES IN CONTAINERS?**
Yes, roses can be grown in containers. Miniature roses and small floribundas are easiest, but even hybrid teas will do nicely in planter boxes. See page 383 for specific container planting ideas.

4. **WHY ARE MY ROSES MORE FRAGRANT AT CERTAIN TIMES?**
Roses are often more fragrant on warm, humid days and during a brief time before a summer storm. Drought, extreme heat, or very cool days diminish their fragrance.

5. **WHAT ARE THE MOST FRAGRANT ROSES?**
Fragrant Cloud, Fragrant Memory, Intrigue, Dolly Parton, and Tropicana are among the most fragrant varieties. For a larger listing see page 385.

6. **HOW DO I KNOW IF ROSES WILL GROW IN MY AREA?**
Roses are extremely hardy plants and will grow in just about any area of North America. In the most northern areas, however, plants may require some winter protection, such as mulching around the roots after the ground freezes.

7. **WHEN IS THE BEST TIME OF YEAR TO TRANSPLANT ROSES?**
The best time to transplant is either in the fall or in the early spring when roses are dormant and the ground is workable.

8. **WHEN IS THE BEST TIME TO PRUNE ROSES?**
The best time for pruning is early spring, sometime after the last killing frost, and just before new growth starts. For more about pruning see page 313.

9. **WHERE CAN I PLANT ROSES?**
Roses can be planted in any location that meets the following three requirements: The spot must receive at least four to six hours of direct sun each day; there must be enough space to allow 18 to 24 inches around the plant for air circulation; and the soil must drain well enough that there is no standing water. For complete planting instructions see page 307–308.

10. **HOW MUCH TROUBLE IS IT TO GROW ROSES?**
Though protected from foraging animals by thorns, the succulent leaves are subject to attack by insects and diseases and a spray program is advisable. A regular feeding program and irrigation also help produce superlative results. For complete care instructions see pages 307–315.

Opposite page: A beautiful close-up of Peace rose, which captivated the hearts of the world after World War II.

CHAPTER TWO

CARE OF ROSES

Good soil is essential for quality rose plants. If the soil is not properly prepared no amount of fertilizing, irrigation, or spraying will yield superior results. Soil not only serves to anchor a rose plant, it provides nutrients to roots. Nutrients enter the roots in *soluble* form; therefore, the soil must have good moisture-holding capacity, yet allow excess water to drain.

SOIL PREPARATION

Soil that puddles because of poor drainage can be improved by laying a bed of crushed stones on top of it and building a raised soil bed with landscape ties above the water table. Another alternative is to drain the area.

Sand, clay, and loam are the three main types of soil. Sand has poor anchorage and lets moisture and nutrients drain away too rapidly; it trickles through the fingers when held in the hand. Clay is thick, sticky, and cold, forming tight wads when squeezed in the hand. Roots find it hard to penetrate the suffocating, airless mass represented by clay. Loam is a happy medium, not too light and not too heavy, containing generous amounts of organic matter to make it fluffy.

To improve a soil that is too sandy or one that is composed of too much clay, the remedy is the same—generous amounts of compost must be added to boost its organic content. Fail-

ing a supply of compost, add well-rotted manure, well-decomposed leaf mold, or bales of peat instead.

Poor soils are best improved in autumn, prior to spring planting, allowing the soil conditioners time to interact with the original soil base and to build up populations of beneficial soil bacteria.

The best test for good soil is the squeeze test. Take a handful of moist soil and squeeze it tight. When you open your hand, the soil should not bind together like clay, nor run through your fingers like sand. It should just remain as loose and crumbly after squeezing as before.

It doesn't pay to be complacent about good soil. The action of wind, rain, and footprints on soil will lead to compaction and the natural feeding of roots will deplete nutrients. Adding a commercial fertilizer each year is not enough; the addition of humus each autumn is also a necessity.

PLANTING ROSES

The best size for a planting hole (except for miniature roses) is 2 feet wide by 1 1/2 feet deep. This represents the removal of approximately forty gallons of soil. A good soil mix for the planting hole is comprised of 20 percent humus in the form of compost, leaf mold or peat; 20 percent well-decomposed horse or cow manure; and 60 percent garden topsoil. In the

PLANTING A ROSE *(Right)*:

1. This is a typical bare-root plant ready for planting.

2. Dig a hole to accommodate the spread and depth of roots. Mound soil in the bottom of the hole and spread the roots over the mound.

3. Leave a 1-inch lip around hole to catch water.

4. Mound wood-chip mulch around the base of the plant.

absence of animal manure, double up on the humus and add a 5-10-5 granular fertilizer to the mix.

With the soil mix described above, build a cone in the bottom of the hole so that the roots of a bare-root plant can be spread evenly and the bud union (an enlarged section between the root section and branches) sits slightly above the level of the soil surface. Keeping the plant upright, shovel soil over the roots and tamp the soil down with your feet to settle it and make contact around the roots.

With a potted rose plant there is no need to build a cone. Simply shovel soil into the bottom of the hole until you can place the top of the root ball level with the soil surface. Fill around the sides, tamping the loose soil so the root ball sits tightly in the hole.

Give each plant four gallons of water. When all settling has stopped it may be necessary to adjust the bud union so it sits above the soil line.

In northern states, where winters are severe and roses are planted in the autumn, it is essential to build a mound of soil to 8 or 9 inches above the bud union for protection against "winterkill"—the drying effects of cold winter winds and glaring sun.

Fertilizing

Before the soil is mounded, a slow-release, high-phosphorus fertilizer (such as 5-10-5) can be added to the soil surface. After the plant has leafed out and finished blooming, a regular feeding schedule can be practiced.

A basic fertilizing program should consist of the following: Surface feeding with a 5-10-5 or 10-20-10 slow release fertilizer at time of planting (spring or fall), and a booster application in spring and autumn each year thereafter. Different brands of fertilizer require different amounts of application, so read the label carefully. In addition to granular fertilizer, it's possible to keep roses fed by foliar feeding by spraying a liquid fertilizer onto leaf surfaces.

The best rose fertilizers have a 1-2-1 ratio of plant nutrients, such as 10-20-10 or 15-30-15. These numbers stand for the percentages of vital plant nutrients, nitrogen, phosphorus, and potassium, in that order. Nitrogen grows lush leaves, phosphorus develops a healthy root system and encourages flower bud formation, and potassium adds overall vigor. The rest is "filler" used as a distributing agent.

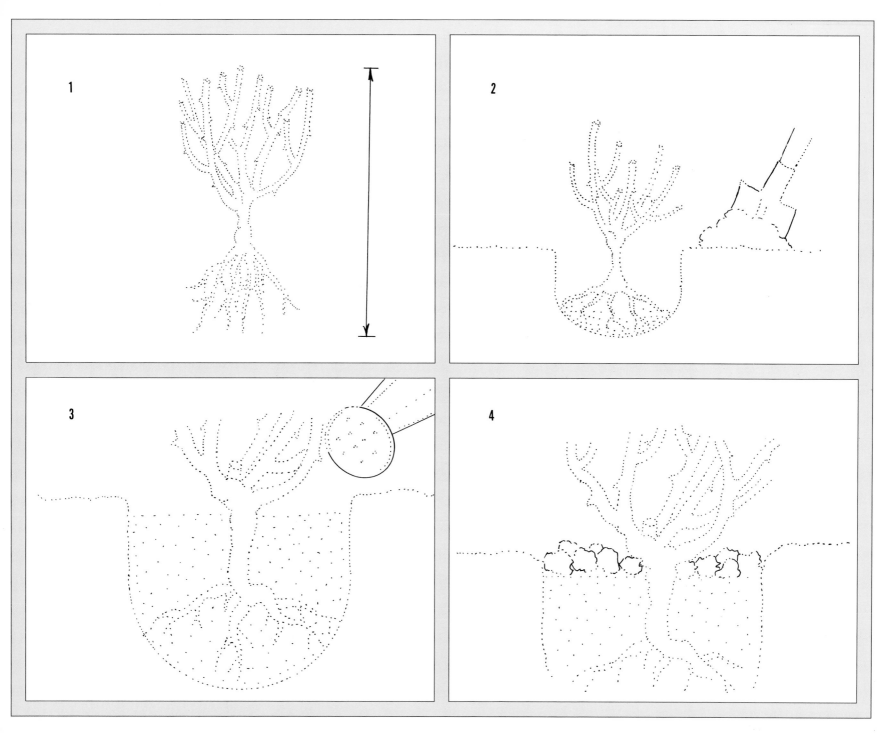

CONTROLLING INSECTS AND DISEASES

Though roses have developed a good defense—their thorns—against foraging animals, the leaves are especially susceptible to attack by insects and diseases. The old saying, "an ounce of prevention is worth a pound of cure," is particularly true with roses, since once a problem occurs it is often difficult to eradicate.

Good soil, topped up annually to maintain its humus content, a regular feeding schedule, and irrigation during dry spells will help give roses a strong constitution to resist diseases, but a precautionary spray program involving the following is also advisable:

Insecticide Harmful insect pests either chew leaves or suck their juices. The biggest enemies of roses are aphids, scale, and Japanese beetles.

Miticide Spider mites are tiny creatures that build fine webbing among foliage and suck a plant's juices. Ordinary insecticides are usually ineffective in controlling them, so a miticide is needed.

Fungicide Roses are attacked mainly by three fungi: mildew, blackspot, and rust. Mildew is a silvery, dusty coating on leaf surfaces that inhibits the manufacture of chlorophyll, thus weakening plants. Blackspot consists of small, black marks covering leaf surfaces and a yellowing of the leaf. Rust is evident by brownish pustules covering leaf surfaces.

Though there are different sprays available for each problem listed above, it is possible to buy chemical controls that are pre-mixed so a general purpose insecticide, miticide, and fungicide can be applied at one time.

It's also possible to use specific organic controls. For example, some roses are resistant to blackspot and mildew. Insecticidal soaps and also pyrethrum/rotenone sprays or dusts are available. These products are not long-lasting in their control, but they are environmentally safe, leaving no harmful residues to contaminate the soil.

Irrespective of what kind of spray product you choose, always read the label carefully before use, since dosages differ and even sprays made from "organic" compounds may be toxic to humans, pets, or fish.

IRRIGATION

Roses require watering during dry spells, and by far the most efficient way to water roses is by means of a drip irrigation system. Many kinds of drip lines are available, costing as little as $25.00 to irrigate 500 square feet, to over $100.00. There are two basic kinds. The "emitter" type has small nozzles spaced at two feet intervals to drip water from each nozzle. Another type has micro-pores along the hose length so it "sweats" beads of moisture from beginning to end.

Most drip irrigation lines can be laid on the soil surface and simply covered with a light layer of mulch to hide them.

Drip lines are connected to a water source, allowing you to turn on a faucet, leave it on overnight, and turn it off in the morning. Some can be fitted with a fertilizer applicator so that the water mixes with plant nutrients to feed plants while they are being watered.

WEED CONTROL

Rose beds should be kept free of weeds. The easiest way to do this is by laying down a mulch around the plants. A mulch is a covering that rests on top of the soil. It can be organic, such as wood chips, pink bark, or shredded leaves, or it can

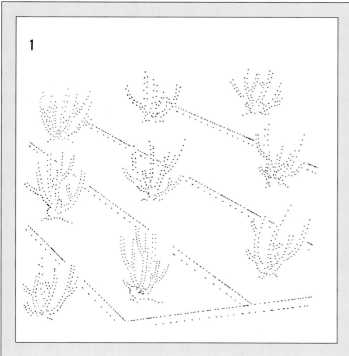

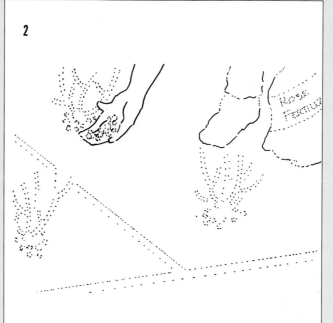

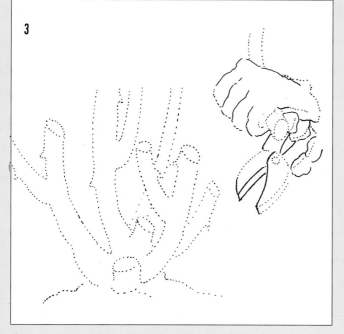

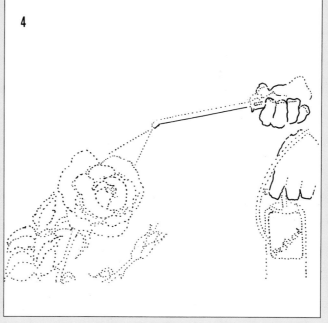

FOUR POINT SCHEDULE FOR CARE OF ROSES

1. WATER: Preferably with a drip irrigation system.

2. FEED: In spring and fall with granular fertilizer.

3. PRUNE: Preferably in early spring.

4. SPRAY: Most important to apply a general purpose fungicide/pesticide during spring and summer months.

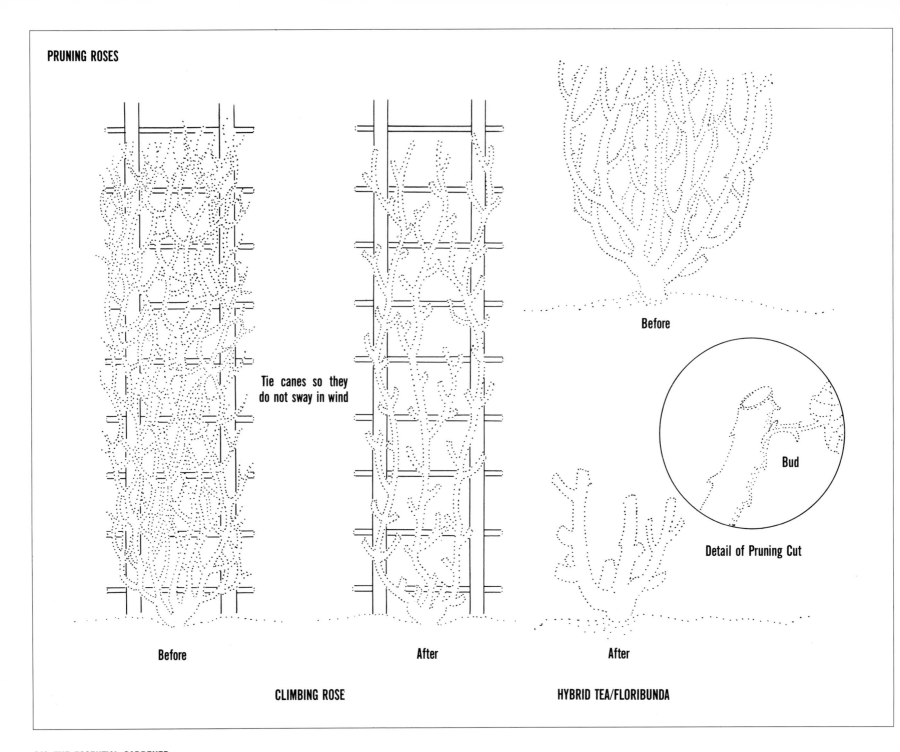

PRUNING ROSES

Tie canes so they
do not sway in wind

Before

Bud

Detail of Pruning Cut

Before

After

After

CLIMBING ROSE

HYBRID TEA/FLORIBUNDA

be non-organic, such as black plastic. Mulching not only acts as a weed barrier, it reduces moisture evaporation and stabilizes soil temperatures, cooling soil in the case of organic mulches like wood chips, heating it up in the case of black plastic. Since roses prefer a cool soil temperature, organic mulches are preferred. If black plastic is used, it should be covered with an organic mulch to break the sun's rays.

Organic mulches may need "topping up" during the growing season, since decomposition depletes the supply, which is itself a benefit since it adds valuable humus to the soil as it decomposes.

PRUNING

It is necessary to prune roses for several reasons: to stimulate the production of new canes, since the best roses tend to be produced on new canes (all desirable new canes are produced *above* the bud union); to eliminate suckers (suckers originate from *below* the bud union), since suckers rob the plant of energy; to control the plant's height or shape; and to remove dead or crowded canes.

Proper pruning keeps the center of the plant open to encourage light penetration and air movement.

It is essential after pruning to remove all canes and fallen leaves to a compost pile, or burn them since this debris can harbor diseases if left around the plants.

Examine the accompanying diagrams showing how to prune a rose for the desired effect.

The best time for pruning depends on where you live. In areas with winter freezes, pruning should begin when the spring thaw begins and before the leaf buds have started to open out. Pruning too early can weaken the plant. In areas with mild winters pruning is generally done in January or February.

The most important tool for pruning roses is a hand pruner, particularly one with a curved "anvil" blade that makes a clean cut and resists tearing tissue. These are good for pruning canes up to $1/2$-inch thickness. Next is a long-handled lopper, good for pruning canes thicker than $1/2$ inch, and also for reaching into dense growth to open up a "window" so a hand pruner can be used.

Many rose growers also like to use a pruning saw especially the kind with a scimitar or crescent-shaped blade that folds into the handle, allowing for precision cuts when removing suckers or canes that are close to the bud union. A heavy pair of gauntlet-type gloves is a necessity for pruning in order to avoid being scratched by large thorns.

When making cuts to canes it is best to make them on a slant, pointing down from the opposite side of a leaf bud in order to shed water away from the bud. A discerning eye is needed before making any drastic cuts. First take out all dead canes, then remove all undersized canes or "whips," canes less than the thickness of a pencil. Next, decide what lateral canes to keep for good shape and which to remove for good air circulation. Try not to cut into the main canes. These are the prime source of energy and new canes, and too heavy a pruning hand on these may drastically weaken the plant. When cutting healthy canes, make the cut no more than 1 inch above a leaf bud. If the cut is made too high, dieback may occur in the exposed stump, and pose a danger of it continuing to the full length of the cane. If cut too close to the leaf bud, a new lateral cane may fail to develop.

When lateral canes emerge from below the main canes, it is generally best to regard these as new main canes and preserve them. At least do not prune them back lower than the level of the original main canes.

Pruning Climbers

The foregoing pruning tips refer especially to hybrid tea roses, polyanthas, grandifloras, and floribundas. With climbing roses, the object is to preserve the length of the best canes and encourage maximum bloom production on these selected canes. Generally speaking, climbers should be pruned of all upright growth except four to six strong, healthy canes after they have gone dormant in autumn. The remaining canes should be secured fast to their support, and in areas with harsh winters, the lower regions should be wrapped in burlap sacking to resist dehydration from cold winds or glaring sun and subsequent dieback.

Left: In late April and early May, the city gardens in Charleston, South Carolina, overflow with roses; here, they are planted in gardens and over a trellis.

HOW TO HYBRIDIZE A ROSE

Roses are one of the easiest of plants to hybridize. You don't need to be a professional rose grower to create a new rose. Here, in words and pictures, is how to do it yourself.

1. First, select your parents. This is the female parent. Take a mature bud and open up the petals to reveal the center circle of pollen-bearing anthers. Using tweezers, remove the ring of anthers (the male part of the flower) so pollen from them does not pollinate the central cluster of stigmas (the female part of the flower). This part is called "the emasculation".

2. Collect pollen from another flower (the male parent) by placing the pollen-laden anthers in a jar and storing them in a refrigerator until ready to use.

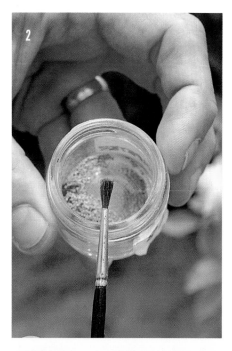

3. Using a camel's hair brush, transfer pollen from the jar to the stigmas of the female parent. This part is called "the cross".

4. Tag the crosses with the names of the parents and dates of the cross. For example, if you crossed 'Iceberg' floribunda rose (the female parent) with 'Showbiz' floribunda rose (the male parent), make a tag saying 'Iceberg (female) x Showbiz' (male).

5. As the seed pods (the hips) ripen, collect the seeds and plant into potting soil. As the seeds germinate, grow them to transplant size and transfer to the garden for evaluation.

6. As the seedlings bloom, check them to see if any are worth saving and propagating. If they are, give each hybrid a name and increase the number of plants by taking cuttings.

CHAPTER THREE

THE ENCYCLOPEDIA OF ESSENTIAL ROSES

P RESENTED IN THIS CHAPTER ARE 100 CHOICE roses, ranging from the large-flowering hybrid teas to the dainty, diminutive miniatures, including old-fashioned roses, wild species roses, and roses for special landscape effects, such as hedging roses.

Heights given are approximate and will vary according to climate and the fertility of the soil. Generally, fertile soils, especially those fertilized with animal manure, can produce much taller plants than specified here.

It is impossible in a book of this scope to include every garden-worthy variety, especially of a class like floribunda roses and hybrid teas, each of which includes more than a thousand varieties still in general commerce. Selections have been made primarily to offer a range of colors, and to provide those which have the greatest popular appeal.

The photographs are mostly close-ups in actual garden settings, in natural light on a slightly overcast day. Bright sunlight and indoor lighting can change the appearance of rose colors dramatically.

The roses in this section are divided alphabetically by major class, as follows:

HYBRID TEA ROSES

The largest-flowering of all roses, growing one big bloom on a single stem, generally held erect. The term "Tea" comes from the distinctive tealike fragrance of the flowers. They are all careful, man-made crosses, usually involving other hybrid tea varieties or else seedlings produced from these varieties. In the garden, hybrid teas are generally used for massing together in a bed or border. The flowers are valued by flower arrangers who like to pick the flowers in what is called the "mature bud" stage—halfway between a tight bud formation and an open flower.

Below is the hybrid tea rose, Heirloom.

NAME Blue Moon

RATING ARS 7.4; Gold Medal Rome, 1964.

TYPE Hybrid Tea

ORIGIN Introduced in 1964. Produced in Germany by the House of Tantau from crossing Sterling Silver and an unnamed seedling.

HEIGHT 5 feet; upright, vigorous habit. Climbing Blue Moon, a mutation of Blue Moon, grows much taller.

FRAGRANCE Pleasant, heavy fragrance.

DESCRIPTION Considered one of the very best blue roses, which are not a true blue, but more of a lavender-blue. The large, 4-inch double blooms are produced singly on strong stems. Foliage is dark green, leathery, and disease-resistant. Makes an attractive cut flower in the mature-bud stage. Seems to prefer warmer climates.

NAME Brandy

RATING ARS 7.3; AARS Award, 1982.

TYPE Hybrid Tea

ORIGIN Introduced by Armstrong Nurseries in 1982. A cross between First Prize and Dr. A. J. Verhage.

HEIGHT 4 to 5 feet; upright, bushy habit.

FRAGRANCE Mild, tealike fragrance.

DESCRIPTION Large, bronze, double, golden-apricot blooms develop from long, streamlined buds. Vigorous plants with semi-glossy, dark green leaves. Disease-resistant. Highly valued by flower arrangers for the perfection of its flowers, especially in the mature-bud stage. Often sold as "sweetheart" roses.

NAME Candy Stripe

RATING ARS 6.5.

TYPE Hybrid Tea

ORIGIN Introduced in 1963 by Conard Pyle Co. A mutation of pink Peace.

HEIGHT Up to 4 feet; bushy habit.

FRAGRANCE Pleasant, heavy fragrance.

DESCRIPTION Large, double blooms of dusky pink streaked almost white, measures up to 6 inches across. Profuse blooming. Glossy, dark green, leathery leaves. No rose breeder has yet developed a really good red-and-white bicolored rose, with uniform candy-cane striping. The public would love it, especially as a climber. Candy Stripe and a similar rose named Candystick (also known as Red 'n White Glory) come the closest in uniformity. Candystick was hybridized by J. B. Williams and released through Lakeland Nursery Sales in 1978.

NAME Chicago Peace

RATING ARS 8.3; Gold Medal Portland, 1961. Deserves to have been much more highly honored.

TYPE Hybrid Tea

ORIGIN Introduced by Conard Pyle Co. in 1962. A sport of the famous Peace Rose discovered among a planting of Peace in the rose garden at Cantigny Museum, near Chicago.

HEIGHT 5 feet; upright, bushy habit.

FRAGRANCE Slight, same as Peace Rose.

DESCRIPTION Large, double blooms are up to 5½ inches across. All the colors of Peace are accentuated by deeper coloring in Chicago Peace—a deeper yellow basic color and deeper pink highlights—contrasting magnificently against large, glossy, leathery, dark green leaves. A true connoisseur's rose considered to be a distinct improvement over the original Peace Rose largely because of its stronger color tones. Plants are vigorous, the blooms are exhibition quality, and flower arrangers adore the swirled, high-centered, mature bud stage as sweetheart roses.

NAME Christian Dior

RATING ARS 7.7; AARS Award, 1962; Gold Medal Geneva, 1958.

TYPE Hybrid Tea

ORIGIN Hybridized by the House of Meilland, in France, and introduced in the United States through Conard Pyle Co. in 1958. A cross between a seedling of Independence x Happiness and a seedling of Peace x Happiness.

HEIGHT 5 feet; bushy, erect habit.

FRAGRANCE Surprisingly slight considering it was named for the head of the House of Dior, famous for fashion and perfume.

DESCRIPTION What this rose lacks in perfume it more than makes up for in quality of its flowers, regarded as one of the best for exhibition. Blood red blooms are up to 4½ inches across, made up of fifty-five petals with a heavy, velvety texture. Glossy, leathery, dark green leaves are a perfect background, though susceptible to mildew. Long-lasting as a cut flower, this is one of America's top-selling roses, appealing to everyone's sense of what a red-red rose should look like.

NAME Chrysler Imperial

RATING ARS 8.3; AARS Award, 1953; Gold Medal Portland, 1951 and other international awards.

TYPE Hybrid Tea

ORIGIN Hybridized by Lammerts, California, and introduced through Germain's in 1952. A cross between Charlotte Armstrong and Mirandy.

HEIGHT Up to 5 feet; upright, bushy habit. May need heavy pruning to keep it compact.

FRAGRANCE Strong and spicy, reminiscent of cloves.

DESCRIPTION One of America's top-selling roses on account of its classic form and heavy substance. The large flowers measure up to 5 inches across, colored a dusky, deep red that darkens with age. The dark green leaves are prone to mildew in humid climates, but otherwise its bloom production is heavy, with flowers that win prizes at shows and are beloved by arrangers.

NAME Color Magic

RATING ARS 8.0; AARS Award, 1978.

TYPE Hybrid Tea

ORIGIN Introduced by Jackson & Perkins in 1978. A cross between Spellbinder and an unnamed seedling.

HEIGHT 5 feet; bushy, upright habit.

FRAGRANCE Slight.

DESCRIPTION An excellent cut flower and show rose. The ivory-pink, 6- to 7-inch double blooms darken to a deep rose color with age. Leaves are glossy, dark green. Vigorous, disease-resistant plants. In cold climates it may need extra winter protection by mounding soil up around the main stems, or heavy mulching after the ground has frozen.

NAME Command Performance

RATING ARS 7.2; AARS Award, 1971.

TYPE Hybrid Tea

ORIGIN Hybridized by Robert V. Lindquist of California, and introduced in 1970. A cross between Tropicana and Hawaii.

HEIGHT 5 to 6 feet; upright, slender habit kept low by pruning.

FRAGRANCE Heavy, intoxicating aroma.

DESCRIPTION Superb, semi-double, 3- to 4-inch orange-red blooms flower from early summer to fall frost, though hot, humid weather puts it under temporary stress. The dark green, leathery leaves are susceptible to mildew, which accounts for its relatively low ARS rating, but its flowers are sensational and it is outstanding for garden display. Flower arrangers, too, admire its shapely, scented blooms.

NAME Confidence

RATING ARS 8.0; Gold Medal Bagatelle, 1951.

TYPE Hybrid Tea

ORIGIN Introduced by the House of Meilland, France, through the Conard Pyle Co. A cross between Peace and Michele Meilland.

HEIGHT Up to 4 feet; upright, bushy habit.

FRAGRANCE Delightful, heavy, satisfying fragrance.

DESCRIPTION The creamy pastel tones of pink, yellow, and peach blend together exquisitely, producing a beautiful contrast to the dark green, leathery leaves. The large, individual flowers are high-centered, up to 5 inches across. Good for garden display on account of its heavy bloom production, also a good show rose and valued by flower arrangers for the high-centered flowers.

NAME Dolly Parton

RATING ARS 7.4.

TYPE Hybrid Tea

ORIGIN Hybridized by Joseph Winchel and introduced by Conard Pyle Co. in 1984. A cross between Fragrant Cloud and Oklahoma.

HEIGHT Up to 5 feet; erect, vigorous habit.

FRAGRANCE Exceptionally heavy fragrance. The rich, fruity, almost intoxicating fragrance is noticeable even before the flowers are fully open.

DESCRIPTION One of the largest flowering hybrid tea roses of all time. Like its namesake, the flamboyant, cheerful country and western singer, the Dolly Parton Rose is bright, colorful, full-formed, and beautiful—a star that commands attention. Individual flowers measure up to 6 inches across, are fully double, and are a luminous orange-red. Thick canes support the heavy, heady blooms without bending.

NAME Double Delight

RATING ARS 8.8; AARS Award, 1977; Gold Medal Rome, 1976 and other international awards.

TYPE Hybrid Tea

ORIGIN Introduced in 1977 by Armstrong Nurseries, California. A cross between Granada and Garden Party.

HEIGHT 4 feet; spreading, bushy habit. Climbing Double Delight, a sport, grows much taller.

FRAGRANCE Heavy, spicy fragrance.

DESCRIPTION The prolific, double, bicolored flowers are up to 6 inches across. They are a glorious combination of creamy white and red petals, with the creamy white ones concentrated towards the center. It is an absolutely uplifting sight to see these in the garden, and also to find they have such a heavenly fragrance! The leaves are a perfect contrast—dark green, disease-resistant, and glossy. Plants are vigorous, though somewhat tender. An incredibly beautiful color combination in a garden display, but also a favorite among flower arrangers. The climber, too, is sensational though rather a shy bloomer compared to other climbers.

NAME Electron

RATING ARS 7.7; AARS Award, 1973 and other international awards.

TYPE Hybrid Tea

ORIGIN Introduced in 1970 by the House of McGredy, New Zealand. A cross between Paddy McGredy and Prima Ballerina.

HEIGHT Up to 4 feet; bushy, erect habit.

FRAGRANCE Delightfully fragrant.

DESCRIPTION Long-lasting, glowing, rose-pink, double blooms range from 3 to 5 inches across. The ideal pink rose that photographers like to work with. Buds open slowly into spectacular flowers of classic form. Lush, dark green leaves cover the plant to the ground. Remarkably heat- and disease-resistant. Very free flowering even under unfavorable conditions. An exceptional rose for both garden display and flower arrangements.

NAME Fragrant Cloud

RATING ARS 8.0; Gold Medal from the National Rose Society, 1963 and other national awards.

TYPE Hybrid Tea

ORIGIN Introduced in 1968 by the House of Tantau, West Germany. A cross between Prima Ballerina and an unnamed seedling.

HEIGHT 5 feet; upright, branching habit.

FRAGRANCE One of the all-time best roses for heavy fragrance. Just a few blooms will fill a room with their aroma.

DESCRIPTION Long-stemmed, 5-inch, double, shapely, coral-red flowers appear singly or in clusters of two's. Dark, glossy leaves help accentuate the beauty of the blossoms. Plants are vigorous and disease-resistant. Excellent for exhibition and highly prized by flower arrangers not only for their intense tea-rose perfume, but also for its shape at all stages of development, from bud to petal drop.

NAME Garden Party

RATING ARS 8.6; AARS Award, 1960; Gold Medal Bagatelle, 1959.

TYPE Hybrid Tea

ORIGIN Introduced in 1959 by Armstrong Roses, California. A cross between Charlotte Armstrong and Peace.

HEIGHT 4 feet; upright, branching habit.

FRAGRANCE Slight.

DESCRIPTION Double, high-centered, ivory buds have a blush of pink on the petal margins. These open into 4- to 5-inch creamy, ivory blossoms on long, strong stems. Luxurious, semi-glossy, dark green leaves are a perfect background to the profuse quantities of flowers. Good winter hardiness and disease resistance, except for mildew. A top exhibition rose and a popular cut flower.

NAME Honor

RATING ARS 8.0; AARS Award, 1980 and other awards.

TYPE Hybrid Tea

ORIGIN Introduced in 1980 by Jackson & Perkins, Oregon. Parents unknown.

HEIGHT 4 feet; upright, slender habit.

FRAGRANCE Light.

DESCRIPTION Pure white, double, 5-inch blooms are held erect on strong stems. Plants are vigorous and disease-resistant, flowering continuously throughout the growing season, even during hot weather. Originally introduced as a threesome with Love (red) and Cherish (coral pink), all developed by the same breeder. Good for garden display on account of its prolific blooming; also an exquisite cut flower.

NAME King's Ransom

RATING ARS 6.7; AARS Award, 1962.

TYPE Hybrid Tea

ORIGIN Introduced in 1962 by Jackson & Perkins, Oregon. A cross between Golden Masterpiece and Lydia.

HEIGHT 3 to 4 feet; erect habit.

FRAGRANCE Moderate.

DESCRIPTION Large, golden yellow, handsome flowers up to 6 inches across, have high centers and prominent darker yellow petal veins. Lower petals have a tendency to curl under and end in a tapered point, giving some of the flowers a distinct spidery effect. Dark green, leathery, glossy leaves accentuate the brilliant colored blossoms. Plants are vigorous, producing long, strong, flowering stems excellent for cutting. Generally considered to be greatly underrated by the ARS rating system.

NAME Medallion

RATING ARS 7.6; AARS Award, 1973.

TYPE Hybrid Tea

ORIGIN Introduced in 1973 by Jackson & Perkins, Oregon. A cross between South Seas and King's Ransom.

HEIGHT 4 feet; bushy, branching habit.

FRAGRANCE Moderate, fruity aroma reminiscent of ripe apples.

DESCRIPTION Long, graceful, buff apricot buds have a hint of pink in their coloration. The dramatic flowers unfold into gigantic, double, pale apricot specimens, up to 8 inches across, borne singly on long, strong stems. Flower color tends to be pinkish in cooler climates, more apricot in warmer areas. Leaves are large and dark green. Plants are vigorous, hardy, and disease-resistant. Frequently produces its best display in autumn. Useful as a hedge or screen. A popular rose for making fresh bouquets on account of the spectacular flower size.

NAME Miss All-American Beauty

RATING ARS 8.7; AARS Award, 1968.

TYPE Hybrid Tea

ORIGIN Introduced by the House of Meilland, France, in 1967. A cross between Chrysler Imperial and Karl Herbst.

HEIGHT Up to 4 feet; bushy habit. Climbing Miss All-American Beauty grows much taller.

FRAGRANCE Moderate to strong tea-rose fragrance.

DESCRIPTION Big, bold, perfectly-shaped, hot pink flowers make this one of the best pink hybrid teas. Retains its rich, deep pink color throughout the flowering cycle, from bud formation, to the opening of the petals, to the disintegration of the flower parts. Individual flowers can measure up to 5 inches across, and are freely produced on hardy, disease-resistant plants. A popular choice for mass planting in beds. A good cut flower—one of America's top-selling roses.

NAME Mister Lincoln

RATING ARS 8.7; AARS Award, 1965.

TYPE Hybrid Tea

ORIGIN Introduced in 1963, and hybridized by Swim & Weeks, California, through the Conard Pyle Co., Pennsylvania. A cross between Chrysler Imperial and Charles Mallerin.

HEIGHT Usually over 4 feet; upright, vigorous, bushy habit.

FRAGRANCE Heavy. One of the best for filling a room with the perfume of roses.

DESCRIPTION Beautiful, long, pointed buds open to dazzling deep red blooms up to 6 inches across. Plants are free-flowering over a long period. Flowers have a velvety texture and the dark red coloring much admired by flower arrangers. The color holds true even in high temperatures. Large, dark green, leathery leaves are a perfect foil to the flowers. Top exhibition quality.

NAME Olympiad

RATING ARS 8.1; AARS Award; 1984.

TYPE Hybrid Tea

ORIGIN Hybridized by the House of McGredy, New Zealand, and introduced in 1984 by Armstrong Nurseries, California.

HEIGHT 3 to 5 feet; bushy, upright habit.

FRAGRANCE Slight.

DESCRIPTION The official rose of the 1984 Olympic Games, and the only deep red rose to win an AARS Award since Mister Lincoln. Large, exhibition quality flowers up to 5 inches across are produced in great profusion on long, strong stems. The vigorous plants are hardy, disease-resistant, and covered with medium green leaves, making Olympiad a popular choice for mass plantings.

NAME Oregold

RATING ARS 7.5; AARS Award, 1975.

TYPE Hybrid Tea

ORIGIN Hybridized by the House of Tantau, West Germany, and introduced in 1975 by Jackson & Perkins, Oregon. A cross between Piccadilly and Konigin der Rosen.

HEIGHT 4 feet; upright, bushy habit.

FRAGRANCE Light, pleasant, tea-rose fragrance.

DESCRIPTION One of the most popular yellow roses because of its extra large flowers, which are a deep golden yellow, up to 6 inches across, and borne singly on long, strong, thorny stems. Profilic repeat bloomer that doesn't fade. The dark green, glossy foliage is a perfect contrast for the bright flowers. Plants are vigorous and disease-resistant, though not reliably hardy where summers are hot and humid and winters are subjected to prolonged freezing periods. Top exhibition quality; the high-pointed flowers are also prized for cutting.

NAME Paradise

RATING ARS 8.5; AARS Award, 1979.

TYPE Hybrid Tea

ORIGIN Hybridized by the House of Weeks, California, and introduced in 1979 by Conard Pyle Co., Pennsylvania. A cross between Swarthmore and an unnamed seedling.

HEIGHT Up to 4 feet; bushy, compact habit.

FRAGRANCE Lightly scented.

DESCRIPTION When the House of Meilland, in France, introduced Princess de Monaco it caused a sensation among flower arrangers who loved its delicate ivory white petals with a blush of pink along the petal tips. Then along came Paradise, with deeper bicolor hues—silvery lavender edged in deep pink. The two make an incredible color combination in a floral arrangement. Individual flowers of Paradise measure up to 5 inches across, and hold their form and color well. Plants are vigorous, disease-resistant, and prolific bloomers.

NAME Pascali

RATING ARS 8.4; AARS Award, 1969 and other awards.

TYPE Hybrid Tea

ORIGIN Hybridized by the House of Dickson, Northern Ireland, and introduced in 1968 by Armstrong Nurseries, California.

HEIGHT 4 feet and more; bushy, upright habit.

FRAGRANCE Slight.

DESCRIPTION Strong, vigorous canes bear glistening, creamy white flowers of medium size, 3 to 4 inches across. The high-centered, double blooms are borne in profusion. An exceptional white rose since it is reasonably free of mildew and holds its color well even under adverse conditions. Good for exhibition and cutting. Makes a beautiful tree-form standard and container patio plant by pruning.

NAME Peace

RATING ARS 8.5; AARS Award, 1946 and many other international awards.

TYPE Hybrid Tea

ORIGIN Hybridized by the House of Meilland, France, and introduced in 1945 by Conard Pyle Co., Pennsylvania (see "The Story of Peace Rose," page 302). Produced by a complex cross involving Margaret McGredy Rose as one parent and a seedling produced from other crosses as the other parent.

HEIGHT Up to 5 feet; erect, bushy habit. Climbing Peace grows taller.

FRAGRANCE Slight tea-rose fragrance.

DESCRIPTION Probably the world's best-known rose and the parent of many other fine roses since its introduction, including Pink Peace and Chicago Peace. The original Peace Rose produces immense blooms up to 6 inches across, with pale yellow petals flushed with deep pink or magenta at the petal tips. Plants are vigorous, hardy, and disease-resistant, growing stiff canes covered with glossy, dark green leaves. An excellent rose to plant as a single specimen. Its beautiful blooms are exhibition quality and prized by floral arrangers from its mature bud stage to petal drop.

NAME Perfume Delight

RATING ARS 7.7; AARS Award, 1974.

TYPE Hybrid Tea

ORIGIN Hybridized by the House of Weeks, California, and introduced in 1973 by Conard Pyle Co., Pennsylvania. Complex crosses that include Chrysler Imperial and Peace Roses in its parentage.

HEIGHT Up to 4 feet; bushy, upright habit.

FRAGRANCE Heavy, spicy, old-fashioned rose scent.

DESCRIPTION Rich, deep pink, double blooms with a satinlike sheen to the petals, grow up to 5 inches across, borne erect on long, strong stems. Flowers continuously throughout the growing season, though heaviest bloom production is in spring and autumn. Large, leathery, dull, olive-green leaves enhance the flowering display. Excellent show rose. Good for cutting—especially in the mature bud stage with their long, pointed shape.

NAME Pink Peace

RATING ARS 7.7; AARS Award, 1974; Gold Medal at Geneva and Rome, 1959.

TYPE Hybrid Tea

ORIGIN Hybridized by the House of Meilland, France, and introduced in 1959 by Conard Pyle Co., Pennsylvania. A cross between Peace x Monique and Peace x Mrs. John Laing.

HEIGHT 4 feet and more; upright, bushy habit.

FRAGRANCE Intense old rose fragrance, much stronger than the original Peace Rose.

DESCRIPTION Identical to the original Peace Rose in shape and size of bloom (up to 6 inches across), but with a sensational, uniform, deep rose coloring and heavenly fragrance to match. Vigorous plants are repeat blooming, though the large, blue-green, leathery leaves are susceptible to mildew. An attractive, show quality rose that can be used alone as a lawn highlight, massed in a bed, or planted in a line to create a hedge.

NAME Pristine

RATING ARS 8.0.

TYPE Hybrid Tea

ORIGIN Hybridized by Bill Warriner and introduced by Jackson & Perkins, Oregon, in 1978. A cross between White Masterpiece and First Prize.

HEIGHT Up to 4 feet; upright, slightly spreading habit.

FRAGRANCE Slight.

DESCRIPTION Large, high-pointed ivory white flowers and the look of fine porcelain characterize this show quality rose. A touch of soft pink colors the petal edges. The hardy, disease-resistant plants produce glossy, dark, reddish green leaves. Very popular among flower arrangers who use it predominently in the mature bud stage.

NAME Red Masterpiece

RATING ARS 7.2.

TYPE Hybrid Tea

ORIGIN Hybridized by Jack Warriner and introduced in 1974 by Jackson & Perkins, Oregon. A cross between Siren x Chrysler Imperial and Carrousel x Chrysler Imperial.

HEIGHT Up to 4 feet; bushy, upright habit.

FRAGRANCE Heavy, old-fashioned rose scent.

DESCRIPTION Long, sturdy stems hold classic, dark red, double blooms measuring up to 6 inches across. Would be much higher rated by the American Rose Society if it were not so prone to mildew. Nevertheless, plants are vigorous, the flowers hold their gorgeous red coloring even under adverse conditions, and the dark, leathery, green leaves complement the flowers, which are of exhibition quality and admired by flower arrangers who especially value the mature bud stage for use as sweetheart roses.

NAME Royal Highness

RATING ARS 8.5; AARS Award, 1963 and other awards.

TYPE Hybrid Tea

ORIGIN Hybridized by Swim & Weeks, California, and introduced in 1962 by Conard Pyle Co., Pennsylvania. A cross between Virgo and Peace.

HEIGHT 3 to 4 feet; low, bushy habit.

FRAGRANCE Pleasant, heavy fragrance.

DESCRIPTION Long, pointed buds open to double, soft pink blooms up to $5\frac{1}{2}$ inches across on long, strong stems. Leathery, dark green leaves are an excellent contrast to the light coloring of the flowers. The delicate pink coloring and classic, high-centered shape of the flowers make this a popular rose to paint, to photograph, and to write poetry about. Exhibition quality; excellent for cutting. A rose with enduring popularity.

NAME Sutter' s Gold

RATING ARS 6.9; AARS Award, 1950 and other international awards.

TYPE Hybrid Tea

ORIGIN Hybridized by Herbert H. Swim, California, and introduced by Armstrong Nurseries, California, in 1950. A cross between Charlotte Armstrong and Signora.

HEIGHT Up to 4 feet; erect, spreading, compact habit. Climbing Sutter's Gold grows much taller.

FRAGRANCE Heavy, fruity scent. Winner of the James Alexander Gamble Award for rose fragrance in 1966.

DESCRIPTION Beautiful, high-centered, 4- to 5-inch double blooms are golden yellow, with a slight tinge of salmon-pink at the petal edges. Vigorous plants are disease-resistant, have dark, glossy green, leathery leaves. Prefers cool weather. In its half-open bud stage it makes a particularly fine cut flower.

NAME Tropicana

RATING ARS 8.4; AARS Award, 1963 and other awards.

TYPE Hybrid Tea

ORIGIN Hybridized by the House of Tantau, West Germany, and introduced in 1960 by Jackson & Perkins, Oregon.

HEIGHT 4 to 5 feet; upright, spreading habit. Climbing Tropicana grows much taller.

FRAGRANCE Heavy, fruity aroma.

DESCRIPTION Considered the best of the orange-red roses. The coral-orange coloring is almost fluorescent, while the double, 4- to 5-inch blooms are exquisitely shaped. Plants are vigorous though prone to mildew. Glossy, leathery, dark green leaves help to accentuate the flowers. Prolific blooming under a wide range of climatic conditions. Exhibition quality and good for cutting.

NAME White Masterpiece

RATING ARS 7.6.

TYPE Hybrid Tea

ORIGIN Hybridized by Eugene Boerner and introduced in 1969 by Jackson & Perkins, Oregon. A cross between two unnamed seedlings of unknown origin.

HEIGHT Up to 4 feet; upright, spreading habit.

FRAGRANCE Light and sweet.

DESCRIPTION Exquisite flower form and large size. The double, pure white blooms measure up to 6 inches across. Considered the best of the pure white hybrid tea roses. Blooms throughout the growing season. Vigorous plants are disease-resistant and can adapt to a wide range of climatic conditions. Glossy, dark green leaves and strong-flowering stems. A superb cut flower and top exhibition quality rose.

FLORIBUNDA ROSES

A modern group of roses more recent than the large-flowered hybrid teas, developed from crossing hybrid tea roses with old-fashioned polyantha (shrub) roses. Floribundas have smaller individual flowers than hybrid teas, but the flowers generally form a big, bold cluster. They are especially valuable for massing in beds and borders where a bold splash of color is needed. The more compact varieties are sometimes grown in tubs for decorating patios and decks. Floribundas are cherished by flower arrangers for informal arrangements and where a stunning mass of color is wanted. A single flowering stem of floribundas will make an instant bouquet.

Below is the floribunda rose, Showbiz.

NAME Accent

RATING ARS 7.0.

TYPE Floribunda

ORIGIN Hybridized by Bill Warriner and introduced in 1977 by Jackson & Perkins, Oregon. A cross between Marlena and an unnamed seedling.

HEIGHT 3 to 4 feet; bushy, compact growth.

FRAGRANCE Slightly fragrant.

DESCRIPTION Double, cardinal red flowers measure up to 2½ inches across and are grouped together in bold clusters, each of which makes an instant bouquet. Small, dark green, leathery leaves. Outstanding for mass bedding and to highlight a mixed shrub or perennial border.

NAME Betty Prior

RATING ARS 8.5; Gold Medal, National Rose Society of Great Britain, 1933.

TYPE Floribunda

ORIGIN Hybridized by Betty Prior, Great Britain, and introduced in 1935 by Jackson & Perkins, then headquartered in New York State. A cross between Kirsten Poulsen and an unnamed seedling.

HEIGHT 4 feet; bushy habit.

FRAGRANCE Very slight.

DESCRIPTION A wonderful, vigorous, free-flowering, single rose that has an appealing, old-fashioned look about it. The carmine-pink flowers have just five petals, and measure up to 3 inches across. They are borne in generous clusters of up to thirty flowers per cluster, in such profusion that they can almost completely hide the foliage. Probably the most prolific flowering floribunda ever developed. Plants are strong growers, hardy, disease-resistant, and display leathery, dark green leaves. Though flowering occurs all at one time—in early summer—Betty Prior makes a wonderful highlight used alone, but is most attractive when planted as a short hedge.

NAME Cathedral

RATING ARS 7.4; AARS Award, 1976 and other awards.

TYPE Floribunda

ORIGIN Hybridized by the House of McGredy, New Zealand, in 1975. A cross between Little Darling x Goldilocks and Irish Mist.

HEIGHT 4 feet; compact, bushy habit.

FRAGRANCE Slight.

DESCRIPTION Apricot to salmon double blooms measure up to 5 inches across, and are borne in small clusters on short stems. Almost a grandiflora in appearance. The glossy, coppery green leaves are disease-resistant, particularly to mildew. An elegant cut flower and an excellent exhibition rose.

NAME Charisma

RATING ARS 8.0; AARS Award, 1978.

TYPE Floribunda

ORIGIN Hybridized by E. G. Hill Co., Indiana, and introduced in 1977 by Conard Pyle Co., Pennsylvania. A cross between Gemini and Zorina.

HEIGHT 4 feet; bushy, erect habit.

FRAGRANCE Slight.

DESCRIPTION Oval buds open into double blooms, 2 to 2½ inches across, with scarlet petal tips. Color intensifies with age. Its glossy, leathery, green leaves, abundant, continuous flowering, and compact growth habit make this an excellent bedding rose. The generous flower clusters can be picked as an instant bouquet. The color is heightened under indoor lighting.

NAME Fashion

RATING ARS 7.7; AARS Award, 1950 and other international awards.

TYPE Floribunda

ORIGIN Hybridized by Gene Boerner and introduced in 1949 by Jackson & Perkins, at that time headquartered in New York State. A cross between Pinocchio and Crimson Glory.

HEIGHT 4 feet; vigorous, bushy habit. Climbing Fashion grows much taller.

FRAGRANCE Moderate.

DESCRIPTION Beautiful coral-peach, double blooms, measuring 3 to 3½ inches across, are borne in tight clusters. Attractive, glossy, bronze-green foliage. A profuse bloomer, Fashion is disease-resistant and holds color well even in hot weather. Outstanding for garden display and bedding. Combines well with yellow, pink, and lavender floribundas.

NAME Fire King

RATING ARS 7.5; AARS Award, 1960.

TYPE Floribunda

ORIGIN Hybridized by the House of Meilland, France, and introduced in 1958 by Conard Pyle Co., Pennsylvania. A cross between Moulin Rouge and Fashion.

HEIGHT Up to 4 feet; upright, bushy habit.

FRAGRANCE Musky fragrance.

DESCRIPTION Fiery scarlet, double flowers up to 3 inches across, are borne in clusters. Plants are vigorous, have dark green, leathery leaves. Especially good for garden display where a mass of red is desirable. Mix with white and yellow floribundas for beautiful border.

NAME First Edition

RATING ARS 8.4; AARS Award, 1977.

TYPE Floribunda

ORIGIN Hybridized by the House of Delbard, France, and introduced in 1976 by Conard Pyle Co., Pennsylvania. Complicated crosses involving Zambra, Orleans x Goldilocks, and an Orange Triumph seedling x Florada.

HEIGHT 4 feet; erect, bushy habit.

FRAGRANCE Slight.

DESCRIPTION Continuous flowering, vigorous plants are highly resistant to both mildew and black spot diseases. Flowers are semi-double, and measure 2½ inches across. They have a brilliant coral color, shading to orange. Color is more vibrant during cool weather. Glossy, leathery, olive-green foliage helps to make this an excellent rose to use as a low hedge or massed in a border. One of the all-time great floribunda roses—useful as a container plant; it is exhibition quality and good for cutting.

NAME French Lace

RATING ARS 7.8; AARS Award, 1982.

TYPE Floribunda

ORIGIN Hybridized by Bill Warriner and introduced in 1982 by Jackson & Perkins, Oregon. A cross between Dr. A. J. Verhage and Bridal Pink.

HEIGHT 4 feet; bushy, erect habit.

FRAGRANCE Slight.

DESCRIPTION Lovely, 3- to 4-inch double, ivory white blooms are delicately flushed with peach, and produce up to twelve flowers to a cluster. Vigorous plants are disease-resistant, and produce glossy, leathery, dark green foliage that helps to display the flowers to perfection. Perpetual flowering from spring until fall frost, with heaviest blooming occurring in cool weather. The exhibition quality blooms make exquisite cut flowers. Good for garden display, too. Worth growing in pots. If you have room for only one white rose, this is it.

NAME Gene Boerner

RATING ARS 8.7; AARS Award, 1969.

TYPE Floribunda

ORIGIN Hybridized by Gene Boerner and introduced in 1969 by Jackson & Perkins, Oregon. A cross between Ginger and Ma Perkins x Garnette Supreme.

HEIGHT 5 feet; bushy, vigorous, erect habit.

FRAGRANCE Slight tea scent.

DESCRIPTION Oval buds with high centers turn into true pink, double blooms, 3 to 3½ inches across, borne in clusters on long, strong stems. Glossy, green leaves are a good complement to the flowers. Disease-resistant plants grow a little taller than most floribundas but the flowers are exhibition quality and greatly admired by flower arrangers not only for their lovely color but also for their elegant shape in the mature bud stage.

NAME Iceberg

RATING ARS 8.9; Gold Medal from the National Rose Society of Great Britain, 1958 and other awards.

TYPE Floribunda

ORIGIN Hybridized by the House of Kordes, West Germany and introduced in 1958. A cross between Robin Hood and Virgo.

HEIGHT 6 to 8 feet; tall, rounded, bushy habit. Climbing Iceberg grows to 10 feet and higher.

FRAGRANCE Sweetly scented.

DESCRIPTION One of the most popular white-flowering floribundas where a torrent of blossoms is desired. An avalanche of pure white double blooms, up to 4 inches across, occurs during the cool weather of early summer and autumn, though the plant is rarely without flowers except when dormant. The huge flower clusters contrast well against the shiny green leaves. Plants are hardy, disease-resistant, and almost thornless. Iceberg needs room to spread its billowing canes, and Climbing Iceberg needs strong support for its heavy mantle of blooms. An essential component of the garden where a "wedding theme" or an "all-white" emphasis is desired. Truly, an incredible sight when in full flower.

NAME Impatient

RATING ARS 8.0; AARS Award, 1984.

TYPE Floribunda

ORIGIN Hybridized by Bill Warriner and introduced in 1984 by Jackson & Perkins, Oregon.

HEIGHT 3 to 4 feet; upright, bushy habit.

FRAGRANCE Slight.

DESCRIPTION The only purpose in life this vigorous rose seems to have is to flower its head off. Semi-double, brilliant, orange-red flowers measure 3 inches across, and are clustered together in huge trusses. Any one flower cluster makes a big bouquet. New foliage growth is mahogany, turning to dark green. Flowers heavily in early summer and again in autumn during cool weather. An outstanding name for this extremely free-flowering floribunda that is now recognized as perhaps the very best for mass bedding. Combines extremely well with yellow roses, such as Sunsprite.

NAME Ivory Fashion

RATING ARS 8.7; AARS Award, 1959.

TYPE Floribunda

ORIGIN Hybridized by Gene Boerner and introduced by Jackson & Perkins, Oregon, in 1958. A cross between Sonata and Fashion.

HEIGHT 3 feet; upright habit.

FRAGRANCE Moderate.

DESCRIPTION Ivory white, semi-double, flat blooms measure up to $4^{1}/_{2}$ inches across, and are borne in large clusters. Leathery, medium green leaves. Vigorous plants are disease-resistant and free-flowering. Long-lasting as a cut flower as only one stem will form a bouquet. Useful for massing in beds and for creating a low hedge.

NAME Marina

RATING ARS 8.0; AARS Award, 1981.

TYPE Floribunda

ORIGIN Hybridized by the House of Kordes, West Germany. A cross between Color Wonder and an unnamed seedling.

HEIGHT 4 feet; upright habit.

FRAGRANCE Lightly scented.

DESCRIPTION Lovely orange flowers are yellow at the petal center, beautifully double. Buds are long and pointed—exquisite for flower arranging. They are often sold as sweetheart roses in the mature bud stage. Foliage is glossy, dark, and leathery. Generous bloom production throughout the season, the flowers grouped in typical floribunda-type clusters.

NAME Showbiz

RATING ARS 8.1; AARS Award, 1985.

TYPE Floribunda

ORIGIN Hybridized by the House of Tantau, West Germany, in 1981. Parentage not disclosed, but obviously a cross involving floribunda roses.

HEIGHT 4 feet; bushy habit.

FRAGRANCE None.

DESCRIPTION Brilliant, medium red, double flowers grow up to 2½ inches across, and are borne in large clusters throughout the growing season, with a particularly strong flush of color in early summer and again in autumn during cool weather. An extravagant flower show on compact, tidy plants, excellent for mass bedding. Dark green, semi-glossy foliage is a perfect background to its spectacular flower clusters.

NAME Simplicity

RATING ARS 8.3; Gold Medal New Zealand, 1976.

TYPE Floribunda, sometimes listed as a shrub or hedge rose.

ORIGIN Hybridized by Bill Warriner and introduced through Jackson & Perkins, Oregon, in 1976. A cross between Iceberg and an unnamed seedling.

HEIGHT Upright, bushy habit; 4 to 5 feet high.

FRAGRANCE Slightly fragrant.

DESCRIPTION Simplicity has become one of the biggest-selling roses of all time, largely due to its value as a hedge rose and the desire among gardeners to use it for screening, edging driveways, and planting as a "living fence". Plants are highly disease-resistant and perpetual blooming, displaying masses of lovely, shell pink, semi-double, 4-inch flowers, grouped in clusters of four or five blooms. Very similar in appearance to Carefree Beauty, a perpetual-flowering hedge rose with good disease resistance, introduced by Conard Pyle Co., Pennsylvania.

NAME Sunsprite

RATING ARS 8.0; Gold Medal Baden Baden, 1972.

TYPE Floribunda

ORIGIN Hybridized by the House of Kordes, West Germany, in 1977 and introduced by Jackson & Perkins, Oregon. A cross between Spanish Sun and an unnamed seedling.

HEIGHT 3 to 4 feet; upright habit.

FRAGRANCE Moderate to strong.

DESCRIPTION Deep yellow, double, cupped blooms are borne in dense clusters, each flower up to 3 inches across. The deep green foliage is a good contrast to the flowers, which are fade-resistant and flower continuously from early summer to fall frosts, with heaviest blooming occurring during cool weather. Plants are vigorous and are good for massed bedding displays. One of the best yellow floribundas, Sunsprite makes a particularly good companion to orange, scarlet, and red floribunda roses.

NAME Vogue

RATING ARS 7.5; AARS Award, 1952 and other awards.

TYPE Floribunda

ORIGIN Hybridized by Gene Boerner and introduced by Jackson & Perkins, Oregon. A cross between Pinocchio and Crimson Glory.

HEIGHT 3 to 4 feet; upright, bushy habit.

FRAGRANCE Pleasant, medium fragrance.

DESCRIPTION Cherry-coral, high-centered, double flowers grow to 3½ to 4½ inches across and are borne in large clusters. Vigorous plants produce attractive, glossy green leaves. Mostly used for bedding because of its capacity to flower so freely in spring and autumn during cool weather. One spray of flowers can make a bouquet. Looks especially good planted in combination with a deep red floribunda, such as Fire King or Impatient.

GRANDIFLORA ROSES

This class was established in the 1950s especially for the rose variety Queen Elizabeth. Grandiflora roses have large blooms like hybrid teas, but they are borne in clusters, like floribundas. In most respects, grandiflora roses should be treated like hybrid teas and used as mass plantings in beds and borders. Since the introduction of Queen Elizabeth, a number of other garden worthy roses have been classified as grandifloras.

Below is the grandiflora rose, Love.

NAME Arizona

RATING ARS 6.2; AARS Award, 1975.

TYPE Grandiflora

ORIGIN Hybridized by the House of Weeks, California, and introduced in 1975 by Conard Pyle Co., Pennsylvania. A cross involving Golden Scepter and Golden Rapture.

HEIGHT 4 to 6 feet; tall, bushy habit.

FRAGRANCE Strong.

DESCRIPTION Double, golden bronze blooms measure up to 4 inches across, and are borne singly and in clusters of two or three on long, thorny stems. Semi-glossy, leathery, bronze-green foliage is disease-resistant. Popular in mass plantings and as a hedging rose. Excellent cut flower.

NAME Love

RATING ARS 7.5; AARS Award, 1980.

TYPE Grandiflora

ORIGIN Hybridized by Bill Warriner and introduced in 1980 by Jackson & Perkins, Oregon. A cross between Redgold and an unnamed seedling.

HEIGHT 3 to 4 feet; bushy, upright habit.

FRAGRANCE Light, spicy fragrance.

DESCRIPTION Plump, pointed buds unfold into magnificent bright red, bicolored double blooms with high centers and silvery white undersides. Flowers are up to 3 1/3 inches across with recurved petals. Seen from above the flowers look all red; from the side or below they show their bicolored effect to perfection. Several blooms may appear in a cluster, contrasting against the medium green foliage. One of the best of all roses for cutting to create stunning arrangements. The blooms are also exhibition quality.

NAME Queen Elizabeth

RATING ARS 9.1; AARS Award, 1955 and other international awards.

TYPE Grandiflora

ORIGIN Hybridized by the House of Lammerts, California, and introduced in 1954 by Germain's Roses, California. A cross between Charlotte Armstrong and Floradora.

HEIGHT 4 to 6 feet; erect, bushy habit. Climbing Queen Elizabeth is much taller, growing up to 10 feet.

FRAGRANCE Moderately fragrant.

DESCRIPTION Profuse double, high-centered blooms are up to 4 inches across. Color is carmine, fading to pale pink. Flowers are borne singly and in clusters of up to five on long, almost thornless stems. Beautiful, dark green, glossy foliage. Plants are vigorous, hardy, and disease-resistant. A classic—the first of the grandiflora roses and still the highest rated. Makes an exceptional hedge, screen, or tall background planting because it blooms continuously. Admired by flower arrangers. One of the all-time top-selling roses in North America. Exhibition quality blooms repeatedly win prizes. One of the roses rated highest by the American Rose Society.

NAME Scarlet Knight

RATING ARS 7.8; AARS Award, 1968 and other awards.

TYPE Grandiflora

ORIGIN Hybridized by the House of Meilland, France, and introduced in 1966 by Conard Pyle Co., Pennsylvania. A cross between Happiness and Independence x Sutter's Gold.

HEIGHT Over 4 feet; upright, bushy habit.

FRAGRANCE Slight.

DESCRIPTION Double, brilliant scarlet blooms measuring 4 to 5 inches across, are borne in clusters of two or three blooms. Petals have a velvety texture. Leaves are leathery, glossy, and medium green. Plants are disease-resistant, and the blooms hold their color well. Good cut flower, especially mixed with pink roses; useful for bedding.

NAME Shreveport

RATING ARS 7.4; AARS Award, 1982.

TYPE Grandiflora

ORIGIN Hybridized by the House of Kordes, West Germany, and introduced in 1981 by Armstrong Roses, California. A cross between Zorina and Uwe Seeler.

HEIGHT 4 feet and more; tall, erect habit.

FRAGRANCE Mild tea fragrance.

DESCRIPTION Orange flowers are double, up to 4 inches across, and grow in clusters. Large, dark green, prickly leaves. Named in honor of the city where the American Rose Society is headquartered. Plants are vigorous and free-flowering; a popular cut flower because of its high, pointed shape in the mature bud stage.

NAME Sundowner

RATING ARS 7.5; AARS Award, 1979.

TYPE Grandiflora

ORIGIN Hybridized by the House of McGredy, New Zealand. A cross between Bond Street and Peer Gynt.

HEIGHT Up to 5 feet; tall, erect habit.

FRAGRANCE Strong, spicy aroma.

DESCRIPTION Golden orange, double blooms, $3^{1}/_{3}$ to 4 inches across are borne singly and occasionally in clusters of two or three, on long stems. Slightly recurved petals. Large, glossy, dark green leaves with copper overtones. Plants are vigorous, hardy, and resistant to blackspot but prone to mildew. Popular for cutting.

NAME White Lightenin'

RATING ARS 7.5; AARS Award, 1981.

TYPE Grandiflora

ORIGIN Hybridized and introduced by Armstrong Nurseries, California, in 1980. A cross between Angel Face and Misty.

HEIGHT 4 feet; upright, bushy habit.

FRAGRANCE Strong, citruslike scent.

DESCRIPTION Pointed, oval buds open out to clear white, double blossoms up to 4 inches across, in clusters. The petals are occasionally tinted at the edges with a blush of pink. Plants bloom profusely, the flowers contrasting beautifully with the glossy, dark green leaves. A sensational cut flower on account of its heavenly aroma and perfection at every stage of development, from bud formation to petal drop.

CLIMBING ROSES

This tall-growing group can include mutations of hybrid teas, floribundas, and miniatures, plus old-fashioned garden roses, species roses, and other groups. They are characterized by long, whiplike canes, which can climb unaided if the hooked thorns have branches and twigs of other woody plants to latch onto. However, in most garden situations, climbers are best grown up trellises, walls, and fences, in which case they need assistance, generally in the form of string or "twist ties" that can secure the cane firmly to a support.

Below is the climbing rose, Constance Spry.

NAME American Pillar

RATING Not yet rated by the American Rose Society.

TYPE Climber

ORIGIN Hybridized by Van Fleet and introduced in 1902 through Conard Pyle Co., Pennsylvania. A cross between *R. wichuraiana* (the Memorial Rose) and *R. setigera* (the Prairie Rose).

HEIGHT 15 to 20 feet; rambling habit.

FRAGRANCE None.

DESCRIPTION Carmine-pink, single flowers measuring up to 1 inch across, are grouped in large clusters 3 to 8 inches wide. One of the best climbing roses for covering arbors. Glossy, medium green, leathery leaves. Plants are vigorous, producing tremendous quantities of flowers over a three-week period in early summer. An especially good planting of American Pillar can be seen in June at Longwood Gardens, Pennsylvania, where they create a tunnel effect, supported on metal arches.

NAME Blaze, also called Improved Paul's Scarlet.

RATING ARS 7.9.

TYPE Climber

ORIGIN Introduced in 1932 by Jackson & Perkins, at that time headquartered in New York State. A cross between Paul's Scarlet and Gruss an Teplitz.

HEIGHT Up to 10 feet. Can be kept low and bushy by pruning, but its natural tendency is to grow long, pliable canes that can be trained vertically or horizontally.

FRAGRANCE Slight.

DESCRIPTION Strong-growing canes are covered with masses of cup-shaped, semi-double, bright red flowers measuring up to 2¼ inches across in early summer. One of America's top-selling roses. A well-grown specimen can produce so many flowers that they almost rub shoulder to shoulder, covering the foliage. Plants have good disease resistance, and display blue-green leaves. Prune by thinning out weak canes and leaving four strong canes, tied to a support during the winter. Especially good for training along fence rails, chain link fences, up trellises, and over arbors.

NAME City of York

RATING Not yet rated by the American Rose Society, though it won a Gold Medal Certificate from them in 1950.

TYPE Climber

ORIGIN Hybridized by the House of Tantau, West Germany, and introduced in 1945 by Conard Pyle Co., Pennsylvania. A cross between Dorothy Perkins and Professor Gnau.

HEIGHT Up to 10 feet; billowing, climbing habit.

FRAGRANCE None.

DESCRIPTION Probably named for its resemblance to old heraldic art associated with the House of York during the War of the Roses. Officially classified as a floribunda rose, but more often used as a climber because of its long canes and capacity to cover itself with an avalanche of flowers for several weeks in late spring. White, semi-double flower clusters measure up to 3 inches across. Dark green, glossy leaves look almost black when the flowers appear. Plants are vigorous, hardy, and appear to have a cast-iron constitution. Mostly used to decorate pergolas, arbors, and trellises. Always produces a stunning display along a high stone wall; an example can be seen in the rose garden at Longwood Gardens, Pennsylvania.

NAME Constance Spry

RATING Not yet rated by the American Rose Society.

TYPE Climber, officially classified as a shrub rose.

ORIGIN Hybridized by David Austin, England, and introduced in 1961. A cross between Belle Isis and Dainty Maid.

HEIGHT 5 to 10 feet; bushy habit, usually trained to climb.

FRAGRANCE Myrrhlike fragrance.

DESCRIPTION Has the appearance of an old-fashioned rose because the large, double, pink blooms are cupped and borne in clusters, with each flower measuring up to 5 inches across. Plants are vigorous, with dark green foliage. A favorite of flower arrangers because of the informal appearance of the flowers and their enchanting aroma. A good rose to decorate old stone walls, ornate ironwork, and picket fences.

NAME Don Juan

RATING ARS 8.3.

TYPE Climber

ORIGIN Hybridized by Michelle Malandrone, Italy, and introduced in 1958 by Jackson & Perkins, Oregon. A cross between a seedling of New Dawn and Detroiter.

HEIGHT 8 feet and more; upright, rambling habit.

FRAGRANCE Heavy.

DESCRIPTION A top-notch climber because of its unusually good fragrance and heavy bloom production. Dark red, double, velvety flowers measure up to 5 inches across, borne both singly and in clusters on long stems. Vigorous plants are hardy and disease-resistant, displaying dark green, leathery leaves. Blooms continuously throughout summer, although the heaviest flush of color occurs during cool weather in early summer and early autumn. The blooms almost pass for hybrid tea roses, and are good for cutting. Mostly used for training along fence rails, up trellises, and wherever a "pillar of fire" is desirable. Not so free-flowering as Blaze, but larger flowered and a darker red, with a much heavier fragrance.

NAME Dortmund

RATING ARS 9.0.

TYPE Climber

ORIGIN Hybridized by the House of Kordes, West Germany, and introduced in 1955. A cross between *R. kordesii* and an unnamed seedling.

HEIGHT Long, trailing canes that can be trained vertically or horizontally to 10 feet.

FRAGRANCE Slight.

DESCRIPTION Pointed buds open out into strawberry red, single flowers with white centers. Each flower measures up to 4 inches across and is borne in a cluster. Starts blooming early and continues throughout the entire summer. Plants are hardy and disease-resistant, and display glossy, light green leaves. Tolerates partial shade. In the landscape it is mostly used as a single specimen since it is such a strong accent it can be overpowering. Can be kept shrub-like by pruning and allowed to trail down slopes as a slope cover, but mostly used as a climber to grow up posts, trellises, and arbors.

NAME Golden Showers

RATING ARS 6.9; AARS Award, 1957 and Gold Medal Portland, 1960.

TYPE Climber

ORIGIN Hybridized by Lammerts, California, and introduced in 1956 through Germain's Roses, California. A cross between Charlotte Armstrong and Captain Thomas.

HEIGHT 8 to 12 feet; tall, rambling habit.

FRAGRANCE Moderate.

DESCRIPTION Pointed, long buds open out into glorious daffodil-yellow, double blooms, 4 inches across. Flowers behave like grandiflora roses, borne singly and in clusters on long, almost thornless stems. The glossy, dark green, leathery leaves contrast well with the flowers. Plants are vigorous, hardy, and disease-resistant, with strong canes that need little support to keep them erect. Blooms throughout the summer. Train along fences, up trellises, and as a pillar.

NAME Joseph's Coat

RATING ARS 7.5; Gold Medal Bagatelle, 1964.

TYPE Climber

ORIGIN Hybridized by Armstrong Nurseries, California, and introduced by them in 1964. A cross between Buccaneer and Circus.

HEIGHT 6 to 8 feet; erect, climbing habit.

FRAGRANCE Slight.

DESCRIPTION Yellow and red bicolored, double blooms measure 3 inches across, and are borne in tight, generous clusters. Plants are vigorous, though somewhat tender, displaying glossy, dark green leaves. Would be much more highly rated if not so susceptible to mildew. Prolific bloomer throughout summer. A versatile rose that can be used as a shrub, pillar, or climber. Though many of the blooms are true bicolors, with red and yellow petals appearing on the same flower, some flowers may be all yellow and others all red, even on the same cluster, giving it its name, Joseph's Coat.

NAME New Dawn

RATING ARS 8.0.

TYPE Climber

ORIGIN A sport of Dr. W. Van Fleet introduced by Dreer Nursery, New York, in 1930.

HEIGHT 12 to 20 feet; tall, upright habit.

FRAGRANCE Slight.

DESCRIPTION Pink, double blooms, 3 inches across, are borne in great profusion, in small clusters on long stems. They are enhanced by glossy, dark green leaves. Continuous flowering, hardy, and disease-resistant. Popular for training over arbors, especially mixed with red, yellow, orange, and white climbers, to create a kaleidoscope of color. Suitable for cutting to make attractive, informal arrangements.

Right: Arches of the climbing rose, American Pillar, surround a sitting area at Longwood Gardens, Pennsylvania.

NAME Piñata

RATING ARS 7.0

TYPE Climber

ORIGIN Hybridized by S. Suzuki, Japan, and introduced in 1978 by Jackson & Perkins, Oregon. A cross between seedlings of unknown parents.

HEIGHT Up to 8 feet; semi-climbing habit.

FRAGRANCE Slight.

DESCRIPTION Oval-shaped buds of light yellow and red open into high-centered blooms of yellow edged in orange, measuring up to 3 inches across. Unusual color for a climber. Easy-to-train plants have semi-glossy, green leaves. Heavy flowering in cool weather. A good rose to train along low fences or up a short trellis.

NAME Red Fountain

RATING ARS 7.0.

TYPE Climber

ORIGIN Hybridized by J. B. Williams, Maryland, and introduced by Conard Pyle in 1975. A cross between Don Juan and Blaze.

HEIGHT 10 to 12 feet; upright, climbing habit.

FRAGRANCE Heavy.

DESCRIPTION Inheriting the best traits of two of the world's best climbing roses in its parentage, including the strong fragrance of Don Juan and the prolific blooming qualities of Blaze, Red Fountain is aptly named since its flowers form an almost solid pillar of cascading blooms right down to the ground. Flowers are dark red, velvety, and double; they grow up to 3 inches wide, and are grouped in clusters. Plants are vigorous and disease-resistant.

MINIATURE ROSES

Miniature roses are generally scaled-down versions of hybrid teas and floribundas, producing their diminutive flowers on dwarf plants that rarely exceed 2 feet in height. Under ideal conditions—filtered sunlight, fertile soil, and irrigation during dry spells—miniatures can be kept in flower twelve months of the year. They are most often used for edging beds and borders, also for growing in containers. Many are suitable for growing indoors as flowering house plants. Miniatures are not judged by All-America Selections, but they are rated by the American Rose Society.

Below is the miniature rose, Woman's Day.

NAME Beauty Secret

RATING ARS 9.3; Award of Excellence 1975, American Rose Society.

TYPE Miniature

ORIGIN Hybridized by Sequoia Nurseries, California, and introduced in 1964. A cross between Little Darling and Magic Wand.

HEIGHT 8 to 12 inches; moderately compact, dwarf, bushy habit.

FRAGRANCE Strong, sweet.

DESCRIPTION Pointed, cardinal red buds open to semi-double, medium red blooms. They are perfect miniatures of the Grandes Dames of roses, the hybrid teas. Glossy, leathery leaves. Prolific bloomer. Hardy. Good in semi-shade. Top cut- and exhibition flower. One of the top-rated miniatures, excellent for growing in pots and hanging baskets and as a low edging in beds and borders.

NAME Gold Coin

RATING ARS 7.5.

TYPE Miniature

ORIGIN Hybridized by Sequoia Nurseries, California, and introduced in 1967. A miniature cross between Golden Glow and Magic Wand.

HEIGHT Up to 12 inches; low-growing, dwarf, compact habit.

FRAGRANCE Moderate.

DESCRIPTION Double, 1½-inch buttercup yellow blooms resemble hybrid tea roses, but miniature. Dark, leathery leaves. Profuse bloomer. Color-fast. Vigorous grower. Good to use as an edging for low beds and borders. Also ideal for growing in pots.

NAME Green Ice

RATING ARS 7.9.

TYPE Miniature

ORIGIN Hybridized by Sequoia Nurseries, California, and introduced in 1971. A miniature cross between *Rosa wichuraiana* (the Memorial Rose) and Floradora x Jet Trail.

HEIGHT 6 to 12 inches; short, spreading, habit.

FRAGRANCE None.

DESCRIPTION Ivory white flowers in the sun turn shades of green and chartreuse in the shade. The double blossoms are 1½ inches wide and are borne in clusters. Leathery, glossy green leaves. Prolific bloomer. Disease-resistant. Easy to grow. Makes a good hanging basket and pot plant. Good cut flower and exhibition rose.

NAME Holy Toledo

RATING ARS 8.5; Award of Excellence, 1980, American Rose Society.

TYPE Miniature

ORIGIN Hybridized by Armstrong Nurseries, California, and introduced by them in 1978. A cross between Gingersnap and Magic Carrousel.

HEIGHT Up to 20 inches; bushy, dwarf habit.

FRAGRANCE Slight.

DESCRIPTION Beautiful, shapely, miniature blooms of deep apricot with a yellow-orange center. Prolific, double, 2-inch flowers. Blooms last throughout the summer. Glossy dark leaves. Vigorous grower. Sharp thorns. Excellent pot plant. Suitable for low bedding. A good plant for grafting to create a tree-form rose.

NAME Honest Abe

RATING ARS 7.3.

TYPE Miniature

ORIGIN Hybridized by Armstrong Nurseries, California, and introduced in 1978. A cross between Fairy Moss and Rubinette.

HEIGHT 10 to 12 inches; bushy, dwarf, compact habit.

FRAGRANCE Slight tea fragrance.

DESCRIPTION Mossy buds open to deep, velvety, crimson-red, double flowers, 1½ inches across, borne on short stems. Leaves are glossy. Vigorous grower. A popular miniature for growing in pots and mass bedding.

NAME Honey Moss

RATING ARS 6.2.

TYPE Miniature

ORIGIN Hybridized by Mrs. Julia A. Sudol, California, and introduced in 1977 by Armstrong Nurseries, California.

HEIGHT 10 to 12 inches; dwarf, spreading habit.

FRAGRANCE Very fragrant.

DESCRIPTION Mossy buds open to small, 1-inch, double, honey-scented white flowers with flat petals. Leaves are dark and leathery. Mostly used as a pot plant for growing indoors. One of the best white-flowering miniatures.

NAME Luvvie

RATING ARS 6.9.

TYPE Miniature

ORIGIN Hybridized by Dee Bennett for Tiny Petals Nursery, California, and introduced in 1980. A cross between Little Darling and Over the Rainbow.

HEIGHT 10 to 12 inches; dwarf, moderately compact habit.

FRAGRANCE Only slight.

DESCRIPTION Deep coral-pink, long-lasting, double blooms measure 5/8 to 1 inch across. Dark green leaves. Good cut flower. Admired by flower arrangers for its perfectly formed mature buds that are exact miniatures of hybrid tea roses. Makes an excellent container plant.

NAME Puppy Love

RATING ARS 8.0; Award of Excellence 1979, American Rose Society.

TYPE Miniature

ORIGIN Hybridized by E. W. Schwartz, Maryland, and introduced in 1978 by Nor'East Miniature Roses, Maryland. A cross between Zorina and an unnamed seedling.

HEIGHT Up to 16 inches; dwarf, compact habit.

FRAGRANCE Slight.

DESCRIPTION Double blossoms 1 1/2 to 1 3/4 inches across are borne singly on long stems. Flower color ranges from orange to pink to coral. Leaves are glossy; plants are free-blooming. Good cut- or exhibition flower. Excellent container plant.

NAME Starina

RATING ARS 9.4; has the highest rating of any miniature rose. Also a winner of more American and international awards than any other miniature, including a 1968 Gold Medal from Japan.

TYPE Miniature

ORIGIN Hybridized by the House of Meilland, France, and introduced in 1965 by Conard Pyle Co., Pennsylvania.

HEIGHT 15 to 18 inches; compact, dwarf, bushy habit. Climbing Starina, a mutation of Starina, grows to 4 feet.

FRAGRANCE None.

DESCRIPTION In the bud stage Starina looks like a perfect miniature of a hybrid tea rose, but opens out into cheerful, flat, double, orange-scarlet flowers that measure up to 2 inches across, borne singly and in clusters. The glossy, dark green leaves are a perfect contrast to the flowers that seem to glow like hot coals. Outstanding from bud formation to petal drop. Faded blooms just seem to stimulate more buds to develop and open for a non-stop flower show even through hot summers. Beautiful cut flower to make dainty arrangements. One of the best roses to consider for edging beds and borders as a low hedge. Makes a stunning pot plant—including hanging baskets.

HEDGE ROSES

This group is not officially recognized by the American Rose Society, since many types of roses can be planted to make a hedge effect, including miniatures and floribundas. In some catalogs and books, hedge roses are listed under shrub roses or polyantha roses. The varieties listed here are particularly good for creating flowering hedges because of the sheer quantity of their blooms. However, readers should look under other classifications for good hedging material, particularly among the species roses where the rugosa and multiflora roses are described.

NAME The Fairy

RATING ARS 8.7.

TYPE Polyanthus rose

ORIGIN Hybridized by Ann and J. A. Bentall and introduced in 1932 by Conard Pyle Co., Pennsylvania. A cross between Paul Crampel and Lady Gay.

HEIGHT 3 feet; bushy, spreading, cascading habit.

FRAGRANCE Moderate.

DESCRIPTION The pale pink flowers are small—just 1 inch across—but are produced in big clusters throughout the summer, with incredible flushes of bloom during the cool weather of early summer and early autumn. A vigorous plant, The Fairy has shiny, bright green leaves. Sometimes planted singly as a flowering shrub in mixed borders, but more often used as a low hedge or trained along fence rails. Also can be used as a slope cover for erosion control.

NAME Robin Hood

RATING ARS 7.1.

TYPE Shrub rose

ORIGIN Hybridized by the House of Pemberton, England, in 1927. A cross between Miss Edith Cavell and an unnamed seedling.

HEIGHT Up to 4 feet; dense, billowing, shrub-like habit.

FRAGRANCE None.

DESCRIPTION Carmine-red flowers about 1-inch across are grouped in large clusters that completely cover the plants in early summer. Extremely free-flowering, though its peak floral display is concentrated to several weeks in late spring and early summer. Arching canes create a dense, impenetrable barrier. Mostly used as a spectacular flowering hedge. Plants are hardy and disease-resistant, displaying small, medium green leaves.

NAME Sea Foam

RATING ARS 7.6; Gold Medal Rome, 1963 and other international awards.

TYPE Shrub rose

ORIGIN Hybridized by E. W. Schwartz and introduced in 1964 by Conard Pyle Co., Pennsylvania. Crosses among White Dawn and Pinocchio x White Dawn, and Pinocchio x White Dawn and Pinnocchio.

HEIGHT 3 to 4 feet; billowing, prostrate habit.

FRAGRANCE Slight.

DESCRIPTION Double white to cream flowers measure up to 2 inches across in dense clusters on arching canes. Leaves are small, shiny, dark green, and leathery. Mostly used as a low hedge, but can also be planted close to terraces and retaining walls where its flower laden canes will cascade onto steps and pathways. Can be planted on slopes for erosion control.

OLD-FASHIONED ROSES

Includes varieties of polyantha roses dating back hundreds of years that became immensely popular about 100 years ago. This popularity waned with the advent of modern hybrid roses, particularly the hybrid teas, floribundas, and grandifloras. Old-fashioned roses as a group also include roses of history, such as the Gallicas, Damask Roses, and Apothecary Roses whose ancestry is lost in antiquity. These roses generally are planted today as a curiosity and for nostaglic reasons. They are much less free-flowering than modern hybrids and too ungainly for most gardens. However, they do have their place in collections of roses and in restored historical gardens.

Below is the old-fashioned rose, Apothecary Rose.

NAME Baronne Prevost

RATING ARS 7.0.

TYPE Hybrid perpetual rose

ORIGIN Introduced in 1842. Descended from other hybrid perpetuals that include Damask, China, and Bourbon Roses.

HEIGHT 4 to 5 feet; bushy, erect habit.

FRAGRANCE Moderate.

DESCRIPTION Hybrid perpetuals are the forerunners of modern roses. They peaked in popularity at the end of the nineteenth century after more than 3,000 varieties were developed. Baronne Prevost is known for its profuse blooming, the main flush of color occurring in early summer, followed by a mild flush in autumn at the return of cool weather. The rose-pink, double flowers usually have an enormous number of petals, and are borne in clusters on erect stems. Plants are vigorous and hardy, with medium green foliage. Mostly used as a specimen shrub in old gardens where a carefree, informal appearance is desired.

NAME Cardinal de Richelieu

RATING ARS 7.1.

TYPE Old-fashioned

ORIGIN Developed from *Rosa gallica* in France by the House of Laffay and introduced in 1840. However, there is some evidence that it may have originated in Holland by Van Sian and named Rose Van Sian.

HEIGHT Up to 4 feet; bushy habit.

FRAGRANCE Slight.

DESCRIPTION One of the most popular old-fashioned garden roses on account of its deep purple coloring. The flowers are cup-sized, double, with in-curving petals, measuring up to 2 inches across, borne in clusters. Mostly grown as a curiosity in historical gardens as a single specimen flowering shrub.

NAME La Reine Victoria

RATING ARS 7.7.

TYPE A Bourbon rose

ORIGIN Introduced in 1872. Derived from crosses between China Roses and Damask Roses.

HEIGHT 6 feet and more; erect, spreading habit.

FRAGRANCE Wonderful apple scent.

DESCRIPTION Pure perfection of what everyone thinks an old-fashioned rose should be. The cupped, double pink flowers grow in generous clusters, each flower up to 3 inches across, nodding forward on slender stems. Plants bloom heavily in early summer, and sporadically through the growing season. Needs support such as a fence or trellis. Flowers are treasured by arrangers. Plants may need protection, such as a mulch of leaves applied after the ground freezes, where winters are severe. Best grown as an espalier, with the main canes splayed out like a fan.

NAME Martha Lambert

RATING Not rated by the American Rose Society.

TYPE Polyanthus rose (forerunner of floribunda rose)

ORIGIN Hybridized by P. Lambert, England, and introduced in 1906. A cross between Thalia and Mme Laurette Messimy.

HEIGHT 3 to 4 feet; bushy habit.

FRAGRANCE None.

DESCRIPTION Coppery rose, double blooms individually measure only 1½ inches across, but together form large clusters of up to twenty-two roses each. An old garden rose used mostly as a short hedge or a specimen in shrub borders.

Left: The climbing rose, American Pillar, forms a colorful arbor framed over metal arches.

NAME *Rosa centifolia*

COMMON NAME Chapeau de Napoleon

RATING ARS 8.7.

TYPE Old-fashioned

ORIGIN Discovered growing on the wall of a ruined Swiss convent. Its parentage is unknown, although the flowers are similar to Moss Roses. Introduced in 1827.

HEIGHT 5 feet; arching, shrubby habit.

FRAGRANCE Moderate.

DESCRIPTION Buds have a heavy, moss-like pubescence along the flower stalks. Perfectly shaped, double pink flowers measure up to 4 inches across, and generally bloom in clusters. Medium green leaves. Plants are hardy and disease-resistant. Mostly planted to climb up a short trellis, or along an old brick or stone wall, or fence. A popular specimen to plant in historic gardens and collections of old roses.

NAME *Rosa centifolia muscosa*

COMMON NAME Moss Rose

RATING Not yet rated by the American Rose Society.

TYPE Old-fashioned

ORIGIN Introduced in the late seventeenth century, its parents descend from *Rosa centifolia,* or Cabbage Rose.

HEIGHT Usually 5 feet, but can reach 10 feet; erect, shrubby habit.

FRAGRANCE Moderate.

DESCRIPTION Named for the minute, moss-like hairs that cover the flower stem below the bud. This growth is sticky and has a fragrance similar to balsam fir. Most varieties have large, globular white, pink, crimson, or purple flowers with in-curving petals. Moss Roses usually bloom once a year, in early summer. The canes turn from red to green with age and have long thorns. Taller varieties need support. Leaves are rough, large, dark blue-green. To encourage a bushy habit cut back canes by one third after plant has flowered. Mostly grown in herb gardens and historical gardens.

NAME *Rosa damascena*

COMMON NAME Damask Rose

RATING Not yet rated by the American Rose Society.

TYPE Old-fashioned European garden rose

ORIGIN Introduced into Europe in the sixteenth century from Damascus, in what is today, Syria. Probably derived from the Red Apothecary Rose.

HEIGHT Generally 4 to 5 feet, but can grow to 8 feet in rich soil; beautiful, arching habit.

FRAGRANCE Classic rose scent. Powerful is the only word to describe it. The variety Kazanlik is the main source in the world for the extracted oil known as "Attar of Roses". More than 32,000 flowers are processed to produce one ounce of attar.

DESCRIPTION The canes are thorny, with weak, pale green stems. The flowers are double, white, pink, or red, up to 4 inches across. They grow in clusters on long stems surrounded by gray-green leaves. It blooms once a year, in early summer, except for the Autumn Damask Rose which repeats its bloom in autumn. The scarlet hips are large and round. Plants are hardy and disease-resistant. To maintain a bushy habit, remove the twiggy growth and cut back the lateral canes to three buds.

SPECIES ROSES

These are wild roses that are useful to consider for special effects and for wild gardens. For example, the sheer profusion and height of bloom from *R. banksiae* (Lady Banks Rose) and *R. laevigata* (Cherokee Rose) endears these roses to Southern gardeners who like to grow them over arbors. The glowing red thorns of *R. sericea pteracantha* (Omei Rose) bring color to bleak winter gardens and the salt tolerance of *R. rugosa* (Rugosa Rose) allows windswept coastal gardens summertime color where few other flowering plants will survive. There are more than 200 species of roses worldwide, most have single flowers possessing five petals, but their diversity is astonishing.

Below is the species rose, *Rosa banksiae* (Lady Banks Rose).

NAME *Rosa alba*

COMMON NAME White Rose of York

RATING Not presently rated by the American Rose Society.

TYPE Species rose

ORIGIN Origin unkown. Cultivated prior to 100 A.D.

HEIGHT 6 to 8 feet; bushy habit.

FRAGRANCE Moderate.

DESCRIPTION The original plant has single, white, five-petaled flowers. Other varieties are semi-double and double, up to 3 inches across, some with petals flushed pink or yellow. The hips are conspicuous and turn scarlet in autumn. Plants are hardy and disease-resistant, with blue-green foliage. Can survive well into Canada without winter protection. Historically, *Rosa alba* is associated with the White Rose of York, made famous as a heraldic symbol during England's War of the Roses.

NAME *Rosa banksiae*

COMMON NAME Lady Banks Rose

RATING ARS 9.0.

TYPE Species rose

ORIGIN Introduced in 1796, from China.

HEIGHT To 20 feet and more; climbing habit. Can be kept bushy and shrub-like by rigorous pruning.

FRAGRANCE Slightly fragrant.

DESCRIPTION One of the few roses that will tolerate shade, though it prefers full sun. Numerous clusters of white or yellow flowers appear on slender stems, each flower no more than 1 inch across. The variety Lutea is a favorite of Southern gardeners, possessing double yellow flowers. Normalis has single white flowers, Albo Plena has double white flowers. Not reliably hardy in the northeastern United States above Washington, DC. Popular for growing over a high wall and covering romantic arbors, flowering in spring. This is the highest-rated of species roses. Plants are highly disease-resistant; evergreen leaves are small and have a medium green color; stems are almost thornless.

NAME *Rosa canina*

COMMON NAME Dog Rose; Briar Rose

RATING Not yet rated by the American Rose Society.

TYPE Species rose

ORIGIN Native to Europe; introduced into the United States prior to 1737.

HEIGHT Up to 10 feet; mounded habit.

FRAGRANCE None.

DESCRIPTION Single, white or pale pink flowers measure up to 2 inches across. They bloom throughout summer on strong, arching canes. Scarlet, conspicuous rose hips cover the plants in autumn. Leaves are medium green. Has naturalized in many parts of North America. Mostly grown as a curiosity in historical gardens. Because of the extreme hardiness of its roots, it is often used as an understock for grafting hybrids.

NAME *Rosa chinensis viridiflora*

COMMON NAME The Green Rose

RATING 7.1.

TYPE Species rose

ORIGIN China, cultivated in Europe and North America prior to 1845.

HEIGHT Usually no more than 2 feet high; weak plants have a low, bushy habit.

FRAGRANCE None.

DESCRIPTION Vivid green, double flowers, with pointed petals, barely distinguishable in color from the leaves when seen from a distance. Some color variation depending on age of plants and exposure to sunlight, some flowers tinged with bronze, others tending towards lime green. Flowers are $1\frac{1}{2}$ inches across, borne in generous clusters. Very little ornamental value. Mostly grown in pots as a novelty or curiosity.

NAME *Rosa foetida*

COMMON NAME Austrian Briar Rose

RATING Though the copper-red colored species has not been rated by the American Rose Society, the bicolor form is rated 8.1 and the yellow form is rated 7.7.

TYPE Species rose

ORIGIN Probably from Persia originally, but has been cultivated in Europe since the thirteenth century.

HEIGHT Up to 8 feet; erect, sparse habit.

FRAGRANCE Sickly sweet, disagreeable odor.

DESCRIPTION Single, cup-shaped, coppery red or bright yellow flowers bloom along slender, arching canes. There is a bicolored form considered to be the first bicolored rose, with the mutation occuring in the thirteenth century. Prone to blackspot disease, which discolors its blue-green leaves. Mostly grown against old stone walls, barn siding, and to disguise garden boundaries where the discoloration of its leaves is not too noticeable.

NAME *Rosa glauca.* Sometimes listed as *Rosa rubrifolia.*

COMMON NAME Redleaf Rose

RATING ARS 8.8.

TYPE Species rose

ORIGIN Introduced in 1830. Native habitat is dry mountain meadows at altitudes of 1,650 to 5,000 feet in central and southern Europe.

HEIGHT 5 feet; arching, shrubby habit.

FRAGRANCE None.

DESCRIPTION Small, single, pink flowers with yellow stamens are borne singly and in clusters of two or three. Flowering occurs in early summer, followed by decorative, bright red rose hips. Reddish tinged foliage is highly decorative, and when in full flower the plant is beautiful. Plants are hardy. The branches are used in floral arrangements.

NAME *Rosa* x *harisonii*

COMMON NAME Harison's Yellow Rose

RATING ARS 7.6.

TYPE Species rose

ORIGIN Probably a natural cross between *R. foetida* (Austrian Briar Rose) and *R. spinosissima* (Scotch Rose). Introduced in 1830 from the garden of Mr. G. F. Harison, located in what is now Midtown Manhattan, New York City, New York.

HEIGHT 6 feet and more; erect, rambling habit.

FRAGRANCE Strong, yeasty aroma.

DESCRIPTION Small, open, semi-double, bright yellow blossoms up to 2 inches across, appear in early summer. Delicate, gray-green foliage. Brownish rose hips. Plants are extremely hardy and loved by gardeners who want to grow a "cottage garden", where informality and bright color is desired. Mostly planted to grow up a trellis as an espalier, also against an old brick wall, and spilling over hedges.

NAME *Rosa multiflora*

COMMON NAME Multiflora Rose

RATING Not presently rated by the American Rose Society.

TYPE Species rose

ORIGIN Originally from China, introduced to the Western world in 1784. Naturalized to such an extent in the Northeastern United States that it is a pest, and local ordinances sometimes forbid its planting.

HEIGHT 10 to 16 feet; aggressive, billowing habit.

FRAGRANCE Slight.

DESCRIPTION Dense clusters of single, white flowers are borne in a cone shape on arching canes. Leaves are attractive, light green. Prefers acid soil. Grows vigorously during wet weather. Though the flowering period is brief, confined to about two weeks in early summer, its flowers are so numerous that the plants can look like mounds of snow. Mostly used as a barrier plant to mark the boundary of a property. Popular for wildlife and meadow gardens because its small orange-red hips attract songbirds, such as cardinals, in winter.

NAME *Rosa pomifera*

COMMON NAME Apple Rose

RATING ARS 6.3.

TYPE Species rose

ORIGIN Originally from Europe and Asia, introduced into cultivation in 1771.

HEIGHT 6 feet; shrub-like, mounded habit.

FRAGRANCE Slight.

DESCRIPTION Small clusters of dusky, pink, single flowers, 1 to 2 inches across, are followed in autumn by large, orange-red rose hips. The skin of the hips is thick and juicy and can be peeled like an orange and eaten raw like an apple, hence its common name. Popular during Colonial times and widely planted at Thomas Jefferson's restored gardens at his home, Monticello. Useful as a specimen in herb gardens, and to train along fence rails surrounding an orchard or vegetable garden.

NAME *Rosa rugosa*

COMMON NAME Rugosa Rose

RATING ARS 7.5.

TYPE Species rose

ORIGIN Native to Japan, introduced into Western gardens in 1845.

HEIGHT 5 to 7 feet; bushy habit.

FRAGRANCE Cinnamon scent.

DESCRIPTION Carmine or white, single or semi-double flowers measure up to $3\frac{1}{2}$ inches across. Large, round, orange-red rose hips appear in autumn. Plants bloom all summer, the blossoms contrasting beautifully with rich, shiny, dark green, textured leaves, even though the flowering display is never profuse. Plants are hardy, disease-resistant, and highly salt tolerant. Popular as a seashore plant, especially to mark a property boundary and to stabilize shifting sand. Naturalized in many coastal areas of the Northeastern United States. Useful as a barrier hedge and windbreak.

CHAPTER FOUR

PLANT SELECTION GUIDE

THE FOLLOWING LIST SHOULD BE HELPFUL IN deciding which roses to choose for a particular purpose. Not only have the top 100 roses in the encyclopedia section been classified according to color, they have been listed according to suitability as bedding plants or container culture, for growing up arbors and trellises, for grounding cover effect, hedging, fragrance, repeat bloom, and many other useful purposes.

RED ROSES

HYBRID TEA
Christian Dior
Chrysler Imperial
Command Performance
Fragrant Cloud
Mister Lincoln
Olympiad
Red Masterpiece

FLORIBUNDA
Accent
Fire King
Impatient
Meidiland Scarlet
Showbiz

GRANDIFLORA
Scarlet Knight

SPECIES ROSES
Rosa foetida (Austrian
  Briar Rose)
Rosa moyesii (Moyes Rose)
Rosa rugosa (Rugosa Rose)

CLIMBING ROSES
Blaze (also called
  Improved Paul's Scarlet)
Don Juan
Dortmund
Red Fountain

MINIATURE ROSES
Beauty Secret
Honest Abe
Starina

HEDGE ROSES
Robin Hood

OLD-FASHIONED
Damask Rose
Moss Rose
Rosa gallica
  (Apothecary Rose)

YELLOW & ORANGE ROSES

HYBRID TEA
Brandy
King's Ransom
Medallion
Oregold
Tropicana

FLORIBUNDA
Cathedral
First Edition
French Lace
Sunsprite

SPECIES ROSES
Rosa banksiae (Lady Banks Rose)
Rosa x *harisonii* (Harison's Yellow Rose)
Rosa hugonis (Father Hugo's Rose)

CLIMBING ROSES
Golden Showers

MINIATURE ROSES
Gold Coin
Holy Toledo

GRANDIFLORA
Arizona
Sundowner

BICOLOR ROSES

HYBRID TEA
Candy Stripe
Confidence
Double Delight
Peace
Pristine
Sutter's Gold

FLORIBUNDA
Charisma

SPECIES ROSES
Rosa foetida (Austrian Briar Rose)

GRANDIFLORA
Love
Shreveport

CLIMBING ROSES
American Pillar
Joseph's Coat
Piñata

MINIATURE ROSES
Magic Carousel
Puppy Love

PINK ROSES

HYBRID TEA
Candy Stripe
Color Magic
Chicago Peace
Electron
Miss All-American Beauty
Perfume Delight
Pink Peace
Royal Highness

FLORIBUNDA
Betty Prior
Fashion
Gene Boerner
Meidiland Bonica
Meidiland Ferdy
Simplicity
Vogue

GRANDIFLORA
Queen Elizabeth

SPECIES ROSES
Rosa canina (Dog Rose, Briar Rose)
Rosa laevigata (Cherokee Rose)
Rosa pomifera (Apple Rose)
Rosa rubrifolia (Redleaf Rose)

CLIMBING ROSES
Constance Spry
New Dawn
Climbing Tropicana

MINIATURE ROSES
Luvvie

HEDGE ROSES
The Fairy

OLD-FASHIONED
Baronne Prevost
Chapeau de Napoleon
Damask Rose
Moss Rose

BLUE & LAVENDER ROSES

HYBRID TEA
Blue Moon

OLD-FASHIONED
Cardinal de Richelieu
Moss Rose

WHITE ROSES

HYBRID TEA
Garden Party
Honor
Pascali
White Masterpiece

FLORIBUNDA
Iceberg
Ivory Fashion
Meidiland White

GRANDIFLORA
White Lightnin'

SPECIES ROSES
Rosa alba (White Rose of York)
Rosa canina (Dog Rose, Briar Rose)
Rosa laevigata (Cherokee Rose)
Rosa multiflora (Multiflora Rose)
Rosa omeiensis (Omei Rose)

CLIMBING ROSES
City of York

HEDGE ROSES
Sea Foam

MINIATURE ROSES
Green Ice
Honey Moss

OLD-FASHIONED
Damask Rose
Moss Rose

ROSES FOR BEDDING

HYBRID TEA
Candy Stripe
Chicago Peace
Christian Dior
Chrysler Imperial
Command Performance
Electron
Garden Party
King's Ransom
Medallion
Miss All-American Beauty
Mister Lincoln
Oregold
Pascali
Peace
Perfume Delight
Royal Highness
Sutter's Gold
Tropicana

SPECIES ROSES
Rosa x *harisonii* (Harison's
   Yellow Rose)
Rosa rugosa (Rugosa Rose)

FLORIBUNDA
Betty Prior
Fashion
Gene Boerner
Iceberg
Vogue

GRANDIFLORA
Arizona
Queen Elizabeth
Scarlet Knight

MINIATURE ROSES
Beauty Secret
Puppy Love
Starina

OLD-FASHIONED
Damask Rose
La Reine Victoria
Chapeau de Napoleon
Martha Lambert

ROSES FOR CONTAINERS

HYBRID TEA
Pascali

FLORIBUNDA
First Edition
French Lace

MINIATURE ROSES
Beauty Secret
Green Ice
Luvvie
Puppy Love

ROSES FOR GROUND COVER

CLIMBING ROSES
Dortmund
New Dawn

HEDGE ROSES
Sea Foam
The Fairy

MINIATURE ROSES
Beauty Secret
Gold Coin
Holy Toledo

ROSES FOR HEDGING

HYBRID TEA
Command Performance
Medallion
Pink Peace

FLORIBUNDA
Betty Prior
Charisma
First Edition
Gene Boerner
Iceberg
Ivory Fashion
Meidiland
Simplicity
Sunsprite
Vogue

GRANDIFLORA
Arizona
Queen Elizabeth

SPECIES ROSES
Rosa alba (White Rose of York)
Rosa x *harisonii* (Harison's Yellow Rose)
Rosa moyesii (Moyes Rose)
Rosa rugosa (Rugosa Rose)

HEDGE ROSES
The Fairy
Robin Hood
Sea Foam

MINIATURE ROSES
Gold Coin
Luvvie
Starina

OLD-FASHIONED
La Reine Victoria
Rosa gallica (Apothecary Rose)
Chapeau de Napoleon
Martha Lambert

Opposite page: The old-fashioned rose, La Reine Victoria, trained against a fence. First introduced in 1872, the delicate, pink-cupped flowers are highly fragrant.

Opposite page: The climbing rose, Tropicana, is trained to climb a pillar by having its long canes tied upright to the support by means of "twist-ties." The original Tropicana is a hybrid tea. Both forms have a delightful fruity fragrance.

ROSES FOR REPEAT BLOOMS

HYBRID TEA
Candy Stripe
Chicago Peace
Christian Dior
Confidence
Double Delight
Electron
Fragrant Cloud
Garden Party
Honor
King's Ransom
Medallion
Meidiland
Miss All-American Beauty
Mister Lincoln
Olympiad
Oregold
Paradise
Pascali
Peace
Perfume Delight
Pink Peace
Red Masterpiece
Simplicity
Sutter's Gold
Tropicana
White Masterpiece

FLORIBUNDA
Betty Prior
Charisma
Fashion
Fire King
First Edition
French Lace
Gene Boerner
Iceberg
Impatient
Sunsprite

GRANDIFLORA
Love
Queen Elizabeth
Scarlet Knight
Sundowner
White Lightenin'

CLIMBING
Blaze
City of York
Dortmund
Don Juan
The Fairy
Golden Showers
Joseph's Coat
New Dawn
Piñata
Red Fountain

MINIATURE
Beauty Scarlet
Green Ice
Holy Toledo
Puppy Love
Starina

HEDGE
Robin Hood

OLD-FASHIONED
Baronne Prevost
La Reine Victoria
Moss Rose

SPECIES
Rosa alba (White Rose of York)
Rosa rugosa (Rugosa Rose)

ROSES FOR ARBORS & TRELLISES

CLIMBING
American Pillar
Blaze
City of York
Don Juan
Dortmund
Fragrant Cloud
Golden Showers
Joseph's Coat
New Dawn
Piñata
Red Fountain

HEDGE
Sea Foam

OLD-FASHIONED
Damask Rose

SPECIES
Rosa foetida (Austrian Briar Rose)
Rosa laevigata (Cherokee Rose)
Rosa moyesii (Moyes Rose)

ROSES FOR FRAGRANCE

HYBRID TEA
Blue Moon
Chrysler Imperial
Command Performance
Confidence
Double Delight
Electron
Fragrant Cloud
Miss All-American Beauty
Mister Lincoln
Perfume Delight
Pink Peace
Red Masterpeice
Royal Highness
Sutter's Gold
Tropicana

FLORIBUNDA
Betty Prior
Cathedral
Fashion
Iceberg
Ivory Fashion
Sunsprite

GRANDIFLORA
Arizona
Queen Elizabeth
Sundowner
White Lightenin'

CLIMBING
City of York
The Fairy
Golden Showers
Red Fountain

MINIATURE
Beauty Secret
Magic Carousel

OLD-FASHIONED
Chapeau de Napoleon
Baronne Prevost
Damask Rose
La Reine Victoria
Moss
Rosa gallica (Apothecary Rose)

SPECIES
Rosa alba (White Rose of York)
Rosa foetida (Austrian
   Briar Rose)
Rosa x *harisonii* (Harison's
   Yellow Rose)
Rosa laevigata (Cherokee Rose)
Rosa rugosa (Rugosa Rose)

ROSES FOR SEASHORE

CLIMBING
American Pillar

SPECIES
Rosa rugosa (Rugosa Rose)

1940
Dicksons Red
Flash
The Chief
World's Fair

1941
Apricot Queen
California
Charlotte Armstrong

1942
Heart's Desire

1943
Grande Duchesse Charlotte
Mary Margaret McBride

1944
Fred Edmunds
Katherine T. Marshall
Lowell Thomas
Mme. Chiang Kai-shek
Mme. Marie Curie

1945
Floradora
Horace McFarland
Mirandy

1946
Peace

1947
Rubaiyat

1948
Diamond Jubilee
High Noon
Nocturne
Pinkie
San Fernando
Taffeta

1949
Forty-niner
Tallyho

1950
Capistrano
Fashion
Sutter's Gold
Mission Bells

1951
No Selection

1952
Fred Howard
Helen Traubel
Vogue

1953
Chrysler Imperial
Ma Perkins

1954
Lilibet
Mojave

1955
Jiminy Cricket
Queen Elizabeth
Tiffany

1956
Circus

1957
Golden Showers
White Bouquet

1958
Fusilier
Gold Cup
White Knight

1959
Ivory Fashion
Starfire

1960
Fire King
Garden Party
Sarabande

1961
Duet
Pink Parfait

1962
Christian Dior
Golden Slippers
John S. Armstrong
King's Ransom

1963
Royal Highness
Tropicana

1964
Granada
Saratoga

1965
Camelot
Mister Lincoln

1966
American Heritage
Apricot Nectar
Matterhorn

1967
Bewitched
Gay Princess
Lucky Lady
Roman Holiday

1968
Europeana
Miss All-American Beauty
Scarlet Knight

1969
Angel Face
Comanche
Gene Boerner
Pascali

1970
First Prize

1971
Aquarius
Command Performance
Redgold

1972
Apollo
Portrait

1973
Electron
Gypsy
Medallion

1974
Bahia
Bon Bon
Perfume Delight

1975
Arizona
Oregold
Rose Parade

1976
America
Cathedral
Seashell
Yankee Doodle

1977
Double Delight
First Edition
Prominent

1978
Charisma
Color Magic

1979
Friendship
Paradise
Sundowner

1980
Love
Honor
Cherish

1981
Bing Crosby
Marina
White Lightenin'

1982
Brandy
French Lace
Mon Cheri
Shreveport

1983
Sun Flare
Sweet Surrender

1984
Impatient
Intrigue
Olympiad

1985
Showbiz

1986
Broadway
Touch of Class
Voo Doo

1987
Bonica
New Year
Sheer Bliss

1988
Amber Queen
Mikado
Prima Donna

1989
Debut
Tournament of Roses
Class Act
New Beginning

Opposite page: Perfect shape is seen in this close-up of a specimen of Christian Dior, a hybrid tea rose.

ESSENTIAL
TREES
AND SHRUBS

INTRODUCTION

COLORFUL, LONG-LIVED PLANTS FOR LITTLE EFFORT

CONTRARY TO POPULAR BELIEF, THE OLDEST life forms on earth are not trees—not the giant redwoods of coastal California or the ancient bristlecone pine of the Rocky Mountains. The appearance of certain shrubs preceded these trees by at least 3,000 years. In California's Sonora Desert, a creosote bush nicknamed 'King Clone' is believed to be over 10,000 years old; in Western Pennsylvania, a box huckleberry is believed to be 13,000 years old. Over the centuries, this plant has established itself across many acres in an ever-spreading clump that began from a seedling.

Shrubs, known as "woody plants", are a large, long-lived group of plants that includes trees, shrubs, and subshrubs. By definition, a shrub is any woody plant that has multiple stems rising from the ground. True shrubs differ from trees in that they have multi-stems or multiple trunks emerging from the soil, and generally remain below 15 feet in height. Trees tend to grow a single, main trunk, and are capable of growing to more than 15 feet. Subshrubs are a group of plants normally considered to be perennials that develop wood parts with age. Examples of subshrubs include candytuft, lavender, and rosemary.

These broad definitions are not clear-cut since there are too many exceptions to establish any rules. For example, if cut to the ground, many trees will sprout multiple stems around the damaged trunk, becoming shrublike. Similarly, even true shrubs and subshrubs, given ideal conditions, can be trained to a single stem and can grow to 15 feet.

CLASSIFYING TREES AND SHRUBS

The three classifications of woody plants—trees, shrubs, and subshrubs—serve different purposes in the landscape.

Shrubs provide decoration at eye level. If these have beautiful flowers or attractive berries they are generally referred to as flowering shrubs, and are used like other flowering plants to provide eye-catching color. Subshrubs are low-growing plants that provide interest at ground level. They are used most commonly in perennial borders. Apart from their flowering effect, shrubs make good hedges, carefree ground covers, and wall-covering vines. Even if they have inconspicuous flowers, decorative leaves often make shrubs worth planting

as camouflage for monotonous expanses of wall or fencing. Some shrubs can take the form of trees, while some trees can take the form of a shrub.

Besides planting trees and shrubs for the shape, texture, and color of their leaves, they can be either deciduous or evergreen. Deciduous trees and shrubs drop their leaves in autumn, sometimes preceded by dramatic fall coloring. Evergreens, which retain their leaves throughout the year, are further classified as narrowleaf evergreens, such as pines, or broadleaf evergreens, such as rhododendrons and hollies.

The fall color of many deciduous trees and shrubs is often dramatic enough to outshine the beauty of flowers. Burning bush *(Euonymous alata)* and many Japanese maples *(Acer japonicum)* have scarlet leaves in fall as red as many azalea flowers. These and other woody plants also have interesting wintry silhouettes, especially when seen against a background of white.

Evergreens can help to form the framework of a landscape design. Plants such as boxwood and yew can form corridors to guide the eye from one space to another; they can form boundaries, outline garden spaces, and define planting beds for flowering plants. And, their growth can be pruned into vertical accents such as cones, spheres, and mounds.

Many woody plants—whether evergreen or deciduous—can be trained to create special decorative effects, such as bonsai, the art of pruning and restricting the roots of shrubs to create miniature forms; espalier, the art of training shrubs to form patterns against a wall or fence; and topiary, the art of pruning shrubs into shapes that have animal and human forms.

Woody plants suitable as hedges can be planted to make screens for privacy, as well as for parterres, low hedges forming patterns and planting spaces; mazes, intricate passages that challenge people to find their way into the middle and out again; and as windbreaks to cushion the force of wind and salt spray.

Considering the years of satisfaction trees and shrubs can give, it is worth taking the time to choose the right plants for your needs, and to understand their needs, including what type of soil they grow best in, whether or not they need sun or can bear wind or salt sprays, and how and when to prune.

Opposite page: Billowing forms of evergreen azalea and rhododendron overhung with spreading branches of deciduous dogwood combine to create a spectacular winter scene.

Left: Here yew, pruned to a cone shape, contrasts with myrtle growing in a planter box and pruned to a "pompon" shape.

CHAPTER ONE

CARING FOR TREES AND SHRUBS

BEFORE PLANTING

THERE ARE SOME FUNDAMENTAL STEPS THAT need to be considered even before you place a tree or a shrub in the ground.

Where and What to Buy

The most convenient place to buy woody plants is from a garden center or nursery located close to your home. On display they are likely to have plants offered in different ways at different price levels. For example, most woody plants are sold "bare-root." Deciduous and evergreen woody plants are dug from the field when dormant. The soil is washed from them, and the roots are wrapped in moist sphagnum moss and enclosed in plastic. Bare-root plants should be purchased and planted in the fall or spring while the plants are still dormant. Prices for bare-root stock tend to be the most economical.

At the next price level are woody plants sold in containers, which can be made of plastic, wood, metal, or fiber. The plants can be slipped out of their containers, usually a one gallon capacity, and planted with large root balls. There is minimal root disturbance and the transplant success rate is high.

At the next price level are trees and shrubs that are "balled and burlapped." These are dug from the fields by a special machine that picks up a large, round root mass and wraps it in burlap. This technique enables extra large specimens and evergreens to survive transplanting. Prices for balled and burlapped plants are higher than for bare-root plants.

Mail-order nurseries provide another source for trees and shrubs. They tend to offer a far wider selection than do garden centers, including rare plants. Also, some catalogs specialize in a particular family of shrubs, such as roses and rhododendrons. A list of mail-order houses can be found in the back of this book, page 679.

Almost all mail-order woody plants are sent bare-root. It is important to open your mail-order shipment immediately and examine the roots and top growth for signs of damage. If there are any broken roots or stems of a superficial nature, just prune them away before planting. However, if the main support branches are broken, if a tap root is snapped in two, or if there are signs of rodent damage—where the bark at the soil line has been nibbled away in complete circle—the shipment should be returned for replacement. For information on planting a bare-root woody plants, see page 397.

Choosing a Site

You must decide whether your planting site is to be in the sun or shade, and whether the drainage of your site is good or poor. It is hard to provide shade for a sunny site, but a shady site can often be improved by simply removing overhanging branches from trees. The choice of trees and shrubs available for planting in the sun is far greater than the choice available for shade.

Poor drainage will severely restrict your choice of plants. However, a poorly drained site can be easily improved by "berming"—mounding top soil over the poorly drained area—or by building a raised bed of landscape ties with top soil dumped in the middle.

If high winds or salt spray are a problem, a shelter of wind-resistant or salt-tolerant windbreak plants can be established on the side exposed to prevailing winds. To establish a windbreak it may be necessary to protect the young plants until they are well-established (a year or two) by erecting a temporary screen using hay bales to form a wall, or rolls of burlap to form a fence.

Soil Conditions

Though many trees and shrubs will survive in poor, infertile soil, best results are achieved by determining the nature of your soil and how to improve it. Poor soil can be classified as sandy or clay. Sandy soil has little moisture or nutrient-holding capacity. Though plant roots can penetrate sand freely, they starve from lack of moisture and nutrients. Soil with a lot of clay is heavy, sticky, and cold, creating an impenetrable barrier for plant roots. The "happy medium" is loam soil. It is not too light or too heavy, it is porous enough to allow excess water to drain away, yet holds moisture and nutrients for feeding roots continuously. The remedy for sandy and clay soil is the addition of humus. By adding humus (composed of decomposed organic matter), sand becomes moisture- and nutrient-retentive and clay becomes aerated with fibers and particles allowing roots freedom to roam.

Soils also can be acidic or alkaline in their chemical balance. The amount of acidity or alkalinity is measured by the pH scale. A rating of seven is neutral—anything above seven is alkaline and below is acidic. Some plants, such as azaleas and hollies, demand a low pH content (acid). Acidity can be reduced by adding lime; alkalinity can be reduced by adding sulphur peat or leaf mold to soil.

Acidic soils generally persist in forested areas with high rainfall. Alkaline soils prevail in areas with low rainfall, such as desert regions. A soil test conducted through a soil laboratory (check your county extension service for the address of the nearest extention) will tell you the nature of your soil and also recommend specific nutrients and soil conditioners for improvement.

PLANTING

Specific planting instructions for trees and shrubs depend mostly on the type of transplant purchased: bare-root, containered, or balled and burlapped.

Bare-Root If the soil is in good condition, composed of fairly loose loam, simply dig a hole deep enough to accommodate the deepest roots. Center the plant in the hole and put the soil back, making sure the roots are splayed out as much as possible, and there is good soil contact. Water and tamp down the soil with your foot, adding more soil to level off any major settling. A slight depression around the rim to help catch rainwater is advisable. Cover the base of the plant with a mulch of wood chips or shredded leaves. Fertilize by sprinkling granular fertilizer over the surrounding soil surface, and again each year in spring.

Containered Plants Try to remove containered plants with as little root disturbance as possible. Fiber containers can be torn open to help slide the root ball out. With tough plastic or metal containers you may need to slide a long-bladed knife around the rim first to loosen the root ball. In good loam soil simply dig a hole slightly larger in size than the root ball and ensure a snug fit by filling the edges with excavated soil.

Leave a slight depression to catch rainwater and place a layer of wood chips or shredded leaves around the plant. Fertilizing can be done by lightly sprinkling a general purpose fertilizer over the soil surface.

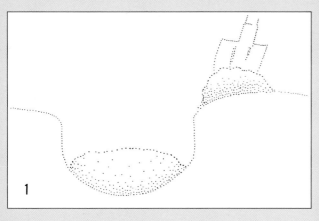

1

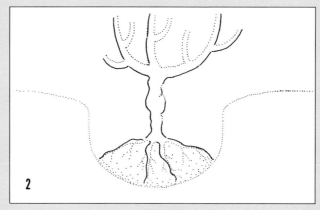

2

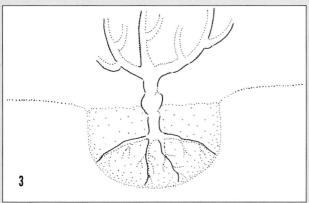

3

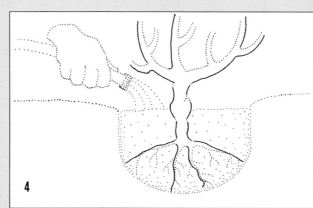

4

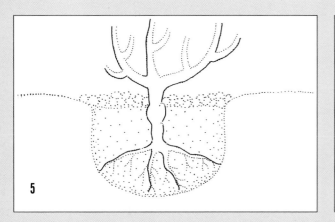

5

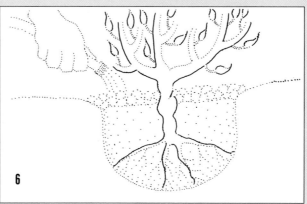

6

PLANTING A BARE-ROOT TREE OR SHRUB

1. Dig a hole deep enough and wide enough to accommodate the roots. Mound the bottom with top soil.

2. Position the shrub in the center of the hole so the roots are splayed out and around the mound.

3. Fill the hole to within 1 inch of the rim.

4. Water and tamp the soil down. Add more soil to compensate for any settling.

5. Lay organic mulch over the hole.

6. Water whenever the soil feels dry.

HOW TO PLANT A TREE OR SHRUB

For the purpose of showing the proper planting of a tree or shrub, we have chosen a rhododendron that has been balled in burlap sacking. (For planting a bare-root tree or shrub, see diagram on page 397.)

1. At the garden center, examine your proposed purchase for healthy green leaves and any signs of bark damage by mice; also check for insect infestations, such as scale and spider mites.

2. Rest the plant on the ground. The string holding the burlap in place must be removed prior to planting.

3. Dig a hole to the depth of the root ball and slightly wider than its diameter. This soil was enriched with compost and peat moss to make it sufficiently moist and acid for a rhododendron.

4. Gently loosen the burlap and use it to maneuver the root ball into the hole. The burlap does not need to be removed completely.

5. Fill the hole and apply a layer of loose organic material, such as a mulch, around the base of the plant to deter weeds and conserve moisture. Pine needles are the mulch material used here.

6. Water thoroughly—at least once a week in the absence of natural rainfall.

7. The newly planted rhododendron looks comfortable in its new home.

8. Within ten days of planting, the rhododendron (variety Vulcan) is flowering profusely.

Balled & Burlapped

These can be extremely heavy and awkward to move because of the size of the root ball. Use a sturdy wheelbarrow to move heavy specimens to the planting site, and enlist help in lifting it into the hole, which should be slightly wider and slightly deeper than the root ball. Loosen any string or wire, remove nails, and unwrap the top of the burlap from around the stems. Do not remove the burlap completely, otherwise the root ball is likely to fall apart and leave you with little more than a bare-root plant. Once the burlap sack is moistened with water and in contact with the soil it soon decomposes. Leave a slight depression around the plant to help catch rainwater, and mulch with wood chips or shredded leaves. If any fertilizer is needed, just sprinkle it lightly in granular form over the soil surface all around the plant extending to slightly beyond the drip line.

AFTER CARE

The following instructions apply after the shrub is comfortably seated in its planting hole.

Staking   Unless shrubs are unusually tall they generally do not need staking to keep them upright. However, if staking is needed, use wire or strong string like guy ropes. Be sure to cushion the part of the plant that comes into contact with the string with pieces of folded cloth.

Watering   The biggest cause of failure with new shrubs is dehydration, either because the plants were not sufficiently watered to begin with, or because they received insufficient amounts of water after they were planted. After planting, water thoroughly. In the event of a week without natural rainfall, try to give newly planted shrubs at least three gallons of water per plant per week.

Winter Protection   Newly planted shrubs—especially those planted in autumn—are susceptible to winter-kill from cold winds that dehydrate bare limbs. In exposed locations, shield valuable new plantings with a burlap screen; mulch plants after the ground has frozen, and keep snow off limbs before the snow has a chance to freeze. Hardy shrubs have

Opposite page: This Japanese cut-leaf maple shows its ornamental value even in winter, as light snowfall accentuates its billowing form and cascading tracery of branches.

Left: A balance between deciduous trees and evergreens in this woodland garden creates a spectacular composition in the fall.

roots that can survive freezing by going dormant, but damage can occur when an early thaw breaks dormancy, followed by a freeze that kills the vulnerable roots. A mulch applied after the ground freezes helps keep the ground frozen until a sustained thaw sets in. Where shrubs are positioned under the eaves of a house—as in foundation plantings—they should be covered with wooden structures that can break the fall of snow from the roof pitch.

Fertilizing   Shrubs benefit from an annual application of fertilizer, particularly a well-balanced fertilizer that provides adequate amounts of nitrogen (to stimulate leafy growth), phosphorus (to stimulate flowering and root development), and potassium (for disease resistance). You can tell whether a fertilizer has a balance of these nutrients by the set of three numbers printed on the label, such as 10-10-10 or 20-20-

Right, top: High hedges demand special pruning techniques to keep them shapely. Here, an electric hedge trimmer is used for speed. A stepladder laid between two 'A-frame' ladders has a plank laid over the rungs to make a "cat-walk," providing a firm walking surface.

Right, bottom: Severe pruning of evergreen shrubs, such as junipers, makes them bushy.

20, meaning each has equal percentages of the three major nutrients, known as NPK for nitrogen, phosphorus, and potassium, in that order.

A light surface feeding of a granular fertilizer at the time you plant and then a regular surface feeding each spring at recommended rates should keep shrubs vigorous and healthy. Make sure that the surface area covered extends slightly beyond the drip line (the area where rain would drip from the leaves around the periphery of the plant) to encourage roots to reach out beyond the growing perimeter. Do not put fertilizer directly into planting holes because the roots may be burned from an overdose. It is not necessary to drill holes deep into the soil for shrub fertilizers to work. Tests have proven that simple surface feeding (except on slopes) is more effective since most feeder roots are close to the soil surface.

Pruning

Once a tree or shrub is established, several ways of pruning should be considered to keep it healthy and attractive. Following are different kinds of pruning techniques and the tools needed:

Shearing This is done to shape a plant to a particular contour—a box shape in the case of a hedge, but also a mound, globe, cone, or column, and even more fanciful shapes like topiary animals. Shearing cuts encourage bushy growth where the cut is made. Shearing is done primarily with a pair of hand pruning shears or by an electric hedge trimmer, which is considerably faster.

Thinning This consists of selectively removing excess branches—especially dead branches—to open up the plant for better air circulation. Thinning cuts should be made at ground level; they do not make the plant bushier. Thinning can be done with scimitar hand pruners for branches up to 1/4-inch thickness, or with a pruning saw for easily reached thicker branches. To cut thick branches that are difficult to reach, a long handled "lopper" works well. Thinning is especially effective for encouraging generous berry clusters and fruit yields.

Rejuvenation (or "Take it to the ground" pruning) Many old shrubs need drastic pruning. When plants like for-

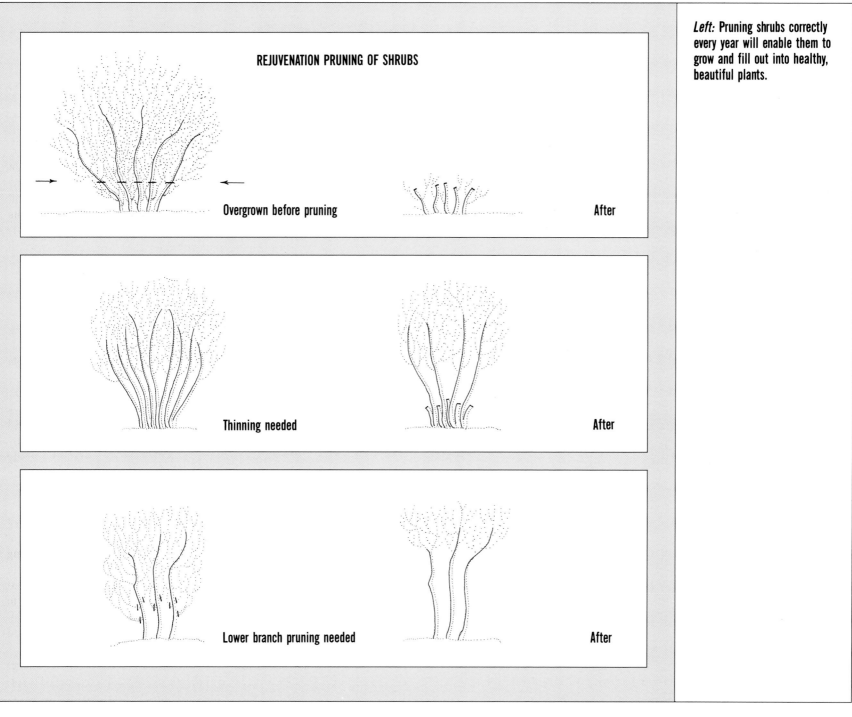

REJUVENATION PRUNING OF SHRUBS

Overgrown before pruning

After

Thinning needed

After

Lower branch pruning needed

After

Left: Pruning shrubs correctly every year will enable them to grow and fill out into healthy, beautiful plants.

Right: There are many common shrub shapes that can be achieved by pruning. Some of the most popular are illustrated here.

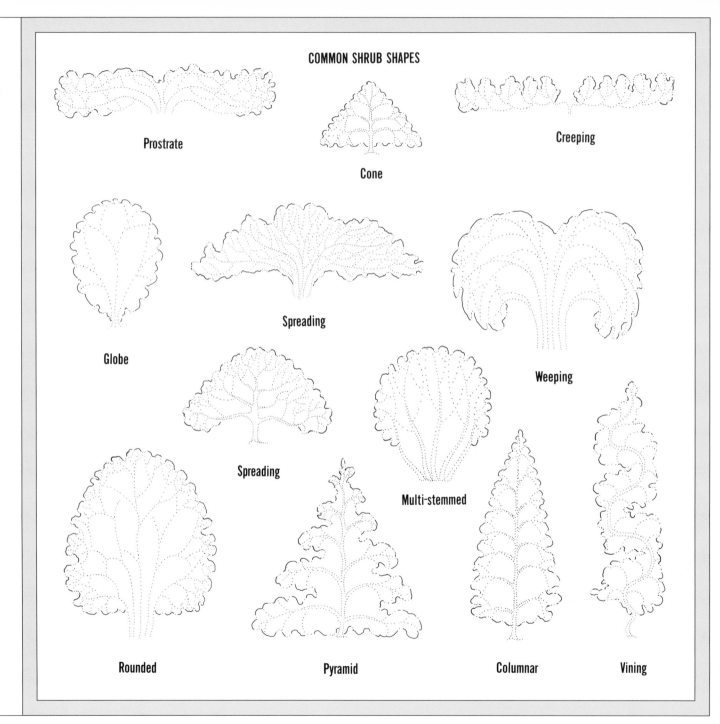

COMMON SHRUB SHAPES

Prostrate

Cone

Creeping

Globe

Spreading

Weeping

Spreading

Multi-stemmed

Rounded

Pyramid

Columnar

Vining

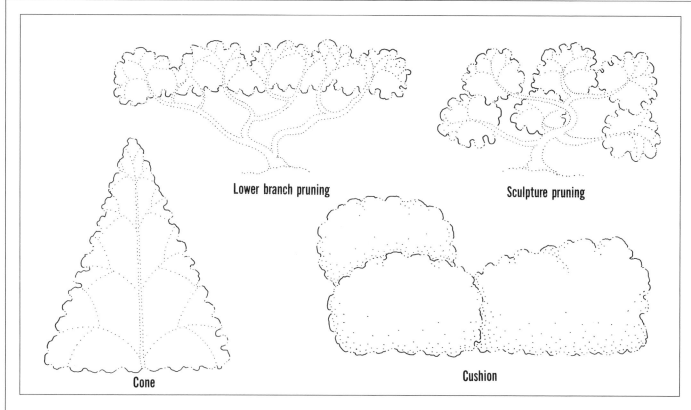

Lower branch pruning

Sculpture pruning

Cone

Cushion

sythia, lilac, and viburnum become overgrown and untidy, they can be cut to within 6 inches of the ground either with a lopper or a swipe of the chain saw. This encourages the plant to send up a host of new shoots that can be shaped as desired.

Weed Control Though some shrubs and most trees will grow through turf, it is always best to keep the area encompassing the drip line clear of sod or competition from weeds. A layer of organic material placed around the plant will help suffocate weeds. The very best mulch materials are shredded leaves or shredded bark. Bark chips and wood chips are not as desirable since they are known to attract fungus that can attack the roots of shrubs.

Shrub Shapes Shrubs are extremely versatile in their growth habit, allowing for many useful functions in the landscape. Above are some basic shapes, along with some design ideas, from low-spreading shrubs suitable as ground covers,

to tall, rambling vines for covering walls and arbors.

Prostrate. Example: *Juniperus horizontalis*, 'Blue Rug Juniper.' Excellent for ground cover and erosion control.

Low-spreading. Example: *Skimmia japonica*, 'Skimmia.' Excellent in rock gardens and low beds.

Weeping. Example: *Spiraea* species, 'Spiraea.' Excellent lawn accent.

Pyramid. Example: *Picea pungens nana*, 'Dwarf Blue Spruce.' Excellent lawn accent.

Columnar. Example: *Taxus cuspidata*, 'Upright Yew.' Excellent for vertical accents and tall hedges.

Globular. Example: *Buxus sempervirens*, 'Boxwood.' Excellent for edging walkways, and for hedges.

Vine. Example: *Wisteria floribunda*, 'Wisteria.' Good to cover walls and arbors.

Mounded. Example: *Hydrangea macrophylla*, 'Hydrangea.' Good lawn accent, foundation highlight, and hedge.

Right, top: The Exbury azalea, 'Golden Sunset', planted along a stream bank.

Right, bottom: The tall, cone-shaped form of an Alberta spruce adds a vertical accent to this shrub border.

STARTING TREES AND SHRUBS FROM SEEDS

1. Materials needed are: peat or plastic trays and pots, packets of seed, and planter mix of equal parts peat, sand, and vermiculite, or purchase a brand-name starter mix.

2. Press moist planter mix into container. The mixture should be sufficiently moist so that when squeezed tightly a few water drops will appear.

3. Sow seed evenly on the surface. The seed packet will specify the recommended depth depending on size.

4. Cover large seeds with a layer of planting mix. Leave fine seeds uncovered, since they generally need light to germinate.

PROPAGATION

Although it's a lot easier to buy ready-grown plants from a nursery or mail-order house, trees and shrubs can be grown inexpensively using a variety of propagating techniques. The process may sometimes be tedious, but the sense of accomplishment gained by raising a beautiful specimen from seed or cuttings can be immensely uplifting. The following techniques are within the capability of most gardeners.

Seeds Though some trees and shrubs are sterile through hybridizing, and do not set viable seed, the vast majority produce large quantities of seed, varying in size from grains of pepper to bean-size. Some are easy to germinate, others have special needs. One interesting aspect involving tree or shrub seeds is that you can never be certain of growing a plant identical to the one from which the seed came. The seedlings can be highly variable in both color and habit. (To be assured of an identical match, you should take cuttings from woody plants.) Some good woody plants to experiment with starting from seed include the hardy-orange *(Poncirus trifoliata)*, the trumpet-vine *(Campsis radicans)*, and camellias *(Camellia japonica)*. These plants are relatively easy to germinate using fresh seeds.

Start the seeds on a tray of flats filled with potting soil composed of equal parts of sand and peat moss. Cover the seeds with about 1 inch of potting soil (smaller seeds need less coverage).

Cover the tray with glass to establish a humid environment, maintaining a soil temperature of about 70°F (this can be done with a heating cable). Once seeds germinate remove the glass cover. Keep the soil moist and in bright light, but out of direct sunlight. A cold frame in a partially shaded area is an ideal place for raising seedlings. Transplant seedlings to individual containers once they are large enough to handle.

Cuttings Many trees and shrubs are easy to root from cuttings. In fact, some will often sprout roots simply by being inserted in water: forsythia and pussy willow, for example. Other woody plants, like roses, lilacs, and honeysuckle, will root quite quickly (within several weeks) in a moist potting soil. Slow-growing plants, like hollies and magnolias, generally take a long time to form roots—up to three months. Some

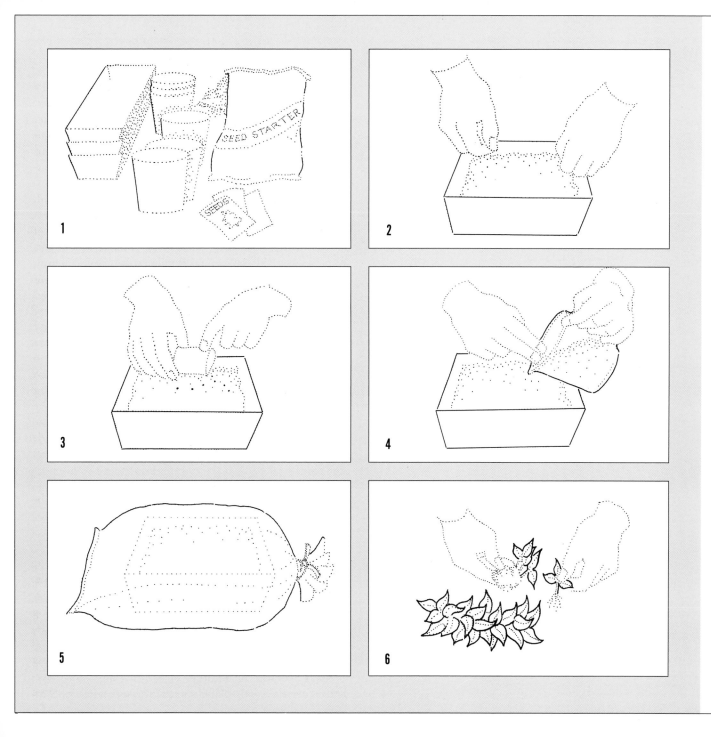

5. Place the container in a polyethylene bag (a kitchen freezer bag), close the end and keep in a warm place (about 70°F) until the seeds germinate. A freezer bag creates a self-contained micro-climate, so leave the container alone until the seeds germinate.

6. When the seeds have germinated, remove the freezer bag and begin watering and fertilizing seedlings with liquid plant food. When they are large enough to handle, separate and transfer them to individual pots.

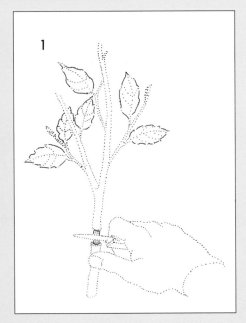

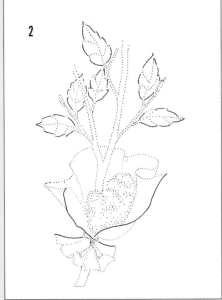

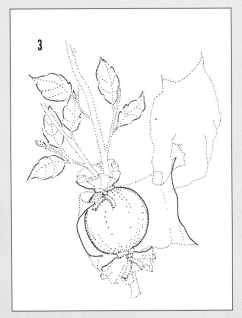

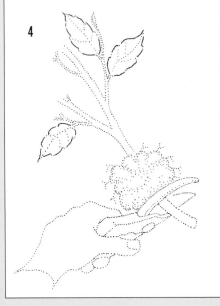

trees and shrubs root best when cuttings are taken off new soft growth in spring, others from mature wood in autumn, referred to as hard wood cuttings. For a complete list of shrubs suitable for taking cuttings, see lists on pages 504-505.

Cuttings are usually 4- to 6-inch sections of stem taken from the branch tips. Do this by cutting the ends on a diagonal and removing the lower leaves. Slit the cut end lengthwise, just enough to expose the inner wood. Once this is done, dip the cut ends in a rooting hormone and stick them upright into a pot or tray of moist starting soil containing equal parts sand, peat, and perlite. Enclose the container of cuttings with a clear plastic bag to create a humid microclimate. Keep the cuttings at room temperature in low light. Kept in moist soil, the cuttings should be well-rooted in three to twelve weeks, depending on variety, after which they can be transferred to individual pots until they are large enough to be transplanted into the garden. Easy woody plants to start from cuttings include pussy willows *(Salix discolor)*, gold-dust shrub *(Aucuba japonica)*, and red-twig dogwood *(Cornus nus sericea)*. If cuttings are started outdoors in a cold frame or specially prepared nursery bed, they should be protected from the direct rays of sun with shade cloth. Regular watering is essential since a cutting without an established root system can dehydrate quickly unless protected by shade and watered daily during dry spells.

Soil Layering The long, pliable branches of certain trees and shrubs can be bent to the ground and pegged into a position so that there is soil contact. A root system will be established where the branch remains in contact with the soil. Rhododendron, forsythia, and viburnum are particularly easy to grow this way. At the point where the branch touches the ground, it is best to scratch away the bark on the underside. This hastens the rooting process. Soil contact can be maintained by pegging the branch in position with a bent wire. A light covering of leaf mold or sphagnum moss will help prevent the layered part from drying out. If the soil is kept moist, within a year the plant will usually be sufficiently well-rooted to be cut from its parent and transplanted to another area of the garden.

Air Layering In addition to soil layering, described above, certain woody plants such as rhododendron (includ-

1

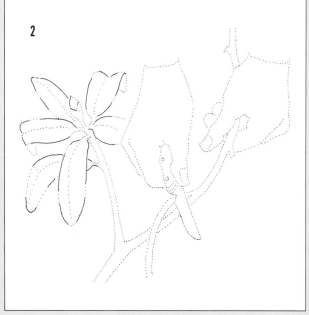

2

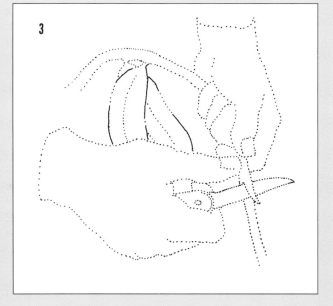

3

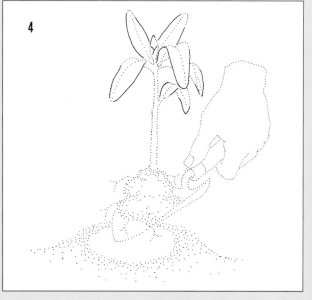

4

AIR LAYERING *(Opposite page)*

1. Scrape away the cambium.

2. Add sphagnum moss and cover with a plastic bag.

3. Cover the plastic with aluminum foil; use a twist tie to attach it to the shrub.

4. Cut off below the new roots and plant in the ground.

SOIL LAYERING (Left)

1. Branch to be layered should be slit to depth of bark where it touches the soil.

2. Pile soil over the cut and anchor with a piece of bent wire.

3. After layered branch is rooted (usually after several months), cut layered branch from parent.

4. Lift rooted end from soil with trowel for transplanting to a new location.

A FOOLPROOF WAY TO GROW TREES AND SHRUBS FROM CUTTINGS—INDOORS

A common plastic freezer bag from your own kitchen can be turned into a mini-greenhouse for root cuttings.

The idea is to create a self-contained environment with its own humid micro-climate. Woody cuttings may take eight weeks to root. Cuttings which lose their leaves, turn brown, or wither should be removed or discarded.

1. Mix together equal parts of peat and sand, or peat and perlite, or peat and vermiculite. Alternatively, use a packaged propagating mix, ready-formulated from your local garden supply center. When using sand it should be salt-free, not the kind found at the beach.

2. Wet the mixture to make it evenly moist, just enough so that when you squeeze it tightly a few drops of water will appear.

ing azaleas), mock-orange *(Philadelphus coronarius)*, and firethorn *(Ptyracantha coccinea)* can be air layered. To do this, simply select a healthy portion of branch and scrape away about 1 inch of bark, completely encircling the branch. Then, take some moist sphagnum moss or a household sponge soaked with water, and cover the cut area. Hold it in place and secure a sheet of clear plastic around it with an elastic band or twist tie. Some air layers started in the spring will have formed a healthy root system by the end of the summer. Others, especially in colder climates, may take up to a year to produce visible roots. When roots are visible through the plastic, cut the rooted branch from the mother plant using a sharp knife or hand pruners, and plant in the garden.

GROWING TREES AND SHRUBS IN CONTAINERS

Even though there are more colorful, longer-lasting plants to consider for decorating containers, many trees and shrubs provide a sophisticated beauty in their shape and form, flowering longevity, and vertical accent. In fact, there has been such a great demand for shrubs and small trees that will grow in containers that special hybrids have been developed for this purpose.

The bigger the container, the easier it will be to grow a woody plant in it. Tubs of all kinds are fine, although a ten gallon minimum capacity is usually needed to accommodate enough soil for the large root system of most woody plants. The best containers to use are made of wood or clay, which help keep the soil cool on hot days when the root systems can be burned. Plastic and metal containers should not be used because they heat up rather than insulate the root system.

A very effective woody plant container is called a "Versailles Planter," so named because it is a popular feature in the Sunken Garden at the Palace of Versailles, located outside of Paris, France. It is a square, wooden planter, painted white or green, and supported on casters so it can be wheeled about. The beautiful and practical Versailles planter is especially good for growing tender trees and shrubs because it is easy to roll indoors during the cold winter

months. For this reason people choose to grow exotic trees and shrubs in it, like dwarf orange trees, angel's trumpets, camellias, and gardenias, which merely require frost exclusion to keep them alive through the winter.

Generally, the commercial soil mixtures used with woody plants are too light on their own to anchor a shrub or small tree in a container. Therefore, it is a good practice to blend these potting mixes with sand to provide a greater density. Two ingredients commonly combined with potting soil are vermiculite, a lightweight, gritty rock, and perlite, a porous, volcanic rock. Beside helping to anchor the plant in its pot, both have the ability to absorb water like a sponge and hold it for long periods of time, preventing rapid dehydration. They also add aeration for healthy development of roots.

3. Take a two quart plastic freezer bag and fill with about four inches of your propagating mixture. The bag must be free of holes so when it is sealed there will be no moisture loss.

4. Insert the cuttings so that they do not touch each other or the sides of the plastic bag.

5. Sprinkle the cuttings lightly with water—just enough to moisten the foliage. This is the last watering they will need until they are rooted.

6. Seal the top of the bag tightly with a rubber band. Place on a windowsill that receives no direct sunlight (north and west exposure). Leave the bag alone until the cuttings have had a chance to root.

Container plants need water regularly, sometimes as much as once a day. You can test for moisture by plunging a finger about 2 inches deep into the pot. If the soil is dry, water it. Container shrubs can be watered with a garden hose, a watering can, or by installing a drip line connected to an irrigation system. Some irrigation systems have sets of long tubes with a nozzle on the end that drips moisture to feed numerous container plants at the turn of a faucet.

Container shrubs also need frequent fertilizing, approximately once every two weeks. Simply mix a liquid fertilizer with a gallon of water, and water as usual, or use a granular, time-released fertilizer. A time-released fertilizer releases its nutrients into the soil slowly (up to several months) and so saves you time.

PEST AND DISEASE CONTROL

In spite of their capacity to live long and healthy lives, trees and shrubs are vulnerable to attack from various pests and diseases. Among the pests that can inflict severe damage are borers, scale insects, spider mites, and whiteflies. The best prevention against problems from insects, pests, and diseases, is healthy plants, kept in good condition by timely watering during dry spells and fertilizing every year.

Pests

Scale Insects commonly infect camellias, aucuba, and Japanese aralia. The most telling symptom is bulbs attached to the succulent part of the stems. These bulbs can be white, brown, gray, red, or yellow in color. If these areas are scaped with a fingernail, the soft underside of the insect will be revealed. Because scale insects suck the juices out of plants, once infected, the leaves generally turn yellow and the branches start to die. One treatment method requires spraying with an insecticide specifically marked "For treatment of scale." An alternative is to dip a cotton swab in rubbing alcohol and swabbing the pests off of the plant. This must be done every week, as eggs are newly hatching.

Borers, usually the burrowing caterpillars of night-flying moths, commonly infect rhododendrons, ornamental

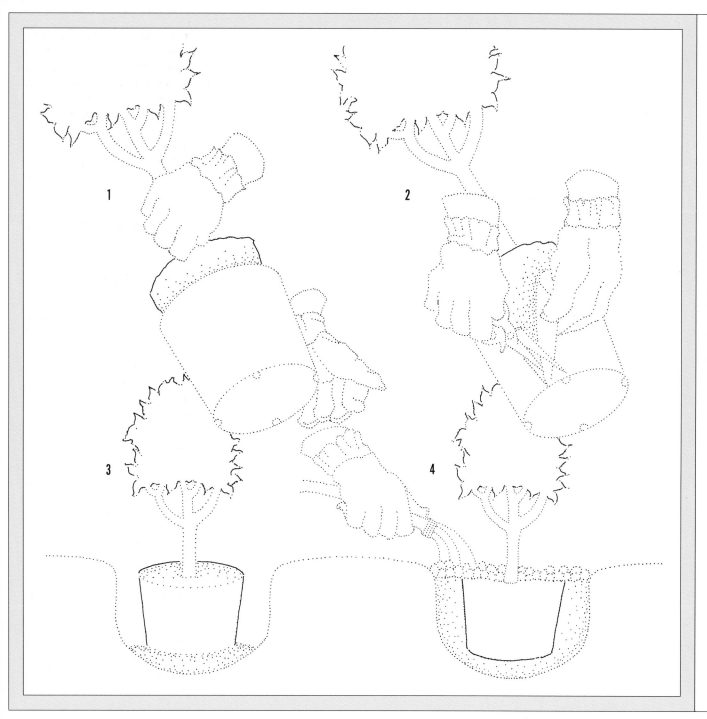

PLANTING TREES AND SHRUBS FROM CONTAINERS

1. Gently tug the root ball to see if it will slide out of the container easily. Run a knife blade around the edge of the container if necessary.

2. If root ball resists, cut the container with a pair of heavy-duty scissors.

3. Place the root ball on a mound of topsoil.

4. Fill the hole to 1 inch of the soil line. Water. Tamp soil down. Supply wood chip mulch to deter weeds and conserve moisture.

Opposite page: A fruiting lemon tree in a terra cotta tub has its trunk ringed with daisies for added ornamental effect.

Right: A beautiful shrub border featuring azaleas and rhododendrons decorates a woodland walk.

Opposite page: Here, a wisteria vine is trained to a single trunk and pruned to three layers of branches to create a tree form. Each layer is held horizontally by an "umbrella" of metal spokes.

almonds, dogwoods, and lilacs. Some infected plants exude a gummy sap where the borer entered, but in many plants it's difficult to detect penetration by borers. Other signs include a branch that suddenly wilts, and bark that flakes away easily, revealing tunnels and holes where the borers are at work. Once these pests have entered a shrub they are extremely difficult to control, especially if they have entered the main trunk or the main multiple trunks. If only one branch seems to be infected, prune it away immediately. There is a compound you can buy in a tube, called Borekil, that you squeeze into the hole, gassing the borers; however, this kind of treatment is usually only good when there are just one or two borers to kill. The best remedy is to spray the base of shrubs with Lindane insecticide which kills the larvae as they hatch, and before they have a chance to enter the plant.

Spider mites are troublesome for rhododendrons, azaleas, camellias, and many other shrubs with fleshy leaves. They colonize plants and debilitate them by draining their juices. Signs of infestation include: yellowing leaves that take on a dusty, dirty appearance and curl at the ends, and a fine webbing on the undersides. If you hold a piece of white paper under a leaf and tap it sharply, tiny red, yellow, and lime green specks will drop down and crawl about.

To be effective, controls must be administered early in the infestation stage. Spray with Kelthane, making sure the pesticide reaches the underside of the leaves and branches. Repeat as needed. Spraying mite populations with a strong jet of water from a garden hose, if done on a regular basis, is also helpful in dislodging webs and colonies.

Whiteflies are small, white winged insects that colonize the underside of leaves. They are a problem mostly for shrubs grown under glass, especially camellias and gardenias. When a branch is shaken they rise in a cloud of white and flutter about. An indication that your shrubs are infested are sickly looking leaves that turn yellow and drop; the leaves may also have a black, sooty mold on them. You will also notice a sticky excrement coating the stems and leaves. If your shrubs do become infected with whiteflies, spray with an insecticide such as Diazinon.

In general, a good way to help combat a recurring pest problem with plants in containers is to repot the plant, as eggs can sometimes remain in the soil.

Diseases

By far the most serious woody plant diseases are caused by fungi either entering the foliage canopy or attacking the roots. Though different strains of fungi attack different areas, the following are generally widespread:

Flower blight is especially troublesome on camellias and azaleas, with different strains affecting each type of plant. However, the symptoms for all strains are similar: The petals will start to turn brown until the entire flower drops off.

To prevent flower blight, spray flowers with Benomyl as soon as they reach the mature bud stage. Spray the ground before flowering begins, and clean up all infected debris. Destroy by burning. This fungus is especially prevalent in the Southern states and other humid climate areas.

Dieback is a fungus that enters the plant through wounds in branches. Usually the lower regions of the plant may look infected first. The leaves will turn brown but remain attached to the plant. Unfortunately, once a plant is infected, cure is impossible, except to prune away and burn the affected areas. The following season, spray with a copper based fungicide after blooming.

Powdery mildew shows itself as gray, powdery patches on leaves. This fungus is troublesome to lilacs, euonymus, and hydrangeas. Though the disease rarely kills a plant, it hampers photosynthesis, thus weakening them. The disease is most prevalent in the summer, during wet weather. It can be combatted by spraying with Benomyl.

Other physiological disorders not caused by pests or diseases, but conditions in the environment, can affect shrubs. These include:

Chlorosis, a yellowing of leaves caused by a deficiency of iron. The leaf veins of a plant with chlorosis will become prominent. To cure, increase soil acidity for such acid-loving plants as azaleas, pieris, and rhododendrons. This is done by adding peat moss or a similar organic content to the soil, or by adding aluminum sulphate according to the label directions. For non-acid-loving plants, increase overall fertility with a general-purpose fertilizer.

Salt burn is evident by the browning of the tips of leaves, especially in older plants. This occurs because salt builds up in soil from over-fertilizing, and the rainfall has not been sufficient to flush away this build up. It may also occur as a result of salt being used on the road or on walkways. Salt burn most often occurs with plants in containers, which are constantly being fed fertilizers. To cure, flush the soil thoroughly.

Windburn can be distinguished from salt burn since it is usually the younger leaves on the plant that suffer first, turning brown and brittle. The side facing prevailing winds will usually show the first symptoms. Windburn takes its heaviest toll in winter, when cold, searing winds chill and dehydrate the plant. To cure, some form of shelter is needed on the side facing prevailing winds. In extremely exposed locations the entire plant may need to be encircled with burlap. A dry Indian summer—where a lack of rainfall occurs prior to cold winter temperatures—makes shrubs particularly susceptible for they may enter winter dormancy lacking moisture. To counteract this, water in fall and even during the winter to replenish much-needed soil moisture.

TEN QUESTIONS FREQUENTLY ASKED ABOUT TREES AND SHRUBS

1. WHY DOESN'T MY FLOWERING TREE OR SHRUB BLOOM?

There are many reasons why a flowering shrub or tree may not bloom. A few follow.

Do not expect flowers too soon after planting, as many trees and shrubs suffer transplant shock and need two years to adjust to their new environment. Another common reason they don't bloom is insufficient sunlight. Is it in a deeply shaded area? Is heavy shade from an adjacent tree falling on it during the day? Perhaps it needs feeding to replenish the nutrients in the soil. When it starts to starve, the first part to suffer is often flower-bud formation.

Quite often, inappropriate pruning may be the culprit of a non-flowering tree or shrub. For example, azaleas set new flower buds soon after flowering, but if the plant is sheared in late summer or early autumn, it will not have enough time

before winter dormancy to initiate more flower buds. Also, winterkill of flowering buds can be a problem. Another problem may be that during an early spring thaw, the buds can begin to swell; but, if a heavy freeze sets in, this can kill the immature flower parts inside the bud. This frequently happens to azaleas, rhododendrons, and forsythia in colder climates.

2. WHAT FLOWERING SHRUBS CAN I PLANT IN SHADE?

By far the best choice would be azaleas, though they like a lot of air circulation, so the shading elements, such as a tree canopy, should be fairly high up. Camellias, rhododendrons, and hydrangeas are also good for shade.

3. WHICH SHRUBS WILL FLOWER ALL SUMMER?

Not many, and those that do generally have small flowers. *Abelia* x *grandiflora* ('Glossy Abelia') is one, as is *Potentilla fruticosa* ('Bush Cinquefoil'). The polyantha rose, 'The Fairy,' and the new 'Meidiland' roses will bloom continuously through the summer. Many roses also have a propensity to "repeat bloom," flowering first in early summer when the nights are cool and then again in autumn when cool conditions return.

4. ARE THERE ANY GOOD FLOWERING GROUND COVERS?

There are some good low-spreading varieties of azaleas suitable for ground cover, including the North Tisbury hybrids. The blue-flowering periwinkle, *Vinca minor*, makes a good durable, ground cover in sun or shade, producing blue, starlike flowers even before the last snows of winter, and continuing to flower for a month or more.

5. ARE THERE EASY-CARE FLOWERING TREES AND SHRUBS THAT DON'T NEED PRUNING?

Many shrubby vines can be left to their own devices, providing they have sufficient room to ramble. The following vines and shrubs require little pruning: *Campsis radicans* ('Trumpetvine'); weeping shrubs, such as *Forsythia spectabilis* ('Forsythia'); and *Prunus subhirtella* 'Pendula' ('Weeping Cherry'). Also, many kinds of slow-growing rhododendrons and azaleas require little or no pruning if they have sufficient room to grow.

6. WHEN A TREE OR A SHRUB LOOKS SICK, HOW CAN I GET THE PROBLEM DIAGNOSED?

Call your local county extension agent and ask for instructions on where to send a specimen of the sickly looking parts; this will usually be a pest identification center often located at your state land-grant university. You will quickly receive a diagnosis and recommended cure.

7. WHAT'S THE BEST WAY TO FERTILIZE TREES AND SHRUBS?

Select a high-nitrogen fertilizer in granular form, and simply sprinkle it over the whole surface, raking it into the topsoil, without disturbing the roots. Rainfall or watering will then carry the nutrients to the feeder roots, mostly located near the soil surface. Extend the fertilizer application to slightly beyond the drip line. Mulching plants each year with organic material, such as well-decomposed leaf mold made from shredded leaves left in a pile for a year to break down, helps to replenish exhausted soil with nutrients. It is rich in plant nutrients and trace elements.

8. WHAT ARE SOME GOOD SHRUBS FOR WINTER COLOR?

Many shrubs that flower in spring or summer produce wonderful berry displays in autumn that often persist well into winter. The best berry-bearing shrubs are *Ilex verticillata* ('Winter-berry'), *Pyracantha coccinea* ('Scarlet Firethorn'), *Berberis koreana* ('Korean Barberry'), and *Ilex* x *meserveae* ('Blue Holly'). For flowering effect, plant *Hamamelis mollis* ('Witch Hazel'), which blooms in late winter and early spring at the first sign of a warming trend, even before early spring-flowering bulbs.

9. WHAT ARE OTHER GOOD FLOWERING SHRUBS, LIKE RHODODENDRONS, THAT BLOOM LATE IN THE YEAR?

Rosea species ('Roses'), *Lagerstroemia indica* ('Crepemyrtle'), *Hydrangea* ('Hydrangea'), and berry-bearing viburnums, like *Viburnum dilatatum*.

10. WHAT'S THE BEST FLOWERING HEDGE?

Probably, types of polyantha roses, such as 'Robin Hood'; also azaleas. Fierthorn *(Pyracantha coccinea)* makes a great decorative hedge because of its beautiful berries, and the leaves of burning bush *(Euonymus alata)* have a brilliant red autumn color as intense as any red azalea, even though its flowers are inconspicuous.

Opposite page: Trees and shrubs planted along a grassy walk create a beautiful vista leading from the house to the bottom of the property. Dogwoods extend color high into the sky.

CHAPTER TWO

DESIGNING WITH TREES AND SHRUBS

IT IS NOT AS EASY FOR TREES AND SHRUBS TO make an impact in the landscape as it is for more colorful and faster-flowering annuals, perennials, and bulbs. Instead of providing color, trees and shrubs are used more for their structural beauty; they add height and form to garden design concepts. Shrubs can highlight the area beneath a canopy of trees, while trees can produce dramatic skyline effects. Certain woody plants are used more for purely functional reasons: They have a desirable quality, such as dense habit, that makes them suitable as permanent plantings. Some of these functions are as sentinels to an entranceway, as hedges delineating corridors and the movement of traffic, and as barriers. No one could argue that in flower or fruit many trees and shrubs match the dramatic color impact of the showiest annuals. What could be more stunning than a golden chain tree, a kurume azalea, or a floribunda rose in flower? The many tree and shrub designs are described below.

Mixed Shrub Borders consist of a collection of plants arranged according to the effect produced by their color, texture, and form. Mixing needle evergreens and broadleaf evergreens with deciduous trees and shrubs of all shapes and sizes produces a pleasant visual effect. Usually, any flowering trees or shrubs are chosen to produce a color impact at a particular time of year—usually spring—so that something is always coming into bloom, except during the winter months. Care must be taken to plant trees and shrubs with the right

spacing so that as they grow and mature they can attain their maximum height and width—kept within bounds, of course, by timely pruning. In mixed shrub borders, plants are chosen for three distinct heights: low-growing, medium height, and tall. Some plants should be left to grow informally to produce an irregular outline, while others should be pruned to create cushions, which have a soothing effect. Others may be pruned into such shapes as cones and spires to achieve height and accentuate the architectural line of a nearby wall or building. Mixed shrub borders tend to be situated away from the house so they can be admired from a window.

Foundation plantings are generally collections of trees and shrubs situated along the foundation of a house. Their purpose is to soften the stark lines of a wall, to disguise monotonous expanses of concrete and brick, and to make the house look attractive from the road or other vantage points. Many foundation plantings are composed entirely of evergreens to make them easy to care for. Their appearance is enhanced by timely pruning, allowing the creation of mounds, spires, cones, and other rounded, vertical, or horizontal shapes. More imaginative foundation plantings include flowering plants, especially azaleas, camellias, and hydrangeas, with enough space left between for a splash of seasonal color from clumps of annuals, perennials, and flowering bulbs. In new houses, debris may have been left by the builders; therefore, it is important to excavate beds to a good soil depth (at least 2 feet) and add quality soil with plenty of humus. Similarly, consideration should be given to exposure: Is the foundation planting on a sunny side of the house or a shaded side of the house? This will help determine what types of trees and shrubs to plant.

Rock Gardens Many kinds of evergreen plants look especially attractive planted in a rock garden, as they serve to break up what might otherwise be a bleak or barren landscape. Tall, spirelike junipers can be planted to provide vertical accents, while low-spreading cotoneasters and hypericum can carpet the ground and cascade over rocks. Mounded shrubs like mugo pines can decorate the landscape like cushions, while billowing forms like rhododendrons can create a beautiful, dark green background or windbreak against which the rock garden can be admired. Usually, rock gardens are situated on slopes with a sunny

Left: A rich assortment of trees and shrubs, specially chosen to present a pleasing arrangement of shapes and textures, decorate a rocky slope at Bishop's Close, a garden overlooking the Wilamette River, Portland, Oregon.

Opposite page: A billowing hedge of English boxwood creates an intimate sitting area between a flower-bordered lawn and the wall of a house.

Right: It is possible to be quite creative when designing with shrubs. Some unusual forms are seen at right.

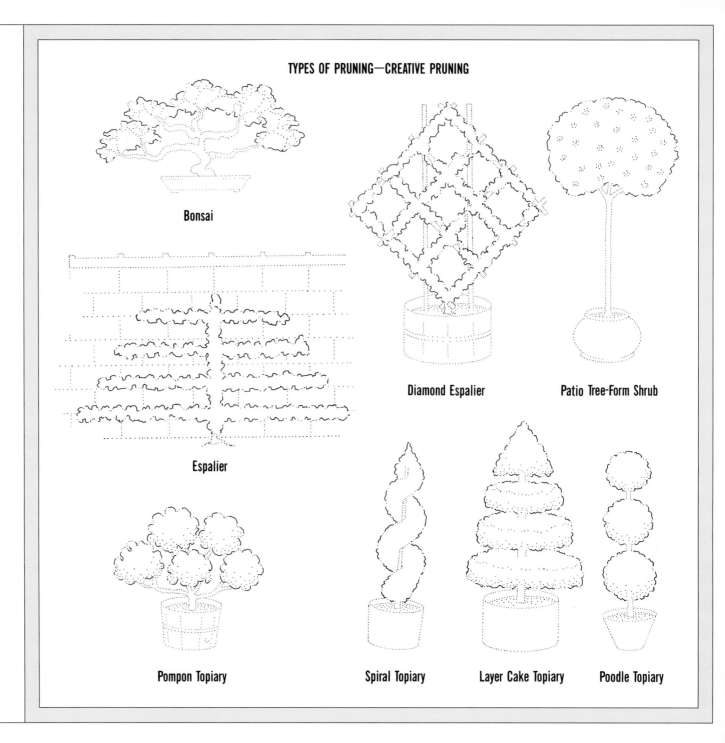

TYPES OF PRUNING—CREATIVE PRUNING

Bonsai

Diamond Espalier

Patio Tree-Form Shrub

Espalier

Pompon Topiary

Spiral Topiary

Layer Cake Topiary

Poodle Topiary

exposure, so the soil is likely to be the dry side, thus demanding plants that tolerate drought. Solutions to this dry soil problem may be to thread the rock garden with streams and waterfalls or irrigate with drip lines, allowing moisture-loving plants to be added to the landscape.

Parterres are low hedges that outline planting beds. Sometimes they are simple, geometric shapes like diamonds and squares; other times they are extremely elaborate swirls, scrolls, and flourishes. Usually a parterre is situated near a tall structure, such as a tower or tall building, so that the decorative outlines can be seen to their best advantage. Effective parterres generally need dwarf shrubs with dense, evergreen growth, like boxwood.

Hedges can be planted in a straight line to make a barrier, or in parallel lines to form corridors directing movement from one area of the garden to another. Hedges can also serve as windbreaks, cushioning the force of winds, and as screens to provide privacy. Tall hedges can be pruned to make windows and archways. Effective hedges need to be fairly fast-growing and capable of forming a dense mass of intermingling branches and branchlets that knit together to make an impenetrable barrier. Though evergreens are generally the preferred choice for hedges, many deciduous shrubs that drop their leaves in autumn can still present an impenetrable living wall from their tightly interwoven twigs; some even have the added distinction of thorns to resist penetration.

Since the idea of a hedge is for each plant to merge into its neighbor, negating any apparent distinction from one plant to another, shrubs grown for this purpose are generally planted closer together than normal. Generally, hedges in small gardens are sheared to maintain straight sides, while hedges that form boundaries of properties are left to grow untamed.

Mazes are hedges planted in parallel lines, either straight or curved, to form a labyrinth. The first hedge maze in the world, constructed at Hampton Court Palace, England, in the 1700s, still exists today. A copy of this famous Tudor-design maze can be seen on the grounds of the Governor's Palace, at Colonial Williamsburg, in Virginia, and at Deerfield Garden, near Philadelphia, Pennsylvania. Usually, a mound is located near the maze so that the people standing on top of the mound can see over the hedges and direct those in the maze to the center and out again. Good hedge material

Right: An English yew splayed out like a fan softens the lines of a stone wall.

Below: Firethorn makes an especially good subject for espalier plantings because of the colorful berries that persist well into winter.

Opposite page: Wisteria vine, trained along metal supports, forms a flowering arbor beside the pond in Claude Monet's garden in Giverny, France. The painter planted this wisteria almost 100 years ago.

for mazes includes holly, hemlock, and Japanese yew, though the very best is generally English boxwood. Unfortunately, English boxwood grows extremely slowly, but when pruned its lines are clean and sharp.

Whether planting a parterre, hedge, or maze, it is extremely important to provide good soil. In the absence of good soil, dig a trench 1 to 2 feet deep and fill it with humus-rich topsoil trucked to the site or taken from another area of your garden. You want every plant to be given an equal chance of survival and to last a long time, so it's worth the extra effort of ensuring good soil. To create your parterre, hedge, or maze layout, use string tied to stakes for a straight design, and a garden hose for a curved design.

Topiary was first used by the Romans, and later popularized by the British. It is the pruning of trees and shrubs into whimsical shapes and figures. Suitable specimens to use for topiary include Japanese yew, hemlock, English boxwood, and holly.

Usually, the tree or shrub is grown in soil and its growth habit is kept compact by continued shearing until it is large enough to cut with pruning shears. Some popular topiary designs are swans, crowns, chess pieces, and even giraffes. A faster way of creating a topiary accent is to make a wire form and fill it with moist sphagnum moss. Then a creeping vine like English ivy is planted to hug the frame and fill out the shape. These "quick" topiaries can be started in pots and moved about from place to place, even indoors.

Espalier is a method of training shrubs or small trees so they make a flat pattern against a wall or fence. Common shrubs to use include dwarf pears, dwarf apples, firethorn, and yew. Care must be taken to ensure that the wall is not too light-reflective. Stucco walls, for example, can be extremely harsh for espaliered fruit trees, burning the embryo fruits so they never mature, and scorching the wood. For fruit trees a brick wall or wooden fence is preferable. Some shrubs, such as apples and pears, have such pliable limbs, they can be trained along wires or wooden rails to form "ropes" (botanically called cordons). The added air circulation of this form of espalier generally encourages fruit. These cordons are especially good for making a low edging or fence to define an herb garden, vegetable garden, or border.

Left: In this garden at Carmel Mission California, bougainvillea and hydrangea combine to make a beautiful and colorful shrub foundation.

SMALL CIRCULAR BED

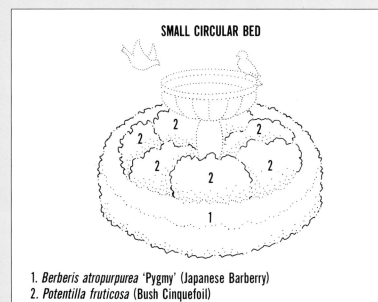

1. *Berberis atropurpurea* 'Pygmy' (Japanese Barberry)
2. *Potentilla fruticosa* (Bush Cinquefoil)

CONTAINER PLANTS FOR A DECK

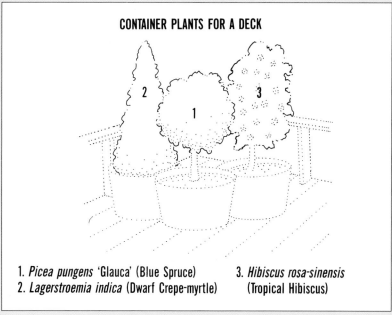

1. *Picea pungens* 'Glauca' (Blue Spruce)
2. *Lagerstroemia indica* (Dwarf Crepe-myrtle)
3. *Hibiscus rosa-sinensis* (Tropical Hibiscus)

DOORWAY PLANTING

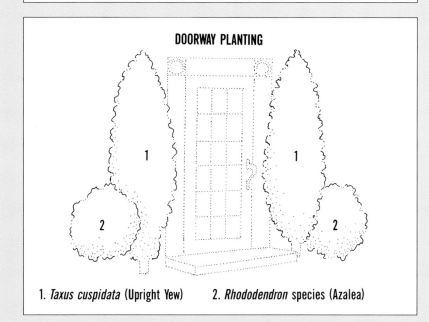

1. *Taxus cuspidata* (Upright Yew)
2. *Rhododendron* species (Azalea)

BORDER PLANTING ALONG A FENCE

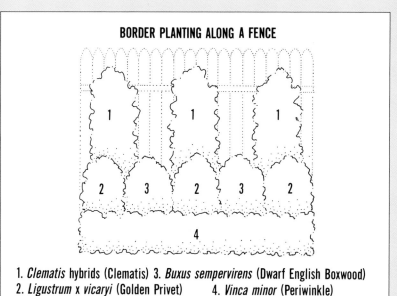

1. *Clematis* hybrids (Clematis)
2. *Ligustrum* x *vicaryi* (Golden Privet)
3. *Buxus sempervirens* (Dwarf English Boxwood)
4. *Vinca minor* (Periwinkle)

Right: An Atlas cedar makes a beautiful bonsai specimen, with copper wire used to hold branches in place.

Far right: A pair of forsythia, planted on either side of a gate, make colorful sentinels in early spring.

Opposite page: A collection of azaleas, pruned to mounded shapes, creates a colorful shrub border.

Avenues are the perfect complement for driveways. Plant the edges of the driveway with cone-shaped trees and shrubs to make a formal entryway, or with billowing shrubs, such as forsythia, spiraea, hydrangea, and azalea, to create a sweep of color.

Archways are best for side entrances and pathways leading through gardens, as they can completely cover the walk with a canopy of leafy and flowering vines. Good shrubs to work with include wisteria, honeysuckle, trumpet creepers, and climbing roses.

Sentinels are pairs of attractive trees or shrubs that stand on either side of a gate or doorway. They can be planted in soil or grown in containers, (see "Growing Trees and Shrubs In Containers," page 411). Some good trees and shrubs to consider as sentinels include upright yews, podocarpus, upright junipers, star magnolias, quince, hemlock, and firethorn espaliered against a wall.

Ground cover Many creeping or low-spreading shrubs can be planted in a mass knit together to form a luxurious, dense mass of leaves through which weeds cannot grow. The very best, durable ground covers for sun include Blue Rug juniper, hypericum, cotoneaster, and red barberry. For shade, consider vinca, English ivy, pachysandra, and dwarf azalea. Consider tough, durable candidates for erosion control on slopes. Low-spreading forms of forsythia, banksia roses, bearberry, azaleas, and ceanothus can be both functional and highly ornamental.

Windbreaks The problem with planting any tree or shrub to create a windbreak is how to get it established. The solution is to build a temporary shelter from bales of hay or burlap sacking stapled to posts, sheltering the windbreak plants from prevailing winds until the plants themselves are sufficiently well-established to resist the wind on their own. Where winds are a constant problem, a double windbreak (consisting of two parallel rows of shrubs) may be necessary to completely dissipate the force of the wind. Usually, evergreens are preferred for windbreaks. Good windbreak plants include holly, pittosporum, rugosa rose, podocarpus, pines, junipers, and beach plum.

Bonsai is a skill requiring great patience, since it involves growing shrubs and trees in special shallow dishes. Confining the roots in this manner tends to restrict the height of the plant; by careful pruning, an illusion of great age and maturity can be created. Limbs can be bent into special contours and fixed in place by wires so that the shrubs take on the appearance of plants that have been weathered by exposure to winds on a mountaintop, or salty air by the ocean. Special instruction by bonsai masters is needed to become adept at this fascinating art form. Some good plants that make terrific bonsai subjects include azaleas, camellias, calamondin orange, pomegranate, and plums. Many evergreens are also favored as bonsai subjects, including pine, spruce, and juniper, sometimes planted as a miniature grove to create an illusionary bonsai forest.

WAYS TO USE TREES AND SHRUBS IN THE LANDSCAPE

Left: Grow shrubs as a hedge along a fence or up a wall. Use shrubs as an island bed surrounded by paving. Grow shrubs in containers.

For an Arbor, use flowering vines such as *Campsis radicans* (Trumpetcreeper), *Wisteria sinensis* (Wisteria), climbing roses, and *Clematis jackmanii*.

For a Hedge, use flowering shrubs, especially *Abelia* x *grandiflora* (Glossy Abelia), *Azalea* hybrids, and *Hibiscus* species.

For Ground Cover Where Grass Will Not Grow, use shade-loving shrubs, such as *Vinca minor* (Periwinkle).

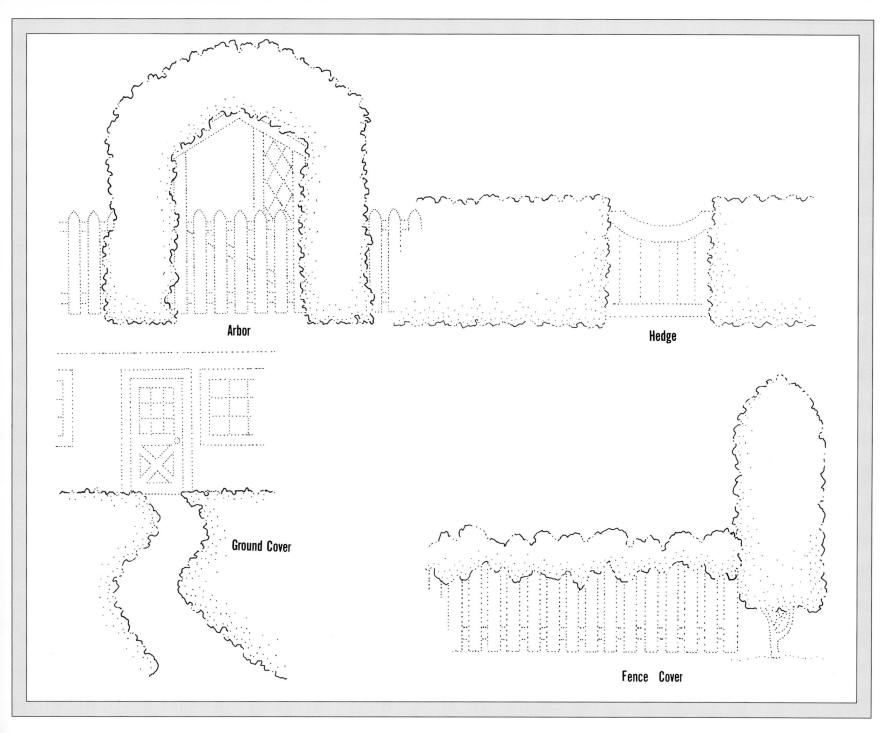

Arbor

Hedge

Ground Cover

Fence Cover

CHAPTER THREE

THE ENCYCLOPEDIA OF ESSENTIAL TREES AND SHRUBS

T
HE FOLLOWING SECTION DESCRIBES THE deciduous and evergreen trees and shrubs most often used in home landscaping. They include true shrubs, some ornamental trees, a number of vines, and several good ground covers. Most are hardy, though a few exotic, tender varieties have been included for those gardeners fortunate enough to live in areas with mild winters. Some of the trees and shrubs featured are noted for their flowering effect; others for functional reasons, such as screening for privacy, hedges, topiary, and covering arbors.

Each woody plant is listed first with its botanical (Latin) name, since this more accurately identifies the plant than does its common name. While many shrubs have popular common names—'Holly' for *Ilex* species—others do not, or else they are known by two or more common names: *Caryopteris* x *clandonensis*, for example, is often called 'Blue Mist Shrub' or 'Bluebeard.'

To find a description for a plant where you know only the common name, simply refer to the index for a quick cross-reference.

The heights given are approximate. Often, with age and in good soil, plants may exceed the heights stated here. Also, the description for habit is the natural habit of the plant left to its own devices. Many trees and shrubs described as 'billowing' or 'mounded' can be pruned into any desirable shape.

BOTANICAL NAME *Abelia* x *grandiflora*

COMMON NAME Glossy Abelia

RANGE Tolerates zone 5 but prefers zone 6 and further south. Stem kill occurs at -5° to -10°F.

HEIGHT 3 to 5 feet tall and equally as wide; medium-sized shrub.

CULTURE Moist, well-drained, acidic soil, in full to partial sun. Propagated by cuttings.

DESCRIPTION Semi-evergreen. Grown primarily for its excellent, lustrous, dark green foliage that is paler green beneath. Leaves are 1 to 1½ inches long and take on a bronze color in the winter months. Flowers bloom from July until frost and are funnel-shaped, 3/4 of an inch long with white to pinkish blossoms. Fairly disease-resistant. Dislikes harsh, strong winds.

LANDSCAPE USE This spreading, dense, multi-stemmed shrub has arching branches that make a good hedge or bank cover. Prune to the height you want. Also used as a background or specimen plant. Plus, it combines well with broadleaf evergreens.

BOTANICAL NAME *Abies concolor*

COMMON NAME White Fir

RANGE Native to Colorado and Southern California. Hardy zones 3 to 7.

CULTURE Transplant young seedlings bare-root, older plants balled and burlapped. Prefers sandy loam soil in full sun, though tolerant of a wide range of soils. Good drought resistance.

DESCRIPTION Medium-fast-growing bluish, dark green needle evergreen to 50 feet high. Attractive conical shape.

LANDSCAPE USE Good lawn highlight and windbreak. Useful as a Christmas tree.

RELATED SPECIES *Abies fraseri* ('Fraser Fir'), not quite so tolerant of dry conditions as the White Fir, but a handsome, spirelike shape and the favored fir as a Christmas tree.

BOTANICAL NAME *Acer palmatum dissectum*

COMMON NAME Japanese Maple

RANGE Zones 5–8. Native to Japan and Korea.

HEIGHT Slow-growing, 15 to 20 feet tall, with a spread equal to or greater than height; mounded form, weeping branches.

CULTURE Thrives in moist, well-drained, and acidic soil in full sun or partial shade if the weather is hot and dry, with constant winds. Propagated by seed and cuttings.

DESCRIPTION Deciduous tree. Provides all-year interest: red growth in the spring, soft green lacey leaves in the summer, scarlet foliage in the fall, and a delicate, leafless silhouette during the winter. Flowers are small and purple, borne in clusters May through June.

LANDSCAPE USE One of the most flexible maple species for landscape uses. Attractive planted as a specimen tree for patios or entryways; in groves as woodland plants; as a background for ferns and azaleas; as an accent plant, shrub border, or bonsai planting. Since it naturally grows layers of leaves at the end of sinuous branches, pruning is rarely needed.

BOTANICAL NAME *Acer rubrum*

COMMON NAME Scarlet Maple; Swamp Maple

RANGE Native to North America. Hardy zones 3 to 9.

CULTURE Perhaps the most widely adapted of all maples, though it is best to select plants grown locally to ensure adequate heat tolerance or cold hardiness. Transplant bare-root or balled and burlapped into acid, moist soil in sun or partial shade.

DESCRIPTION Usually pyramidal in shape, fast growing to 60 feet. Leaves are three-cornered, turn from dark green to brilliant orange or red in autumn.

LANDSCAPE USE Excellent lawn highlight. Good to decorate parks, streets, and golf courses.

RELATED SPECIES *A. saccharinum* ('Silver Maple') has leaves that shimmer with silvery undersides turning yellow in autumn; *A. saccharum* ('Sugar Maple') has leaves that turn bright orange in autumn, and are valued as a source of maple sugar.

BOTANICAL NAME *Actinidia chinensis*

COMMON NAME Kiwi

RANGE Zone 7. Native to east Asia.

HEIGHT To 30 feet tall; twining vine, requires support.

CULTURE Prefers rich, sandy soil in full sun or partial shade. Rapid grower that needs regular pruning to hold shape or pattern. Propagated by seed.

DESCRIPTION Deciduous vine that is highly adaptable. Leaves are heart-shaped, lustrous, and dark green above with white, downy undersides. New growth looks like it is covered with a rich looking red fuzz. Flowers are 1 to 1 1/2 inches wide with creamy white blooms that appear throughout May. Fruits are covered with brown fuzz and are somewhat egg-shaped. The lime-green flesh of the fruit is reminiscent of the taste of melon and banana. Both a male and a female plant are necessary for fruit set. A hardier species, *A. arguta* ('Bower Actinidia') has equally attractive leaves, and bears small, edible, green, grape-sized fruits.

LANDSCAPE USE Excellent quick vine cover that grows well in problem areas. Train to cover walls and fences or supply sturdy supports such as trellis, arbor, or patio, overhead.

BOTANICAL NAME *Aesculus pavia*

COMMON NAME Red Buckeye

RANGE Native to North America. Hardy zones 3 to 8.

CULTURE Prefers fertile, humus-rich loam soil in full sun. Transplant from containers or balled.

DESCRIPTION Beautiful, upright billowing habit. Large, oval, serrated leaves arranged in a fan turn brown in autumn. Decorative red flower clusters appear in spring, followed by spiny seed cases containing large, shiny brown seeds. Reasonably fast growing—up to 3 feet a year; can grow to 80 feet.

LANDSCAPE USE Excellent lawn highlight. Tolerates high heat. Popular in the South.

RECOMMENDED VARIETY *Aesculus* x *carnea* ('Red Horse Chestnut') is a hybrid between *A. pavia*, and *A. hippocastanum*, the common horsechestnut. Plants grow to 80 feet and are popular for lining avenues.

BOTANICAL NAME *Albizia julibrissin*

COMMON NAME Silk Tree

RANGE Native to China. Hardy zones 6 to 9.

CULTURE Easily transplanted from containers. Tolerates a wide range of soil types including alkaline soil, providing drainage is good and the tree is in full sun. Highly wind resistant.

DESCRIPTION A graceful, small deciduous tree creating a mounded, airy leaf canopy, allowing grass to grow up to its trunk. Beautiful pink flowers shaped like powderpuffs cover branches in midsummer. Fast growing to 35 feet.

LANDSCAPE USE Excellent lawn highlight. Good to shade decks, terraces, and patios.

BOTANICAL NAME *Allamanda cathartica* 'Williamsi'

COMMON NAME Yellow Allamanda; Henderson Common Allamanda

RANGE Zone 9. Native to Brazil.

HEIGHT Climbs to 10 feet or spreads as a shrub depending on pruning.

CULTURE Prefers rich soil in full sun. Feed regularly. Grows in only the warmest, most frost-free areas. Can be grown as a greenhouse plant. Propagated by cuttings.

DESCRIPTION Broadleaf evergreen. Dense foliage of thick, 6-inch long, roundish, dark green leaves. Yellow, saucer-shaped flowers, up to 4 inches across, bloom in June.

LANDSCAPE USE Evergreen vining shrub. Good to grow up a trellis or allow to cascade over low walls.

BOTANICAL NAME *Amelanchier arborea*

COMMON NAME Serviceberry

RANGE Zones 4–9. Native to North America.

HEIGHT Generally 15 to 25 feet tall with a variable spread, can grow as high as 40 feet; tree-like habit.

CULTURE Prefers well-drained, moist, acidic soil in full sun or partial shade. Commonly found in nature along woodland borders, streambanks, and fencerows in open meadows. Intolerant of pollution. Rarely needs pruning. Propagated by seed or division.

DESCRIPTION Deciduous shrub or small tree. Provides all season interest: showy clusters of white flowers appear in mid to late April; small, edible, purplish black round fruits ripen in June; medium to dark green leaves turn yellow, orange, and red in the fall; an attractive winter branch and twig pattern occurs in the winter. Rounded habit.

LANDSCAPE USE Widely used in landscaping. Stunning planted against a dark evergreen background to emphasize its delicate flowers and foliage. Excellent used for naturalistic plantings near the edges of woodlands, ponds, or streambanks. Berries attract birds.

BOTANICAL NAME *Ardisia japonica*

COMMON NAME Marlberry; Japanese Ardisia

RANGE Zones 8–9. Native to Japan and China.

HEIGHT 8 to 18 inches high; low-spreading shrub.

CULTURE Prefers an organic, moist, well-drained, acidic soil in partial or full shade. Propagated by division.

DESCRIPTION Broadleaf evergreen. Leathery, dark green leaves. White, star-shaped flowers bloom July through August, followed by brilliant scarlet fruits that last throughout the winter. Spreads rapidly.

LANDSCAPE USE Excellent shrub or ground cover to use in shady areas. Ideal choice for a woodland setting.

BOTANICAL NAME *Aucuba japonica* 'Variegata'

COMMON NAME Gold-dust Plant

RANGE Zones 7–10, not reliably winter hardy in Zone 6. Native to Japan.

HEIGHT 5 to 10 feet tall; bushy habit.

CULTURE Prefers well-drained, moist, high organic soil in dappled shade. May need some winter protection. Can be grown as a houseplant. Propagated by root cuttings.

DESCRIPTION A tidy, broadleaf evergreen, upright, rounded shrub that is usually multi-stemmed. Dark, lustrous, showy leaves with yellow flecking. Small, purple flowers bloom March through April and are ornamentally unimportant. Red berries mature in October and November, and persist until spring.

LANDSCAPE USE An attractive understory plant. Good foundation planting on the north or east side of a home. If protected, it can make an effective evergreen border. Spruces up a dark corner and adds color to an all-green landscape.

BOTANICAL NAME *Beaumontia grandiflora*

COMMON NAME Herald's-trumpet; Easter Lily Vine

RANGE Zone 9; hardy to 28°F. Native to South America.

HEIGHT Up to 30 feet with equal spread; vine.

CULTURE Prefers deep, rich, moist soil in full sun. Heavy feeder. Prune back two and three-year old wood to preserve shape. Flowers are borne on old growth. Prune after flowering. Propagated by cuttings.

DESCRIPTION Broadleaf evergreen. Large lush, dark green, roundish leaves are shiny above with downy undersides. Fragrant, white, green-veined, 5-inch trumpet-shaped blooms resemble Easter lilies. Flowers bloom April through September.

LANDSCAPE USE Espalier on a wall sheltered from wind; train on a sturdy support or along the eaves of a house.

BOTANICAL NAME *Berberis thunbergii atropurpurea*

COMMON NAME Japanese Barberry

RANGE Zones 4–8. Native to Japan.

HEIGHT 4 to 6 feet tall with equal spread; bushy habit.

CULTURE Grows in a variety of soils and climates. Very hardy. Excellent for harsh climates. Shear to maintain a tidy shape. Prune to ground level in late winter to rejuvenate plants. Propagated by cuttings.

DESCRIPTION Compact, rounded, deciduous shrub that can look untidy if not pruned. Vigorous grower that requires full sun to develop leaf color. One of first shrubs to leaf out in spring. Green leaves turn a bronzy to purplish red in the summer. Inconspicuous, small yellow flowers bloom mid April through May. Attractive red fruit persists through winter and attracts birds.

LANDSCAPE USE Planted for its foliage color, fruit, and its rounded, multi-stemmed shape. Tolerates urban conditions quite well. Use as a hedge, barrier, and in groupings.

RELATED SPECIES *Berberis koreana*, ('Korean Barberry'), whose bright red berries persist into winter.

BOTANICAL NAME *Betula papyrifera*

COMMON NAME White Birch

RANGE Native to North America. Hardy zones 2 to 7.

CULTURE Prefers fertile loam soil in full sun. Plant from containers or balled and burlapped.

DESCRIPTION Slender, upright, deciduous tree usually grows a cluster of several trunks with white bark and black patches. Bright green, oval, serrated leaves change to yellow in autumn. Yellow catkinlike flowers appear in spring. Slow growing, up to 50 feet high.

LANDSCAPE USE Good lawn highlight. Effective in groves and planted between needle evergreens.

RELATED SPECIES *B. pendula* ('Weeping White Birch') has silvery bark and black patches like the regular white birch, but graceful pendant branches like a weeping willow, but with triangular, serrated leaves.

BOTANICAL NAME *Bougainvillea spectabilis*

COMMON NAME Bougainvillea; Brazil Bougainvillea

RANGE Zone 9–10. Hardy in tropical climates.

HEIGHT Grows to 20 feet high; shrubby vine.

CULTURE Prefers well-drained, good garden soil in full sun; light shade in hottest areas. Protect from wind. If planted in a container, use rich soil. Where frost is expected, grow the vine in the warmest spot in the garden or on a protected wall. Plant in early spring to give longest possible growing season before frost. **Caution:** Plants don't like to be moved or repotted as this disturbs their root system. Handle with extreme care by cutting open the pot or cutting out the bottom before placing plants in a larger container or in the ground. Prune to renew, shape, or direct growth of plants. Propagated by cuttings.

DESCRIPTION Showy, trailing shrub grown for its vibrant yellow to purplish magenta colors. The small white flowers are ornamentally unimportant and are almost hidden between the showy, colorful bracts. Leaves are medium green or variegated on thorny stems.

LANDSCAPE USE Heavily pruned plants can be used as container shrubs for patio or terrace. Otherwise, use as a sprawling vine on a sturdy structure or as a sprawling shrub for banks and ground covers. Grow under glass where freezing winters occur.

BOTANICAL NAME *Brunfelsia calycina floribunda*

COMMON NAME Yesterday, Today, Tomorrow

RANGE Zone 9. Native to Brazil.

HEIGHT About 10 feet, but may be held to 3 feet by pruning; bushy habit.

CULTURE Rich, well-drained, moist, acidic soil in partial shade. Heavy feeder during growing season. Prune in spring to hold shape and to remove untidy growth. Propagated by cuttings.

DESCRIPTION Named after the quick color change of its blossoms: purple ("yesterday"), lavender ("today"), and white ("tomorrow"). Tubular-shaped flowers, borne in clusters, bloom profusely in the spring. Broadleaf evergreen shrub that loses most of its foliage for a short period of time in non-tropical climates. Leaves are about 4 inches long, dark green above, pale green below.

LANDSCAPE USE Good for use in containers or as a showy specimen plant. Grows under glass where freezing winters occur.

BOTANICAL NAME *Buddleia davidii*

COMMON NAME Butterfly Bush

RANGE Zones 5–9. In cold climates the soft wood freezes to the ground but roots remain hardy. Native to China.

HEIGHT 3 to 10 feet high; bushy habit.

CULTURE Prefers well-drained, fertile soil in full sun. Propagated by cuttings.

DESCRIPTION Deciduous shrub. Vigorous grower that is almost weedlike. Lance-shaped leaves are dark green above, downy white below. In mid-summer, dense, arching, spikelike clusters appear with small, fragrant lilac flowers with orange eyes. Attracts butterflies.

LANDSCAPE USE Good summer-flowering specimen plant. Attractive in shrub or perennial borders. Suitable for containers.

BOTANICAL NAME *Buxus sempervirens*

COMMON NAME English Boxwood

RANGE Zones 5–9. Native of southern Europe, northern Africa, and western Asia.

HEIGHT Generally 15 to 20 feet tall with equal spread but can grow to 30 feet; bushy habit.

CULTURE Adaptable but prefers warm, moist climates. Likes moist, well-drained, high organic soil. Tolerates full sun to partial shade. Keep roots cool. Some winter protection is often necessary. Keep the evergreen leaves cleared of ice and snow to prevent "browning". Prune by shearing to maintain shape. Propagated by cuttings.

DESCRIPTION Slow-growing broadleaf evergreen shrub. Easy to maintain. Grown for its dense foliage of medium-sized, lustrous, dark green, oval leaves. Flowers and fruit are ornamentally unimportant.

LANDSCAPE USE An excellent plant for foundations, formal gardens, hedges, and edging.

BOTANICAL NAME *Calliandra haematocephala*

COMMON NAME Powderpuff Shrub

RANGE Zones 9–10. Native to Bolivia.

HEIGHT 16 feet high, 10 feet wide; mounded, bushy habit.

CULTURE Moist, well-drained, average soil in full sun. Propagated by seed.

DESCRIPTION Evergreen. Grown for its brilliant, scarlet, large powderpuff of silky flowers that bloom October through March. The fruit consists of a flat pod with thickened margins. Dark green, velvety, rich leaves.

LANDSCAPE USE Popular accent shrub in California, southern Florida, and Hawaii. Prefers a warm, sunny site and makes an ideal plant for espalier.

BOTANICAL NAME *Callicarpa japonica*

COMMON NAME Japanese Beauty Berry

RANGE Zones 5-8. Native to Japan.

HEIGHT 6 to 10 feet tall, but is usually pruned to hold shape at 3 feet; bushy, arching habit.

CULTURE Grows in any well-drained soil in full sun. Tolerates light shade. Propagated by cuttings or ground layering.

DESCRIPTION Deciduous shrub. Grown primarily for its colorful, purple berries that are borne in clusters along arching stems in the fall. Berries last two to three weeks after the leaves fall. Small white or pink flowers bloom in midsummer and are hidden beneath 2- to 4-inch green leaves. Leaves turn a golden color in autumn. Plant is often pruned in the spring to 4 to 6 inches from the ground in order to produce a bountiful crop of berries. In colder climates, plant freezes to the ground and reappears in the spring as a young shoot.

LANDSCAPE USE Effective planted in groups in a shrub border. Berries attract birds.

BOTANICAL NAME *Callistemon citrinus*

COMMON NAME Lemon Bottlebrush

RANGE Zones 9–10. Native to Australia.

HEIGHT Grows to 10 to 15 feet tall. With pruning and staking, can be trained to a narrow, roundish tree, 20 to 25 feet tall. Massive shrub.

CULTURE Prefers moist, well-drained, sandy soil in full sun. Tolerates drought, wind, neglect, salt air, and alkaline soil. Propagated by seed.

DESCRIPTION Broadleaf evergreen. Vivid green leaves are 3 inches long, willow-like. Leaves are lightly fragrant, emitting a faint lemon scent when bruised. Pendant, 6-inch crimson flower clusters are showy with conspicuous yellow stamens. A hard, rounded fruit surrounds the flowering stems.

LANDSCAPE USE This spreading shrub can be trained as a street or garden tree. Good used as a windbreak hedge, screen, or espalier; versatile. Can be grown under glass in colder climates.

BOTANICAL NAME *Calluna vulgaris*

COMMON NAME Scotch Heather

RANGE Zones 4–7. Native to Europe, Asia Minor, and has naturalized in northeastern North America.

HEIGHT 15 to 30 inches tall; upright, bushy habit.

CULTURE Prefers sandy, organic, moist, well-drained, acidic soil that is not too fertile, in full sun or partial shade. Avoid sweeping winds as plants are susceptible to drying. Prune by shearing in early spring before new growth starts. Mulch to retain moisture. Propagated by seed or cuttings.

DESCRIPTION There are hundreds of cultivars. Upright, branching, small broadleaf evergreen. Dense leaves and stems form thick mounds. Leaf color may vary from a medium green to orange-red. The urn-shaped flowers bloom from July to September. Flower color includes white, rose, and purplish pink.

LANDSCAPE USE Attracts bees. Excellent ground cover. Good for edging and slope cover.

BOTANICAL NAME *Camellia japonica*

COMMON NAME Camellia

RANGE Zones 8–9. Native to the central coast of Japan, South Korea, and Taiwan.

HEIGHT 15 to 45 feet, spreading to 6 to 15 feet; generally kept to 6 to 12 feet by pruning; upright, bushy habit.

CULTURE Prefers well-drained, moist, acidic, humus-rich soil rich in organic material, in full sun. Prune after flowering to hold form. Shorten lower branches to encourage upright growth. Prune dead or weak growth to open up dense foliage and to enhance the showy blooms. Propagated by cuttings.

DESCRIPTION Broadleaf evergreen. Easy to grow. Many varieties are available. Smooth twigs have oval, glossy, deep green leaves. Flowers are $2\frac{1}{2}$ to 4 inches wide and have single or double petals similar in shape to a rose or peony. They vary in color from white to deep rose-pink and dark red.

LANDSCAPE USE Popular as a specimen plant or planted as an informal hedge. Good to espalier against a sheltered wall. Good to grow under glass in colder climates.

BOTANICAL NAME *Campsis radicans*

COMMON NAME Trumpetcreeper; Trumpetvine; Hummingbird Vine.

RANGE Zones 4–9. Native from Pennsylvania to Missouri, Florida to Texas.

HEIGHT 30 to 40 feet high; climbing vine.

CULTURE Rampant grower in any soil. Prefers full sun or partial shade. Prune back to a few buds in the spring. Propagated by seed.

DESCRIPTION Deciduous vine. Easy to grow. Two-and-a-half inch long, lustrous, dark green leaves change to yellow-green in the fall. Late leafer. Orange and scarlet trumpet-shaped flowers bloom on new growth from July to September. Fast grower (up to 10 feet per season) bursting with health and vitality.

LANDSCAPE USE Clings to wood, brick, and stucco surfaces with aerial rootlets. Good for screening. Use on trellises and lath structures. Attracts hummingbirds.

RECOMMENDED VARIETY 'Madame Galen', a hybrid cross between *C. radicans* and *C. grandiflora*.

BOTANICAL NAME *Carissa grandiflora*

COMMON NAME Natal-Plum

RANGE Zones 9–10. Native to South Africa.

HEIGHT 5 to 7 feet, but occasionally grows to 18 feet; low, spreading habit.

CULTURE Prefers well-drained, sandy or loam soil in full sun. Adapts to poor soil and to dry sites; will tolerate partial shade. Enjoys a warm south or west facing wall, preferably with an overhang to protect it from frost. Propagated by cuttings.

DESCRIPTION Broadleaf evergreen. Lustrous, leathery green leaves are 3 inches long. Fragrant white flowers are star-shaped, 2 inches wide. Flowers appear intermittently throughout the year, followed by red, plum-shaped, edible fruit.

LANDSCAPE USE Use as a low screen or hedge. Spines on stems discourage trespassers.

BOTANICAL NAME *Caryopteris* x *clandonensis*

COMMON NAME Blue-mist shrub; Bluebeard

RANGE Zones 6–9. Hybrid developed from species native to Asia.

HEIGHT 2 feet tall with equal spread; low-growing shrub.

CULTURE Prefers light, loamy, well-drained soil in full sun. Cut back nearly to the ground in spring to encourage new growth. Flowers grow only on new shoots. Propagated by cuttings.

DESCRIPTION Generally grown as a deciduous, shrubby perennial. Valued for its powder blue, mistylike flowers. Blooms August to frost. Leaves are medium green and narrow.

LANDSCAPE USE Lovely late-blooming garden shrub.

BOTANICAL NAME *Castanea mollissima*

COMMON NAME Chinese Chestnut

RANGE Native to China. Hardy zones 4 to 8.

CULTURE Transplant young seedlings bare-root, larger plants from containers. Prefers well-drained loam soil in full sun. Heat and drought tolerant.

DESCRIPTION Attractive nut-bearing deciduous tree introduced as a disease-resistant substitute when the American chestnut began dying off from chestnut blight. Plants are slow-growing to 40 feet, creating a mounded habit. Long, pointed, serrated green leaves turn bronze in autumn. Conspicuous white flower clusters cover the tree in summer, followed by prickly nut cases that split open when ripe and spill large shining brown nuts onto the ground for easy harvesting. Fruits after four to five years.

LANDSCAPE USE Good lawn highlight; suitable for planting in groves.

BOTANICAL NAME *Ceanothus thyrsiflorus*

COMMON NAME California Lilac; Blue Blossom Ceanothus

RANGE Zones 8–10. Native to western coastal ranges from Santa Barbara, California to southern Oregon.

HEIGHT Usually 4 to 8 feet tall; but sometimes seen as tall as 20 feet; bushy, spreading habit.

CULTURE Prefers well-drained, average garden soil in full sun. Drought tolerant. Propagated by cuttings.

DESCRIPTION Broadleaf evergreen shrub or small tree. Glossy, dark green leaves. Flowers bloom March or April and are light to dark blue, displayed in dense clusters.

LANDSCAPE USE Good specimen plant. Usually planted against a wall or fence.

BOTANICAL NAME *Cedrus atlantica*

COMMON NAME Atlas Cedar

RANGE Native to Atlas Mountains, North Africa. Hardy zones 6 to 9.

CULTURE Prefers a well drained, moist loam soil in sun or partial shade. Transplant from containers.

DESCRIPTION Hardy evergreen conifer with beautiful blue needles forms a pyramid shape. Pliable branches shed heavy loads of snow. Slow growing to 60 feet.

LANDSCAPE USE Good lawn highlight; excellent tree to espalier against a wall.

RECOMMENDED VARIETY *Cedrus glauca pendula* is a magnificent weeping form with horizontal branches that can extend to 40 feet.

RECOMMENDED SPECIES *C. libani* ('Cedar of Lebanon') is more hardy, grows more massive, has dark green needles; *C. deodora* ('Deodora Cedar') has more graceful, pendulous branches and a more pronounced pyramidal habit, but is less hardy.

BOTANICAL NAME *Celastrus scandens*

COMMON NAME American Bittersweet

RANGE Zones 3–8. Native to North America, including Canada.

HEIGHT 20 feet or higher; vine.

CULTURE Grows well in any soil in full sun. Needs both a male and female plant for fruit set. Propagated by seed and cuttings.

DESCRIPTION Vigorous and twining deciduous vine with ropelike branches. Needs strong support. Grown for yellow to orange fruit clusters, which split open revealing brilliant red-coated seeds inside. Flowers are white and bloom in June. Deep, glossy green leaves turn yellowish green in winter.

LANDSCAPE USE Use in poor soils on fences and old trees. Branches with fruit are popular for indoor winter arrangements. Considered a pest in some New England states. **Caution:** Fruit is poisonous.

BOTANICAL NAME *Cercis chinensis*

COMMON NAME Chinese Redbud; Chinese Judas-tree

RANGE Zone 6. Native to central China.

HEIGHT Less than 10 feet; multi-stemmed shrub.

CULTURE Adaptable to many well-drained soil types including acidic and alkaline soils, in full sun to light shade. Propagated by cuttings.

DESCRIPTION Deciduous. Showy, purple, pealike flowers, less than an inch long, bloom in March or April. New leaf growth emerges as reddish purple, changing to a dark, lustrous green in the summer. Fall color is yellow to yellowish green.

LANDSCAPE USE Attractive as a specimen plant, in groupings and in a shrub border.

BOTANICAL NAME *Chaenomeles speciosa*

COMMON NAME Flowering Quince

RANGE Zones 5–9. Native to China, Tibet, and Burma.

HEIGHT 6 to 10 feet high, 8 to 12 feet wide; mounded, bushy habit.

CULTURE Tolerant of most climatic conditions, although prefers an acidic soil in full sun. Blooms reluctantly in warm winter areas. Prune at any time to control shape or growth. Flowers bloom on new growth. Propagated by cuttings.

DESCRIPTION Deciduous. Grown primarily for the flowers that can be forced indoors as early as January. Flowers, ranging in color from white to pink to scarlet red, are up to 2 inches long, and bloom in early May. Occasional fragrant, yellowish, globe-shaped fruit appears in autumn. Shiny green leaves grow on thorny stems.

LANDSCAPE USE A popular, showy, flowering, deciduous shrub. Bare branches suggest an oriental look.

BOTANICAL NAME *Chamaecyparis pisifera*

COMMON NAME False Cypress

RANGE Zones 5–9. Native to Japan.

HEIGHT 20 to 30 feet with 20 feet spread; upright habit.

CULTURE Tolerant of a variety of conditions. However, plants dislike dry, alkaline, or heavy clay soils and strong, cold winds. Tolerates shade and pollution. Prune heavily to maintain a compact, tidy shape. Propagated by cuttings.

DESCRIPTION Narrowleaf evergreen. Loose, open growth with spiny, scale-like, rough leaves that are dark green above and lighter green below. Light bearer of cones.

LANDSCAPE USE Excellent in Oriental gardens. Good as a specimen plant, and in a foundation or boundary planting.

BOTANICAL NAME *Cistus ladanifer*

COMMON NAME Crimson-spot Rock-rose; Gum Rock-rose

RANGE Zone 7 south. Native to Mediterranean.

HEIGHT 3 to 5 feet tall; compact, shrubby habit.

CULTURE Prefers average, well-drained soil in full sun. Tolerates drought, poor, dry soil, cold ocean winds, sea spray, or desert heat. Pinch the tips of young plants to encourage thick growth. Propagated by seed and cuttings.

DESCRIPTION Deciduous leaves are 3 to 4 inches long, and are dark green above and whitish below. Fragrant, large, 3-inch wide white flowers have dark crimson spots at the base of the petals. Blooms in June and July.

LANDSCAPE USE Use as a dry bank cover, in rock gardens, along drives, and in mixed borders.

BOTANICAL NAME *Clematis* species and hybrids

COMMON NAME Clematis

RANGE Zones 3–9. Wild species are distributed mostly in North America and China.

HEIGHT 5 to 18 feet tall. Fast grower, up to 5 to 10 feet a year; vigorous vining habit.

CULTURE Mulch so that the roots stay cool while the tops are in partial shade or full sun. Plant in rich, loose, well-drained soil. Prefers a neutral to acidic soil. Varieties that bloom only in the spring should be pruned severely after flowering. Varieties that bloom in the summer, bloom only on new wood and should be cut back in the spring about 6 to 12 inches off the ground. Varieties that bloom in the spring and in the summer should be pruned lightly after flowering, as the blooms appear both on old and new wood. Propagated by seed and cuttings.

DESCRIPTION Deciduous. Not a difficult herbaceous vine to grow. Leaves are green. Flowers are 3 to 7 inches across and vary from white and pink to purple and blue.

LANDSCAPE USE Stems twist and twine around trellises, fences, walls, or any structure that offers a good support. Popular for covering arbors.

BOTANICAL NAME *Cornus florida*

COMMON NAME Flowering Dogwood

RANGE Zones 3–9. Native to North America.

HEIGHT 5 to 30 feet tall and to 30 feet wide; small tree.

CULTURE Deciduous. Easy to grow in neutral to acidic soil in sun or light shade. Tolerates pollution. To prevent anthracnose disease (also called lower branch dieback) keep plants watered during dry spells and feed by sprinkling a general purpose granular fertilizer around the drip line each spring. Propagated by cuttings.

DESCRIPTION Highly ornamental with white or pink star-shaped flowers, showy red fruit, and dramatic fall leaf colorings. Plants bloom in spring, outshining everything else in the garden. Fruit is favored by birds and squirrels. Pointed, oval green leaves have veins running parallel to the leaf margins. The autumn color varies among red, purple, and bronze foliage.

LANDSCAPE USE Excellent specimen tree to use as a lawn highlight. Popular for foundation plantings and as a canopy for mass plantings of azaleas.

BOTANICAL NAME *Cornus kousa*

COMMON NAME Korean Dogwood

RANGE Zones 5–8. Native to Korea.

HEIGHT Up to 30 feet; mounded, spreading habit.

CULTURE Prefers humus-rich, acidic loam soil in full sun. Has better disease resistance than the native flowering dogwoods. Propagated from cuttings.

DESCRIPTION Deciduous. Spectacular flowering display similar to the native flowering dogwoods, except it blooms several weeks later, in early summer, and while the plant is in full leaf. The leaves are bright green, pointed, and serrated, and turn scarlet in autumn. Flowers are followed by edible fruits that resemble large raspberries.

LANDSCAPE USE Excellent lawn highlight and foundation accent. Exquisite planted as an avenue along a driveway.

BOTANICAL NAME *Cornus mas*

COMMON NAME Cornelian-cherry

RANGE Zones 5–9. Native to Europe and Asia.

HEIGHT 20 to 25 feet, equal spread; rounded habit.

CULTURE Easy to grow in any well-drained loam soil in full sun. Propagated mostly from cuttings. Transplant bare-root or from containers. Pollution resistant.

DESCRIPTION Small, deciduous tree valued for its yellow, early spring flowers, borne in clusters before the leaves appear. Leaves are oval, serrated, pointed, dark green. Oblong, cherry-red fruit appears in summer and is edible, generally eaten by birds as it ripens.

LANDSCAPE USE Good lawn highlight. Popular as an accent in beds and borders planted with daffodils and early-flowering perennials, such as pansies.

BOTANICAL NAME *Cornus sericea*

COMMON NAME Red-twig Dogwood

RANGE Zones 3-9. Native to North America.

HEIGHT Up to 8 feet, generally kept below 6 feet by pruning; erect habit.

CULTURE Tolerates a wide range of soil conditions, including wet soil, in full sun. Propagated by cuttings. Plant bare-root or from containers. Prune to the trunk after flowering to encourage a new set of juvenile stems.

DESCRIPTION Deciduous. Whiplike stems grow skyward. In the juvenile stage these are a brilliant red color and stand out as a beautiful ornamental accent in winter when the leaves have fallen. White flowers are borne in flat clusters, and appear soon after the leaves in spring. The bright green leaves are oval, pointed, and serrated, with prominent leaf veins typical of dogwoods.

LANDSCAPE USE Popular for massing on berms, raised mounds of soil built for screening. Good accent in mixed shrub borders and foundation plantings, especially planted against white stucco walls or white picket fences where the red winter bark color stands out dramatically.

BOTANICAL NAME *Corylopsis glabrescens*

COMMON NAME Fragrant Winterhazel

RANGE Zones 5–9. Native to China.

HEIGHT To 5 feet and as wide; mounded habit.

CULTURE Prefers well-drained, moist, acidic garden soil in partial shade or in a sheltered location in sun.

DESCRIPTION Deciduous. Valued for the soft yellow, fragrant flowers that bloom in March on bare stems. Dark green, oval-shaped leaves turn golden in the fall. Open, attractive, branching habit.

LANDSCAPE USE One of the earliest blooming shrubs. Branches are often cut and taken indoors in the spring to use in floral arrangements. Popular as a foundation shrub and as a winter accent in mixed shrub borders.

BOTANICAL NAME *Cotinus coggygria*

COMMON NAME Smoketree

RANGE Zones 5–8. Native to southern Europe and central China.

HEIGHT 10 to 15 feet with spread of 10 to 20 feet; upright, spreading, loose, open habit.

CULTURE Adaptable to a wide range of soil types in full sun. Readily transplanted. Can be pruned in March down to 5 to 6 feet to get a shrub effect. Propagated by seed and cuttings.

DESCRIPTION Deciduous. Brown or purplish bark with bluish green leaves. Ornamentally unimportant, small yellow flowers bloom in June and July. However, starting in July and lasting through September, clusters of flower stems burst into a spectacular show of soft, smokey pink hairs, resembling clouds hovering over the foliage. Small, kidney-shaped fruit develops after the show. Some varieties have purple leaves and purple flower stems.

LANDSCAPE USE Effective as a lawn accent and as a foundation plant.

BOTANICAL NAME *Cotoneaster horizontalis*

COMMON NAME Rock Spray

RANGE Zones 5–10. Native to China.

HEIGHT 3 to 4 feet high, spreading to 8 to 10 feet; low, spreading habit.

CULTURE Prefers well-drained soil in full sun. Likes good air circulation. Propagated by seed and cuttings.

DESCRIPTION Deciduous. Green, round, 1/2-inch long leaves turn a lovely bronze color in the fall. Branches spread by side shoots and give the overall appearance of a fish bone pattern. The early summer pink flowers are ornamentally unimportant but are followed by bright red berries that last through the fall, into the winter months.

LANDSCAPE USE Excellent ground cover that is often used in rock gardens to spill over boulders and retaining walls.

BOTANICAL NAME *Crataegus phaenopyrum*

COMMON NAME Washington Hawthorn

RANGE Native eastern United States. Hardy zones 3 to 8.

CULTURE Transplant from containers or balled and burlapped. Prefers fertile loam soil in full sun.

DESCRIPTION Upright, rounded, deciduous tree admired for its abundance of white blossoms in spring and brilliant red berry displays in autumn. Reasonably fast-growing to 40 feet.

LANDSCAPE USE Excellent lawn highlight. Can be pruned heavily to make an attractive flowering hedge. Sharp thorns on branches deter intruders.

RECOMMENDED VARIETIES There are more than 100 different species of hawthorn native to North America. Extensive hybridizing has been done with European species to produce superior varieties. A related species, *C. viridis* ('Green Hawthorn'), especially the variety 'Winter King', is also a valuable hawthorn for home landscapes.

BOTANICAL NAME *Cytisus scoparius*

COMMON NAME Scotch Broom

RANGE Zones 5–8. Native to central and southern Europe.

HEIGHT 5 to 6 feet tall, spreading equal to or greater than height; bushy, mounded habit.

CULTURE Easy to grow, drought tolerant. Prefers well-drained, garden soil in full sun. Propagated by seed or softwood cuttings.

DESCRIPTION Deciduous. Rounded shrub with upright, slender, medium green stems and twigs that keep their color throughout winter. Leaves are a light to medium green with no fall color. Bright yellow pea flowers bloom profusely on old wood in May and June. Fruit is a fuzzy brown pod of no ornamental importance.

LANDSCAPE USE Excellent plant for poor soil. Often seen dotting coastal highways. Good in mixed shrub borders and as a hedge plant.

BOTANICAL NAME *Daphne* x *burkwoodii*

COMMON NAME Burkwood Daphne

RANGE Zones 4–8. Wild species native to China.

HEIGHT 3 to 4 feet tall; mounded habit.

CULTURE Prefers well-drained, moist, slightly acidic to alkaline soil. Prefers some shade. Propagated by cuttings.

DESCRIPTION Tends to be semi-evergreen. Leaves are lustrous dark green above and lighter green beneath. The outstanding feature of this plant is the heavy, fragrant, pinkish white flower clusters that bloom in May. Flowers are followed by bright red berries, also borne in clusters.

LANDSCAPE USE Good in a shrub border, foundation planting, or near a walkway, where the fragrant flowers can be enjoyed.

BOTANICAL NAME *Deutzia gracilis*

COMMON NAME Slender Deutzia

RANGE Zones 4–8. Native to Japan.

HEIGHT 2 to 4 feet high, but can grow to 6 feet tall and 3 to 4 feet wide; compact, mounded habit.

CULTURE Prefers any good garden soil in full sun or very light shade. Transplant in the spring. Prune after flowering. Propagated by cuttings.

DESCRIPTION Deciduous. Graceful, wide-spreading, arching branches. Leaves are flat green in the summer, and turn slightly bronze in the fall. Flowers profusely in May in a mass of fragrant, white, star-shaped blooms.

LANDSCAPE USE A popular, easy-to-grow accent, hedge, or border plant.

BOTANICAL NAME *Enkianthus campanulatus*

COMMON NAME Redvein Enkianthus

RANGE Zones 4–7. Native to Japan.

HEIGHT 8 to 15 feet; upright, bushy habit.

CULTURE Prefers acidic soil in sun or partial shade. Propagated by seed or cuttings.

DESCRIPTION Deciduous. Beautiful, creamy yellow flowers resembling lily-of-the-valley, are tinged orange or pink, appear in spring. Small, pointed, dark green leaves resemble azaleas, turn orange and red in autumn.

LANDSCAPE USE Good for foundation plantings, containers, bonsai, and hedges. Twiggy silhouette looks beautiful against winter landscape.

BOTANICAL NAME *Escallonia exoniensis*

COMMON NAME Escallonia

RANGE Zones 7–10. Native to South America.

HEIGHT Up to 10 feet, spreading 10 feet; dense, mounded habit.

CULTURE Prefers moist, acidic loam soil in full sun. Best planted from containers. Propagated by cuttings.

DESCRIPTION Weeping branches have dark green, heart-shaped leaves. Masses of small, rose-pink flowers cover the plant in spring.

LANDSCAPE USE Beautiful lawn highlight and billowing, informal hedge.

BOTANICAL NAME *Euonymus alata*

COMMON NAME Burning Bush; Winged Euonymus

RANGE Zones 4-7. Native to northeastern Asia and central China.

HEIGHT 7 to 10 feet high; 10 to 15 feet spread; mounded, bushy habit.

CULTURE Grows well in any well-drained soil in full sun to light shade. Propagated by cuttings.

DESCRIPTION Deciduous, dense shrub with side-spreading stiff branches that have corklike protrusions called "wings". Main interest comes in the fall when the medium- to deep green oval leaves turn a brilliant crimson so intense the plant seems to be on fire. If planted in partial shade the leaves turn a purplish red, never attaining their full, dazzling glory. Inconspicuous, tiny, greenish flower clusters bloom in May to be followed by a sparse crop of orange-red berries.

LANDSCAPE USE A popular plant with several seasons of interest. Stunning planted against dark evergreens. Use as background, screen, hedge, or specimen plant.

BOTANICAL NAME *Euonymus japonicus*

COMMON NAME Japanese Euonymus

RANGE Zones 7–9. Native to Japan.

HEIGHT 5 to 15 feet high, narrower in width. Prune for a low height; upright, shrubby habit.

CULTURE Adaptable to a variety of soils and conditions. Tolerates clay soil and ocean spray, and full sun to heavy shade. Propagated by division and cuttings.

DESCRIPTION Broadleaf evergreen. Attractive, deep green, glossy, leathery, oval leaves. Small, greenish white flowers appear in June, followed by pinkish orange berries. Varieties with variegated gold and silver leaves are offered.

LANDSCAPE USE Popular for its ability to grow well in unfavorable conditions. Effective as a hedge. Can be used as a houseplant.

BOTANICAL NAME *Exochorda racemosa*

COMMON NAME Pearlbush

RANGE Zones 5–9. Native to China.

HEIGHT 10 to 15 feet tall, spreading as wide; mounded, bushy habit.

CULTURE Grows well in almost any well-drained soil in full sun. Hard to establish in garden if planted bare-root. Buy as a container- grown plant or balled and burlapped. Prune off stem tips to maintain compact habit. Propagated by cuttings.

DESCRIPTION Deciduous. Although the flowers only last for about seven to twelve days in midspring, they are worth planting for the spectacular show of white, pearl-shaped buds that open into gorgeous flower clusters. Pointed, oval, attractive green leaves.

LANDSCAPE USE Use as a small specimen tree, or plant in groupings of three or more for an effective shrub border. Makes an attractive display planted against an evergreen background.

BOTANICAL NAME *Fagus sylvatica*

COMMON NAME European Beech

RANGE Native to Europe. Hardy zones 4 to 7.

CULTURE Prefers deep loam soil in full sun. Transplant from containers or balled and burlapped.

DESCRIPTION Large, billowing, deciduous tree grows to 90 feet with an equal spread. Bright green, oval leaves are serrated and have prominent leaf veins, changing to parchment brown in autumn. Inconspicuous green flowers followed by small, nut-like seed capsules enjoyed by squirrels. Massive dove-gray trunk. Slow growing.

LANDSCAPE USE Magnificent lawn highlight. Can be trained and pruned to make an arbor or to create a tunnel effect. Also a dense hedge.

RECOMMENDED VARIETY There is a weeping form, 'Pendula', and purple-leafed form, 'Trifolia'.

BOTANICAL NAME *Fatsia japonica*

COMMON NAME Japanese Aralia

RANGE Zones 8–10. Native to Japan.

HEIGHT Up to 10 feet; upright habit.

CULTURE Prefers moist, sandy, humus-rich soil in a lightly shaded location. Plant from containers. Propagated by cuttings.

DESCRIPTION Tender, evergreen shrub. Its large, handsome, figlike leaves give the plant a tropical appearance. Greenish yellow flower clusters occur in summer, enhancing the ornamental appearance of the leaves.

LANDSCAPE USE Mostly used in the southern United States and California to create a dramatic accent among foundation plantings, as well as in atriums and mixed shrub borders.

BOTANICAL NAME *Forsythia* x *intermedia*

COMMON NAME Forsythia

RANGE Zones 5–9. Hybrid cross from Germany.

HEIGHT 7 to 10 feet tall, with an equal spread; upright, arching, spreading habit.

CULTURE Accepts any well-drained soil condition in full sun or light shade. Propagated by seed and cuttings.

DESCRIPTION Deciduous. Grown for its prolific, deep yellow 1-inch flowers that bloom throughout March and April. The medium green leaves are long and somewhat oval shaped. In the fall, the foliage turns a yellow-green.

LANDSCAPE USE Valued for its early spring blooms. Effectively used in shrub borders, massings, groupings, and as a slope cover to control erosion.

RECOMMENDED VARIETY 'Lynwood Gold,' a mutation discovered in Ireland.

BOTANICAL NAME *Fothergilla gardenii*

COMMON NAME Dwarf Fothergilla

RANGE Zones 5-8. Native to Virginia and Georgia.

HEIGHT 2 to 3 feet high with similar or greater spread; upright, twiggy habit.

CULTURE Prefers well-drained, peaty, sandy, acidic soil in full sun or partial shade. Propagated by cuttings.

DESCRIPTION Deciduous. Can be difficult to establish. White fragrant flower spikes resemble pussy willows, burst into bloom on naked branches in April and May. Attractive dark green leaves are leathery and turn a brilliant yellow to orange-scarlet in the fall. Has a bare, twiggy, winter silhouette.

LANDSCAPE USE Good planted in combination with rhododendrons and azaleas. Excellent choice as an accent in tulip beds. Frequently used in foundation plantings, borders, and masses. Flowering stems are good for cutting to make attractive indoor floral arrangements.

BOTANICAL NAME *Fuchsia hybrida*

COMMON NAME Hybrid Fuchsia; Lady's Ear Drops

RANGE Zones 6–10. Native to South America.

HEIGHT 3 to 12 feet tall, depending upon variety; habit varies from erect shrub to trailing types.

CULTURE Prefers well-drained, humus-rich garden soil in partial shade. Enjoys cool summer temperatures where there is a lot of moisture and salt in the air, such as coastal locations. Prune by snipping off tips of branches to discourage legginess. Propagated by cuttings.

DESCRIPTION Fuchsias bloom from early summer to late frost. Over 500 varieties are grown, mostly on the West Coast of the United States. Flowers are mostly bicolored. The outer part of the flower is always white, red, or pink. The inner flower color can be any combination of white, blue-violet, purple, pink, red, and orange-red. The flowers are not fragrant. The green leaves are usually small, oval-shaped. Fuchsias wilt easily from lack of moisture and are prone to whiteflies and spider mites.

LANDSCAPE USE Makes an attractive hanging basket, and a small to large shrub, espalier, or standard form. Nectar of flowers is relished by hummingbirds.

BOTANICAL NAME *Gardenia jasminoides*

COMMON NAME Gardenia; Cape-jasmine

RANGE Zones 8–10. Native to China.

HEIGHT 3 to 5 feet tall with equal spread; mounded, bushy habit.

CULTURE Prefers a well-drained, moist, fertile, acidic soil in partial shade or full sun in coastal areas. Feed regularly with fertilizer during the growing season. Treat chlorosis with iron sulfate or iron chelate. Prune to remove faded blooms and wayward branches.

DESCRIPTION Broadleaf evergreen. Grown for its heavy fragrance and the beautiful, 3-inch wide, solitary, waxy white flowers which appear from late spring through summer. The glossy, thick, leathery, dark green leaves add to the overall beauty of the shrub. Intolerant of ocean spray.

LANDSCAPE USE Commonly used as a houseplant. Attractive in containers, raised beds, hedges, low screens, and as a specimen plant. Can be grown outdoors only in frost-free areas.

BOTANICAL NAME *Gelsemium sempervirens*

COMMON NAME Carolina Jessamine

RANGE Zones 6–9. Native to North America from Virginia to Florida.

HEIGHT 10 to 20 feet; vine.

CULTURE Prefers moist, well-drained, humus-rich soil in full sun, but will flower in partial shade. Propagated by seed and cuttings.

DESCRIPTION Broadleaf evergreen, twining vine. Shiny, bright green leaves are 1 to 4 inches long and run in pairs along thin, green to brown stems. Fragrant, tubular yellow flowers are 1 to 1 1/2 inches long; bloom late winter through early spring.

LANDSCAPE USE Grows on trellises, stone walls, up small trees, and on fences and mailboxes. Can be used as a slope cover to control erosion. Will survive hard pruning to within 3 feet of the soil line to control its aggressive habit. **Caution:** All parts are highly poisonous.

BOTANICAL NAME *Ginkgo biloba*

COMMON NAME Ginkgo; Maidenhair Tree

RANGE Native to China. Hardy zones 3 to 9.

CULTURE Transplant from containers or balled and burlapped. Prefers sandy loam soil in full sun. Male trees are more desirable than females, since the females develop plum-like fruits that are malodorous.

DESCRIPTION Plants are deciduous and grow slowly to 80 feet, with an upright, pyramidal habit becoming more wide-spreading with age. Fan-shaped leaves turn golden yellow in fall.

LANDSCAPE USE Popular street tree and lawn highlight, especially the male form, which does not produce malodorous fruit.

RECOMMENDED VARIETY 'Autumn Gold' is an attractive, spreading, male form.

BOTANICAL NAME *Halesia carolina*

COMMON NAME Carolina Silverbell

RANGE Native to the eastern seaboard of North America. Hardy zones 4 to 8.

CULTURE Transplant balled and burlapped. Prefers fertile, humus-rich, acid soil in sun or partial shade.

DESCRIPTION Medium-fast growing to 40 feet with an upright, spreading habit. Beautiful pendant, bell-shaped flowers crowd the branches in spring. Oval, dark green leaves change to lime-green in fall.

LANDSCAPE USE Beautiful lawn highlight. Effective planted in woodland gardens.

RELATED SPECIES A related species, *Halesia monticola* ('Mountain Silver-bell'), also native to North America, is much taller, growing to 100 feet and not such a good plant for small gardens.

BOTANICAL NAME *Hamamelis mollis*

COMMON NAME Chinese Witch-hazel

RANGE Zones 5–8. Native to China.

HEIGHT 10 to 15 feet tall with equal spread; rounded, sparse habit.

CULTURE Prefers moist, well-drained, acidic soil in full sun or partial shade. Temperatures below -15°F will cause damage. Propagated by seed or cuttings.

DESCRIPTION Deciduous. Ascending branches with soft, downy, new stems. Stark winter silhouette. The sweet, fragrant flower clusters are borne on naked stems and begin to bloom as early as January, through early March. The yellow flowers have a red base and are $\frac{1}{2}$ inch wide. The 5-inch leaves are roundish, short, and pointed; medium green above and downy gray below. Leaves turn yellow in the fall.

LANDSCAPE USE Mainly planted for its early, fragrant bloom and its winter habit.

RECOMMENDED VARIETY 'Arnold's Promise,' a clear yellow.

BOTANICAL NAME *Hedera helix*

COMMON NAME English Ivy

RANGE Zones 5–10. Native to Europe and western Asia.

HEIGHT Up to 20 feet high; woody vine.

CULTURE Thrives in any good garden soil with average moisture in full sun. Propagated by cuttings.

DESCRIPTION Broadleaf evergreen. Thick, leathery, dark green leaves are lobed in the juvenile stage and smooth once adult. Some leaves may turn purplish in the fall in exposed areas. Small, greenish white flowers borne in clusters attract insects in the spring. In warm climates, black fruit is produced.

LANDSCAPE USE Terrific ground cover or climber. Ivy holds soil, discouraging erosion and slippage on slopes. Ivy tendrils cling to almost any vertical surface including walls, trellises, and fences. Also used in topiary designs.

BOTANICAL NAME *Hibiscus syriacus*

COMMON NAME Rose of Sharon; Shrub Althea

RANGE Zones 5–9. Native to China and India.

HEIGHT 6 to 20 feet tall and 8 to 10 feet wide; bushy, mounded habit.

CULTURE Prefers moist, fertile soil in full sun. Adaptable to most soil types and to partial shade in the hottest climates. Tolerates pollution and seashore conditions. Prune to maintain compact shape. Propagated by seed or cuttings.

DESCRIPTION Deciduous. Compact, much branched, and erect. Charming, hibiscus-like, unscented flowers, up to 3 inches across, bloom late July through August. Colors include white, red, purple, and blue with a crimson "eye." They can be single or double. Leaves are generally less than 3 inches long, oval-shaped, with a deep green to grayish green color. Drab autumn color.

LANDSCAPE USE Prune to a single trunk to make a small, flowering tree or sheer multiple trunks to make a screen or hedge. Well-grown specimens can produce masses of flowers to create a lawn highlight.

BOTANICAL NAME *Hydrangea macrophylla*

COMMON NAME Hydrangea

RANGE Zones 6–9. Native to Japan.

HEIGHT 5 to 8 feet tall, spreading 6 to 10 feet; symmetrical, rounded habit.

CULTURE Succeeds in any average soil in full sun or light shade. The blue to pink flower color is controlled by soil pH. Neutral or alkaline soil produces pink or red flowers. Acidic soil (prepare neutral or alkaline soils with aluminum sulfate) produces blue flowers. Tolerates seashore conditions. Propagated by cuttings.

DESCRIPTION Deciduous. Profuse bloomer in mild winter areas; likes the protection of a wall or fence where plants freeze to the ground in winter. The unscented, large, globular, lacy clusters of blue, pink, red, or white flowers bloom July through September and are reminiscent of flowers grown in an old-fashioned garden. Bright green leaves are oval-shaped, 4 to 8 inches long, with no fall color. Close to 400 cultivars are available.

LANDSCAPE USE Popular florist plant available around Easter and Mother's Day. Makes a good shrub border or accent plant.

RECOMMENDED VARIETY 'Annabelle,' a large-flowered, free-flowering, white variety.

BOTANICAL NAME *Hypericum calycinum*

COMMON NAME St.-John's-wort

RANGE Zones 4–8. Native to southeastern Europe and Asia Minor.

HEIGHT Up to 24 inches tall; dense, compact habit.

CULTURE Prefers well-drained, moist, loamy garden soil in full sun or partial shade. Tolerant of sandy soil. Invasive in good growing conditions. In colder climates needs protected site. Cut back any dead stems after new growth appears in early spring. Propagated by division or cuttings.

DESCRIPTION Evergreen except in colder climates. Grown for its prolific, glistening yellow flowers in mid- to late summer. Slender, oval, green leaves have conspicuous veins.

LANDSCAPE USE Versatile. Excellent ground cover. Good for erosion control on slopes. Desirable to use as a foundation planting near a house or as an edging to a shrub border.

RECOMMENDED VARIETY 'Hidcote'.

BOTANICAL NAME *Ilex* x *meserveae*

COMMON NAME Blue Holly; Meserve Hybrids

RANGE Zones 5–9. Hybrid cross developed in New York state.

HEIGHT 6 to 10 feet tall with equal width; upright habit.

CULTURE Prefers loose, well-drained, acidic soil in full sun or partial shade. Protect from wind in colder climates. Need both a male and a female plant to produce fruit. One male will pollinate up to eight females. Tip-prune to encourage new growth and maintain density. Propagated by cuttings.

DESCRIPTION Broadleaf evergreen. Valued for its beautiful, bluish green leaf tone. The glossy, leathery 2-inch leaves are wavy with spines. New stems have a purplish caste. Bright red fruit is persistent, remaining on the plant through autumn and winter. Generally more attractive than *I. aquifolia* ('English Holly'), and bears more berries.

LANDSCAPE USE Excellent choice for hedges, foundation plantings, and as a lawn highlight. Can be pruned into cones to make sentinels on both sides of a gate or doorway. Attracts birds.

BOTANICAL NAME *Ilex opaca*

COMMON NAME American Holly

RANGE Native to North America, mostly along the eastern seaboard. Hardy zones 5 to 9.

CULTURE Transplant balled and burlapped. Prefers moist, sandy, or loam, acid soil in sun or partial shade. One male plant is needed for every six females in order to produce berries.

DESCRIPTION Beautiful pyramid shape with spiny, evergreen, dark green leaves; inconspicuous white flowers followed by bright red berries in fall and winter. Slow growing, up to 50 feet high.

LANDSCAPE USE Good evergreen lawn highlight. Popular as sentinels to an entrance. Plants can be heavily pruned to make a dense, impenetrable hedge.

RECOMMENDED VARIETIES 'Jersey Knight'—a male—and 'Jersey Princess'—a female—both display handsome dark green leaves more attractive than the yellow-green coloring of the species.

RECOMMENDED SPECIES *Ilex aquifolium* ('English Holly') generally displays a more attractive form, with glossy, darker green leaves and richer berry display, but is not so hardy. *Ilex* x *meserveae* ('Hybrid blue Hollies') are even more beautiful, with handsome blue-green coloring and heavy berry displays.

BOTANICAL NAME *Ilex verticillata*

COMMON NAME Winterberry

RANGE Zones 3–9. Native to swamps along the Eastern seaboard of North America.

HEIGHT 6 to 10 feet tall with equal spread; dense, multi-stemmed habit.

CULTURE Prefers moist, acidic, rich soil in full sun or partial shade. Tolerates light and heavy soils. Adaptable to wet conditions. Transplant balled and burlapped or as a container plant. Propagated by cuttings.

DESCRIPTION Broadleaf evergreen. Small, smooth, oval, dark green leaves are hairy below. Slender, angled, brown stems. Showy, bright red fruit appears August through January. Best to plant one male for every eight females in order to ensure a good berry display.

LANDSCAPE USE Choice plant along lakes and ponds where water can reflect fruit. In the winter, stunning as a mass planting where the red fruit contrasts against snowy lawns. Good foundation plant and lawn highlight. Attracts birds.

BOTANICAL NAME *Juniperus horizontalis*

COMMON NAME Creeping Juniper

RANGE Zones 3–9. Native to North America.

HEIGHT 1 to 2 feet tall, spreading 4 to 8 feet; low, creeping habit.

CULTURE Prefers well-drained, stony or sandy, slightly alkaline soil in full sun. Tolerates exposure and hot, dry climates. Propagated by layering or cuttings.

DESCRIPTION Narrowleaf evergreen. Low-growing shrub with long trailing branches forming large mats. Leaves vary from green to steel blue, depending on the variety, with a purplish caste in the winter. Flowers and cones are ornamentally unimportant.

LANDSCAPE USE A popular, low ground cover that persists in poor situations, including seashore plantings. Good slope cover to control erosion. Effective for rock gardens and as an edging to foundation plantings.

BOTANICAL NAME *Kalmia latifolia*

COMMON NAME Mountain-laurel

RANGE Zones 4–9. Native to eastern North America.

HEIGHT 4 to 8 feet; upright, bushy habit.

CULTURE Prefers cool, moist, well-drained, acidic soil in full sun or partial shade. Flowers best in full sun, but one of the best flowering shrubs for deep shade. Easy to transplant. Mulch to keep soil moist. Propagated by cuttings.

DESCRIPTION Broadleaf evergreen. Slow-grower. In youth, symmetrical and loose; old age, open with gnarled trunks and limbs. One-half-inch hexagonal-shaped flowers are borne in large, showy clusters up to 5 inches across. Colors include white, pink, red, and purple. The buds, too, are extremely attractive, folded in intricate patterns. Two-to-5 inch leathery, dark green leaves arranged in a whorl. Brown seed capsules last throughout the winter, but are best removed before they develop seeds to encourage flowering for the next season.

LANDSCAPE USE One of the best-loved native flowering shrubs. Excellent for naturalizing. Good specimen for shady borders and mass plantings.

BOTANICAL NAME *Kerria japonica*

COMMON NAME Japanese Kerria

RANGE Zones 4–9. Native to China.

HEIGHT 5 to 8 feet, 6 to 9 feet wide; spreading habit.

CULTURE Prefers loamy, well-drained soil of moderate fertility in full shade. Transplant balled and burlapped or from a container. Prune away any dead branches. Propagated by cuttings.

DESCRIPTION Deciduous. Densely branched and twiggy with yellowish to bright green stems that spread by suckering. Bright green leaves turn yellow in the fall. The golden yellow, single, cup-shaped flowers bloom April through May, and are $^1/_2$ to 2 inches across. The variety 'Pleniflora' has double flowers.

LANDSCAPE USE Tough plant. Effective as an informal hedge. Tolerates light shade and for this reason plants look good massed in a woodland garden.

BOTANICAL NAME *Koelreuteria paniculata*

COMMON NAME Golden Rain

RANGE Native to China. Hardy zones 5 to 9.

CULTURE Deciduous tree best transplanted balled and burlapped. Adaptable to a wide range of soils and climate conditions. Tolerates heat, drought, alkaline soil. Prefers full sun.

DESCRIPTION Beautiful, rounded, shade tree, reasonably fast-growing to 40 feet. Rich green, deeply serrated, compound leaves. Masses of yellow flower clusters in midsummer are followed by attractive seed cases resembling Chinese lanterns that change from green to parchment brown.

LANDSCAPE USE Excellent lawn highlight. Good choice to provide shade for a deck, patio, or terrace.

RELATED SPECIES A related species, *Koelreuteria bipinnata* ('Coral Tree') is preferred for the southwestern states. Similar to *K. paniculata* ('Golden Rain') in appearance, its decorative seed capsules change to a beautiful pink in fall.

BOTANICAL NAME *Kolkwitzia amabilis*

COMMON NAME Beauty Bush

RANGE Zones 5–8. Native to China.

HEIGHT 7 to 15 feet high and 5 to 10 feet wide; erect, dense, compact habit.

CULTURE Prefers well-drained loam soil in full sun or partial shade. Easy to grow. Propagated by cuttings.

DESCRIPTION Deciduous. Graceful, many-branched, fountainlike shrub. Dark green leaves are fuzzy and turn a dull red in autumn. The 3-inch flower clusters bloom profusely in late May. The bell-shaped flowers are bright pink with yellow throats. Tiny, hairy seed heads are noticeable in late June. Decorative brown bark peels in large strips and flakes on older stems.

LANDSCAPE USE Good screen or border plant. Excellent lawn highlight and foundation specimen.

BOTANICAL NAME *Laburnum* x *watereri*

COMMON NAME Golden Chain

RANGE Hybrid of species native to Europe. Hardy zones 5 to 7.

CULTURE Transplant balled and burlapped. Prefers moist loam soil with good drainage, in sun or light shade. Medium-fast growing to 15 feet.

DESCRIPTION Upright habit with oval, pointed, green leaves arranged in threes, has gorgeous "chains" of yellow pea-like flowers hanging from the branch tips.

LANDSCAPE USE Beautiful lawn highlight. Can be trained over metal arches to create a flowering tunnel.

RECOMMENDED VARIETY The variety 'Vossii', raised in Holland, has extra long "chains" up to 2 feet long.

BOTANICAL NAME *Lagerstroemia indica*

COMMON NAME Crape-myrtle

RANGE Zones 7–10. Native to China and Korea.

HEIGHT 12 to 20 feet tall, 8 to 12 feet wide; tree-like habit.

CULTURE Prefers a moist, well-drained, rich organic soil in full sun. Tolerates dry, poor soil, pollution, and extreme heat. Transplant when balled and burlapped or from a container. Propagated by cuttings.

DESCRIPTION Deciduous. Dense shrub can develop into a small, flowering tree. Bud clusters, 6 to 12 inches long, burst into wrinkled, 1-inch, pink, purple, or white flowers resembling lilacs. Young leaves are bronze, maturing to medium or dark green. Vivid show of orange, red, and yellow fall color. Attractive, smooth, brownish gray bark peels to reveal maroon and pinkish blotches.

LANDSCAPE USE Use as a lawn accent and to create an avenue framing a path. Suitable for planting in containers. Extremely popular in hot climates because it is heat and drought resistant.

BOTANICAL NAME *Lantana camara*

COMMON NAME Shrub Verbena; Common Lantana

RANGE Zones 8–10. Native to the West Indies.

HEIGHT To 6 feet; upright, spreading habit.

CULTURE Tolerates any well-drained garden soil. Excess water and fertilizer inhibits blooms. Prune in spring to remove dead wood and to maintain a compact habit. Propagated by cuttings.

DESCRIPTION Vining shrub grown for profuse, all-year bloom in frost-free areas. Rough, dark green leaves. One-to-2-inch flower clusters bloom yellow, orange, or red.

LANDSCAPE USE Use for low hedges and foundation plantings. An extremely versatile plant that can be sheared to keep it low and bushy, or trained to climb up a trellis. In areas with severe winters, it is often grown in pots, pruned to a single trunk, and moved indoors.

BOTANICAL NAME *Leucothoe fontanesiana*

COMMON NAME Drooping Leucothoe

RANGE Zones 4–6. Native to mid-Atlantic and southeastern United States.

HEIGHT 3 to 6 feet tall with equal spread; spreading, arching habit.

CULTURE Prefers loose, moist, well-drained, acidic, high-organic soil in partial shade. Protect from full sun and wind. Propagated by seed or cuttings.

DESCRIPTION Broadleaf evergreen. Majestic, long, arching, leathery green leaves stir with the slightest breeze. Leaves turn bronze in the fall. Fragrant, white, pendulous flowers bloom in May.

LANDSCAPE USE All season interest. Excellent cover for banks or cascading over retaining walls. An interesting, graceful plant for massing along woodland walks and driveways. Contrasts well with rhododendrons.

BOTANICAL NAME *Ligustrum* x *vicaryi*

COMMON NAME Vicary Golden Privet

RANGE Zones 6–10. Native to England.

HEIGHT 3 to 12 feet tall, 4 to 15 feet wide; dense, rounded habit.

CULTURE Adaptable to a variety of soils in full sun or partial shade. Its coloring is more effective in sun. Propagated by cuttings.

DESCRIPTION Deciduous. Slow-growing. Leaves are green with an overlay of bright gold or yellow-green if planted in a shady area. Small, white clusters of flowers bloom in July and are ornamentally unimportant.

LANDSCAPE USE Attractive specimen for a shrub border. Good container plant. Makes an unusual hedge, especially when alternated with a regular green privet for a "checkered" effect.

BOTANICAL NAME *Liquidambar styraciflua*

COMMON NAME Sweetgum

RANGE Native to North America. Hardy zones 5 to 9.

CULTURE Transplant balled and burlapped. Prefers moist loam soil in full sun.

DESCRIPTION Fast-growing to 60 feet, developing an attractive pyramidal shape. The glossy-green, star-shaped leaves turn yellow and reddish tones in autumn. Hard, brown, spiney seed cases hang from the tree in winter.

LANDSCAPE USE Superb lawn highlight. Good street tree.

RECOMMENDED VARIETY Various named varieties are available, some selected for exceptional fall coloring, including 'Burgundy,' which displays deep reddish purple hues.

BOTANICAL NAME *Liriodendron tulipifera*

COMMON NAME Tulip Tree

RANGE Native to North America. Hardy zones 4 to 9.

CULTURE Prefers deep, acid, loam soil in full sun. Transplant young from containers. Plants have a long taproot that is easily broken, making transplanting difficult after two years.

DESCRIPTION Tall, fast-growing, deciduous tree with trunks as straight as telephone poles and large, bright green, almost square leaves. Beautiful tulip-like yellow flowers the size of teacups occur after ten years. Leaves change to butter-yellow in autumn.

LANDSCAPE USE Good lawn highlight. Can grow up to 6 feet a year in its juvenile years. Makes a beautiful wooded lot.

BOTANICAL NAME *Lonicera japonica* 'Halliana'

COMMON NAME Japanese Honeysuckle

RANGE Zones 5–10. Native to Japan.

HEIGHT To 15 feet tall; vine.

CULTURE Adaptable to any soil in sun or shade. Tolerates poor drainage. Prune back almost to the ground once a year to keep plants bushy. Propagated by cuttings.

DESCRIPTION Evergreen to wholly deciduous in coldest regions. Rampant grower. Oval green leaves. Sweet, fragrant white flowers that change to yellow or take on a purplish tinge, are borne in profusion in early summer.

LANDSCAPE USE Good climber that is used for bank and ground cover. Effective for erosion control. Train on screen or fence. Somewhat invasive if not kept within bounds. Plants that escape into the wild can suffocate small trees.

BOTANICAL NAME *Magnolia grandiflora*

COMMON NAME Southern Magnolia

RANGE Native to southeastern United States. Hardy zones 6 to 9.

CULTURE Prefers sandy loam soil in sun or partial shade. Transplant from containers or balled and burlapped.

DESCRIPTION Magnificent broadleaf evergreen tree hardy from western Canada and as far east as Philadelphia. Handsome, glossy green, leathery leaves have brown, feltlike undersides, creating a perfect foil for the huge, waxy, white flowers up to 10 inches across. Slow growing to 80 feet.

LANDSCAPE USE Use as a lawn highlight, as a grand avenue, or espaliered against a wall.

RECOMMENDED VARIETY 'Southern Cross' is a dwarf variety good for small spaces.

BOTANICAL NAME *Magnolia stellata*

COMMON NAME Star Magnolia

RANGE Zones 3-8. Native to Japan.

HEIGHT 15 to 20 feet tall with spread of 15 feet; compact, wide spreading habit.

CULTURE Prefers peaty, highly rich soil in full sun or light shade. Flowers are injured by frost. Transplant balled and burlapped or from containers. Propagated by cuttings.

DESCRIPTION Deciduous. Slow-growing. Low-branched, multi-stemmed shrub that can be trained into a tree. White, many petaled, fragrant, star-shaped flowers bloom in early April. Thick green leaves turn yellow to bronze in autumn. Bark is smooth, gray.

LANDSCAPE USE Pointed, downy flower buds add interest during winter months. Excellent single specimen or accent plant. Good integrated into foundation plantings.

BOTANICAL NAME *Malus sargentii*

COMMON NAME Sargent Crabapple

RANGE Native to Europe. Hardy zones 4 to 8.

CULTURE Transplant from containers or balled and burlapped. Plants tolerate a wide range of soil types providing it is acid and well drained, in full sun.

DESCRIPTION Beautiful, rounded, deciduous tree bearing masses of light pink flowers in early spring, the petals changing to white. Plants grow to 40 feet. The flowers are followed by decorative, round red fruits in autumn.

LANDSCAPE USE Spectacular lawn highlight in flower; good to plant in groves and as avenues.

RECOMMENDED VARIETIES Many more species and hybrids exist, some with red flowers and yellow fruits. 'Snowdrift' is a particularly good white flowering hybrid; 'Radiant' is a magnificent carmine-red with bronze foliage.

BOTANICAL NAME *Metasequoia glyptostroboides*

COMMON NAME Dawn Redwood

RANGE Native to China. Hardy zones 5 to 8. Thought to be extinct until a grove was discovered growing wild in China.

CULTURE Transplant bare-root or from containers. Prefers a moist, loam, acid soil in full sun.

DESCRIPTION Deciduous conifer with tall, spirelike habit. Fast growing up to 120 feet high. Reddish brown, fluted trunk is buttressed. Dark green needlelike leaves turn russet brown in autumn.

LANDSCAPE USE Suitable for planting as a windbreak, to create a grove, and as a tall lawn highlight. Especially effective planted near water, along streams, and beside lakes or ponds.

BOTANICAL NAME *Myrica cerifera*

COMMON NAME Southern Wax-myrtle

RANGE Zones 7–10. Native from New Jersey to Florida and west to Texas.

HEIGHT 35 feet tall, 20 feet wide; open habit.

CULTURE Prefers moist, peaty, or wet, sandy soil in full sun. Transplants easily. Good seashore plant. Propagated by cuttings.

DESCRIPTION Deciduous. Clump-forming shrub grown for its waxy, fragrant, green, narrow leaves; and for its fragrant, waxy, gray-green fruit. Flowers are ornamentally unimportant. Easy to grow.

LANDSCAPE USE Good border plant. Often used in seashore plantings. The berried branches are beautiful used in both fresh and dried winter floral arrangements.

BOTANICAL NAME *Nandina domestica*

COMMON NAME Heavenly-bamboo; Nandina

RANGE Zones 6–9. Native to China.

HEIGHT 6 to 8 feet tall; upright, loose habit.

CULTURE Prefers loose, well-drained, moist, fertile soil in full sun or partial shade. Spreads by rhizomes. Propagated by cuttings.

DESCRIPTION Deciduous. Overall oriental appearance. Open, fine-textured, 2-inch long leaves are arranged in threes on slender stems resembling bamboo. Autumn foliage is plum-red. Clusters of white flowers bloom in summer. Handsome, bright red berries appear August through October and last well into winter.

LANDSCAPE USE Mainly used as a screen, background, and foundation planting. Can be grown as a container plant. Effective under deciduous trees like oak and maple. Dwarf forms are suitable as a ground cover. The generous berry clusters make beautiful holiday decorations and arrangements.

BOTANICAL NAME *Nerium oleander*

COMMON NAME Oleander

RANGE Zones lower 8–10. Native to Southern Asia and the Mediterranean region.

HEIGHT 6 to 20 feet tall with equal spread; upright, rounded, bushy habit.

CULTURE Prefers well-drained, loam or sandy soil in sun or partial shade. Tolerant of seashore and dry conditions and pollution. Transplants easily. Propagated by cuttings.

DESCRIPTION Broadleaf evergreen, rapid-growing, many branched shrub. Large, leathery, pointy, dark gray-green leaves can grow up to 10 inches long. Pretty, fragrant, single or double flowers borne in clusters, bloom from June to August. Color range includes white, pink, and red.

LANDSCAPE USE Effective as a tall hedge, massed for erosion control, and in border, screen, and foundation plantings. In Northern states and other areas with freezing winter temperatures, plants are grown in containers so that they can be moved indoors. **Caution:** All parts are poisonous if eaten.

BOTANICAL NAME *Osmanthus heterophyllus*

COMMON NAME Holly Osmanthus

RANGE Zones 7–9. Native to China.

HEIGHT 8 to 10 feet tall with similar spread; dense, spreading habit.

CULTURE Prefers moist, well-drained, rich, acidic soil in full sun. Will withstand heavy pruning. Propagated by cuttings.

DESCRIPTION Broadleaf evergreen. Grown for its lustrous, dark green, spiny leaves. Heavily scented white flowers bloom September through November and are hidden by foliage.

LANDSCAPE USE Use as an elegant, formal specimen planted near walkways. Also effective as a screen, barrier, or hedge. Similar in appearance to holly, capable of being trimmed into cones and mounded shapes.

BOTANICAL NAME *Oxydendrum arboreum*

COMMON NAME Sourwood; Sorrel Tree

RANGE Native to North America. Hardy zones 4 to 9

CULTURE Transplant from containers or balled and burlapped into acid, humus-rich, loam soil in full sun. Prefers dry soil rather than moist soil.

DESCRIPTION Deciduous, pyramidal tree with gracefully curved branches, large, oval green leaves, and attractive clusters of white flowers blooming in late summer. Leaves turn yellow, red, or purple in autumn. Plants grow to 30 feet high.

LANDSCAPE USE Excellent lawn highlight. Good for planting along the house foundation. Attractive planted along an avenue.

BOTANICAL NAME *Paeonia suffruticosa*

COMMON NAME Tree Peony

RANGE Zones 5–8. Native to China.

HEIGHT 3 to 6 feet high, up to 12 feet across; loose, mounded habit.

CULTURE Prefers a well-drained, moist, rich soil in a sheltered position. Likes its feet in the shade and its head in the sun, though it will tolerate partial shade. Propagated by cuttings.

DESCRIPTION Deciduous. Beautiful, maple-shaped leaves and huge single or double flowers up to 10 inches across make this one of the most spectacular of all flowering shrubs. Color range includes white, yellow, pink, red, crimson, and purple to almost black, all with a prominent, powdery yellow crest of stamens in the center.

LANDSCAPE USE A good family of plants to collect, planted spontaneously throughout the garden as lawn accents, in mixed shrub borders, and as a foundation planting.

BOTANICAL NAME *Parthenocissus quinquefolia*

COMMON NAME Virginia Creeper

RANGE All zones. Native to North America.

HEIGHT Up to 30 feet; tall, vigorous vine.

CULTURE Prefers well-drained, moist loam soil in full sun or partial shade.

DESCRIPTION Deciduous. Clinging vine that attaches itself to walls and other structures by its tendrils. Grown for its beautiful orange to scarlet fall leaf color. Leaves are saw-toothed, lustrous green in summer, divided into five leaflets. Difficult to remove once established. Looser habit than Boston ivy, to which it is closely related.

LANDSCAPE USE Good vine for covering walls and tall structures. Use as a ground cover on slopes.

BOTANICAL NAME *Paulownia tomentosa*

COMMON NAME Empress Tree

RANGE Native to China. Hardy zones 5 to 9.

CULTURE Tolerates a wide range of soils. Takes heat and drought. Transplant bare-root or from containers. Hardy to western Canada and as far east as Philadelphia.

DESCRIPTION Fast-growing deciduous tree that grows up to 60 feet at the rate of 8 feet a year. Large, bright green, heart-shaped leaves appear after the ornamental flowers resembling blue foxgloves.

LANDSCAPE USE Excellent lawn highlight. Good for avenues.

BOTANICAL NAME *Philadelphus coronarius*

COMMON NAME Sweet Mock-orange

RANGE Zones 5–8. Native to southeastern Europe and Asia Minor.

HEIGHT 7 to 10 feet and as wide; rounded habit.

CULTURE Prefers well-drained, moist, rich soil in full sun or partial shade. Tolerates dry conditions. Prune after flowering to prevent legginess. Propagated by seed or cuttings.

DESCRIPTION Vigorous, erect, and dense with oval, dark green leaves, 2 to 3 inches long. Leaf stalks are hairy. Grown for its fragrant clusters of 1- to 1½-inch wide white flowers that appear in early June. Both single and double forms are available.

LANDSCAPE USE An old-fashioned favorite as a lawn accent and reliable foundation plant. Good to create informal screens and windbreaks.

BOTANICAL NAME *Photinia* x *fraseri*

COMMON NAME Fraser Photinia; Red Tips

RANGE Zones 7–10. Originated in Alabama through hybridizing.

HEIGHT 20 feet high and half as wide; upright, bushy habit.

CULTURE Prefers well-drained, rich, loam soil in full sun or partial shade. Intolerant to wet soils. Transplants easily. Takes heavy pruning. Propagated by cuttings.

DESCRIPTION Broadleaf evergreen. Vigorous. Grown for its bright coppery red new foliage. The slender, pointed mature leaves are glossy and dark green. Clusters of white flowers bloom in the spring.

LANDSCAPE USE Stunning hedge or container plant. Good lawn highlight. Also can be espaliered.

BOTANICAL NAME *Picea pungens* 'Glauca'

COMMON NAME Blue Spruce

RANGE Native to Colorado. Hardy zones 2 to 7.

CULTURE Transplant balled and burlapped or as bare-root seedlings. Prefers a fertile, moist loam soil in full sun, though tolerant of adverse conditions. Slow growing to 100 feet and more.

DESCRIPTION Evergreen conifer. Beautiful conical shape and blue needlelike foliage endear this to homeowners.

LANDSCAPE USE Good lawn highlight; excellent windbreak; can be heavily pruned to create a tall hedge.

RECOMMENDED VARIETIES This plant is actually a variety of Colorado Spruce *(Picea pungens)*, which has plain green foliage. A dwarf variety, 'Glauca Globosa', has a mounded, spreading shape popular for edging and rock gardens.

BOTANICAL NAME *Picea pungens nana*

COMMON NAME Dwarf Blue Spruce

RANGE Zones 3–8. Native to Wyoming, Utah, Colorado, and New Mexico.

HEIGHT 3 to 5 feet tall; densely pyramidal habit.

CULTURE Prefers moderately rich, well-drained, gravelly soil in full sun. Tolerates dry and moist soil. Propagated by cuttings.

DESCRIPTION Slow-growing narrowleaf evergreen. Rigid, horizontal branching. Grown for its adaptability. Sharp $1/2$- to $1\,1/4$- inch gray to gray-green needles adorn this prickly plant. Shiny, oblong cones are 2 to 4 inches long.

LANDSCAPE USE Good seashore plant. Excellent planted near a house or in a rock garden. If regularly pruned, it can be shaped into mounds and made into a low hedge.

BOTANICAL NAME *Pieris japonica*

COMMON NAME Japanese Andromeda

RANGE Zones 5–8. Native to Japan.

HEIGHT 9 to 12 feet high with 6 to 8 feet spread; upright, dense habit.

CULTURE Prefers loose, moist, well-drained, acidic soil in full sun or partial shade. Shelter from winds. Prune after flowering to maintain a compact habit. Transplant balled and burlapped or as a container plant. Propagated by cuttings.

DESCRIPTION Broadleaf evergreen. Bushy habit with spreading branches and rosettelike foliage. New leaves are a rich bronze which change to a lustrous, dark green at maturity. Large, drooping clusters of slightly fragrant, white, urn-shaped flowers bloom March through April. Flower buds add winter appeal since they are formed the summer prior to flowering.

LANDSCAPE USE Excellent lawn specimen or foundation plant. Effective in shrub borders mixed with other broadleaf evergreens, such as azaleas and rhododendrons.

BOTANICAL NAME *Pinus mugo*

COMMON NAME Mugo Pine; Swiss Mountain Pine

RANGE Zones 2–7. Native to central and southern Europe from Spain to the Balkans.

HEIGHT 15 to 20 feet with 25 to 30 feet spread; low-spreading or pyramidal habit.

CULTURE Prefers moist loam soil in sun or partial shade. Transplant balled and burlapped or buy container plants. Prune to thicken plant and to keep a dwarf habit. Propagated by seed and cuttings.

DESCRIPTION Narrowleaf evergreen. Slow-growing, variable plants. Mostly forms a low, mounded shape. Needles vary in color from medium green in summer to yellowish green in winter. The grayish brown, 1- to 2-inch cones stand erect.

LANDSCAPE USE Best used in groups of three or more plants as a dwarf planting in foundations and rock gardens.

BOTANICAL NAME *Pinus strobus*

COMMON NAME Eastern White Pine

RANGE Native to North America. Hardy zones 3 to 8.

CULTURE Transplant seedlings bare-root or older trees balled and burlapped. Tolerates a wide range of acid soil conditions, including dry and moist soils. Prefers full sun, but tolerates light shade.

DESCRIPTION Fast-growing needle evergreen grows to 80 feet with a pyramidal habit and soft-textured appearance on account of its long, blue-green needles.

LANDSCAPE USE Best used as a windbreak; also can be heavily pruned to make a dense hedge.

RECOMMENDED VARIETIES Many dwarf varieties have been developed that are suitable for rock gardens and small spaces. A weeping form, 'Pendula', has long, arching branches that sweep to the ground.

BOTANICAL NAME *Pittosporum tobira*

COMMON NAME Japanese Pittosporum

RANGE Zones 8–10. Native to Japan, Formosa, Korea, and China.

HEIGHT 6 to 12 feet high and 4 to 5 feet wide; dense, broad-spreading habit.

CULTURE Prefers any well-drained soil in full sun or shade. Enjoys dry locations. Tolerates salt spray. Easy to transplant. Tip-prune to encourage bushiness or to control height. Propagated by cuttings.

DESCRIPTION Broadleaf evergreen. Lustrous, blunt, wide, dark green leaves are set in whorls on brown stems. When crushed, leaves produce a disagreeable odor. Creamy white to yellow fragrant flower clusters open in April and May. Green, pear-shaped fruit turns to brown at maturity in September and October.

LANDSCAPE USE Popular in mass plantings, foundations, and as drifts under trees. Suitable for hedges, screens, and barrier plantings. Interesting container plant. Foliage used in both fresh and dried floral arrangements.

BOTANICAL NAME *Podocarpus macrophyllus*

COMMON NAME Yew Podocarpus

RANGE To 50 feet tall; stiff, upright habit.

HEIGHT Zones 8–10. Native to Japan, southern China.

CULTURE Prefers well-drained, loam or sandy garden soil in full sun or partial shade. Tolerant of salt spray. Easily pruned to form a column shape. Propagated by cuttings.

DESCRIPTION Narrowleaf evergreen. Versatile plant with good-looking foliage. Lustrous, dark green, narrow leaves. Flowers bloom in April and May, followed by small, edible, bluish fruit.

LANDSCAPE USE Grows indoors and out in tubs and open ground. Use for espalier, screen plantings, topiary, and clipped hedges. A popular street tree in warm climates.

BOTANICAL NAME *Poncirus trifoliata*

COMMON NAME Hardy-orange

RANGE Zones 6–9. Native to Northern China and Korea.

HEIGHT 10 to 15 feet tall with almost equal spread; oval-shaped, twiggy habit.

CULTURE Prefers a well-drained, acidic soil in full sun. Easily transplanted. Propagated by seed or cuttings.

DESCRIPTION Deciduous. Low-branching shrub or small tree with green, sharp spines. Young bark is green; older bark is slightly furrowed. Oval leaves are light green and are in sets of threes. Foliage turns to yellow in autumn. Fragrant, white, single flowers are 1 to 2 inches across, resemble orange-blossoms and appear in April and May. Attractive, small, downy, yellow, golf-ball-sized fruit appears in September and October. Extremely fragrant. Fruit is highly astringent, remains on the tree a short time after the leaves have dropped.

LANDSCAPE USE Effective for screen, privacy, and security. Use as a hedge or a barrier plant. Unusual, high interest plant suitable for containers and foundation accent.

BOTANICAL NAME *Populus hybrida*

COMMON NAME Hybrid Poplar

RANGE Hybrids of species native to North America and Europe. Hardy zones 4 to 9.

CULTURE These fast-growing deciduous trees grow in poor soils where other trees will not—acid or alkaline, dry or moist—providing they are in full sun. Developed to re-forest impoverished soils exposed to harsh conditions by strip mining, the plants are best transplanted bare-root. Some mail-order specialists also sell unrooted cuttings at an economical price for rooting in moist soil.

DESCRIPTION Mostly upright, spirelike in habit, with pointed oval green leaves that shimmer and shine with a silvery sheen in the slightest breeze.

LANDSCAPE USE Popular for creating a property boundary, windbreak, or avenue along a driveway—wherever a tall, fast-growing tree is needed for screening and erosion control. Keep away from pipes and drains on account of its vigorous root system.

RECOMMENDED VARIETY 'Androscoggin' is the most widely available of the hybrids recommended for home landscapes.

BOTANICAL NAME *Potentilla fruticosa*

COMMON NAME Bush Cinquefoil

RANGE Zones 2–8. Native to Europe and Asia.

HEIGHT 2 to 4 feet high with equal spread; rounded habit.

CULTURE Adaptable to dry and wet soil, also heavy and sandy soil in full sun to light shade. Drought tolerant. Propagated by cuttings.

DESCRIPTION Hardy, deciduous, dense shrub that has a fine-textured appearance. The long-stalked, bright green leaves consist of five oval leaflets about 1/2 inch long. Flowers are creamy white to bright yellow and look like miniature, single-flowered roses. They bloom intermittently, starting in late May. Bark is flaky and deep brown.

LANDSCAPE USE Good for ground covers and accents in borders. Pink- and red-flowering varieties are available, but these tend to be plants suitable only for areas with cool, moist summers, such as the Pacific Northwest.

BOTANICAL NAME *Prunus glandulosa* 'Alboplena'

COMMON NAME Flowering Almond

RANGE Zones 4–8. Native to China and Japan.

HEIGHT 3 to 5 feet tall with equal spread; upright habit.

CULTURE Prefers well-drained, moist, humus-rich soil in full sun. Prune after flowering to increase new stem development. Propagated by cuttings.

DESCRIPTION Deciduous. Somewhat rounded shrub with slender, multi-stems. The most popular variety, 'Rosea,' has lovely 1-inch double flowers crowded along the stems like pink powderpuffs, appearing in early spring. Foliage is oval, light green, and provides no autumn interest.

LANDSCAPE USE Specimen shrub used for flowering display in mixed borders. Popular for planting in the middle of tulip displays and beds of early perennials, such as pansies, to provide a spectacular color highlight.

BOTANICAL NAME *Prunus subhirtella* 'Pendula'

COMMON NAME Weeping Higan Cherry

RANGE Native to Japan. Hardy zones 4 to 9.

CULTURE Transplant from containers or balled and burlapped. Prefers a fertile, loam, acid soil in full sun. Protect trunk from borers with tree wrap until well established.

DESCRIPTION Reasonably fast-growing deciduous tree, to 40 feet with an equal spread. Magnificent billowing, weeping habit. Small, oval, serrated leaves open bright green, usually after masses of pale pink, 1/2-inch diameter flowers have covered the branches in early spring at the first hint of a warming trend.

LANDSCAPE USE Exceptionally beautiful as a lawn highlight; also good to plant in groves and as avenues.

BOTANICAL NAME *Pseudotsuga menziesii*

COMMON NAME Douglas Fir

RANGE Native to Colorado and the Pacific Northwest. Hardy zones 4 to 7.

CULTURE Best transplanted balled and burlapped into acid, loam, fertile soil. Prefers full sun.

DESCRIPTION Tall, spirelike, needle evergreen that is long-lived in good soil. Makes a good Christmas tree. Can grow to 300 feet and more.

LANDSCAPE USE Makes a good lawn highlight and windbreak.

RECOMMENDED VARIETIES There are two strains of Douglas Fir with varying degrees of hardiness, one from the Rocky Mountains of Colorado and the other from the Pacific Northwest. *Pseudotsuga menziesii* 'Glauca' ('Rocky Mountain Douglas Fir') is more widely adapted, hardier, and slower growing.

BOTANICAL NAME *Pyracantha coccinea*

COMMON NAME Scarlet Firethorn

RANGE Zones 6–9. Native to Italy and the Caucausus mountain region.

HEIGHT 6 feet high and 10 feet wide; erect habit.

CULTURE Prefers well-drained, sandy or loam soil in full sun or partial shade. Difficult to transplant. Propagated by seeds or cuttings. Plants are susceptible to fireblight disease, a bacteria that turns the fruit black as if scorched.

DESCRIPTION Broadleaf evergreen. Open shrub with stiff, thorny branches. Lustrous, dense, dark green leaves may turn brown during winter in unprotected areas. Malodorous, profuse, white, showy flowers bloom in April and June. Spectacular, orange-red berry-like fruit persists through the winter.

LANDSCAPE USE Grown primarily for showy fruit. Use as an informal hedge or barrier plant. Good for espaliers on walls and trellises. Some varieties have yellow berries.

BOTANICAL NAME *Pyrus calleryana 'Bradford'*

COMMON NAME Bradford Pear

RANGE Native to China. Hardy zones 4 to 8.

CULTURE Transplant young, bare-root cuttings or older plants balled and burlapped. Tolerates a wide range of soils, in full sun. Highly resistant to fire-blight disease so common to other ornamental pears.

DESCRIPTION A tree for all seasons: beautiful white blossoms in early spring; mint-green leaves during summer; gorgeous orange leaves in autumn and an attractive wintry silhouette when it loses its leaves. Tolerates pollution.

LANDSCAPE USE Popular lawn highlight and street tree.

RECOMMENDED VARIETIES Although the 'Bradford' pear is itself a variety of *Pyrus calleryana*, other good forms have been introduced. Particularly desirable is 'Aristocrat,' a pyramidal form, and 'Chanticleer,' an upright form.

BOTANICAL NAME *Quercus palustris*

COMMON NAME Pin Oak

RANGE Native to North America. Hardy zones 4 to 8.

CULTURE Transplant seedlings bare-root or larger plants balled and burlapped. Tolerates a wide range of acid soil conditions, including swampy soil.

DESCRIPTION Fastest growing oak, up to 3 feet a year, grows to a mature height of 60 feet. Beautiful pyramidal habit. Dark green, sharply pointed leaves turn parchment brown in autumn, persist on the tree through winter.

LANDSCAPE USE Good lawn highlight and street tree; a popular tree to make a "wooded lot".

RECOMMENDED VARIETY A related variety, *Quercus coccinea* ('Scarlet Oak') is almost identical in appearance to the Pin Oak, but has beautiful red fall leaf coloring. Scarlet Oak is not as widely adapted as the Pin Oak.

BOTANICAL NAME *Raphiolepis indica*

COMMON NAME Indian Hawthorn; India Raphiolepis

RANGE Zones 7–10. Native to Japan and Korea.

HEIGHT 4 to 5 feet high with equal spread; dense, mounded habit.

CULTURE Prefers well-drained loam soil in full sun. Tolerates occasional drought, and seashore conditions. Prune after flowering to retain shape. Propagated by seed and cuttings.

DESCRIPTION Broadleaf evergreen. Spectacular show of flowers from late fall through mid-winter. Colors range from white to a light red. Attractive dark blue berries follow, persisting through winter. New leaves in tones of bronze and red also add ornamental interest. Adult foliage is glossy, dark green, and pointed. Habit can be sturdy, bushy, and compact or a natural spreading, open shape.

LANDSCAPE USE A great basic landscape shrub. Makes a good, dense mass planting, large-scale ground cover, low divider, or informal hedge. Especially popular in drought-prone areas.

BOTANICAL NAME *Rhododendron* species (Azalea)

COMMON NAME Azalea

RANGE Zones 1–10. Native to China and Japan, also North America.

HEIGHT Generally 2 to 15 feet high and 3 to 9 feet wide, depending on variety; rounded, spreading habit.

CULTURE Prefers well-drained, moist, rich, acidic soil in partial shade or full sun in cool summer areas. Protect from strong, cold winds. Tolerates air pollution. Easy to transplant. Tip-prune plant after bloom period to maintain compact habit. Propagated by seed and cuttings.

DESCRIPTION Azaleas are really rhododendrons, but differ from the generally accepted notion of a rhododendron in having smaller leaves and flowers, and a more compact, low-spreading habit. Mostly deciduous but some species are evergreen. Flowers are generally funnel-shaped, in white, pink, red, purple, yellow, and orange. Prime bloom time is from spring to early summer. The leathery leaves are rounded, smooth-edged, and set in whorls. Leaves are frequently hairy.

LANDSCAPE USE Attractive, versatile plant. Perfect for shrub borders, groupings, massings, and foundation plantings.

BOTANICAL NAME *Salix* x *chrysocoma*

COMMON NAME Weeping Willow; Golden Willow

RANGE A hybrid between species native to North America and China. Hardy zones 2 to 9.

CULTURE Deciduous tree best transplanted bare-root or from containers. Cuttings root readily in moist soil. Prefers moist soil in full sun along streams and pond margins. Plant away from the house since the vigorous root system can interfere with sewer lines and drains.

DESCRIPTION Fast-growing to 100 feet. Majestic, billowing, weeping habit. Branches have a pronounced yellow coloring that intensifies in early spring just before leaves emerge.

LANDSCAPE USE Best used away from the house at the edge of a property and along stream banks or pond margins, where its massive, billowing outline can be best admired.

RELATED SPECIES & HYBRIDS Many other willows have a weeping habit, including forms of *Salix alba* ('White Willow') and *Salix babylonica*, ('Babylon Weeping Willow'). A new hybrid willow from Australia using *Salix tortuosa* ('Corkscrew Willow') in its parentage grows at the astonishing rate of 12 feet a year, and is becoming popular as a windbreak. It has an upright, rather than weeping, habit.

BOTANICAL NAME *Salix discolor*

COMMON NAME Pussy Willow

RANGE Zones 2–9. Native to the eastern United States.

HEIGHT To 20 feet tall; upright, twiggy habit.

CULTURE Prefers moist, humus-rich soil in full sun. Readily transplanted. Propogated by cuttings.

DESCRIPTION Deciduous. Fast-grower with invasive roots. Slender, brownish red stems with 2- to 4-inch oval leaves that are bright green above, and bluish below. Beloved for their soft, silky, pearl-gray flowers called catkins that measure up to 1 1/2 inches long on the male plants.

LANDSCAPE USE Old-fashioned favorite. Plant as a single specimen or combine it with other plants in borders. Branches may easily be forced for indoor winter bloom. Keep plants pruned hard so flowering branches are always easily within reach.

BOTANICAL NAME *Skimmia japonica*

COMMON NAME Japanese Skimmia

RANGE Zones 6–9. Native to Japan.

HEIGHT 1 to 5 feet tall with similar spread; mounded, dense habit.

CULTURE Prefers loose, moist, well-drained, humus-rich acidic soil in partial shade. Propagated by seed and cuttings.

DESCRIPTION Broadleaf evergreen. Flower sexes are on separate plants. Male plant is smaller and can service about a dozen female plants for berry production. The purple-red buds open to sweetly scented, creamy white flowers in March and April. In October, festive, bright red clusters of berries appear on the female plants. Leaves are green above, lighter green below, oblong, and smooth.

LANDSCAPE USE Beautiful, dainty evergreen shrub. Use as a ground cover, in foundation plantings, or planter boxes. Also popular in rock gardens.

BOTANICAL NAME *Spiraea* x *vanhouttei*

COMMON NAME Bridalwreath; Vanhoutte Spirea

RANGE Zones 5–10. Developed from species native to China.

HEIGHT 6 to 8 feet tall and 8 to 10 feet wide; fountainlike habit.

CULTURE Tolerant of many fertile soils in full sun. Easy to transplant. Propagated by cuttings.

DESCRIPTION Deciduous. Graceful, round-topped, arching branches fall to the ground, giving a broad, mounded appearance. Fast-growing and durable. Leaves are a dull bluish green with grayish undersides. Some slight autumn leaf color ranging from red to orange. The showy white flower clusters bloom in April and May.

LANDSCAPE USE Widely used as a lawn highlight, hedge, or screen planting.

BOTANICAL NAME *Syringa vulgaris*

COMMON NAME Lilac

RANGE Zones 3–7. Native to the Balkan penninsula.

HEIGHT 8 to 15 feet tall and 6 to 12 feet wide; upright habit.

CULTURE Prefers a moist, humus-rich, neutral soil in full sun. Prune to revitalize overgrown or damaged plants. Propagated by cuttings.

DESCRIPTION Deciduous. Grown for the pleasant, gratifying fragrance of its flowers, which appear mid-May to early June, in dense, erect clusters of lavender-blue, purple, red, and white. The almost bluish green leaves are semi-glossy and heart-shaped.

LANDSCAPE USE An old-fashioned favorite. As the seasonal interest is limited to length of bloom time, plant sparingly. Use in a shrub border or in foundation plantings. The flowers make exquisite indoor arrangements.

BOTANICAL NAME *Tamarix ramosissima*

COMMON NAME Tamarix; Five Stamen Tamarisk

RANGE Zone 2 south. Native to southeastern Europe and central Asia.

HEIGHT 10 to 15 feet tall with narrower spread; loose, open habit.

CULTURE Prefers well-drained, acidic soil in full sun. Tolerates sandy soil and seashore conditions. Easy to grow. Propagated by seed and cuttings.

DESCRIPTION Deciduous. Fast-growing, spreading shrub with attractive, bright green, feathery foliage. The dense clusters of tiny, pale pink flowers bloom June through July.

LANDSCAPE USE Grown primarily for its adaptability to saline environments. Use in mixed plantings, such as mixed shrub borders, and along the side of a wall or fence where its arching stems and light, airy flower clusters can cascade over the top.

BOTANICAL NAME *Taxus cuspidata*

COMMON NAME Japanese Yew

RANGE Zones 4–7. Native to Japan, Korea, and Manchuria.

HEIGHT 50 feet high, spreading 25 feet wide; upright habit.

CULTURE Prefers well-drained loam soil in full sun or part shade. Tolerant of both drought and cold. Propagated by cuttings.

DESCRIPTION Rapid-growing, hardy, narrowleaf evergreen. Can reach tree size but usually remains a sturdy, multi-stemmed shrub. Twigs are yellow-green with broad, leathery, 1¼-inch dull green needles, with conspicuous, yellow-green undersides. Leaves form a distinct V-shaped pattern as they lay flat in two rows along the stem. Stem bark is reddish to grayish brown and flakes off with age. Oval red berries appear in autumn.

LANDSCAPE USE The tall varieties make good accents as sentinels to doorways and garden entrances. Also valuable as a hedge. Dwarf, spreading kinds can be sheared into mounds.

BOTANICAL NAME *Trachelospermum jasminoides*

COMMON NAME Star or Confederate Jasmine; Chinese Star-jasmine

RANGE Zones 7–9. Native to China.

HEIGHT To 20 feet tall; vine.

CULTURE Prefers well-drained, moist loam soil in full sun or partial shade in hottest areas. Once established it grows moderately fast. Prune to hold shape. Cut back older plants by one-third each year to spruce up plant. Propagated by cuttings.

DESCRIPTION Broadleaf evergreen, sprawling vine. The lustrous, dark green leaves are 3 inches long. The clusters of sweetly fragrant white flowers bloom profusely in June and July.

LANDSCAPE USE Can be trained as a spreading shrub or ground cover. Mostly used as a decorative vine to camouflage walls and fences. Suitable for containers or trained up a short trellis.

BOTANICAL NAME *Tsuga canadensis*

COMMON NAME Canadian Hemlock

RANGE Native to North America. Hardy zones 3 to 8.

CULTURE Prefers humus-rich, acid soil in sun or shade. Transplant bare-root, from container, or balled.

DESCRIPTION Tall, slow-growing, pyramid-shaped needle evergreen up to 100 feet high. Fine needles give it a soft appearance. Small brown cones hang from the branch tips.

LANDSCAPE USE Good lawn highlight. Excellent windbreak. Superb hedge.

RECOMMENDED VARIETY 'Sargents Weeping Hemlock' spreads sideways with arching branches, creating a fountainlike effect.

BOTANICAL NAME *Tsuga canadensis* 'Sargentii'

COMMON NAME Weeping Hemlock

RANGE Zones 3–7. Native to eastern United States.

HEIGHT 2 to 3 feet high and twice as wide; low, broad habit.

CULTURE Prefers moist, acidic soil with high humidity in partial shade. Protect from hot sun and wind. Propagated by layering, seed, and cuttings.

DESCRIPTION Narrowleaf evergreen. Drooping branches with flat, narrow needles are dark green above and white-banded below. Small, oval, brown cones hang from branches in autumn.

LANDSCAPE USE Excellent plant to use as an accent in large rock gardens. Can look sensational as a lawn highlight. The branches and leaves seem to cascade like a waterfall.

BOTANICAL NAME *Viburnum opulus sterile*

COMMON NAME European Snowball Bush

RANGE Zones 3–8. Native to Europe, northern Africa, and northern Asia.

HEIGHT 8 to 12 feet tall and 10 to 15 feet wide; upright, spreading habit.

CULTURE Prefers well-drained loam soil in full sun, but tolerates boggy soil. Propagated by seed and cuttings.

DESCRIPTION Deciduous. Maple-shaped leaves, 2 to 4 inches long, are dark green and glossy. Inconsistent fall coloring, but when the leaves turn, they range from yellow-red to a reddish purple. The immature flower clusters are green before turning globular and white, thus resembling snowballs; they bloom during the month of May.

LANDSCAPE USE Grown for its showy flower display. Use in shrub borders and as a screen. Popular for planting against low fences and walls so the heavily laden flowering stems can spill over the top.

BOTANICAL NAME *Vinca minor*

COMMON NAME Periwinkle; Myrtle

RANGE Zones 4–9. Native to northeastern United States.

HEIGHT 3 to 4 inches high, spreading 3 feet and more; low, ground-hugging habit.

CULTURE Prefers moist, well-drained acid soil in shade or full sun. Propagated by cuttings and by division.

DESCRIPTION Broadleaf evergreen. Dark green, glossy, oval leaves form a low, dense, decorative ground cover, especially popular for shaded areas. Decorative, star-shaped, 1-inch blue flowers appear in early spring and continue for several months. A similar species, *Vinca major*, has slightly larger flowers. It is not so hardy, but is popular in the South and mild-winter areas.

LANDSCAPE USE Good weed-smothering ground cover, particularly in deep shade where other ground covers will not grow. Also suitable for planting in window boxes so the creeping stems can hang down the sides.

BOTANICAL NAME *Vitex agnus-castus*

COMMON NAME Chaste-tree

RANGE Zones 7–10. Native to the Mediterranean.

HEIGHT 10 to 20 feet high with equal spread; loose, spreading habit.

CULTURE Prefers moderately dry, fertile, well-drained soil in full sun. Enjoys seashore conditions. Propagated by cuttings.

DESCRIPTION Deciduous. Multiple trunks. Twigs and leaves are pleasantly aromatic. Leaves are divided fan-wise into five to seven leaflets and are dark green above and gray beneath. Fragrant, long-lasting spikes of lavender-blue flowers, 7 inches long, bloom August through October.

LANDSCAPE USE Good in a shrub border for late-summer flowering. Popular in hot climates because it is heat-resistant. North of zone 7, top growth may be killed to the ground in winter, but new growth with flowering stems will sprout in the spring.

BOTANICAL NAME *Weigela florida*

COMMON NAME Weigela

RANGE Zones 5–8. Native to Japan.

HEIGHT 6 to 9 feet tall and 9 to 12 feet wide; spreading habit.

CULTURE Prefers well-drained loam soil in full sun. Tolerant to air pollution. Prune to retain compact shape. Propagated by cuttings.

DESCRIPTION Deciduous, dense, old-fashioned shrub. Grown primarily for its profuse show of reddish to rose-pink blossoms in May and June. Flowers are 1 1/4 inches long and grow in groups of three or four on short, grayish twigs. The oval-shaped leaves are light green and 2 to 4 inches long. No fall color.

LANDSCAPE USE Frequently used in shrub borders, groupings, massings, or foundation plantings. Resembles an azalea, but is later-flowering.

BOTANICAL NAME *Wisteria floribunda*

COMMON NAME Wisteria

RANGE Zones 4–9. Native to Japan.

HEIGHT Up to 30 feet; vine.

CULTURE Prefers well-drained, loamy garden soil in full sun. Propagated by seed.

DESCRIPTION Deciduous vine that can be shaped into a tree or shrub. Prune back stems that interfere with framework of desired form. The main stem will become a good-sized trunk. Provide good support and train developing stems to enhance desired shape. Bright green leaves are 12 to 16 inches long and are divided into fifteen to nineteen leaflets. Long, 18-inch clusters of fragrant violet to violet-blue flowers burst into bloom in April and May.

LANDSCAPE USE Excellent flowering vine. Good to train over arbors, along balconies, and the top of walls. There is a double-flowered form. A blue and white intertwined has an especially beautiful flowering effect.

CHAPTER FOUR

PLANT SELECTION GUIDE

THE FOLLOWING LISTS SHOULD BE HELPFUL in deciding which shrubs to choose for a particular purpose. Here you will find shrubs suitable for hedging, ground cover effects, vining habit, and a multitude of other purposes.

*indicates a tree

LOW SHRUBS FOR GROUND COVERS

Allamanda cathartica (Yellow Allamanda)
Ardisia japonica (Marlberry)
Calluna vulgaris (Scotch Heather)
Cotoneaster horizontalis (Rock Spray)
Gelsemium sempervirens (Carolina Jessamine)
Hedera helix (English Ivy)
Hypericum calycinum (St.-John's-wort)
Leucothoe fontanesiana (Drooping Leucothoe)
Lonicera japonica (Japanese Honeysuckle)
Parthenocissus quinquefolia (Virginia Creeper)
Potentilla fruticosa (Bush Cinquefoil)
Trachelospermum jasminoides (Star or Confederate Jasmine)

NARROWLEAF EVERGREENS

*Abies concolor (White Fir)
*Cedrus atlantica (Atlas Cedar)
Chamaecyparis pisifera (False Cypress)
Juniperus horizontalis (Creeping Juniper)
*Picea pungens 'Glauca' (Blue Spruce)
Picea pungens nana (Dwarf Blue Spruce)
Pinus mugo (Mugo Pine)
*Pinus strobus (White Pine)
Podocarpus macrophyllus (Yew Podocarpus)
*Pseudotsuga menziesii (Douglas Fir)
Taxus cuspidata (Japanese Yew)
*Tsuga canadensis (Eastern Hemlock)
Tsuga canadensis 'Sargenti' (Weeping Hemlock)

VINES

Actinidia chinensis (Kiwi)
Allamanda cathartica (Yellow Allamanda)
Beaumontia grandiflora (Easter Lily Vine)
Bougainvillea spectabilis (Bougainvillea)
Celastrus scandens (American Bittersweet)
Clematis species and hybrids (Clematis)
Gelsemium sempervirens (Carolina Jessamine)

VINES (con't.)

Hedera helix (English Ivy)
Lantana camara (Shrub Verbena)
Lonicera japonica (Japanese Honeysuckle)
Parthenocissus quinquefolia (Virginia Creeper)
Trachelospermum jasminoides (Star or Confederate Jasmine)
Wisteria floribunda (Wisteria)

SHRUBS TO GROW FROM SEED

Although most shrubs can be grown from seed, it is usually faster to propagate them from cuttings. The following kinds of shrubs are particularly easy to grow from seed, and they are reasonably fast-growing. Besides being inexpensive, growing shrubs from seed offers the chance of producing an unusual new variety since seed-grown shrubs often differ from the parent plant, as opposed to cuttings, which are identical.

Acer palmatum dissectum (Japanese Maple)
Aucuba japonica (Gold-dust Plant)
Azalea kaempferi (Kaempferi Azalea)
Azalea mollis (Mollis Azalea)
Berberis thunbergii atropurpurea (Japanese Barberry)
Buddleia davidii (Butterfly Bush)
Calluna vulgaris (Scotch Heather)
Camellia japonica (Camellia)
Campsis radicans (Trumpetcreeper; Trumpetvine; Hummingbird Vine)
Caryopteris x *clandonensis* (Blue-mist Shrub; Hybrid Bluebeard)
Ceanothus species (California Lilac)
Cistus ladanifer (Crimson-spot Rock-rose; Gum Rock-rose)
Clematis paniculata (Sweet Autumn Clematis)
Cornus florida (Flowering Dogwood)
Cornus kousa (Korean Dogwood)
Cotinus coggygria (Smoketree)
Cotoneaster horizontalis (Rock Spray Cotoneaster)
Cytisus scoparius (Scotch Broom)
Daphne species (Daphne)
Enkianthus campanulatus (Redvein Enkianthus)
Euonymus alata (Burning Bush; Winged Euonymus)

Fuchsia species and hybrids (Fuchsia)
Hamamelis species (Witch-hazels)
Hibiscus species (Hibiscus)
Ilex species (Hollies)
Kalmia latifolia (Mountain-laurel)
Kolkwitzia amabilis (Beautybush)
Lonicera species (Honeysuckle)
Paeonia suffruticosa (Tree Peony)
Parthenocissus quinquefolia (Virginia Creeper)
Picea species (Spruce)
Pinus species (Pines)
Pyracantha coccinea (Scarlet Firethorn)
Rhododendron species and hybrids (Rhododendrons and Azaleas)
Rosa species (Roses)
Skimmia japonica (Japanese Skimmia)
Syringa species (Lilacs)
Viburnum opulus sterile (European Snowball Bush)
Wisteria species (Wisteria)

TREES AND SHRUBS FOR THE SEASHORE

*Albizia julibrissin (Silk Tree)
Callistemon citrinus (Lemon Bottlebrush)
Ceanothus thyrsiflorus (California Lilac)
Cistus ladanifer (Crimson-spot Rock-rose)
*Crataegus phaenopyrum (Hawthorn)
Cytisus scoparius (Scotch Broom)
Hibiscus syriacus (Rose of Sharon)
*Ilex opaca (American Holly)
Juniperus horizontalis (Creeping Juniper)
Myrica cerifera (Southern Wax-myrtle)
Nerium oleader (Oleander)
*Pinus strobus (White Pine)
Pittosporum tobira (Japanese Pittosporum)
Raphiolepis indica (Indian Hawthorn)
Tamarix ramosissima (Tamarix)
Vitex agnus-castus (Chaste-tree)

BROADLEAF EVERGREENS

Abelia x *grandiflora* (Glossy Abelia)
Allamanda cathartica (Yellow Allamanda)
Ardisia japonica (Marlberry)
Aucuba japonica 'Variegata' (Gold-dust Plant)
Beaumontia grandiflora (Herald's-trumpet)
Brunfelsia calycina floribunda (Yesterday, Today, Tomorrow)
Buxus sempervirens (English Boxwood)
Calliandra haematocephala (Powderpuff Shrub)
Callistemon citrinus (Lemon Bottlebrush)
Camellia japonica (Camellia)
Carissa grandiflora (Natal-Plum)
Cotoneaster horizontalis (Rock Spray)
Euonymus japonicus (Japanese Euonymus)
Gardenia jasminoides (Gardenia)
Gelsemium sempervirens (Carolina Jessamine)
Hedera helix (English Ivy)
Hypericum calycinum (St.-John's-wort)
Ilex x *meservae* (Blue Holly)
*Ilex opaca (American Holly)
Ilex verticillata (Winterberry)
Kalmia latifolia (Mountain-laurel)
Leucothoe fontanesiana (Drooping Leucothoe)
Ligustrum x *vicaryi* (Vicary Golden Privet)
*Magnolia grandiflora (Southern Magnolia)
Mahonia aquifolium (Oregon Holly-grape)
Mahonia bealei (Leatherleaf Mahonia)
Nerium oleander (Oleander)
Photinia x *fraseri* (Red Tips)
Pieris japonica (Japanese Andromeda)
Pittosporum tobira (Japanese Pittosporum)
Pyracantha coccinea (Scarlet Firethorn)
Raphiolepis indica (Indian Hawthorn)
Rhododendron species (Rhododendron)
Rhododendron (Azalea)
Skimmia japonica (Japanese Skimmia)
Trachelospermum jasminoides (Star or Confederate Jasmine)

Opposite page: Chinese snowball bush (*Viburnum macrocephalum*) is much larger flowered than the more common European snowball bush (*Viburnum opulus* 'sterile'), but is not reliably hardy north of Wilmington, Delaware.

SHRUBS FROM CUTTINGS

Where there is a preference between a softwood or hardwood cutting, it is given in parentheses.

Abelia x grandiflora (softwood)
Acer palmatum
Actinidia chinensis
Allamanda carthartica
Amelanchier arborea (softwood)
Aucuba japonica
Beaumontia grandiflora
Berberis thunbergii
Bougainvillea spectabilis
Brunfelsia calyana floribunda
Buddleia davidii (hardwood)

Buxus sempervirens (hardwood)
Calliandra haematocephala (hardwood)
Callicarpa japonica (softwood)
Callistemon citrinus
Calluna vulgaris (softwood)
Camellia japonica (softwood)
Campsis radicans (softwood)
Carissa grandiflora
Caryopteris x *clandonensis* (softwood)
Ceanothus thyrsiflorus
Celastrus scandens (softwood)
Cercis chinensis (semi-hardwood)
Chaenomeles speciosa (semi-hardwood)
Chamaecyparis pisifera
Cistus ladanifera
Clematis species
Cornus florida (softwood)
Cornus kousa (softwood)
Cornus mas (softwood)
Corus sericea (softwood)
Corylopsis glabrescens (softwood)
Cotinus coggygria (softwood)
Cotoneaster horizontalis (softwood)
Cytisus scoparius (hardwood)
Daphne x *burkwoodii* (semi-hardwood)
Deutzia gracilis (softwood)
Enkianthus campanulatus (softwood)
Escallonia exoniensis
Euonymus alata (softwood)
Euonymus japonicus
Exochorda racemosa (semi-hardwood)
Fatsia japonica (semi-hardwood)
Forsythia x *intermedia* (softwood)
Fothergilla gardenii (softwood)
Fuchsia hybrida (softwood)
Gardenia jasminoides (softwood)
Gelsemium sempervirens (hardwood)
Hamamelis mollis (semi-hardwood)
Hedera helix (softwood)
Hibiscus syriacus (hardwood)
Hydrangea macrophylla (softwood)
Hypericum calycinum (softwood)

Ilex x *meserveae*
Ilex verticillata (softwood)
Juniperus horizontalis (softwood, but difficult)
Kalmia latifolia
Kerria japonica
Kolkwitzia amabilis (softwood)
Lagerstroemia indica (softwood)
Lantana camara
Leucothoe fortanesiana
Ligustrum x *vicaryi*
Lonicera japonica
Magnolia stellata (softwood)
Myrica cerifera
Nandina domestica
Nerium oleander (softwood)
Osmanthus heterophyllus
Paeonia suffruticosa
Parthenocissus quinquefolia (softwood)
Philadelphus coronarius (softwood)
Photinia x *fraseri* (softwood)
Picea pungens
Pieris japonica
Pinus mugo
Pittosporum tobira (hardwood)
Podocarpus macrophyllus (hardwood)
Potentilla fruticosa (softwood)
Prunus glandulosa
Pyracantha coccinea (softwood)
Rhododendron (hardwood)
Salix discolor
Skimmia japonica
Spiraea x *vanhouttei* (softwood)
Syringa vulgaris (softwood)
Taxus cuspidata
Trachelospermum jasminoides (softwood)
Tsuga canadensis (difficult)
Viburnum opulus (softwood)
Vinca minor
Vitex agnus-castus (softwood)
Weigela florida (softwood)
Wisteria floribunda

TREES AND TALL SHRUBS FOR SCREENING

Abies concolor (White Fir)
Berberis thunbergii atropurpurea (Japanese Barberry)
Buxus sempervirens (English Boxwood)
Camellia japonica (Camellia)
Carissa grandiflora (Natal-Plum)
Ceanothus thyrsiflorus (California Lilac)
Chaenomeles speciosa (Flowering Quince)
*Crataegus phaenopyrum (Washington Hawthorn)
*Ilex opaca (American Holly)
*Magnolia grandiflora (Southern Magnolia)
Osmanthus heterophyllus (Holly Osmanthus)
Photinia x fraseri (Red Tips)
*Picea pungens 'Glauca' (Blue Spruce)
Pieris japonica (Japanese Andromeda)
*Pinus strobus (White Pine)
Pittosporum tobira (Japanese Pittosporum)
Podocarpus macrophyllus (Yew Podocarpus)
*Pseudotsuga menziesii (Douglas Fir)
Raphiolepis indica (Indian Hawthorne)
Rhododendron species (Rhododendron)
Taxus cuspidata (Japanese Yew)
Viburnum opulus sterile (European Snowball Bush)

HEDGES

Abelia x grandiflora (Glossy Abelia)
Amelanchier arborea (Serviceberry)
Aucuba japonica 'Variegata' (Gold-dust Plant)
Berberis thunbergii atropurpurea (Japanese Barberry)
Buxus sempervirens (English Boxwod)
Camellia japonica (Camellia)
Callistemon citrinus (Bottlebrush)
Carissa grandiflora (Natal-plum)
Cercis chinensis (Chinese Redbud)
Cytisus scoparius (Scotch Broom)
Deutzia gracilis (Slender Deutzia)
Enkianthus campanulatus (Redvein Enkianthus)
Euonymus alata (Burning Bush)
Euonymus japonica (Japanese Euonymus)
Forsythia x intermedia (Forsythia)
Ilex x meserveae (Blue Holly)
*Ilex opaca (American Holly)
Kerria japonica (Japanese Kerria)

Kolkwitzia amabilis (Beautybush)
Lantana camara (Shrub Verbena)
Ligustrum x vicaryi (Vicary Golden Privet)
Nerium oleander (Oleander)
Osmanthus heterophyllus (Holly Osmanthus)
Photinia x fraseri (Red Tips)
*Picea pungens 'Glauca' (Blue Spruce)
Picea pungens nana (Dwarf Blue Spruce)
*Pinus strobus (White Pine)
Podocarpus macrophyllus (Yew Podocarpus)
Poncirus trifoliata (Hardy-orange)
*Pseudotsuga menziesii (Douglas Fir)
Raphiolepis indica (Indian Hawthorn)
Spirea x vanhouttei (Bridalwreath)

SHRUBS SUITABLE FOR LAYERING

Amelanchier arborea (Serviceberry)
Azalea (Azalea)
Berberis thunbergii (Japanese Barberry)
Bougainvillea spectabilis (Bougainvillea)
Chaenomeles speciosa (Flowering Quince)
Cornus sericea (Red-twig Dogwood)
Cotoneaster horizontalis (Rock-spray)
Cytisus scoparius (Scotch Broom)
Enkianthus campanulatus (Redvein Eukianthus)
Euonymus japonica (Japanese Euonymus)
Exochorda racemosa (Pearlbush)
Fothergilla gardenii (Dwarf Fothergilla)
Hamamelis mollis (Witch-hazel)
Ilex x meserveae (Blue Holly)
Ilex verticillata (Winterberry)
Juniperus horizontalis (Creeping Juniper)
Kalmia latifolia (Mountain Laurel)
Magnolia (Magnolia)
Philadelphus coronarius (Sweet Mock-orange)
Photinia x fraseri (Red Tips)
Pieris japonica (Andromeda)
Potentilla fruticosa (Bush Cinquefoil)
Pyracantha coccinea (Firethorn)
Raphiolepsis indica (Indian Hawthorn)
Rhododendron (Rhododendron)
Syringa vulgaris (Lilac)
Viburnum opulus sterile (European Snowball Bush)

Right, top: Topiary hounds clipped out of Japanese yew at the Ladew Topiary Gardens, near Monkton, Maryland.

Right, bottom: Azaleas flank a stairway. Such severe pruning must be done after the plants have finished flowering, but before September, in order to give the plants sufficient time to set flower buds for the following season's bloom.

AUTUMN FOLIAGE COLOR

Acer palmatum dissectum (Japanese Maple)
Acer rubrum (Red maple)
Amelanchier arobira (Serviceberry)
Berberis thunbergii atropurpurea (Japanese Barberry)
Betula papyrifera (White Birch)
Callicarpa japonica (Japanese Beauty Berry)
Campsis radicans (Trumpetcreeper)
Cercis chinensis (Chinese Redbud)
Cornus species (Dogwood)
Corylopsis glabrescens (Fragrant Winterhazel)
Cotinus coggygria (Smoketree)
Enkianthus campanulatus (Redvein Enkianthus)
Euonymous alata (Burning Bush)
Fothergilla gardenii (Dwarf Fothergilla)
Gingko biloba (Maidenhair Tree)
Hamamelis mollis (Chinese Witch-hazel)
Kerria japonica (Japanese Kerria)
Kolkwitzia amabilis (Beautybush)
Lagerstroemia indica (Crape-myrtle)
Liquidamber styraciflua (Sweetgum)
Liriodendrum tulipifera (Tulip Tree)
Magnolia stellata (Star Magnolia)
Metasequoia glyptostoboides (Dawn Redwood)
Nandina domestica (Heavenly-bamboo)
Oxydendrum arboreum (Sourwood)
Parthenocissus quinquefolia (Virginia Creeper)
Prunus subhirtella 'Pendula' (Weeping Cherry)
Pyrus calleryana (Bradford Pear)
Quercus palustris (Pin Oak)
Spiraea x *vanhouttei* (Bridalwreath)
Viburnum opulus sterile (European Snowball Bush)

TOPIARY

Buxus sempervirens (English Boxwood)
Hedera helix (English Ivy)
Ilex opaca (American Holly)
Podocarpus macrophyllus (Yew Podocarpus)
Taxus cuspidata (Japanese Yew)
Tsuga canadensis (Eastern Hemlock)

ESPALIER

Beaumontia grandiflora (Herald's-trumpet)
Calliandra haematocephala (Powderpuff Shrub)
Callistemon citrinus (Lemon bottlebrush)
Cedrus atlantica (Atlas Cedar)
Fuchsia hybrida (Fuchsia)
Podocarpus macrophyllus (Yew Podocarpus)
Pyracantha coccinea (Scarlet Firethorn)

SHOWY FRUITS AND BERRIES

Actinidia chinensis (Kiwi)
Amelanchier arborea (Serviceberry)
Ardisia japonica (Marlberry)
Aucuba japonica 'Variegata' (Gold-dust Plant)
Berberis thunbergii atropurpurea (Japanese Barberry)
Callicarpa japonica (Japanese Beauty Berry)
Carissa grandiflora (Natal-plum)
Celastrus scandens (American Bittersweet)
Chaenomeles speciosa (Flowering Quince)
Cornus species (Dogwood)
Cotoneaster horizontalis (Rock Spray)
Crataegus phaenopyrum (Hawthorn)
Daphne x *burkwoodii* (Burkwood Daphne)
Ilex x *meservae* (Blue Holly)
Ilex opaca (American Holly)
Ilex verticillata (Winterberry)
Kalmia latifolia (Mountain-laurel)
Malus sargentii (Sargent Crabapple)
Myrica cerifera (Southern Wax-myrtle)
Nandina domestica (Heavenly-bamboo)
Pyracantha coccinea (Scarlet Firethorn)
Raphiolepis indica (Indian Hawthorn)
Skimmia japonica (Japanese Skimmis)
Viburnum opulus sterile (European Snowball Bush)

Left: Hardy orange (*Poncirus trifoliata*) planted beside a pond at the Morris Arboretum, near Philadelphia, Pennsylvania.

SHOWY FLOWERING

Abelia x *grandiflora* (Glossy Abelia)
*Aesculus pavia (Red Chestnut)
*Albizia julibrissin (Silk Tree)
Allamanda cathartica (Yellow Allamanda)
Beaumontia grandiflora (Herald's-trumpet)
Bougainvillea species (Bougainvillea)
Brunfelsia calycina floribunda (Yesterday, Today, Tomorrow)
Buddleia davidii (Butterfly bush)
Calliandra haematocephala (Powderpuff Shrub)
Callistemon citrinus (Lemon Bottlebrush)
Calluna vulgaris (Scotch Heather)
Camellia japonica (Camellia)
Campsis radicans (Trumpetcreeper)
Caryopteris x *clandonensis* (Blue-mist Shrub)
Castanea millissima (Chinese Chestnut)
Ceanothus thyrsiflorus (California Lilac)
Cercis chinensis (Chinese Redbud)
Chaenomeles speciosa (Flowering Quince)
Cistus ladanifer (Crimson-spot Rock-rose)
Clematis species and hybrids (Clematis)
*Crataegus phaenopyrum (Washington Hawthorn)
Cornus species (Dogwood)
Corylopsis glabrescens (Fragrant Winterhazel)
Cotinus coggygria (Smoketree)
Daphne x *burkwoodii* (Burkwood Daphne)
Deutzia gracilis (Slender Deutzia)
Enkianthus campanulatus (Redvein Enkianthus)
Exocorda racemosa (Pearlbush)
Forsythia x *intermedia* (Forsythia)
Fothergilla gardenii (Dwarf Forthergilla)
Fuchsia hybrida (Hybrid Fuchsia)
Gardenia jasminoides (Gardenia)
Gelsemium sempervirens (Carolina Jessamine)
Hamamelis mollis (Chinese Witch-hazel)
*Halesia carolina (Silverbell)
Hibiscus syriacus (Rose of Sharon)
Hydrangea macrophylla (Hydrangea)
Hypericum calycinum (St.-John's-wort)
Kalmia latifolia (Mountain-laurel)
Kerria japonica (Japanese Kerria)
Kolkwitzia amabilis (Beautybush)
*Koelreuteria paniculata (Golden Rain Tree)
*Laburnum waterii (Golden Chain Tree)

Lagerstroemia indica (Crape-myrtle)
Lantana camara (Shrub Verbena)
Leucothoe fontanesiana (Drooping Leucothoe)
Lonicera japonica (Japanese Honeysuckle)
*Magnolia grandiflora (Southern Magnolia)
Magnolia stellata (Star Magnolia)
*Malus sargentii (Crabapple)
Nandina domestica (Heavenly-bamboo)
Nerium oleander (Oleander)
Osmanthus heterophyllus (Holly Osmanthus)
Philadelphus coronarius (Sweet Mock-Orange)
Photinia x *fraseri* (Red Tips)
Pieris japonica (Japanese Andromeda)
Pittosporum tobira (Japanese Pittosporum)
Poncirus trifoliata (Hardy-orange)
Potentilla fruticosa (Bush Cinquefoil)
Prunus glandulosa 'Alboplena' (Flowering Almond)
Pyracantha coccinea (Scarlet Firethorn)
Raphiolepis indica (Indian Hawthorn)
Rhododendron species (Rhododendron)
Rhododendron (Azalea)
Skimmia japonica (Japanese Skimmia)
Spiraea x *vanhouttei* (Bridalwreath)
Syringa vulgaris (Lilac)
Tamarix ramosissima (Tamarix)
Trachelospermum jasminoides (Star or Confederate Jasmine)
Viburnum opulus sterile (European Snowball Bush)
Vitex agnus-castus (Chaste-tree)
Weigela florida (Weigela)
Wisteria floribunda (Wisteria)

SHRUB FLOWERING GUIDE

		January	February	March	April	May	June	July	August	September	October	November	December
Abelia x *grandiflora*	(Glossy Abelia)						▓	▓	▓	▓			
Acer palmatum dissectum	(Japanese Maple)			E	V	E	R	G	R	E	E	N	
Actinidia chinensis	(Kiwi)									▓	▓		
Allamanda cathartica 'Williamsi'	(Yellow Allamanda)						▓			▓			
Amelanchier arborea	(Serviceberry)			▓	▓								
Ardisia japonica	(Marlberry; Japanese Ardisia)	▓	▓	▓	▓								
Aucuba japonica 'Variegata'	(Gold-dust Plant)			E	V	E	R	G	R	E	E	N	
Beaumontia grandiflora	(Herald's-trumpet)					▓							
Berberis thunbergii atropurpurea	(Japanese Barberry)			E	V	E	R	G	R	E	E	N	
Bougainvillea spectabilis	(Bougainvillea)	▓	▓	▓	▓	▓	▓	▓	▓	▓	▓	▓	▓
Brunfelsia calycina floribunda	(Yesterday, Today, Tomorrow)				▓	▓							
Buddleia davidii	(Butterfly Bush)								▓	▓			
Buxus sempervirens	(English Boxwood)			E	V	E	R	G	R	E	E	N	
Calliandra haematocephala	(Powderpuff Shrub)			▓	▓								
Callicarpa japonica	(Japanese Beauty Berry)									▓	▓		
Callistemon citrinus	(Lemon Bottlebrush)				▓	▓							
Calluna vulgaris	(Scotch Heather)								▓	▓			
Camellia japonica	(Camellia)	▓	▓	▓									
Campsis radicans	(Trumpetcreeper)							▓	▓				
Carissa grandiflora	(Natal-Plum)	▓	▓	▓	▓	▓	▓	▓	▓	▓	▓	▓	▓
Caryopteris x *clandonensis*	(Blue-mist shrub; Bluebeard)								▓	▓			
Ceanothus thyrsiflorus	(California Lilac)			▓	▓								
Celastrus scandens	(American Bittersweet)										▓	▓	
Cercis chinensis	(Chinese Redbud)				▓	▓							

		Jan	Feb	Mar	Apr	May	Jun	Jul	Aug	Sep	Oct	Nov	Dec
Chaenomeles speciosa	(Flowering Quince)			■	■								
Chamaeceyparis pisifera	(False Cypress)			E V E R G R E E N									
Cistus ladanifer	(Crimson-spot Rock-rose)						■	■	■	■			
Clematis species and hybrids	(Clematis)						■	■	■	■			
Cornus florida	(Flowering Dogwood)					■							
Cornus kousa	(Korean Dogwood)						■						
Cornus mas	(Cornelian-cherry)			■									
Cornus sericea	(Red-twig Dogwood)	■	■	■								■	■
Corylopsis glabrescens	(Fragrant Winterhazel)			■	■								
Cotinus coggygria	(Smoketree)							■	■				
Cotoneaster horizontalis	(Rock Spray)										■	■	■
Cytisus scoparius	(Scotch Broom)				■	■							
Daphne x *burkwoodii*	(Burkwood Daphne)					■							
Deutzia gracilis	(Slender Deutzia)					■							
Enkianthus campanulatus	(Redvein Enkianthus)					■							
Escallonia exoniensis	(Escallonia)					■	■	■					
Euonymus alata	(Burning Bush)			E V E R G R E E N									
Euonymus japonicus	(Japanese Euonymus)			E V E R G R E E N									
Exochorda racemosa	(Pearlbush)					■							
Fatsia japonica	(Japanese Aralia)			E V E R G R E E N									
Forsythia x *intermedia*	(Forsythia)			■	■								
Fothergilla gardenii	(Dwarf Fothergilla)				■	■							
Fuchsia hybrida	(Hybrid Fuchsia)						■	■	■	■	■	■	
Gardenia jasminoides	(Gardenia; Cape-jasmine)			■	■								

		January	February	March	April	May	June	July	August	September	October	November	December
Gelsemium sempervirens	(Carolina Jessamine)			▓	▓								
Hamamelis mollis	(Chinese Witch-hazel)		▓	▓									
Hedera helix	(English Ivy)				E V	E R	G R	E E	N				
Hibiscus syriacus	(Rose of Sharon; Shrub Althea)								▓	▓			
Hydrangea macrophylla	(Hydrangea)						▓	▓					
Hypericum calycinum	(St.-John's-wort)						▓						
Ilex x *meserveae*	(Blue Holly; Meserve Hybrids)	▓	▓	▓									▓
Ilex verticillata	(Winterberry)										▓	▓	▓
Juniperus horizontalis	(Creeping Juniper)				E V	E R	G R	E E	N				
Kalmia latifolia	(Mountain-laurel)						▓						
Kerria japonica	(Japanese Kerria)					▓							
Kolkwitzia amabilis	(Beauty Bush)												
Lagerstroemia indica	(Crape-myrtle)							▓	▓	▓			
Lantana camara	(Shrub Verbena)						▓	▓	▓	▓	▓		
Leucothoe fontanesiana	(Drooping Leucothoe)					▓							
Ligustrum x *vicaryi*	(Vicary Golden Privet)				E V	E R	G R	E E	N				
Lonicera japonica 'Halliana'	(Japanese Honeysuckle)						▓	▓					
Magnolia stellata	(Star Magnolia)			▓									
Myrica cerifera	(Southern Wax-myrtle)												
Nandina domestica	(Heavenly-bamboo; Nandina)	▓	▓	▓								▓	▓
Nerium oleander	(Oleander)						▓	▓	▓	▓	▓		
Osmanthus heterophyllus	(Holly Osmanthus)				E V	E R	G R	E E	N				
Paeonia suffruticosa	(Tree Peony)					▓							
Parthenocissus quinquefolia	(Virginia Creeper)				E V	E R	G R	E E	N				

		January	February	March	April	May	June	July	August	September	October	November	December
Philadelphus coronarius	(Sweet Mock-orange)						■						
Photinia x *fraseri*	(Fraser Photinia; Red Tips)					■							
Picea pungens nana	(Dwarf Blue Spruce)			E V E R G R E E N									
Pieris japonica	(Japanese Andromeda)			■	■								
Pinus mugo	(Mugo Pine)			E V E R G R E E N									
Pittosporum tobira	(Japanese Pittosporum)			E V E R G R E E N									
Podocarpus macrophyllus	(Yew Podocarpus)			E V E R G R E E N									
Poncirus trifoliata	(Hardy-orange)										■		
Potentilla fruticosa	(Bush Cinquefoil)					■	■	■	■	■			
Prunus glandulosa 'Alboplena'	(Flowering Almond)				■	■							
Pyracantha coccinea	(Scarlet Firethorn)										■	■	■
Raphiolepis indica	(Indian Hawthorn)			■	■					■	■		
Rhododendron species (Azalea)	(Azalea)					■							
Salix discolor	(Pussy Willow)			■									
Skimmia japonica	(Japanese Skimmia)										■	■	■
Spiraea x *vanhouttei*	(Bridalwreath; Vanhoutte Spirea)					■	■						
Syringa vulgaris	(Lilac)					■							
Tamarix ramosissima	(Tamarix)					■							
Taxus cuspidata	(Japanese Yew)			E V E R G R E E N									
Trachelospermum jasminoides	(Star or Confederate Jasmine)						■	■	■				
Tsuga canadensis 'Sargentii'	(Weeping Hemlock)			E V E R G R E E N									
Viburnum opulus sterile	(European Snowball Bush)					■	■						
Vinca minor	(Periwinkle; Myrtle)			■	■	■							
Vitex agnus-castus	(Chaste-tree)							■					

		January	February	March	April	May	June	July	August	September	October	November	December
Weigela florida	(Weigela)						▓						
Wisteria floribunda	(Wisteria)					▓	▓						

Left: Japanese cut-leaf maple, artistically pruned of lower branches, exposes an exotic tracery of twisted trunks and sinuous branches, in the Japanese Garden of Swiss Pines, near Philadelphia, Pennsylvania.

PART SIX

ESSENTIAL

HERBS AND VEGETABLES

INTRODUCTION

HERBS AND VEGETABLES

BOTANICALLY SPEAKING, THERE IS NO CLEAR-cut classification between a vegetable and an herb. "Herb" is simply an accepted term used to describe a group of plants with useful properties. In addition to their other culinary uses, herbs are sources for dyes, medicines, and insect repellents.

Some horticulturists like to define an herb as any annual, perennial, or biennial that provides useful benefits and can be grown from seed. They consider everything else that doesn't grow readily from seed, such as bulbs (saffron) and even woody plants (bay laurel tree), spices.

There is a fine distinction between the accepted notion of a "vegetable" and that of an "herb." Most vegetables are a complete food in themselves (lettuce, tomatoes, peas), while herbs generally enhance or complement the flavor of meat, poultry, and fish, among other things. It is generally believed that the first gardens were grown as food gardens, producing essential grains and vegetables, but there is evidence to sup-

port the notion that man's first cultivated crop was an herb, probably a medicinal or hallucinogenic one. We do know herbs have a rich history. From ancient times through the nineteenth century, herbs were an essential element in civilized society, helping mask unpleasant household odors before the invention of modern plumbing, and disguising and enhancing the flavor of bland or putrid foodstuffs before the advent of modern refrigeration. Prior to modern medicinal treatments, herbs were often the only form of relief known for all manner of ailments.

The terms "herbs" and "spices" are often used interchangeably, though spices normally refer to culinary powders and small fragrant pieces, such as ginger, that originate from woody plants. For example, black pepper, cinnamon, and cloves are all derived from tropical trees. It was the high value placed on these spices that inspired Christopher Columbus to seek a shorter route to the Far East, where these precious commodities grew. Although Columbus found

Right: This classical knot garden design at Well-Sweep Herb Farm in New Jersey takes on autumnal hues following fall frosts.

Opposite page: Parallel beds of silvery lamb's ears *(Stachys olympica)* line a walkway leading to a Colonial-style outhouse at Well-Sweep Herb Farm in Port Murray, New Jersey.

many interesting and valuable new plants when he discovered the Americas, including potatoes, tobacco, and cocoa trees, relatively few native American plants (such as allspice, chili peppers, and bergamot) have added to the list of important herbs and spices.

Merchants seeking sources of herbs—especially for spices and to use as perfumes—found them growing all over the world. Sage, for example, was found along the shores of the Mediterranean; tarragon was first discovered in Siberia; and ginger is believed to have been brought from China. Native American herbs include bergamot and sassafras, both popular flavorings for tea.

The costliest spice in the world is undoubtedly saffron, gathered from the glowing red stigmas, or female flower parts of *Crocus sativus.* In value, it is worth more than its weight in gold—an ounce currently costs more than $2,000.00! Not easy to flower, difficult to grow in colder climates, it is a commercial crop in parts of Spain and Kashmir. Harvested by hand, it requires up to 100,000 blossoms to yield one pound of dried saffron stigmas. Though a beautiful yellow dye can be made from saffron, its principal use is in flavoring Mediterranean and Oriental dishes, especially French bouillabaisse soup, Spanish paella, and Italian risotto.

English lavender is another valuable herb crop, grown mostly in the county of Norfolk, northeast of London. Unlike the shy-blooming saffron crocus, English lavender is relatively easy to grow throughout North America. It flowers for most of the summer and looks highly decorative in a flower border; it also produces one of the most cherished fragrances in the world.

Because vegetable and herbs are such diverse plants, they can serve many functions in the landscape. Some, such as chamomile and thyme, can be grown as ground covers; others, such as pole beans and nasturtium, can be trained as vines; and still others, such as chives, ruby chard, and foxglove, will serve well as ornamentals.

Presented here are some ideas for growing vegetables and herbs in imaginative ways, including some classic herb garden designs, plus instructions for propagating the most useful vegetables and herbs, lists for many varied uses, and a concise encyclopedia section.

CHAPTER ONE

GROWING HERBS AND VEGETABLES

PROPAGATING HERBS AND VEGETABLES

THE MAJORITY OF HERBS CAN BE PROPAGATED in at least one of three ways: by seed, by cuttings, and by root division. Some herbs, such as lavender and mint, are easily propagated by all three methods.

Vegetables are propagated mostly from seeds, though some perennial vegetables, such as asparagus and artichokes, can also be propagated from roots.

STARTING FROM SEED

For those vegetables and herbs that grow easily from seed, this is the best and most inexpensive way to grow large numbers of plants. A packet of lavender seed, for example, is sufficient to grow hundreds of plants. There are three seed-starting systems to consider: direct-seeding into the garden, in which the seeds are sown where plants are to mature; the two-step method, whereby seeds are started in a peat pot or peat pellet and then transplanted into the garden; and the three-step method, whereby plants are first started in a seed tray, then transplanted into a peat or plastic pot, and then finally transferred to the garden. The following seed-starting techniques for growing most vegetables and many herbs are illustrated with diagrams in the section on growing Annuals (see page 22).

Direct-Seeding generally requires reading the packet instructions to see how deeply the seeds must be sown. If the packet does not specify a planting depth, sow seeds at a depth three times the diameter of the seed. Scratch a furrow to the required depth and sow the seeds along it. Then simply cover the seed with soil, making sure to keep the seed bed moist and weed-free until seeds germinate. When the young seedlings are large enough to handle, thin them so they do not compete against each other for space. If fertile soil is called for, it is best to fertilize the bed about ten days before sowing the seeds so that the fertilizer does not "burn" the delicate seedlings.

Two-Step Seed-Starting requires peat pots and potting soil or a Jiffy-7 or Jiffy-9 peat pellet. The peat pots need to be filled with potting soil. The peat pellets do not need soil and will expand to several times their size once immersed in water. Press the seeds into the growing medium and keep the pot or pellet moist. An ideal temperature is 70°F. Allow the seeds to germinate and then thin out the seedlings in stages until just one healthy plant remains to fill the pot or pellet. When it is time to transplant, dig a hole for the pellet or pot, place the transplant into the hole, and firm the soil around it to anchor the plant in its location. For best root development, the bottom of the peat pot should be peeled away, releasing the roots; and if the pellet has a net holding it together, carefully remove it.

Three-Step Seed-Starting consists of filling a seed tray made from peat or plastic with potting soil. Scatter the seeds over the soil surface and lightly cover them—there should be enough soil on top of them to anchor the seeds. Moisten the soil and keep the tray inside a clear plastic bag until the seeds germinate. The plastic bag prevents rapid drying out of the soil and creates a humid micro-climate, ideal for germinating seeds. The optimum temperature for germination is 70°F.

When the seeds have germinated, use a sharp pencil and your forefinger to raise the seedlings out of the seed tray and into individual peat pots. Keep the pots warm and in bright light (but *not* direct sunlight) until they are large enough to tolerate transplanting into the garden. If the transplants are in individual plastic pots, try to disturb the roots as little as possible. Tender varieties may need frost protection if frost threatens; this can be done by covering over with "hot-caps" or floating on covers.

Taking Cuttings Herbs such as mint and lavender are very easy to propagate by cutting off a 4- to 6-inch stem section, making sure to include a node at the base of the cutting. Root it in a moist, sandy potting soil. Some herbs, such as mint, will root in just plain water. Others, such as lavender, will enjoy a greater success rate if the cut end is first dipped in a rooting hormone, such as Rootone, before placing the cutting in potting soil. Bury the cut end with at least one inch of soil. Batches of cuttings can be started in seed trays and

the container enclosed in a clear plastic bag to create a humid micro-climate.

Multiplying by Division Many perennial herbs, including mints, sage, and chives, spread over an area and sometimes become invasive. Once established, these plants can be divided every year to keep them from becoming unruly. These divisions are an excellent source of new plants for filling in other parts of the garden, or for trading with friends. Division is best done in the fall or the spring using a sharp, heavy-duty trowel to break up clumps. Sometimes the planting is so tightly matted that a garden fork may be required to break clumps apart.

Some herbs, such as mint, root so easily from division that even a 3-inch section of root will sprout a new plant. Botanically, these are called "root cuttings." Many other herbs, such as orris root (an iris), multiply by a bulb or rhizome produced by the mother plant, and it is relatively easy to dig them up, break them apart, and replant them.

Left: A windowsill planting of assorted herbs and leaf lettuce growing indoors during winter.

Right: A raised planter over-flows with basil and chives in this combination vegetable and herb garden designed by horticulturalist Ed Toth.
Opposite page: Here, herbs are planted in decorative pots and placed around a sundial.

GROWING HERBS AND VEGETABLES IN CONTAINERS

Most vegetables and herbs grow well in containers; in fact, this is often the best way to stop the aggressive kinds of herbs from being too invasive. Many herbs, particularly culinary favorites such as chives, parsley, and thyme, can be grown in small containers. They develop their pungency early, and even a 4-inch pot can accommodate a healthy clump that will be sufficient to provide a light supply of fresh seasonings. Obviously, the bigger the pot the more you can grow, and the less likelihood of having the container dry out.

Though some vegetables, such as dwarf tomatoes, can be grown in pots (even hanging baskets), vegetables are best grown in raised planter beds, whereby long wooden boards are used to raise the soil level above the existing soil surface or paved surface.

Vegetables and herbs grown in pots need a potting soil that is on the heavy side (with garden loam added) to provide good anchorage. Many peat based potting soils are too light and fluffy unless mixed with garden loam. Containerized plants—especially hanging baskets—need watering almost daily and regular amounts of fertilizer, which is best applied in a weak strength at the time of watering. Hanging baskets usually need more moisture because they are subjected to excessive air circulation.

Whatever type of pot you choose to use, it must have good drainage. Most commercial plant pots already have drainage holes punched in the bottom and some even come with a useful drainage tray to collect excess water. To stop the potting soil from falling through the drainage holes—and also to prevent them from clogging up by soil compaction—it is best to place a few pebbles or convex pieces of broken clay pots over the holes. Some commercial containers come with a device built into the bottom to keep the holes cleared, such as a raised wire platform.

Most herbs will tolerate being pot-bound, and can be kept compact by pruning, but eventually they will benefit from being transplanted into a larger pot. Salt build up from the

use of chemical fertilizers should be watched. When the soil surface is caked with salts, consider re-potting. If you live in an area with a cold climate, try growing some tender herb species that can be moved outdoors during warm weather. Lemon trees, bay laurel, ginger, and basil are examples of tender plants that can be overwintered in pots.

Another group of herb plants can be trained into interesting shapes, such as topiary, bonsai, and espalier forms. Myrtle, for example, can be grown so it has a slender, straight trunk and a rounded top. Quince makes an exquisite bonsai subject—and, even though you can dwarf the plant by restricting its roots and by pruning, the fruit will always be full size. The multiple branches of rosemary can be trained to splay out like a fan (a popular form of espalier).

Growing Herbs Indoors To grow herbs successfully indoors, they are best cultivated in containers (see above) and provided with bright light, but not direct sunlight, which can cause rapid moisture loss and "sunscorch." Try to give plants light that is not too direct. A plant placed too far back from a bright window, for example, will have a tendency to stretch and exhaust itself. A good way to ensure an even distribution of light in a window location is to purchase a window greenhouse that works like a bay window, projecting out from the house one or two feet, with several rows of shelves to grow a wide assortment of plants.

When there is a total absence of natural daylight it's possible to use grow lights. For most herbs, pairs of grow lights should be set 6 to 8 inches above the plants, under a reflector canopy. Check garden supply houses for specific brands and complete growing instructions. These fluorescent lights will enable you to grow herbs even in a dark basement. They generally need to burn sixteen hours a day for optimum growth and are best set on timers so the lights switch on and off automatically.

How to Buy Herbs There is such a great year-round demand for herbs that even discount stores may have a selection to offer, although a garden center, florist, or houseplant outlet may carry a better selection. For the best selection, however, try locating a local "herb farm." Herb farms are now a popular cottage industry, and you will find a good selection offered for sale in pots varying in size from young transplants to mature potted topiaries and hanging baskets.

Some of these herb farms do a mail-order trade and by checking the source list on page 679 you will find names of some reliable mail order herb specialists you can write to for their catalog. The success rate from mail-order herbs is quite good. Only herbs that travel safely through the mail are offered. Generally, they are shipped in small pots; the soil is prevented from shaking loose by a tight plastic wrapper. Sometimes—if the plant is shrubby—you may receive a bare-root cutting with the roots wrapped in moist sphagnum moss for protection, and occasionally you will receive dormant bulbs, as in the case of saffron crocus and orris root. When buying from mail-order sources, read the order form carefully for instructions on how to enter your order and the waiting period to expect. When plants arrive, examine the package immediately and request a replacement if there is evidence of serious damage or wilt, and plant as soon as weather conditions allow.

DESIGNING WITH HERBS

Herbs work best in the landscape when they are grown in a special area (preferably close to the kitchen) where there is a strong sense of design to the overall layout since many herbs are not sufficiently ornamental to dress up an uninspired landscape like colorful annuals and perennials. Herbs look particularly good in highly formal designs, such as parterre gardens and knot gardens, where they can be used to delineate planting beds. The "cartwheel design" in particular is a great favorite, whereby paths radiate from a center point like the spokes of a wheel, the pie-shaped areas between the spokes serving as planting beds. For blueprints of specific garden designs, see Part 7, "Garden Designs."

Once you have a highly formal layout in place, the plantings can be extremely informal. In fact, the very best herb gardens generally combine a strong formal design with a deliberate softening of the edges accomplished with plants that spill into the pathways, create billowing cushions, or punctuate the design with tall flower spikes.

While it is possible to have an herb garden with a preponderance of flowering plants, the best herb gardens rely more heavily on creating subtle and subdued color by concentrating more on texture, form, and gradations of green, silver,

and purple—hues commonly found in their leaves. Texture comes from recognizing the beauty of leathery, shiny leaves like bay laurel, and contrasting them with the woolly, glistening leaves of lamb's ears. Form is introduced by accentuating the shapes of plants, for example exposing the strong, spreading multiple stems of a quince tree by pruning away lower side branches and ringing it with the low-growing, ground-hugging, cushionlike form of thyme or santolina.

It's possible to create theme gardens using herbs. For example, an herb garden can look "Ecclesiastical" by placing a font or other religious artifact at the center as a focal point. It can be given a "Gothic" or "Medieval" look by using low wattle fences to divide planting beds; these wattle fences are made by weaving together pliable branches.

POPULAR HERB GARDEN DESIGN THEMES:

Beehive Herb Garden: uses a beehive as a focal accent.

Biblical Herb Garden: shaped like a cross, contains plants of the Bible.

Butterfly Herb Garden: layout simulates the outstretched wings of a butterfly.

Cameo Herb Garden: herbs planted by use—dye plants together, etc.

Cartwheel Herb Garden: spaces between spokes become planting beds.

Elizabethan Herb Garden: hexagonal cartwheel design with brick paths.

Knot Garden: herbs planted as low hedges to make parterre designs.

Medieval Herb Garden: low wattle fences used as an edging to a geometric design.

Monastery Herb Garden: includes a well head as a focal accent.

POPULAR STRUCTURES FOR HERB GARDENS:

Arbors	Fonts
Benches	Gazebos
Birdbaths	Outhouses
Birdhouses	Sculpture: especially St. Fiacre,
Brick Paths	the patron saint of gardeners
Flagstones	Terra-cotta containers

A "Butterfly" herb garden can be created by introducing herbal plants, such as beebalm, that attract butterflies, and by laying out the garden in the shape of a butterfly's outstretched wings.

Another enterprising herb garden design is the "Cameo" garden, whereby herbs for special purposes are grouped together. For example, herbs with culinary qualities could be grouped in one section, insect repellent plants in another, and herbs used for perfumes in another. Another type of Cameo garden includes garden beds that represent different themes. For example, an oval space edged with a low wattle fence and a unicorn statue in the middle can represent a "medieval garden;" a bed of plants attractive to bees can feature a beehive in the middle to create a "beehive garden," and so on.

Care should be taken when designing with herbs to ensure that tall plants, such as dill, do not obscure shorter ones, such as lavender.

An especially attractive type of herb garden is the knot garden which uses dwarf herbs to create miniature hedges that can be planted in merging swirls and circles (see sample designs, pages 672 to 673). Generally, three foliage colors are used—dark green, silver, and purple—as are shrubby plants that can tolerate repeated shearing to keep the outlines sharp and well-defined. Usually, santolina is used for a silver effect, germander for the dark green, and pygmy barberry for the purple. Use different colored gravel in the geometric spaces created by the hedges.

SOIL PREPARATION

Herbs generally do not demand as rich a soil as do other garden plants, such as vegetables, flowering annuals, and perennials. Many herbs grow in the most inhospitable places—sage on rocky hillsides bordering the Mediterranean Sea, scented geraniums in the desertlike areas of South Africa, and tarragon on the bleak steppes bordering the Arctic Circle. Herbs are tough survivors that developed strong fragrances and flavors as protection against insects or foraging animals. Where soil conditions are too difficult for vegetables or ornamentals, you might succeed with selections of easy-to-grow herbs such as sage, lavender, and thyme.

In general, herbs prefer a soil pH that is slightly acidic. If you are unsure about the nature of your soil, contact your local County Extension Agent for instructions on how to take a soil sample and mail it to a soil testing laboratory for analysis. The lab will respond with a report that tells you what your soil needs to grow a particular crop.

Soil generally can be classifed as sand, clay, or loam. The particles in sandy soil do not retain moisture or nutrients.

Clay soil is thick and impervious to moisture. Rainwater will lie on the surface of clay soil for a long time. It is cold and lumpy, and sticks together in a mass when you pick up a handful and squeeze it in your hand.

Loam soil is loose and crumbly. Even when moist you can squeeze it in your hand and it will fall apart when released. Loam soil has a high humus content (decomposed organic matter) which gives the soil the ability to hold moisture like a sponge, while still allowing excess moisture to drain away.

Soils that are too light and sandy or too heavy and contain too much clay can be improved by adding organic matter to create humus. Well-decomposed animal manure, leaf mold (the product of well-decomposed leaves), garden compost, and peat are all good sources of organic matter.

To prepare a new site for planting herbs, mark out the area with string to make squares and rectangles, or coils of garden hose to make circles, ovals, or kidney shapes. Remove sod from the surface, shake it free of soil, which can be returned to the site, and discard the sod onto a compost pile. Dig the site over to a depth of 12 inches and add generous amounts of compost, even if the soil is good quality garden loam. If the site drains poorly, or has hard subsoil difficult to dig, consider laying down a foundation of broken stones or large pieces of gravel to create a raised bed. Fill it with topsoil brought from elsewhere in the garden.

If a soil test has determined that the soil is too alkaline (as in desert regions), building a raised bed with corrected soil trucked in may be preferable to correcting the existing soil through amendments. Where soil is only slightly alkaline, correction can be achieved by adding sulphur at the rate recommended by the soil analysis. Where soil is acidic, correction is generally possible by adding lime at the rate recommended by the soil test.

Opposite page: In the herb garden at The Cloisters in New York City, wattle fences are used to edge the herb beds; the stone font helps to recreate the medieval design typical of ancient monastery gardens.

USING HERBS AND VEGETABLES

H ERBS CAN BE USED FRESH, DRIED, OR BOTH. The time of harvesting depends on the individual herb and the use to be made of it. For example, parsley and chives are prized for fresh use and pieces of leaf as a garnish can be harvested at any time, providing plants are not weakened by over-picking. Usually, for fresh use, the younger leaves on the plant provide the best flavor. With mint, for example, the first whorl of leaves (no lower than the first six leaves from the tip) provides the best flavor.

Many herbs cannot be used instantly; they must be left to mature. Either the flowering part (as with lavender) or the root (as with ginseng) is valued, so patience is needed until a particular plant part is ready for harvest (usually one growing season in the case of lavender, but as much as three years in the case of ginseng). The individual descriptions in the encyclopedia section of this book (beginning on page 538) provide specific information on each herb.

Vegetables are used mostly fresh or cooked. They generally are divided into three groups: leaf vegetables, like lettuce or spinach, popular for salads; root crops, such as carrots and beets, that are usually boiled; and fruits, such as tomatoes and melons, usually eaten raw. Since most people are familiar with the ways to prepare and eat popular vegetables, this section will deal mainly with the many uses of herbs.

USING FRESH HERBS

When an herb is to be used fresh for culinary purposes (such as adding to a salad, flavoring a soup, or making a refreshing tea) it should be picked just prior to use; once picked, never leave it in the sun for any length of time, or deprive it of water so it wilts. If there might be any delay between the time the herb is picked and the time it is used, just pop the stems in a jar of water. Herbs such as watercress, mint, parsley, and basil will even look decorative sitting in a jar on a kitchen windowsill until ready to be used.

DRYING HERBS

Generally, herbs are dried for two reasons: to preserve the herb for storage until you are ready to use it, or to preserve the herb for decoration, generally for use in potpourri and wreaths. Many herbs dried for culinary use (such as sage, rosemary, bay, and thyme) retain their flavors a long time and can be stored in jars. When choosing herbs to dry for wreaths and potpourri we generally like to retain as much fragrance and color as possible. In both cases the method of drying is extremely important.

Methods of Drying Herbs

Drying methods depend on whether you are drying short-stemmed or long-stemmed herbs. Usually, short-stemmed herbs must be dried over screens so air circulates freely. Herbs can be dried indoors or outdoors providing they are kept out of direct sunlight. Long-stemmed herbs are best gathered into small bunches of a dozen stems each, held together by twist-ties or elastic bands, and suspended upside down from a rafter or a clothesline.

Where the intention is to harvest seeds (such as anise and caraway), the seed heads are best gathered when the seeds are ripe. Once ripe, the seed head is shaken over newspaper pages to catch the seeds as they fall. A curing period of about seven days on the newspaper is needed to reduce the moisture content for long storage. To speed up this drying process, the seeds can be placed on pie trays or cookie sheets and left in the back of a car with the windows down. Sun shining through the windows will heat up the car quickly and cure the seeds in a day. After drying the seeds, any chaff should be carefully separated out and the seeds stored in air-tight containers.

Long-stemmed herbs can be highly ornamental while they are in the process of being dried. A good place to dry them is in a kitchen or around a fireplace. Bunches of blue lavender, red chili peppers, yellow yarrow, and silvery artemisia can not only provide an uplifting sight when visitors enter the room, but also fill the air with pleasant aromas. Even if you never find the time to chop the dried leaves and store them in jars for future use, the sheer visual delight that is a part of drying herbs is reason enough to grow and harvest them.

WAYS TO USE HERBS

Most people are familiar with the culinary uses of herbs. Usually, very small amounts of a particular herb are needed to enhance the flavor of any dish. Mint sauce is to lamb what apple sauce is to pork; saffron is a vital ingredient in the preparation of the famous French soup, *bouillabaisse,* and many people feel that dill is indispensable in fish dishes. Similarly, with beverages, herbs are used as flavor enhancers. Ginger is a prime ingredient in ginger ale and ginger beer; woodruff is synonymous with May wine, and mint enlivens the taste of ice tea. Following are a few familiar and not-so-familiar ways to use herbs around the house.

Herb Teas

Some of the best herbal teas are chamomile, mint, lavender, and lemon verbena. Many herb teas are claimed to have therapeutic properties—such as calming a nervous stomach, improving digestion, and sharpening the senses—but even without those benefits they just taste good. The method for brewing herbal teas is very easy—simply place a few sprigs of the herb in a teapot and pour in boiling water. Allow the herb to steep for two minutes; pour into cups through a strainer and serve with a dash of sugar, if desired. Herbs to make teas can be used fresh or dried.

Herb Vinegars

Though herbs can be used fresh or dried to flavor vinegar, fresh herbs are best. Some of the finest herbs to use include tarragon, rosemary, and fennel. The best vinegars to use are cider vinegar, and white- and red wine vinegars purchased in gallon containers.

To make herb vinegar, insert a few sprigs of the particular herb into a glass bottle, then pour the vinegar into it so the sprigs float in the liquid. The amount of herb used depends on how strong a flavor you want. Herbal vinegars are great gifts if you use fancy glass bottles with corks as stoppers.

Herb Butters

Herb butters taste so much better than plain butter that they can almost become addictive. Particularly good herbs to consider include parsley, tarragon, chives and basil—fresh or dried, though fresh herbs are preferred, and more colorful.

To make herb butter simply take a stick (one-quarter pound) of butter and place it in a bowl. Chop the herb leaves very fine into small pieces and mix the two together by hand or with an electric beater. Pat into molds or scoop into balls and refrigerate for several hours to allow the flavor to permeate.

Candied Herbs

The flowers, petals, and leaves of certain herbs are good to candy. These include violet flowers, rose petals, and scented geranium leaves. They are mostly used to decorate cakes, cookies, and desserts. Pick only firm, blemish-free blossoms and leaves to be candied.

To candy herbs, follow this procedure: Wash the herbs and pat them dry with a paper towel. Beat one egg white until it is foamy. Hold the leaf or flower in one hand and, using a camel hair brush, gently dab it all over with the egg white. Make sure you push the brush into all the nooks and crannies above and under the flower or leaf surface. Then, sprinkle it with superfine granulated sugar. To enhance the flower color you may wish to use colored sugar (for example, blue on violets, pink on rose petals) by adding a little food coloring to the sugar. Place the flowers or leaves on waxed paper and leave them to dry for two days. Then store in tight, dry containers in layers, with a piece of wax paper separating each layer.

Herb Potpourri

The word "potpourri" is derived from the French word *pourir*, meaning to rot, since highly fragrant, long-lasting herbal mixes were made by infusing semi-dried herbs with alcohol, such as brandy. Today, however, the easiest method for making potpourri is the dry method, allowing the aromatic leaves and petals of herbs to dry thoroughly, and mixing them into a bowl. Usually, the best potpourri allow a particular herbal fragrance to dominate—for example, the aroma given off by the petals of a rose, a lemony aroma achieved by drying lemon grass and lemon verbena, or a pineapple aroma achieved through the use of pineapple sage and pineapple-scented geraniums. To help the potpourri retain its aroma for an extended period of time, it's best to mix an essential oil (such as oil of violet or oil of lavender) with a fixative (such as powdered orris root) and blend it with the dried herbal ingredients.

For the strongest aroma, store the mixture in a tight container and place it in a dark closet for about six weeks to allow the ingredients to mingle their fragrances and mature. Then, the potpourri mixture can be transferred to a decorative bowl, emptied into an attractive spice jar, or stuffed into pillows and sachets.

CHAPTER THREE

THE ENCYCLOPEDIA OF ESSENTIAL HERBS AND VEGETABLES

THE FOLLOWING LISTING OF POPULAR VEGETAbles and herbs is arranged alphabetically by latin name. If you know only the common name of a plant and want to find its listing, simply check in the cross reference of botanical and common names at the back of the book (page 686) and it will refer to the page number where the common name can be found.

For all entries, heights given are average, and under certain conditions, such as high rainfall and high soil fertility, vegetables and herbs may grow taller than suggested. Under "uses," the listing will give not only the culinary use, if the plant is known for one, but, in the case of herbs, also whether the herb is used for a dye, for insect repellent, for fragrance in potpourri, and any other significant use. Where a therapeutic remedy is given, such as "clearing the sinuses" in the case of mint leaves, and "aiding the digestion" in the case of anise seeds, these claims are made on the basis of common knowledge or widely accepted herbal literature. Where herbs are recommended for making tea, these should be imbibed in small amounts only, as modern medical research is finding that overdoses of certain herbs can be harmful.

No medical claims are made for any herbs in this book. Where a medical use is given, as in the case of foxglove (*Digitalis purpurea*), the use of that herb should be only in the form of a prescription and under a physician's supervision. Such herbs are recommended only for their ornamental or historical value.

BOTANICAL NAME *Abelmoschus esculentus*

COMMON NAME Okra

CULTURE Sow seed directly into the garden 1/2-inch deep in fertile loam soil after all danger of frost. Thin seedlings to 12 inches apart in rows 3 feet apart. Germination is improved if the bullet-hard seeds are soaked overnight in luke warm water. Tolerates hot, humid weather.

DESCRIPTION A tall-growing crop, up to 6 feet high, related to hibiscus, okra produces edible green or red pods that are tender and succulent when small, but become fibrous, and even woody, if allowed to dry.

HARVEST AND USE A popular Southern vegetable cooked into soups and stews and boiled as a side dish. Popular ingredient of vegetable curry. Excellent for freezing. Good for pickling.

RECOMMENDED VARIETY 'Blondy' is an award-winning dwarf variety producing tender pods earlier than tall kinds.

BOTANICAL NAME *Agastache foeniculum*

COMMON NAME Anise Hyssop

HEIGHT 3 to 4 feet; clump-forming, shrubby habit.

CULTURE Hardy perennial. Propagated mostly from seed. Thrives in fertile loam soil and full sun, but tolerates partial shade.

DESCRIPTION Aromatic, erect plants have round, gray-green leaves and prominent spikes studded with purple flowers, similar to lavender. All plant parts are anise scented.

USES Leaves mostly used air-dried in teas and potpourri, but can be used fresh to flavor drinks and fruit salads, or as a substitute for authentic anise seed by steeping in water, then using the liquid in cakes, muffins, and cookies.

BOTANICAL NAME *Agave americana*

COMMON NAME Century Plant; American Aloe

HEIGHT Up to 5 feet, taller when flowering; rosette-forming habit.

CULTURE Tender perennial succulent plant mostly grown in pots so can be taken indoors during freezing weather. Propagated by division. Demands excellent drainage, sunny location. Tolerates poor soil and drought.

DESCRIPTION Thick, triangular, pointed blue-green leaves, with spines along the edges, emerge from a basal crown. At maturity (sometimes 100 years), a flower spike resembling an asparagus spear will emerge, opening out to reveal greenish yellow flowers attractive to hummingbirds. After flowering, plant dies but leaves "pups" or offsets around the base which will continue to grow.

USES Leaves used medicinally by Indians of the Southwestern United States. Also a modern source of steroids.

BOTANICAL NAME *Agrimonia eupatoria*

COMMON NAME Agrimony

HEIGHT 2 to 3 feet; wide, spreading habit.

CULTURE Hardy perennial. Propagated by seed and cuttings. Prefers partial shade in dry, well-drained soil.

DESCRIPTION Leaves and stalks are deep green and downy, with slender spikes of yellow flowers. All plant parts are slightly aromatic, with the flowers emitting an apricot-like spicy scent.

USES After drying, the stems, leaves, and flowers can be used to make tea. The whole plant is also used to make a yellow dye.

BOTANICAL NAME *Allium cepa*

COMMON NAME Onion

CULTURE Start seed indoors to produce transplants six weeks before outdoor planting, or sow seed directly into the garden, 1/4 inch deep. Thin seedlings to 4 inches apart in rows at least 12 inches apart. Alternatively plant "sets" so that only half the bulb is covered with soil. Prefers fertile loam soil with a high humus content. Onions respond well to soil enriched with animal manure and regular watering.

DESCRIPTION Bulbous plants grow from seeds, sets (small immature onions), and transplants. Seeds and transplants produce the largest bulbs, since onions are biennials and the first year's growth goes into the onion bulb. Sets are easy to plant but part of their energy goes into growing a flowering stem.

HARVEST AND USE Onions are responsive to day length and will not start to "size up" until midsummer. Harvest bulbs when tops have started to die down.

RECOMMENDED VARIETIES 'Spartan Sleeper' is a long-storage onion—won't soon spoil even at room temperature. 'Giant Walla Walla' is a giant-size, sweet-flavored onion.

BOTANICAL NAME *Allium cepa proliferum*

COMMON NAME Egyptian Top Onion

HEIGHT 3 feet; erect, clump-forming habit.

CULTURE Perennial bulb propagated mostly from bulblets that form on top of pungent, hollow, onionlike stalks. Plants are extremely hardy, and multiply by forming bulblets in the soil.

DESCRIPTION Clusters of bulbs sprout slender, pointed onion-like leaves and a hollow stem topped by a cluster of inconspicuous white flowers that quickly turn into groups of three to five bulbs.

USES Both the bulbs in the soil, and the bulblets that form on the flowering stems are edible, mostly grated to substitute for onions as a seasoning in soups, sandwiches, and salads.

BOTANICAL NAME *Allium fistulosum*

COMMON NAME Welsh Onion

HEIGHT 2 to 3 feet; upright, clump-forming habit.

CULTURE Hardy perennial bulb. Propagated mostly from the seeds that follow the flowering in the second season of growth. Also propagated by division of underground bulbs. Prefers moist, fertile loam soil in full sun or partial shade.

DESCRIPTION Rounded white flower clusters are borne on hollow green stems with new leaves forming at the base of the plant.

USES Young leaves are chopped into rings and used as a garnish like chives. The bulbs are used in cooking.

BOTANICAL NAME *Allium schoenoprasum*

COMMON NAME Chive

HEIGHT 12 to 18 inches; clump-forming habit.

CULTURE Hardy perennial bulb. Propagated by seed and by dividing established clumps. Easy to grow in any well-drained loam soil in full sun or partial shade.

DESCRIPTION Rounded pink or purple flowers appear on top of slender stalks above clumps of arching, hollow, pointed leaves. Both leaves and flowers emit a mild onion flavor.

USES Leaves are chopped and used fresh, frozen, or dried as a garnish in cooking and on salads. Highly ornamental, and popular to use as an edging.

BOTANICAL NAME *Allium tuberosum*

COMMON NAME Chinese Chive; Garlic Chive

HEIGHT 2 feet; upright, clump-forming habit.

CULTURE Hardy perennial bulb. Propagated by seed and by dividing established clumps. Easy to grow in any well-drained loam soil, in full sun or partial shade.

DESCRIPTION Vigorous plants produce spikey leaves and masses of showy, white, rounded blossoms. The flowers are sweetly scented, while the leaves and bulb have a garlic odor. Highly ornamental when in bloom.

USES Leaves are snipped into salads, soups, and sauces. The dried, green seed head makes an excellent garlic vinegar. Good to use as a ground cover for erosion control on banks. Blooms midsummer.

BOTANICAL NAME *Aloe barbadensis* (formerly *Aloe vera*)

COMMON NAME Healing Plant; Barbados Aloe

HEIGHT 1 foot usually, 2 feet when flowering; rosette-forming habit.

CULTURE Tender perennial. Propagated from seed or from young side-shoots called "pups." May be grown outdoors year-round only in frost-free areas. Prefers well-drained loam or sandy soil. In northern states, popular as a houseplant grown in pots on a sunny windowsill.

DESCRIPTION White-freckled, succulent leaves have spiny edges that are broad at the base and taper to a point. Well-established plants will develop spikes of yellow flowers.

USES A moist gel on the inside of the leaves is used to relieve the pain of burns, including sunburn. Also used as a skin moisturizer and in cosmetics—especially shampoo and soaps.

BOTANICAL NAME *Aloysia triphylla*

COMMON NAME Lemon Verbena

HEIGHT 2 to 10 feet; bushy habit.

CULTURE Tender perennial becoming woody with age. Propagated mainly by root division and stem cuttings. Grown outdoors as a shrub in frost-free areas; otherwise plants are overwintered by growing in pots and taking them indoors. Prefers fertile, moist loam soil in sun or partial shade.

DESCRIPTION Inconspicuous panicles of pale lavender blossoms appear along the stems in summer. Green, heavily veined leaves are pointed, with scalloped edges. The leaves are highly fragrant, releasing a pleasant, clean, lemon scent when bruised.

USES Dried leaves retain their delightful scent for years and are used in teas, also potpourri. The extracted oil is prized for its scent and is often used in perfumery.

BOTANICAL NAME *Amaranthus hybridus hypochondriacus*

COMMON NAME Prince's-feather; Green Amaranth

HEIGHT Up to 5 feet; erect habit.

CULTURE Tender annual. Propagated by seed. Prefers fertile loam soil with plenty of organic matter, in full sun.

DESCRIPTION Deep crimson flowers are densely packed on erect spikes. Veined, pointed leaves have purple undersides. Highly ornamental when in flower.

USES Both the seeds and the leaves are edible, the seeds as a grain and the leaves as a spinach substitute. Also, the dried flower heads are popular for floral arrangements.

BOTANICAL NAME *Amorpha fruticosa angustifolia*

COMMON NAME Indigo Bush; Bastard Indigo

HEIGHT 6 to 20 feet, with 5 to 15 feet spread; shrub or tree-like.

CULTURE Hardy deciduous shrub. Tolerates poor soil, including dry, sandy soil, in full sun. Best pruned in winter or early spring to discourage a leggy, untidy appearance.

DESCRIPTION Spikes of small, purplish blue flowers bloom June through July. Small, bright green leaves in summer turn yellow in autumn. Hardy in zones 4 to 9.

USES Source of dye. Good landscape plant for poor soils where few other ornamentals will grow.

RELATED SPECIES *Amorpha nana*, known as 'Fragrant False Indigo,' grows just 3 feet high and is cultivated for its spicy fragrance.

BOTANICAL NAME *Anethum graveolens*

COMMON NAME Dill

HEIGHT 3 to 4 feet; upright habit.

CULTURE Hardy annual. Propagated by seed. Prefers moist, fertile, acid soil in full sun.

DESCRIPTION Flowers are yellow in broad, flat umbels. The aromatic seeds are flattened with a conspicuous rib. Leaves are narrow, fern-like, blue-green.

USES All parts of the plant are aromatic. The leaves and seeds in particular are used for flavoring pickles, sauerkraut, and beets. The feathery leaves are most often used to flavor fish dishes.

BOTANICAL NAME *Angelica archangelica*

COMMON NAME Angelica

HEIGHT Up to 6 feet tall, 3 feet wide; clump-forming habit.

CULTURE Hardy biennial which produces foliage the first year and flowers the second. Propagated from seed. Prefers cool, moist, alkaline soils, in sun or partial shade.

DESCRIPTION Spectacular clusters of yellow-green flowers bloom in summer. Dark green leaves are 2 to 3 feet long, with toothed edges, borne on hollow stems that are purplish at the base. All plant parts are fragrant.

USES The entire plant—finely chopped—is used mainly as a garnish with rhubarb, salads, fish, and poultry. Tea made from the root is supposed to be a tonic and stimulant. Oils are extracted from the seeds for use as a perfume fragrance and for flavoring.

BOTANICAL NAME *Anthemis nobilis* (see also *Chamaemelum nobilis*)

COMMON NAME Chamomile

HEIGHT 6 to 12 inches; low, mat-forming habit.

CULTURE Evergreen hardy perennial. Propagated by seed and by division of established clumps. Easy to grow in well-drained loam soils in full sun.

DESCRIPTION Small, yellow, buttonlike blossoms appear in summer. Leaves are light green and segmented. All parts are highly fragrant.

USES Flowers can be used fresh or dried in tea, reputed to have a calming effect on the senses.

RELATED SPECIES *Matricaria recutita*, the 'Pineapple Weed,' and other species of *Matricaria* and *Anthemis*, possess a similar fragrance and are also referred to as chamomile.

BOTANICAL NAME *Anthriscus cerefolium*

COMMON NAME Chervil

HEIGHT 2 to 3 feet; erect, clump-forming habit.

CULTURE Hardy annual. Propagated from seed. Prefers moist, fertile, loam soil in full sun.

DESCRIPTION Dainty white flower clusters appear on thin, brittle stems in summer. Leaves are bright green and resemble parsley. Flavor is sweet and mild, with a hint of anise.

USES Young leaves can be used fresh, dried, or frozen as a garnish, especially on fish and fruit salads. It is an essential ingredient in bearnaise sauce and in the "Fines Herbs" mixture of chives, plus marjoram or tarragon. Also used on salads, in soups and marinades, and combined with butter for a chicken or fish baste.

BOTANICAL NAME *Apium graveolens dulce*

COMMON NAME Celery

CULTURE Celery needs at least 100 days to develop its crisp, crunchy green stalks. Start seed indoors six to eight weeks before planting outdoors, well after danger of frost, since exposure to frosty nights causes plants to bolt to seed. Celery is a heavy feeder and heavy drinker. Water heavily whenever a week passes without natural rainfall. Fertilize soil prior to planting with a high nitrogen fertilizer, and provide booster feedings every three to four weeks during growing season. Plants grow best in soil with high humus content, especially soil that is well manured.

DESCRIPTION Plants grow clumps of upright, edible green stalks topped by indented leaves.

HARVEST AND USE Harvest in late summer or fall during cool weather. The familiar white or "blanched" celery is produced by placing paper collars around the green stalks to exclude light.

RECOMMENDED VARIETY 'Tendercrisp' is a home garden favorite.

BOTANICAL NAME *Armoracia rusticana*

COMMON NAME Horseradish

HEIGHT 2 to 3 feet; clump-forming, upright habit.

CULTURE Hardy perennial. Propagated from root cuttings in spring. Prefers fertile, well-drained loam soil in full sun.

DESCRIPTION Large, dark green paddle-shaped leaves, with wavy edges, rise erect from deep, thick taproots. Small, white flowers appear in clusters among the leaves. Best confined to a special corner, otherwise plants can become invasive.

USES The white taproots are uprooted from the soil, washed clean, and dried to release the hot, pungent aroma that flavors condiments and sauces for beef, pork, and seafood.

BOTANICAL NAME *Artemisia absinthium*

COMMON NAME Wormwood

HEIGHT 4 to 5 feet; erect, clump-forming habit.

CULTURE Hardy perennial becoming woody with age. Propagated by seed, by division of established clumps, and by cuttings. Thrives in clay soils and tolerates drought. Prefers full sun. Can become leggy and untidy if not trimmed back in spring. Best divided every two to three years to encourage vigorous new growth.

DESCRIPTION Leaves are its most ornamental feature—silvery grey in appearance, slender and fuzzy. Inconspicuous yellow flowers appear in midsummer.

USES The aperitif, absinthe, was made from this plant. Also used as a main ingredient in Vermouth. Ingestion of excessive amounts is believed to cause brain damage. Diluted wormwood tea is thought to stimulate the appetite. The dried herb is popular as a moth repellent.

BOTANICAL NAME *Artemisia dracunculus sativa*

COMMON NAME French Tarragon

HEIGHT 2 to 3 feet; erect, clump-forming habit.

CULTURE Hardy perennial. Propagated by division or cuttings. There is a related variety, *Artemisia dracunculus inodora* ('Russian Tarragon'), that can be grown from seeds, but it is inferior in quality to the true French Tarragon, which is sterile. Prefers fertile, well-drained loam soil in full sun or partial shade. Plants need dividing every three years to maintain vigor.

DESCRIPTION Narrow, anise-flavored shiny green leaves are willow-like. Inconspicuous greenish white blooms are produced sporadically.

USES Essential culinary herb used to flavor vinegar and also to season spinach, mushrooms, chicken, beef, or fish.

BOTANICAL NAME *Asparagus officinalis*

COMMON NAME Asparagus

CULTURE Start seeds indoors at least eight weeks before outdoor planting after frost danger is past, or plant one-year-old roots into fertile loam soil. Do not begin cutting spears until third season, when a light harvest can be made. Do not cut all stems even from an established bed, since the green fronds keep the roots healthy. Plant roots 12 inches apart in rows spaced 3 feet apart.

DESCRIPTION Succulent pointed stems as thick as a thumb emerge in spring from fleshy roots that live from year to year. The stems quickly elongate and produce fern-like fronds. After frost kills the tops, plants survive winter as dormant roots.

HARVEST AND USE Cut stems soon after they emerge from the soil, using a sharp knife. Ideal stem length is five to six inches. Boil stalks in water for five minutes. Blanched stalks are good for freezing.

RECOMMENDED VARIETIES Choose an "all-male" hybrid such as 'Jersey Giant' or 'Ben Franklin'. These produce up to three times heavier yields than standard varieties that produce thin, seed-bearing stems.

BOTANICAL NAME *Beta vulgaris*

COMMON NAME Beet

CULTURE Sow seed directly into the garden several weeks before the last frost date, since seedlings tolerate mild frosts. Cover with 1/4 inch of soil and thin seedlings to 3 inches apart in rows spaced 2 feet apart. In the absence of natural rainfall, keep plants watered since lack of moisture causes toughness. Preferred soil is sandy loam with high humus content.

DESCRIPTION Beets are root vegetables that like to mature during cool weather. They produce succulent, edible, dark green leaves that are an excellent substitute for spinach, and round or cylindrical roots that are usually purple in color, but can be golden yellow or white. Swiss chard is a beet that does not produce roots, but grows large, decorative, succulent leaves with crisp, edible stalks.

HARVEST AND USE Baby beets can be harvested when golf-ball size, or left to reach baseball-size. Baby beets are delicious boiled until tender, canned, or frozen.

RECOMMENDED VARIETIES 'Pacemaker' is a hybrid with extra-tender roots. 'Burpee's Golden Beet' has delicious tops and tasty round roots that don't bleed like red beets.

BOTANICAL NAME *Borago officinalis*

COMMON NAME Borage

HEIGHT 2 to 3 feet; sprawling habit.

CULTURE Tender annual. Propagated by seed. Re-seeds itself readily. Easy to grow in most well-drained loam soils in full sun.

DESCRIPTION Pretty bicolored flowers (pink and blue) are star-shaped, borne on velvety blue-green succulent stems. Highly ornamental.

USES Borage has a cooling effect in fruit punches and wine drinks. Its leaves and flowers have a distinct cucumber flavor. Can be substituted for cucumbers in salads and drinks. Before using scrape the fresh leaves free of hairs. This also helps release the flavor. The flowers are used to decorate cakes.

BOTANICAL NAME *Brassica oleracea botrytis*

COMMON NAME Broccoli

CULTURE Start seeds six to eight weeks before outdoor planting—several weeks before the last frost date. Seedlings tolerate mild frosts and plants grow best during cool weather. For fall harvest, start seeds in midsummer. Plants prefer a firm loam soil. In loose soil, such as sand, heads may not mature properly.

DESCRIPTION A relative of the cabbage, producing heads of tight green bud clusters up to 12 inches across on 2-foot high plants. When main head is picked, smaller heads form on side shoots. Hot weather induces the tight head to burst and go to seed.

HARVEST AND USE Harvest heads while bud clusters are tight and show no hint of yellow petal color. Cut stalk several inches below the head. Broccoli is edible raw, boiled, and steamed. The blanched heads freeze well.

RECOMMENDED VARIETIES 'Green Comet' hybrid is one of the earliest (fifty-five days after transplanting); 'Premium Crop' grows the biggest heads.

BOTANICAL NAME *Brassica oleracea botrytis*

COMMON NAME Cauliflower

CULTURE Start seeds indoors six weeks before outdoor planting; move to garden after frost danger in spring. Plant in fertile, nitrogen-rich loam soil, spaced 2 feet apart, in rows spaced 2 feet apart. For fall harvest, start seed indoors in midsummer and transplant seedlings when nights turn cool. When the heads are the size of a baseball, draw up the largest jacket leaves over the head and secure with a rubber band to exclude sunlight so the curds (heads) do not discolor.

DESCRIPTION A member of the cabbage family and similar in appearance to broccoli, except the heads are white rather than green, made up of tightly packed bud clusters. Cauliflower is not as easy to grow as broccoli, usually requiring leaves to be drawn up over the heads to maintain an attractive white color. Plants are sensitive to heat and moisture stress.

HARVEST AND USE Harvest heads when bud clusters are tight and before the onset of warm weather, which causes an undesirable "ricey" texture. Curds can be eaten raw, boiled for a few minutes until tender, or frozen for long storage. Canning and pickling are also popular methods of storage.

RECOMMENDED VARIETY 'Snow Crown' hybrid for its large, early, well-rounded heads.

BOTANICAL NAME *Brassica oleracea capitata*

COMMON NAME Cabbage

CULTURE Start seed indoors six weeks before outdoor planting, and several weeks before the last frost date. Seedlings tolerate mild frosts and grow best while nights are cool. Space plants 2 feet apart in rows 2 feet apart. Plants prefer a humus-rich loam soil and high nitrogen fertilizer. Protect plants from caterpillars and other chewing insects by covering with floating row covers.

DESCRIPTION There are several kinds of cabbage, including green cabbage, red cabbage, savoy cabbage, and Chinese cabbage. Green cabbage is the most popular, growing solid, round heads up to the size of basketballs; red cabbage is similar. Savoy has heavily crinkled leaves and a buttery yellow center. Chinese cabbage has an elongated head with crinkled leaves and a buttery yellow center. A non-heading variety, Bok Choy, has crispy white stems and dark green, spinach-like leaves.

HARVEST AND USE Harvest heading cabbage when heads are large and firm. Heads will store for a month or more in the vegetable bin of a refrigerator. Cabbage is also stored frozen as coleslaw.

RECOMMENDED VARIETIES 'Stonehead' hybrid is a disease-resistant green cabbage; 'OS Cross' hybrid grows extra-large heads; 'Ruby Ball' is a top quality red cabbage; 'Jade Pagoda' is the earliest heading variety of Chinese cabbage.

BOTANICAL NAME *Brassica oleracea gemmifera*

COMMON NAME Brussels Sprouts

CULTURE Plants require a long growing season (usually 100 days) and are best planted in early summer to mature in the fall when cool weather favors heavy yields. Start seeds six to eight weeks before outdoor planting. Space plants at least 2 feet apart in rows 3 feet apart. Control caterpillars with Bacillus Thuringiensis (an organic bacterial control) and aphids by washing off colonies with jets of water.

DESCRIPTION Related to cabbage, brussels sprouts develop firm, round bud clusters called "sprouts", up to the size of a golf ball, along a tall stem that can reach 3 to 4 feet in height.

HARVEST AND USE Abundant moisture and sharp frosts improve the flavor of brussels sprouts. Pick from the bottom first. To speed bud development, cut off growing tip. The sprouts are best eaten fresh, boiled until tender. They also freeze well.

RECOMMENDED VARIETY 'Jade Cross' hybrid produces high yields on short plants earlier than most other varieties.

BOTANICAL NAME *Brassica oleracea gongylodes*

COMMON NAME Kohlrabi

CULTURE Sow seed directly in the garden, 1/4 inch deep, after last frost date. Though seedlings are hardy and tolerate mild frosts, seed needs 70°F temperature to germinate. For earlier sowing, pregerminate seed indoors in moist paper towels. Thin seedlings to stand 4 inches apart in rows spaced 2 feet apart. Plants prefer moist, fertile loam soil to grow rapidly during cool spring or fall weather.

DESCRIPTION A fast-growing member of the cabbage family, producing a round, turnip-flavored, bulbous stem, edible raw or cooked. Cabbage-like leaves sprout from the top of the bulb.

HARVEST AND USE Thinly sliced kohlrabi bulbs are edible raw. Skin needs peeling first. Diced and boiled in water until tender, kohlrabi is a good substitute for turnips.

RECOMMENDED VARIETIES White and purple-colored varieties are available. 'Grand Duke' is an award-winning hybrid.

BOTANICAL NAME *Brassica rapa rapifera*

COMMON NAME Turnips

CULTURE Sow seed directly into the garden 1/4 inch deep in rows spaced at least 12 inches apart, several weeks before last frost date, since plants tolerate frost and need cool weather to grow well. Thin seedlings to 3 inches apart. Plants prefer fertile loam soil and plenty of moisture for rapid growth.

DESCRIPTION A popular, fast-growing root crop producing edible green tops and rounded white, purple, or bicolored swollen roots.

HARVEST AND USE Harvest tops when large enough to pick, taking leaves from different plants so the roots can continue to grow. Turnips grown as a fall crop can be left in the ground until freezing weather.

RECOMMENDED VARIETY 'Tokyo Cross' a white-rooted hybrid, produces tender golf-ball size turnips within fifty days of sowing seed.

BOTANICAL NAME *Capsicum annum*

COMMON NAME Hot Pepper; Chili Pepper

HEIGHT 1 to 2 feet; compact, bushy habit.

CULTURE Tender annual. Propagated from seed, first started indoors and then transplanted to the garden after all danger of frost has passed. Prefers a fertile loam soil high in calcium, in full sun.

DESCRIPTION Small, white, starlike flowers cover the plants in summer, produce showy, curved, pointed fruits that change color from green to bright red when fully ripe.

USES Valued in cooking for adding a fiery, hot flavor to soups, stews, and many ethnic dishes such as Indian curries and Mexican salsas. Good to grow in containers.

BOTANICAL NAME *Capsicum annuum grossum*

COMMON NAME Bell Pepper

CULTURE Start seed indoors eight weeks before outdoor planting, after all frost danger in spring. Plants prefer fertile, loam, humus-rich soil. Planting through black plastic encourages highest yields. Space plants at least 2 feet apart in rows 2 feet apart.

DESCRIPTION Bushy plants produce starry white flowers followed by sweet, crunchy, hollow, lobed fruits that ripen from green to red, yellow, black, or chocolate-brown, depending on variety.

HARVEST AND USE Harvest fruit when it has reached its mature size. Use sliced in salads, stuffed and steamed, or roasted. Excellent for freezing.

RECOMMENDED VARIETIES 'Big Bertha' grows extra large fruits up to 10 inches long. 'Golden Goliath' is a giant yellow. 'Sweet Chocolate' is a cold-tolerant brown pepper sweet enough to eat fresh like an apple. In addition to sweet peppers there are "hot" kinds, also called chili peppers, though not nearly as popular as sweet bell peppers.

BOTANICAL NAME *Carthamus tinctorius*

COMMON NAME Safflower

HEIGHT 3 feet; erect, branching habit.

CULTURE Tender annual. Propagated from seed. Tolerates a wide range of soils, including impoverished, dry soil, in full sun.

DESCRIPTION Bright orange thistlelike flowers appear in summer. Indented, shiny green leaves are covered in spines.

USES The white seeds are harvested commercially to make safflower oil for cooking. Seeds are frequently incorporated into wild bird foods. The dried petals are used to color food, and can be substituted for saffron powder in a variety of dishes. The petals also yield a natural dye for cloth.

BOTANICAL NAME *Carum carvi*

COMMON NAME Caraway

HEIGHT 3 feet; feathery habit.

CULTURE Hardy biennial. Seed should be sown directly into the garden, since seedlings do not take to transplanting. Seed sown in fall bears flowers and edible seeds the following summer. Spring-sown plants bear the second year. Prefers moist, fertile, loam soil in full sun. Roots need mulching to protect them from freezing.

DESCRIPTION The finely cut leaves resemble carrot tops. White flower umbels appear in midsummer, followed by gray-brown seeds.

USES The seeds are pleasantly aromatic and popular to flavor vegetable soups, meat stews, sauerkraut, coleslaw, and fish casseroles. The oil from caraway seeds is used to flavor many liqueurs.

BOTANICAL NAME *Chamaemelum nobile*

COMMON NAME True Chamomile; Roman Chamomile

HEIGHT 1 inch; low, spreading, carpetlike habit.

CULTURE Hardy perennial that remains evergreen in winter except under severe conditions. Propagated from seed and division. Prefers a well-drained, sandy or loam soil in full sun. Difficult to maintain except in cool coastal areas.

DESCRIPTION There are many "false" chamomiles, including *Anthemis tinctoria* ('Golden Marguerite') and *Matricaria recutata* ('German chamomile'). The true chamomile is a much lower-growing plant, rarely exceeding 1 inch high, covering the ground like moss with tiny, green, slender leaves. Small, yellow, buttonlike flowers occur in summer. The entire plant is aromatic, and walking on it not only releases the apple-scented fragrance, it seems to stimulate the plant to grow thicker.

USES Prized for planting between flagstones, especially close to a bench where people can sit and appreciate the uplifting aroma of its bruised leaves. The flowers can be harvested and dried to make a refreshing tea.

BOTANICAL NAME *Chenopodium bonus-henricus*

COMMON NAME Good-King-Henry Goosefoot

HEIGHT 1½ to 2 feet; clump-forming habit.

CULTURE Hardy perennial. Propagated from seed. Prefers fertile loam soil in full sun.

DESCRIPTION Upper surface of the spear-shaped leaves are dark green with a lighter, slightly downy underside. Insignificant green flowers appear in spring.

USES Young leaves are harvested and cooked like spinach.

BOTANICAL NAME *Chrysanthemum balsamita*

COMMON NAME Costmary; Bible Leaf

HEIGHT 2 to 3 feet; upright, clump-forming habit.

CULTURE Hardy perennial. Propagated by root cuttings. Prefers fertile loam soil in sun or partial shade. Plant dies out in the middle after several years. Top-dressing soil with compost helps keep plants looking attractive.

DESCRIPTION Grown for its minted-scented leaves and flowers. Blossoms resemble pale yellow buttons on leggy stems that are best removed to keep plants looking attractive. The leaves are oblong and pointed with serrated edges.

USES The young leaves are used fresh or dried as a substitute for mint. Small quantities can be sprinkled on salads, also to flavor soups, poultry, and bread. The common name Bible Leaf refers to the custom among early settlers to use the dried, leathery leaves as page markers in the Bible.

BOTANICAL NAME *Chrysanthemum coccineum*

COMMON NAME Pyrethrum; Painted Daisy

HEIGHT 2 to 3 feet; bushy habit.

CULTURE Hardy perennial. Propagated from seed. Easy to grow in most well-drained loam soils in full sun. After flowering in late spring, stems can be cut back to the soil line to encourage a second flush of flowers as cool weather returns in autumn.

DESCRIPTION Beautiful daisylike flowers have yellow centers, with outer petals colored red, pink, and white. Highly ornamental. Leaves are silvery green, feathery.

USES Powdered petals are a source of an effective natural insecticide. Beautiful landscape plant for the perennial border and cutting garden.

BOTANICAL NAME *Cichorium intybus*

COMMON NAME Chicory

HEIGHT 2 to 3 feet; upright, branching habit.

CULTURE Hardy perennial. Propagated from seed. Prefers a deep, fertile loam soil in full sun.

DESCRIPTION Cheerful light blue bossoms are produced on sparse plants that are mostly stems with a few wavy green leaves. Native to Europe, plants have escaped to the wild and have become a common wayside weed.

USES Medicinally, the blue flowers were at one time distilled to make soothing eye drops. The young leaves are edible as a salad green. Also, the root can be ground to make a flavoring for coffee.

RELATED SPECIES *Cichorium endivia*, also known as 'Escarole' or 'Endive,' a high-quality salad green.

BOTANICAL NAME *Citrullus lanatus*

COMMON NAME Watermelon

CULTURE Sow seed directly into the garden in groups of three to five, thinning plants to one healthy vine, spaced 4 feet apart in rows spaced 4 feet apart. Plants must be watered if a week goes by without natural rainfall. Soil should be sandy loam high in humus, especially in the form of well-decomposed animal manure. High phosphorus fertilizer improves fruit yields. Planting through black plastic encourages highest yields and earliness.

DESCRIPTION Vining plants make strong, rapid growth during hot, sunny days, and oval or round green fruit ripen within seventy days of sowing seeds. Interior flesh color can be red or yellow, depending on variety.

HARVEST AND USE Test for ripeness by examining tendril closest to fruit. A shrivelled, brown tendril indicates ripeness. Also, tapping the fruit can determine ripeness. A dull sound means underripe, a hollow sound ripe, and a soft sound overripe.

RECOMMENDED VARIETIES 'Yellow Baby', an icebox size watermelon, has 50 percent fewer seeds than other icebox watermelons and is cold-tolerant. Award-winning 'Sweet Favorite' grows large, oblong fruits even in Northern climates.

BOTANICAL NAME *Coriandrum sativum*

COMMON NAME Coriander; Chinese Parsley; Cilantro

HEIGHT 1½ to 3 feet; upright habit.

CULTURE Hardy annual. Propagated by seed. Easy to grow in any well-drained loam soil in full sun.

DESCRIPTION White, umbrella-like flower clusters appear in summer, produce pungent seeds. Young leaves are oval with toothed edges. The name coriander usually refers to the seeds, which are used sparingly to flavor many ethnic dishes, particularly Chinese, Mexican, and Italian. The names Chinese parsley and cilantro refer to the leaves, which are generally chopped fine as flavoring to soups and stews.

BOTANICAL NAME *Crocus sativus*

COMMON NAME Saffron

HEIGHT 4 to 6 inches; low, clump-forming habit.

CULTURE Hardy perennial bulb. Propagated by corms. Difficult to grow. Prefers a well-drained, fertile loam or sandy soil in full sun. Corms are usually planted in early summer, first producing spiky leaves and then fall-blooming flowers.

DESCRIPTION Blue or purple crocus flowers have conspicuous orange stigmas that hang over the petals. The long, pointed leaves are dark green, grasslike.

USES Cultivated for the orange stigmas that are cut, dried, and crushed into powder; used to flavor many ethnic foods, such as Indian (saffron rice), French (bouillabaisse), Spanish (paella), and Swedish (saffron bread). Since 10,000 flowers are needed to make one pound of saffron it is an extremely expensive herb. Saffron imparts an attractive yellow color to the dish being prepared, and was a source of beautiful yellow dye.

BOTANICAL NAME *Cucumis melo reticulatus*

COMMON NAME Cantaloupe

CULTURE Sow seed directly into the garden after frost danger, in groups, 1 inch deep, and at least 4 feet between each group. Thin seedlings to one strong vine per group. Plants prefer a humus-rich loam or sandy soil and should be watered at least once a week in the absence of natural rainfall. Planting through black plastic, which keeps the soil warm, encourages extra earliness and heaviest yields.

DESCRIPTION Tender vines up to 10 feet long produce both male and female yellow flowers, the females growing large oval or rounded fruits with sugar-sweet orange or green flesh.

HARVEST AND USE Harvest melons when blossom end of fruit feels slightly soft. Best eaten fresh off the vine. Can be frozen by making "melon balls."

RECOMMENDED VARIETIES 'Burpee Hybrid' grows attractive, heavily netted fruit up to 10 pounds each. Choose 'Sweet 'n Early' hybrid for fruit that is ripe extra early.

BOTANICAL NAME *Cucumis sativus*

COMMON NAME Cucumber

CULTURE Sow seed directly into the garden after all danger of frost has passed, in groups spaced at least 3 feet apart, in rows spaced 3 feet apart. Thin seedlings to one plant per group. Since cucumber beetles introduce wilt diseases, discourage them with organic sprays. Also, plant disease-resistant varieties for extra protection. Plants prefer a fertile, sandy loam soil with high humus content. Plants will climb by tendrils if planted against trellis.

DESCRIPTION Spreading vines up to 6 feet long produce yellow male and female flowers; the females grow cylindrical green fruits after pollination. The white interior is full of moisture. Cucumbers are classified as "slicing" or "pickle" types according to size.

HARVEST AND USE Pick fruit before it turns yellow—an indication of overripeness. "Burpless" varieties have tender skins and can be eaten raw without peeling. Mostly used sliced fresh in salads, cucumbers are also popular as pickles.

RECOMMENDED VARIETIES Although some varieties of cucumber are "all-female", setting a high percentage of female flowers, home gardeners are better off planting standard hybrid varieties such as 'Marketmore 80', which have extremely good disease resistance.

BOTANICAL NAME *Cucurbita pepo*

COMMON NAME Pumpkin; Squash

CULTURE Sow seed directly into fertile loam soil, in groups spaced 3 to 4 feet apart in rows 3 to 4 feet apart. Thin seedlings to one strong vine. Planting through black plastic encourages highest yields.

DESCRIPTION Vigorous vines develop quickly during warm, sunny weather, producing fruit of different shapes, sizes, and colors. Pumpkins and winter squash are slow-growing, ripen their fruits in autumn. Boston marrow, butternut, and acorn are examples of winter squash. Hard skins aid long storage. Summer squash are faster-growing, some producing compact bush vines, yielding soft-skinned fruit early, within fifty days of sowing seeds. Zucchini, crooknecks, and patti-pans are examples of summer squash.

HARVEST AND USE Harvest summer squash while skin is soft and tender. Harvest pumpkins and winter squash when skin shows ripe color and hardness. To facilitate storage leave several inches of dry stem attached to the fruit. Interior flesh can be scooped out and boiled like potatoes.

RECOMMENDED VARIETIES 'Cinderella' is an award-winning, short-vine pumpkin. 'Golden Acorn' is a compact bush-type winter squash. 'Richgreen' zucchini squash produces more female flowers than males and is extra heavy yielding since only female flowers will bear fruit.

BOTANICAL NAME *Cymbopogon citratus*

COMMON NAME Lemon grass

HEIGHT 3 to 6 feet; clump-forming, upright habit.

CULTURE Tender perennial grass from the tropics. Propagated by division of the clumps in spring. Can be grown year-round outdoors only where winters are mild and frost-free. Usually grown in containers and taken indoors during winter. Before dividing, cut leaves back to just above the soil line. Prefers a well-drained, fertile loam soil in partial shade. Trim leaves to encourage tender new growth.

DESCRIPTION Rarely flowers. Leaves are long, slender, bright green, and slightly ridged.

USES Commercially cultivated in Florida for its strong, lemon-scented oil. Used in making many kinds of lemon-flavored candy. Leaves steeped in boiling water make a refreshing tea. Popular in Oriental cooking as a flavor enhancer and substitute for lemon.

BOTANICAL NAME *Cynara scolymus*

COMMON NAME Artichoke

CULTURE Thrives where summers are cool. Start seeds indoors about eight weeks before outdoor planting after all danger of frost has passed. Prefers fertile loam soil and regular watering during dry spells. Space plants at least 4 feet apart in rows spaced 4 feet apart.

DESCRIPTION Thistlelike plants produce up to fifty edible flower buds on reasonably hardy plants with silvery green leaves. Plants grow to 5 feet high, spread 5 feet. Top growth dies down in winter after frost. Roots sprout new shoots in spring unless severe winter weather kills them.

HARVEST AND USE The green buds are covered in succulent scales, should be picked with 2 inches of leaf stalk and boiled until tender (about fifteen minutes). The overlapping scales are then peeled away, dipped in melted butter, and the succulent lower portion scraped from the hard part of the scale by pulling it between the teeth. The extra-tender, tightly packed inner leaves form a gourmet delicacy called the artichoke heart.

RECOMMENDED VARIETY 'Green Globe' will reliably produce edible buds from seed the first year.

BOTANICAL NAME *Daucus carota sativa*

COMMON NAME Carrot

CULTURE Sow seed directly into the garden several weeks before the last frost date, covering with 1/4 inch of fine soil. Carrot seed is tiny and needs careful sowing to avoid overcrowded rows. Thin seedlings so carrots stand 1 to 2 inches apart in rows spaced at least 12 inches apart. Several thinnings may be needed to get the carrots properly spaced.

DESCRIPTION An easy-to-grow root crop producing mostly tapered, cone-shaped roots below ground and bright green, fern-like leaves above ground. Carrot shape can vary from long tapered varieties, shaped like icicles, suitable for deep sandy soil to rounded types suitable for shallow loam soils.

HARVEST AND USE "Baby carrots" can be pulled from the soil as soon as the carrot roots show a deep orange color. The roots can be washed and eaten raw or cooked in boiling water until tender. Freezing and canning are good methods of storage.

RECOMMENDED VARIETIES 'Short 'n Sweet' has small cores for extra tenderness. Any of the 'Spartan' hybrids from Michigan State University are outstanding for uniformity and tenderness.

BOTANICAL NAME *Dianthus gratianopolitanus*

COMMON NAME Cheddar Pink

HEIGHT 6 to 10 inches; low, mounded habit.

CULTURE Hardy perennial usually remaining evergreen through winter. Propagated by seed, cuttings, and division. Prefers a well-drained, sandy to loam soil in full sun.

DESCRIPTION Slender, blue-gray grasslike leaves form a dense mat creating an attractive ground cover. The showy, rosy pink flowers occur in spring.

USES The clove-scented flowers are used fresh and dried for potpourri. Popular ornamental for rock gardens and rock walls, also containers.

RELATED SPECIES *D. caryophyllus* ('Carnations') grown in Europe for perfumes.

BOTANICAL NAME *Dipsacus sylvestris*

COMMON NAME Teasel

HEIGHT 2 to 3 feet; upright, branching habit.

CULTURE Hardy biennial. Propagated from seed. Easy to grow in a wide range of soils, including impoverished soil. A common wayside weed throughout North America.

DESCRIPTION Cone-shaped flower heads studded with tiny lilac flowers appear in midsummer. The seed head dries, becomes hard, and is covered with curly spines. Leaves are pointed, thistlelike. Both stems and leaves are prickly.

USES The dried, prickly seed heads are used as a comb. They are also ornamental in dried flower arrangements.

BOTANICAL NAME *Elettaria cardamomum*

COMMON NAME Cardomon

HEIGHT 2 feet; spreading habit.

CULTURE Tender perennial. Propagated by division of rhizomes. Prefers fertile, moist loam soil in partial shade. Survives outdoors in winter only in mild-climate areas with little or no frost. Usually overwintered indoors in pots in Northern states.

DESCRIPTION Member of the ginger family. Broad, pointed, smooth green leaves hug the stem like a sheath. Small cream-colored flowers are borne on long horizontal stems, followed by seed cases that are triangular in shape and contain reddish brown seeds that emit a powerful, aromatic odor.

USES Mainly used as an ingredient in curry powder. Also pleasant to chew. In Russia, Norway, and Sweden cardomon is popular for flavoring cakes.

BOTANICAL NAME *Euphorbia lathyris*

COMMON NAME Mole plant

HEIGHT Up to 3 feet; stout, leafy, upright habit.

CULTURE Tender annual or biennial. Seed should be sown directly into the garden after danger of frost has passed, or from transplants started six weeks before outdoor sowing.

DESCRIPTION Stiff, erect, succulent stems are crowded with narrow, pointed leaves arranged in regimented alignment, one above the other. Inconspicuous flowers are nested in small bracts towards the top of the plant.

USES Its main value is as a repellent against infestations of moles, voles, gophers, and other animal soil pests. Generally planted in clumps around the perimeter of herb gardens and food plots. **Caution:** All parts of this plant should be considered poisonous.

BOTANICAL NAME *Ficus carica*

COMMON NAME Edible Fig

HEIGHT To 30 feet, usually, kept below 6 feet by pruning; shrub or treelike habit.

CULTURE Tender shrub or small tree mostly grown in tubs so it can be taken indoors during winter. Prefers fertile, well-drained loam soil in full sun. Heat and drought tolerant.

DESCRIPTION Large indented green leaves have prominent veins, are highly ornamental. Edible fruits are produced in the leaf joints, ripen in autumn, turning yellow, black, or brown depending on variety.

USES Grown extensively in herb gardens because of its presence in ancient monastery gardens and associations with the Bible. The ripe fruit is delicious eaten fresh, dried, and used in preserves.

RECOMMENDED VARIETIES 'Brown Turkey' (hardiest fig known—survives with protection to zone 5) and 'Mission' for mild winter areas.

BOTANICAL NAME *Foeniculum vulgare azoricum*

COMMON NAME Florence Fennel; Finocchio

HEIGHT 2 to 3 feet; feathery, upright habit.

CULTURE Hardy annual. Propagated from seed sown directly into the garden or started indoors six weeks before outdoor planting. Prefers a light, fertile soil in full sun. Cool weather is needed to form the bulbous lower stem section prized by gourmet cooks.

DESCRIPTION Resembles dill, except for its pale bulbous base and more compact growth habit. Slender, branching stems have fine, feathery leaves and yellow flower umbels. Its stems, leaves, and flowers are slightly more sweetly flavored than common fennel (*F. vulgare*).

USES Valuable flavor enhancer, especially in Italian cooking, imparting an aniselike flavor. With common fennel the seeds, leaves, stems, and flowers can be used to flavor soups, stews, and fish dishes. With Florence fennel, the crunchy bulbous base is used mostly to flavor salads, sliced like pieces of celery and used sparingly with salad greens.

BOTANICAL NAME *Fragraria fragraria* and hybrids

COMMON NAME Strawberry

CULTURE The easiest to grow of all berry fruits. Purchase dormant roots by mail order or from local nurseries, setting into fertile loam soil in spring or fall. Prefers full sun and a mulch of hay, shredded leaves, or black plastic to control weeds. Space plants 12 inches apart in rows spaced 3 feet apart. From a spring planting, flowers should be removed the first season to encourage a bushier plant and extra heavy yields the next season.

DESCRIPTION Low, mounded plants produce masses of small, starlike flowers in spring, followed by luscious, cone-shaped red berries that grow up to the size of golf balls. There are June-bearers that fruit only in June and grow the largest berries; Everbearers that fruit in June and again in fall; and Day-Neutrals (or All-Season) that bear continuously from June until fall frost.

HARVEST AND USE Pick berries when color is deep red. Eat fresh off the vine or freeze. Plants may need covering with netting to prevent rodents and birds from eating the harvest.

RECOMMENDED VARIETIES 'Earliglow' produces extra large berries (June-bearer); 'Tri-star' is a heavy yielding day-neutral with disease resistance; 'Sweetheart' is a day-neutral ground cover strawberry that produces a dense knit of runners and tasty fruit midway in size between an alpine strawberry and regular June-bearer.

BOTANICAL NAME *Galium odoratum* (also known as *Asperula odorata*)

COMMON NAME Sweet Woodruff

HEIGHT Up to 6 inches; low, ground-hugging habit.

CULTURE Hardy perennial. Propagated mostly by dividing clumps in spring or fall. Prefers a moist, humus-rich, loose soil in partial shade.

DESCRIPTION Small clusters of tiny, starry white flowers appear in spring among whorls of pointed leaves. The plant spreads rapidly and maintains a uniform height, making it a decorative ground cover.

USES An essential flavor enhancer for "May" wine. Once used for scattering on floors to sweeten musty rooms. Ornamentally, a valuable ground cover for shady areas. In autumn, when the leaves wilt and dry they pervade the air with a sweet hay-scented aroma.

BOTANICAL NAME *Heliotropium arborescens*

COMMON NAME Sweet Heliotrope; Common Heliotrope

HEIGHT 12 to 18 inches; erect habit.

CULTURE Tender annual. Seed should be started indoors and transplanted to the garden after danger of frost has passed. Prefers a fertile, moist, well-drained loam soil in full sun.

DESCRIPTION Clusters of fragrant violet-blue flowers are borne on brittle stems. Leaves are glossy, dark green, heavily veined, pointed. Flowers last all summer.

USES The vanilla scented flowers are used in the perfume industry. Plants are highly ornamental and popular for cutting.

BOTANICAL NAME *Hyssopus officinalis*

COMMON NAME Hyssop

HEIGHT 2 feet; shrubby, clump-forming habit.

CULTURE Hardy perennial. Propagated by seed sown directly into the garden or from cuttings. Prefers fertile, well-drained loam soil in full sun or light shade. If dry stems persist through winter, cut back to soil level in early spring.

DESCRIPTION Lavender-like flower spikes in blue, pink, or white bloom throughout summer. Aromatic leaves are narrow with a slightly musky aroma.

USES Oil from the leaves is used mostly in scented soaps and in potpourri. It is an important ingredient in Chartreuse liqueur. The strong aroma is considered a repellent against the cabbage butterfly. A tea from the leaves is said to ease discomfort from colds and indigestion. A popular component of herb gardens because of its ornamental flowers.

BOTANICAL NAME *Ipomoea batatus*

COMMON NAME Sweet Potato

CULTURE Mostly grown from transplants started from seed or separated from a "seedling" tuber that produces shoots with roots at every growing point. Set transplants out into garden after frost danger in spring. At least 100 frost-free days are needed to form edible tubers which mature in the soil. Plant 2 feet apart in rows 3 feet apart.

DESCRIPTION Related to morning glories, sweet potatoes grow vigorous, ground-hugging vines with heart-shaped leaves and large tubers usually red, orange, or yellow in color.

HARVEST AND USE Dig up tubers in fall after vines have died down. Brush away soil and store in a cool, frost-free location. Mostly boiled or baked.

RECOMMENDED VARIETIES 'Centennial' grows extra-large orange-red tubers. 'Porto Rico' grows more compact vines suitable for raising in containers.

BOTANICAL NAME *Iris germanica* 'Florentina'

COMMON NAME Orris Root

HEIGHT 2 feet; clump-forming habit.

CULTURE Hardy perennial spreading by means of rhizomes. Propagated mostly by division of the rhizomes in autumn. Prefers a moist, well-drained soil in sun or partial shade.

DESCRIPTION Decorative flowers resemble those of *Iris germanica* ('Bearded iris'), usually white with a pale blue tint, possessing a spicy, pleasant fragrance. Slender, sword-shaped leaves emerge from the rhizomes in early spring, followed by flowers that may last two weeks.

USES When chopped into small pieces, or powdered and dried, the odorless rhizome becomes highly aromatic, with a sweet vanilla-like or violet-like fragrance. Mostly used as a fixative to preserve the fragrances of other herbs in potpourri and dried arrangements.

BOTANICAL NAME *Latuca sativa*

COMMON NAME Lettuce

CULTURE Sow seed directly into the garden several weeks before last frost date, since seedlings tolerate mild frosts. Thin seedlings to 6 inches apart for loose-leaf types, 12 inches apart for heading varieties. Sowings made in late summer will mature in fall.

DESCRIPTION Fast-growing leaf crop that prefers cool weather. Loose-leaf types mature within forty days of sowing seed; heading types need at least ten days longer. Leaf color can be green or red.

HARVEST AND USE Harvest outer leaves of loose-leaf kinds and plants will grow more inner leaves to prolong harvest. Heading types can be harvested when the tight cluster of inner leaves feels firm.

RECOMMENDED VARIETIES 'Buttercrunch' is an award-winning head lettuce; 'Green Ice' is a popular loose-leaf type. 'Red Sails' is a decorative, award-winning loose-leaf with red-tinted, frilly leaves.

BOTANICAL NAME *Laurus nobilis*

COMMON NAME Sweet Bay; Laurel

HEIGHT Normally kept under 6 feet high by pruning, but in the wild it grows up to 40 feet high; forms an attractive bushy habit or tree.

CULTURE Tender evergreen shrub that must be overwintered under glass except in frost-free areas. Propagated by seed and by cuttings, though ready-grown plants are available from houseplant outlets. Best grown in a container with at least a one gallon capacity, using a fertile soil composed of equal parts of garden loam and potting soil.

DESCRIPTION Its tiny yellow flowers are borne in dainty clusters, though it rarely flowers in cold climates. The leaves are leathery in texture, shiny above, oval, and pointed, usually 3 to 4 inches long. Stems are upright, woody, and pliable. Often confused with California-laurel (*Umbellularia californica*) which has a stronger, harsher flavor and is not as desirable for culinary use.

USES Mostly used to flavor soups, stews, and sauces, one leaf to each gallon of liquid, simmered slowly to release its distinctive flavor. Traditionally used for "victory wreaths" to crown the heads of athletes and other people deserving high honors. The dried leaves have insect repellent properties and are popular for adding to potpourri.

BOTANICAL NAME *Lavandula angustifolia* (also known as *L. vera* and *L. officinalis*)

COMMON NAME English Lavender; True Lavender

HEIGHT 2 to 3 feet; bushy habit.

CULTURE Hardy perennial. Propagated from seed and cuttings. Easy to grow in any well-drained loam or sandy soil in full sun. Space plants 3 feet apart.

DESCRIPTION Lavender, pink, blue, or white flower clusters are borne on slender stems. Gray-green leaves are narrow, pointed. All plant parts are highly fragrant. Highly ornamental.

USES Mostly used air-dried to add distinctive fragrance to potpourri. Stems may also be steeped in boiling water to make a delicious tea. Lavender oil distilled from the flowering stems is used as a scent in soaps and perfumes.

RECOMMENDED VARIETIES 'Hidcote' (deep blue) and 'Jean Davis' (pink).

RELATED SPECIES *L. stoechas* ('French Lavender').

BOTANICAL NAME *Levisticum officinale*

COMMON NAME Lovage

HEIGHT Up to 6 feet; upright, clump-forming habit.

CULTURE Hardy perennial. Best grown by seeds sown directly into the garden in autumn, or started indoors six weeks before outdoor planting in spring. Prefers a deep, fertile, moist loam soil in full sun.

DESCRIPTION Small flower umbels, resembling dill flowers, are produced on celery-like plants in spring; become much taller and more invasive than garden celery. Produces brown seeds, thick roots.

USES All parts of the plant, including leaves, stems, roots, and seeds have culinary value, mostly as a flavor enhancer for salads, soups, stews, meat, and poultry. The roots can be steeped in boiling water to make a refreshing tea. Its reputation as a love potion is questionable. The flavor resembles celery.

BOTANICAL NAME *Lycopersicum esculentum*

COMMON NAME Tomato

CULTURE Start seed indoors eight weeks before outdoor planting; plant after frost-danger in spring. Space plants 2 feet apart in rows 3 feet apart. Planting through black plastic encourages highest yields and earliness. Irregular watering and lack of calcium in the soil can cause blossom-end rot, controlled by irrigating if a week goes by without natural rainfall, and adding lime to acid soil. High phosphorus fertilizer encourages early, heavy yields.

DESCRIPTION There are two classifications of tomatoes—short-lived bush types (called determinate), which ripen their fruits at one time, and vining kinds (called indeterminate), which need staking to keep them growing, and which ripen their fruit over an extended period of time. Fruit color is mostly red, but yellow, orange, pink, white, and striped varieties are available ranging in size from a cherry to two-pound giants as big as grapefruits.

HARVEST AND USE Harvest before frost when fruits turn from green to red (or other ripe coloring). Green fruits harvested before frost may ripen indoors at room temperature. Canning is the most popular form of storage.

RECOMMENDED VARIETIES 'Supersteak VFN' grows extra-large fruits; 'Early Pick' hybrid has medium-large fruits and ripens early; 'Supersonic' is a high-yielding, tasty, medium-size hybrid.

BOTANICAL NAME *Malus*, *Pyrus*, and *Prunus* hybrids

COMMON NAME Dwarf Fruit Trees (Apples, Pears, Peaches)

CULTURE These plants need a chilly winter in order to prepare themselves for fruit-bearing. They all prefer fertile, loam, weed-free soil in full sun. Some varieties can be grown easily in tubs.

DESCRIPTION Plant breeders have worked miracles with fruit trees such as apples, pears, peaches, and cherries. By skillful selection of trees that are genetically compact in growth habit, and by grafting standard-size onto special rootstocks that cause "dwarfing," home gardeners can find dwarf varieties to fit the smallest amount of garden space, even training these mighty midgets flat against a sunny wall.

HARVEST AND USE Dwarf fruit trees are not only space-saving, they are easier to care for than standard-size trees, requiring less pruning, no staking, and no ladder to reach the fruit; also, the fruit bears sooner—sometimes the next season after planting.

RECOMMENDED VARIETIES Dwarf 'Granny Smith' apple; Dwarf 'Bartlett' pear; 'Stella' sweet cherry; 'Bonanza' nectarine; 'Sensation' peach.

BOTANICAL NAME *Marrubium vulgare*

COMMON NAME White Horehound; Candy Horehound

HEIGHT 2 feet; erect, clump-forming habit.

CULTURE Hardy perennial. Propagated mostly by seed. Tolerates poor, impoverished soils in full sun. Shear old plants in spring for a compact, bushy appearance. Divide overgrown clumps every three years.

DESCRIPTION Small white flowers bloom along the stems in summer. Gets its common name from the wrinkled, hoary appearance of the gray-green leaves, which have crinkled edges and curl down.

USES Mostly used to flavor candy. Leaves can be steeped in boiling water to make a refreshing tea said to relieve colds and sore throats. Popular in herb gardens because of its added ornamental value, especially as an edging or container planting.

RELATED SPECIES *Ballato nigra* ('Black Horehound') is much stronger in flavor and too harsh for most tastes, except as a strong tea.

BOTANICAL NAME *Melissa officinalis*

COMMON NAME Lemon-balm

HEIGHT 2 to 3 feet; mounded habit.

CULTURE Hardy perennial. Propagated by seed, cuttings, or root division. Prefers fertile, moist loam soil in full sun.

DESCRIPTION Related to mint, and very mintlike in general appearance. Leaves are bright green, heart-shaped, serrated, and heavily-veined. Small white flowers are borne along the stems in summer. Young plants form attractive compact mounds, but left unchecked it can become invasive.

USES The lemon-scented leaves make a delicious, refreshing tea steeped in boiling water. The leaves rubbed on hands act as a deodorizer, covering unpleasant smells such as fish and garlic. Dried leaves retain their aroma and are popular for adding to potpourri.

BOTANICAL NAME *Mentha piperita*

COMMON NAME Peppermint

HEIGHT Up to 3 feet; upright, clump-forming habit.

CULTURE Hardy perennial. Propagated mostly by cuttings and division of overgrown clumps. Prefers moist loam soil in full sun or light shade. Spreads quickly by underground rhizomes.

DESCRIPTION Erect, square stems with oval, pointed, serrated leaves. Pale lavender flower spikes appear in summer.

USES Commercially grown for its oil which is used to flavor candy, perfume, and potpourri. Rubbing the leaves between the palms covers objectionable odors, and inhaling the aroma clears the sinuses. Leaves steeped in boiling water make a refreshing tea.

BOTANICAL NAME *Mentha pulegium*

COMMON NAME Pennyroyal

HEIGHT 12 inches; spreading habit.

CULTURE Hardy perennial. Propagated by seed and by division of overgrown clumps. Tolerates a wide range of well-drained soils in full sun.

DESCRIPTION A member of the mint family. Leaves are small, oval, pointed, spaced evenly along slender stems with a dainty crown of pink flowers clustered at each leaf node.

USES Strong mint flavor reminiscent of peppermint. Its culinary use has diminished in recent years following reports that it can be toxic if used in excess. The leaves steeped in boiling water make a refreshing tea. Also adds a pleasant mint flavor to iced tea. Good to use as a natural insect repellent, dried and stuffed into sachets, or sprinkled over pet bedding.

BOTANICAL NAME *Mentha spicata*

COMMON NAME Spearmint

HEIGHT 3 feet; erect, bushy habit.

CULTURE Hardy perennial. Propagated by seed and root division. Any 3- to 4-inch section of root will produce a new plant. Prefers a moist loam soil in full sun or partial shade.

DESCRIPTION Pink flower clusters are borne at the top of erect stems in long, tapering spikes, usually in early summer. Narrow, pointed, bright green serrated leaves have conspicuous veins and are highly fragrant when bruised.

USES Spearmint is similar to peppermint in appearance and its list of uses, though it is milder. The oil is used as a flavoring by the cosmetics industry for everything from shampoo to toothpaste. Its culinary uses include flavoring iced tea, vinegar, fruit punch, and jelly. Mint cordials are common, as is mint tea.

RECOMMENDED VARIETY *Mentha spicata* 'Crispa' ('Curly-leaf Mint') has curly, quilted leaves that have ornamental value.

BOTANICAL NAME *Mentha suaveolens* (also known as *M. rotundifolia*)

COMMON NAME Apple Mint

HEIGHT 3 feet; upright, spreading habit.

CULTURE Hardy perennial. Propagated from seed, cuttings, and root division. Prefers moist loam soil in full sun. Tolerates dry conditions better than most other mints. Spreads by vigorous underground rhizomes, and generally needs thinning every year once a clump is established.

DESCRIPTION Typical mintlike appearance with heart-shaped, serrated leaves and square stems, though leaves are more rounded and have a woolly appearance with a distinct applelike aroma.

USES Mostly used in potpourri for its apple fragrance. Leaves can be candied and also used fresh or dried in cooking.

BOTANICAL NAME *Monarda citriodora*

COMMON NAME Lemon Mint; Lemon Bee-balm

HEIGHT 3 to 5 feet; bushy, clump-forming habit.

CULTURE Hardy perennial. Propagated mostly by division or cuttings taken in spring. Prefers moist, fertile soil in partial shade. Usually needs dividing every year after the third year.

DESCRIPTION Pale pink tubular flowers are arranged in a crown at the top of stiff, square stems. Leaves are oval and pointed and release a lemony aroma when bruised.

USES The fresh or dried leaves can be used as a flavoring in salads or steeped in boiling water to make a refreshing tea. Good also for potpourri. The flower display, which occurs in summer, is highly ornamental, attracting butterflies, hummingbirds, and bees.

BOTANICAL NAME *Monarda didyma*

COMMON NAME Scarlet Bee-balm; Bergamot; Oswego Tea

HEIGHT 3 to 5 feet; bushy; clump-forming habit.

CULTURE Hardy perennial. Propagated by seed, cuttings, and root division in spring or fall. Prefers fertile, moist, loam soil in full sun. Established clumps generally need dividing each year.

DESCRIPTION Red, tubular flowers are arranged in a crown on top of the plant in profusion; blooms July and August. Dark green, oval, pointed leaves have a citruslike aroma.

USES Mostly used for its leaves, which make a refreshing tea when steeped in boiling water. A prime ingredient in the making of Earl Grey tea. Highly ornamental for display. Attractive to butterflies, hummingbirds, and bees.

BOTANICAL NAME *Myrrhis odorata*

COMMON NAME Sweet Cicely; Myrrh

HEIGHT 5 feet; erect, branching habit.

CULTURE Hardy perennial. Propagated by seed or root division. Prefers a moist, humus-rich soil in partial shade. Plants self-seed easily.

DESCRIPTION The tall, sprawling plants somewhat resemble dill, but with white flower umbels. Related to parsley, the entire plant is aromatic, with a licorice-like flavor. In autumn the seed heads turn almost black, indicating ripeness. These are especially valued for culinary uses.

USES Pick young leaves for adding flavor to summer salads, and for steeping in boiling water to make a refreshing tea. The seeds can be used in baking to flavor pastries, and the fleshy root can be shredded to eat raw in salads or added to stir-fried vegetables.

BOTANICAL NAME *Nepeta cataria*

COMMON NAME Catnip; Catmint

HEIGHT 3 feet; upright, branching habit.

CULTURE Hardy perennial. Propagated mostly by seed. Easy to grow even in poor soils, in full sun.

DESCRIPTION Masses of white flower spikes cover the gray-green plants in midsummer. Leaves are soft to touch, up to 2 inches long, pointed with toothed edges.

USES Cats enjoy sniffing and rubbing in catnip, which acts as a temporary euphoric on their senses. The leaves are sometimes dried and steeped in boiling water to make a soothing tea for humans.

BOTANICAL NAME *Nepeta mussinii*

COMMON NAME Catmint

HEIGHT 12 to 15 inches; low, spreading habit.

CULTURE Hardy perennial. Propagated by seed. Easy to grow in most well-drained loam soils in sun or partial shade.

DESCRIPTION Flowers consist of blue blossoms in tight clusters, appearing mostly in spring or early summer. Grayish leaves are rounded and soft to the touch.

USES Its gray foliage and ornamental blue flowers combine well, making catmint a good edging plant. The scent deters garden pests, but is attractive to bees. Commercially grown for its oil as an insect repellent. Unlike catnip, cats are indifferent to catmint.

RELATED SPECIES *Nepeta* x *faassenii* ('Ornamental catnip'): its deeper blue flowers produce an even better ornamental effect.

BOTANICAL NAME *Ocimum basilicum*

COMMON NAME Sweet Basil

HEIGHT 1 to 3 feet, depending on variety; bushy habit.

CULTURE Tender annual. Propagated by seed, best started indoors and transplanted into the garden after all danger of frost has passed. Easy to grow in any reasonably fertile, well-drained garden soil in full sun.

DESCRIPTION Common sweet basil has glossy, dark green, spear-shaped leaves with prominent leaf veins. Some varieties have curling, ruffled leaves, others tiny, rounded leaves forming a perfect mound. White flowers are borne in clusters on short spikes.

USES Fresh and dried leaves are used in a multitude of culinary dishes. It is the primary ingredient of pesto sauce and makes an excellent vinegar flavoring; it also goes well as a garnish with tomatoes.

RELATED SPECIES *Ocimum basilicum* 'Purpurascens,' (Dark Opal basil), a purple-leaf type popular as an ornamental in annual flower borders.

BOTANICAL NAME *Olea europaea*

COMMON NAME European Olive; Common Olive

HEIGHT 20 feet; bushy, multi-stemmed small tree.

CULTURE Tender evergreen tree that must be grown indoors in tubs over the winter in areas with freezing temperatures. Propagated mostly by cuttings. Tolerates poor soil in full sun.

DESCRIPTION Many varieties of European olive have been developed, including dwarf forms that can be trimmed into mounds and hedges. However, the common form is mostly grown in herb gardens to add height, particularly from its upright, twisting branches. The slender, willowlike leaves are an attractive gray-green. Tiny white flowers are followed by oval fruits that turn black when ripe.

USES Since the olive has strong associations with the Bible, it is popular in herb garden designs with an ecclesiastical emphasis. The oil from the pressed fruit produces olive oil enjoyed on salads. The fruit also makes tasty preserves for garnishing Greek and Italian dishes.

BOTANICAL NAME *Origanum majorana*

COMMON NAME Sweet Marjoram

HEIGHT 12 inches or more; tall, upright, bushy habit.

CULTURE Tender perennial usually grown as an annual. Propagated by seed, cuttings, and division. Prefers moist, reasonably fertile soil in full sun.

DESCRIPTION Small, oval green leaves are pungent and sweet, and are frost-hardy, but roots are sensitive to freezing. Clusters of small white flowers grow at the top of soft stems that turn woody with age.

USES Fresh or dried leaves are good to flavor omelettes and other egg dishes, also dishes involving mixed vegetables such as soups and stews.

BOTANICAL NAME *Origanum vulgare*

COMMON NAME Oregano; Wild Marjoram

HEIGHT 12 to 18 inches; bushy, erect habit.

CULTURE Hardy perennial. Propagated by seed, cuttings, and root divisions. Easy to grow in most well-drained loam soils in full sun.

DESCRIPTION Native American wayside plant. Similar in appearance to marjoram, except the small pink flower clusters are less conspicuous.

USES Fresh or dried leaves are used in a variety of dishes, especially pizza, cheese casseroles, and pastas, also tomato and spaghetti sauces.

BOTANICAL NAME *Panax quinquefolius*

COMMON NAME Ginseng

HEIGHT 12 to 18 inches; low, ground-cover effect.

CULTURE Hardy perennial. Propagated mostly by seed, though it is one of the slowest growing herbs in cultivation, requiring four years to flower and seed. Demands a moist, humus–rich soil in partial shade. A challenge to grow. Native to the Appalachian forest regions.

DESCRIPTION Five-pointed leaves surround a basal stem. Small greenish flowers appear on mature plants, followed by bright red berries. The plant develops a curious, fleshy tap-root often resembling a human form.

USES The powdered or shredded roots are dried to make a refreshing tea. The Chinese attribute mythical powers to ginseng as a medicinal cure-all for sexual potency; it is also a stimulant.

BOTANICAL NAME *Pastinaca sativa*

COMMON NAME Parsnip

CULTURE Sow seed directly into the garden, 1/2 inch deep in a loose loam or sandy soil several weeks before last frost date, since seedlings tolerate frost. Sowings timed to mature during cool, moist fall weather yield best crops since flavor of roots is improved by frost.

DESCRIPTION A root crop similar in appearance to a carrot, but with white roots and a sweet, nutty flavor. Takes twice the growing time of carrots.

HARVEST AND USE Use a garden fork to loosen soil and unearth the long roots. Parsnips can be left in the ground until the ground freezes. Roots are boiled and used like potatoes as a side dish.

RECOMMENDED VARIETY 'Hollow Crown' has large roots and small cores.

BOTANICAL NAME *Pelargonium graveolens*

COMMON NAME Rose-scented Geranium; Deodorizer Plant

HEIGHT 12 inches or more; low, bushy habit.

CULTURE Tender perennial killed when ground freezes. Propagated mostly by stem cuttings. Grows in a wide range of garden soils in full sun or partial shade, as long as drainage is adequate. Mostly grown in containers so plants can be moved indoors over the winter. Can be kept compact and bushy by pruning.

DESCRIPTION Dark green, ruffled leaves are downy, soft to the touch, and release a spicy, rose-scented aroma. Flowers are borne in small clusters, in shades of pink.

USES The leaves are good, either fresh or dried, to flavor jellies, cakes, fruit punch, tea, and vinegars. Oil extracted from the leaves is distilled to make perfume. Popular for adding to potpourri. Leaves rubbed on hands mask unpleasant smells.

RELATED SPECIES There are hundreds of varieties of scented-leaf geraniums, including: *P. tomentosum* ('Wooly Pelargonium'), a peppermint-scented geranium; *P. odoratissimum* ('Apple Pelargonium'), an apple-scented geranium; *P. crispum* ('Finger Bowl Pelargonium'), a lemon-scented geranium; *P. fragrans* ('Fragrant Geranium'), a nutmeg-scented geranium; and *P. grossularoides*, a coconut-scented geranium.

BOTANICAL NAME *Perilla frutescens*

COMMON NAME Perilla; Beefsteak Plant

HEIGHT 3 to 4 feet; bushy habit.

CULTURE Tender annual. Seed can be sown directly in the garden or started indoors and transplanted after all danger of frost has passed. Tolerates poor soil, needs full sun or partial shade. Pinch growing tips to keep plants compact. Self-seeds easily. Tolerates high heat.

DESCRIPTION Shining, heavily-veined purple leaves resemble coleus. There is also a green-leafed variety that resembles nettle. Inconspicuous pale pink flowers may appear late in the season.

USES Young leaves are edible in salads, soup, and as a spinach substitute.

BOTANICAL NAME *Petroselinum crispum*

COMMON NAME Parsley

HEIGHT 12 inches; mound-like habit.

CULTURE Hardy biennial that sometimes remains evergreen even during freezing weather. Propagated by seed. Prefers a cool, humus-rich moist soil in sun or partial shade.

DESCRIPTION Dark green leaves are finely divided and curly, sometimes resembling a tight cushion of moss. Tiny clusters of greenish yellow flowers are produced on tall stems in the spring of the second year, setting seed and then dying.

USES An extremely popular garnish for all manner of culinary dishes, especially fish and potatoes. Sometimes used as an ornamental for edging flower beds.

RELATED SPECIES *Petroselinum crispum* 'Neopolitanum,' also known as 'Italian Parsley.'

BOTANICAL NAME *Phaseolus limensis*

COMMON NAME Lima Bean

CULTURE Plant seeds directly into the garden 1 to 2 inches deep, after all frost danger is past. Thin seeds so plants are spaced at least 6 inches apart, in rows spaced at least 2 feet apart. Plants prefer a humus-rich, fertile loam soil with high phosphorus content. Keep plants free of bean beetles by spraying with a rotenone-pyrethrum organic insecticide.

DESCRIPTION There are two kinds of lima beans: pole limas capable of growing to 30 feet high, and bush limas that stay under 2 feet. Pods are large, green, and leathery; they grow up to 5 inches long and more than 1 inch wide, with large pale green beans that turn white when dried.

HARVEST AND USE Harvest pods when they feel plump with seeds. The pods are tough and inedible, but the seeds can be eaten fresh, boiled in water for a few minutes until tender, or dried. Blanched limas freeze well.

RECOMMENDED VARIETIES 'Fordhook 242' is a disease-resistant bush variety; 'Prizetaker', a vigorous pole variety, yields up to five enormous beans per pod.

BOTANICAL NAME *Phaseolus vulgaris*

COMMON NAME Snap Beans

CULTURE Sow seed directly into the garden after frost danger in spring. Plant seeds 1 inch deep in fertile loam soil. Allow 12 inches between plants in rows spaced 2 feet apart. Bean beetles can be a serious pest; spray plants with a rotenone-pyrethrum organic insecticide once a week and after rainfall to control them.

DESCRIPTION Plants are classified as pole beans (10 feet tall) and bush beans (12 to 24 inches). Edible pods can be green, yellow, or purple. Pole varieties need strong supports.

HARVEST AND USE As pods mature, keep plants picked since this stimulates maximum yields. A few minutes boiling in water makes the pods tender. Dried pods can also be shelled to produce shell beans for storage. The green pods are good for freezing and canning.

RECOMMENDED VARIETIES 'Goldcrop' a yellow-podded bush bean and 'Bush Blue Lake,' a green-podded variety, are extra-heavy yielding and delicious.

BOTANICAL NAME *Pimpinella anisum*

COMMON NAME Anise

HEIGHT 2 feet; upright, slender habit.

CULTURE Hardy annual propagated from seed. Prefers a moist loam soil in full sun. Tolerates crowding.

DESCRIPTION Feathery green leaves resemble those of wild carrot. Umbels of white flower clusters resemble dill or Queen Anne's Lace, appear in summer. Entire plant has a licorice aroma.

USES The seeds can be collected and chewed to sweeten the breath and as a digestive aid. The seeds also yield a flavorful oil used in beverages, to add a licorice-like taste to candies and cookies, also to make a refreshing tea.

BOTANICAL NAME *Pisum sativum*

COMMON NAME Pea

CULTURE Sow seeds directly into the garden 1 inch deep, 2 inches apart, in rows 3 feet apart, as soon as soil can be worked in spring. Seeds germinate at low temperatures and seedlings will tolerate frost. Soaking seeds for an hour in water prior to planting aids germination. Plants will only yield satisfactorily while nights are cool. Sowings made to mature in fall generally succumb to mildew disease unless a disease-resistant variety is used.

DESCRIPTION Hollow-stemmed vines with pairs of oval leaves have tendrils that allow the fast-growing plants to climb up supports. White flowers are self-pollinating and form green pods with up to ten succulent, sweet green peas to each pod.

HARVEST AND USE Harvest pods when plump with peas. Freeze or can for storage. Sugar peas, a special edible pod variety popular in Chinese cooking, should be harvested before peas swell the pod. Snap peas, another special edible pod variety, can be harvested when peas are plump.

RECOMMENDED VARIETIES 'Green Arrow' grows extra long pods with up to ten peas per pod. 'Sugar Snap' produces fat, edible pods, extra sweet, extra crunchy, and delicious.

BOTANICAL NAME *Poterium sanguisorba*

COMMON NAME Salad Burnet

HEIGHT 12 inches; low, mounded habit.

CULTURE Hardy perennial. Propagated by seed and division. Tolerates dry, sandy soil in full sun. Tolerates crowding. Self-seeds easily.

DESCRIPTION Long cascading stems splay out from the center of the plant, presenting the toothed, green leaves in matched pairs along each stem. Greenish flowers, small and inconspicuous, are produced in late summer.

USES The cucumber-flavored leaves are used in salads and vinegars.

BOTANICAL NAME *Punica granatum*

COMMON NAME Pomegranate

HEIGHT Up to 15 feet, usually kept below 6 feet by pruning; shrub or tree-like habit.

CULTURE Tender shrub or small tree. Propagated by cuttings. Tolerates a wide range of garden soils providing drainage is good, in full sun. Hardy to zone 7 outdoors, but mostly grown in tubs so it can be moved indoors for the winter.

DESCRIPTION Dark green, narrow, oblong leaves produced on woody stems. Lovely orange-red funnel-form flowers occur in summer, followed by shiny red fruit the size of tennis balls. A pulpy, succulent, fleshy area under the skin, surrounding the seeds, is edible.

USES Like figs, pear trees, and quince trees, the pomegranate was grown in ancient monastery gardens, and has become a traditional container plant for modern herb gardens. Considered a delicacy as a dessert fruit. Modern herbalists prize its long-lasting red fruits for decorating herbal wreaths.

BOTANICAL NAME *Raphanus sativus*

COMMON NAME Radish

CULTURE Sow seed directly into the garden several weeks before last frost date in spring, since seedlings tolerate mild frost. Cover seed with 1/4 inch of soil and thin seedlings to 1 inch apart in rows 1 foot apart.

DESCRIPTION A fast-growing root crop that produces round, oblong, or icicle-shaped roots within twenty days during cool, moist weather.

HARVEST AND USE Pull roots from soil when they reach bite-size. Best eaten fresh as a snack and sliced into salads.

RECOMMENDED VARIETIES 'Cherry Belle', a round, red radish, is the earliest; Japanese 'Dikon' white radish is more pungent; and Spanish "black" radish grows large and needs a longer growing season.

BOTANICAL NAME *Rheum rhabarberum*

COMMON NAME Rhubarb

HEIGHT 2 to 3 feet or more; clump-forming habit.

CULTURE Hardy perennial. Propagated by seed and by root cuttings. Prefers moist, humus-rich, fertile soil in full sun. Thick clumps should be divided every four years.

DESCRIPTION Large, glossy, floppy leaves are borne on thick succulent stems colored green or red according to variety. Though the green part of the leaf is poisonous, the stem portion is edible if it is cooked. Flower spikes are large, bearing masses of creamy white blossoms.

USES The stems are generally cubed, boiled, and made into pie filling with sugar added to reduce the tartness.

BOTANICAL NAME *Rosmarinus officinalis*

COMMON NAME Rosemary

HEIGHT Up to 6 feet tall; shrubby habit.

CULTURE Tender perennial that remains evergreen in areas with mild winters. Develops woody stems with age and needs pruning to keep it compact. Prefers well-drained light soil in full sun. Popular container plant so it can be taken indoors over the winter.

DESCRIPTION Many ornamental varieties have been developed, including some with a weeping habit and others with a low, spreading habit. In the common variety, stems are stiff, upright, covered in needlelike leaves emitting a resinous, pinelike scent when rubbed. White or blue blossoms are small.

USES Popular herb garnish to flavor pork or ham. Steep leaves in boiling water to make a refreshing tea. Rosemary oil distilled from the leaves is used in perfume and shampoo. Many other uses are claimed medicinally. Good ingredient in potpourri.

BOTANICAL NAME *Rumex scutatus*

COMMON NAME French Sorrel

HEIGHT 2 feet; upright, clump-forming habit.

CULTURE Hardy perennial. Propagated by seed or root division. Tolerates poor soil, but flavor is enhanced by moist, fertile soil in full sun. To promote leafy growth, remove any flowers that form. Divide plants every three years.

DESCRIPTION Light green, spear-shaped leaves are wavy, growing upright from a basal clump. Flowers are greenish white, borne in loose spikes. The leaves are high in vitamins and impart a tangy, lemony flavor.

USES The leaves are chopped small to flavor soups and salads.

BOTANICAL NAME *Ruta graveolens*

COMMON NAME Rue

HEIGHT 2 to 3 feet; erect, bushy habit.

CULTURE Hardy perennial that sometimes remains evergreen throughout winter. Propagated by seed, by root cuttings, and by division. Prefers an acidic soil in full sun or partial shade. Tolerates poor soil.

DESCRIPTION Beautiful, indented blue-green leaves form attractive moundlike plants in spring, becoming more bushy and open as the season advances. Bright yellow flower clusters appear in midsummer.

USES Many of the medicinal claims made of rue are not now recognized as true. Today dried rue is used mostly as an insect repellent. The roots produce a rosy red dye. Popular in herb gardens for the ornamental value of its leaves, particularly the variety 'Blue Mound' and a variegated form with green and white leaves.

BOTANICAL NAME *Salvia elegans*

COMMON NAME Pineapple Sage

HEIGHT 2 to 3 feet; upright habit.

CULTURE Tender perennial. Propagated mostly from cuttings. Easy to grow in any well-drained garden soil in full sun. Needs pinching back to keep plants bushy and compact. Best grown in pots so it can be moved indoors during winter.

DESCRIPTION Beautiful tubular red flowers are borne on slender flower spikes in late summer. Stems turn woody with age. Green, spear-shaped leaves impart a pineapple fragrance.

USES Dried foliage is used in tea, potpourri, jam, and jelly. Flowers attractive to hummingbirds. Highly ornamental in bloom.

BOTANICAL NAME *Salvia officinalis*

COMMON NAME Garden Sage

HEIGHT 2 to 3 feet; bushy habit.

CULTURE Hardy perennial. Propagated by seed and by cuttings. Easy to grow in any well-drained garden soil.

DESCRIPTION Slender, oval leaves are gray, with a quilted texture, and highly aromatic when touched. Decorative flower spikes in white, pink, or light blue appear in spring.

USES Fresh sage leaves are more pungent than the dried leaves and should be used sparingly to flavor stuffing, sausage, vegetable dishes, and many other foods. Oil distilled from the leaves is used to make perfume.

RECOMMENDED VARIETIES 'Purpurescens' has purple leaves, and 'Tricolor' features white, pink, and purple leaves.

BOTANICAL NAME *Santolina chamaecyparissus*

COMMON NAME Gray Santolina; Lavender-cotton

HEIGHT 2 to 2¹/₂ feet; low, mound-shaped habit.

CULTURE Hardy perennial. Propagated by seed and cuttings. Prefers fertile, moist, well-drained acidic loam soil in full sun. During periods of high heat and humidity foliage may turn black. Roots need mulch protection during severe winters.

DESCRIPTION Attractive, silvery foliage is finely cut, making a mosslike cushion. In summer, masses of yellow, buttonlike blooms appear on slender stalks. Leaves are highly aromatic when touched.

USES Dried foliage repels insects, especially moths. Sensational edging plant for beds and borders.

RELATED SPECIES *Santolina virens,* 'Green santolina,' has dark green leaves and is hardier.

BOTANICAL NAME *Satureja hortensis*

COMMON NAME Summer Savory

HEIGHT 18 inches; bushy, spreading habit.

CULTURE Hardy perennial. Propagated by seed. Prefers fertile, well-drained loam soil in full sun. Self-seeds easily. Grows to be top-heavy as the season advances and may need staking for support.

DESCRIPTION Leaves are dark green, needlelike, crowded along wiry stems that become woody with age. Spikes of small pink flowers bloom in summer.

USES Fresh or dried leaves have a peppery flavor and are more potent than the related species, 'Winter Savory.' Used to flavor salad, vinegar, vegetable soup, and poultry.

RELATED SPECIES *S. douglasii* ('Yerba Buena'), a native of California.

BOTANICAL NAME *Satureja montana*

COMMON NAME Winter Savory

HEIGHT 8 to 12 inches; low, spreading habit.

CULTURE Hardy perennial that stays evergreen except during severe winters. Prefers moist, sandy soil that is not too fertile, in full sun. The root crown is susceptible to rot in moist soils. Prune tops back in spring to keep the plant looking tidy.

DESCRIPTION Narrow, pointed green leaves are crowded along wiry stems. Plant is slow-growing and spreading. Short spikes of white flowers appear in late summer.

USES Milder flavor than Summer Savory, and is used the same way—to flavor salad, vegetable soup, vinegar, and poultry.

BOTANICAL NAME *Sesamum indicum*

COMMON NAME Sesame

HEIGHT 3 feet; upright, clump-forming habit.

CULTURE Tender annual. Propagated by seed. Prefers well-drained loam or sandy soil in full sun. Fast growing and difficult to grow in states with cool summers.

DESCRIPTION Resembles a giant nettle. Small, tubular, cream-colored flowers have broad, serrated, pointed leaves. Seeds, which are prized as a flavoring for Oriental dishes, soups, and cookies, are harvested when ripe, about five weeks after the flowers appear.

USES Soups and bakery products rely heavily on sesame seeds for their flavor. Seeds can be used whole, mixed into soups and stews, or crushed.

BOTANICAL NAME *Solanum melongena esculentum*

COMMON NAME Eggplant

CULTURE Start seed indoors six to eight weeks before outdoor planting after all danger of frost. Protect plants from flea beetles with organic sprays. Plants prefer fertile loam soil and watering during dry spells. Planting through black plastic to warm the soil promotes heavy yields and earliness.

DESCRIPTION Bushy plants up to 3-feet high produce purple star-shaped flowers and oval fruits that vary in size from a chicken's egg to an ostrich's egg. Fruit color is usually purple or black, but in some varieties, white and bicolored.

HARVEST AND USE Pick fruits when shiny and before they turn brown or yellow. They are generally sliced and fried to serve as a side dish. Diced eggplant can be frozen for storage.

RECOMMENDED VARIETY 'Dusky' hybrid produces handsome pear-shaped fruit within fifty-six days of transplanting.

BOTANICAL NAME *Solanum tuberosum*

COMMON NAME Irish Potato

CULTURE Grown from seeds or "seedling" tubers, with tubers the most common method. Any part of the potato tuber with an "eye" (growing point) can be used. Plant in spring after danger of frost, covering with 1 inch of soil. Space plants at least 2 feet apart in rows spaced 2 feet apart. Plants grow best when nights are cool.

DESCRIPTION Plants resemble bush tomatoes, grow white, star-shaped flowers and small, round, poisonous fruit resembling a tomato. **Caution:** All parts of plant are poisonous except the tubers, which can be brown, white, red, or blue in color, depending on variety.

HARVEST AND USE Harvest "new" potatoes the size of golf balls within eighty-five days. Harvest mature potatoes when stems have died down. Mostly eaten boiled or fried.

RECOMMENDED VARIETIES 'Katahdin' is a high-yielding, white-skinned potato; 'Red Pontiac' a red-skinned variety.

BOTANICAL NAME *Spinacea oleracea*

COMMON NAME Spinach

CULTURE Sow seed directly into the garden 1/4 inch deep, in rows spaced at least 12 inches apart. Harvest is improved if seeds are first germinated indoors in a moist paper towel and transferred to the planting row, spaced 6 inches apart. Plants tolerate frost.

DESCRIPTION A fast-growing leaf crop that needs cool weather. Oval or pointed dark green leaves are best grown in early spring or fall.

HARVEST AND USE Harvest leaves before hot weather causes plants to bolt to seed. Good to eat fresh in salads or boiled as a side dish. Spinach also freezes well.

RECOMMENDED VARIETY 'Melody' is an award-winning hybrid.

BOTANICAL NAME *Stachys byzantina, S. olympia*

COMMON NAME Lamb's-ears; Wooly Betony

HEIGHT 12 to 18 inches; low, ground-hugging habit.

CULTURE Hardy perennial. Propagated by division in spring. Prefers well-drained, fertile loam soil in full sun. Clear away winter-damaged foliage in spring.

DESCRIPTION Mats of soft, wooly, grayish white leaves resemble lamb's ears. In summer, spikes of pale pink flowers appear above the foliage.

USES Excellent for ground cover and edging. Grown mostly for its appealing silver color and velvety texture. Used extensively to help enhance herbal wreaths.

RECOMMENDED VARIETIES 'Silver Carpet,' a non-flowering form that remains low and spreading.

BOTANICAL NAME *Symphytum officinale*

COMMON NAME Comfrey

HEIGHT 3 to 4 feet; clump-forming habit.

CULTURE Hardy perennial. Propagated by seed and division. Prefers moist, fertile loam soil in full sun.

DESCRIPTION Big, dramatic leaves are dark green, heavily-veined, arching out from a basal crown. Pale pink tubular flowers are borne in summer on long stems. Needs pruning back after flowering.

USES A great number of medicinal remedies are attributed to comfrey, including relief from ulcers. In recent years, however, overdoses of chemical substances found in comfrey have caused cancer in rats. Its place in the herb garden today, therefore, has changed to emphasize its ornamental value, though traditional herbalists still do not hesitate to brew a cup of comfrey tea or add a chopped leaf to a spring salad.

BOTANICAL NAME *Tanacetum vulgare*

COMMON NAME Tansy

HEIGHT 4 feet; dense, clump-forming habit.

CULTURE Hardy perennial. Propagated by seed and division. Easy to grow even in poor soil; prefers full sun. Spreads rapidly by underground rhizomes. Needs dividing annually after third year.

DESCRIPTION Dark green leaves are fernlike, pungent. Yellow buttonlike flowers appear in summer. Common wayside plant throughout North America.

USES Fresh and dried flower heads and foliage have insect repellent properties. Both leaves and flowers are beautiful in fresh or dried arrangements.

BOTANICAL NAME *Teucrium chamaedrys*

COMMON NAME Germander

HEIGHT 12 to 15 inches; low, bushy habit.

CULTURE Hardy perennial that stays evergreen in winter. Propagated by cuttings or division. Prefers fertile loam soil in full sun. In areas where winters are severe, plants benefit from mulching around roots.

DESCRIPTION Mature plants develop woody stems crowded with small, oval green leaves. Dainty pink flowers resembling thyme occur in midsummer. Plants tolerate crowding and can be planted to create a dwarf hedge.

USES A tea brewed from its leaves was thought to relieve gout. Today, its main value is as an edging plant for beds and borders; also to create knot designs and parterres.

BOTANICAL NAME *Thymus vulgaris*

COMMON NAME English Thyme; Common Thyme

HEIGHT 12 inches; mounded, shrubby habit.

CULTURE Hardy perennial that remains evergreen in winter. Cultivated by seed, cuttings, and division. Prefers a well-drained, garden loam soil in full sun.

DESCRIPTION Small, rounded green leaves create a bushy mound, covered in spring with clusters of showy pink flowers. Mature stems turn woody. Leaves are aromatic when touched.

USES The most popular culinary use for thyme is as a seasoning for vegetable, meat, and fish dishes. An essential ingredient in "Bouquet Garni," a cluster of five essential herbs tied together and steeped in soup or stew.

RELATED SPECIES *T. praecox* ('Creeping Thyme'), good for planting between flagstone; and *T. serpyllum* ('Lemon Thyme'), imparting a lemonlike aroma.

BOTANICAL NAME *Trigonella foenum-graecum*

COMMON NAME Fenugreek

HEIGHT 18 to 24 inches; erect habit.

CULTURE Tender annual propagated from seed. For curry-flavored sprouts, germinate seeds indoors on a moist paper towel in bright light. Outdoors, plants prefer fertile loam soil in full sun. Cold or moist soil induces root rot.

DESCRIPTION The brown, square-shaped seeds germinate quickly indoors and produce succulent sprouts with a mild curry flavor. Outdoors, mature plants produce cloverlike leaves and cream colored flowers in midsummer, followed by beaklike seed pods.

USES A primary ingredient of curry powder. Prized in Middle-Eastern cuisine to flavor curries, chutney, and candy. The sprouted seeds are good for sandwich fillings and salads. The ancient Egyptians attributed many medicinal benefits to fenugreek, including relief from colds and fever.

BOTANICAL NAME *Tropaeolum majus*

COMMON NAME Nasturtium

HEIGHT 2 feet for dwarf types, 6 feet for vining types; spreading habit.

CULTURE Tender annual grown from seed sown directly into the garden after danger of frost has passed. Flowers best when nights are cool. Tolerates a wide range of soil conditions in full sun. Rich soils produce more leaves, fewer flowers.

DESCRIPTION Bright green leaves resemble parasols. Flowers prolifically during cool weather. Color range includes yellow, orange, red, pink, and white. Dwarf cultivars trail beautifully to cover slopes. Climbing cultivars can be used on trellises.

USES Flowers and leaves are edible and impart a peppery flavor to salads. Seeds are edible, pickled as capers.

BOTANICAL NAME *Valeriana officinalis*

COMMON NAME Garden Valerian

HEIGHT 4 to 5 feet; erect habit.

CULTURE Hardy perennial. Propagated by seed and division. Prefers moist, well-drained loam soil in full sun or partial shade. Self-seeds easily. Sometimes needs staking.

DESCRIPTION Clusters of attractive white or pink flowers are borne on stiff stems in spring, imparting a vanilla-like fragrance. Finely divided leaves are blue-green and ornamental.

USES In ancient times the root was used medicinally to treat problems of the heart and central nervous system, such as hypertension and epilepsy. Today, the plant is used mostly for its ornamental effect.

BOTANICAL NAME *Vicia faba*

COMMON NAME Fava Bean

CULTURE Plants demand cool weather and will burn up quickly in summer heat. Plant seeds directly into the garden, in spring as soon as soil can be worked; cover with 2 inches of soil. Thin plants to 6 inches apart in rows at least 2 feet apart. Fastest germination is assured if bottomless milk cartons are placed over groups of seeds to act as soil warmers. Control aphids by dislodging colonies with jets of water.

DESCRIPTION Fava beans, or broad beans, have the biggest pods of any garden bean—up to 10 inches long, with fat, cream-colored beans, nestled in a velvetlike, silvery lining. The pods are not edible.

HARVEST AND USE Harvest as soon as pods feel plump. Boil in water for a few minutes until tender and serve with butter. **Caution:** Some people are allergic to Fava beans.

RECOMMENDED VARIETY 'Long Pod' yields heavily within sixty-five days.

BOTANICAL NAME *Viola odorata*

COMMON NAME Sweet Violet

HEIGHT 4 to 12 inches; low, clump-forming habit.

CULTURE Hardy perennial. Propagated from seed and division. Prefers moist, fertile loam soil in full sun or partial shade. Flowers best in spring and fall when nights are cool.

DESCRIPTION Showy flowers resemble miniature pansies, deep violet-blue in color. The dark green, heart-shaped leaves are also ornamental.

USES Oil distilled from the flowers is used in perfume. The candied flowers are sold commercially. Flowers are also added to jelly, salad, and fruit punch.

RECOMMENDED VARIETY 'Royal Robe,' growing large, long-stemmed purple flowers.

BOTANICAL NAME *Zea mays rugosa*

COMMON NAME Sweet Corn

CULTURE Sow seeds directly into the garden after danger of frost, covering with 1 inch of soil. Thin to stand 12 inches apart in rows spaced at least 2 feet apart. Alternatively, pre-germinate seeds indoors on moist paper towels and transplant the young seedlings. Plants prefer nitrogen-rich loam soil, and regular amounts of water at time of "tasselling" to develop ears filled to the tips with creamy, sweet kernels.

DESCRIPTION Member of the grass family, growing tall, bamboo-like stalks and arching, green leaves. Ears of corn are produced at the leaf nodes when the "silks" (the female flower) are pollinated by pollen grains falling on it from the "tassel," the male flower that emerges at the top of the stalk.

HARVEST AND USE Harvest ears when silks have turned brown and ears feel plump. Strip away leaves surrounding the kernels and cook by roasting or boiling. Sweet corn also freezes well.

RECOMMENDED VARIETY 'Silver Queen', a white mid-season variety, matures in ninety-five days, has large ears and sweet flavor. Many new "Super Sweet" corns, such as 'How Sweet It Is', hold their sweetness for up to a week after picking. These generally need isolating from other corns to produce their super sweetness.

BOTANICAL NAME *Zingiber officinale*

COMMON NAME Ginger

HEIGHT 3 to 4 feet; erect, shrubby habit.

CULTURE Tender perennial native to the tropics. Propagated mostly by rhizomes and division. Mostly grown in tubs so it can be taken indoors during the winter. Prefers moist, fertile, humus-rich soil in sun or partial shade.

DESCRIPTION Slender, canelike stems grow erect, with broad, arching sword-shaped leaves. Yellow-green flowers with purple lips are arranged in a poker-straight spike. The fleshy underground rhizome is a source of ginger spice.

USES Invaluable flavor enhancer for spicy foods, particularly in Indian and Chinese cuisine. Also used to flavor drinks (ginger ale) and as candied preserves.

Right: The kitchen garden at the Governor's Palace in Williamsburg, Virginia features both salad greens and herbs. The white flower heads of chervil are conspicuous in the foreground.

CHAPTER FOUR

HERB SELECTION GUIDE

Note: This section deals mostly with those plants classified as herbs, which are less familiar to people than vegetables. Most vegetables are generally grown from seed, demand good sunlight, and soil that drains well.

HERBS TO GROW FROM SEEDS

Achillea filipendulina (Yarrow)
Agrimonia eupatoria (Agrimony)
Allium species (Onion)
Aloysia triphylla (Lemon Verbena)
Anethum graveolens (Dill)
Angelica archangelica (Angelica)
Anthemis nobilis (Chamomile)
Anthriscus cerefolium (Chervil)
Artemisia absinthium (Wormwood)
Baptisia australis (False Indigo; Blue Wild Indigo)
Calendula officinalis (Pot-marigold)
Capsicum annuum (Hot Pepper, Chilli Pepper)
Carthamus tinctorius (Safflower)
Chenopodium bonus-henricus (Good-King-Henry Goosefoot)
Chrysanthemum species (Costmary; Pyrethrum; Feverfew)
Cichorium intybus (Chicory)
Coriandrum sativum (Coriander)
Digitalis species (Foxglove)
Dipsacus sylvestris (Teasel)
Elettaria cardamomum (Cardamon)

Foeniculum vulgare azoricum (Florence Fennel)
Galium odoratum (Sweet Woodruff)
Hyssopus officinalis (Hyssop)
Iris germanica 'Florentina' (Orris Root)
Lavandula angustifolia (English Lavender; True Lavender)
Marrubium vulgare (White Horehound; Candy Horehound)
Melissa officinalis (Lemon-balm)
Monarda citriodora (Lemon Mint; Lemon Bee-balm)
Monarda didyma (Scarlet Bee-balm; Bergamot; Oswego Tea)
Myrrhis odorata (Sweet Cicely; Myrrh)
Nasturtium officinale (Watercress)
Nepeta cataria (Catnip)
Nepeta mussinii (Catmint)
Ocimum basilicum (Sweet Basil)
Origanum majorana (Oregano; Wild Marjoram)
Panax quinquefolius (Ginseng)
Petroselinum crispum (Parsley)
Pimpinella anisum (Anise)
Poterium sanguisorba (Salad Burnet)
Rheum rhabarbarum (Rhubarb)
Rosmarinus officinalis (Rosemary)
Rumex scutatus (French Sorrel)
Salvia elegans (Pineapple Sage)
Salvia officinalis (Garden Sage)
Satureja hortensis (Summer Savory)
Satureja montana (Winter Savory)
Tagetes species (Marigold)

HERBS TO GROW FROM SEEDS (cont.)

Tanacetum vulgare (Tansy)
Teucrium chamaedrys (Germander)
Thymus species (Thyme)
Trigonella foenum-graecum (Fenugreek)
Valeriana officinalis (Garden Valerian)
Viola odorata (Sweet Violet)

HERBS FOR SUN

Achillea filipendulina (Yarrow)
Agastache foeniculum (Anise Hyssop)
Agrimonia eupatoria (Agrimony)
Allium cepa proliferum (Egyptian Top Onion)
Allium fistulosum (Welsh Onion)
Allium schoenoprasum (Chive)
Allium tuberosum (Chinese Chive)
Aloe barbadensis (Healing Plant; Barbados Aloe)
Aloysia triphylla (Lemon Verbena)
Amaranthus hybridus hypochondriacus (Prince's-feather;
    Green Amaranth)
Armoracia rusticana (Horseradish)
Amorpha fruticosa angustifolia (Indigo Bush; Bastard
    Indigo)
Anethum graveolens (Dill)
Angelica archangelica (Angelica)
Anthemis nobilis (Chamomile)
Anthriscus cerefolium (Chervil)
Artemisia absinthium (Wormwood)
Artemisia dracunculus sativa (Tarragon)
Baptisia australis (False Indigo; Blue Wild Indigo)
Calendula officinalis (Pot-marigold)
Camassia quamash (Quamash)
Capsicum annuum (Hot Pepper, Chilli Pepper)
Carthamus tinctorius (Safflower)
Chrysanthemum balsamita (Costmary; Bible leaf)
Chrysanthemum coccineum (Pyrethrum; Painted Daisy)
Chrysanthemum parthenium (Feverfew)
Cichorium intybus (Chicory)
Coriandrum sativum (Chinese Parsley; Cilantro;
    Coriander)
Crocus sativus (Saffron)
Digitalis species (Foxglove)
Dipsacus sylvestris (Teasel)
Elettaria cardamomum (Cardamon)

Foeniculum vulgare azoricum (Florence Fennel)
Hyssopus officinalis (Hyssop)
Laurus nobilis (Laurel; Sweet Bay)
Lavandula angustifolia (English Lavender;
    True Lavender)
Levisticum officinalis (Lovage)
Marrubium vulgare (Candy Horehound;
    White Horehound)
Melissa officinalis (Lemon-balm)
Mentha peperita (Peppermint)
Mentha pulegium (Pennyroyal)
Mentha spicata (Spearmint)
Mentha suaveolens (Apple Mint)
Monarda citriodora (Lemon Mint)
Monarda didyma (Scarlet Bee-balm; Bergamot; Oswego
    Tea)
Nepeta cataria (Catnip)
Nepeta mussinii (Catmint)
Pelargonium graveolens (Rose-scented Geranium;
    Deodorizer Plant)
Petroselinum crispum (Parsley)
Pimpinella anisum (Anise)
Poncirus trifoliata (Hardy-orange)
Poterium sanguisorba (Salad Burnet)
Rheum rhabarbarum (Garden Rhubarb)
Rosarinus officinalis (Rosemary)
Rumex scutatus (French Sorrel)
Ruta graveolens (Rue)
Salvia elegans (Pineapple Sage)
Salvia officinalis (Garden Sage)
Santolina chamaecyparissus (Gray Santolina;
    Lavender-cotton)
Satureja hortensis (Summer Savory)
Satureja montana (Winter Savory)
Tagetes species (Marigold)
Tanacetum vulgare (Tansy)
Thymus praecox (Creeping Thyme)
Thymus serpyllum (Lemon Thyme)
Thymus vulgaris (English Thyme; Common Thyme)
Trigonella foenum-graecum (Fenugreek)
Valeriana officinalis (Garden Valerian)
Viola odorata (Sweet Violet)

Opposite page: This ecclesiastical herb garden at Carmel Mission, Carmel, California contains many of the herbs mentioned in the Bible. It features a fountain as a focal point.

Opposite page: An island bed of decorative summer-flowering herbs features silvery lamb's ears, yellow-flowering rue, white-flowering feverfew, and purple-flowered hyssop.

HERBS FOR SHADE

Agrimonia eupatoria (Agrimony)
Angelica archangelica (Angelica)
Anthriscus cerefolium (Chervil)
Armoracia rusticana (Horseradish)
Artemisia absinthium (Wormwood)
Chenopodium bonus-henricus (Good-King–Henry Goosefoot)
Cichorium intybus (Chicory)
Cymbopogon citratus (Lemon Grass)
Digitalis purpurea (Foxglove)
Galium odoratum (Sweet Woodruff)
Hyssopus officinalis (Hyssop)
Iris germanica 'Florentina' (Orris Root)
Laurus nobilis (Sweet Bay; Laurel)
Levisticum officinalis (Lovage)
Melissa officinalis (Lemon-balm)
Mentha piperita (Peppermint)
Mentha pulegium (Pennyroyal)
Mentha spicata (Spearmint)
Monarda didyma (Scarlet Bee-balm; Bergamot; Oswego Tea)
Myrrhis odorata (Sweet Cicely; Myrrh)
Nasturtium officinale (Watercress)
Nepeta cataria (Catnip)
Panax quinquefolius (Ginseng)
Rosmarinus officinalis (Rosemary)
Salvia elegans (Pineapple Sage)
Salvia officinalis (Garden Sage)
Tanacetum vulgare (Tansy)
Teucrium chamaedrys (Germander)
Valeriana officinalis (Garden Valerian)
Viola odorata (Sweet Violet)

HERBS WITH ATTRACTIVE FLOWERS

Achillea filipendulina (Yarrow)
Allium schoenoprasum (Chive)
Amaranthus hybridus hypochondriacus (Green Amaranth; Prince's-feather)
Baptisia australis (False Indigo; Blue Wild Indigo)
Calendula officinalis (Pot-marigold)
Cichorium intybus (Chicory)
Coriandrum sativum (Coriander)
Dianthus granitus (Spice Pink)
Digitalis species (Foxglove)
Dipsacus sylvestris (Teasel)
Hyssopus officinalis (Hyssop)
Iris germanica 'Florentina' (Orris Root)
Lavandula angustifolia (True Lavender; English Lavender)
Levisticum officinalis (Lovage)
Mentha suaveolens (Apple Mint)
Myrrhis odorata (Sweet Cicely; Myrrh)
Origanum vulgare (Oregano; Wild Marjoram)
Pelargonium graveolens (Rose-scented Geranium; Deodorizer Plant)
Poterium sanguisorba (Salad Burnet)
Rosmarinus officinalis (Rosemary)
Ruta graveolens (Rue)
Salvia officinalis (Garden Sage)
Satureja hortensis (Summer Savory)
Satureja montana (Winter Savory)
Tagetes species (Marigold)
Tanacetum vulgare (Tansy)
Thymus serpyllum (Lemon Thyme)
Valeriana officinalis (Garden Valerian)
Viola odorata (Sweet Violet)

HERBS FOR CONTAINERS

Allium schoenoprasum (Chive)
Aloe barbadensis (Barbados Aloe; Healing Plant)
Aloysia triphylla (Lemon Verbena)
Amaranthus hybridus hypochondriacus (Prince's-feather;
    Green Amaranth)
Anethum graveolens (Dill)
Anthemis nobilis (Chamomile)
Anthriscus cerefolium (Chervil)
Artemisia dracunculus sativa (Tarragon)
Calendula officinalis (Pot-marigold)
Cichorium intybus (Chicory)
Coriandrum sativum (Coriander)
Euphorbia lathyris (Mole plant)
Foeniculum vulgare azoricum (Florence Fennel)
Galium odoratum (Sweet Woodruff)
Hyssopus officinalis (Hyssop)
Laurus nobilis (Laurel; Sweet Bay)
Lavandula angustifolia (English Lavender;
    True Lavender)
Marrubium vulgare (White Horehound;
    Candy Horehound)
Melissa officinalis (Lemon-balm)
Mentha species (Mint)
Nepeta cataria (Catnip)
Nepeta mussinii (Catmint)
Ocimum basilicum (Sweet Basil)
Origanum majorana (Sweet Marjoram)
Origanum vulgare (Oregano; Wild Marjoram)
Pelargonium graveolens (Rose-scented Geranium;
    Deodorizer Plant)
Petroselinum crispum (Parsley)
Poterium sanguisorba (Salad Burnet)
Rosmarinus officinalis (Rosemary)
Rumex scutatus (French Sorrel)
Ruta graveolens (Rue)
Salvia elegans (Pineapple Sage)
Salvia officinalis (Garden Sage)
Satureja hortensis (Summer Savory)
Satureja montana (Winter Savory)
Tagetes species (Marigold)
Teucrium chamaedrys (Germander)
Thymus species (Thyme)

HERBS FOR CULINARY USE

Agastache foeniculum (Anise Hyssop)
Allium species (Onion)
Anethum graveolens (Dill)
Angelica archangelica (Angelica)
Anthemis nobilis (Chamomile)
Anthriscus cerefolium (Chervil)
Armoracia rusticana (Horseradish)
Artemisia dracunculus sativa (Tarragon)
Borago officinalis (Borage)
Capsicum annuum (Hot Pepper; Chilli Pepper)
Carthamus tinctorius (Safflower)
Chenopodium bonus-henricus (Good-King-Henry
    Goosefoot)
Chrysanthemum balsamita (Costmary)
Cichorium intybus (Chicory)
Coriandrum sativum (Coriander)
Crocus sativus (Saffron)
Elettaria cardamomum (Cardamon)
Foeniculum vulgare azoricum (Fennel)
Laurus nobilis (Sweet Bay; Laurel)
Levisticum officinale (Lovage)
Melissa officinalis (Lemon-balm)
Mentha species (Mint) except *M. pulegium* (Pennyroyal)
Monarda didyma (Scarlet Bee-balm; Bergamot; Oswego
    Tea)
Nasturtium officinale (Watercress)
Ocimum basilicum (Sweet Basil)
Olea europaea (Common Olive; European Olive)
Origanum majorana (Sweet Marjoram)
Origanum vulgare (Oregano; Wild Marjoram)
Pelargonium graveolens (Rose-scented Geranium;
    Deodorizer Plant)
Petroselinum crispum (Parsley)
Pimpinella anisum (Anise)
Poterium sanguisorba (Salad Burnet)
Rheum rhabarbarum (Rhubarb)
Rosmarinus officinalis (Rosemary)
Rumex scutatus (French Sorrel)
Salvia officinalis (Garden Sage)
Satureja hortensis (Summer Savory)
Satureja montana (Winter Savory)
Thymus species (Thyme)
Trigonella foenum-graecum (Fenugreek)
Viola odorata (Sweet Violet)

Opposite page: A pair of scented-leaf geraniums in pots crown the stone walls; other potted herbs provide culinary flavors for the kitchen, located right off of the patio. The close proximity of the garden to the kitchen makes it easier for the cook to clip the herbs needed for the dish being prepared.

HERBS FOR FLAVORING

Angelica *(Angelica archangelica):* breads, fruit, jellies, teas

Basil *(Ocimum basilicum):* breads, butters, cheeses, eggs, meats, salads, sauces, vegetables, vinegars

Burnet *(Poterium sanguisorba):* cheeses, eggs, salads, vegetables, vinegars

Caraway *(Carum carvi):* breads, cheese, meats, vegetables

Chervil *(Anthriscus cerefolium):* breads, butters, cheeses, eggs, fish, meats, vegetables

Chives *(Allium schoenoprasum):* breads, butters, cheeses, eggs, fish, meats, salads, sauces, teas

Sweet Cicely *(Myrrhis odorata):* breads, butters, cheeses, eggs, fish, fruits, jellies, meats, salads, sauces, tea, vegetables

Dill *(Anethum graveolens):* breads, butters, cheeses, eggs, fish, meats, salads, sauces, vegetables, vinegars

Fennel *(Foeniculum vulgare azoricum):* meats, sauces, vegetables

Lovage *(Levisticum officinale):* salads, sauces, vegetables, vinegars

Marjoram *(Origanum* species): breads, butters, cheeses, meats, salads, sauces, vegetables

Mint *(Mentha* species): breads, butters, fruits, jellies, meats, salads, sauces, vegetables

Oregano *(Origanum vulgare):* breads, butters, cheeses, eggs, meats, salads, sauces, vegetables

Parsley *(Petroselinum crispum:* breads, butters, cheeses, eggs, fish, salads, sauces, vegetables

Rosemary *(Rosmarinus officinalis):* breads, butters, cheeses, eggs, fish, fruits, meats, sauces, teas, vegetables

Sage *(Salvia officinalis):* breads, butters, cheeses, meats, sauces, teas

Savory *(Saturea hortensis* or *S. montana):* breads, butters, cheeses, eggs, meats, salads, sauces, vegetables

Tarragon *(Artemisia dracunculus sativa):* breads, butters, cheeses, eggs, fish, meats, salads, sauces, vegetables, vinegars

Thyme *(Thymus* species): breads, butters, cheeses, eggs, fish, meats, salads, sauces, vegetables, vinegars

HERBAL BUTTERS

Allium schoenoprasum (Chive)
Anethum graveolens (Dill)
Anthriscus cerefolium (Chervil)
Armoracia rusticana (Horseradish)
Artemisia dracunculus sativa (Tarragon)
Mentha species (Mint)
Myrrhis odorata (Sweet Cicely; Myrrh)
Ocimum basilicum (Sweet Basil)
Origanum majorana (Sweet Marjoram)
Origanum vulgare (Oregano; Wild Marjoram)
Petroselinum crispum (Parsley)
Rosmarinus officinalis (Rosemary)
Salvia officinalis (Garden Sage)
Satureja hortensis (Summer Savory)
Satureja montana (Winter Savory)
Thymus species (Thyme)

HERBS FOR TEA

Achillea filipendulina (Yarrow)
Agrimonia eupatoria (Agrimony)
Anthemis nobilis (Chamomile)
Borago officinalis (Borage)
Cymbopogon citratus (Lemon Grass)
Foeniculum vulgare azoricum (Florence Fennel)
Hyssopus officinalis (Hyssop)
Laurus nobilis (Sweet Bay; Laurel)
Marrubium vulgare (White Horehound; Candy Horehound)
Melissa officinalis (Lemon-balm)
Mentha species (Mint)
Monarda citriodora (Lemon Mint)
Monarda didyma (Scarlet Bee-balm; Bergamot; Oswego Tea)
Nepeta cataria (Catnip)
Ocimum basilicum (Sweet Basil)
Origanum vulgare (Wild Marjoram)
Salvia officinalis (Pineapple Sage)
Satureja hortensis (Summer Savory)
Satureja montana (Winter Savory)
Symphytum officinale (Comfrey)
Thymus species (Thyme)

HERBS FOR VINEGARS

Allium schoenoprasum (Chives)
Anethum graveolens (Dill)
Artemisia dracunculus sativa (Tarragon)
Levisticum officinale (Lovage)
Ocimum basilicum (Sweet Basil)
Origanum majorana (Sweet Marjoram)
Origanum vulgare (Wild Marjoram)
Petroselinum crispum (Parsley)
Poterium sanguisorba (Salad Burnet)
Rosmarinus officinalis (Rosemary)
Salvia officinalis (Garden Sage)
Thymus species (Thyme)

HERBS FOR FRAGRANCE AND POTPOURRIS

Agastache foeniculum (Anise Hyssop)
Agrimonia eupatoria (Agrimony)
Angelica archangelica (Angelica)
Anthemis nobilis (Chamomile)
Artemisia absinthium (Wormwood)
Chrysanthemum balsamita (Costmary)
Coriandrum sativum (Coriander)
Foeniculum vulgare azoricum (Florence Fennel)
Iris germanica 'Florentina' (Orris Root)
Laurus nobilis (Sweet Bay; Laurel)
Lavandula angustifolia (English Lavender)
Melissa officinalis (Lemon-balm)
Mentha species (Mint)
Monarda citriodora (Lemon Mint)
Monarda didyma (Scarlet Bee-balm; Bergamot;
    Oswego Tea)
Myrrhis odorata (Sweet Cicely; Myrrh)
Nepeta cataria (Catnip)
Ocimum basilicum (Sweet Basil)
Origanum majorana (Sweet Marjoram)
Pelargonium graveolens (Rose-scented Geranium;
    Deodorizer Plant)
Pimpinella anisum (Anise)
Rosmarinus officinalis (Rosemary)
Salvia elegans (Pineapple Sage)
Salvia officinalis (Garden Sage)

Santolina chamaecyparissus (Gray Santolina;
    Lavender-cotton)
Satureja hortensis (Summer Savory)
Satureja montana (Winter Savory)
Thymus species (Thyme)
Viola odorata (Sweet Violet)

HERBS FOR DRYING

Amaranthus hybridus hypochondriacus (Prince's-feather;
    Green Amaranth)
Anthemis nobilis (Chamomile)
Anthriscus cerefolium (Chervil)
Artemisia dracunculus sativa (Tarragon)
Carthamus tinctorius (Safflower)
Chrysanthemum balsamita (Costmary)
Chrysanthemum parthenium (Feverfew)
Coriandrum sativum (Coriander)
Dipsacus sylvestris (Teasel)
Iris germanica 'Florentina' (Orris Root)
Lavandula angustifolia (English Lavender; True
    Lavender)
Laurus nobilis (Sweet Bay; Laurel)
Levisticum officinale (Lovage)
Melissa officinalis (Lemon-balm)
Mentha species (Mint)
Monarda citriodora (Lemon Mint)
Monarda didyma (Scarlet Bee-balm; Bergamot; Oswego
    Tea)
Ocimum basilicum (Sweet Basil)
Origanum majorana (Sweet Marjoram)
Origanum vulgare (Oregano; Wild Marjoram)
Nepeta cataria (Catnip)
Pimpinella anisum (Anise)
Rosmarinus officinalis (Rosemary)
Ruta graveolens (Rue)
Salvia elegans (Pineapple Sage)
Salvia officinalis (Sage)
Satureja hortensis (Summer Savory)
Satureja montana (Winter Savory)
Symphytum officinale (Comfrey)
Tanacetum vulgare (Tansy)
Thymus species (Thyme)
Trigonella foenum-graecum (Fenugreek)
Valeriana officinalis (Garden Valerian)

Opposite page: Beds of herbs planted to overflowing at Wave Hill Garden, near New York City.

Opposite page: A garden statue flanked by potted bay laurel is a good accent for decorating herb gardens.

HERBS FOR DYES

HERB	COLOR
Achillea fillipendulina (Yarrow)	green
Agrimonia eupatoria (Agrimony)	yellow
Alchemilla mollis (Lady's Mantle)	green
Allium cepa proliferum (Egyptian Top Onion)	yellow-orange
Anethum graveolens (Dill)	green
Anthemis nobilis (Chamomile)	buff to gold
Baptisia australis (Blue Wild Indigo)	blue
Carthamus tinctorius (Safflower)	pink, orange, yellow
Chamaemelium nobile (Chamomile)	yellow
Crocus sarvus (Saffron)	yellow
Foeniculum vulgare azoricum (Florence Fennel)	bright yellow, gold
Galium odoratum (Sweet Woodruff)	yellow
Iris germanica 'Florentina' (Orris Root)	blue
Nepeta cataria (Catnip)	light yellow, gray-gold
Origanum vulgare (Wild Marjoram)	red
Petroselinum crispum (Parsley)	golden green yellow
Ruta graveolens (Common Rue)	yellow, green
Symphytum officinale (Comfrey)	green
Tagetes species (Marigolds)	lemon-yellow, bright orange
Tanacetum vulgare (Common Tansy)	green, yellow, brown

HERBS FOR MEDICINAL USES

Aloe barbadensis (Healing Plant; Barbados Aloe)
Anthemis nobilis (Chamomile)
Borago officinalis (Borage)
Cichorium intybus (Chicory)
Digitalis species (Foxglove)
Hyssopus officinalis (Hyssop)
Marrubium vulgare (Horehound; Candy Horehound)
Melissa officinalis (Lemon-balm)
Mentha species (Mint)
Ocimum basilicum (Sweet Basil)
Panax quinquefolius (Ginseng)
Pimpinella anisum (Anise)
Poterium sanguisorba (Salad Burnet)
Rheum rhabarbarum (Rhubarb)
Rosmarinus officinalis (Rosemary)
Ruta graveolens (Rue)
Satureja hortensis (Summer Savory)
Thymus species (Thyme)
Valeriana officinalis (Garden Valerian)

PART SEVEN

ESSENTIAL

GARDEN DESIGNS

DESIGN IDEAS

Presented here is a selection of classical garden designs. Some have been chosen to feature a particular plant group. The cartwheel design on page 670, for example, happens to be especially good for herbs, however, it can also serve as a good rose garden design.

Similarly, the cutting garden design on page 677, while especially good for displaying annuals, can also be used to grow a mixed flower garden featuring annuals, perennials, flowering bulbs, and even some shrubs and herbs.

All the designs are easily adapted to suit a variety of locations. Just take a piece of graph paper and pencil in different dimensions using the featured design as a base.

ISLAND BED; RECTANGLE WITH BULL'S-EYES

SUN

1. Gray dusty miller (*Senecio cineraria*)
2. Red salvia (*Salvia splendens*) or zinnia (*Zinnia elegans*)
3. Gold marigold (*Tagetes erecta*), calendula (*Calendula officinalis*), or crested celosia (*Celosia cristata*)
4. Blue salvia (*Salvia farinacea*) or blue ageratum (*Ageratum houstonianum*)
5. Hot pink zinnia (*Zinnia elegans*), aster (*Callistephus chinensis*), petunia (*Petunia* x *hybrida*), or cosmos (*Cosmos bipinnatus*)

SHADE

1. White impatiens (*Impatiens wallerana*)
2. Scarlet impatiens (*Impatiens wallerana*) or red wax begonia (*Begonia* x *semperflorens*)
3. Mimulus (*Mimulus* x *hybridus*), apricot viola (*Viola tricolor*), Chinese forget-me-not (*Cynoglossum amabile*)
4. Blue browallia (*Browallia speciosa*), viola (*Viola tricolor*), or Chinese forget-me-not (*Cynoglossum amabile*)
5. Hot pink impatiens (*Impatiens wallerana*)

Left: Shown here is a good companion planting featuring scarlet sage and dusty miller.

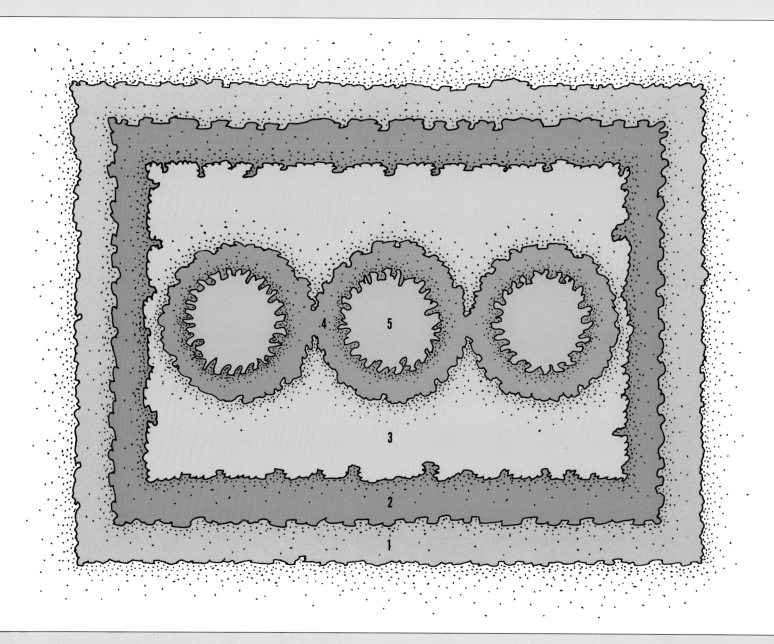

ISLAND BED; RECTANGLE

SUN

1. Dusty miller (*Senecio cineraria*) or white geranium (*Pelargonium* x *hortorum*)
2. Blue petunia (*Petunia* x *hybrida*), ageratum (*Ageratum houstonianum*), pansies (*Viola tricolor*), or blue salvia (*Salvia farinacea*)
3. Blue canterbury bells (*Campanula media*), delphinium (*Delphinium elatum*), or larkspur (*Consolida ambigua*)
4. White cosmos (*Cosmos bipinnatus*)

SHADE

1. White impatiens (*Impatiens wallerana*)
2. Blue forget-me-not (*Myosotis sylvatica*), pansies (*Viola tricolor*), or cambridge blue lobelia (*Lobelia erinus*)
3. Deep blue browallia (*Browallia speciosa*) or crystal palace lobelia (*Lobelia erinus*)
4. White foxglove (*Digitalis purpurea*)

Left: White and blue salvia farinacea mixed with red celosia create an informal effect against mass plantings of white and yellow gazania.

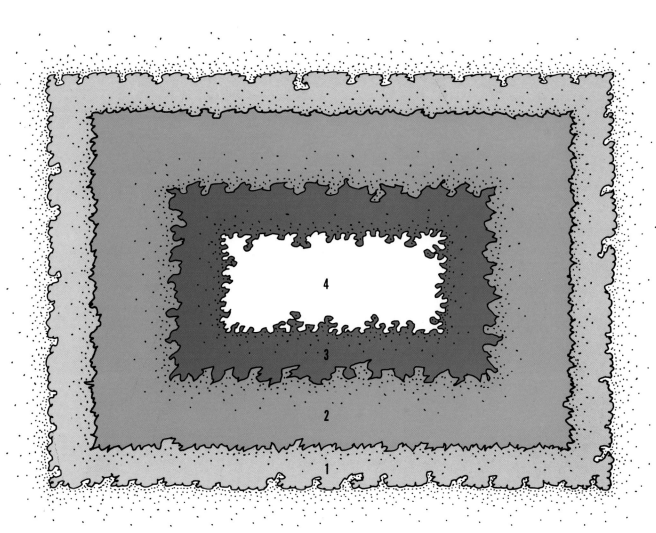

ISLAND BED; RECTANGLE

SUN

1. Gray dusty miller (*Senecio cineraria*)
2. Peach geranium (*Pelargonium* x *hortorum*)
3. Pink geranium (*Pelargonium* x *hortorum*) or aster (*Callistephus chinensis*), Shirley poppies (*Papaver rhoeas*), or petunias (*Petunia* x *hybrida*)
4. White cosmos (*Cosmos bipinnatus*) or hollyhocks (*Alcea rosea*), stock (*Matthiola incana*) or delphinium (*Delphinium elatum*)

SHADE

1. White impatiens (*Impatiens wallerana*)
2. Peach impatiens (*Impatiens wallerana*)
3. Pink impatiens (*Impatiens wallerana*) or coleus (*Coleus* x *hybridus*)
4. White impatiens (*Impatiens wallerana*)

Left: Here, a bed of impatiens is used as an edging between the lawn and a brick path, with hanging baskets in the background.

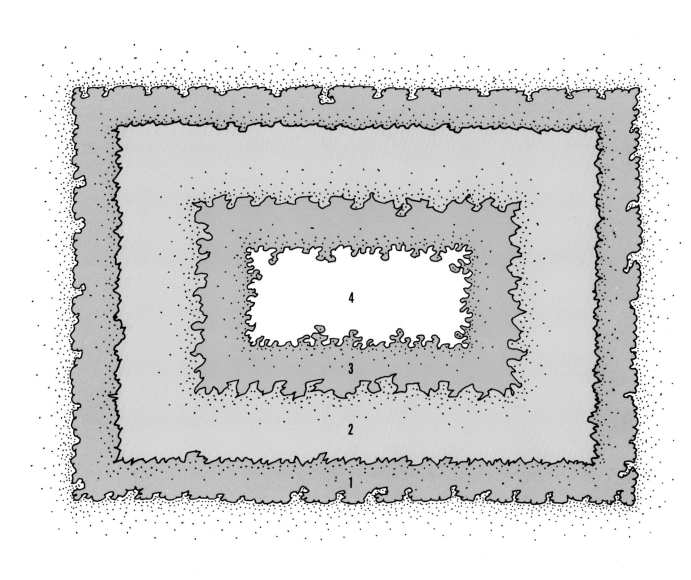

ISLAND BED; RECTANGLE

SUN

1. White geranium (*Pelargonium hortorum*), petunia (*Petunia* x *hybrida*), allysum (*Lobularia maritima*), or dusty miller (*Senecio cineraria*)
2. Pink geranium (*Pelargonium hortorum*), aster (*Callistephus chinensis*), petunia (*Petunia* x *hybrida*), zinnia (*Zinnia elegans*), statice (*Limonium sinuatum*), phlox (*Phlox drummondii*), or dianthus (*Dianthus chinensis*)
3. Lavender petunia (*Petunia* x *hybrida*), aster (*Callistephus chinensis*), statice (*Limonium sinuatum*), ageratum (*Ageratum houstonianum*), candytuft (*Iberis umbellata*), or ornamental kale (*Brassica oleracea*)

SHADE

1. White impatiens (*Impatiens wallerana*), geranium (*Pellargonium* x *hortorum*), or wax begonia (*Begonia sempervirens*)
2. Pink impatiens (soft and hot pink can be interplanted) (*Impatiens wallerana*) wax begonia (*Begonia* x *semperflorens*), nicotiana (*Nicotiana alata*)
3. Lavender impatiens (*Impatiens wallerana*)

Left: Cheerful pink petunias and ornamental fountain grass, *Pennisetum setaceum*, decorate a flower bed.

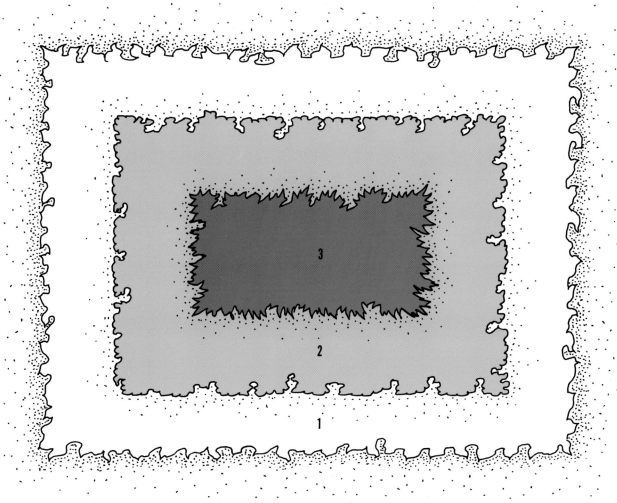

"COLONIAL" FORMAL GARDEN; WILLIAMSBURG DESIGN

SHADE—BRIGHT COLORS

1. Orange, yellow, or scarlet mix of nasturtium (*Trapaeolum majus*)
2. Mimulus (*Mimulus* x *hybridus*) or nemesia (*Nemesia strumosa*), mixed colors
3. Scarlet impatiens (*Impatiens wallerana*)

Left: A mass planting of nasturtiums decorates this California garden.

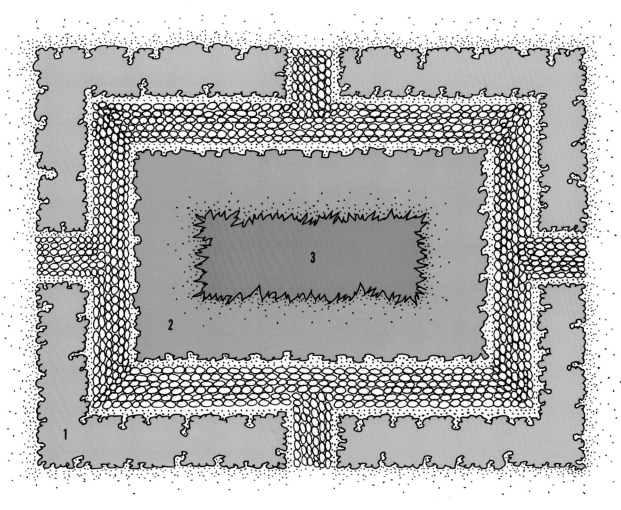

"COLONIAL" FORMAL GARDEN; WILLIAMSBURG DESIGN

SHADE—SOFT COLORS

1. White impatiens (*Impatiens wallerana*)
2. Coral and peach impatiens (*Impatiens wallerana*)
3. Soft blue forget-me-not (*Anchusa capensis*) or white and pink nicotiana (*Nicotiana alata*), or White foxgloves, mixed colors (*Digitalis purpurea*)
4. Optional sundial, fountain, or deeper lavender flowers: tall foxglove (*Digitalis purpurea*) or larkspur (*Consolida ambigua*)

Left: A formal garden at the headquarters of the Pennsylvania Horticultural Society in downtown Philadelphia, Pennsylvania, features petunias, coleus, and portulaca in geometrically shaped beds.

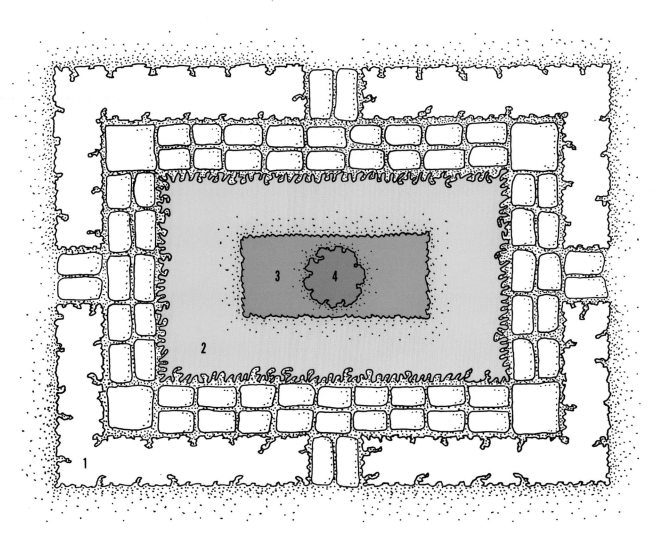

"COLONIAL" FORMAL GARDEN; WILLIAMSBURG DESIGN

SUN—SOFT COLORS FOR CUTTING

1. White cosmos (*Cosmos bipinnatus*)
2. Pink asters (*Callistephus chinensis*)
3. Pink cockscomb (*Celosia cristata*) or pink stock (*Matthiola incana*)
4. Pink phlox (*Phlox drummondii*)
5. Pink snapdragon (*Antirrhinum majus*)
6. Yellow snapdragon (*Antirrhinum majus*)
7. Yellow hollyhocks (*Alcea rosea*)
8. Lemon yellow American marigold (*Tagetes erecta*)
9. Bright yellow zinnia (*Zinnia angustifolia*) or dahlia (*Dalia* x *hybrida*)

Path: pink pea gravel path
Option: If you want to border in yellow, use marigolds (*Tagetes erecta*)

SUN—BRIGHT COLORS FOR CUTTING

1. Hot pink cosmos (*Cosmos bipinnatus*) interplanted with gold helianthus (*Helianthus annuus*)
2. Deep lavender asters (*Callistephus chinensis*)
3. Hot pink phlox (*Phlox drummondii*)
4. Deep lavender asters (*Callistephus chinensis*)
6. Pink snapdragons (*Antirrhinum majus*) or asters (*Callistephus chinensis*)
7. Pink cockscomb (*Celosia cristata*)
8. Lavender stock (*Matthiola incana*) or snapdragons (*Antirrhinum majus*)

Left: Zinnias and marigolds make a good companion planting in a flower bed.

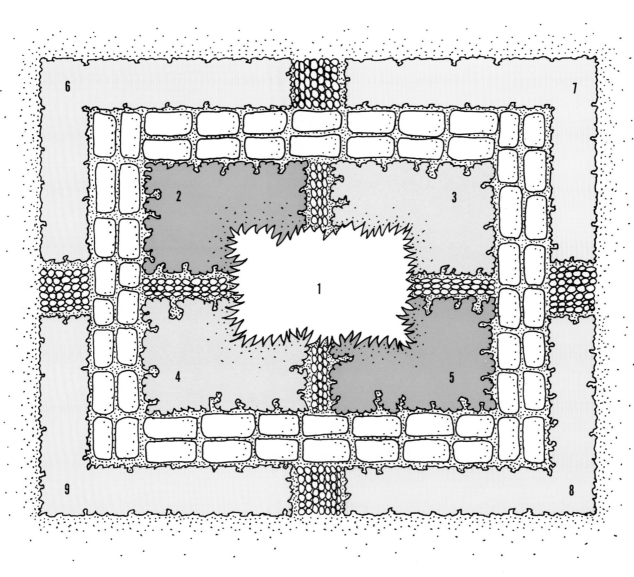

SUN—HOT COLORS FOR CUTTING

1. Pink cosmos (*Comos bipinnatus*)
2. Red salvia (*Salvia splendens*) or red zinnia (*Zinnia elegans*)
3. Mexican sunflowers (*Tithonia rotundifolia*) or orange marigolds (*Tagetes erecta*)
4. Blue salvia (*Salvia farinacea*) and/or cornflowers (*Centaurea cyanus*)
5. Lemon yellow marigolds (*Targetes patula*) or gold strawflowers (*Helichrysum bracteatum*)

SUN—SOFT COLORS

1. Soft pink or peach phlox (*Phlox drummondii*)
2. Blue salvia (*Salvia farinacea*)
3. Blue delphinium (*Delphinium elatum*), scabiosa (*Scabiosa atropurpurea*), or cornflowers (*Centaurea cyanus*)
4. Pink ornamental kale (*Brassica oleracea*) or asters (*Callistephus chinensis*)
5. Pink snapdragon (*Antirrhinum majus*) or pale pink zinnias (*Zinnia elegans*) or pink nicotiana (*Nicotiana alata*)

Left: Scarlet sage rings a pine tree at Cantigny Museum, near Chicago. The circular bed is rimmed with wax begonias.

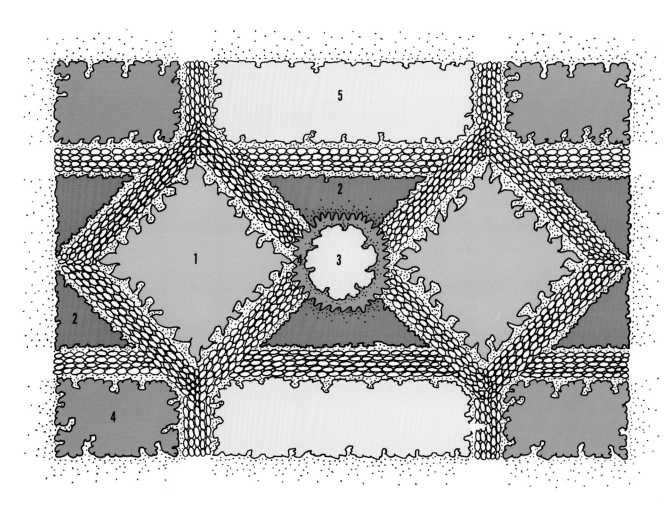

"FRENCH" FORMAL GARDEN; DIAMOND DESIGN

SHADE—BRIGHT COLORS

1. Hot pink impatiens (*Impatiens wallerana*)
2. White impatiens (*Impatiens wallerana*)
3. Tall, powder blue ageratum (*Ageratum houstonianum*)
4. Crystal palace lobelia (*Lobelia erinus*)
5. Lavender or crimson impatiens (*Impatiens wallerana*)

SHADE—SOFT COLORS

1. White impatiens (*Impatiens wallerana*)
2. Coral impatiens (*Impatiens wallerana*)
3. Blue salvia (*Salvia farinacea*) or Chinese forget-me-not
    (*Cynoglossum amabile*)
4. Pink w/white edge fibrous begonias (green foliage)
    (*Begonia* x *semperflorens*)
5. Cambridge blue lobelia (*Lobelia erinus*) or soft
    lavender impatiens (*Impatiens wallerana*)

Left: A mixture of 'Futura' hybrid impatiens in a shady area.

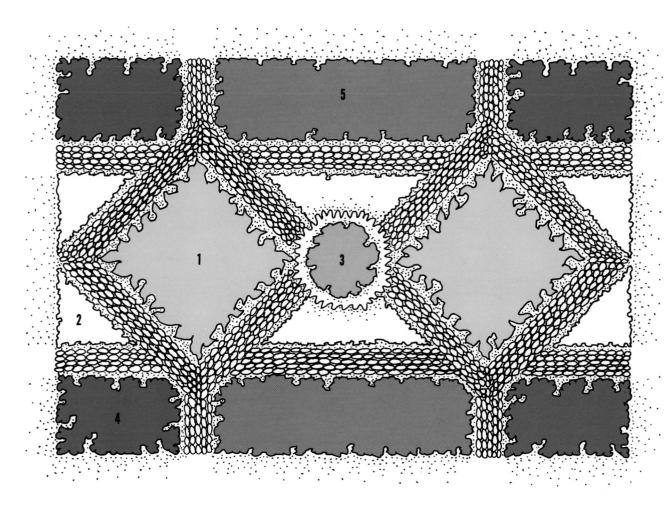

"ENGLISH" FORMAL GARDEN; CARTWHEEL DESIGN

SUN—COLOR WHEEL CUTTING GARDEN

1. Red snapdragons (*Antirrhinum majus*) or red phlox (*Phlox drummondii*), zinnia (*Zinnia elegans*), or cockscomb (*Celosia cristata*)
2. Orange American marigolds (*Tagetes erecta*) or Mexican sunflowers (*Tithonia rotundifolia*)
3. Gold helianthum (*Helianthum annuus*), coreopsis (*Coreopsis tinctoria*), or gloriosa daisies (*Rudbeckia hirta burpeeii*)
4. Lemon yellow snapdragon (*Antirrhinum majus*) or marigolds (*Tagetes erecta*)
5. Blue cornflowers (*Centaurea cyanus*)
6. Purple or violet aster (*Callistephus chinensis*), stock (*Matthiola incana*), or snapdragon (*Anthirrhinum majus*)
7. Hot pink cosmos (*Cosmos bipinnatus*)

SUN—SOFT, COLORS FOR A CUTTING GARDEN

1. Pink stock (*Matthiola incana*)
2. Pink snapdragons (*Antirrhinum majus*)
3. Pink zinnias (*Zinnia elegans*)
4. Pink phlox (*Phlox drummondii*) or pink cosmos (*Cosmos bipinnatus*)
5. Dusty miller (*Senecia cineraria*)
6. Lavender larkspur (*Consolida ambigua*)
7. White cosmos (*Cosmos bipinnatus*) and blue delphinium (*Delphinium elatum*) or cornflowers (*Centaurea cyanus*)

Left: Dwarf hybrid zinnias make spectacular bedding plants. This variety is 'Border Beauty Rose.'

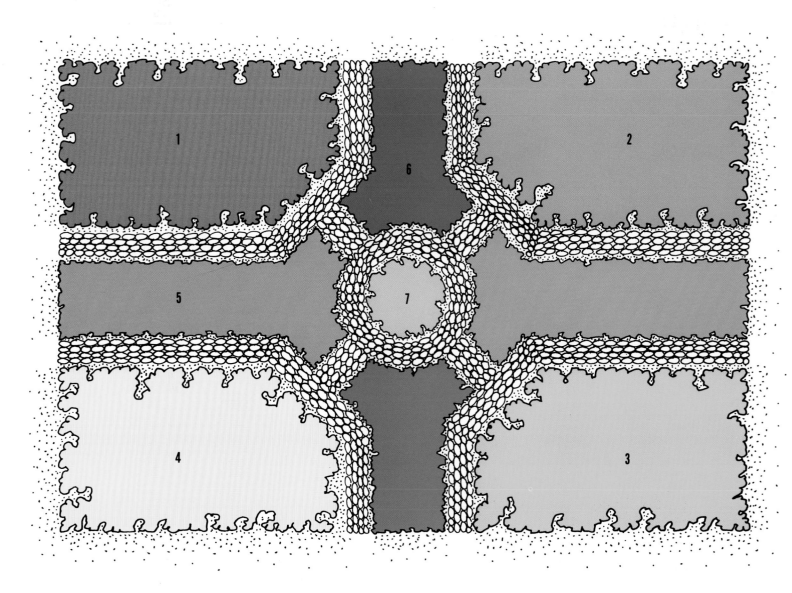

Though the following recommendations are all annuals, an early spring flowering display can be created by planting tulips in different colors. The same applies to all the formal designs that follow.

SHADE—SOFT COLORS

1. Peach or salmon impatiens (*Impatiens wallerana*)
2. Soft pink or rose impatiens (*Impatiens wallerana*)
3. Lavender impatiens (*Impatiens wallerana*)
4. Cambridge blue lobelia (*Lobelia erinus*)
5. White impatiens (*Impatiens wallerana*)

SHADE—WARM, SUNNY COLORS

1. Red impatiens (*Impatiens wallerana*)
2. Scarlet impatiens (*Impatiens wallerana*)
3. Yellow and orange mimulus (*Mimulus* x *hybridus*)
4. Yellow coleus (*Coleus* x *hybrida*)
Gray gravel path

Left: Beds filled with impatiens radiate from a circular pool, with brick paths accentuating its "cartwheel" design.

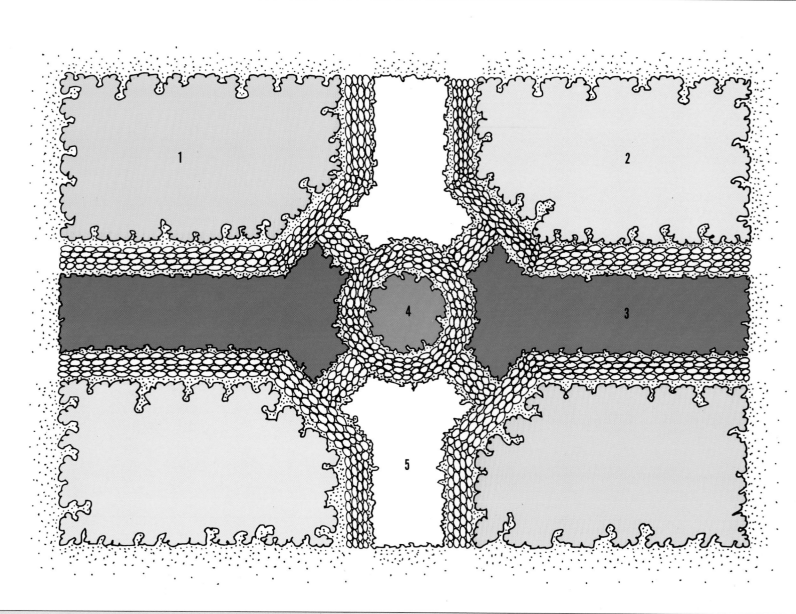

BUTTERFLY GARDEN (TO ATTRACT BUTTERFLIES)

Though the following plants are all annuals, this design can feature flowering bulbs, such as tulips, daffodils, and grape hyacinths, for an early spring display. Overplant this design with annuals for a mid-summer display.

1. Lavender stock (*Matthiola incana*)
2. Pink stock (*Matthiola incana*)
3. Hollyhocks, mixed colors (*Alcea rosea*)
4. Scabiosa, mixed colors (*Scabiosa atropurpurea*)
5. White alyssum (*Lobularia maritima*)
6. Rose asters (*Callistephus chinensis*)
7. Lavender verbena (*Verbena* x *hybrida*)
8. Yellow American marigolds (*Tagetes erecta*)
9. Red zinnias (*Zinnia elegans*)
10. Strawflowers, mixed colors (*Helichrysum bracteatum*)
11. Coreopsis (*Coreopsis tinctoria*)
12. Hot pink cosmos (*Cosmos bipinnatus*)
13. Lavender asters (*Callistephus chinensis*)

Stone paths with lavender and white alyssum growing in between stones.

Left: An informal cutting garden planted with cosmos, zinnias, and celosia.

SPRING PERENNIAL BORDER

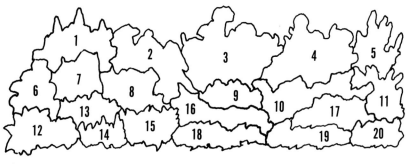

1. Russell Lupines (*Lupinus* hybrids)
2. Common Bleeding-heart (*Dicentra spectabilis*)
3. Oriental Poppy (*Papaver orientale*)
4. Herbaceous Peony (*Paeonia officinalis*)
5. Blue Wild Indigo (*Baptisia australis*)
6. Dogbane (*Doronicum cordatum*)
7. Blue-star Amsonia (*Amsonia tabernaemontana*)
8. Columbine (*Aquilegia* x *hybrida*)
9. Globeflower (*Trollius europaeus*)
10. Chilean Avens (*Geum chiloense*)
11. Primrose (*Primula* species)
12. Johnny Jump-Ups (*Viola cornuta*)
13. Great Solomon's-seal (*Polygonatum commutatum*)
14. Blue Bugle (*Ajuga reptans*)
15. Common Thrift (*Armeria maritima*)
16. Cottage Pink (*Dianthus plumarius*)
17. Perennial Candytuft (*Iberis sempervirens*)
18. Moss-pinks (*Phlox subulata*)
19. Perennial Alyssum (*Aurinia saxatilis*)
20. Forget-me-not (*Myosotis sylvatica*)

Other perennials not represented here, but that also look wonderful in a spring perennial border are: *Achillea tomentosa, Aubrieta deltoida, Bergenia cordifolia, Caltha palustris, Dictamnus albus, Digitalis* species, *Euphorbia epithymoides, Geranium sanguineum, Helleborus niger,* and *Penstemon hartwegii.*

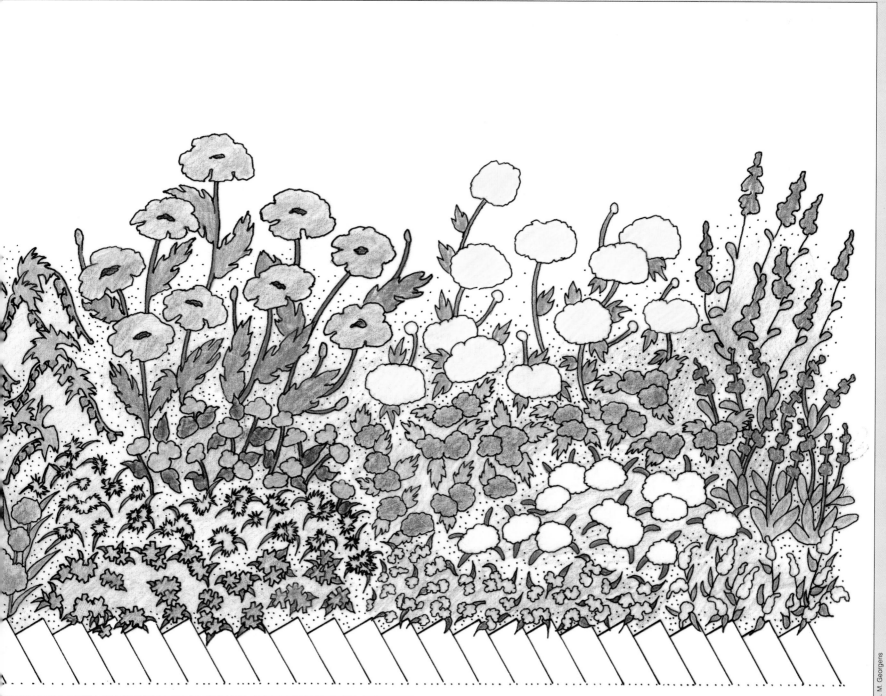

A. M. Georgens

EARLY SUMMER PERENNIAL BORDER

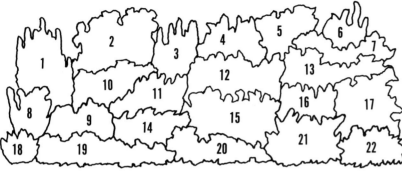

1. Foxglove (*Digitalis purpurea*)
2. Lily (*Lilium* hybrids)
3. Snakeroot (*Cimicifuga racemosa*)
4. Larkspur (*Delphinium elatum*)
5. Rose Mallow (*Hibiscus moscheutos*)
6. Purple Loosestrife (*Lythrum salicaria*)
7. Summer Phlox (*Phlox paniculata*)
8. Siberian Iris (*Iris sibirica*)
9. Spirea (*Astilbe* hybrids)
10. Feverfew (*Chrysanthemum parthenium*)
11. Red-hot Poker (*Kniphofia uvaria*)
12. Japanese Iris (*Iris kaempferi*)
13. Bee-balm (*Monarda didyma*)
14. Black-eyed Susan (*Rudbeckia hirta*)
15. Daylilies (*Hemerocallis* hybrids)
16. Bottlebrush (*Liatris spicata*)
17. Purple Coneflower (*Echinacea purpurea*)
18. Spanish Dagger (*Yucca filimentosa*)
19. Lance-leaf Coreopsis (*Coreopsis lanceolata*)
20. Blanket-flower (*Gaillardia* x *grandiflora*)
21. Plaintain-lily (*Hosta seiboldiana*)
22. Lily-turf (*Liriope muscari*)

A. M. Georgens

LATE SUMMER PERENNIAL BORDER

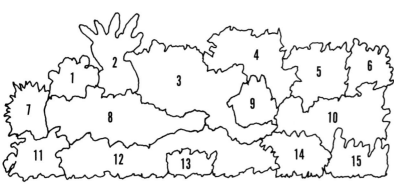

1. Japanese Anemone (*Anemone* x *hybrida*)
2. Pampas Grass (*Cortadera selloana*)
3. Michaelmas Daisy (*Aster novae-anglae*)
4. Sunflower (*Helianthus decapetalus*)
5. Sneezeweed (*Helenium autumnale*)
6. Perennial Ageratum (*Eupatorium fistulosum*)
7. Eulalia Grass (*Miscanthus sinensis*)
8. Sedum 'Autumn Joy'
9. Obedient Plant (*Physostegia virginiana*)
10. Stonecrop (*Sedum spectabile*)
11. Chinese Lanterns (*Physalis alkekengi*)
12. Garden Mum (*Chrysanthemum* x *morifolium*)
13. Artemisia 'Silver Mound'
14. Fountain Grass (*Pennisetum setaceum*)
15. Betony (*Stachys lanata*)

Other perennials not represented here, but that will look wonderful in a late-summer perennial border include: *Hosta* hybrids and *Solidago* hybrids.

A. M. Georgens

ISLAND BED OF SUMMER-FLOWERING BULBS

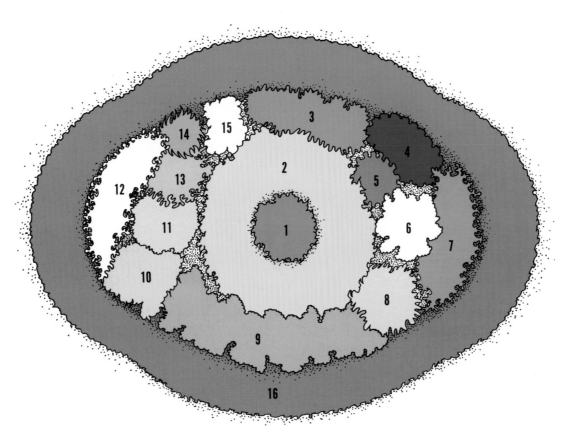

This design also works well with annuals and perennials, and a combination of the two.

1. Elephant ear (*Colocasia esculenta*)
2. Dahlia, mixed colors (*Dahlia pinnata*)
3. Orange-red Montbretia (*Crocosmia crocosmiiflora*)
4. Blue bearded iris (*Iris germanica*)
5. Red spider lily (*Lycoris radiata*)
6. White trumpet lily (*Lilium longiflorum*)
7. Blue African lily (*Lilium* species)
8. Pink gladiola (*Gladiolus africanus*)
9. Orange daylily (*Hemerocallis* hybrids)
10. Tiger-flowers, mixed colors (*Tigridia pavonia*)
11. Pink Nerine (*Nerine bowdenii*)
12. White calla lily (*Zantedeschia aethiopica*)
13. Pink amaryllis (*Crinum* x *powelii*)
14. Lime green pineapple lily (*Billbergia pyramidalis*)
15. White peacock flower (*Acidanthera bicolor*)
16. Rainbow plant, mixed colors (*Caladium* x *hortulanum*)

Left: These tulip borders in a woodland garden feature the Darwin hybrid tulip, 'Beauty of Apeldoorn', at the entrance to a driveway in Atlanta, Georgia.

INFORMAL BULB BORDER

This design can feature annuals or perennials, and a combination of both.

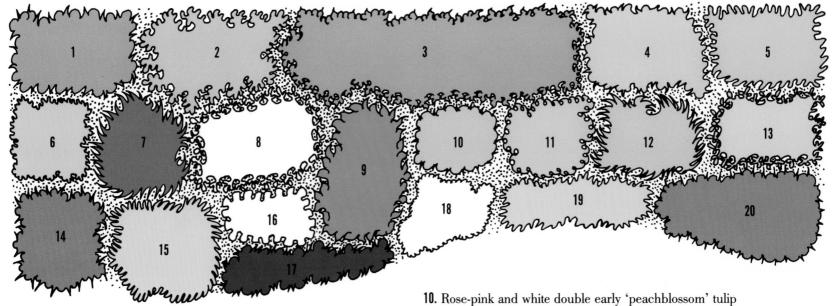

1. Orange General de Wet tulip (*Tulipa* species)
2. Rose pink on white garden party triumph tulip (*Tulipa* species)
3. Orange crown imperial (*Fritillaria imperialis*)
4. Soft apricot pink triumph tulip (*Tulipa* species)
5. Yellow and scarlet single early keizerschoon tulip (*Tulipa* species)
6. Yellow with orange cup Birma daffodil (*Narcissus* species)
7. Scarlet double early 'Stockholm' tulip (*Tulipa* species)
8. White and cream ice follies daffodil (*Narcissus* species)
9. Porcelain blue Bismark hyacinth (*Hyacinthus* species)
10. Rose-pink and white double early 'peachblossom' tulip (*Tulipa* species)
11. Deep yellow golden harvest daffodil (*Narcissus* species)
12. Rose-pink Princess Margaret hyacinth (*Hyacinthus* species)
13. Yellow double early tulip (*Tulipa* species)
14. Red foster tulip (*Tulipa fosteriana*)
15. Yellow and red parrot Texas flame tulip (*Tulipa* species)
16. White hyacinth (*Hyacinthus* species)
17. Grape hyacinth (*Muscari armeniacum*)
18. White with huge yellow and orange crown roulette daffodil (*Narcissus* species)
19. Yellow tarda tulip (*Tulipa tarda*)
20. Red emperor foster tulip (*Tulipa fosteriana*)

Left: This rainbow tulip border features different colors of Darwin hybrid tulips.

WINTER-FLOWERING BULB GARDEN

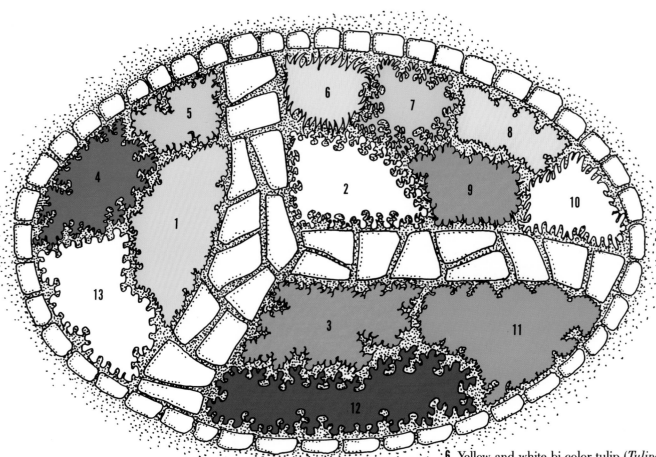

This design can feature herbs, annuals, or perennials, and a combination of all three.

1. Yellow aconite (*Eranthis hyemalis*)
2. White snowdrop (*Galanthus elwesii*)
3. Early dwarf blue Iris (*Iris reticulata*)
4. Purple snow crocus (*Crocus tomasinianus*)
5. Yellow tulip (*Tulipa daysystemon*)

6. Yellow and white bi-color tulip (*Tulipa kaufmanniana*)
7. February gold daffodil (*Narcissus* species)
8. Dwarf yellow iris (*Iris pseudacorus*)
9. Blue Siberian squill (*Scilla sibirica*)
10. White windflower (*Anemone blanda*)
11. Red foster tulip (*Tulipa fosteriana*)
12. Blue glory of the snow (*Chinodoxa lucilae*)
13. White spring snowflake (*Leucojum vernum*)

A. M. Georgens

Left: A sunny slope at Lentenboden Bulb Garden near New Hope, Pennsylvania, planted with early flowering tulips and hyacinths, beneath the flower-laden branches of a crabapple tree.

FREE-FORM BED OF SPRING AND SUMMER-FLOWERING BULBS

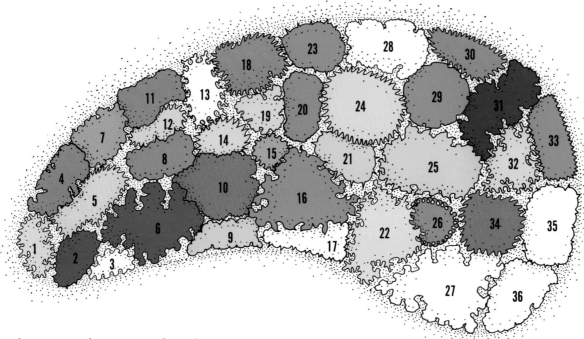

This design can feature annuals or perennials, and a combination of the two.

1. Yellow aconite (*Eranthis hyemalis*)
2. Purple crocus (*Crocus tomasinianus*)
3. White snowdrop (*Galanthus elwesii*)
4. Dwarf blue iris (*Iris reticulata*)
5. Golden yellow February gold daffodil (*Narcissus* species)
6. Purple common crocus (*Crocus vernus*)
7. Orange crown imperial (*Fritillaria imperialis*)
8. Red emperor tulip (*Tulipa* species)
9. Yellow tulip (*Tulipa tarda*)
10. Red and yellow bi-colored double-fringed beauty tulip (*Tulipa* species)

11. Blue hyacinth (*Hyacinthus hispanica*)
12. Yellow crocus (*Crocus flavus*)
13. White wildflower (*Anemone blanda*)
14. Yellow lily leek (*Allium moly*)
15. Orange crown imperial (*Fritillaria imperialis*)
16. Red and yellow bi-color Queen of Sheba tulip (*Tulipa* species)
17. White striped squill (*Puschkinia scilloides*)
18. Blue wild hyacinth (*Hyacinthus* species)
19. Yellow with orange cup roulette daffodil (*Narcissus* species)
20. Red and yellow bi-color Queen of Sheba Tulip (*Tulipa* species)
21. Yellow King Alfred daffodil (*Narcissus* species)

22. Pink lady derby hyacinth (*Hyacinth* species)
23. Red darwin hybrid Oxford tulip (*Tulipa* x *hybrida* 'Darwin')
24. Darwin hybrid golden springtime tulip (*Tulipa* x *hybrida* 'Darwin')
25. Yellow with gold cup 'Sempre Avanti' daffodil (*Narcissus* x *hybrida* 'Sempre Avanti')
26. Grape hyacinth (*Muscari armeniacum*)
27. White triumph tulip (*Tulipa* species)
28. White Mount Hood daffodil (*Narcissus* species)
29. Red parrot tulip (*Tulipa* species)
30. Blue wedgewood iris (*Iris* species)
31. Dark blue Bismark hyacinth (*Hyacinthus* species)
32. Yellow and red Texas flame tulip (*Tulipa* species)
33. Red devon daffodil (*Narcissus* species)
34. Red Darwin hybrid tulip (*Tulipa* x *hybrida* 'Darwin')
35. White spring snowflake (*Leucojum aestivum*)
36. White hyacinth L'Innocence (*Hyacinthus* x *hybrida* 'L'Innocence')

ROCK GARDEN FOR SPRING-FLOWERING BULBS

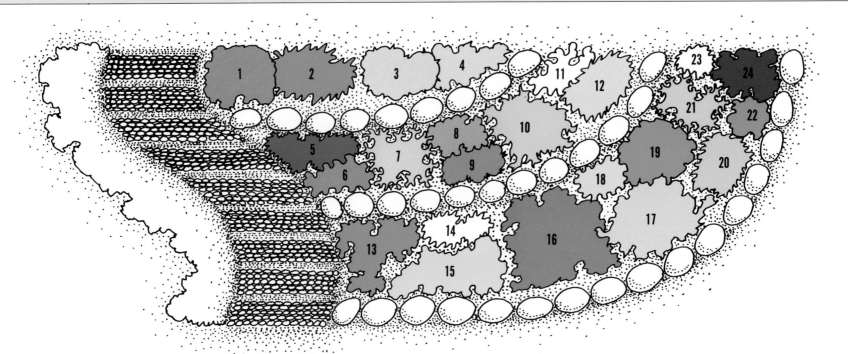

This design can feature herbs, annuals, or perennials, plus a combination of all three.

1. Delft blue hyacinth (*Hyacinthus orientalis*)
2. Red riding hood tulip (*Tulipa* species)
3. Pink pearl hyacinth (*Hyacinthus* species)
4. Yellow and red bi-color stresa Tulip (*Tulipa* species)
5. Giant purple crocus (*Crocus* species)
6. Blue Siberian squill (*Scilla sibirica*)
7. Gold coin tulip (*Tulipa* species)
8. Orange crown imperial (*Fritillaria imperialis*)
9. Grape hyacinth (*Muscari armeniacum*)
10. Yellow King Alfred daffodil (*Narcissus* species)
11. White windflower (*Anemone blanda*)

12. Yellow tulip (*Tulipa daysystemon*)
13. Red Apeldoorn tulip (*Tulipa* species)
14. White Mount Hood daffodil (*Narcissus* species)
15. Yellow aconite (*Eranthis hyemalis*)
16. Red emperor tulip (*Tulipa* species)
17. Pink ballade tulip (*Tulipa* species)
18. Yellow with gold cup Suzy daffodil (*Narcissus* species)
19. Red and white bi-color kees nelis tulip (*Tulipa* species)
20. Apricot beauty tulip (*Tulipa* species)
21. Yellow with gold cup Suzy daffodil (*Narcissus* species)
22. Red-and-white striped peppermint stick tulip (*Tulipa* species)
23. White snowdrop (*Galanthus elwesii*)
24. Dwarf blue iris (*Iris reticulata*)

A. M. Georgens

Left: Lily-flowered tulips and *Phlox divaricata* make good companions in this New Orleans garden.

ISLAND BED OF FALL-FLOWERING BULBS

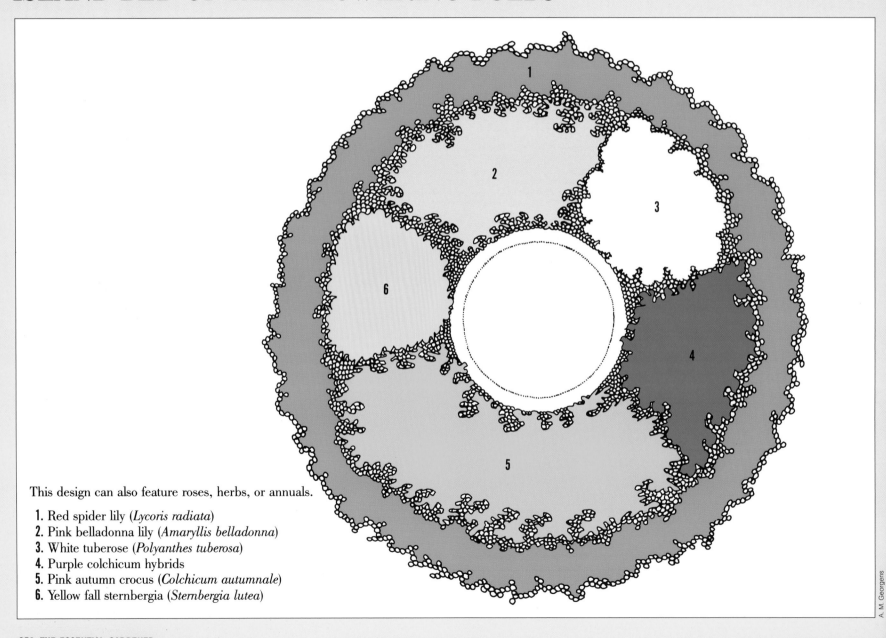

This design can also feature roses, herbs, or annuals.

1. Red spider lily (*Lycoris radiata*)
2. Pink belladonna lily (*Amaryllis belladonna*)
3. White tuberose (*Polyanthes tuberosa*)
4. Purple colchicum hybrids
5. Pink autumn crocus (*Colchicum autumnale*)
6. Yellow fall sternbergia (*Sternbergia lutea*)

A. M. Georgens

Left: The tulip 'Printemps' is thriving in light shade under this crabapple tree.

FORMAL BULB GARDEN

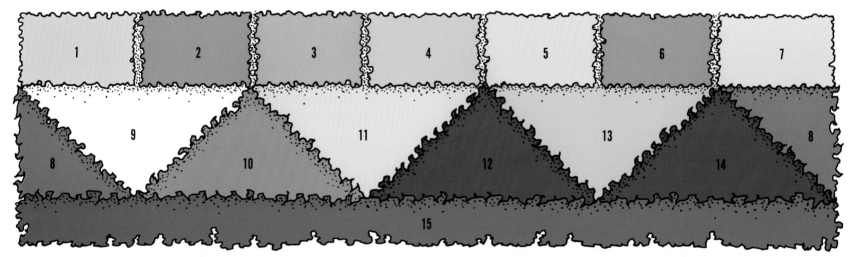

After the bulbs have finished blooming, the spaces can be planted with summer-flowering annuals to provide a succession of color.

1. Golden springtime Darwin hybrid tulip (*Tulipa* x *hybrida* 'Darwin')
2. Red General Eisenhower Darwin hybrid tulip (*Tulipa* x *hybrida* 'Darwin')
3. Orange sun Darwin hybrid tulip (*Tulipa* x *hybrida* 'Darwin')
4. Rose flushed pink Big Chief Darwin hybrid tulip (*Tulipa* x *hybrida* 'Darwin')
5. Yellow and carmine beauty of Apeldoorn, Darwin hybrid tulip (*Tulipa* x *hybrida* 'Darwin')
6. Red volcano Darwin hybrid tulip (*Tulipa* x *hybrida* 'Darwin')

7. Pink Elizabeth Arden Darwin hybrid tulip (*Tulipa* x *hybrida* 'Darwin')
8. Deep carmine rose Jan Bos hyacinth (*Hyacinthus* species)
9. Pure white 'L'Innocence' hyacinth (*Hyacinthus* x *hybrida* 'L'Innocence')
10. Porcelain blue Bismark Hyacinth (*Hyacinthus* species)
11. Soft yellow city of Haarlem hyacinth (*Hyacinthus* species)
12. Deep blue ostara hyacinth (*Hyacinthus* species)
13. Pale pink lady derby hyacinth (*Hyacinthus* species)
14. Sapphire blue Delft hyacinth (*Hyacinthus orientalis*)
15. Grape hyacinth (*Muscari armeniacum*)

Left: This small-space bulb garden features borders of tulips, daffodils, and grape hyacinths surrounding a lawn.

WATER GARDEN FEATURING SPRING AND SUMMER BULBS

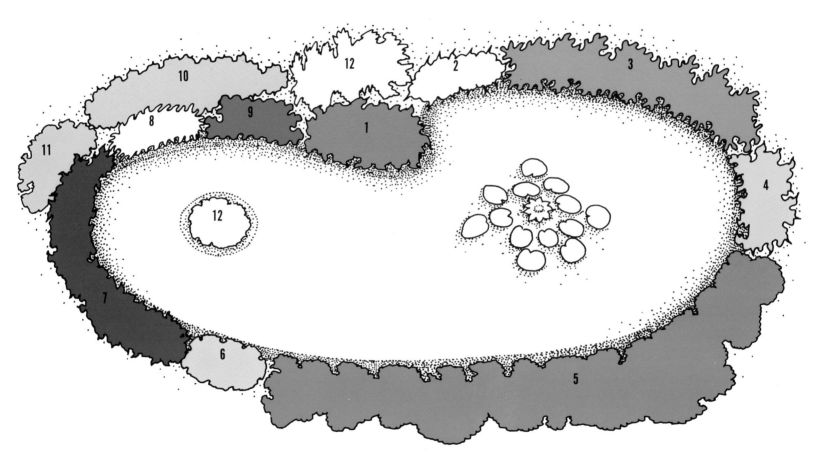

This design can also be planted with perennials and annuals, and a combination of the two.

1. Elephant ear (*Colocasia esculenta*)
2. White daffodil (*Narcissus* species)
3. Red canna (*Canna generalis*)
4. Yellow flag iris (*Iris pseudacorus*)
5. Rainbow plant, mixed colors (*Caladium* x *hortulanum*)
6. Yellow daffodil 'Sempre Avanti' (*Narcissus* species)

7. Blue Siberian iris (*Iris sibirica*)
8. White triumphator tulip (*Tulipa* species)
9. Purple Japanese iris (*Iris kaempferi*)
10. Peony-flowered tulip, mixed colors (*Tulipa* x *hybrida* 'Peony-flowered')
11. Yellow unsurpassable daffodil (*Narcissus* species)
12. White calla lily (*Zantedeschia aethiopica*)

A. M. Georgens

Left: A border of daffodils brighten a formal bulb garden at the Keukenhoff estate, Holland. This variety is called 'Flower Record'.

CUTTING GARDEN FOR ROSES

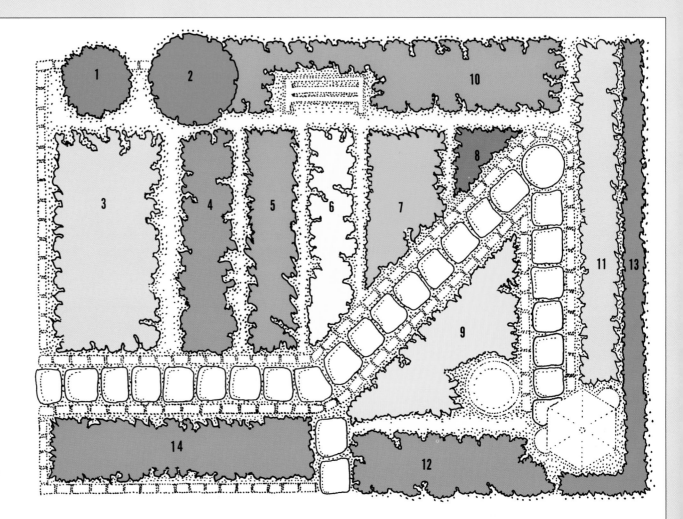

1. Grandiflora, Love
2. Climbing Rose, Blaze
3. Floribunda, Carefree Beauty
4. Floribunda, Impatient
5. Floribunda, French Lace
6. Floribunda, Marina
7. Grandiflora, Queen Elizabeth
8. Hybrid Tea, Peace
9. Hybrid Tea, Fragrant Cloud
10. Floribunda, Simplicity
11. Hybrid Tea, Dolly Parton
12. Climbing America on trellis
13. Hybrid Tea, Tropicana
14. Hybrid Tea, Tropicana

Left: A corner of the author's rose garden, featuring the hedge rose Robin Hood and climbing Blaze.

FLORIBUNDA ROSES

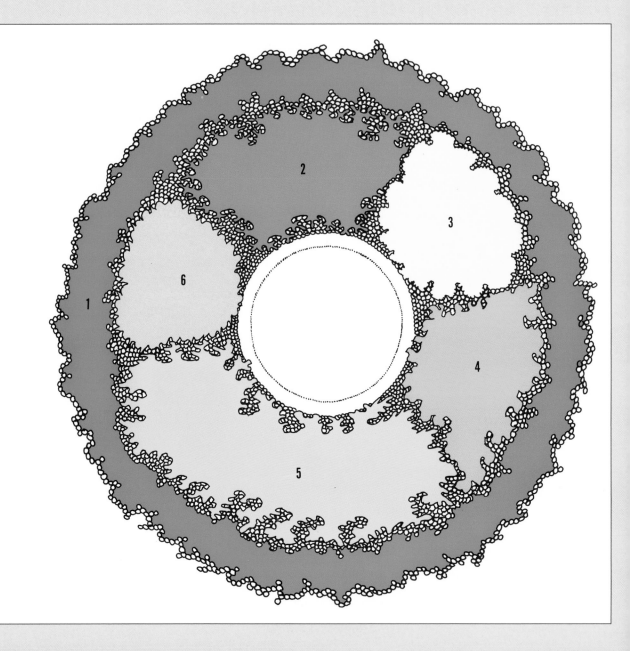

1. Miniature Starina for edging
2. Impatient
3. French Lace
4. Tropicana
5. Sun Flare
6. Gene Boerner

Left: Otto Linne, classified as a shrub rose, creates a wonderful hedge in the International Rose Test Garden, Portland, Oregon.

Right: The climbing rose, Blaze, is a favorite for covering garden structures, such as this archway, leading into a home garden.

Opposite page: Roses can play many different roles in the landscape. Just a few of these are: as a fence cover, espaliered against a wall, as a mass planting, in containers, and climbing up a wall.

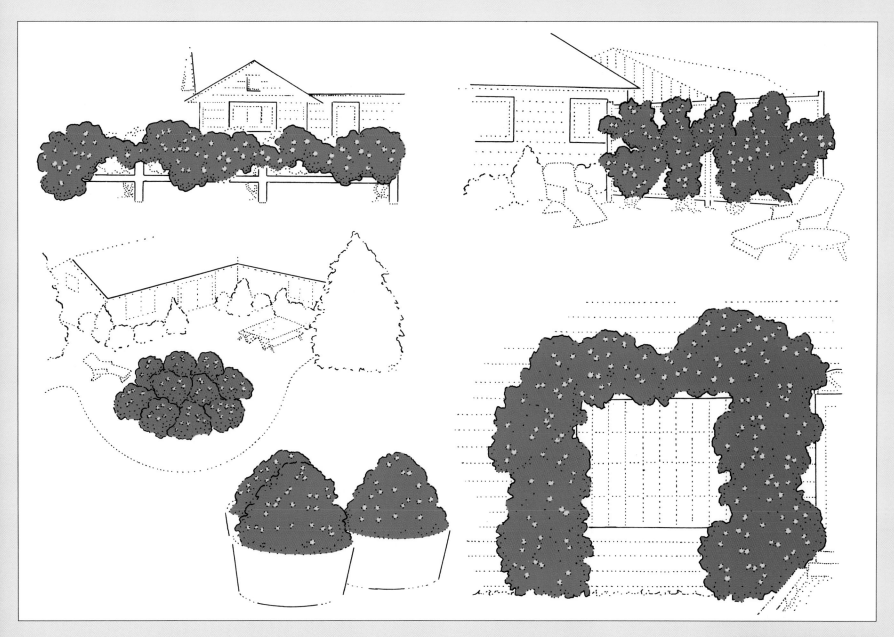

FORMAL PARTERRE GARDEN OF HERBS

This design also works well planted exclusively with roses, flowering bulbs, or annuals.

1. Germander (*Teucrium chamaedrys*)
2. Garden Sage (*Salvia officinalis*)
3. Chervil (*Anthriscus cerefolium*)
4. English Lavender (*Lavandula angustifolia*)
5. Parsley (*Petroselinum crispum*)
6. Rue (*Ruta graveolens*)
7. English Thyme (*Thymus vulgaris*)
8. Orris Root (*Iris germanica*)
9. True Chamomile (*Chamaemelum nobile*)
10. Dill (*Anethum graveolens*)
11. Lamb's-ears (*Stachys byzantina*)
12. Rosemary (*Rosmarinus officinalis*)
13. Spearmint (*Mentha spicata*)
14. Rose-scented Geranium (*Pelargonium graveolens*)
15. French Sorrel (*Rumex scutatus*)
16. Chive (*Allium schoenoprasum*)
17. Chinese Chive (*Allium tuberosum*)

Left: A classical cartwheel design incorporates an intricate knot garden of herbs at the Matthaei Botanical Garden, Ann Arbor, Michigan. Green germander and silvery lavender form the dwarf hedges for the knot design. Yellow yarrow blooms in the foreground and rear.

KNOT GARDEN DESIGNS

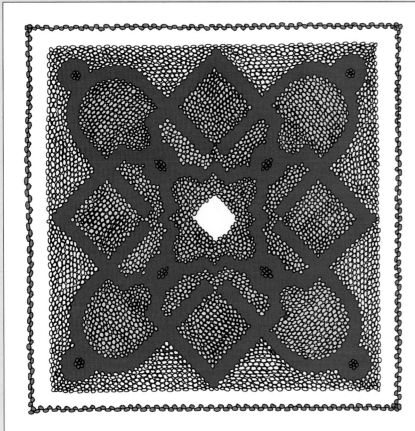

The two designs featured above appeared in a 1638 gardening book, entitled *The Country Housewife's Garden*, by William Lawson.

The following herbs, which are either low-growing or can be heavily pruned to form miniature hedges, are perfect for use in knot gardens.

Cheddar Pink *(Dianthus gratianopolitanus)*
Basil, especially Green Globe variety *(Ocimum basilicum)*
English Lavender *(Lavandula angustifolia)*

Rue *(Ruta graveolens)*
Garden Sage *(Salvia officinalis)*
Lavender-cotton *(Santolina chamaecyparis)*
English Thyme *(Thymus vulgaris)*
Germander *(Teucrium chamaedrys)*

In addition to the above herbs, certain dwarf shrubs are also included in herbal knot gardens, including Dwarf Red Barberry *(Berberis buxifolia)* and Dwarf English Boxwood *(Buxus sempervirens)*.

Left: This walled herb garden at Agecroft Hall, Virginia, features Elizabethan-style knot gardens. Germander and lavender are used to form the knot patterns, while silvery lamb's ears edge the beds in the rear.

CULINARY HERB GARDEN

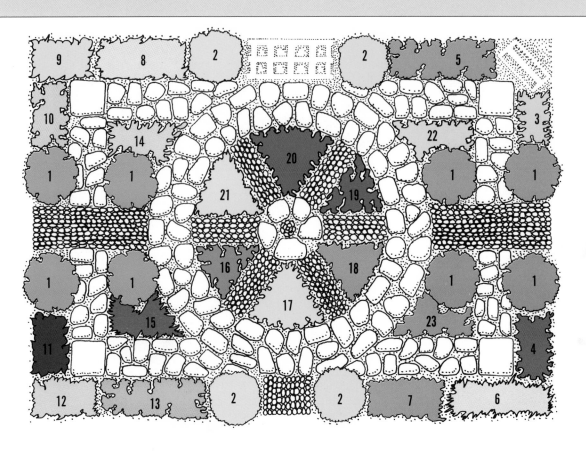

This garden plan also works well planted exclusively with roses or perennials.

1. Hardy-orange (*Poncirus trifoliata*)
2. Sweet Bay (*Laurus nobilis*)
3. Yarrow (*Achillea filipendulina*)
4. English Lavender (*Lavandula angustifolia*)
5. Chili Pepper (*Capsicum annuum*)
6. Chive (*Allium schoenoprasum*)

7. Garlic Chive (*Allium tuberosum*)
8. English Thyme (*Thymus vulgaris*)
9. Pyrethrum (*Chrysanthemum coccineum*)
10. Cheddar Pink (*Dianthus gratianopolitanus*)
11. Foxglove (*Digitalis purpurea*)
12. Teasel (*Dipsacus sylvestris*)
13. Butterfly Milkweed (*Asclepias tuberosa*)
14. Golden Marguerite (*Anthemis tinctoria*)
15. Pineapple Sage (*Salvia elegans*)
16. Rosemary (*Rosmarinus officinalis*)
17. American Marigold (*Tagetes erecta*)
18. Garden Valerian (*Valeriana officinalis*)
19. Scarlet Bee-balm (*Monarda didyma*)
20. Sweet Heliotrope (*Heliotropum arborescens*)
21. Dill (*Anthem graveolens*)
22. Nasturtium (*Tropaeolum majus*)
23. Lamb's-ears (*Stachys byzantina*)

GARDEN OF HERBS, VEGETABLES, AND FRUITS

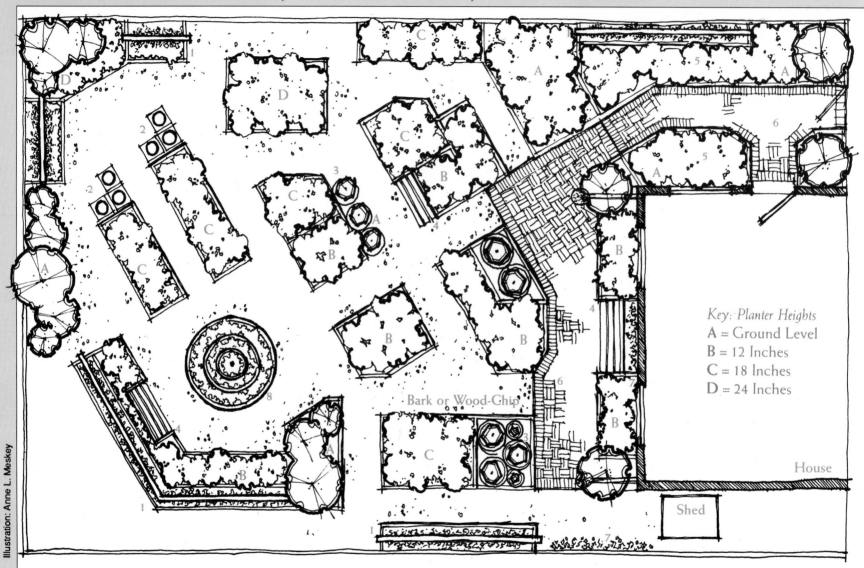

Illustration: Anne L. Meskey

Key: Planter Heights
A = Ground Level
B = 12 Inches
C = 18 Inches
D = 24 Inches

Bark or Wood-Chip

House

Shed

1. Trellis for pole beans
2. Columns, varied heights with potted plants
3. Pots or tubs
4. Bench

5. Herb gardens
6. Red brick terrace
7. Vine or espaliered fruit tree
8. Strawberry (*Fragraria fragraria*)
   three-tiered planter

This backyard garden, designed by Joan Pierson, uses raised beds to grow mostly herbs, fruits, and vegetables.

VEGETABLE AND HERB GARDEN FOR SPRING, SUMMER, AND FALL HARVESTS

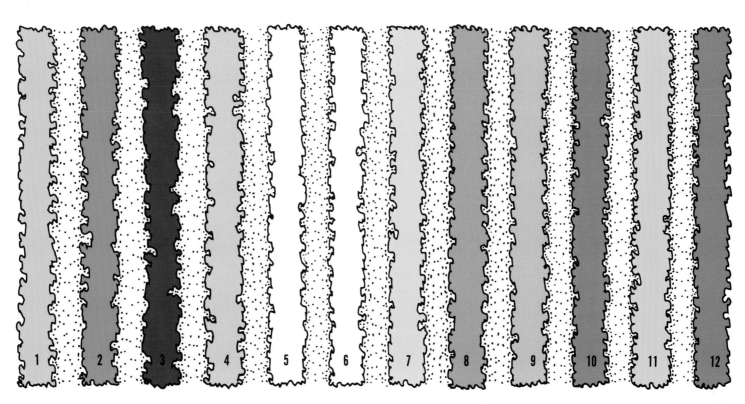

1. Asparagus (*Asparagus officinalis*)
2. Tomatoes (*Lycopersicum esculentum*)
3. Peppers (*Capsicum annuum grossum*)
4. Cabbage (*Brassica oleracea capitata*)
5. Bush snap peas (*Pisum sativum*)
6. Lettuce (*Latuca sativa*) followed by brussels sprouts (*Brassica oleracea gemmifera*)
7. English peas (*Pisum sativum*), followed by zucchini squash (*Cucurbita* species)
8. Spinach (*Spinacea oleracea*) followed by carrots (*Daucus carota sativa*)
9. Irish (*Solanum tuberosum*) or sweet potatoes (*Ipomoea batatus*)
10. Broccoli (*Brassica oleracea botrytis*) and cauliflower (*Brassica oleracea botrytis*), followed by beets (*Beta vulgaris*)
11. Cucumber (*Cucumis sativus*)
12. Mixed row of herbs: parsley (*Petroselinum crispum*), chives (*Allium schoenoprasum*), basil (*Ocimum basilicum*), and sage (*Salvia officinalis*)

HARDINESS ZONE MAP

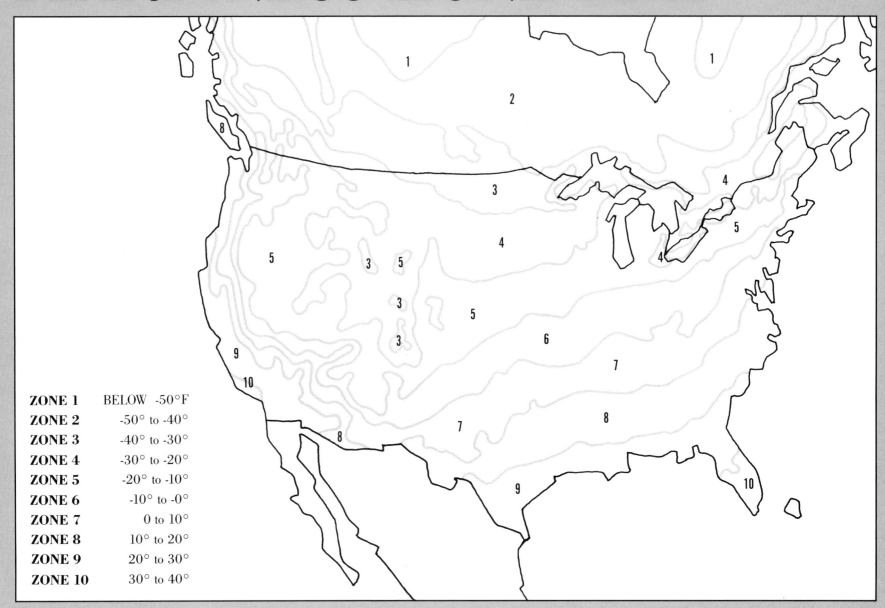

ZONE 1	BELOW -50°F
ZONE 2	-50° to -40°
ZONE 3	-40° to -30°
ZONE 4	-30° to -20°
ZONE 5	-20° to -10°
ZONE 6	-10° to -0°
ZONE 7	0 to 10°
ZONE 8	10° to 20°
ZONE 9	20° to 30°
ZONE 10	30° to 40°

MAIL-ORDER SOURCES

ANNUALS

Applewood Seed Co.
Box 10761, Edgemont Station
Golden, CO 80401

W. Atlee Burpee
300 Park Ave.
Warminster, PA 18974

Comstock Ferre & Co.
263 Main St.
Wethersfield, CT 06109

Dominion Seed House
115 Guelph St.
Georgetown, Ontario
Canada L7G 4A2

Henry Field Seed & Nursery Co.
407 Sycamore St.
Shenandoah, IA 51602

Gurney Seed & Nursery Co.
Yankton, SD 57079

Joseph Harris Co.
Moreton Farm
Rochester, NY 14624

H.G. Hastings Co.
Box 4274
Atlanta, GA 30302

The Charles Hart Seed Co.
Main & Hart Streets
Wethersfield, CT 06109

J.L. Hudson, Seedsman
Box 1058
Redwood City, CA 94064

Johnny's Selected Seeds
Albion, ME 04910

J.W. Jung Seed Co.
Randolph, WI 53956

Laval Seeds Inc.
3505 Boul St. Martin
Chomedey Laval
Quebec, Canada H7V 2T3

Orol Ledden & Sons
Center St.
Sewell, NJ 08080

Earl May Seed & Nursery Co.
Shenandoah, IA 51603

McLaughlins Seeds
Box 550
Mead, WA 99021

Mellingers Inc.
North Lima, OH 44452

Nichol's Herbs & Rare Seeds
1190 N. Pacific Hwy.
Albany, OR 97321

L.L. Olds Seed Co.
2901 Packers Ave.
Madison, WI 53707

George W. Park Seed Inc.
Greenwood, SC 29647

W.H. Perron & Co. Ltd.
515 Labelle Blvd.
Chomedey Laval
Quebec, Canada H7V 2T3

Plants of the Southwest
1812 Second St.
Santa Fe, NM 87501

Clyde Robin Seed Co.
Box 2366
Castro Valley, CA 94546

Stokes Seed Inc.
Box 548
Buffalo, NY 14240

Thompson & Morgan
Box 1308
Jackson, NJ 08527

Otis S. Twilley Seed Co.
Box 65
Trevose, PA 19047

PERENNIALS

UNIQUE AND RARE

Andre Viette Nursery
Route 1, Box 16
Fisherville, VA 22939

Kurt Bluenol, Inc.
2543 Hess Road
Fallston, MD 21047

Bluestone Perennials
7211 Middle Ridge Rd.
Madison, OH 44057

Canyon Creek Nursery
3527 Dry Creek Rd.
Oroville, CA 95965
Catalog $1

Carroll Gardens
P.O. Box 310
Westminster, MD 21157

Heaths & Heathers
Box 850
Elma, WA 98541

Holbrook Farm & Nursery
Route 2, Box 223B
Fletcher, NC 28732

Stallings Nursery
910 Encinitas Blvd.
Encinitas, CA 92024
Catalog $2

Wayside Gardens
Hodges, SC 29695-0001

Western Hills Nursery
16250 Coleman Valley Rd.
Occidental, CA 95465
Plant list $2

White Flower Farm
Litchfield, CT 06759
Catalog $5

Wildwood Farm
10300 Highway 12
Kenwood, CA 95452

Yerba Buena Nursery
19500 Skyline Blvd.
Woodside, CA 94062

BULBS

SPRING- AND SUMMER-BLOOMING
Bakker of Holland
Box 50
Louisiana, MO 63353
Catalog free

Brecks
Box 1757
Peoria, IL 61656
Catalog free

Burpee Bulbs
300 Park Ave.
Warminster, PA 18974
Catalog free

Peter De Jager Bulb Co.
Box 2010
South Hamilton, MA 01982
Catalog free

Dutch Gardens
Box 200
Adelphia, NJ 07710
Catalog $1.00

Gurney Seed & Nursery
Second & Capital Streets
Yankton, SD 57078
Catalog free

International Growers Exchange
Box 52248
Livonia, MI 48152
Catalog $5.00

J.W. Jung Co.
335 S. High St.
Randolph, WI 53957
Catalog free

Earl May Nursery Co.
Box 500
Shenandoah, IA 51603
Catalog free

Messelaar Bulb Co.
Box 269
Ipswich, MA 01938
Catalog free

Michigan Bulb Co.
1950 Waldorf NW
Grand Rapids, MI 49550
Catalog free

Park Seed Co.
Box 46
Greenwood, SC 29648
Catalog free

Pinetree Garden Seeds
Rte. 100N
Gloucester, ME 04260
Catalog free

John Scheepers Inc.
63 Wall St.
New York, NY 10005
Catalog free

Ty Ty Plantation
Box 159
Ty Ty, GA 31795
Catalog free

K. Van Bourgandien & Sons, Inc.
Box A
Babylon, NY 11702
Catalog free

Van Engelen, Inc.
307 Maple St.
Litchfield, CT 06759
Catalog free

Waushara Gardens
Box 570
Plainsfield, WI 54966
Catalog $1.00

Wayside Gardens
Box 1
Hodges, SC 29695
Catalog $1.00

White Flower Farm
Rte. 63
Litchfield, CT 06759
Catalog $5.00

AMARYLLIS (HIPPEASTRUM)
Amaryllis Inc.
Box 318
Baton Rouge, LA 78021
Catalog $1.00

BEGONIAS
Antonelli Brothers
2545 Capitol Rd.
Santa Cruz, CA 95062
Catalog $1.00

Fairyland Begonia Garden
1100 Griffith Rd.
McKinleyville, CA 95521
Catalog 50¢

Kartuz Greenhouses
1408 Sunset Dr.
Vista, CA 92083
Catalog $2.00

DAHLIAS
Blue Dahlia Gardens
Box 316
San Jose, IL 62682
Catalog free

Connell's Dahlias
10216 40th Ave.
Tacoma, WA 98446
Catalog $1.00

Dahlias by Phil Traff
1316 132nd Ave.
Summer, WA 98390
Catalog free

Legg Dahlia Gardens
1069 Hastings Rd.
Geneva, NY 14456
Catalog free

Swan Island Dahlias
Box 800
Canby, OR 97013
Catalog $2.00

GLADIOLUS
Flad's Glads
2109 Cliff Ct.
Madison, WI 53713
Catalog $1.00

Gladside Gardens
61 Main St.
Northfield, MA 01360

HEMEROCALLIS (DAYLILIES)
American Daylily & Perennials
Box 7008
The Woodlands, TX 77380
Catalog $3.00

Daylily World
Box 1612
Sanford, FL 32771
Catalog free

Greenwood Nursery
Box 1610
Goleta, CA 93116
Catalog $3.00

Klehm Nursery
Box 197
South Barrington, IL 60010
Catalog $2.00

Gilbert H. Wild & Son, Inc.
P.O. Box 338
1112 Joplin Street
Sarcoxie, MO 64862
Catalog $2.00

IRIS
Comanche Acres Iris Gardens
Box 258
Gower, MO 64454
Catalog $1.00

Cooley's Gardens
Box 126
11553 Silverton Rd., NE
Silverton, OR 97381
Catalog $2.00

French Irish Gardens
621 S. 3rd Ave.
Walla Walla, WA 99362
Catalog $2.00

Garden of the Enchanted Rainbow
Box 439
Killeen, AL 35645
Catalog $1.00

Maple Tree Gardens
Box 278
Ponca, NE 68770
Catalog free

McMillens Iris Garden
R.R. #1
Norwich, ONT Canada, N0J 1P0
Catalog free

Shreiners Gardens
3625 Quinaby Rd. NE
Salem, OR 97303
Catalog $2.00

LILIUM
Oregon Bulb Farms
14071 N.E. Arndt Rd.
Aurora, OR 97002
Catalog $2.00

Rex Bulb Farms
Box 774
Port Townsend, WA 98368
Catalog free

NARCISSUS
The Daffodil Mart
Box 794
Gloucester, VA 23061
Catalog free

Grant Mitsch Novelty Daffodils
Box 218
Hubbard, OR 97032
Catalog $3.00

Charles H. Mueller
River Rd.
New Hope, PA 18938
Catalog free

Oakwood Daffodils
2330 W. Bertrand Rd.
Niles, MI 49120
Catalog free

TULIPS
Veldheer Tulip Gardens
12755 Quincy St.
Holland, MI 49424
Catalog free

ROSES

MODERN
Armstrong Roses
P.O. Box 1020
Somis, CA 93066
Catalog free

BDK Nursery
P.O. Box 628
2091 Haas Rd.
Apopka, FL 32712
Catalog free

Emlong Nurseries
2671 W. Marquette Woods Rd.
Stevensville, MI 49127
Catalog free

Gurney Seed & Nursery Co.
2nd & Capital
Yankton, SD 57078
Catalog free

Hastings
P.O. Box 4274
Atlanta, GA 30302-4274
Catalog free

Hortico, Inc.
723 Robson Rd., R.R.1
Waterdown, ON, Canada L0R2H0
Catalog free

Jackson & Perkins Co.
P.O. Box 1028
Medford, OR 97501
Catalog free

Krider Nurseries
P.O. Box 29
Middlebury, IN 46540
Catalog free

McConnell Nurseries, Inc.
R.R.1
Port Burwell, ON, Canada N0J1T0
Catalog free

Milaeger's Gardens
4838 Douglas Ave.
Racine, WI 53402-2498
Catalog $1.00

Rose Acres
6641 Crystal Blvd.
Diamond Springs, CA 95619
Catalog free with 9½" long self-addressed envelope.

Roses by Fred Edmunds
6235 S.W. Kahle Rd.
Wilsonville, OR 97070
Catalog free

Savage Farms Nursery
P.O. Box 125
Highway 56 South
McMinnville, TN 37110
Catalog free

Spring Hill Nurseries Co.
P.O. Box 1758
Peoria, IL 61656
Catalog free

Stark Brothers Nurseries &
Orchard Co.
Highway 54 West
Louisiana, MO 63353-0010
Catalog free

Thomasville Nurseries
P.O. Box 7
1842 Smith Ave.
Thomasville, GA 31799-0007
Catalog free

Wayside Gardens
P.O. Box 1
Hodges, SC 29695-0001
Catalog $1.00

MINIATURE

Justice Miniature Roses
5947 S.W. Kahle Rd.
Wilsonville, OR 97070
Catalog free

MB Farm Miniature Roses
Jamison Hill Rd.
Clinton Corners, NY 12514
Catalog free

McDaniel's Miniature Roses
7523 Zemco St.
Lemon Grove, CA 92045
Catalog free

Mini-Roses
P.O. Box 4255, Sta.A
Dallas, TX 75208
Catalog free

Miniature Plant Kingdom
4125 Harrison Grade Rd.
Sebastopol, CA 95472
Catalog $2.50

Nor'East Miniature Roses
58 Hammond St.
Rowley, MA 01969
Catalog free

The Rose Garden &
Mini Rose Nursery
P.O. Box 560
SC Highway 560 (Austin Street)
Cross Hill, SC 29332-0560
Catalog free

Rosehill Farm
Gregg Neck Rd.
Galena, MD 21635
Catalog free

Tiny Petals Nursery
489 Minot Ave.
Chula Vista, CA 92010
Catalog free

ANTIQUE

Antique Rose Emporium
Route 5, Box 143
Brenham, TX 77833
Catalog $2.00

Greenmantle Nursery
3010 Ettersburg Rd.
Garberville, CA 95440
Catalog $3.00

Heritage Rosarium
211 Haviland Mill Rd.
Brookville, MD 20833
Catalog $1.00

Heritage Rose Gardens
16831 Mitchell Creek Dr.
Ft. Bragg, CA 95437
Catalog $1.00

High Country Rosarium
1717 Downing St.
Denver, CO 80218
Catalog $1.00

Historical Roses
1657 W. Jackson St.
Painesville, OH 44077
Catalog free with 9½" long self-addressed envelope.

Lowe's Own-Root Roses
6 Sheffield Rd.
Nashua, NH 03062
Catalog $2.00

Pickering Nurseries Inc.
670 Kingston Rd. (Hwy. 2)
Pickering, ON, Canada L1V1A6
Catalog $2.00

Roses of Yesterday & Today
802 Brown's Valley Rd.
Watsonville, CA 95076-0398
Catalog $2.00

TREES AND SHRUBS

Beaver Creek Nursery
7526 Pelleaux Rd.
Knoxville, TN 37938
Specializes in collector's trees
and shrubs.
Catalog $1.00

The Bovees Nursery
1737 S.W. Coronado
Portland, OR 97219
Specializes in species and hybrid
rhododendrons.
Catalog $2.00

W. Atlee Burpee Co.
300 Park Ave.
Warminster, PA 18974
Offers plants, seeds, books, supplies,
tools, and bulbs.
Catalog free

Carroll Gardens
P.O. Box 310
444 East Main St.
Westminster, MD 21157
Large selection including hollies,
yews, viburnums, and much more.
Catalog $2.00

Gardens of the Blue Ridge
P.O. Box 10
U.S. 221 N.
Pineola, NC 28662
Good selection of native shrubs.
Catalog $2.00

Girard Nurseries
P.O. Box 428
6801 North Ridge (US 20)
Geneva, OH 44041
Broad selection of flowering shrubs,
dwarf conifers, rhododendrons,
azaleas, and hollies.
Catalog free

Gurney Seed & Nursery Co.
2nd and Capital
Yankton, SC 57078
Offers broad selection of plants
and seeds.
Catalog free

Hall Rhododendrons
1280 Quince Dr.
Junction City, OR 97448
Offers broad selection of species and
hybrid rhododendrons and azaleas.
Catalog $1.00

Hortico, Inc.
723 Robson Rd., R.R.1
Waterdown, ON, Canada
L0R2H0
Specializes in a broad selection of
garden perennials along with ornamental trees, shrubs, ferns, wildflowers, and conifers.
Catalog free

Krider Nurseries
P.O. Box 29
Middlebury, IN 46540
Broad selection of fruit trees, ber-
ries, ornamental trees, shrubs, and
roses.
Catalog free

Lawyer Nursery, Inc.
950 Highway 200 West
Plains, MT 59859
Many types of ornamental trees, fruit
and nut trees, rootstock for fruit
trees, conifers, and shrubs.
Catalog free

Musser Forests, Inc.
P.O. Box 340
Route 119 North
Indiana, PA 15710-0340
Supplies trees, shrubs, and
ground covers.
Catalog free

Spring Hill Nurseries Co.
P.O. Box 1758
Peoria, IL 61656
Broad selection of perennials, flower-
ing shrubs, ground covers.
Catalog free

Wayside Gardens
P.O. Box 1
Hodges, SC 29695-0001
Offers ornamental trees and shrubs.
Catalog $1.00

HERBS

Abundant Life Seed Foundation
Box 771
1029 Lawrence
Port Townsend, WA 98368
Offers a wide selection of
herb seeds.
Catalog $1.00

W. Atlee Burpee Co.
300 Park Ave.
Warminster, PA 18974
Offers both herb seeds and plants.
Catalog free

Caprilands Herb Farm
Silver St.
North Coventry, CT 06238
Offers herb plants. Display gardens
open to the public.

Carroll Gardens
Box 310
Westminster, MD 21157
Offers perennial herb plants.
Catalog $2.00

Comstock, Ferre & Company
Box 125
Wethersfield, CT 06109
Offers herb seeds.
Catalog free

The Cook's Garden
Box 65
Moffits Bridge
Londonderry, VT 05148
Offers an extensive selection
of herbs.
Catalog $1.00

Fox Hill Farm
440 West Michigan Ave.
Parma, MI 49269
Offers 350 varieties of herbs and
scented geraniums.
Catalog $1.00

Le Jardin du Gourmet
Box 44 West
Danville, VT 05873-0044
Features packets of herb seed at
low cost.
Catalog 50¢

Nichols Garden Nursery
1190 North Pacific Hwy.
Albany, OR 97321
Offers herbs to grow from seed.
Catalog free

Geo. W. Park Seed Co.
Box 31
398 Cokesbury Rd.
Greenwood, SC 29647
Features herbs to grow from seed.
Catalog free

Pinetree Garden Seeds
Route 100 North
New Gloucester, ME 04260
Features many herbs to grow
from seed.
Catalog free

Redwood City Seed Co.
Box 361
Redwood City, CA 94064
Offers herbs to grow from seed.
Catalog 50¢

Roses of Yesterday & Today
802 Brown's Valley Rd.
Watsonville, CA 95076
Offers fragrant and old fashioned
roses for potpourri.
Catalog $1.00

Thompson & Morgan
Box 1308
Jackson, NJ 08527
Offers herb seeds.
Catalog free

Well-Sweep Herb Farm
317 Mt. Bethel Rd.
Port Murray, NJ 07865
Offers herb plants. Display gardens
open to the public.
Catalog $1.00

CROSS-REFERENCE OF BOTANICAL AND COMMON NAMES

Amazon-lily. *See Eucharis grandiflora*
Amelanchier arborea (s/t), 440
American aloe. *See Agave americana*
American bittersweet. *See Celastrus scandens*
American holly. *See Ilex opaca*
American marigold. *See Tagetes erecta*
American pillar (r), 351
Amphora fruticosa angustifolia (h/v), 546
Amsonia tabernaemontana (p), 130
Anaranthus hybridus hypochondriacus (h/v), 545
Anchusa azurea (p), 130
Anchusa capensis (a), 33
Andromeda. *See Pieris japonica*
Anemone. *See Anemone coronaria; Anemone x hybrida*
Anemone blanda (b), 225
Anemone coronaria (b), 226
Anemone x hybrida (p), 131
Anemone pulsatilla (p), 131
Anethum graveolens (h/v), 546
Angelica. *See Angelica archangelica*
Angelica archangelica (h/v), 547
Angel's-tears. *See Narcissus triandrus*
Angel's trumpet. *See Datura metel*
Anise. *See Pimpinella anisum*
Anise hyssop. *See Agastache foeniculum*
Anthemis nobilis (h/v), 547
Anthemis tinctoria (p), 132
Anthriscus cerefolium (h/v), 548

Antirrhunum majus (a), 33
Apium graveolens dulce (h/v), 548
Apple mint. *See Mentha suaveolens*
Apple rose. *See Rosa pomifera*
Apple tree. *See Malus* hybrids
Aquilegia hybrids (p), 132
Arabis caucasia (p), 133
Aralia. *See Fatsia japonica*
Arctotis stoechadifolia (a), 34
Ardisia. *See Ardisia japonica*
Ardisia japonica (s/t), 440
Arizona (r), 346
Armeria maritima (p), 133
Armoracia rusticana (h/v), 549
Artemesia absinthium (h/v), 549
Artemesia dracunculus sativa (h/v), 550
Artemesia ludoviciana (p), 134
Artichoke. *See Cynara scholymus*
Arum. *See Arum italicum*
Arum italicum (p), 134
Asclepias tuberosa (p), 136
Asiatic hybrid lilies. *See Lilium hybrida 'asiatic'*
Asparagus. *See Asparagus officinalis*
Asparagus officinalis (h/v), 550
Asperula odorata (h/v), 567
Aster. *See Callistephus chinensis; Stokesia laevis*
Aster novae-angliae (p), 136
Astilbe x arendsii (p), 137
Atamasco lily. *See Zephyranthes atamasco*
Atlas cedar. *See Cedrus atlantica*

Aubrieta deltoide (p), 137
Aucuba japonica 'Variegata' (s/t), 441
Aurinia saxatilis (p), 138
Austriah briar rose. *See Rosa foetida*
Autumn-crocus. *See Colchcum autumnale*
Avens. *See Geum chiloense*
Azalea. *See Rhododendron* sp.

B

Babiana stricta (b), 226
Baboon flower. *See Babiana stricta*
Baby-blue-eyes. *See Nemophila menziesii*
Baby's-breath. *See Gypsophilia elegans; Gypsophilia paniculata*
Bachelor's-button. *See Centaurea cyanus*
Balloonflower. *See Platycodon grandiflorus*
Balsam. *See Impatiens balsamina*
Bamboo. *See Nandina domestica*
Baptisia australis (p), 138
Barbados aloe. *See Aloe barbadensis*
Barberry. *See Berberis thunbergii atropurpurea*
Baronne Prevost (r), 367
Basi. *See Ocimum basilicum*
Basket of gold. *See Aurinia saxatilis*
Bastard indigo. *See Amphora fruticosa angustifolia*

Bay. *See Laurus nobilis*
Bean. *See Phaseolus limensis; Phaseolus vulgaris; Vicia faba*
Bear's-breech. *See Acanthus mollis*
Bearded iris. *See Iris germanica*
Bearded tongue. *See Penstemon gloxinoides*
Beaumontia grandiflora (s/t), 441
Beauty berry. *See Callicarpa japonica*
Beauty bush. *See Kolkwitzia amabilis*
Beauty secret (r), 359
Bedding dahlias. *See Dahlia x hybrida*
Bee-balm. *See Monarda citriodora; Monarda didyma*
Beech. *See Fagus sylvatica*
Beefsteak plant. *See Perilla frutescens*
Beet. *See Beta vulgaris*
Begonia. *See Begonia x semperflorens; Begonia x tuberhybrida*
Begonia x semperflorens (a), 34
Begonia x tuberhybrida (b), 227
Belamcanda chinesis (b), 227
Belladonna lily. *See Amaryllis belladonna*
Bellflower. *See Campanula glomerata; Campanula percisifolia*
Bell pepper. *See Capsicum annuum grossum*
Bells-of-Ireland. *See Moluccella laevis*
Berberis thunbergii atropurpurea (s/t), 442
Bergamot. *See Monarda didyma*
Bergenia. *See Bergenia cordifolia*

Candytuft. *See Iberis sempervirens; Iberis umbellata*
Canna. *See Canna x generalis*
Canna x generalis (b), 229
Cantaloupe. *See Cucumis melo reticulatus*
Cape-jasmine. *See Gardenia jasminoides*
Cape lily. *See Veltheimia viridifolia*
Cape marigold. *See Dimorphoteca sinuata*
Capsicum annuum (h/v), 555
Capsicum annuum (a), 37
Capsicum annuum grossum (h/v), 555
Caraway. *See Carum carvi*
Cardinal de Richelieu (r), 367
Cardiocrinum giganteum (b), 230
Cardomon. *See Elettaria cardamomum*
Carissa grandiflora (s/t), 448
Carnation. *See Dianthus caryophyllus*
Carolina jessamine. *See Gelsemium sempervirens*
Carolina silverbell. *See Halesia carolina*
Carrot. *See Daucus carota sativa*
Carthamus tinctorius (h/v), 556
Carum carvi (h/v), 556
Caryopteris x clandonensis (s/t), 448
Castanea mollissima (s/t), 449
Castor bean plant. *See Ricinus communis*
Catananche caerulea (p), 141
Catharanthus roseus (a), 38
Cathedral (r), 337

Catmint. *See Nepeta cataria; Nepeta mussinii*
Catmint, ornamental. *See Nepeta mussinii*
Catnip. *See Nepeta cataria*
Cauliflower. *See Brassica oleracea botrytis*
Ceanothus. *See Ceanothus thyrsiflorus*
Ceanothus thyrsiflorus (s/t), 449
Cedar. *See Cedrus atlantica*
Cedrus atlantica (s/t), 450
Celery, *See Apium graveolens dulce*
Celosia oristata (a), 38
Centaurea cyanus (a), 39
Centranthus ruber (p), 141
Century plant. *See Agave americana*
Cerastium tomentosum (p), 142
Cercis chinensis (s/t), 451
Chaenomeles sp. (s/t), 451.
Chamaecyparis pisifera (s/t), 452
Chamaemelum nobile (h/v), 557
Chamaemelum nobilis (h/v), 547
Chamomile. *See Anthemis nobilis; Chamaemelum nobile*
Chapeau de Napoleon. *See Rosa centifolia*
Charisma (r), 337
Chaste-tree. *See Vitex agnus-castus*
Checkered lily. *See Fritillaria meleagris*
Cheddar pink. *See Dianthus gratianopolitanus*
Chenopodium bonus-henricus (h/v), 557

Cherry. *See Cornum mas; Prunus subhirtella* 'Pendula'
Chervil. *See Anthriscus cerefolium*
Chestnut. *See Castanea mollissima*
Chicago peace (r), 320
Chicory. *See Cichorium intybus*
Chilean avens. *See Geum chiloense*
Chili pepper. *See Capsicum annuum*
China aster. *See Callistephus chinensis*
Chincherinchee. *See Ornithogalum thyroides*
Chinese chestnut. *See Castanea mollissima*
Chinese chive. *See Allium tuberosum*
Chinese Forget-me-not. *See Cynoglossum amabile*
Chinese Judas-tree. *See Cercis chinensis*
Chinese lanterns. *See Physalis alkekengi*
Chinese orchid. *See Bletilla striata*
Chinese parsley. *See Coriandrum sativum*
Chinese redbud. *See Cercis chinensis*
Chinese star-jasmine. *See Trachelospermum jasminoides*
Chinese witch-hazel. *See Hamamelis mollis*
Chionodoxa lucilae (b), 230
Chive. *See Allium schoenoprasum; Allium tuberosum*
Christian Dior (r), 321
Christmas-rose. *See Helleborus niger*

Chrysanthemum balsamita (h/v), 558
Chrysanthemum carinatum (a), 39
Chrysanthemum coccineum (h/v), 558
Chrysanthemum x morifolium (p), 142
Chrysanthemum parthenium (p), 143
Chrysanthemum x superbum (p), 143
Chrysler imperial (r), 321
Cichorium intybus (h/v), 559
Cilantro. *See Coriandrum sativum*
Cimicifuga racemose (p), 144
Cinquefoil. *See Potentilla fruticosa*
Cistus ladanifer (s/t), 452
Citrullus lanatus (h/v), 559
City of York (r), 352
Clarkia amoena (a), 40
Classic zinnia. *See Zinnia angustifolia*
Clematis sp. (s/t), 453
Cleome hasslerana (a), 40
Clivia miniata (b), 231
Cobaea scandens (a), 41
Cockscomb. *See Celosia cristata*
Colchicum autumnale (b), 231
Coleus. *See Coleus x hybrida*
Coleus x hybrida (a), 41
Colocasia esculenta (b), 232
Color magic (r), 322
Columbine. *See Aquilegia* hybrids
Comfrey. *See Symphytum officinale*
Command performance (r), 322
Common allamanda. *See Allamanda cathartica* 'Williamsi'
Common crocus. *See Crocus vernus*

Hardy-orange. *See Poncirus trifoliata*
Hardy prickly-pear. *See Opuntia humifusa*
Harison's yellow rose. *See Rosa x harisonnii*
Harlequin flower. *See Sparaxis tricolor*
Hawthorn. *See Crataegus phaenopyrum; Raphiolepis indica*
Healing plant. *See Aloe barbadensis*
Heartleaf bergenia. *See Bergenia cordifolia*
Heather. *See Calluna vulgaris*
Heavenly-bamboo. *See Nandina domestica*
Hedera helix (s/t), 466
Helenium autumnale (p), 153
Helianthemum nummularium (p), 153
Helianthus annuus (a), 51
Helianthus x multiflorus (p), 154
Helichrysum bracteatum (a), 52
Heliopsis helianthoides (p), 154
Heliotrope. *See Heliotropium arborescens*
Heliotropium arborescens (h/v), 568
Helleborus niger (p), 155
Hemerocallis hybrids (p), 155
Hemlock. *See Tsuga canadensis; Tsuga canadensis 'Sargentii'*
Henderson common allamanda. *See Allamanda cathartica 'Williamsi'*

Herald's-trumpet. *See Beaumontia grandiflora*
Herbaceous peony. *See Paeonia officinalis*
Heuchera sanguinea (p), 156
Hibiscus moscheutos (p), 156
Hibiscus syriacus (s/t), 467
Higan cherry. *See Prunus subhirtella 'Pendula'*
Himalayan lily. *See Cardiocrinum giganteum*
Hippeastrum hybrida (b), 243
Holly. *See Ilex x meserveae; Ilex opaca*
Hollyhocks. *See Alcea rosea*
Holly osmanthus. *See Osmanthus heterophyllus*
Holy Toledo (r), 360
Honest Abe (r), 361
Honey moss (r), 361
Honeysuckle. *See Lonicera japonica 'Halliana'*
Honor (r), 326
Horehound. *See Marrubium vulgare*
Horseradish. *See Armoracia rusticana*
Hosta seiboldiana (p), 157
Hot pepper. *See Capsicum annum*
Hummingbird vine. *See Campsis radicans*
Hunnemannia fumariifolia (a), 52
Hyacinth. *See Camassia scilloides; Hyacinthus orientalis; Muscari armeniacum*
Hyacinthoides hispanica (b), 244

Hyacinthus orientalis (b), 244
Hybrid fuchsia. *See Fuchsia hybrida*
Hybrid lilies. *See Lilium hybrida 'asiatic'*
Hybrid poplar. *See Populus hybrida*
Hydrangea. *See Hydrangea macrophylla*
Hydrangea macrophylla (s/t), 467
Hymenocallis narcissiflora (b), 245
Hypericum calycinum (s/t), 468
Hyssop. *See Agastache foeniculum; Hyssopus officinalis*
Hyssopus officinalis (h/v), 568

I

Iberis sempervirens (p), 157
Iberis umbellata (a), 53
Iceberg (r), 340
Iceland poppy. *See Papaver nudicaule*
Ilex x meserveae (s/t), 468
Ilex opaca (s/t), 469
Ilex verticillata (s/t), 469
Immortelle. *See Xeranthemum annuum*
Impatiens balsamina (a), 53
Impatiens wallerana (a), 54
Impatient (r), 341
Improved Paul's scarlet (r), 351
Incarvillea delvayii (b), 245
Indian hawthorn. *See Raphiolepis indica*

India raphiolepis. *See Raphiolepis indica*
Indigo. *See Baptisia australis*
Indigo bush. *See Amphora fruticosa angustifolia*
Ipomoea alba (a), 54
Ipomoea batatus (h/v), 569
Ipomoea tricolor (a), 55
Iris. *See Iris cristata; Iris danfordiae; Iris germanica; Iris hollandica; Iris kaempferi; Iris reticulata; Iris sibirica*
Iris cristata (b), 246
Iris danfordiae (b), 246
Iris germanica (p), 158
Iris germanica 'Florentina' (h/v), 569
Iris hollandica (b), 247
Irish potato. *See Solanum tuberosum*
Iris kaempferi (b), 247
Iris reticulata (b), 248
Iris sibirica (p), 158
Ismene. *See Hymenocallis narcissiflora*
Italian arum. *See Arum italicum*
Italian bugloss. *See Anchusa azurea*
Ivory fashion (r), 341
Ivy. *See Hedera helix*
Ixia maculata (b), 248

aethiopica; *Zephyranthes*
atamasco
Lily-flowered tulip. *See Tulipa* x *hybrida*
'Lily-flowered'
Lily leek. *See Allium moly*
Lily-of-the-Nile. *See Agapanthus*
africanus
Lily-of-the-valley. *See Convallaria*
majalis
Lily-turf. *See Liriope muscari*
Lily vine. *See Beaumontia grandiflora*
Lima bean. *See Phaseolus limensis*
Limnanthes douglasii (a), 57
Limonium sinuatum (a), 57
Linaria maroccana (a), 58
Linum perenne (p), 161
Liquidambar atyraciflua (s/t), 475
Liriodendron tulipifera (s/t), 475
Liriope muscari, 162
Lisianthus russulanus (a), 58
Livingstone daisy. *See Dorotheanus*
bellidiformis
Lobelia cardinalis (p), 162
Lobelia erinus (a), 59
Lobularia maritima (a), 59
Lonicera japonica 'Halliana' (s/t), 476
Loosestrife. *See Lysimachia punctata;*
Lythrum salicaria
Lovage. *See Levisticum officinale*
Love (r), 346
Lovely browallia. *See Browallia* sp.
Lupinus hybrids (p), 163
Luvvie (r), 362

Lychnis chalcedonica (p), 163
Lycopersicum esculentum (h/v), 572
Lycoris radiata (b), 252
Lycoris squamigera (b), 252
Lysimachia punctata (p), 164
Lythrum salicaria (p), 164

M

Machaeranthera tanacetifolia (a), 60
Madonna lily. *See Lilium candidum*
Magnolia. *See Magnolia grandiflora;*
Magnolia stellata
Magnolia grandiflora (s/t), 476
Magnolia stellata (s/t), 477
Maidenhair tree. *See Ginkgo biloba*
Mallow. *See Hibiscus moscheutos*
Maltese Cross. *See Lychnis*
chalcedonica
Malus hybrids (h/v), 572
Malus sargentii (s/t), 477
Maple. *See Acer palmatum dissectum;*
Acer rubrum
Marigold. *See Calendula officinalis;*
Caltha palustris; Dimorphoteca
sinuata; Tagetes erecta; Tagetes
patula; Tagetes tenuifolia
Marina (r), 342
Marjoram. *See Origanum majorana;*
Origanum vulgare
Marlberry. *See Ardisia japonica*
Marrubium vulgare (h/v), 573

Marsh-marigold. *See Caltha palustris*
Martha Lambert (r), 368
Matthiola incana (a), 60
Meadow-foam. *See Limnanthes*
douglasii
Medallion (r), 327
Melissa officinalis (h/v), 573
Mentha piperita (h/v), 574
Mentha pulegium (h/v), 574
Mentha rotundifolia (h/v), 575
Mentha spicata (h/v), 575
Mentha suaveolens (h/v), 575
Meserve hybrids. *See Ilex* x *meserveae*
Metasequoia glyptostroboides (s/t), 478
Mexican sunflower. *See Tithonia*
rotundifolia
Mexican tulip poppy. *See*
Hunnemannia fumariifolia
Michaelmas daisy. *See Aster*
novae-angliae
Mignonette. *See Reseda odorata*
Milkweed. *See Asclepias tuberosa*
Mimulus x *hybridus* (a), 61
Miniature daffodil. *See Narcissus*
minimum
Mirabilis jalapa (a), 61
Miss All-American beauty (r), 327
Mister Lincoln (r), 328
Mock-orange. *See Philadelphus*
coronarius
Mole plant. *See Euphorbia lathyris*
Moluccella laevis (a), 62

Monarch-of-the-veldt. *See Venidium*
fastuosum
Monarda citriodora (h/v), 576
Monarda didyma (h/v), 576
Monkey flower. *See Mimulus* x *hybridus*
Montbretia. *See Crocosmia* x
crocosmiiflora
Moonflower. *See Ipomea alba*
Morning glory. *See Ipomoea tricolor*
Moss-pinks. *See Phlox subulata*
Moss rose. *See Portulaca grandiflora;*
Rosa centifolia muscosa
Moutain-laurel. *See Kalmia latifolia*
Moutain pine. *See Pinus mugo*
Mugo pine. *See Pinus mugo*
Multiflora rose. *See Rosa multiflora*
Mum. *See Chrysanthemum* x
morifolium
Muscari armeniacum (b), 253
Myosotis scorpiodes (p), 165
Myosotis sylvatica (a), 62
Myrica cerifera (s/t), 478
Myrrh. *See Myrrhis odorata*
Myrrhis odorata (h/v), 577
Myrtle. *See Lagerstroemia indica;*
Vinca minor

Perennial sunflower. *See Helianthus* x
    multiflorus
Perennial sweet pea. *See Lathyrus*
    latifolius
Perfume delight (r), 331
Perilla. *See Perilla frutescens*
Perilla frutescens (h/v), 582
Periwinkle. *See Catharanthus roseus;*
    Vinca minor
Perovskia atripicifolia (p), 168
Persian buttercup. *See Ranunculus*
    asiaticus
Peruvian daffodil. *See Hymenocallis*
    narcissiflora
Peruvian lily. *See Alstroemeria*
    aurantiaca
Peruvian squill. *See Scilla peruviana*
Petroselinum crispum (h/v), 582
Petunia. *See Petunia* x *hybrida*
Petunia x *hybrida* (a), 67
Phaseolus limensis (h/v), 583
Phaseolus vulgaris (h/v), 583
Pheasant's eye. *See Narcissus poeticus*
Philadelphus coronarius (s/t), 482
Phlox. *See Phlox drummondii; Phlox*
    paniculata
Phlox drummondii (a), 68
Phlox paniculata (p), 168
Phlox subulata (p), 169
Photinia. *See Photinia* x *fraseri*
Photinia x *fraseri* (s/t), 483
Physalis alkekengi (p), 169
Physotegia virginiana (p), 170

Picea pungens 'Glauca' (s/t), 483
Picea pungens nana (s/t), 484
Pieris japonica (s/t), 484
Pimpinella anisum (h/v), 584
Piñata (r), 357
Pincushion flower. *See Scabiosa*
    atropurpurea; Scabiosa
    caucasica
Pine. *See Pinus mugo; Pinus strobus*
Pineapple lily. *See Eucomis comosa*
Pineapple sage. *See Salvia elegans*
Pink peace (r), 331
Pin oak. *See Quercus palustris*
Pinus mugo (s/t), 485
Pinus strobus (s/t), 485
Pisum sativum (h/v), 584
Pittosporum. *See Pittosporum tobira*
Pittosporum tobira (s/t), 486
Plantain-lily. *See Hosta seiboldiana*
Platycodon grandiflorus (p), 170
Pleione formosa (b), 258
Podocarpus. *See Podocarpus*
    macrophyllus
Podocarpus macrophyllus (s/t), 486
Poet's daffodil. *See Narcissus poeticus*
Poker. *See Kniphofia uvaria*
Polemonium reptans (p), 171
Polianthus x *tuberosa* (b), 258
Polyantha primrose. *See Primula* x
    polyantha
Polygonum bistorta (p), 171
Pomegranate. *See Punica granatum*
Poncirus trifoliata (s/t), 487

Poor man's orchid. *See Schizanthus* x
    wisetonensis
Poplar. *See Populus hybrida*
Poppy. *See Eschscholzia californica;*
    Hunnemannia fumariifolia;
    Papaver nudicaule; Papaver
    orientale; Papaver rhoeas
Poppy anemone. *See Anemone*
    coronaria
Populus hybrida (s/t), 487
Portulaca grandiflora (a), 68
Potato. *See Solanum tuberosum*
Potentilla fruticosa (s/t), 488
*Poterium sanguisorba (h/v), 585
Pot-marigold. *See Calendula officinalis*
Powderpuff shrub. *See Calliandra*
    haematocephala
Prairie gentian. *See Lisianthus*
    russulanus
Prickly-pear. *See Opuntia humifusa*
Primrose. *See Primula japonica;*
    Primula x *polyantha*
Primula japonica (p), 172
Primula x *polyantha* (p), 172
Prince's-feather. *See Anaranthus*
    hybridus hypochondriacus
Pristine (r), 332
Privet. *See Ligustrum* x *vicaryi*
Prunus glandulosa 'Alboplena' (s/t),
    488
Prunus hybrids (h/v), 572
Prunus subhirtella 'Pendula' (s/t), 489
Pseudotsuga menziesii (s/t), 489

Pumpkin. *See Cucurbita pepo*
Punica granatum (h/v), 585
Puppy love (r), 362
Purple coneflower. *See Echinacea*
    purpurea
Purple loosestrife. *See Lythrum*
    salicaria
Puschkinia scilloides (b), 259
Pussy willow. *See Salix discolor*
Pyracantha coccinea (s/t), 490
Pyrethrum. *See Chrysanthemum*
    coccineum
Pyrus calleryana 'Bradford' (s/t), 490
Pyrus hybrids (h/v), 572

Q

Queen Elizabeth (r), 347
Quercus palustris (s/5), 491
Quince. *See Chaenomeles* sp.

R

Radish. *See Raphanus sativus*
Rainbow daisy. *See Gazania ringens*
Rainbow plant. *See Caladium* x
    hortulanum
Ranunculus asiaticus (b), 259
Raphanus sativus (h/v), 586
Raphiolepis indica (s/t), 491
Red buckeye. *See Aesculus pavia*

White rose of York. *See Rosa alba*
White trumpet lily. *See Lilium
    longiflorum*
Wild hyacinth. *See Camassia scilloides*
Wild indigo. *See Baptisia australis*
Wild marjoram. *See Origanum vulgare*
Willow. *See Salix* x *chrysocoma; Salix
    discolor*
Willow-leaf bellflower. *See Campanula
    percisifolia*
Windflower. *See Anemone blanda*
Winged euonymus. *See Euonymus
    alata*
Winter aconite. *See Eranthis hyemalis*
Winterberry. *See Ilex verticillata*
Winterhazel. *See Corylopsis
    glabrescens*
Winter savory. *See Satureja montana*
Wishbone flower. *See Torenia fournieri*
Wisteria. *See Wisteria floribunda*
Wisteria floribunda (s/t), 499
Witch-hazel. *See Hamamelis mollis*
Woodruff. *See Galium odoratum*
Wooly betony. *See Stachys byzantina*
Wormwood. *See Artemesia absinthium*

X

Xeranthemum annuum (a), 80

Y

Yarrow *See Achillea filipendulina*
Yellow allamanda. *See Allamanda
    cathartica* 'Williamsi'
Yellow crocus. *See Crocus flavus*
Yellow loosestrife. *See Lysimachia
    punctata*
Yellow rose. *See Rosa* x *harisonnii*
Yellow yarrow. *See Achillea
    filipendulina*
Yesterday, today, tomorrow. *See
    Brunfelsia calycina floribunda*
Yew. *See Taxus cuspidata*
Yew podocarpus. *See Podocarpus
    macrophyllus*
Yucca filamentosa (p), 177

Z

Zantedeschia aethiopica (b), 270
Zea mays rugosa (h/v), 598
Zephyranthes atamasco (b), 271
Zephyr lily. *See Zephyranthes atamasco*
Zingiber officinale (h/v), 598
Zinnia. *See Sanvitalia procumbens;
    zinnia angustifolia; Zinnia
    elegans*
Zinnia angustifolia (a), 80
Zinnia elegans (a), 81

SUBJECT INDEX